THE
HUNGRY
YEARS

THE
HUNGRY
YEARS

——◆——

A Narrative History of the
Great Depression in America

T. H. Watkins

A Marian Wood Book
Henry Holt and Company ◆ New York

Henry Holt and Company, LLC
Publishers since 1866
115 West 18th Street
New York, New York 10011

Henry Holt® is a registered trademark of
Henry Holt and Company, LLC.

Library of Congress Cataloging-in-Publication Data
Watkins, T. H. (Tom H.), date.
The hungry years : A narrative history of the Great
Depression in America / by T. H. Watkins.—1st ed.
        p.   cm.
"A Marian Wood book."
ISBN 0-8050-1675-9 (alk. paper)
1. United States—History—1933–1945. 2. United States—
History—1919–1933. 3. Depressions—1929—United States.
4. Depressions—1929—United States—Personal narratives. 5. United
States—Social conditions—1933–1945. 6. United States—Social
conditions—1918–1932. I. Title.
E806.W35   1999   99-10391
973.91'6—dc21   CIP

Henry Holt books are available for special promotions and
premiums. For details, contact: Director, Special Markets.

First Edition 1999

Designed by Kelly Soong Too

Printed in the United States of America
All first editions are printed on acid-free paper. ∞

1   3   5   7   9   10   8   6   4   2

For Joan. In fact, all of them are.
And to Ralph Hone, guiding spirit.

Ours is a story mad with the impossible, it is by chaos out of dream, it began as dream and it has continued as dream down to the last head-line you read in a newspaper, and of our dreams there are two things above all others to be said, that only madmen could have dreamed them or would have dared to—and that we have shown a consider-able faculty for making them come true.

—*Bernard DeVoto to*
Catherine Drinker Bowen
(ca. 1940)

CONTENTS

FOREWORD

◆

A generation of witnesses is passing. The men and women who came to maturity during the years of one of the most transforming decades in the American chronicle are swiftly being lost to time, and the Great Depression, for so long a genuine memory in the lives of millions, will soon become merely folklore—or folklore's more respectable cousin, history. *The Hungry Years* provides some of both, for its main intent is to pay tribute to those who lived through these times by offering a portrait of the era that is as rich and full and true as I can make it.

That tribute is necessary, I think. Something very important took place in this decade of change, something that made us very different as a people and as a nation. I am not talking here about just the New Deal, with all its engines of institutional metamorphosis. Indeed, the New Deal does not even enter this chronicle until a third of the way through the book. One cannot escape the New Deal in any book about the thirties in America, of course, nor should the attempt be made. The "dreamers and dealers" of the age, as historian (and former New Dealer)

Joseph Lash described them, rattled the cage of government more violently than any other single group of human beings in our history. Not
only did they make it answerable to the needs of the people to a degree
never before imagined but profoundly enlarged the power of the presidency and created a bureaucratic structure of unprecedented size and
Byzantine complexity, all of which was designed to better the national
estate and improve the quality of life for all the country's citizens. This
has not always been viewed as a good thing. Much revisionist history—
particularly that from the disillusioned Left—has pointed to the contra-
dictions, frequent incompetence, continuing fealty to capitalism, and
unmet expectations of the New Deal as evidence that the whole business was at heart a cynical failure perpetrated by essentially conservative
ideologues. Contrarily, those on the political Right hold that the New
Deal was such a triumph of radical liberal excess that its legacy must be
dismantled before the Republic sinks beneath its weight. In spite of
both persuasions, I hope I have made a case in these pages for what I
believe was a nobility of purpose that few governments have ever entertained, and that if much of what the New Dealers hoped to accomplish
fell far short of their often bloated expectations, it was, at least, a magnificent failure. And to the extent that some residue of that original
purpose still lurks somewhere in our government, however battered it
may be by the passing winds of expedience and unenlightened self-
interest, by just that much can the nation continue to lay claim to
greatness.

    Still, this is less a book about the New Deal and the New Dealers—
the focus of my previous book, *The Great Depression: America in the
1930s*—than it is about the people whose lives were changed by what
the Great Depression brought. Their response to the crisis helped to
shape the character of the age, and that, too, is a major theme in this
book. The programs and policies of the New Deal, after all, were not
carried to Washington, D.C., and imposed on an uncomprehending citizenry by a cabal of individuals who had been secretly planning such a
coup for decades (though there were—and still are—those ready to
believe it). Those individuals emerged from a stew of discontent and
occasional violence, diverse progressive instincts, anarchism, socialism,
communism, intermittent populist eruptions, philosophical disputes,
and political realignments that had characterized the national life ever

since the end of the Civil War and the triumph of industrial capitalism. The dreams, schemes, hopes, frustrations, incompetence, and genius of the New Dealers were those of the people themselves; directly or indirectly, the people had put them there in Washington, had demanded that they do something, and to a substantial degree continued to support them in their efforts throughout much of the decade.

While I take the reader into the sometimes murky world of national policy and politics as necessary, my ambition in this book is to take it as far beyond Washington, D.C., as I can get it, and wherever possible present the story from the ground up—showing how individual lives were affected, how individual decisions were made, how individual hope, despair, confusion, humor, and bravery were reflected in action and emotion across as wide a spectrum of geography and society as I can capture between these covers.

To do so, I have abandoned ordinary narrative structure in much of the book, which is arbitrarily divided into three main sections. The first, "In the Crucible," is generally chronological, taking the story from the Crash of 1929 to the dark heart of the early Depression years and the eve of the New Deal. That point reached, the presentation divides into two related sections. The first of these, "Holding Up the Walls," is largely urban in character, concentrating on the early efforts of the New Dealers to get a grip on the economy and come up with workable relief and social welfare systems, while a resurgent labor movement, both encouraged and frustrated by programs being developed in Washington and seething with contradictory internal forces, erupted spectacularly in the streets of Minneapolis and Toledo, the waterfronts of the Pacific Coast, the mines and mill towns of Appalachia, the shop floors of Detroit and Chicago, and hundreds of other sites of industrial America.

The final division of the book, "The Ploughland Curve," shows how the same anguish of the Depression years played out in the rural areas of the nation, from the Farm Holidays and "penny auction" riots of the Midwest to the industry-wide strikes of Mexican migrant workers in California's Imperial and San Joaquin valleys, from the New Deal's visions of a new Arcadia in the river basins of the West to the lonely and little-known struggle of black sharecroppers in the Black Belt of Alabama, from the ravages of the Dust Bowl to the failed dream of Utopia called the Tennessee Valley Authority.

Whether in a rural or an urban context, it is the people in whom I find the heart of the depression story. I am no more interested, for example, in the agonizing details of how the union-validating elements of Section 7(a) of the National Industrial Recovery Act were fabricated into law than I am in what the section meant to workers who had been locked in the darkness of repression for a decade—and in what they did with their new opportunity. If the story of welfare from Hoover to Roosevelt is fascinating (and it is), I am every bit as entranced by what the social workers in the field had to deal with and how the programs they represented were experienced by those they were created to help. And if I discuss the economic causes and consequences of the Great Depression in suitably objective terms throughout, it is the human dimension of those objective realities that subjectively fascinates me—particularly when it is remembered that those consequences included some of the most deadly social violence in our history. To this day, no one knows precisely how many people died in the decade's hunger marches and farm revolts and urban riots and explosive strikes, and it would be a disservice to history to let the anguish of class warfare—for that is what much of it was—be muffled in an arid exegesis of politics and policy.

I could say much the same about the role of communism. The Communist Party/USA plays an important part in this book, particularly with regard to the first half of the decade. The CP/USA was no model of revolutionary efficiency and altruism; usually, it was the witting tool of the Comintern, whose ignorance of how America really worked was as deep as its adherence to Stalinist rigidity was unshakable; its American leadership was raddled by fractious and often preposterous internal squabblings; and it was prey to extraordinary levels of opportunism and cynicism that took the bloom off much of its presumed glory. In spite of all this, in the dedication and often stunning courage of its rank and file—particularly in the Deep South, the farm fields of California, and in other arenas of class conflict—the CP/USA sometimes gave radicalism a good name, and I pay appropriate tribute to what its people achieved.

In this emphasis on the power of the grass roots and radicalism, I hope to demonstrate that if the years of the Great Depression were indeed a time of unprecedented change that helped to make us what we are today, the transformation was not only *in* the people but, to an extent never quite duplicated before or since, *of* the people. Much conventional historical wisdom suggests that what was especially remarkable about the early years of the depression was the level of apathy in the public's response to a disaster whose causes could all too easily be found in an economic system unfettered by controls, riddled with excess, and often dominated by corporate monsters with no more finely tuned a sense of social responsibility than a bag of rocks. In its most extreme manifestations, such an observation seems to imply that since the people did not rise up en masse and trample their oppressors (as many feared and predicted they would in fact do in violent imitation of the Bolshevik Revolution of 1917), there was something spineless or at least morally confused in the national character.

It is true enough that there was no national Armageddon and that the vast majority of Americans tried to muddle through the worst of times without recourse to street violence or the hanging of capitalists. There was nothing new in this. Americans commonly are politically inert. At the same time, hundreds of thousands of citizens—proportionately more than at any time in our post–Civil War history—*did* rise up at one time or another to challenge the system that had brought them so low, and if they hung no capitalists, they threatened to from time to time, marched in plenty of streets, and gave indispensable emotional weight to the movement for change. The willingness of people like these to put their lives on the line—sometimes quite literally on the line—still bears a moral authority deserving of our respect.

But an even more powerful argument against the charge of apathy is the fact that millions of voters—more millions than ever before—exercised their demand for a profound change in how their government did business with them in not one but three national elections. Pundits and politicians prattle on these days about "mandates" when only a fraction of the electorate expresses its opinion one way or the other, but the two most definitive elections of the thirties—the presidential election of 1932 and the congressional election of 1934—were not paltry turnouts open to convenient ideological interpretation; they were true mandates that overwhelmingly represented "the voice of the people," that hackneyed and usually corrupted phrase. And if the presidential election of 1936 was more an endorsement of Roosevelt and what he and his people already had done than a call for more of the same—as many New Dealers mistakenly assumed—it nevertheless adds weight to my belief that only part of the responsibility for the dimensions of change in American society, politics, and economic life that took place in the thirties could be credited to the artful bureaucrats and hardworking drones of the New Deal; the rest of it belonged to the people.

Such levels of involvement did not survive even the thirties, of course. While the structure of a new kind of interdependence between the citizenry and the government had been set firmly in place, the energy of reform slowly began to dissipate after the 1936 elections, diminished by another, if briefer, period of economic slippage, in combination with a political shift to the right in the Congress. And by the end of the decade the most compelling fear driving both the people and their government was not that of economic deprivation but of war.

That ending, like so much else from this compelling and troubled era, reverberates in the national consciousness with a terrible vividness still—and perhaps the intensity of that recollection represents not just the dreadful uncertainty that war always brings but an inchoate sense of loss. For a time, millions of Americans—white, black, and brown, male and female, urban and rural, young and old, white-collar and blue-collar—had been given a sense of their own worth and power, the notion that by joining together they could control at least some portion of their lives, however imperfectly, however briefly. But the needs of war demanded that the collectivism of social change be subsumed in the larger collectivism of survival—necessary, perhaps, but ultimately bleak and dehumanizing, bringing with it an ineffable sadness.

—T. H. Watkins
Washington, D.C.,
and Bozeman, Montana
1990–1998

THE
HUNGRY
YEARS

CAREENING DOWN MAIN STREET, 1929

At four o'clock in the morning of January 2, 1929, a mass of men began to form in the enormous car park across Miller Road from Gate No. 3 of the Ford Motor Company's plant on the banks of the River Rouge near Dearborn, Michigan. The sky was overcast and the predawn night was black, but the men were given a faintly sinister presence by the eerie glow from interior factory lights filtered through blue-tinted windows and the pulsing foundry and blast furnace fires of the largest industrial complex in the world—ninety individual buildings totaling 229 acres of floor space scattered over two thousand acres. Two of the buildings exceeded 1,500 feet in length—the equivalent of five football fields—each one seemingly made entirely of windows. River Rouge also had its own deepwater port to accommodate ships from the Great Lakes laden with coal and iron ore, and its own railroad system, with ninety-three miles of track to shuttle supplies and products to and from railheads in and around Detroit. There were twenty-seven miles of conveyors—every kind of conveyor known to industrial engineering—many of which stretched from building to building like covered bridges, linking operations in an angular web of clattering productivity. In this complex alone, more than forty thousand employees manufactured the parts for and assembled Model A Fords, Fordson tractors, and Ford Trimotor airplanes. It took five thousand maintenance workers just to clean the place.

"The nearest thing to the sublime in Michigan," Leonard Lanson Cline had written in *The Nation* back in November 1922, "is the Ford factory. See it at dusk some October afternoon, from a distance away, a vast squat looming monster, glinting a shrill blue light from its windows into the shadows, gibbering, ominous. Out of the tall chimneys drifts black smoke. It smuts one's nose and collar, and the soot of it cakes over one's imagination and is too heavy for wings."[1] Cline could have written such a description again this January morning a little over six years later, but it was fourteen degrees below zero out in the car park now, and the men pulling up their collars, clutching their coats closed at the neck, jamming their free hands into their pockets, trying not to inhale the gelid air too deeply, stamping in several inches of rigid, crackling snow to keep their feet from freezing—these men probably were not worrying about soot in their noses or on their collars, few of which were clean to begin with. As dawn began to reveal the stark geometry of buildings that rose like prison blocks in the thin light, what they were worrying about was whether they would soon become one of the chosen: a Ford employee.

There were an estimated 32,000 job seekers crammed into the car park, waiting to be hired, having responded to an invitation broadcast by the company at the year's end. The men ranged the demographic spectrum from white, native Anglo-Saxons out of Tennessee to first-generation Polish immigrants out of Pittsburgh; from African American cotton pickers who had escaped the Mississippi Delta to Mexican American beet field workers who had crossed into the United States, legally and otherwise, at the Rio Grande. Ford's employment division had promised that local men from Detroit, Dearborn, and other nearby cities would be given preference, but the sheer numbers

---

1. Leonard Lanson Cline, "Michigan." In Daniel H. Borus, ed., *These United States: Portraits of America from the 1920s*, p. 184. Full bibliographic citations for all titles are found in "Sources" at the end of the book.

involved made such fine distinctions impossible. "We are from other states," one of the men admitted to a reporter for *The New Republic*, "but if we are asked about it, we've been in Detroit all our lives. What we want is a job."[2]

What they got was a grim human lottery. Burly hiring agents stood at the plant's gate, letting in the first ten men, dismissing the following ten, letting in the next ten, and so on, a bleak assembly-line process that continued, hour after hour. When fights broke out among men jostling for position at the front of the mass, Ford's security guards turned fire hoses on them. Drenched and miserable, men collapsed from exhaustion, exposure, and hypothermia; some were taken to local hospitals, though a few with a little change in their pockets staggered into a nearby ten-cent movie house to thaw out. Most remained where they stood, hoping to become one of the 30,000 new employees the company said it would need over the next several weeks to bring its total workforce to more than 150,000 and raise production by 20 percent to meet demand.

The company was accustomed to dealing in such outsized numbers. A little over a year and a half before, the last Model T Ford had rattled off the production line, and the company had shut down completely for several months to develop the Model A. Some 60,000 workers in the Detroit area alone were let go, with thousands more laid off in parts and assembly plants around the country. Henry Ford, founder of both the feast and then the sudden famine, thought the layoffs would be psychologically beneficial for his workers. "I know it's done them a lot of good," he told a reporter for the *Survey Graphic*, "to let them know that things are not going along too even always."[3]

The scene that greeted Ford as he arrived at the River Rouge plant this January morning, then, probably gave him considerable satisfaction. The extraordinary number of men huddled in the cold and freezing slush of the car park under the lowering clouds, elbowing and

<hr />

2. Quoted in William K. Klingaman, *1929: The Year of the Great Crash*, p. 121. For more on River Rouge hiring this day, see Gordon Thomas and Max Morgan-Witts, *The Day the Bubble Burst*, pp. 37–39; Robert Conot, *American Odyssey*, p. 255; and Peter Collier and David Horowitz, *Fords*, p. 90.
3. Quoted in Warren Sloat, *1929: America Before the Crash*, p. 43.

fighting one another and the hiring agents to become one of those selected, shivering violently in the terrible blasts from fire hoses when they got too restive—for him, the very number of such men could only have validated the power of the magic he had given the nation.

Certainly, no individual and no industry so precisely illustrated the extraordinary covenant between productivity and consumerism that had characterized the postwar years. Even before President Warren G. Harding died in August 1923, leaving the nation in the hands of his vice president, Calvin Coolidge, the era of what would come to be called "Coolidge Prosperity" already had begun its dizzy spin. Americans as a whole had emerged from the years of the war richer, healthier, and living more comfortable lives than ever before, technological genius and business instinct combining to produce a material abundance quite unlike anything the world had ever known. Between 1915 and 1920, the gross national product had risen by more than $51 billion (about $414 billion in equivalent 1998 dollars), the largest five-year increase in history, and while production declined sharply during a brief postwar recession, it began to climb again in 1925, until by the end of 1928 it stood at $97 billion. During the war years, disposable personal income had grown from a yearly average of $33.3 billion to more than $61 billion, and by the end of 1928 it had reached $77.5 billion.[4]

To the distress of the few preachers of frugality left in the land, a postwar boom in installment buying—a dollar down and a dollar a week at its most primitive level—let millions of Americans have immediately what they might have waited years for in prewar decades. Instant gratification in the matter of clothes and gadgets and even automobiles bloated consumer credit from $2.6 billion in 1920 to $7.1 billion in 1929, the largest jump in the country's history. "[This] plan of merchandising," the editors of The American Year Book for 1928 announced with some satisfaction, "is now recognized as an integral part of our economic life. In short, installment buying has settled down to a more or less normal existence."[5]

4. For all comparisons of dollar values then and today (1998), see "A Note on Statistics and Money" at the end of the book.
5. Albert Bushnell Hart and William M. Schuyler, eds., The American Year Book: A Record of Events and Progress for the Year 1928, pp. 314–15.

Such a development, its adherents insisted, was not just a mindless indulgence in materialism. It was, instead, an integral part of the very democratic process and the nation's inexorable drift toward perfection. Nor was this dogma professed only by the kinds of dense and righteous go-getting businessmen who inhabited Sinclair Lewis's satirical 1922 novel, *Babbitt*. From "social economist" Simon Patten at the Wharton School of Economics in Philadelphia to sociologist Franklin Giddings at Columbia University in New York, there had developed a body of philosophical theory that maintained, as Patten put it in 1912, that "the non-saver is now the higher type of man than the saver, just as the saver was an elevation of type above the extravagance of more primitive man."[6] People *should* spend, he said, and every instinct of society's industry, government, and culture should be devoted to encouraging a "desire for goods" and then making it possible for more and more people to satisfy those sudden consumptive urges by providing them with easily available standardized products. They should be standardized, according to Giddings in 1922, because the conformity of goods was a necessary step toward the achievement of a conformity of values: "Chief among the assimilative forces . . . [is] standardized consumption. . . . As consumers of wealth we exhibit mental and moral solidarity. We want the same things. We have the same tastes. So far as this part at least of our life is concerned we have the basis and the fact of a highly general consciousness of kind."[7]

Henry Ford had played a central role in the flowering of this new age of assimilative consumerism. Ever since its first appearance in 1908, his Model T, with its modest price and equally modest aspect, became in the minds of many the most purely democratic machine in history. Ford himself had been fond of saying, "a Ford will take you anywhere except into Society."[8] The Model T was sturdy, reliable, quirky, and through the years much loved. By 1927, when Ford finally ceased production of this heroic machine in order to go into production of the Model As, the company had sold more than fifteen million, many to the

6. Quoted in William Leach, *Land of Desire: Merchants, Power, and the Rise of a New American Culture*, p. 239.
7. Quoted in ibid., p. 243.
8. Quoted in Robert Lacey, *Ford: The Men and the Machine*, p. 286.

very working people who had built them. If someone had gathered all
the vehicles together, then distributed them throughout the country in
that one year, 1927, there would have been one Model T for every eight
people in the United States—and the vehicle's reputation suggested
that almost every single one of the cars would still have been in working
condition.

Ford was hardly free of competitors. There were forty-four other
automobile-makers in business by 1929, although the big three of
Ford, General Motors, and Chrysler were responsible for the manufacture and sale of more than 80 percent of the nearly 4.5 million cars built
in the United States every year. Chrysler's little Plymouth would give
the Model A a run for its axle grease, and GM, which produced the Buick,
the Oldsmobile, and the Cadillac, also had developed the Chevrolet,
another powerful contender for Ford's basic market.

Still, Ford was the colossus who bestrode the industry—indeed, the
nation: in 1924 there had even been talk of his running for president, an
ambition he eventually disowned. Behind the man, however, lay a paradox to which he apparently was blind. This pioneer who had guided the
nation into the rumble and stink of the automobile age held firm to the
notion that almost everything in the rural past that his industry had
done so much to change, even destroy, was better, cleaner, purer than
the world he had helped to make. Since 1915, his film division had been
grinding out a series of short inspirational movies celebrating the life,
culture, and morality of rural America, inventing scenes where they
could not be found in reality, offering flickering images of sturdy farmers plowing with mules, of cheerful farm women churning butter at the
hearthstone, of families gathering for meals and simple games played
by lamplight, of hoedowns and square dances and church socials. He
promoted country music, sponsored an annual fiddler's contest, and
"encouraged" his executives to attend company-sponsored evening
dance parties like those he remembered from his youth. (He was an
excellent dancer himself, moving about the floor with the bony grace of
a praying mantis.) He spent tens of thousands of dollars annually on all
the life-sized puzzle pieces of "Greenfield Village," a reconstruction
near Dearborn, Michigan, that offered authentic old houses (including
his own birthplace), shops, barns, buggies, and other paraphernalia

plucked from everywhere in the country and brought to Michigan to make a rural dreamland. "I'm trying in a small way," he once explained to a curious *New York Times* reporter, "to help America take a step, even if it is a little one, toward the saner and sweeter idea of life that prevailed in prewar days."[9]

If Ford had ever discerned a contradiction between what he had created and what his heart yearned for, it has not been recorded, so he probably was equally oblivious to the significance of the 32,000 men gathered outside River Rouge Gate No. 3 on the morning of January 2, 1929. Were he a reflective man, the scene might have prompted in him a question—and an answer—that might have made him rest less easily in his certitude that all was well in the world he had helped to conjure: if prosperity ruled the nation, as virtually every industrialist, banker, merchant, politician, financier, educator, and churchman in the land had been trumpeting for most of the decade—if this country was doing so well, why was it that 32,000 men needed work so badly that they had been willing to travel many thousands of miles by whatever means they could and suffer misery and the risk of death in order to find it?

ON INAUGURATION MORNING, March 4, Herbert Hoover, the former secretary of commerce and now president-elect of the United States, put on his top hat and, with his wife and family, set off for the White House. There, he met with outgoing President Calvin Coolidge, exchanged pleasantries briefly, then joined him in the back of the inaugural limousine for the short journey down Pennsylvania Avenue to the Capitol building. The tall, white-haired, and somewhat portly president-elect was no stranger to the crowds that lined the route this morning. He had been a public figure for a long time now and had won national regard as a man of granite integrity and intellectual brilliance. He had earned his first reputation (and his first $4 million, it was said) as an international mining engineer after graduating from Stanford University in 1895. Then, during the first three years of World War I, he had directed various international relief efforts for the people of Belgium. When the

9. Quoted in Walter Karp, "Greenfield Village," *American Heritage* (December 1980).

United States entered the war in 1917, President Woodrow Wilson had chosen him to head up the U.S. Food Administration and after the armistice appointed him to direct the American Relief Administration. President Warren Harding had made him secretary of commerce in 1921, a position he had continued to hold under Coolidge until winning, almost by acclamation, the nomination of the Republican Party in the summer of 1928.

Hoover's Democratic opponent had been Alfred E. Smith, the governor of New York. A colorful, experienced, and appealing candidate, Smith was not without significant financial support: his campaign manager was none other than retired General Motors executive John J. Raskob. But Smith did not have a prayer. He was, after all, Irish and Catholic and had earned his political stripes as a "Happy Warrior" (as his admirer and political protégé Franklin D. Roosevelt had dubbed him) for the mavens of Tammany Hall, an institution universally despised as a sinkhole of corruption by reform-minded folk of all persuasions. Moreover, Smith had to face Hoover's extraordinary popularity among most Americans, particularly after the "Great Humanitarian" took charge of directing Red Cross relief efforts during the horrendous Mississippi flood of 1927—a task so handsomely publicized (though accomplished, as things usually were with Hoover, with a cool, almost coldhearted dedication to efficiency) that Hoover was fully justified when he told his friend, humorist Will Irwin, in May 1927 that "I shall be the nominee, probably. It is almost inevitable."[10] Smith also had to deal with the tide of optimism and prosperity with which Hoover was identified—a connection his opponent did not deny. "Given a chance to go forward with the policies of the last eight years," Hoover had said upon accepting the nomination, "we shall soon with the help of God be in sight of the day when poverty will be banished from the nation."[11] "I might," advertising man Bruce Barton remarked, "get more fun out of having Smith around, but I'd make more money with Hoover."[12] That certainly had been the expectation of the 58 percent of the electorate

10. Quoted in John M. Barry, *Rising Tide: The Great Mississippi River Flood of 1927 and How It Changed America*, p. 289.
11. Quoted in Richard Norton Smith, *An Uncommon Man: The Triumph of Herbert Hoover*, p. 105.
12. Quoted in ibid., p. 104.

who had voted for Hoover in November 1928, giving him 444 electoral votes compared to a paltry 88 for Smith.

One would not have guessed at the enormity of his victory by looking at the man. Except for evincing a brief twitch of warmth when they shook hands and the occasional, almost reluctant smile at the crowds along the route, his death mask of a face was a match for that of Coolidge (in public, both men appeared to favor an institutional glumness, though each had a wry sense of humor when moved to express it). Their expressions were complemented by the weather. It was a typical late-winter day in Washington, and a gray drizzle had been falling for hours. In spite of the rain, a good crowd was on hand in the Capitol Plaza to witness the quadrennial ritual of inauguration. On the platform, with the enormous Chief Justice (and former President) William Howard Taft presiding, the somber-faced Hoover put his hand on a new bible, which had been opened to the Sermon on the Mount, and took the oath of office. Then, beneath an umbrella in the increasingly heavy rain, he turned to face a rank of radio microphones to deliver his inaugural address.

It was not likely that anyone in the crowd or on the platform or in the radio audience was expecting fire and brimstone, or much else in the way of oratorical excess. Hoover was admired as a man of great intelligence, but no one would have accused him of flamboyance in either action or speech. He surprised no one this morning. As his thematic Bible verse for the inaugural address, he had chosen Proverbs 29:18: "Where there is no vision, the people perish; but he that keepeth the law, happy is he." Hoover's own public vision was certainly happy enough:

Ours is a land rich in resources; stimulating in its glorious beauty; filled with millions of happy homes; blessed with comfort and opportunity. In no nation are the fruits of accomplishment more secure. In no nation is the government more worthy of respect. No country is more loved by its people. I have an abiding faith in their capacity, integrity and high purpose. I have no fears for the future of our country. It is bright with hope.[13]

13. Quoted in Harris Gaylord Warren, *Herbert Hoover and the Great Depression*, p. 53.

Coolidge, sitting on the platform behind the new president, may not have been so sure of that. He had, after all, chosen not to run for a second full term and was, insiders said, glad to get out of town. As early as April 1928, *The Kiplinger Washington Letter* had reported that "from a political angle, it is frequently said that the party which is in power between 1929 and 1933 will have more than its share of troubles, and will have difficulty maintaining itself in the presidential elections of 1932. There are those who say that Mr. Coolidge recognizes this, and therefore will not consent to serve another term."[14] Nor did Hoover's own feelings necessarily match the finely tuned optimism of his official words. "My friends," he had complained gently in December, apparently forgetting that he had done nothing to discourage such hyperbole, especially during the 1927 flood, "have made the American people think me a sort of superman, able to cope successfully with the most difficult and complicated problems. . . . They expect the impossible of me and should there arise in the land conditions with which the political machinery is unable to cope, I will be the one to suffer."[15]

LESS THAN EIGHT months after the inauguration, lyricist Jack Yellen bore witness to the validity of Hoover's worries and Coolidge's wisdom. It was October 24, and the elegant dinner-dance ballroom of the Hotel Pennsylvania in Manhattan had only a smattering of patrons. As Yellen, a sprightly, compact elf of a man, handed several sheets of music and lyrics to lead singer George Olsen to pass out among the other singers and the band members, he was worried that this might not be just the right crowd for the premiere of a new song—especially this song. He and his partner, composer Milton Ager, had written the thing in Hollywood a few months earlier as part of an MGM musical called *Chasing Rainbows*, produced by Irving Thalberg but not yet released. The movie, Yellen said later, "was an incredible piece of cheese."[16]

14. The Kiplinger Washington Editors, *Kiplinger's "Looking Ahead": 70 Years of Forecasts from "The Kiplinger Washington Letter,"* p. 17.
15. Quoted in Warren, op. cit., p. 103.
16. Quoted in *Buffalo Courier-Express* (March 5, 1975).

Thalberg, for his part, had hated most of the music the duo had composed and had demanded that they produce one truly good song within twenty-four hours or he would start a court fight that would keep them from publishing anything else they had written for the movie. "MGM had given me a little office on the studio grounds," Yellen remembered, "and I never left it to go to the set or meet with Ager. Milton spent most of his time playing golf. . . . I finally got in touch with Ager, and dragged him off the golf course and into my office to write a song. . . . The whole thing took us under a half an hour to write."[17] With the movie still sitting on the shelf, the only hope for the song's success was to get it into circulation as soon as possible, and the best way to do that was to get it introduced here, at the Hotel Pennsylvania, within a magnum's throw of Tin Pan Alley and the Broadway theater district.

Now, in the sparsely occupied dining room, Yellen looked out worriedly on what he remembered as "a handful of gloom-stricken diners . . . feasting on gall and wormwood." Olsen laughed when he looked at the song's title, then passed out the sheets to the singers and the band. "Sing it for the corpses," he said. They did, and after a while, Yellen remembered, "the corpses" joined in, "sardonically, hysterically, like doomed prisoners on their way to the firing squad."[18]

The song was "Happy Days Are Here Again."

To Yellen's eventual delight, the song would become the anthem of the Democratic Party, an enduring musical symbol of the relentless optimism with which the party became identified. That night, however, the patrons of the Hotel Pennsylvania had plenty of reason to think of it more as an ironic dirge, the proper accompaniment to the bitter end of an age that had flowered with near-mythic splendor. As journalist Frederick Lewis Allen would recall, the period between early 1923 and late 1929 represented "nearly seven years of unparalleled plenty; nearly seven years during which men and women . . . believed that at the end of the rainbow there was at least a pot of negotiable legal

17. Quoted in ibid.
18. Quotes in Klingaman, op. cit., p. 270.

tender. . . . For nearly seven years the prosperity bandwagon [had] rolled down Main Street."[19]

The pot at the end of that rainbow had been a democratic urn— anyone could hope to find it, seize it, and use its contents to finance other pot-hunting expeditions. So the litany of opportunity insisted, at any rate, and at one time or another during the decade, search parties bravely marched down every garden path of perceived opportunity.

In California, for instance. The state already was earning its reputation as a bellwether for the nation, particularly in southern California, where, in the sprawling village of Los Angeles, the dream of possibility had taken on a manic-depressive sheen. "The people on the top in Los Angeles, the Big Men," radical writer and sometime social worker Louis Adamic wrote in 1925, "are the businessmen, the Babbitts. . . . And trailing after the big boys is a mob of lesser fellows . . . all driven by the same motives of wealth, power, and personal glory."[20] These were the types who had ballyhooed the glories of the California climate into a boom at the beginning of the decade, when tens of thousands of new residents, most of them middle-class Midwesterners, streamed west every year. Traveling by train or by car along primitive highways into the broad environs of Los Angeles, they were drawn by a relentless siren song of advertising from organizations like the All-Year Club of southern California, which insisted that this paradise was just as benign in the summer as in the winter: "Sleep under a blanket every night all summer in Southern California."[21]

Waiting for the sunseekers was an army of real estate agents 43,000 strong, ready to sell lots as if they were lottery tickets. More than fourteen hundred new housing tracts sprang up, or were projected to spring up, approved by the Los Angeles Planning Department at the rate of forty a week by the middle of 1924. The value of real estate permits jumped from $28 million in 1919 to more than $200 million by 1924—about $1.9 billion in modern dollars.

19. Frederick Lewis Allen, *Only Yesterday*, p. 160.
20. Quoted in Carey McWilliams, *Southern California Country: An Island on the Land*, page 160.
21. Quoted in ibid., p. 137.

And then the boom died. By the end of 1924 there were more lots than there were people willing to buy them; banks, previously eager to make real estate loans, grew suddenly cool to new promotions and began calling in their money. Scores of subdivisions stood empty in the semi-arid plain and on the chapparal-covered hills of the Los Angeles Basin, their traffic-free streets and empty lots sprouting Russian thistle and gathering dust until whipped clean by the perennial Santa Ana winds.

Never mind. There was always oil. "Yes it's oil, oil, oil / That makes L.A. boil!" the members of the Uplifters Club of Los Angeles caroled in the club's roisterous official drinking song.[22] And there *was* oil, a great deal of oil, more oil in one region of the country than had ever before been found: beneath the sands of Huntington Beach, for example, where in November 1920 Standard Oil's Bolsa Chica No. 1 well began producing 20,000 barrels a day; or below the brushy slopes of Signal Hill over in Long Beach, where in June 1921 a gusher sent a spout of "black gold" 114 feet into the air; or under the alluvial soil of Santa Fe Springs out near Whittier, where in October 1921 a Union Oil Company drilling team brought in the first well in what one geologist would describe as "the greatest outpouring of mineral wealth the world has ever known.[23]

Where there was oil, however, there also were oil promoters. One of the most talented of them all was a Canadian-born real estate speculator named Courtney Chauncey Julian. In 1922, Julian bought four acres of Santa Fe Springs oil land and immediately started selling stock in the Julian Petroleum Company—"Julian Pete" it would come to be called—with a blizzard of extraordinarily effective newspaper advertisements. ("Julian Refuses to Accept Your Money Unless You Can Afford

22. Quoted in Kevin Starr, *Material Dreams: Southern California through the 1920s*, p. 85. One of this booster organization's most prominent members, Starr notes, was L. Frank Baum, author of *The Wizard of Oz*. "Los Angeles," Starr writes, ". . . was Oz come true; Southern California as a whole was Baum's Oz dream materialized" (p. 66).
23. Quoted in Jules Tygiel, *The Great Los Angeles Stock Swindle: Oil, Stocks, and Scandal During the Roaring Twenties*, p. 16.

to Lose!" one bellowed piously. "Widows and Orphans, This is No Investment for You!").[24]

In just six days, the campaign had brought in more than $60,000. Julian bought more advertisements, which generated more money, which inspired more advertisements, which brought in more money. By the time his company had actually struck oil in measurable (if less than colossal) amounts, Julian was well on his way. By the end of the year, his promotion had sucked in $11 million from 40,000 subscribers. He leased more oil property, sold even more stocks, bought and constructed gasoline stations around the Los Angeles Basin, and initiated a personal spending and boozing spree, throwing spectacular parties, commandeering nightclubs, bribing his way out of drunk-driving arrests, and in general heaping noisy contempt upon respectable Los Angeles society.

He continued to produce oil, but mostly he produced stock certificates, which soon represented more in face value than any of his assets could possibly hope to satisfy. Before either the California State authorities, with whom he was engaged in almost constant squabbles over his methodology, or his own creation could bring him down, he cannily sold Julian Pete to oil speculator Sheridan C. Lewis in 1924 and went off to promote a bloated lead-mining scheme in Death Valley. Lewis and his principal colleague, Jacob Berman, went to work swiftly. Julian Petroleum had been authorized to issue only 159,064 shares each of preferred and common stock. This was an inconvenient number for expansion plans; consequently, month after month, Berman manufactured carloads of stock certificates, and Lewis and his people peddled them frantically. Before they were done, Berman and Lewis had issued certificates representing about 3.7 million shares, at least 3.2 million of which were unauthorized.

This was simple, unadorned counterfeiting, which did not seem to discourage scores of investors, who simply pretended not to know about the ever-growing overissue. Forming huge investment pools—one of which reached a total value of $150 million—they demanded enormous returns on their money from the two promoters in exchange for their continued participation, taking their usurious profits, swiftly reinvest-

24. Quoted in ibid., p. 40. Tygiel's book is the best single source for this sorry episode in history.

ing much of these same profits in even more counterfeit stock. And on it went in a maddeningly complicated minuet of unbridled greed that ultimately included the governors of the Los Angeles Stock Exchange, much of the local brokerage industry, entire accounting firms, city and state officials, Hollywood moguls like Louis B. Mayer (who at one point flew into a snit when he was shorted $39.50 in a stock transaction involving thousands), underworld characters, political mavens, and many, many officers of many, many banks, not to mention tens of thousands of small investors who wanted a piece of the big petroleum pie.

Onward and upward and, ultimately, as always, downward. In 1927, the gore of the inevitable crash splattered some of the most important political, financial, and social figures in California. The fraud was estimated at $150 million, and several of the principals—though not C. C. Julian, originator of the feeding frenzy—went to jail amid a stew of charges ranging from stock fraud to mail fraud, conspiracy to usury. One banker was assassinated, while one fringe participant was shot to death in a gunfight with another fringe participant.

For audacity, avarice, complexity, color, and plain larceny, only the Florida real estate boom and bust of 1925–26 compares to the Julian Pete fiasco. Even more money was involved in the Florida boom. One estimate had it that, in 1925 alone, $450 million in outside money had poured into Florida, while the value in building permits throughout the state had soared to astronomical dimensions between July 1924 and July 1925—from $549,100 to $3.5 million in Miami Beach; $348,031 to $2.9 million in Tampa; and $48,500 to nearly $1.2 million in Hollywood, to name a few.[25] Ballyhoo proliferated, with none of it generated with more calculation than that spewing forth from the publicity machine of Addison Mizner, who purchased 16,000 undeveloped waterfront acres in Boca Raton and declared his intention to build a 1,000-room hotel, polo fields, golf courses, a "Venetian" canal, lagoons, lakes, tennis courts, and "the world's most beautiful boulevard." This was to accompany the growth of a great resort city on thousands of

25. Figures in Frank Parker Stockbridge and John Holliday Perry, *Florida in the Making*, pp. 290, 309. This 1925 screed was a shameless promotional device, but the figure of $450 million compares well with other estimates—and the building permit figures apparently were taken from public records. The equivalent today? About $4.2 billion.

available lots whose future value could only be imagined. Banks in Florida and neighboring Georgia were only too happy to loan him the money to finance this dream, and there were plenty of high society types who were eager to get in on the ground floor of this wonderfully exclusive opportunity. "Get the big snobs," Mizner said, "and the little snobs will follow."[26]

So they did, in Boca Raton and elsewhere, their eagerness fueled everywhere by tales of sudden and extraordinary luck. There was the story of the man who couldn't get $4,000 for his 80-acre tract in Sarasota in 1923. After he died, his inheritors sold it for $45,000—and a year later it went for $240,000. Or the story of the Chicago woman who had inherited a chunk of land near St. Petersburg that had cost $400. At the height of the boom, she visited the state, took a look at her property, and sold it for $600,000. "Exclamation points lose their emphasis when relating incidents like that," the authors of *Florida in the Making* wrote thrillingly in 1925. "Some of the stories of big money made in Florida real estate seem almost unbelievable, yet it seems likely that they will dwindle into insignificance beside the fortunes still to be made.[27] These were the kind of stories broadcast by the former secretary of state and greatest orator of his age, William Jennings Bryan, who was paid $100,000 a year by the developer of the new town of Coral Gables to publicize Florida's glories and tell the folks to come on down, take a look, and invest for themselves. Miami, Bryan declaimed in the middle of the boom, was "the only city in the world where you can tell a lie at breakfast that will come true by evening."[28]

Bryan died in 1925, a few days after his brave creationist testimony at the famous Scopes trial in Dayton, Tennessee, so he was not around to see all the lies bring the boom down in 1926. Collapse was accompanied by a hurricane that killed an estimated 400 people, left at least 25,000 homeless (and additional tens of thousands merely lotless), and created a landscape of physical ruin that provided an appropriate backdrop for the financial devastation many considered even worse. Bank

26. Quotes and Boca Raton story in Raymond B. Vickers, *Panic in Paradise: Florida's Banking Crash of 1926*, pp. 21–22.
27. Stockbridge and Perry, op. cit., pp. 295–96.
28. Quoted in Vickers, op. cit., p. 19.

transactions, which had swelled to more than a billion dollars a year by the end of 1925, dropped to a pitiful $143.3 million by 1928—and along the way, 150 banks in Florida and Georgia failed, taking with them more than $30 million in deposits.

Whatever their individual logistics, whether in land, oil, or any other form of flimflammery, whether in Los Angeles, Miami, Boston, or elsewhere, the speculative fevers were symptomatic of an economy so innocent of restraint and so prone to avarice that its acolytes either could not understand or chose to ignore the fact that fever, in economies as in humans, is not ordinarily a symptom of rampant good health. Thus was undertaken the definitive speculative adventure of the age, in which the "bandwagon of prosperity," having survived California and Florida, continued to career bravely through Main Street, America, only to veer recklessly into the New York Stock Exchange, where it was demolished in the most spectacular financial smashup in modern history.

FOR JOHN B. WATSON, one of the country's leading behavioral psychologists and a specialist in matters of the libido, the Wall Street fever of the twenties may have had something like a biological origin. In the relatively goatish atmosphere of the period, he maintained, "sex has become so free and abundant . . . that it no longer provides the thrill it once did. . . . [G]ambling in Wall Street is about the only thrill we have left."[29] While it is unlikely most investors actually believed that buying on margin and selling on the rise was better than sex, there is no denying the intensity with which they embraced this particular dalliance.

The affair can be said to have begun in earnest in 1924, when stock prices took a sudden sharp spurt upward, particularly after Coolidge's presidential victory in November. The comfort level that the business-minded Coolidge promised may not have been the only reason. The Federal Reserve Board had lowered its rediscount rate—the interest charged by the twelve individual banks in the Federal Reserve System to their member banks—in an effort to make money available for domestic industrial expansion and to encourage foreign investment in

29. Quoted in J. C. Furnas, *Great Times*, p. 523.

the United States. This, the theory went, would help stabilize the British pound, which the strains of World War I and its consequent debt load had left in a shaky condition. Stabilization of the pound might then strengthen attempts to reestablish gold as the linchpin of international commerce. The intricate dance of cooperation and communication among nations that a gold standard required had been all but obliterated during the war years, and the western nations were making every effort to get back to the relatively serene trade relationships that had preceded the war. Still, the gold standard would not be fully reinstated in the United States, Great Britain, and Europe until the middle of the decade—and it would prove to be not the foundation for future stability but one of the most prominent rocks upon which the economy of the age was wrecked.[30]

One unforeseen result of the Federal Reserve Board's action was to make more money available for investment in an increasingly attractive stock market. This was not what the Fed had in mind. "Stock market boom worries officials here," *The Kiplinger Washington Letter* reported on November 22, "but they can't do much about it. . . . You ask what Washington thinks of the stock market. Well, this is a situation in which Washington opinion is not worth much; Washington did not think the market would go as long and as high as it has; now thinks surely the break is near."[31] The break was not near. In May, the *New York Times* had reported the average price of twenty-five selected industrial stocks to be $106 a share; by the end of the year, it was $134, and a year later, $181.[32] During the same period, the volume of sales on the New York Stock Exchange rose from 54 million to 236 million.

Sales evened out in 1926, but the following year saw the Federal Reserve Board drop its rediscount rates once more, which pleased Treasury Secretary Andrew W. Mellon, who wanted easy credit for domestic expansion. This action, like that of 1924, was not solely responsible for

30. For the excruciatingly complex relationship between the Federal Reserve, rediscount rates, the gold standard, and the international economy in the early twenties, see Robert Sidelsky, *John Maynard Keynes: The Economist as Savior*, pp. 195–200, and Barry Eichengreen, *Golden Fetters: The Gold Standard and the Great Depression*, pp. 100–24 and 153–86.
31. The Kiplinger Washington Editors, op. cit., p. 11.
32. Statistics from John Kenneth Galbraith, *The Great Crash: 1929*, pp. 12–13.

the outsized proportions of the subsequent boom. Previous stock market eruptions had taken place regardless of the price of money, and there was plenty of capital available even without borrowing; between 1925 and 1929, the value of the nation's industrial output would rise from $60.8 billion to $67.7 billion, while savings and other time deposits would increase from $26.6 billion to $34.5 billion—the equivalent in modern dollars of more than $328 billion. But unquestionably the Fed's reduction did make it easier to borrow, and more and more such capital was being sucked off by the lure of the market; in 1927, sales on the New York Exchange climbed to an unprecedented 577 million shares.

There would soon be more. What came to be called the great "bull market" by enthusiasts and a "mass escape into make-believe" by economic historian John Kenneth Galbraith, began in early March 1928, fueled by the combination of a thirty-day jump in the *New York Times* industrial average of nearly 25 points and a parallel increase in the decibel level of stock promoters like Charles E. Mitchell.[33] "Sunshine Charlie" Mitchell was president of the National City Bank of New York, but in heart and experience he was less a banker than a high-octane financial pitchman who devoted the energies of his bank and its ever-growing number of branches to the selling of stocks and bonds in both National City and other corporations and investment operations. "Look down there," he would tell the bank's team of 350 salesmen during pep-talk lunches, rhetorically inviting them to get up from their creamed corn and rubbery chicken and look out from the windows of the Bankers Club in Manhattan on the noontime crowds scurrying antlike many floors below. "There are six million people with incomes that aggregate thousands of millions of dollars. They are just waiting for someone to come and tell them what to do with their savings. Take a good look, eat a good lunch, and then go down and sell them."[34]

And sell they did—they and thousands more like them in New York and anywhere in the nation where two or more were gathered in possibility's name, aided in their promotions by an enormous public-relations campaign directed by such consultant firms as the one-man operation called the McMahon Institute of Financial Research, or the

33. Ibid., p. 16.
34. Quoted in Klingaman, op. cit., p. 56.

equally ponderous Institute of Economic Research whose lone operator,
A. Newton Plummer, would later be accused by a congressional committee of having given more than a quarter of a million dollars to financial writers on the *Wall Street Journal*, the *New York Times*, and the *New
York Herald Tribune* in order to assure favorable comments on various
stocks.[35]

With promotional fuel fed to the fire regularly, the bull market
continued on into June, individual stocks like RCA and General Motors
gaining as much as 15 points in any given day. Then, on June 12, the
market suddenly appeared to break disastrously. "Wall Street's bull
market," the *New York Times* reported with unaccustomed liveliness the
next morning, "collapsed yesterday with a detonation heard round the
world. . . . It was a day of tumultuous, excited market happenings,
characterized by an evident effort on the part of the general public to
get out of stocks at what they could get. Individual losses were staggering."[36] Not staggering enough, apparently, to do anything but slow the
market down momentarily. By the end of November, half the losses of
June had been regained and by the end of the year, the *New York Times*
industrials had risen 86.5 points. The price of individual stocks bloated
beyond all expectation: on March 3, 1928, RCA had been going for $77
a share, but on December 31 it was over $400; so was Montgomery
Ward, which had started at $133.

All through this dizzying year the market had twitched in response
to every economic stimulus, however vague; stock after stock rose, then
fell, then rose again to new heights. Inspired by the same lambent greed
that had made California's Julian Pete adventure so distended and
fragile, brokers formed and massaged huge stock pools that, if not
flawed by the production of counterfeit stock certificates, were no less
inflated and profoundly risky. Nor were they any less tantalizing to
many who could not bring themselves, as one observer put it, to resist
"the lure of action, of quick profit, the thrill of battle, the call of the
chase . . . the glamor of admission into a charmed circle, the attraction
of a mysterious enterprise, and the social aura of association with the

35. See M. R. Werner, *Privileged Characters*, pp. 445–48.
36. Quoted in John Brooks, *Once in Golconda: A True Drama of Wall Street, 1920–1938*,
p. 95.

elect."[37] Perhaps the biggest pool of all was formed by William Crapo Durant, founder of General Motors, who was said to be manipulating as much as a billion dollars in pool investments by the end of 1928.

Pools were not the only games in town. Scores of equally rickety investment trusts and holding companies were created to speculate in nothing but stocks—and many of these, in turn, sold shares in themselves, building enormous paper pyramids whose only foundation was an abiding faith in permanent prosperity and the cleverness of their operators. Out in Chicago, utilities king Samuel Insull put together a complex structure of ownerships under the rubric of a trust called Insull Utilities Investments, and by the end of August had seen the trust's stock rise from $12 to more than $150, helping to bring his personal assets to $150 million. "My God," he exclaimed to a colleague. "A hundred and fifty million dollars! Do you know what I'm going to do? I'm going to buy me an ocean liner."[38] In January 1929 even the relatively staid officers of J. P. Morgan and Company authorized the issuance of 4.5 million shares of common stock in a holding company called the Allegheny Corporation; the shares opened at $37 and soon shot up to $56—an especially happy increase for those few, like John J. Raskob, chairman of the Democratic National Committee and principal backer of Alfred E. Smith's presidential candidacy, who had been privileged to buy the stock at $20. "Many thanks for your trouble and for so kindly remembering me," Raskob wrote his benefactor, Allegheny representative George Whitney, after being offered 2,000 shares at that price. "My check for forty thousand dollars is enclosed. . . . I appreciate deeply the many courtesies shown me by you and your partners, and sincerely hope the future holds opportunities for me to reciprocate."[39] Alas, Smith lost the election in November, depriving Raskob of some truly magnificent courtesies he might have been able to provide as the president's good right arm.

As 1928 turned, so did the market, upward at an increasingly vertiginous rate. Though there probably were less than a million actual participants, stocks had become the central issue of the day, even for

37. Quoted in ibid., p. 72.
38. Quoted in Forrest McDonald, *Insull*, p. 282.
39. Quoted in Werner, op. cit., p. 449.

those who had nothing directly at stake.[40] "You could talk about prohibition, or Hemingway, or air-conditioning, or music, or horses," a visiting British journalist reported, "but in the end you had to talk about the stock market, and that was when the conversation became serious."[41] Most of the players were men, but there were estimates that by 1929, 20 percent of them now were women. "For a year," journalist Eunice Fuller Barnard wrote in the April issue of the *North American Review*,

> indeed, all through the recent bull market, women by the hundreds have sat, and even stood in tense rows in the special stock-brokers' rooms set aside for them in various hotels of Upper Broadway [in New York City]. Day in and day out through a long five hours, aggressive, guttural dowagers, gum-chewing blondes, shrinking spinsters, who look as if they belonged in a missionary-society meeting, watch, pencil in hand, from the opening of the market till the belated ticker drones its last in the middle of the afternoon.[42]

Whether male or female, in hotel rooms redolent of perfume and powder in midtown Manhattan or in brokerage offices rank with cigar smoke on State Street in Chicago, Montgomery Street in San Francisco, Spring Street in Los Angeles, or similar enclaves of commerce around the country, thousands of players were able to participate only because they bought their chips on margin—paying anywhere from 10 percent to 20 percent of the face value of their stocks to a broker; the remainder of the stock's value stood as a loan from the broker (for which the borrower's certificates served as collateral). Brokers, in turn, got the money

40. Some particularly inflated contemporary estimates put the number of participants at 17 million, a figure no one now accepts. My estimate comes from Lewis Corey's 1934 book, *The Decline of American Capitalism*, a didactic, sometimes shrill, but uncommonly well-documented analysis of capitalism's most glaring flaws. "In 1928," Corey wrote, "470,889 out of 4,070,851 income-taxpayers reported profits from the sale of stocks, bonds, and real estate, another 27,704 reported capital net gains, and 72,829 reported speculative losses. The total is 571,422 persons, not all of whom were necessarily active speculators, offset by others who did not report. In all probability the number of speculators was 750,000 and definitely not over 1,000,000" (p. 176).
41. Quoted in Klingaman, op. cit., p. 54.
42. Eunice Fuller Barnard, "Ladies of the Ticker," *North American Review* (April 1929).

to finance such loans from the banking community, which found little to complain about in a system that allowed it to borrow money from the Federal Reserve banks at 5 percent and loan it out at 12 percent, or from capital-rich industrial corporations like Standard Oil of New Jersey, which in 1929 devoted $97.8 million of its profits to such "call money" loans—and earned $4.9 million in interest from the practice.[43] More millions were poured into the brokerage market from abroad, especially from Great Britain—even though the drain of money seriously depleted that country's gold reserves, making it increasingly difficult to keep the gold standard raft from foundering.

More than $6.4 billion in broker's loans had been made by the end of 1928 (by contrast, the income of the entire federal government for that year was only $3.9 billion). This began to worry the Federal Reserve Board, which had already raised the rediscount rate, albeit somewhat timidly, in an effort to slow speculation. It had not helped. "So far as the board is concerned," one financial writer explained early in 1929, "it does not view the broker loans themselves as dangerous. But the diversion of funds to speculative channels which ought to be available for the normal needs of the country, especially in harvest seasons and in periods of necessary constructive activity, is regarded as a menace to the whole economic structure."[44]

The Fed's anxiety was echoed in Great Britain, where the Bank of England raised its own interest rates from 4.5 percent to 5.5 percent in an effort to stem the hemorrhaging of reserves. The Federal Reserve did not follow suit. Instead, on February 2, 1929, the board chose to scold the financial community. The Federal Reserve Act, the board insisted, "does not . . . contemplate the use of the resources of the Federal Reserve System for the creation or extension of speculative credit." When that admonition seemed to alarm the financial world, however, the board issued an assurance a few days later that it had "no disposition to assume authority to interfere with the loan practices of member banks so long as they do not involve the Federal Reserve banks."[45] Thereafter, the board maintained a silence that many interpreted as

43. See Werner, op. cit., p. 443.
44. Quoted in Klingaman, op. cit., p. 113.
45. Both quotes from Brooks, op. cit., pp. 99–100.

ominous; money suddenly became tight, and the market took a dramatic lurch downward at the end of March—until "Sunshine Charlie" Mitchell announced that National City Bank would continue to pump money into the call market no matter what the Fed might think, and backed up his words with $25 million in loans. The market quickly recovered. Between the end of May and the end of July, the *New York Times* industrial averages rose 77 points. More than $5.8 billion in brokers' loans had been made just in July (by year's end the total would be more than $8.5 billion). The gains of some individual stocks were nearly incomprehensible; National City stock leaped $500 a share in value in a single day in July; on another day that month, the total value of American Telephone and Telegraph (AT&T) stock increased by more than $75.8 million. On August 8, the Federal Reserve finally did what speculators had been fearing for months: it raised its rediscount rate from 5 percent to 6 percent.

The squeeze came too late to have much effect. Once again, the market stumbled briefly, then recovered. By the end of the month, more than 95.7 million shares had been exchanged and the *New York Times* reported that the value of its 240 representative stocks had risen by more than $4.4 billion. "Wall Street has become another world power," Lord Rothermere, proprietor of the *London Daily Mail*, wrote in July, "with more authority than the League of Nations, and more subtlety than Bolshevism."[46] Perhaps, perhaps not—but it was clear that the arcane world of Wall Street speculation was now the main arena in which the great game of prosperity was being played, however ambiguous the rules, however unthinking the hope. And there would be nothing subtle about its collapse.

THERE HAD BEEN plenty of Cassandras to provide a litany of pessimism throughout the boom years, of course. As far back as January 1925, Senator Henrik Shipstead of Minnesota had spoken out against the loose money policies of the Federal Reserve: "[T]he greatest menace which I see in the present situation is the effect upon [a] hundred million minds . . . when it at last dawns upon the common man . . . that our

46. Quoted in Klingaman, op. cit., p. 159.

boasted national prosperity hangs, not upon the productive industry and wage earning toil but upon the use of government financial functions in aiding the stock market operations."[47] Shipstead was one of the youngest of a collection of midwestern and western senators who cheerfully accepted their description as "The Sons of the Wild Jackass," chief among them Hiram Johnson of California, William E. Borah of Idaho, George Norris of Nebraska, and "Young Bob" La Follette of Wisconsin, the inheritor of the reformist mantle of his father, "Fighting Bob," who had died a few months after being defeated in the 1924 presidential elections. These men and their supporters remained generally true to the principles of liberal progressivism all through the decade of Coolidge Republicanism, constituting a narrow but vital philosophical and political bridge between the turn-of-the-century "Square Deal" of Theodore Roosevelt and the "New Deal" years of Franklin Roosevelt that were still to come. Among their most enduring targets was the stock market.

While the opposition of the "Wild Jackasses" was dismissed by most of those on the Street as the reflexive sputtering of hayseed demagogues, Shipstead and his colleagues were not the only ones beginning to suspect that the great bubble of Wall Street was doomed sooner or later to be pricked. Financier Paul M. Warburg, who had helped to write the legislation that created the Federal Reserve System in 1913 and had served on the first Federal Reserve Board from 1914 to 1918, found himself in general agreement with critics of both the stock market and the board. It was time to act, he wrote on March 7, 1929: "If orgies of unrestrained speculation are permitted to spread too far . . . the ultimate collapse is certain not only to affect the speculators themselves, but also to bring about a general depression involving the entire country."[48] Warburg was immediately excoriated by his Wall Street compatriots, who accused him of "sandbagging American prosperity" and hinted darkly that he might be involved in a short-selling scheme.[49]

---

47. Quoted in Cedric B. Cowing, *Populists, Plungers, and Progressives: A Social History of Stock and Commodity Speculation, 1890–1936*, p. 133.
48. Quoted in Ron Chernow, "Father of the Fed," *Audacity* (Fall 1993).
49. Quoted in Galbraith, op. cit., p. 77.

Neither complaint nor warning from any quarter had any appreciable effect on the constantly rising market, however, until financial analyst Roger Babson made a noontime speech before the annual meeting of the National Business Conference in New York on September 5. Babson, who had been "bearish" with regard to the market for two years, was even more gloomily specific than Warburg. "Sooner or later a crash is coming," he announced baldly, "and it may be terrific." He estimated that the Dow-Jones average would plummet anywhere from 60 to 80 points and that "factories will shut down . . . men will be thrown out of work . . . the vicious circle will get in full swing, and the result will be a serious business depression."[50] Nonsense, cried the ever-optimistic Professor Irving Fisher of the Harvard Economic Society: "There may be a recession in stock prices, but not anything in the nature of a crash."[51]

For a while, it seemed as if the professor would be proved right. True, on the afternoon of September 5, after news flashes spread Babson's doomsday remarks around the country and reporters started calling brokers for comment, the market slumped sharply, sell orders coming in faster than brokers could handle them. By the end of the day, the New York Times industrials had dropped a full 10 points and more than 5.5 million shares had been traded. But the next day, after Fisher's remarks had been given equal time, the market began what appeared to be a strong recovery; this time, industrials gained an average of 10 points. The market, nonetheless, remained in an unsettled condition from that point on, rises and declines following one another repeatedly over the next several weeks, putting the glow of nervous sweat on the foreheads of brokers from Atlanta to Seattle. Professor Fisher hastened to assure everyone that the ragged performance of the market during September and the first half of October had been a temporary thing. On October 16, he told inquiring reporters that prices had reached "what looks like a permanently high plateau" and that he fully expected to see the market go "a good deal higher than it is today."[52]

It did not. Beginning on Monday, October 21, the New York Stock Exchange and all its fellow exchanges helplessly witnessed an eight-day

50. Quoted in ibid., pp. 89–90.
51. Quoted in ibid., p. 91.
52. Quoted in Frederick Lewis Allen, *Only Yesterday*, p. 323.

Armageddon during which the gross value of Investment America was nearly exsanguinated. Monday and Tuesday saw steady declines and rising volume, most of which activity was fretfully explained away as "technical readjustment," but on Wednesday the true shape of disaster began to reveal itself. Economic reporter Matthew Josephson was only a modest player, but he remembered that day for the rest of his life: "I heard—and I can still hear it—the sound of running feet, the sound of fear, as people hastened to reach posts of observation before the gong rang for the opening of trading. Hypnotized by their panic, the crowds in the boardrooms stared in horror at the stockboards or the tape recording their progressive ruin."[53]

The tape was 104 minutes late when the gong echoed from the walls of the Exchange on the twenty-third. More than 6 million shares had been traded, many of them in liquidation sales. The *New York Times* industrial averages had started the day at 415 and ended at 384. The next day—Thursday, October 24—started out even worse. The ticker tape was already forty-eight minutes late by 11:30 in the morning as sell orders on the floor of the Exchange sent up an incomprehensible din of entreaty—often greeted by no response at all from buyers. Nevertheless, some five million shares had already been traded by then and eight million dollars a minute was being exchanged. Wastebaskets overflowed with call slips. Prices were sliding with every passing moment. Crowds began to gather out on Wall Street.

At noon, when trading shut down for lunch, a hastily convened gathering of the country's leading bankers took place in the velvet-draped offices of the House of Morgan at 20 Wall Street. After the meeting, Thomas W. Lamont held a brief press conference. "There has been a little distress selling on the Stock Exchange," he said calmly, "and we have held a meeting of the heads of several financial institutions to discuss the situation."[54]

What the bankers had decided to do was to stem the bleeding by packing the wound with money. At 1:30 P.M., their emissary, Richard Whitney, acting (and soon to be permanent) president of the Exchange,

53. Matthew Josephson, *The Money Lords*, pp. 89–90.
54. Quoted in Tom Shachtman, *The Day America Crashed: A Narrative Account of the Great Stock Market Crash of October 24, 1929*, p. 168.

strode manfully onto the floor and started bidding on stocks: U.S. Steel, RCA, General Motors, AT&T, and others. Within minutes he had pumped somewhere between twenty and thirty million dollars into the market. It worked—at least for the day. Sell orders slowed, buy orders increased, some stocks began to creep up. Industrial averages declined only twelve points, less than half that of the previous day—and U.S. Steel actually gained a couple of points. But there had been too much activity for anyone to take real hope: when the gong sounded, the ticker was more than four hours behind, and when it clicked out the last transaction of the day at a little after 7:00 P.M., the total volume traded had exceeded 12.8 million shares. Those few diners sitting next to the dance floor to hear the debut of "Happy Days Are Here Again" in the Hotel Pennsylvania that night had plenty of reason to bring raw mockery to their sing-along.

Volume remained high on Friday and during the half day of trading on Saturday, but prices seemed to stabilize. "We believe," a broker told reporters in time for the Monday morning papers, "that the investor who purchases securities at this time . . . may do so with absolute confidence."[55] Not really. Selling began in earnest at 10:00 A.M. on Monday and continued on into the next day—"Black Tuesday," October 29. No one had ever witnessed anything like this day of trading. People began to collect under the big brooding statue of Alexander Hamilton in front of the Exchange building as word of what was happening on the Exchange floor drifted like rancid wood smoke through downtown New York. Soon there were ten thousand people in the narrow street. Some took to religion, wandering to sit numbly in the pews of nearby Trinity Church. There was reason enough for prayer. Inside the Exchange, brokers stood on the floor gape-mouthed and weeping while the losses mounted in a frenzy of sales that by closing had surpassed 16.4 million shares. The *Times* industrials had sunk 43 points, obliterating every gain made since the Bull Market of 1929 had begun. Most of the 751 fabulous trusts that had been created since 1927 were ruined, and with them hundreds of thousands of investors.

More than $10 billion in market value—about $95 billion in today's money—had vanished in a mere five hours of trading. The full

55. Quoted in Galbraith, op. cit., p. 112.

scope of the catastrophe would not be known until the following morning, when all the tallies were done, but only fools pretended the wounds
were not mortal. You do not need an autopsy to determine the fact of a
death, only the cause, and there was no escaping the brute certainty of
this day's extinction: the chimera of limitless prosperity that had colored the age had vanished like the hallucinations of a drunk on the
morning after, the dream's bright substance draining away at the rate of
$2 billion an hour.

I

IN THE CRUCIBLE

[W]ith the breakdown of our economic life, we had no sense of national destiny. It was not enough to know that we were always to be rich and lead the world in comfort, and the inadequacy . . . was, of course, most apparent when it was proved that it had led us astray. We had for twenty years been throwing overboard the burden of libertarian ideals; we were not the country of free speech or free press or free assembly; we were not the country of the rights of labor; we were not free of religious prejudice; we were not interested in social justice . . . we heard of starvation wages and child labor and barbarous cruelty in chain gangs as if these were natural episodes in the brilliant newsreel of our lives. So long as they passed quickly, they did not matter.

—Gilbert Seldes,
from *The Years of the Locust*
(*America, 1929–1932*), 1932.

1

Boundaries of Havoc

Conventional interpretation maintains that at few times in American history has the human tendency to stare economic catastrophe straight in the face without recognizing it been demonstrated more precisely than in the year or so that followed the stock market crash of October 1929. As a naturalized Central European immigrant working in the Overland automobile works asked a companion, "What t'ell does the stock market have to do with us Overland hunkies? I ain't buyin' no General Motors common or Willys-Overland preferred, are you?"[1] Among those who should have known better, Herbert Hoover himself appeared to be one of the blind leading the blind. "The fundamental business of the country, that is, production and distribution, is on a sound and prosperous basis," the president had announced on October 25, 1929, the day after the stock market debacle of "Black Thursday," as the day already was known.[2] And he kept a generally cheerful face turned to the public (or at least as cheerful as his physiognomy allowed), even after "Black Thursday" was followed by "Black Tuesday,"

1. Quoted in Jack Conroy, "Hard Winter," *The American Mercury* (February 1931).
2. Quoted in Smith, op. cit., p. 116.

October 29, and then by a period in the first two weeks of November during which "the market continued to act like a rubber ball bounding down statistical stairs," in the memorable phrase of historian Harris Gaylord Warren, and the *New York Times* industrial averages dropped by another 87 points.[3]

But during a series of conferences with leading industrialists that began in November, Hoover made it clear that his insistence on public optimism derived less from his inability to comprehend facts than from his firm belief that if melancholy were allowed to overcome the public mind, the situation would become infinitely worse than it already was. "Fear, alarm, pessimism, and hesitation," he told the December 14 meeting of the Gridiron Club in Washington in explaining why public optimism had been vital (carefully putting the unpleasantness in the past tense), "swept through the country, which, if unchecked, would have precipitated absolute panic throughout the business world with untold misery in its wake."[4] At the same time, when confronting business leaders privately, Hoover warned them that the nation's economy was on the edge of the abyss and that public cheerfulness would have to be wedded to action by them if a major depression was to be avoided. Most promised faithfully to continue investing in their own and other industries and to maintain wages at current levels. Henry Ford, for one, said he would not only maintain wages but raise them to $7 a day and at the same time increase his capital investment by $25 million in 1930, while the president of the National Electric Light Association told Hoover that the members of the association would commit themselves to an investment of at least $110 million more than they had spent the previous year.

On the face of it, the business community seemed to share Hoover's faith in the healing powers of public optimism. "A serious depression is not on the business horizon," noted *The Kiplinger Washington Letter* with emphasis on December 9. "Indeed, there were plenty of hardheaded unsentimental men at this conference [a Washington, D.C., gathering] who sincerely believe that 1930 will be what they call a 'good year.'"[5]

3. Warren, op. cit., p. 117.
4. Quoted in ibid., p. 114.
5. The Kiplinger Washington Editors, op. cit., p. 19.

Wall Street appeared to believe it. Richard Whitney, for example, now president of the New York Stock Exchange, wore confidence like an expensive aftershave lotion and simply refused to let gloom overtake him or his bank's brokers. "Now get your smiles on, boys!" he would cry before sending them off to their sales chores every morning.[6] "With satisfaction that a degree of sanity appears to be returning to our investment community," *Nation's Business* editorialized a little smugly in its December 1929 issue, "and with sympathy for those whose losses have been the sacrificial instruments of restoration, we may view the matter as a manifestation of herd psychology . . . the mob was obsessed."[7] By the end of the year, the market had recovered so markedly that Whitney and the Exchange board threw an even bigger New Year's Eve party than usual, featuring the 369th Infantry band playing patriotic airs and other uplifting music right in the middle of the floor while trading was still going on. Friends and relatives of the members were invited and noisemakers handed out. "Pinning tails on the traders," the *New York Times* reported on January 1, 1930, "became the popular sport of the afternoon." When the gong was sounded, the *Times* continued, "the members broke into a pandemonium of noise, everything in the Exchange that had noisemaking possibilities being utilized. The din could be heard as far away as Broadway."

The "Little Bull Market" continued through the spring, bringing forth all manner of brave statements. In May, Secretary of Commerce William Doak allowed as how "normal business conditions should be restored in two or three months," and in June, when a group of clergy arrived at the White House with some suggestions on how the government should respond to the depression, Hoover told them, "Gentlemen, you have come six weeks too late."[8] Writing in the elegant June 1930 issue of the brand-new *Fortune* magazine—just the fifth number in Henry Luce's attempt to give business America its own flagship publication—analyst Merryle Stanley Rukeyser gave Hoover high marks: "I am one of those who think that the engineer in the White House made

6. Quoted in Brooks, op. cit., p. 128.
7. Quoted in Warren, op. cit., p. 112.
8. Quoted in Smith, op. cit., p. 117.

a magnificent gesture to stem psychological panic and to demonstrate that the human will could be an effective contributing cause in shaping the course of the business cycle."[9]

Six months later, *Fortune* cheerily announced that "the year 1930 . . . left behind it impressive monuments to U.S. industrial confidence"—RCA Victor's new radio manufacturing plant in Camden, New Jersey, for example, built at a cost of $5.5 million that year; or Continental Can Company's brand-new $1.25 million plant in Oakland, California; or the huge, new $30 million complex built by Allied Chemical & Dye in Hopewell, Virginia; or the $2 million plant for the manufacture of mechanical rubber goods put up in Passaic, New Jersey, by U.S. Rubber. And there was much, much more, *Fortune* promised: "To compute the total construction investment of U.S. industry in 1930 would be a mathematical undertaking of colossal complexity and of small importance. The enormous total *could* be set down on paper. The important, the significant fact is that these buildings now stand and project themselves into the solvent decades of the future as monuments and implements of the age."[10]

In spite of all the optimism from nearly every quarter, however, one wonders whether the business community truly believed its own rhetoric. Some corporations did attempt to hold wage levels and increase investment, but most paid little more than lip service to the promises they had made to Hoover, even when they had the resources to do so. This was especially true of investments. Between the end of 1929 and the end of 1930, in fact, gross domestic investment by the private sector declined from $35 billion to $23.6 billion and would fall to a low of $3.9 billion by the end of 1932—a drop of more than 88.6 percent in just three years. Investment in producers' durable equipment and non-residential construction—which meant business and industrial plant construction, for the most part—dropped from $23.3 billion in 1929 to $19.2 billion in 1930, and all the way down to $10.1 billion in 1932.[11] Even Henry Ford's vaunted $7-a-day promise was not everything it seemed. First, he did not even put it into effect until 1931; sec-

9. Merryle Stanley Rukeyser, "Current Styles," *Fortune* (June 1930).
10. "The Major Industrial Monuments of the Year," *Fortune* (December 1930).
11. Investment statistics from Lester V. Chandler, *America's Greatest Depression*, pp. 21–22.

ond, to hold that wage level he had to fire thousands of his own workers, then subcontract much of Ford's work out to independent companies that paid as little as 12.5 cents an hour.

  Industrial America could hardly be blamed for hedging its bets. Except for those few brief months of optimism on the floor of the New York Stock Exchange, there was not that much to cheer about. Earnings for the first quarter of 1930 told much of the story. Two hundred companies surveyed by the National City Bank had earned $362 million in the first quarter of 1929; in 1930, the figure was $293.3 million, an average decline of about 19 percent. The hardest hit was the automotive industry, where 34 companies showed an overall slide of 40 percent. General Motors fell from $61.9 million to $44.9 million, and Hudson from $4.5 million to $2.1 million. Railroad profits were cut anywhere from 12 percent (Boston & Maine) to a horrific 84 percent (Chicago, Rock Island & Pacific). The only major corporations that actually increased profits significantly in 1930 were those in the fields of advertising, radio, and motion pictures (and their day of reckoning would come).[12] Given the fact that hundreds of millions of dollars had been invested and lost in the stock market during the weeks of the great panic—much of this money carved out of 1929's superb profit figures—and the fact that the decline in overall profits would keep on plunging after the first quarter of 1930 until for many companies they sank clear through the bottom of the statistical page into the realm where deficits lay, the average businessman or private investor no longer had that much money on hand to invest—and those who did have it were suddenly reluctant to part with it. There would be even less on hand as the months of disaster rolled on, one after the other, each month adding to a gray pyramid of statistics no one could have imagined and few wanted to believe. Not Hoover, not the business community, not anyone.

HOWEVER STUBBORNLY THE nation's sundry leaders tried to defy reality by sending up increasingly gaseous balloons of optimism, what happened to the financial structure of this country between the early winter of 1929 and the summer of 1933 was nothing less than the single worst recession in the economic history of the United States. Both the speed

12. Statistics in "Corporation Earnings," *Fortune* (June 1930).

and character of the decline had never been experienced before and have not since.

Consider the banking industry. Previous to World War I, bank failures were relatively uncommon affairs; between 1865 and 1920, there had been only 3,108 banks whose operations had been suspended—and 326 of those had closed during the terrible panic of 1893. But between the end of 1920 and the end of 1929, an average of 635 banks had failed *every year*, 976 in the boom year of 1926 alone, with a total loss that year of $1.6 billion in deposits (nearly $15 billion in 1998 dollars). If those numbers suggested a certain instability in the banking system throughout the boom years of the twenties—poor regulation, incompetent management, thoughtless investment in the California and Florida real estate booms, an increasing infatuation with the seductions of the broker's-loan market come to mind—that deduction was given even more validity in 1930. That year, the number of failures shot up to 1,352—256 of them in the single month of November, and even more on December 11, when the United States Bank, with deposits of more than $200 million, went under.

"It was a terrible time," one depositor remembered of the day the United States Bank closed. "You felt as though the bottom had dropped out of your life, and I guess the thing that bothered me most was the fact that there had been no notice. . . . [Many] people felt that one reason the other banks didn't want to [help] was because that was a minority bank—it was owned by and run by Jewish stockholders and a Jewish president."[13] There was reason to speculate along such lines. When the New York State superintendent of banks proposed that the House of Morgan take the United States Bank under its wing in order to save it—a service the nearly impregnable firm had provided other banks in trouble—his appeal was rejected, quite possibly because, as Morgan partner Russell Leffingwell described the firm, it was "an uptown bank with many branches and a large clientele among our Jewish population of small merchants, and persons of small means and small education."[14]

Whether class prejudice and genteel anti-Semitism prevented the rescue of the United States Bank or not, its subsequent collapse was at

13. Pearl Max, Blackside interview (January 23, 1992).
14. Quoted in Ron Chernow, *The House of Morgan*, pp. 326–27.

the time the largest single bank failure in American history, bringing a certain drama to the situation. Congress passed joint resolutions, held hearings, debated legislation. "In the meantime," C. D. Bremer, a Columbia University professor of economics, wrote in 1935, "while our financial soothsayers continued to deliver themselves of their Delphic oracles, failures were rapidly increasing." In all, $3.26 billion in deposits had been lost in just three years.[15]

"Since 1930," a British visitor to the United States wrote in 1932,

> the most despised and detested group of men in the Union is the bankers. . . . A story has been going the rounds to the effect that a certain lady, distressed to know that her daughter was about to become the mother of a fatherless infant, was told that its parentage had been accepted by a banker. She at once refused to admit any such acknowledgment. "Rather a bastard than a banker," she declared, with a spirit in which the voice of the nation is audible.[16]

If bankers had earned a special niche in the disregard of most Americans, however, the statistical epidemic ran just as swiftly through the rest of the business community in the years of havoc. The 1,372 bank failures of 1930 represented only a fraction of the 26,355 businesses that collapsed that year, and the rate of 122 failures per 10,000 businesses was the highest in history. Then the rate jumped to 133 in 1931, with 28,285 failures, and to 154 in 1932 with 31,822 failures—numbers that have yet to be equaled. Altogether, the number of businesses in the country dropped from a total of 2.2 million in 1929 to 1.9 million by 1933. The combined deficit of American corporations was $5.64 billion in 1932. In agriculture, the parity index—the prices farmers received for the products they sold, as compared to the prices they had to pay for everything they needed—fell from 89, already a negative figure, to 55. The value of farm property declined from $57.7 million in 1929 to $36.2 million in 1933. Unemployment, estimated

---

15. C. D. Bremer, *American Bank Failures*, p. 13; all bank failure statistics I cite are from this source.
16. Mary Agnes Hamilton, "In America Today"; in Allen Nevins, ed., *America through British Eyes*, p. 443.

at 1.5 million in 1929, rose to 4.3 million in 1930, 8 million in 1931, 12 million in 1932, 12.8 million in 1933—24.9 percent of the civilian labor force. Wages in the manufacturing sector dropped from $16 billion in 1929 to less than $7.7 billion in 1932, and in all industries from $50.4 billion to $30 billion. Per capita income, adjusted for inflation, fell from $681 in 1929 to $495 in 1933, and at one point 28 percent of the population—34 million people—had no income at all. The gross national product plunged from $104 billion in 1929 to $41 billion in 1933.[17]

In some cities and regions the situation for workers was a good deal worse than even the national averages suggested. As early as February 1930, the state of Oregon had already reached 25 percent unemployment, according to the state labor commissioner—three years before the nation as a whole achieved that pinnacle.[18] In Jefferson County, Alabama, there were about 108,000 salaried workers. "Of that number," Congressman George Huddleston told a congressional committee in January 1932, "it is my belief that not exceeding 8,000 have their normal incomes. At least 25,000 men are altogether without work. Some of them have not had a stroke of work for more than twelve months, maybe 60,000 or 75,000 are working from one to five days a week, and practically all have had serious cuts in their wages and many of them do not average over $1.50 a day."[19]

Two months earlier, it had been even more grim in Detroit, where more than 30 percent of the labor force—223,000 people—were without work; and a little over a year later, the figures had gone up to 50

17. Some statistics from Chandler, op. cit.; remainder from *The Statistical History of the United States*. Again, some comparisons are useful here. The $200 million in lost deposits of the Bank of the United States in December 1930 translates to nearly $2 billion in 1998 dollars—a figure that can hold its own against some of the most appalling wrecks that characterized the S & L crisis of the 1990s. And consider the impact on today's economy if the gross national product were to lose more than 60 percent of its value in just four years. Even in the most severe recessions of recent time, economic decline has never come close to reaching such depths. If it should, a national debt now approaching $5 *trillion*—so large as to be little more than an abstraction in the mind of anyone but an economist—would seem but a trifle when put against the very real financial devastation that could be measured in terms of simple human misery.
18. See William H. Mullins, *The Depression and the Urban West Coast, 1929–1933: Los Angeles, San Francisco, Seattle and Portland*, p. 24.
19. Quoted in Chandler, op. cit., p. 43.

percent and 350,000, respectively. Chicago was not much better off; about 624,000 people were unemployed in October 1931—40 percent of the labor force. In Colorado, the State Federation of Labor estimated that some 90 percent of the state's workers were getting less than three days of work a week and that 50 percent "or more are not working even part-time."[20] In West Virginia, coal production—the state's biggest industry—dropped from 145.1 million tons in 1927 to 83.2 million tons in 1932; more than half of all the mines in the state had closed, throwing so many people out of work that more than 135,000 families were said to be in a destitute condition by 1933.[21] In Boston, between July 1931 and December 1932, unemployment averaged 29.72 percent, representing anywhere from 90,000 to 100,000 people.[22]

And stock speculation, that magic carpet of the twenties? The "Little Bull Market" of late 1929 and early 1930 did not survive the spring. Losses among many individual stocks were as monstrous as many of their earnings had been during the "Big Bull Market" days. Consider what happened to Goldman, Sachs & Company, originators of one of the biggest of all the investment trusts. Its fate was revealed in a colloquy in June 1932 between Senator James Couzens of Michigan and Walter Sachs of Goldman, Sachs during a congressional hearing into the stock market crash:

"Did Goldman, Sachs and Company organize the Goldman, Sachs Trading Corporation?" Senator Couzens asked.

"Yes, sir," Mr. Sachs replied.

"And it sold its stock to the public?"

"A portion of it. The firm invested originally in 10 percent of the entire issue for the sum of $10 million."

"And the other 90 percent was sold to the public?"

"Yes, sir."

"At what price?"

"At 104. That is the old stock . . . the stock was split two for one."

20. Quoted in Stephen J. Leonard, *Trials and Triumphs: A Colorado Portrait of the Great Depression*, p. 23.

21. Figures in James S. Olson, "The Depths of the Great Depression: Economic Collapse in West Virginia, 1932–1933," *West Virginia History* (April 1977).

22. See Charles H. Trout, *Boston: The Great Depression and the New Deal*, p. 81.

"And what is the price of the stock now?"

"Approximately 1¾."[23]

"It took me twenty years to figure out what happened," one victim
remembered of those days. "I always figured there was some kind of
logic I didn't understand. Maybe it was some kind of lack in me. 'Cause
I was brought up in a middle-class family: all the privileges, the house
with the servant—all of a sudden, one day it's all gone."[24]

This individual was hardly alone, in either his misery or his mystification. For him and most others who lived through it, the misery would
pass by the end of the decade, but much of the mystification remained.
How was it that an economy that had been riding so high for so long
could be brought so low? Who was to blame? It certainly was not
their fault, the engineers of the stock market wanted everyone to
know, as reporter Matthew Josephson discovered when he interviewed
Richard Whitney in December 1931. "He was enthroned in the regal
presidential suite on an upper floor of the Exchange," Josephson
remembered, "dressed in a black cutaway, and carried himself with
reserve as he spoke. I found his smile an affair of facial muscles, and his
eyes cold; he was tense underneath." The stock market "would come
back," Whitney insisted, "it always does." As for finding blame within
the market for the debacle that followed October 1929, that was nonsense, he said. "The public," Whitney explained impatiently, "is looking for a goat."[25]

It is true enough that the stock market crash of 1929 was not the
single primary "cause" of the relentless spiral of decline that characterized the worst years of the Great Depression. Nevertheless, its role in
helping to shape the dimensions of the catastrophe should not be
underestimated. It not only loosed the virus of depression by imposing
a trauma on the entire financial system so devastating that it was left in
a state of shock, but it also accelerated the spread of economic decline.
This was due to the fact that the failure of the greatest speculative fever

23. Quoted in Galbraith, op. cit., pp. 64–65.
24. Quoted in Studs Terkel, *Hard Times: An Oral History of the Great Depression*, p. 519.
25. Quoted in Josephson, op. cit., pp. 104–5. Whitney himself would become something of a "goat," as he might have put it, when, later in the decade, he was convicted
of grand larceny and sent to Sing-Sing prison.

in American history profoundly weakened confidence in the basic soundness (as politicians liked to put it) of the nation's economic foundations—its abundance of natural resources, its wealth of available labor, its demonstrated genius for industrial innovation and productivity, its pool of capital reserves, all the tangible and intangible assets that go to make up the gross national product. "If you consider the universality of the speculative mania of the later days of the last boom," banker J. M. Barker remembered in 1936,

> you will see how completely the people of this country, to say nothing of the world, were under the influence of the mob psychology of unreasoning, emotional cupidity. When the break came, cupidity turned into unreasoning, emotional, universal fear. . . . In every city of this country, business men, hard hit or already wiped out in the stock market in the earlier part of the crash, were still watching the quotations every day to see how things were going. They saw the market dropping, dropping, dropping. Is there any doubt they made their decisions from day to day under the influence of the emotional backgrounds formed by their observations of the falling security prices?[26]

Still, the argument is frequently made that the principal significance of the crash was its role as the first dramatic symptom of an underlying weakness in the economy. Certainly, there can be no denying the weakness—illustrated perhaps most precisely by the fact that because both wage levels and agricultural income remained low for so many throughout the decade, the disparity between the haves and the have-nots grew during even the biggest boom years, until, as historian Robert McElvaine has noted, "the share of disposable income going to the top 1 percent jumped from 12 percent in 1920 to 19 percent in 1929. . . . This represented the highest concentration of wealth at any time in American history."[27]

Such disparities were harmful not merely because they violated democratic ideals but because what they signified was that, at the same

26. Quoted in Milton Friedman and Anna Jacobson Schwartz, *The Great Contraction, 1929–1933*, p. 127.
27. Robert McElvaine, *The Great Depression*, pp. 38–39.

time industrial productivity continued to increase throughout the twenties, the pool of domestic consumers with the means available to buy all the goods and services being offered grew smaller and smaller. By 1929, some estimates have it, the excess of capacity over potential consumption had risen to an extraordinary 17 percent; in brief, 17 percent of everything that had been produced could not be sold.[28] Indeed, during the two months before the stock market crash, production rates had begun to decline at an estimated annual average of 20 percent and inventories had begun to grow, while wholesale prices dropped at an annual rate of 7.5 percent and personal income by 5 percent. The slide, in effect, had started even before the crash. "Gosh, wasn't we crazy there for a while?" Will Rogers asked in his newspaper column in 1932. "Did the thought ever enter our bone head that the time might come when nobody would want all these things we were making?"[29]

Some have suggested that it was not just lower relative incomes that produced the gap between capacity and consumption. After World War I, this argument goes, there was a worldwide decline in population growth among the developed nations (hardly surprising, given the millions of young men who had been slaughtered during the war, thus depleting the reproduction pool).[30] In the United States, this resulted in a commensurate decline in the number of nonfarm households and the consequently diminishing need for nonfarm housing construction, one of the most important sectors of any nation's economy. After a tremendous spurt in suburban construction in the immediate postwar years, the amount of money invested in the construction of residences in the United States had declined from a high of $5.16 billion in 1925 to just $3.38 billion in 1929—and by the end of 1933 would fall to a devastating $435 million (while the growth rate of nonfarm households that year sank to less than one-half of one percent). "Thus the rapid and

28. See Clarence L. Barber, "On the Origins of the Great Depression," *Southern Economic Journal* (January 1978).
29. In Bryan B. Sterling and Frances N. Sterling, eds., *Will Rogers: Reflections and Observations*, p. 201.
30. "The destructiveness of the First World War, in terms of the number of soldiers killed," Martin Gilbert writes in *The First World War: A Complete History*, "exceeded that of all other wars known to history" (p. 540). An average of 5,600 soldiers were killed every day, he says, for a total of 8.6 million men. This figure does not include

very large decline in the rate of growth of nonfarm households," economic historian Clarence L. Barber has theorized, "was clearly the major reason for the decline that occurred in residential construction in the United States from 1926 on. And this decline . . . may well have been the most important single factor in turning the 1929 downturn into a major depression."[31]

Then there was the agonizing labyrinth of monetary policy to consider, particularly as it related to foreign markets. The boom years of the twenties may have erected a comfortable facade of prosperity in the United States, but it was not mirrored in much of Europe, which remained in a recessionary bog during most of the decade. Great Britain's decision not only to return to the gold standard in 1925 but to maintain the exchange rate of $4.87 to the pound sterling was designed to pull that country out of the postwar doldrums; it turned out to be a little less beneficent than Chancellor of the Exchequer Winston Churchill had hoped when he announced that the economies of the civilized world would now "vary together, like ships in harbor whose gangways are joined and who rise and fall together with the tide."[32] There was movement, right enough, but in Britain it was mostly downward. Maintaining the gold standard and the exchange rate at high levels simply made the country's exports too expensive for most nations to buy. That forced a drop in prices, which forced a drop in already minimal wages, which inspired all manner of labor unrest, including a long general strike that left the economy staggering through the rest of the decade and on into the years of the Great Depression.

The twenties had been kinder to France. The terrible loss of life during World War I may have caused a decline in housing construction there as elsewhere, but it also ensured that there would be relatively little unemployment. Her financial institutions, under the nearly absolute control of the Bank of France (itself under the nearly absolute control of but 200 families), had not been as deeply involved in the purchase of

those who died of their wounds after the war, sometimes many years later, or the hundreds of thousands who were so terribly maimed that they would never be able to live as fully functional human beings. Finally, to these estimates we must add the many millions of potential fathers who died in the influenza pandemic of 1918.

31. Clarence L. Barber, op. cit.

32. Quoted in John Kenneth Galbraith, *A Journey Through Economic Time*, p. 53.

American stocks as those of the British (the crash, one French observer noted icily, was basically an "abscess" that had been "lanced"), nor was her economy as closely tied to industry.[33] Nevertheless, by 1930, production had begun to decline, unemployment had begun to rise, and the French budget showed the first of an upcoming series of deficits.

Germany, of course, was an economic charnel house throughout much of the decade. It could hardly have been otherwise. Defeated in war, Germany was even more profoundly defeated by the retributive peace that followed it. Many people in Great Britain had demanded that Germany be forced to pay the entire cost of the war, estimated at some $120 billion, vowing to "squeeze Germany until the pips squeak." Ravaged Belgium tended to agree, and France was hardly more charitable. "We have been attacked," Foreign Minister Stéphen Pinchon announced, "we want security"—and the Treaty of Versailles got France the Rhineland to ensure that German industry could not recover. "We have been devastated," he added, "we want reparation"—and reparation France got, or at least the promise of it.[34] The combination left the German economy in tatters. By 1923, inflation had so completely devalued the German mark that it took a wheelbarrel full to buy a loaf of bread, and it cost an industrial worker twenty weeks of wages to buy a suit of clothes. Only when enforced austerity and the invention of a new form of currency called the rentenmark—ostensibly backed entirely by the country's landed wealth, not by gold—were instituted by the Reichsbank at the end of 1923 did Germany's inflationary spiral slow. Nevertheless, her economy continued moribund through the rest of the decade, stirring the increasingly fetid stew of anguish, resentment, desperation, fury, and ancient prejudices that ultimately would bubble up Adolf Hitler and the Nazi party.

During most of the twenties, then, it had been virtually impossible to sustain the cooperation necessary to hold the gold standard and keep the balance of payments among the various nations at rational levels—a situation that the onset of sudden recession in this country exacerbated profoundly, with consequences to all. Before the war, Britain had been

33. Quotes in John A. Garraty, *The Great Depression*, p. 39.
34. Both quotes in Quincy Howe, *The World Between the Wars: From the 1918 Armistice to the Munich Agreement*, pp. 4–5.

the world's banker. During the war and the years that followed, that position was occupied by the United States, which doled out nearly $27 billion in foreign loans between 1914 and 1929—much of it going to Germany in the postwar years, on the theory that these loans would enable that nation to make its reparations payments to Great Britain, France, and Belgium. The reparations payments, it was supposed, would then enable the other European countries to purchase American manufactured goods and agricultural produce and repay American war loans. But with or without American loans, Germany was simply incapable of meeting the obligations the peace had imposed on her, and during a League of Nations meeting in Lausanne, Switzerland, in 1932, Germany's creditor nations finally bowed to the inevitable and reduced her indebtedness to a token of 3 billion marks (even that would never be paid).

By then, the world's economic die had long since been cast. American loans to Germany or any other nation all but ceased after the crash of 1929, which made it increasingly difficult for European countries to purchase American goods. With a shrinking market across the seas and a continuing decline in domestic consumption, American industry demanded protectionism to keep European goods from undercutting its sales in the United States. In 1930, Congress complied with the Hawley-Smoot Tariff Act; its restrictive tariffs on most imported goods crippled the ability of European nations to sell what little they were able to produce, which gave them even less money with which to purchase American goods. Furthermore, as American industrial production began its long slide, the demand for raw materials from foreign sources fell commensurately, eliminating much potential additional revenue that might have gone to purchase American goods and repay American loans. The numbers speak precisely to cause and effect: between 1929 and the end of 1932, United States exports fell from $5.2 billion to $1.6 billion, and imports from $4.4 billion to $1.3 billion.

Defaults on American loans proliferated in South America, Central Europe, and Germany. British and American lending fell off to new lows. Currency devaluation accelerated. Germany was forced off the gold standard in the summer of 1931, and by the end of the year the British pound sterling had declined so markedly that even Great Britain finally abandoned its desperate efforts to stay with gold. The

Scandinavian countries and the Dominion nations quickly followed suit. Fearing that the United States would do the same, many foreign interests that had not already done so began pulling their money from American banks, lowering American gold reserves, putting even greater pressure on an already tottering banking system, and giving an altogether stark validity to an observation made by British economist John Maynard Keynes in December 1932: "The course of exchange, as we all know, moves round a closed circle. When we transmit the tension, which is beyond our own endurance, to our neighbour, it is only a question of a little time before it reaches ourselves again traveling round the circle."[35]

35. Quoted in Sidelsky, op. cit., p. 441.

2

The Graveyard of Hope

The worldwide circle of contention, uncertainty, retribution, and protectionism between 1929 and 1933 helped produce a seemingly uncontrollable disintegration that defied comprehension, much less recovery. Calvin Coolidge, whose faith in the protocols of laissez-faire economics had been exemplary, contemplated the situation a few days before his death in January 1933 and told a reporter that even he had abandoned hope. "In other periods of depression," he mused gloomily, "it has always been possible to see some things which were solid and upon which you could base hope. But as I look about, I now see nothing to give ground for hope, nothing of man."[1] Writing in 1934, economist and social theorist George Soule trotted out his own collection of dismal facts relevant to the depression, then concluded: "Neither this nation nor any other had ever in the last century been submitted to such economic strain in time of peace. The imagination

1. Quoted in Ronald Steel, *Walter Lippmann and the American Century*, p. 286.

simply cannot encompass the dislocation and suffering, physical and mental, which is symbolized in these abstract figures."[2]

If the politicians and the pundits felt confused, others felt betrayed. Perhaps the most fully deceived were those hostages to a middle-class dream gone bad—salesmen, promoters, businessmen, brokers, boosters, middle-management executives, Rotarians, Lions, Toastmasters. They had all played by the rules, had joined enthusiastically in the great game of consumerism and limitless potential. Now there was nothing to sell, nothing to boost, nothing to dream on. "The kind of readjustment they are called upon to make is heroic," Episcopal Bishop John Paul Jones observed in the pages of the *Survey Graphic* in 1933. "Vast multitudes of them have lost financial security forever. In bewilderment and bitterness they will seek a sign of hope, and no sign will be given. Some will give up and end it all, but a great majority will go on living some kind of broken and frustrated lives."[3]

The suicide rate between 1929 and the end of 1932 did indeed rise: from 13.9 per 100,000 in population to an all-time high of 17.4, and in some places even higher. The survivors could be seen everywhere, resolutely dressing for business each morning, reading the classified ads, penciling circles around likely items, leaving their homes or apartments with the marked-up newspapers folded under their arms, mimicking the attitudes of success as they purposefully marched off to stand in line in employment agencies and business firms, waiting hours for interviews during which both parties understood the emptiness of the ritual but dared not let truth steal in for fear it could not be endured. Each day, their suits grew a little more worn, a little less clean, their shoes a little less bright, their strides a little less brisk.

Soon, they no longer bothered to gather in the overheated rooms of the agencies where gray cigarette smoke hung near the ceiling, where the smell of desperation grew more rank, where the tempers of the clerks became increasingly frayed, where the stoic, patient faces of the supplicants became thin and pinched with repressed anxiety. More often than not, now, jobless middle-class refugees just walked the streets or sat

2. George Soule, *The Coming American Revolution*, p. 184.
3. Quoted in George K. Pratt, M.D., "Morale: The Mental Hygiene of Unemployment," p. 12.

unmoving on park benches, trying not to look with too much obvious hunger at the begging pigeons, wondering what they could find to say when they finally stood, discarded the useless newspapers they had carried with them all day, and returned to their families.

The feeling of helplessness was a caul whose weight could bring the strongest man down in tears, as a boy discovered when he came upon his father in the empty coal bin of the family's house in Brookline, Massachusetts. The father was crying. "We had owned a small bakery that had failed a few months before," the boy remembered. "Things would get worse for us later on, and for a couple of years we were in really bad shape, but to me the low point of the depression will always be the sight of my father that day, crying in the coal bin."[4]

Probably what haunted that father was the reality that lurked just beyond the door, described vividly by writer Sherwood Anderson, who had seen, he said, "men who are heads of families creeping through the streets of American cities, eating from garbage cans; men turned out of houses and sleeping week after week on park benches, on the ground in parks, in the mud under bridges. . . . Our streets are filled with beggars, with men new to the art of begging."[5] The streets were also full of men new to the agonies of psychological depression, expressed in fatigue that, as a Harvard psychiatrist maintained, "sometimes represents, not overwork, but discouragement, inability to meet situations, lack of interest in the opportunities available. Unsociability, marital incompatibility, alcoholism, an aggressive and embittered social attitude; all these may indicate a disorder of the mental balance."[6] The consequent stress on family structure could be terrible, another psychiatrist emphasized, as many men and women "are inwardly frantic with fear and are nearing the end of their rope in the struggle to adjust their needs for food and shelter, as well as their conceptions of themselves, their normal wills to power, and their self-esteem to the thwarting that loss of job necessitates."[7]

Some decided that family responsibility was beyond them. There were 250,000 fewer marriages in 1932 than in 1929, and the per capita

4. Quoted in Charles A. Jellison, *Tomatoes Were Cheaper: Tales from the Thirties*, p. 14.
5. Ibid.
6. Quoted in George K. Pratt, op. cit., p. 12.
7. Ibid., p. 13.

number of births declined—not merely because people were afraid they could not support children (though this must have been the primary reason) but because impotence among unemployed men rose through the decade. "[Sex] life decreased,"[8] one researcher of the time stated flatly, and at the end of the decade sociologist Mira Komarovsky still reported high levels of impotence in men without jobs and linked cause and effect with no hesitation: "The feeling of disturbance and humiliation apparently exists irrespective of the intellectual convictions of the man. . . . [I]n his own estimation he fails to fulfill . . . the very touchstone of his manhood—the role of family provider."[9]

It was not the middle class alone whose families could be ripped to shreds by such pressures. As a social worker in New York in 1931, Louis Adamic encountered many working-class people no less ravaged. One husband, he reported, a truck driver by trade, lost his job in April 1930 when his employer went bankrupt. Afterward, he found employment for only two weeks before that job, too, disappeared. In December he lost his savings of $350 in a bank failure, possibly the collapse of the United States Bank. Two of his four children took sick, and he and his wife had to pawn many of their possessions, including his wife's wedding ring, to pay the bills. By September 1931 the rent was three months in arrears and the landlord was threatening eviction. Joining with two other unemployed men in the apartment building, the husband pulled off a robbery that netted only $33—and arrest. He was convicted and sent to Sing-Sing, where every now and then he would start banging his forehead against the concrete walls. The wife got enough money from organized charity to keep herself and the children in a tiny one-room flat where Adamic found her in December. "Unable to restrain herself," he wrote in his report, "Mrs. F—— wept a great deal, and the children bawled with her. There were nights when all five of them cried for hours. . . . When I visited the family one child was in bed with a cold; two other children were in the same bed—the only one—'to keep warm.' There was no heat in the dwelling. Mrs. F—— said to me, 'We'd all be better off dead.'"[10]

8. Quoted in Dixon Wecter, *The Age of the Great Depression*, p. 32.
9. Quoted in Harvey Green, *The Uncertainty of Everyday Life, 1915–1945*, p. 88.
10. Quoted in Harvey Swados, ed., *The American Writer and the Great Depression*, pp. 212–13.

The detritus of such social horror was scattered everywhere. In Chicago, social worker Louise Armstrong remembered, "We saw the city at its worst. We saw Want and Despair walking the streets, and our friends, sensible, thrifty families, reduced to poverty. . . . One vivid, gruesome moment of those dark days we shall never forget. We saw a crowd of some fifty men fighting over a barrel of garbage that had been set outside the back door of a restaurant. American citizens fighting for scraps of food like animals!"[11] In 1931, some 1,400 families in the city had been evicted, and Chicago municipal court judge Samuel A. Heller recalled the desperation that infested the daily scene in his landlords and tenants court: "I had an average of four hundred cases a day. It was packed. People fainted, people cried: 'Where am I going?'"[12] Such evictions gave birth to at least one popular joke: "Who was that lady I seen you with last night at the sidewalk café?" a man is asked. "That was no lady; that was my wife. That was no sidewalk café; that was our furniture."[13] In winter 1930–31, a reporter of the time wrote, "You can ride across the lovely Michigan Avenue bridge at midnight with the . . . lights all about making a dream city of incomparable beauty, while twenty feet below you, on the lower level of the same bridge, are 2,000 homeless, decrepit, shivering and starving men, wrapping themselves in old newspapers to keep from freezing, and lying down in the manure dust to sleep."[14]

In Philadelphia, a social worker reported in the summer of 1930, "We didn't know that one of the fathers in our . . . neighborhood was out of work until we wondered why his small son's legs grew thin." The father, his wife said, was "always walking or looking. The places are so far apart that his feet get sore. He's been everywhere—the day shifts and the night shifts. We had to put cotton in the heels of his shoes. Sometimes he don't know where he's walking. He's been back so often they hold up their hands when they see him coming."[15] There were so many evictions in the city—up to 1,300 a month—that children in a day-care

11. Louise Armstrong, *We Too Are the People*, p. 10.
12. In Studs Terkel, op. cit., pp. 471–72.
13. Quoted in J. C. Furnas, *Stormy Weather: Crosslights on the Nineteen Thirties*, p. 288.
14. Quoted in Harold M. Mayer and Richard C. Wade, *Chicago: Growth of a Metropolis*, p. 358.
15. Quoted in Milton Meltzer, *Brother, Can You Spare a Dime?* p. 36.

center fashioned a game out of the experience, piling all their toy furniture in one corner of the room, then picking it up and moving it to another corner. "We ain't got no money for the rent," one of the children explained to the teacher, "so's we've moved into a new house. Then we got the constable on us, so we's movin' again."[16]

In Youngstown, Ohio, an old friend called on Mayor Joseph L. Heffernan one day. "My wife is frantic," the man said calmly. "After working at the steel mill for twenty-five years I have lost my job, and I'm too old to get other work. If you can't do something for me, I'm going to kill myself." Heffernan found the man a minor job, but there were too many more like him in the steel town. Every night, the homeless and unemployed crowded into the city incinerator building for warmth, sleeping among piles of garbage and probably feeding from them as well. The mayor talked the city council into letting him convert an abandoned police station into a flophouse. It was filled immediately and remained so. "I heartily wish," the mayor said of his frequent visits to the place,

> that those folk who have made themselves comfortable by ignoring and denying the suffering of their less fortunate neighbors could see some of the sights I saw. There were old men gnarled by heavy labor, young mechanics tasting the first bitterness of defeat, clerks and white-collar workers learning the equality of misery, derelicts who fared no worse in bad times than in good. Negroes who only a short time before had come from southern cotton fields, now glad to find any shelter from the cold, immigrants who had been lured to [the] "land of youth and freedom"—each one a personal tragedy and all together an overwhelming catastrophe for the Nation.[17]

In Virginia, a former Petersburg trunk maker began to cry when he confessed his family's plight. "I have enough clothes for my wife and family to last until June and enough money to buy food," he said, "but when they get hungry and I have no money, I am going down on

16. Quoted in Edward Robb Ellis, *A Nation in Torment*, p. 233.
17. Joseph L. Heffernan, "The Hungry City: A Mayor's Experience with Unemployment," *Atlantic Monthly* (May 1932).

Sycamore Street, break a store window and get them something to eat."[18] A failed Newport News business executive found himself hunting rabbits to feed himself and his family. In Texas, "A week ago today," an anonymous college professor wrote in *The New Republic* on May 6, 1931,

> my brother, utterly disheartened by his prolonged search for employment, went to his lonely room in a shabby hotel . . . and blew his brains out. After nearly thirty years of toil as a college professor, I myself had great difficulty in raising the money to pay for the modest kind of burial befitting the gentleman that my brother was. I could not go to his funeral; I could not pay for both the burial expenses and the railway fare.[19]

In Detroit, eight destitute families who had crowded into a heatless, gasless, waterless partitioned loft were presented with Christmas chickens by the city in December 1930. There was no way to cook them. The families—thirty-six people in all—went next door to an abandoned house, ripped the wood from it with their bare hands, stacked the purloined lumber in a pile, and made a bonfire, warming themselves while roasting the chickens at the ends of sticks. The warmth increased when the abandoned house itself caught fire from stray sparks.[20]

In New York City by the end of 1931, it was estimated that 85,000 meals a day were being served in the city's eighty-two breadlines—characterized by the kind of cheap, filling food, as the recipients would say, "that don't stand by you."[21] The most visible of all breadlines were two that newspaper mogul William Randolph Hearst had set up at the opposite ends of Times Square; there, Louis Adamic wrote, "[t]he wretched men, many without overcoats or decent shoes, usually began

18. Quoted in Ronald L. Heinemann, *Depression and New Deal in Virginia: The Enduring Dominion*, p. 26.
19. "My Brother Commits Suicide," *The New Republic* (May 6, 1931); condensed in *Reader's Digest* (July 1931).
20. This story is told in Robert Conot, *American Odyssey*, pp. 270–71.
21. Quoted in Mary Heaton Vorse, "School for Bums," *The New Republic* (April 29, 1931); condensed in *Reader's Digest* (June 1931).

to line up soon after six o'clock—in good weather or bad, rain or snow."[22] This did not sit well with the nearby theater owners, who feared that the appearance of as many as two thousand hungry, destitute men, shuffling to get their crusts of bread and cups of Hearstian gruel in snakelike lines hundreds of yards long, would further discourage attendance at a time when the industry already was suffering badly. "Seven or eight years ago," James Thurber wrote in the January 1932 issue of *Fortune*, "a just-average comedy or drama often had a fairly good run—two to three months, let us say, anyway; the same kind of play nowadays is likely to close in a week."[23] (It was perhaps symptomatic that if Ethel Merman could still belt out the relentlessly cheerful lyrics of "Life Is Just a Bowl of Cherries" in *George White's Scandals* in 1931, her ebullience would be countered in 1932 by Rex Weber's warbling the haunting lamentations of "Brother, Can You Spare a Dime?" in J. P. McEvoy's *New Americana*.)[24] In 1931, the city experienced an estimated 200,000 evictions, many of them similar in character to that described by one social worker:

> Mrs. Green left her five small children alone one morning while she went to have her grocery order filled. While she was away, the constable arrived and padlocked her house with the children inside. When she came back, she heard the six-weeks-old baby crying. She did not dare to touch the padlock for fear of being arrested, but she found a window open and climbed in and nursed the baby and then climbed out and appealed to the police to let her children out.[25]

Many of the homeless—there were 15,000 in New York City by the spring of 1931—simply wandered the streets of the city like particles in liquid suspension, seeking shelter however they could—sometimes with ludicrous results. "There was a bunch of us in the men's room in the railroad station," an unemployed worker reported.

22. Quoted in Ellis, op. cit., p. 129.
23. James Thurber, "New York in the Third Winter," *Fortune* (January 1932).
24. For Broadway shows, see Stanley Green, *Ring Bells! Sing Songs! Broadway Musicals of the 1930s*, pp. 53–69.
25. Quoted in Ellis, op. cit., p. 233.

After a while a couple of cops came in. One of 'em, said: "All right, boys, break it up! Break it up!" and began pushing the guys out. I beat it into the can. I was pretty cold and wanted to stick around. One of the cops came in. I stood over a latrine. He stood behind me. After a while he said: "Okeh, bud, long enough, you've broken all the records already." I had to laugh at that. I buttoned my pants and went out of the station.[26]

At night, some 3,300 street people, including as many as 100 women, found sleep on the beds, benches, and floors of the six-story Municipal Lodging House on East Twenty-fifth Street. Thousands more clustered wherever they could in what would come to be called "Hoovervilles," in bitter mockery of the president, shantytowns constructed of everything that came to hand, from packing crates to hundreds of tin cans flattened out and nailed to boards. "Along the Hudson, below Riverside Drive," Robert Bendiner remembered, "I daily passed the tarpaper huts of a Hooverville, where scores of families lived the lives of reluctant gypsies. . . . Dozens of such colonies had sprung up in the city—along the two rivers, in the empty lots of the Bronx, and on the flats of Brooklyn, but not nearly enough to accommodate the swelling army of the . . . dispossessed."[27]

The Hoovervilles were not exclusive to the boroughs of New York City. They were everywhere, gangs of desperate squatters cobbling together bitterly ramshackle imitations of real villages in vacant lots and building sites in virtually every community in the country. In Seattle, the homeless created a city within the city on the flats between the Connecticut Street dock and the central terminal of the port of Seattle, within the view of those working in downtown office buildings. The city fathers were distressed enough to burn the sprawling settlement to ashes not once, but twice. The residents rebuilt it each time. A social worker counted 639 of them still living on the flats in 1934.

Similar enclaves sprouted in Chicago, where a settlement at Harrison and Canal streets sported its own flagpole; in Denver, Colorado,

26. Quoted in Susan Winslow, *Brother, Can You Spare a Dime? America from the Wall Street Crash to Pearl Harbor*, p. 19.
27. Robert Bendiner, *Just Around the Corner: A Highly Selective History of the Thirties*, p. 4.

where an old enclave of shacks and primitive adobe dwellings along the Platte River called Petertown was swiftly enlarged to Hoovervillean dimensions; in Portland, Oregon, where in Sullivan's Gulch more than three hundred people settled down; in Oakland, California, where in one area so many people set up housekeeping in huge abandoned concrete sewer pipes that the place came to be called Pipe City; in San Francisco, where dozens of discarded trolley cars south of the city were occupied in what was nicknamed Carbarn City; in Los Angeles, where a colony of more than seven hundred at 85th and Alameda streets was fed daily at the soup kitchen maintained at the nearby Angelus Temple of Aimee Semple McPherson's Four Square Gospel Church.

There were plenty who did not have even soup kitchens. In the shantytowns of the Appalachian highlands, it was said, people lived off dandelions, pokeweed, and blackberries, and children often grew so hungry they chewed on their hands until they drew blood—though no one could corroborate rumors that some children had eaten the flesh clear off the bones of their fingers. Everywhere, it was the children who seemed to suffer first and most. In Chicago in January 1932, a school principal informed a congressional committee, "I said to the teachers last fall, 'Whenever you have a discipline case, ask this question first, What has he had for breakfast?' Which usually brings out the fact that he has had nothing at all."[28]

Robert J. Hastings remembered the winter day in Marion City, Illinois, when the Marion City Dairy announced that it would offer an entire bucket of skim milk for only a nickel on Saturday mornings. You had to bring your own bucket. "Come Saturday morning, Mom sent me off to the dairy," he wrote. "I held our enamel water bucket in one gloved hand, and a nickel in the other. I took my place in the long line. It was unbelievable. When your turn came, regardless of how big your bucket, you held it under the faucet of the big, stainless steel drum while that great white river just ran and ran."[29]

For those among the urban black population, the levels of poverty most had learned to endure fell to depths for which even long experience could not prepare them. In Chicago's "Bronzetown," the South

28. Quoted in Meltzer, op. cit., p. 43.
29. Robert J. Hastings, *A Nickel's Worth of Skim Milk*, pp. 5–6.

Side, where some 236,000 African Americans lived, the depression had come early; by the end of the summer of 1929—more than two months before the Wall Street disaster—every bank had closed and layoffs begun. They lived 90,000 to the square mile, the blacks of the South Side—as compared to 20,000 to the square mile for the non-black population—many of them in what crudely disingenuous white landlords called "kitchenettes." These were decrepit apartments into each of whose single rooms one or two families were crowded at exorbitant rents, all of the families sharing a single bathroom and kitchen. The resulting feculence was typified by life in the seven-story "Angelus Building," as described by roving journalist and critic Edmund Wilson: "Its owner has turned it over to the Negroes, who flock into the tight-packed apartments and get along there as best they can. . . . Relief workers . . . have come away so overwhelmed with horror that they have made efforts to have the whole place condemned—to the piteous distress of the occupants."[30]

In New York City's Harlem, the situation was hardly better. More than ten thousand people, African American social worker Anna Arnold Hedgman remembered, "lived in cellars and basements which had been converted into makeshift flats. Packed in damp, rat-ridden dungeons, they existed in squalor not too different from that of the Arkansas sharecroppers. Floors were of cracked concrete, and the walls were whitewashed rock, water-drenched and rust-streaked. There were only slits for a window and a tin can in a corner was the only toilet." There was no heat in the winter, no air in the summer; packing crates and cardboard boxes served as the only tables, crumpled newspapers and rags the only beds.[31]

In Harlem as elsewhere, crowded, filthy living conditions and economic deprivation made for social unrest, family disintegration, and a rise in crime rates and illegitimate births, but there was more than psychological misery and community disruption at work here. Death was a commonplace, some of it from the sort of violence such conditions normally breed (in Chicago's South Side, for instance, the homicide rate

30. Edmund Wilson, *The American Earthquake*, p. 462.
31. Quoted in Meltzer, op. cit., p. 55. See also "The Depression in Harlem" in Bernard Sternsher, ed., *Hitting Home: The Great Depression in Town and Country*, pp. 107–8.

averaged six times the rate as that for whites throughout the decade).[32] Most of the mortality, however, was from disease that undernourishment, lack of sanitation, ignorance, and substandard medical care combined to lift to virulent levels. "The kitchenette is our prison," black novelist Richard Wright (*Native Son*) would lament of life in Chicago:

> The kitchenette, with its filth and foul air, with its one toilet for thirty or more tenants, kills our black babies so fast that in many cities twice as many of them die as white babies.
>
> The kitchenette is the seed bed for scarlet fever, dysentery, typhoid, tuberculosis, gonorrhea, syphilis, pneumonia, and malnutrition.
>
> The kitchenette scatters death so widely among us that our death rate exceeds our birth rate.[33]

Wright was not exaggerating. The infant death rate from all causes among blacks in six northern cities (Chicago, New York, Cleveland, Detroit, Philadelphia, and Pittsburgh) between 1928 and 1933 ranged from a little under 80 per 1,000 births in Chicago to a shade under 100 per 1,000 in Pittsburgh, while for white children in the same cities the rate averaged only a little over 55. In the black population as a whole, the biggest killer of all was the era's version of the plague—tuberculosis. Among all whites in the same northern cities during the same years, the average rate of tuberculosis death per 100,000 of population was about 55. Among blacks, the rate averaged about 305, almost five times as high as the rate for whites, and in Detroit, to which so many African Americans had migrated during the boom years of the automobile industry, the rate was 373—almost seven times as high as that for whites. In Pittsburgh in 1933, 17.7 percent of all African American deaths were caused by tuberculosis.[34]

Small wonder, then, that Wright could lament that "the kitchenette is the funnel through which our pulverized lives flow to ruin and

32. See statistics in St. Clair Drake and Horace R. Clayton, *Black Metropolis: A Study of Negro Life in a Northern City*; footnote, p. 202.
33. Richard Wright, *12 Million Black Voices: A Folk History of the Negro in the United States* (Viking Press, 1941), pp. 106–7.
34. Infant mortality and disease death rate statistics from Elsie Witphen, *Tuberculosis and the Negro in Pittsburgh: A Report of the Negro Health Survey* (1934), pp. 1–11.

death on the city pavements."[35] His words carried particular sorrow for young black women, whom the kitchenette life had jammed "while still in their teens, into rooms with men who are restless and stimulated by the noise and lights of the city; and more of our girls have bastard babies than the girls in any other section of the city."[36] The kitchenette life, he said, "creates thousands of one-room homes where our black mothers sit, deserted, with their children about their knees."[37]

Poor black women shared at least one attribute with their relatively better-off white counterparts: near-invisibility. The statistics regarding unemployed and homeless "respectable" single women in the early years of the depression were at best vague. These women existed—they had to exist—but virtually nothing was known about them. "It is one of the great mysteries of the city where women go when they are out of work and hungry," radical journalist Meridel LeSueur wrote from Minneapolis at the end of 1931. "There are not many women in the breadline. There are no flophouses for women as there are for men, where a bed can be had for a quarter or less. You don't see women lying on the floor at the mission in the free flops. . . . Yet there must be as many women out of jobs and suffering extreme poverty as there are men. What happens to them? Where do they go?"[38] Writer Emily Hahn investigated the situation in New York City—where one estimate held that 75,000 homeless single women existed as late as 1934[39]—and concluded that the simple disgrace of poverty kept many women from advertising their condition by applying for charity or even standing in breadlines. To admit failure, Hahn wrote, "is still the greatest shame of all" for such a woman:

> She lives as long as possible on her savings, trying all the time to find more work and going without food to save money for clothes. Then she turns to her friends—private borrowing is not quite so shameful—until she becomes too much of a burden. . . . One by one they give up, slowly and reluctantly, or they go too far even to give up, like

35. Wright, op. cit., p. 111.
36. Ibid., p. 110.
37. Ibid., p. 109.
38. Meridel LeSueur, "Women on the Breadlines," *New Masses* (January 1932).
39. See Sara M. Evans, *Born for Liberty: A History of Women in America*, p. 203.

the fifty-year-old woman who confessed: "I had $60, but I spent it. I didn't even try to save it. I thought perhaps God would be good to me and let me die."[40]

Climate aside, life was similarly hard on women in Los Angeles, Adela Rogers St. Johns discovered. Daughter of the celebrated attorney Earl Rogers, confidant of the rich and famous, Hollywood screenwriter, and one of the best-paid feature writers for William Randolph Hearst's *Los Angeles Examiner*, the singularly undestitute reporter put on a thin dress and a threadbare coat, slid on a pair of horn-rimmed glasses—all of this borrowed from the wardrobe section at MGM—armed herself with a single dime, and as "May Harrison" set out in the middle of December 1931 to experience what it was like to be female, homeless, and unemployed in the City of the Angels.

"One thin dime," she wrote in the first of a series of articles for the *Examiner*. "By my honor as a reporter, that was all I had as I went to seek work. Starting from scratch. No money. No baggage. No friends. The hard way. Over a year after Black Thursday, there were thousands of women doing the same." She made a list of employment agencies while sitting in Pershing Square in downtown Los Angeles, then she began to walk in her thin-soled shoes from agency to potential job, agency to potential job. No work anywhere, and at the end of the day there was nothing for her trouble but aching feet.

After a roll and coffee for lunch, she was down to a nickel. A strange man who only wanted company—though she feared the worst—bought her dinner. Afterward, she could find no room in the Christ Faith Mission, the only mission she discovered that catered to women—though the Midnight Mission in downtown Los Angeles was taking care of more than three hundred men a night—so after walking until two in the morning, she slept in the backseat of an unlocked limousine parked at the rear of a downtown garage. In the morning, she sat at the counter of a coffee shop, ordering toast and coffee. She still had her nickel, but the check was fifteen cents. "I haven't any money," she told the owner at the cash register. He sighed with disgust and slammed her unpaid check on a spindle. "That's only the two hundred and tenth of them I've got," he

40. Quoted in Meltzer, op. cit., pp. 37–40.

said. "You might as well owe me another quarter, I'm going broke, any-
how. Tell [the waitress] to give you an egg and another cup of coffee."

From December 14 until after Christmas, the reporter wandered
Los Angeles (sometimes surreptitiously accompanied by an *Examiner*
photographer), standing in breadlines, begging strangers for money
and food, getting advice from taxi dancers and prostitutes—"the sister-
hood of the damned," she wrote—haunting the airless, overcrowded
rooms of the employment offices, the community chest offices, the
county charities offices, killing entire days in the reading room of the
Los Angeles public library, sleeping on the floor of a new acquaintance's
tiny apartment, finding room for a few nights at the Christ Faith Mission, then at the Salvation Army Home for Women—"I don't know
how they could love me but they did. Like God. And the lassies had
breakfast with me and cheered me on my way." St. Johns got work all
too briefly as a "mother's helper," vainly struggling to stay clean—
"Cleanliness is next to godliness but there does not seem to be any godliness around for it to be next *to*, so we smell of sweat, our nails are never
quite clean, neither are our necks, no needle marks of drugs, but pin-
pricks of dirt in your pores"—and often walked clear out to West Hollywood and back on tortured feet: "Nothing, *nothing* seems to take away
the agony and symbolic ravage of aching, sore burning feet. Grotesque,
isn't it? Oh Lord help me to walk with bleeding feet my guts are bleeding too, listen to the purr of tires, the cling-clang-clang of the trolleys,
I'll be all right if my feet hold out, they say."

Except for the kind words for the Salvation Army, she had little
good to report about the big organized charities and the mainstream
religions, all of whom she found niggardly and arrogant. But not Aimee
Semple McPherson, that free-spirited bane of orthodox Christianity,
whose big white Angelus Temple, topped by an illuminated cross and
spiked by two radio broadcast towers like the horns of righteousness
(KFSG—Kall Four Square Gospel), rose like an exhalation on Glendale
Boulevard: "God bless her," St. Johns wrote. "Feeding, encouraging,
giving hope hope hope to the poor, and faith and strength as they
jammed Angelus Temple and slept there if they had no place else to go.
I saw her begging for them, insulting those with folding money into
parting with it for their destitute brothers. Sick women on the floor of
her home, old men in her garage, families sleeping in the pews."

Returned to her family—"Shaken with joy at sight of them, of my home, hardly able to believe I was back safely and all was well"—St. Johns sat behind her typewriter and pounded out the stories, one by one, sixteen in all. The experience, she said, had changed her view of woman's lot:

> As I walked the long road from Los Angeles to West Hollywood—the hole in my shoe let the wet in and then sizzled . . . my head swam already. Good luck, sister, that gal in an agency had said—well, sisters, I thought as I trudged—we asked for it. We sure liberated hell out of women. True, part of this is the Depression but where were we when that happened, did we try to calm it down any or spend less or—I am wondering as I walk whether our part of it is part of the price we women are paying for this freedom.[41]

Few women trapped indefinitely in a life St. Johns had endured for only a little over two weeks had the time or psychic energy for such artful speculations. Survival was too important, and too hard, and many would more quickly have shared the feelings expressed by Meridel LeSueur, who believed the task of survival had honed young women down to a bitterness that rejected all that traditional values held dear: "I don't want to marry. I don't want any children. So they all say. No children. No marriage. They arm themselves alone, keep up alone. The man is helpless now. He cannot provide. If he propagates, he cannot take care of his young. The means are not in his hands. So they live alone. Get what fun they can. The life risk is too horrible now. Defeat is too clearly written on it."[42]

INCREASINGLY, AMERICANS TOOK to the roads or the rails, seeking escape, relief, hope. We had always been a people given to moving around the landscape, whether chasing the Lorelei call of one frontier after another

---

41. All quotes from Adela Rogers St. Johns, *The Honeycomb*, pp. 284–99. Some quotes are from the newspaper series of 1931 as reprinted in the book, some from the text of the book itself.
42. Meridel LeSueur, op. cit., p. 190.

as the population pushed westward in the nineteenth century or simply moving from region to region, city to city, job to job, opportunity to opportunity as impulse or necessity drove us. Millions of migrant farm laborers, of course, did it for a living and had for many years, following the crops from potatoes in Maine to tomatoes in Florida, the wheat harvest from Kansas to the Canada line, working the cranberry bogs of Wisconsin, the cotton fields of Arizona, the beet fields of Michigan, wandering from one truck crop to another up and down the fertile valleys of the Pacific Coast states. There also were those wanderers for whom work was merely incidental. These were the "hoboes," transients by choice who vanished into a subculture of no fixed address that could trace its origins back to the post–Civil War years, with its own social order and traditions and systems of communication and brotherhood— including an annual "National Hobo Convention" that began gathering in Britt, Iowa, in 1933. "The hobo was what he was because that was what he wanted to be," Maury ("Steam Train") Graham, who had gone "on the bum" in 1931, remembered. "It was his calling, his profession, his reason for being."[43]

During the depression, however, the currents of traditional migration were profoundly swollen by the flow of the desperate. No one knew how many men—indeed, entire families—now sneaked into railroad yards at night and clambered into empty boxcars, destination anyplace else. In one year alone, officials of the Southern Pacific Railroad reported, 683,000 transients had been found riding their freights up and down and back and forth in California and the interior West, and similar numbers could be extrapolated for the other big lines—the Santa Fe, the Union Pacific, the Great Northern—as well as scores of smaller branch lines that tied towns and regions together in a network of steel. Any given transcontinental freight rattler would be carrying more people at any given time than such sleek cross-country passenger trains as the Twentieth Century Limited or the California Zephyr. "The men who rode the freights during the Depression," Graham remembered, "often roamed mindlessly across the country, with no destination to reach and no schedule to keep. It was not at all unusual to see a train

43. "Steam Train" Maury Graham and Robert J. Hemming, *Tales of the Iron Road: My Life as King of the Hobos*, p. 20.

headed in one direction, loaded with transients traveling in search of work, pass another train, with just as many job seekers aboard, going in the opposite direction, neither group knowing that there was no work either way."[44]

For a while, one of the wanderers was the future broadcast journalist Eric Sevareid, twenty years old and unemployed, who entered, he recalled fifteen years later,

> a new social dimension, the great underground world, peopled by tens of thousands of American men, women, and children, white, black, brown, and yellow, who inhabit the "jungle," eat from blackened tin cans, find warmth at night in the boxcars, take the sun by day on the flat cars, steal one day, beg with cap in hand the next, fight with fists and often razors, hold sexual intercourse under a blanket in a dark corner of the crowded car, coagulate into pairs and gangs, then disintegrate again, wander from town to town, anxious for the next place, tired of it in a day, fretting to be gone again, happy only when the wheels are clicking under them, the telephone poles slipping by.[45]

Despite whatever attraction pure wanderlust may have held for some of them, most moved from one town to another because they had little choice. Many towns refused to feed or shelter transients for more than a day. (Atlanta, Georgia, more practical in such matters, offered them a generous thirty days of meals and lodging—on chain gangs rented out to the highway department or local farms and private quarries.)

More and more of the total number of transients, like Sevareid, were young, some of them barely into their teens. In 1932, the National Children's Bureau estimated that as many as a quarter of a million youngsters under the age of twenty-one had joined what *Fortune* magazine called "the vast, homeless horde."[46] In the summers of 1932 and

44. Ibid., p. 57.
45. Eric Sevareid, "Not So Wild a Dream" (in Don Congden, ed., *The '30s: A Time to Remember*, p. 109).
46. Quoted in Meltzer, op. cit., p. 49.

1933, University of Minnesota sociologist Thomas Minehan went on the bum to discover the character of their lives. Most of those he interviewed, he found, were refugees just as certainly as if they had been fleeing the flames of war, the battlegrounds here being families riven by despair and anger and brutality at the hands of violent, frustrated fathers. *"Why did they leave home?"* he asked rhetorically in *Boy and Girl Tramps of America* (1934), then presented a mosaic of stories whose common theme was expressed in a single term: "Three hundred and eighty-seven out of four hundred and sixty-six boys and girls stated definitely that hard times drove them away from home."[47]

Most, he found, had been on the road an average of fourteen months and traveled within a radius of only about five hundred miles from where they had started, learning the ins and outs of the towns and villages of the region, finding out where the best missions were, the most generous housewives, the least antagonistic cops, the least vicious yard bulls. Many were young women—indeed, Minehan seems to have encountered "girl" tramps quite as often as "boy" tramps in his own travels. Most spent the bulk of their time walking, not riding the rails or hitchhiking, but many, especially the women, had learned the safety of numbers that could be found only on the boxcars: "In boxcars . . . boys and girls are able to associate in large numbers and protect themselves. Girls in boxcars are not entirely at the mercy of any man on the road, whatever their relations with the boys may be. In event of loneliness or illness, the boys and girls have friends to comfort and care for them. Fear of being alone, fear of being spied on and seized by the first cop who comes along is absent."[48] The women were not the only ones who needed protection, for the world of the road also was populated by those whom the children called "wolves," older homosexuals who were as capable of seduction or rape as any heterosexual. "It is to protect themselves from the approaches of such men," Minehan wrote, "as well as for other reasons, that boys travel in pairs or gangs. . . . A man attempting to seduce a boy is set upon and trounced severely by any gang of boy tramps that comes along."[49]

47. Thomas Minehan, *Boy and Girl Tramps of America*, pp. 47–48.
48. Ibid., p. 61.
49. Ibid., p. 142.

In spite of its hardships and dangers, "the old road looks good to me," one young man told Minehan. "Square meals don't come every day, but I eat better than I ate at home and no grief about the old man being out of work all the time."[50] And Sevareid could remember "glorious days of sunshine, days when we stretched out nude on a flat car cooled by chunks of ice someone tossed down from the 'reefer' adjoining, days when we swung our legs idly and yelled to the girls working in the passing fields, days when we abandoned the trains and swam naked in deep mountain pools of cold, clear water."[51]

Still, the reality of these lives too often mirrored the transient's hell described in Tom Kromer's 1935 novel, *Waiting for Nothing*, a dark place where past, present, and future joined in a terrible nexus of hopelessness:

> It is night and we are in this jungle. This is our home tonight. Our home is a garbage heap. Around us are piles of tin cans and broken bottles. Between the piles are fires. . . . I look around at this jungle filled with fires. They are a pitiful sight, these stiffs with their ragged clothes and their sunken cheeks. . . . They huddle around their fires in the night. Tomorrow they will huddle around their fires, and the next night, and the next. . . .
>
> When I look at these stiffs by the fire, I am looking at a graveyard. There is hardly room to move between the tombstones. . . . The tombstones are men.[52]

Not many people read Thomas Minehan's relentless account of life on the road, and still fewer ever read Kromer's bleak novel. But as individuals, communities, and governments struggled to come to grips with disaster, it would become increasingly difficult to ignore the questions that both implied: What sort of world was it that could produce such scenes? What sort of country was it that could send its children there?

50. Quoted in ibid., pp. 43–44.
51. Sevareid, op. cit., p. 114.
52. In Harvey Swados, ed., op. cit., pp. 253–54.

3

The Dance of Self-Reliance

However terrible the circumstances, even among many of those who had been driven to the wandering life, dependence upon others for help was accepted as a temporary expedient at best and looked upon as a demonstration of moral weakness at worst. And if individuals were not encouraged to turn to their neighbors and communities for aid, those neighborhoods and communities were just as firmly abjured not to look outside themselves to provide what help they could not decently refuse to the truly desperate. Self-reliance, rugged individualism, and the primacy of local rule were articles of faith rarely questioned by most middle- and upper-class Americans at the beginning of the 1930s.

This deeply held belief in the perceived virtues of self-reliance helped shape much of the individual and community response to the Great Depression—at least, in the beginning. The attitudes prevalent in Muncie, Indiana, as revealed in a newspaper editorial of January 1930, could be taken as typical of those of most American communities as the effects of the economic disaster began to manifest themselves:

> It is an open secret that there has been considerable suffering. . . .
> This situation calls for considerable forbearance on the part of credi-
> tors of men out of jobs a well as the continuance of the laudable works
> of charity by the Social Service Bureau and other agencies. Now is a
> good time for people who can afford it to have all their odd jobs done
> to help the unemployed. The best help is helping others help
> themselves.[1]

The avoidance of "outright charity" took various forms in the early
years of the depression, and as the Muncie editorial suggested, one of
the most popular was the creation of "make-work," based on the theory
that those who were not hit too hard always had something they needed
to have done around the house. "The next six to eight weeks are critical
ones for families that have long been unemployed," the editors of *The
American Home*, one of the country's most popular home-improvement
magazines, noted in February 1932. "Bitter cold sharpens the pinch of
want and may bring tragedy to those who lack food, fuel, and adequate
clothing." The same six weeks, the editors continued, were "the most
monotonous days for many families in better circumstances," so perhaps
the time was ripe to launch home-improvement projects with labor
supplied by the unemployed. They followed this suggestion with a list
of one hundred home projects, including everything from building a
breakfast nook to installing asbestos covering around heating pipes.
"[We] urge your consideration of the entire list of one hundred suggestions," the editors emphasized, "to find a few . . . items that you can
carry out now not only for your own sake but for the benefit of those to
whom charity is an unwelcomed last recourse."[2] To that very end,
Boston's civic leaders had sent letters to 150,000 local homeowners asking them to undertake home repair projects, while in Portland, Oregon,
local newspapers crusaded for a citywide private "fix-it-up" campaign,
and in Washington, D.C., the board of trade launched a "Renovize
Washington" effort, not only urging homeowners to start fixing things

1. Quoted in Robert S. Lynd and Helen Merrell Lynd, *Middletown in Transition*, p. 105.
2. *"The American Home* Employment Plan," *The American Home* (February 1932). Ironically, four months later the magazine announced that because of a decline in advertising revenue, it was going to have to combine its next four issues into two
numbers—June/July and August/September.

up but offering low-interest loans of up to $500 from a pool of $500,000 established by the District Bankers' Association.[3] Similar campaigns sputtered along in many cities between 1930 and 1933.

At the same time, millions of suffering individuals exercised their responsibility to avoid outright charity with astonishing perseverance and sometimes ingenious strategies. In Los Angeles, for example, Robert Hine's father had lost both his job and the apartment complex he had built. For a while, the family sold soda pop from a "counter" attached to their automobile window and rented umbrellas to sun-bathers down at Ocean Park Beach. An even better business was found up in the San Gabriel Mountains:

> We had heard of an isolated county campground at Crystal Lake on one of the forks of the San Gabriel River above Azusa. As a cheap vacation, camping was a growing recreation. . . . We started with a few cases of iced soda pop (Coca-Cola, grape or creme Nehi). We soon learned that campers frequently ran out of basic supplies like bread or milk and would be happy to buy them at pretty good prices. So we built a small two-wheeled trailer which we loaded in Azusa and used at the camp for the store counter. My aunt, always a good cook, started frying hamburgers over a Coleman stove and selling them with a nice profit at something like a quarter. We did this for three or four years.[4]

Some of the self-reliant sought hope in endurance, entering grueling contests whose popularity had spilled over from the frenetic twenties but whose character now reeked of desperation. There were six-day bicycle races and 4,000-mile "roller derbies," pie-eating marathons, talking marathons, and walking marathons. But most memorable of all were the dance marathons, pitiable exercises that drove couple after couple to drop from exhaustion as tinny recorded music echoed in rented halls and auditoriums day after day, often week after week, while

3. For Boston, see Trout, op. cit., p. 97; for Portland, see William H. Mullins, *The Depression and the Urban West Coast, 1929–1933*, p. 82; for Washington, D.C., see Constance Green, *Washington: Capital City, 1879–1950*, pp. 378–80.
4. Robert V. Hine, "Foreclosure in Los Angeles," *The Pacific Historian* (Winter 1983).

masters of ceremonies goaded the dancers on in a grim parody of fun, and spectators paid to watch. Typically, the surviving couple would crawl away with enough cash to get them through another month or two, at best. The marathons, one critic said, "reveal human nature at its worst," spectators wallowing in the "greedy delight" provided by the "sight of others in mental and physical anguish"; another described the dances as the "macabre modern equivalent of a Roman Gladiatorial spectacle."[5]

In October 1930, thousands more entered the annals of folklore as apple-sellers—less a spontaneous movement among the unemployed than a calculated effort by the International Apple Shippers' Association to get rid of a surplus of Pacific Northwest apples. In theory, every morning an individual could buy, on credit, a box of 72 apples for $1.75 at a shipping warehouse in his city, spend the day selling them on the street for a nickel apiece, return to the warehouse, pay off his debt, and walk away with a profit of $1.85. "Buy an apple a day and eat the depression away!" the association proclaimed in advertisements, and for a time the downtown sidewalks of most of the major cities of the country blossomed with apple-sellers, six thousand of them in New York alone.[6] The system worked reasonably well for the Apple Shippers' Association, somewhat less well for the sellers. In November, the price of a box of apples was raised to $2.25, reducing the profit potential to $1.35, and when one took into consideration the inevitable two or three or four bad apples in each box and the expense for bus or subway transportation, the more likely margin could be reduced to less than a dollar. Still, enough people were engaged in the business to persuade the Labor Department to remove them from the official ranks of the unemployed and to bring Herbert Hoover to the preposterous statement that "many persons left their jobs for the more profitable one of selling apples."[7]

Many chose shoe-shining over fruit sales. By the summer of 1932, there were an estimated seven thousand bootblacks in Manhattan, the *New York Times* said: "In one block, on West Forty-third Street, a recent count showed nineteen shoe-shiners. They ranged in age from a sixteen-

5. Both quotes in Gary Dean Best, *The Nickel and Dime Decade*, p. 25.
6. Quoted in Ellis, op. cit., p. 126.
7. Quoted in ibid., p. 127.

year-old . . . to a man of more than seventy. . . . Some sit quietly on
their little wooden boxes and wait patiently for the infrequent customers. Others show true initiative and ballyhoo their trade, pointing
accusingly at every pair of unshined shoes that passes."[8]

Everywhere, door-to-door salesmen proliferated, peddling on commission everything from soap to bibles (sales of the Fuller Brush Company, for one, grew at the rate of a million dollars a year throughout the
depression). There were so many that numerous towns attempted to
license and fingerprint salesmen and prohibit them from coming to the
door without a specific invitation.[9] Others, particularly adolescent boys,
took to tree sitting for a living, climbing to the highest branches of a
suitably toplofty tree and sitting there for days on end, hoping—like
the flag-sitters of the twenties—to break a tree-sitting record, get some
local notoriety, and, not incidentally, garner some income from a coin
box conveniently placed at the foot of the tree. There were other sources
as well. The *Literary Digest* noted in 1930 that "bank accounts of the
numerous contestants from the sale of autographs, publicity mediums
[local merchants often used the tree-sitters to advertise their wares], and
outright donations at coin boxes are not to be dismissed with a shrug."[10]

In many communities, but especially among those with significant
populations of black people, the Saturday night "rent party" became
a common money-raising device. An old tradition among African
Americans in many southern towns, "who sought to confine their troubles with a little joy," in the words of black sociologist Ira Reid, the rent
party had been raised to the level of a major cultural phenomenon in
Harlem by the time of the depression. Invitations were handed out on
the street or stuffed into mailboxes—"Shake it in the morning. Shake it
at night at a Social Matinee Party," a typical invitation read; "Music too
tight. Refreshments just right"—and for an admission fee of anywhere
from ten cents to a dollar the party-goer might even get the chance to
hear such artists as Fats Waller or Duke Ellington sitting in to help out
a friend.[11]

8. The *New York Times* (June 5, 1932).
9. See Caroline Bird, *The Invisible Scar*, pp. 46–47.
10. Quoted in Best, op. cit., p. 22.
11. Quotes from Jervis Anderson, *This Was Harlem,* pp. 152–53.

In the anthracite coal country of the Appalachian Mountains, some overworked and underpaid or unemployed miners stretched the notion of free enterprise a little beyond respectability. They bootlegged coal, smuggling it out of working mines a piece at a time in their clothes or lunch buckets, secretly mining it themselves from company claim land, or stealing it at night from storage areas. It was said that some four million tons of coal a year was bootlegged, and for a time as much as 10 percent of all coal sold in New York City was stolen. There were at least 6,500 bootleggers, one estimate had it, and, being Americans, they formed their own organization, the Independent Anthracite Miners Association, complete with articles of incorporation whose preamble explained their motivation with admirable clarity: "We must dig the coal out of these mountains as a means of supplementing our measly income that we receive in the form of relief, in order to keep the wolf from our doorsteps. Knowing that the coal which is in these mountains was put there by our Creator and that this mineral wealth was stolen away from us by the greedy rich class, the coal operators and the bankers . . ."[12]

Other kinds of mining, more legitimate if no less desperate than coal thievery, took place in the mother lode country of California's Sierra Nevada. It was here that the discovery of gold in unheard-of quantities had started the gold rush of 1849 and changed forever the world's economy. By the time of the depression, California's mining industry had fallen on times quite as hard as any in the country, but the hills now swarmed with a new generation of miners acting out a sad parody of the frenzy of '49. Among them was Eric Sevareid, fresh off a transcontinental freight. "We were more like scavengers," he remembered. "The hope of finding gold, which almost none of us ever did, was more of an excuse to live in the hills where life was cheap, than anything else."[13]

Similarly, in Arizona, where falling prices had closed or severely reduced operations in most of the state's copper mines, hundreds drifted north in the summer months to paw through old placer claims where gold had been worked in the latter third of the nineteenth century. The Yavapai County Chamber of Commerce offered to teach them the rudiments of placer mining, and local banks and a few firms in Prescott

12. Quote and bootlegging discussion from Bird, op. cit., pp. 47–48.
13. Sevareid, op. cit., pp. 107–9.

agreed to trade gold nuggets for cash. "Sometimes they really do pan out a few cents—or once in a while get a dollar or more," one observer in Prescott reported in the summer of 1931, "but the old diggings are very lean of gold—having been worked over and over all these years."[14]

Things were hardly better for erstwhile placer miners up in Colorado, where in the spring and summer of 1932, creeks and rivers in the front range of the Rockies were overrun by so many prospectors that the mayor of Breckenridge, worried that his little town might have hundreds of destitute people on its hands come winter, warned that "it is quite impossible for anyone to pan enough gold to make a living," and asked the governor to send along a couple of tons of flour.[15] In Virginia City, Nevada, where the discovery of the great Comstock lode in 1859 had rivaled the impact of the California gold rush, a writer for *Popular Science* found "a little, middle-aged man shoveling dirt in a very businesslike fashion:

"Me a minin' man?" he answered my query, leaning on his spade. "Yes, I'm a miner—all of ten weeks now. Before that, I'd been a sailor all my life. Now it's a simple case of 'root, hog, or die!' so I'm rootin'. . . ."

He exhibited a small bottle containing a few flat nuggets and some dust, totaling perhaps an ounce or two.

"Not much for the work, but I don't mind that. The worst is the fare I have to eat. It's beans for dinner, for supper, for breakfast and between meals. It's hard, even for a sea-farin' man. It's only hope that keeps us going."[16]

IN THE END, of course, there were never enough renovation projects, dance marathon prizes, apples, oranges, unshined shoes, unsold Bibles and brushes, unsat trees, illicit pieces of coal, placer gold deposits—or

14. Quoted in Margaret F. Maxwell, "The Depression in Yavapai County," *Journal of Arizona History* (Summer 1982).
15. Quoted in Leonard, op. cit., p. 38.
16. Sterling Gleason, "The New Gold Rush," *Popular Science* (August 1932); condensed in *Reader's Digest* (September 1932).

hope—to keep all the hungry families alive. Sooner or later, individuals
were forced to swallow pride and look to their neighbors for simple survival. Most communities made at least an effort to meet the need,
though usually with great reluctance and almost always with the fear
that by doing so they were in grave danger of nourishing the creation of
a permanent class of relief-dependent paupers. And no matter how dire
the circumstances, it was firmly held almost everywhere, no town
should even think to turn to the federal government for direct aid. This
was entirely in keeping with the views of President Hoover, who in
December 1930 emphasized that in the face of the crisis every citizen
should "maintain his self-reliance. . . . [T]he vast majority whose
income is unimpaired . . . should seek to assist . . . neighbors who may
be less fortunate. . . . [E]ach industry should assist its own employees . . . each community and each State should assume its full responsibilities for organization of employment and relief of distress with that
sturdiness and independence which built a great Nation."[17]

This is not to say that Hoover believed that the federal government
should merely fiddle while the national economy went up in flames. As
early as April 1929, he had persuaded Congress to authorize the creation of a farm board whose members would seek (vainly) to craft a
cooperative marketing strategy among farmers that might lift the
already beleaguered agricultural industry out of the red. In June 1930,
although with misgivings about budget-busting, he endorsed the con-
gressionally authorized expenditure of more than $2.3 billion in federal
public works projects in order to create jobs. In October, he formed the
President's Emergency Committee for Employment, whose thirty-two
volunteer members were enjoined to discover the depth and character
of the unemployment problem; they were given very little money to
work with, however, and were reduced to issuing recommendations
regarding home-improvement projects, low-cost food shopping opportunities, and other informational pabulum. In August 1931, Hoover
changed the entity's name to the President's Organization on Unemployment Relief (POUR) and gave it enough money to launch a major
advertising campaign. "Between October 19 and November 25," one
breathless handout sang, "America will feel the thrill of a great spiritual

17. Quoted in Warren, op. cit., p. 193.

experience. In those few weeks millions of dollars will be raised . . . and the fear of cold and hunger will be banished from the hearts of thousands!"[18] (The validity of such effusions may have been undermined by the spectacular ignorance of POUR's director, Walter S. Gifford, who once burbled to a congressional committee, "I think that what we need is that everybody go back to work and have full pay for all jobs."[19])

Two months later, the president browbeat the banking community into setting up a National Credit Corporation with $500 million of the bankers' own money. The NCC would then make loans to troubled financial institutions and presumably muffle the sound of falling banks. Ultimately, it loaned only $153 million to just 575 banks, while scores continued to crash every month. Of greater significance was the Reconstruction Finance Corporation, which Hoover persuaded Congress to create in January 1932. An exercise in pure "state capitalism," the RFC was a quasi-independent body authorized to issue federal loans to banks, credit unions, mortgage loan companies, and other businesses— not merely to shore them up but to inspire them to get more money out into the loan market to stimulate investment and spending. To charges that his devotion to the principle of self-reliance apparently did not preclude federal relief to the rich, Hoover replied stiffly: "As I have stated before, in the shifting battle against depression, we shall need to adopt new measures and new tactics as the battle moves on. The essential thing is that we should build soundly and solidly for the future."[20] The first loan—$15 million to A. P. Giannini's Bank of America National Trust and Savings Association in San Francisco—was made on February 15, and by the end of the summer the RFC would hand out more than a billion dollars. Success was limited, however; while many banks were saved (armed with an additional $49.5 million, Giannini's was among them; as the Bank of America, it would go on to become the second-largest bank in the United States by the end of the decade), many were not, and in spite of the injection of money, most lending institutions,

18. Quote in ibid., p. 196. My summary of Hoover's antidepression measures is taken largely from this source.
19. Quoted in ibid., p. 197.
20. Quoted in James S. Olson, *Saving Capitalism: The Reconstruction Finance Corporation and the New Deal, 1933–1940*, p. 16.

with the fear of ruin hanging over them, stubbornly clutched their growing capital reserves to their fiduciary bosoms.[21]

As for direct aid to human beings, Hoover remained persuaded that communities should be held responsible for their own people, that most aid should come from charitable institutions, not government, and that the federal role should be advisory, as with the cheerful adumbrations issuing almost daily from the offices of POUR. "I'll see it through if *you* will!" exclaimed the illustration of a troubled but stalwart unemployed man in a typical POUR-sponsored magazine advertisement:

> Understand, we're not begging. We'd rather have a job than anything else you can give us. We're not scared, either. If you think the good old U.S.A. is in a bad way more than temporarily, just try to figure out some other place you'd rather be.
>
> Now, don't send me any money—that isn't the idea. Don't even send any to the Committee which signs this appeal. The best way to help us is to give as generously as you can to your local welfare and charity organizations, your community chest or your emergency relief committee if you have one.[22]

The president remained true to his convictions even when human need crossed community, county, and state lines—as it did with terrible impact in the Mississippi Delta, where the economic crisis was as nothing compared to the creeping horror of drought. The region had not fully recovered from the murderous flood of 1927 that had helped to put Hoover in office when a drought in the spring of 1930 began drying up creeks, streams, and ponds, killing fish and wildlife and desiccating commercial crops and kitchen gardens alike. It also succeeded in bankrupting many cotton plantations and leaving sharecroppers and tenant farmers in a condition suggested all too clearly by one woman's letter: "We can't make the winter [we] are all bare foot. The 13 years boy and the 7 years old is just naked, no shoes, nor clothes. We lost all we had

21. For a good firsthand account of the RFC's early months, see Jesse H. Jones, with Edward Angly, *Fifty Billion Dollars: My Thirteen Years with the RFC (1932–1945)*, pp. 13–18.
22. Ad in *The Ladies' Home Journal* (November 1930).

three years ago and have made crop failure ever since. . . . I can't see how we will get by."[23]

Volunteerism, that was the thing, Hoover decided, and instructed drought sufferers to turn to the Red Cross for relief, as they had during the 1927 floods. For the president's part, he used the prestige of his office to promote Red Cross fund-raising efforts, reluctantly approved the use of about $20 million in rehabilitation money for the purchase of food and seed (though only in the form of loans to those with visible collateral, which did not include the families of tens of thousands of sharecroppers and tenant farmers), and sternly resisted efforts by various members of Congress to appropriate money for direct food relief. If the federal government gave drought victims food, he worried, how long would it be before the victims of economic crisis all over the country began to look to Washington for direct aid?

The Red Cross ultimately spent a little under $11 million to feed 2.7 million people at a bare subsistence level in the South during the worst months of the drought. This, and the pittance in federal rehabilitation loans that ever got translated into food for people to eat, were monumentally inadequate under the best of circumstances. The Red Cross program, itself administered at the local level by local people, was generally sporadic, sometimes rigid and miserly, often prejudiced against black applicants, and in many places simply incompetent; as a result, hundreds of thousands of people staggered through winter with almost nothing in the way of food, clothing, heating fuel, or medicine. No accurate count has ever been made of those who died from exposure or starvation. Presumably, their friends and relatives could take comfort in the fact that the moral fiber of the victims had not been corrupted by direct federal aid.

In spite of the drought's terrible consequences, Hoover's insistence on local hegemony was accepted as gospel by most southern communities, as it was elsewhere in the country. Local problems, the litany proclaimed, should be dealt with locally—and if the sheer enormity of the disaster ultimately defeated them, some communities compiled truly admirable records of civic gumption. "I feel that the time has come to

23. Quoted in Nan Elizabeth Woodruff, *As Rare as Rain: Federal Relief in the Great Southern Drought of 1930–1931*, p. 27.

face the situation as it stands," Mayor George Baker told the citizens of
Portland, Oregon, at the end of October 1930. "[The] condition is general and we must call a spade a spade and prepare to meet the problem."
He ordered immediate cuts in city budgets, specified that all money
saved should go into a relief fund for the unemployed, told city departments to create public works jobs, and to that end instituted an urban
renewal project that demolished old buildings and replaced them with
new construction. "I'll wreck the town if it will give employment," he
said.[24] A Civic Emergency Committee was formed to administer the
distribution of emergency relief funds. It ultimately included representatives from 106 different organizations, including county and city officials, church leaders, and businessmen. In April 1931, citizens went to
the polls and by a margin of more than two to one approved a $2 mil-
lion bond issue for relief purposes, a more than respectable commitment
from a town of only about 300,000 residents. A community chest fund
drive in the fall of 1931 raised another $744,000, and the *Portland
Journal* felt that congratulations were in order: "Portland can report to
President Hoover . . . 'We are doing our bit. We as a community have
assumed the responsibility for this community.'"[25]

Few communities matched Portland's level of commitment, but
most at least tried. Civic leaders in Fort Wayne, Indiana, were especially
determined to deal with their city's problems without help from the
outside—preferably, without help from any government entity whatever. "No one," insurance executive Arthur F. Hall declared at one
point, "wants Governmental Taxation or Governmental Supervision for
the care of the unfortunate."[26] And, as in Portland, one of the first
actions taken was to form a committee to raise and administer voluntary
relief funds. Beginning in December 1930, the Allen County Emergency Unemployment Committee called for contributions from across
the community's population of 115,000. Its first drive brought in
$360,000, about 40 percent from the town's richest citizens; working
people who made more than fifty dollars a month were asked to con-

24. Both quotes in Mullins, op. cit., p. 42.
25. Quoted in ibid., p. 82.
26. Quoted in Iwan Morgan, "Fort Wayne and the Great Depression: The Early Years,
1929–1933," *Indiana Magazine of History* (June 1984).

tribute half a day's pay every month for six months, while those who made more than one hundred dollars were asked for a full day's pay. On the basis of that success, the ACEUC launched a second drive in the spring of 1931 to bring in another $385,000. More than a thousand volunteers went to work, and the final tally was $415,000. "We are protecting our city and our community," Hall declaimed once again, "against the perils of social destruction inherent in poverty, idleness, ill health, dependence and discontent."[27]

James Michael Curley, the politically powerful mayor of Boston, on the other hand, was among the few city officials anywhere at the beginning of the depression who did not fully honor the sanctity of local relief. He spent a good deal of time in 1930 trying to get relief funds and public works money out of both the Massachusetts State government and Washington, D.C. Not that it did much good. The Republican-dominated state senate was dead set against giving money to any municipality, much less one in the hands of a reputedly corrupt Democrat—and an Irish Catholic to boot. And, as was to be expected, Hoover was also cool to Curley's importunations. "President Hoover," the mayor complained after an unproductive meeting in September 1930, "is very voluminous in his proclamations regarding the emergency. If proclamations could settle industrial depressions, then we would be the most prosperous of peoples."[28]

Forced to rely on his own city's resources, Curley established an unemployment fund in April 1931. All but the lowest-paid city employees were asked to contribute the equivalent of a day's pay. Curley himself contributed $4,000 of his own salary. Various fund-raising events were staged, including concerts for the jobless given by the civic symphony and a charity football game between Boston College and Holy Cross University in Harvard stadium. In December 1931, the inevitable Emergency Unemployment Relief Committee was formed; to promote its efforts, an effigy labeled "General D. Pression" was put in a coffin, paraded through the streets to Battery Wharf, and, to the accompaniment of tap-dancing chorus girls and a brass band blaring a

27. Quoted in ibid.
28. Quoted in Jack Beatty, *The Rascal King: The Life and Times of James Michael Curley, 1874–1958*, p. 291.

rendition of "Happy Days Are Here Again," put on board a barge, and sent off into Boston harbor. The recession, the mayor announced, was "well buried for all time."[29] The campaign that followed brought in more than $3 million by February 1932.

Doing violence to effigies was a generally popular business; in Norfolk, Virginia, three dummies called "Mis-For-tune," "Pessimism," and "Depression" were paraded through the streets, lynched, put into coffins, and cast out to sea, while in New York City the opening of a new subway line in 1931 seemed like a good time to hang in effigy "Old Man Depression."[30] More practically, New York's civic leaders borrowed from a device invented in upstate Buffalo to institute a "Block-Aid" campaign, enrolling 200,000 working people to go out to get minimum pledges of one dollar a week from their neighbors on the block. "The block population," the *New York Times* mused in support of this effort, "is often not unlike a small town with wealth and modest means in close proximity. To bring them close together in a common interest is something worthwhile in itself."[31] The campaign raised about $18 million, far more of it from working people than from those of wealth. In the meantime, private and public agencies joined to launch a $40 million citywide fund-raising drive ballyhooed at the top of his own considerable lungs by unsuccessful presidential candidate Al Smith.[32] In Kansas City, where Mayor Tom Pendergast's political machine ruled the city like a sledge, voters approved by a four-to-one margin a $32 million bond issue to finance a "Ten-year Plan" for public works designed to stimulate employment and beautify the city.[33] The city and county of Los Angeles spent $10 million for direct relief and put 60,000 men to work building firebreaks, while voters approved a $38 million bond sale to finance work on the Owens Valley Aqueduct, the city's main water supply, that would provide more jobs, and city employees sponsored a job-fund campaign in which voluntary monthly

29. Story and quote in Trout, op. cit., pp. 93–94.
30. See Gilbert Seldes, *The Years of the Locust (1929–1932)*, p. 70.
31. Quoted in ibid., p. 161.
32. For New York relief fund campaign, see Bendiner, op. cit., p. 6.
33. See William K. Reddig, *Tom's Town: Kansas City and the Pendergast Legend*, pp. 179–82.

salary donations of 1 percent per worker raised $114,469.[34] In Butte, Montana, those few copper miners still working the ore bodies of the Anaconda Mining Company (it had laid off about eight thousand men between the end of 1929 and the beginning of 1931) subscribed 2 percent of their monthly salaries to the general relief fund administered by the newly formed Silver Bow County Emergency Relief Administration.[35] Wealthy Philadelphians rallied around the Committee of One Hundred, which in turn formed a Committee for Unemployment Relief and ultimately distributed $29.5 million in private and public funds.[36]

In May 1932, Pittsburgh spent more than $600,000 for relief, and San Francisco more than $550,000. In Chicago, the figure was $2.5 million; in Birmingham, Alabama, $79,374. Tulsa, Oklahoma, spent $20,471; Louisville, Kentucky, $41,805; Topeka, Kansas, $14,478.[37] In spite of Hoover's dictum that the states should assume part of the burden, little, if any, help came from the state governments, most of which, like Massachusetts, were as firm as the national government in their conviction that relief was strictly a local responsibility and whose record of aid, *Fortune* magazine said, was, one "broadly considered, of inaction and failure." Only eight states ever appropriated significant money for the relief of their citizens, and most of that came from only two—Illinois ($18.75 million) and New York ($20 million). California, Maryland, Tennessee, and Wisconsin appointed "investigating committees."[38] For the most part, the cities and counties were on their own, reaching into their collective pockets in the finest American tradition of sturdiness and independence, resolutely stacking up sandbags of money against the rising waters of desperation.

34. See Mullins, op. cit., pp. 33–36.
35. See Mary Murphy, *Mining Cultures: Men, Women, and Leisure in Butte, 1914–1941,* pp. 200–204.
36. See Bonnie Fox Schwartz, "Unemployment Relief in Philadelphia, 1930–1932: A Study of the Depression's Impact on Volunteerism," *Pennsylvania Magazine of History and Biography* (January 1969).
37. All figures from "'No One Has Starved,'" *Fortune* (September 1932).
38. Quotes and figures from "'This State Will Care for Its Own,'" *Fortune* (September 1932).

· · ·

IF TOWNS AND cities everywhere struggled to meet the crisis with varying degrees of commitment and energy, their religious communities
left an equally mixed record. Churches of a Fundamentalist stripe
tended to look upon the depression not only as the visitation of God's
well-deserved wrath but as a dress rehearsal for the cleansing Apoca-
lypse and Final Judgment. Under the circumstances, it seemed to them,
charitable work of any significant dimension was hardly worth the
effort, and little came from such quarters. At the other end of the theological spectrum, the radical Methodist Federation of Social Service
believed that little could be done without a revolutionary change of the
entire social structure into a new world order that would repudiate
greed and embrace redemption. Until that day, the depression was the
fire through which the world would have to pass on the way to the new
millennium, and direct charity from this wing, too, was thin.[39]

Between these two extremes lay a sea of conflicting attitudes, complicated in no small part by what some were calling a "religious depression," the big mainstream churches of the nation having experienced a
falling off in both membership and money. The decline, however, was
not caused primarily by the national depression. The fact was, church
attendance and financial support had been dropping for years, beginning in the early twenties. Between 1921 and 1929, one report estimated, per capita gifts to charity fell from $5.57 to $3.43. In 1920,
2,700 students had offered themselves up for service to the Foreign
Missions Conference of North America; in 1928, the figure had been
252. "Almost all major denominations are now in a period of financial
stringency in the conduct of mission work," the Home Missions Council had reported as early as 1927. "We are in the days of falling
budgets."[40]

The twenties, on the whole, were a particularly secular age. In *Middletown*, the Lynds reported that by 1924 church attendance in Muncie,

39. See Donald Meyer, *The Protestant Search for Political Realism, 1919–1941*, pp.
166–67.
40. Quote and statistics in Robert T. Handy, "The American Religious Depression,
1925–1935," *Church History* (Winter 1976–1977).

Indiana, had fallen by as much as half what it had been in 1890, much of the decline the result of a postwar disillusion with religion in general. "We don't go," one woman remarked. "I believe the church is a good thing for the community, and the beliefs it stands for are probably a good thing, but I've just pretty well lost any belief in church and God and immortality I ever had. If you do the very best you can, that's all anybody can do anyway."[41]

Businessmen were too busy for church, teenagers were too caught up in the excitements of a new age of ostensible freedom, intellectuals spurned religion's "superstitions," and families found that a Sunday drive was more entertaining than a Sunday sermon. Many of the mainstream churches had responded to such apathy by attempting to become more worldly and practical, relaxing their standards regarding public and private behavior and generally embracing the culture of prosperity. This neither brought back membership nor pleased those who would resist the winds of fashion. "America has become almost hopelessly enamoured of a religion that is little more than a sanctified commercialism," Charles Fiske complained in his 1929 book, *Confessions of a Puzzled Parson* (1929). "Our conception of God is that He is a sort of Magnified Rotarian. . . . I hope I may be forgiven . . . when I say that Protestantism in America seems to be degenerating into a sort of Babsonian cult, which cannot distinguish between what is offered to God and what is accomplished for the glory of America and the furtherance of business enterprise."[42] Attendance continued to decline, and as traditional churches drifted further from the certitudes of morality and dogma, people who sought such things in their lives increasingly succumbed to such evangelical offshoots as Aimee Semple McPherson's Four Square Gospel.

While they lamented the depression's impact, many of the traditional churches had actually perceived a solution to their dilemma, hoping that as the crisis deepened, people would turn to religion for solace and reassurance, as they had in past moments of national turmoil and disaster, and that a nationwide wave of revivals would swiftly follow.

41. Quoted in Robert S. Lynd and Helen Merrell Lynd, *Middletown: A Study in Contemporary American Culture*, p. 368.
42. Quoted in Handy, op. cit.

But there was no great revival. The depression clearly was not an act of God, and one observer noted that it might have been "the first time that men have not blamed God for hard times."[43] If it was not caused by God, then there was no compelling reason to turn to Him for help.

For the most part, the traditional religions floundered, their attitudes ranging from that of Pittsburgh's towering and richly endowed new East Liberty Presbyterian Church, whose minister let a waiting world know that in spite of all his church's conspicuous opulence, "there will also be a place where any poor person may be temporarily cared for,"[44] to that of New York's Rabbi Rosenblum, who lectured worshipers on what he perceived to be their clear duty:

> To-day there are nearly twelve hundred thousand persons out of work in our city, which means that three or four times that number, or at least half the population of New York, are on the danger line. Fifty thousand children are in need of feeding. What are the synagogues going to do about it? We cannot keep them alive on prayers. We must give them bread. It is well enough for those who come to our synagogues to fast. Most of them fast by choice, but it will be a sacrilege if out of our worship there does not come the urge to keep the other half from starving.[45]

The social service programs of the Federal Council of Churches, the National Catholic Welfare Council, and the Central Committee of American Rabbis all sponsored their own money drives, worked closely with community chests, encouraged local churches and synagogues to institute odd-job and make-work projects, and engaged in direct charitable work of one kind or another. "This is a world," the Reverend Harry Emerson Fosdick of New York's Riverside Church reminded his parishioners, "where in the long run we cannot keep for ourselves anything we desire unless we share it with the whole body of the people,"

43. Quoted in Martin Marty, *Modern American Religion. Volume II: The Noise of Conflict, 1919–1941*, p. 253.
44. Quoted in ibid.
45. Quoted in Seldes, op. cit., p. 297.

and his somewhat genteel and practical version of charity was echoed in most of the temples of mainstream Protestantism, Catholicism, and Judaism.[46]

Others, less orthodox and timid, were willing to go a little further. There was, for example, the Peace Mission movement of Father Divine, one of the most extraordinarily charismatic religious figures of this century. He had been born George Baker Jr. in Rockville, Maryland, in 1879, and had been drawn into the evangelical tradition of black Methodism at an early age. By the time he reached his twenties, he had decided to spread the gospel himself, turning to the storefront churches of Baltimore for his venue. There he found a stew of Protestantism in all its forms, some of it enriched by New Thought, the mid–nineteenth century movement whose doctrine that the mind controlled health was the root of Mary Baker Eddy's Christian Science. New Thought also informed Charles Fillmore's Unity School of Christianity, which held that God—Father-Mother-God, in Fillmore's cosmology—was not a separate entity but existed in all people; if that presence were properly "channeled," human beings themselves could literally become one with God, and thus divine.

Within a few years, Baker had digested all this and more and from it had concluded that the divine spirit had in fact settled only in him, not everyone, and that it was his mission to bring his personal godhead to the multitudes. He changed his name to the Reverend Major Jealous Divine. "God is here on earth today," his followers sang. "Father Divine is his name," and Father Divine is how he would be known by most of the world.[47] By the time of the depression, Peace Missions devoted to his teachings and to the relief of the poor had spread to many cities, and the number of his followers may have reached as many as two million— many of them white people, since Father Divine preached a militantly nonracial, nondenominational dogma. What he offered to whites and blacks alike was a chance at immortality—and, in the meantime, some

46. Quoted in ibid., p. 298.
47. Quoted in Jill Watts, *God, Harlem, U.S.A.: The Father Divine Story*, p. 48. My discussion of Father Divine is based on this source and on Sara Harris, *Father Divine: Holy Husband*.

good hot food to anyone who needed it, served up in his nationwide network of Peace Mission banquet halls. "Do not fast!" he would cry over platters of beef and chicken and bowls of stew in his own missions in Newark, New Jersey, or Harlem.[48] "Sisters and Brothers," poet Langston Hughes remembered his saying, "I want you to eat and eat and eat, and dine and dine and dine. And when you have eaten and eaten and eaten, and dined and dined and dined, I want you to get up and give your places to others that they might eat and eat and eat, and dine and dine and dine. Peace! It's truly wonderful."[49] So it was, and for most of the people who chose to follow his teachings, that was enough. It was even enough for those who were not followers. "Oh, my Lord, he fed a lot of people," longtime Harlem resident Naomi Washington remembered. "And when I tell you, it was good food—I went. As much as you could eat. If you were hungry when you went in, when you came out, if you didn't eat for two days, you had enough."[50]

In Washington, D.C., Elder Lightfoot Solomon Michaux acquired a following that rivaled the local Peace Mission congregation of Father Divine and, through his radio audience, a "congregation" that surpassed Divine's national following, although Michaux's Church of God dogma was of a more traditional Christian character. He had come to the nation's capital early in the depression years, set up a storefront Church of God on Georgia Avenue, and launched a daily morning radio broadcast on WJSV—whose call letters, he said, were an acronym for "Willingly, *Jesus* *S*uffered for *V*ictory over the grave." Translating the term "gospel" as "happy news" (an interpretation with which most religious scholars, in fact, would have been perfectly comfortable), the "Happy am I" preacher's message of joy over local morning radio became so popular that he was soon broadcasting to a nationwide audience of both black and white people over the CBS and Mutual networks. Nor was his version of Christianity confined to individual spiritual salvation. When Bernarr McFadden, the health faddist, magazine publisher, and sporadic philanthropist, gave a penny lunchroom to the church, Michaux

48. Quoted in Harris, op. cit., p. 54.
49. Quoted in Bendiner, op. cit., p. 142.
50. Quoted in Jeff Kisseloff, *You Must Remember This: An Oral History of Manhattan from the 1890s to World War II*, p. 292.

named it the "Happy News Café" and fed hundreds of hungry people every day. He also acquired a large, rent-free building at Seventh and T Streets NW, where in exchange for providing renovation work, he was able to house forty homeless families.[51]

IF INSTITUTIONAL RELIGION had largely failed, novelist Pearl Buck thought, the spiritual core of most Americans had not. "I am amazed at all the religion I see everywhere," she wrote in 1933. "I am speaking . . . of those men and women who cannot endure the suffering of others, who feel it as their own suffering, and who give out of their own longing to see the world better. . . . They have the living spirit of religion."[52] Some found that spirit in the communitarian efforts of a self-help movement that spread as groups of the unemployed joined together in their own dance of Hooverian self-reliance. Even if *Judge*, the humor magazine, defined it as "giving somebody a pig and a couple of ducks they don't want in exchange for an overcoat that doesn't fit," simple barter between individuals was common in many towns.[53] Some also engaged in more elaborate "self-help" schemes in which labor and goods were exchanged according to complex organizational structures, often with "scrip" used in place of legal currency. Called "an IOU with a pedigree" by one observer, scrip could take some imaginative forms.[54] A cooperative in Blaine, Washington, for instance, issued wooden nickels, while one in Hood River, Oregon, put out "rubber checks" worth the equivalent of a dollar and embossed on (what else?) rubber.[55] "It is important to note," wrote Clark Kerr, a young social economist (and future chancellor of the University of California) who studied such groups in California in 1932 and 1933, "that the self-help idea was not the product of a careful analysis of conditions, but the spontaneous

---

51. See Constance McLaughlin Green, *The Secret City: A History of Race Relations in the Nation's Capital*, pp. 222, 238–49. In 1942, Michaux erected Mayfair Gardens, a 595-unit apartment complex for middle-class black families.
52. Pearl S. Buck, "What Religion Means to Me," *Outlook* (October 1933).
53. Quoted in Arthur Holch, "When Rubber Checks Didn't Bounce," *American Heritage* (June 1961).
54. Quoted in ibid.
55. Scrip information in ibid.

response of the unemployed working class to a given condition. It was not conceived in the minds of economists, or business men, or politicians, but emanated from the 'rank and file.' . . . Self-support sprang from the actions and the minds of the unemployed. They originated it. They put it into operation. They developed it."[56] Stuart Chase, an older and ordinarily fairly circumspect progressive economist, saw in all this not merely the resourcefulness of the unemployed but the outlines of a world finally free of capitalist shackles. "Some millions of Americans," he predicted, "are going to re-educate themselves by embarking upon the largest programme of organized barter and 'wooden money' exchanges that America has ever seen. They do not propose to lie down and starve so long as some have commodities and other services to exchange among themselves."[57]

The more likely number of those who ever involved themselves seriously in barter or exchange systems was, Kerr estimated, in the vicinity of a million. That was not an insignificant figure, however, and in some towns and areas such systems proliferated, at least during the worst years. Dayton, Ohio, for example, developed not one but two distinct systems, though only one truly qualified as a "rank and file" operation. In the summer of 1932, female residents of "Tin Town," the African American section of the city, where only one man had been able to find work in two years, organized themselves as a "production unit." In cooperation with the city's Relief Store, the women obtained raw materials in exchange for finished clothing, bread, soap, and other handcrafted goods; the difference between the cost of raw materials and the value of the finished goods then provided a "profit," which the women could exchange for food and other necessities at the store. The idea caught on and spread beyond Tin Town (renamed Home View by its newly proud residents), and Dayton soon enjoyed twelve production units with a total membership of 650 families. The largest was the East Dayton production unit, which was given an abandoned factory building as its headquarters; here, members of the unit's one hundred partic-

56. Clark Kerr, "Self-Help: A Study of the Cooperative Barter Movement of the Unemployed in California, 1932–1933," p. 19.
57. Quoted in George R. Leighton, "Doing Business Without Money," *Harper's Magazine* (July 1933).

ipating families could find a barbershop, a beauty shop, a sewing center, a carpentry shop, and a shoe-repair factory, while in another building the unit's bakery produced an average of 1,200 loaves of bread a day for sale to the relief store.

The production units were essentially communal enterprises in which proceeds were shared according to need among the participating families. The Dayton Mutual Exchange, however, organized at the same time by local businessmen, was more like a free-enterprise cooperative designed to operate, as its own description had it, "without requiring that individualism as a basis for the general economic organization be abandoned."[58] Membership was not required, and any money realized from the sale of goods or services to the exchange was paid to the individual in a form of scrip called "goods certificates," which could then be used to buy items at the exchange store.

In nearby Antioch that same summer, civic leaders established the Midwest Exchange, whose plan, a spokesman said, "includes the development of a laboratory of socially motivated industry, and in partial fulfillment of our aim, Antioch has undertaken to attack unemployment and frozen resources in its territory." Its subsidiary, on the other hand, the Yellow Springs Exchange, administered by Antioch College, began offering goods and services as a cooperative similar to Dayton's Mutual Exchange, including its use of scrip.[59] In Waterloo, Iowa, unemployed people, struggling businessmen, and farmers established the Unemployed Relief Club of Waterloo. In Omaha, Nebraska, the cooperative idea took the form of the Unemployed Married Men's Council; in Minneapolis, Minnesota, it emerged as the Organized Unemployed of Minneapolis; in New York City, there was the Emergency Exchange Association, and in Salt Lake City, Utah, the Natural Development Association, sponsored by the Mormon church, itself a prime example of cooperative enterprise.

In no city was the self-help movement as prominent, even dominant, as in Seattle, Washington, and in no state was it as widespread

58. Quoted in George K. Leighton, "Doing Business Without Money," *Harper's Magazine* (July 1933). My discussion of the Dayton self-help enterprises is based on this source.
59. Quoted in George R. Leighton, "They Call It Barter: The New Economics in Ohio and Iowa," *Harper's Magazine* (August 1933).

as in California. Seattle's venture may indeed have been the first such in the country. On an evening in July 1931, a group of about forty unemployed men had gathered in a meeting hall in west Seattle to discuss their situation and at the end of it had emerged as the Unemployed Citizens' League. The founders set to work recruiting others from the ranks of the unemployed, and the membership soon swelled to somewhere between 40,000 and 50,000. It was, one supporter remarked, a "Republic of the Penniless" where "honorable employment was all that passed for currency."[60] Over the next several months, the UCL's workers cut 10,000 cords of firewood, plucked 120,000 pounds of fish from the waters of Puget Sound, and harvested eight carloads of agricultural produce from cooperating farms—all of which was distributed to the families of the unemployed by the UCL itself. A barter system among the members was established where work could be exchanged for everything from haircuts to shoe repair, with *Venture*, the organization's official newsletter, serving as a kind of clearinghouse for exchangeable work and goods. When a family was evicted, the UCL would be likely to send a crew over to move the unfortunates—complete with furniture—right back into the house, doing so repeatedly, and with such perseverance, that in many instances landlords simply abandoned eviction proceedings as a waste of time.

The UCL was so successful that the city's official unemployment committee, the Mayor's Commission on Improved Employment, joined hands with the self-help organization. Together, the two bodies established five depots around the city where food and clothing were collected, then distributed to the needy—much of which were given in exchange for work on city projects at a salary of $4.50 a day—and early in 1932 the day-to-day operations of the city's Direct Relief Organization were placed under the control of the UCL. From then until internal squabbling and an increasingly militant leftward tilt depleted the organization's power, the self-help UCL *was* Seattle's relief system.[61]

---

60. Quoted in Murray Morgan, *Skid Road: An Informal Portrait of Seattle*, p. 231.
61. See William H. Mullins, "Self-Help in Seattle, 1931–1932: Herbert Hoover's Concept of Cooperative Individualism and the Unemployed Citizens' League," *Pacific Northwest Quarterly* (January 1981). Also, by the same author: *The Depression and the Urban West Coast*, pp. 77–110.

No individual self-help organization in California ever achieved the importance of Seattle's UCL, but there were, Clark Kerr estimated, about 340,000 members in more than two hundred self-help groups in the state by the middle of 1933, far and away the largest self-help population of any state in the nation and one that represented just under 6 percent of its total population of 5.7 million. Kerr had spent months immersed in the sociology of this huge subculture, sharing, he wrote, "in the life of the movement by becoming a member of four units, attending meetings, going to 'unemployed dances,' aiding in the opposition of evictions, working with the men in the fields, visiting the members in their homes and partaking of the rancid butter, bacon rinds and liberal seasoning of the 'barter meals' in communal kitchens."[62]

The extraordinary size of the movement in California may have been a distorted reflection of the state's outward agricultural richness, surpassed only by that of Iowa—rich not merely in the quantity of things grown on its county-sized industrial farms but in their variety, which included everything from cantaloupes in the Imperial Valley to cotton in the San Joaquin Valley, from lemons in the San Fernando Valley to almonds in the Sacramento Valley, and a stunning cornucopia of cultivated species in between. But in the depression years there was little market for all this home-grown wealth, and the consequent waste was appalling—especially to the hungry, who saw food going to destruction all around them every day. In 1932 in the Imperial Valley alone, 1.4 million crates of cantaloupes, 2.8 million watermelons, and 700,000 lugs of tomatoes had been destroyed because they could not be sold. In the orange groves that stretched nearly unbroken for more than seventy miles from Arcadia to beyond Riverside, hundreds of tons of unsold oranges a week were piled up in huge mounds, covered in thick heating oil to discourage pilfering, and left to rot in the full view of those who could have used them.[63]

The California State Food Administration, the Parent-Teacher Association, various private charities, and the state chamber of commerce managed to persuade some of the less pathologically selfish growers to part with at least some of this surplus for school lunches and relief

62. Kerr, op. cit., p. iv.
63. Figures from ibid., p. 18.

packages; in 1932, about 1,500 tons of surplus food were thus distributed in Los Angeles County. That was a trifling amount compared to
what should have been made available, and there still was so much
going to waste that William Downing, owner of a Compton storage and
moving company, was inspired to invite a few army friends over for a
meeting in his warehouse in March 1932. The men formed the Compton Veterans' Relief Association, the state's first self-help group, with
the goal of working with cooperating farmers in the region to gather
and distribute surplus produce to the needy, including their own families. "We started with nothing," Downing told Kerr. "We didn't have a
car nor a truck to haul our stuff in, nor if we could haul it, we had no
place to put it after we got it, and we didn't get much in those days. We
had to sell the idea to everyone we came in contact with."[64] The veterans persevered, and the group was soon collecting meat from packing-
houses, surplus milk from dairies, and day-old bread from bakeries,
while engaging in work-for-goods bartering on an increasing scale.

Within a few months of its beginning in Compton, the movement
spread throughout Los Angeles County, where 110 individual self-help
groups were functioning by the middle of 1933, then into most of the
counties in the state. There were so many groups, in fact, that in southern California an umbrella organization, the Unemployed Cooperative
Relief Association (UCRA), united ninety-five of them into a single
loosely knit entity. The self-help groups were soon joined by a number
of exchanges that, like those in Ohio and other parts of the country,
used scrip for money and brokered goods and services among their
members—with a fee of 10 percent of the value of every transaction
typically charged to pay for overhead. The largest of these groups was
the Los Angeles Cooperative Exchange, whose operations were touted
in regular advertisements in the Los Angeles Daily News. "One hundred
music teachers are members of the Exchange," one such read.

> A typical case of how the Exchange has helped them follows. One of
> the teachers who is a member owed a $200 doctor bill but didn't have
> the cash to pay it. The doctor was induced to join the Exchange. The
> Exchange sent the teacher three pupils who paid her in credits. The

64. Quoted in Kerr, op. cit., p. 18.

physician agreed to use the $200 worth of credits. He was given the services of a stenographer for his office, a seamstress for his wife, a maid for his housework, and his automobile was equipped with tires.[65]

In both the exchanges and the self-help groups, anyone was welcome, since, as one leader explained, "a democrat can be as hungry as a communist, a painter as naked as an engineer and a negro can have as little over his head as a white American."[66] Yet despite the radical tone of that declaration—and the increasing militancy of such organizations as Seattle's UCL—most of the self-help groups that arose in the darkest moments of the depression were shining examples of the kind of cooperative individualism that Herbert Hoover espoused. "By cooperatively helping themselves," a handout for the UCRA of California boasted, "the unemployed keep their self-respect and when the present crisis is past, these men will face renewed activity with unlowered morale, perhaps with even greater wisdom and resourcefulness."[67]

Perhaps. But one truly radical observer may have been closer to the truth when he remarked that self-help was a form of relief "comparable to the relief that a starving dog might get by eating his own tail,"[68] and at the end of his study of the California self-help groups, Clark Kerr found himself questioning the true effectiveness of even the best of them. "Self-help," he concluded, "has afforded no more than supplemental assistance for most participants . . . and a starvation living for those few families striving to subsist by its methods. . . . Furthermore, it is unlikely that self-help ever will be able to support adequately any large number of unemployed persons."[69] As it was in California, so it was in other parts of the country in which self-help groups and exchange cooperatives had blossomed. While many continued to function well into the decade, few ever became truly self-supporting, and for all the sense of brotherhood and pride of independence they may have nurtured, they were never able to alleviate true deprivation even among

65. Quoted in ibid., p. 131.
66. Quoted in ibid., p. x.
67. Quoted in ibid., p. 227.
68. Communist Herbert Benjamin, quoted in Franklin Folsom, *Impatient Armies of the Poor: The Story of Collective Action of the Unemployed*, p. 281.
69. Kerr, op. cit., p. 228.

their own members. Many of the movement's leaders knew it. Sadly
watching his organization begin its disintegration at the end of 1932,
one of the founders of Seattle's UCL, sixty-nine-year-old former newspaperman John F. Cronin, celebrated its bravery while recognizing its
ultimate futility. "We fail to understand," he told a reporter,

> how men in dominating political, financial, and industrial positions
> can ignore the necessity for fundamental change if the present world-
> wide breakdown is to be corrected. We're doing our best to meet a
> situation not of our own making. . . . Most of our members are good
> people. Good people! I never knew until I got into this work how
> good people can be. Most of us in this work are near life's halfway
> mark or beyond. What happens to us doesn't matter very much. But
> it's hard for the youngsters to understand. Human life is terribly
> short and tomorrow comes soon. We'd like to see it dawn a little
> brighter for the children.[70]

WHAT OF MORE traditional community efforts? By the summer of 1932,
virtually every city and county in America had, by their own lights,
done everything they could—and, like the efforts of the self-help
groups, their best efforts were woefully inadequate. There was no tax
base broad enough or deep enough, no bond-issuing potential capacious
enough, no body of private citizens charitable enough, no city council
generous-hearted enough (or, as conservatives would have it, fiscally
irresponsible enough) to support at anywhere near decent levels of subsistence the growing millions who needed help. Unemployment rates
continued to climb, relief caseloads swelled by 200, 300, or even 400
percent, individual relief allotments grew smaller and smaller, while
larger and larger portions of city budgets went to finance them (in
1932, $256 million—67 percent of all nonfederal public money—
would go for relief), until there was little or nothing left of either
resources or energy.[71] Voluntary relief efforts, commentator Gilbert
Seldes wrote in 1932, "were bucket brigades fighting a skyscraper

70. Quoted in Morgan, op. cit., pp. 231–32.
71. Figures in Mullins, *The Depression and the Urban West Coast*, p. 85.

fire. . . . The reason is that they all tried to make individual kindness cope with a national calamity which had gone far beyond the point at which kindness, even of the noblest sort and highest degree, could function."[72] For two years, Youngstown Mayor Joseph Heffernan wrote early in 1932, "local communities have carried the burden unassisted, and many of them, like Youngstown, have prostrated themselves doing it. We of the cities have done our best. . . . But . . . we must now admit that we have failed miserably. . . . Our one great achievement in response to this national catastrophe has been to open soup kitchens and flophouses."[73]

On June 20, 1932, the *Philadelphia Record* could have been speaking for any city in the country when it parodied one of Hoover's much-quoted assurances regarding imminent prosperity to announce that Philadelphia's Committee of One Hundred had failed: "For fifty-seven thousand families to whom the Committee has meant life itself, STARVATION is 'just around the corner.' The Committee for two years has fought the wolf away from the doorsteps of Philadelphia's worthy poor. It has tapped and exhausted every available source of succor. And now its funds are gone."[74]

And with such funds, for the most part, went the ideology of community self-reliance among civic leaders. "If the modern state is to rest upon a firm foundation," the head of the Children's Bureau of Philadelphia told a congressional committee, "its citizens must not be allowed to starve. Some of them do. They do not die quickly. You can starve for a long time without dying."[75] Horatio Gates Lloyd, a partner in the Morgan Bank, president of Philadelphia's nearly defunct Committee of One Hundred, and once a steadfast advocate of local responsibility, had now changed his tune: "The present need," he said, "is on a scale that calls not for more charity but for governmental action to save the health and indeed the lives of a large portion of the citizenry," a sentiment that was shared by social workers all over the country by the winter of 1932.[76] "[W]e are in the midst of an emergency, now in its third and

72. Seldes, op. cit., p. 162.
73. Heffernan, op. cit.
74. Quoted in Schwartz, op. cit.
75. Quoted in Ellis, op. cit., p. 243.
76. Ibid.

cumulative winter," Paul Kellogg, a New York social worker and editor of *Survey*, wrote in February, "and when industry has failed to take time by the forelock and where private charitable help falls short, the general public cannot dodge its responsibility to act through government."[77] That government should be the federal government, Pennsylvania Governor Gifford Pinchot had declared in January: "I cannot believe that a national government will stand by while its citizens freeze and starve, without lifting a hand to help. I do not see how it can refuse to grant that relief which it is in honor, in duty, and in its own interest bound to supply."[78]

Hoover was not listening, not yet—the administration's "fundamental policy is not to be changed," he insisted—but Congress was, finally.[79] In February 1932, the first federal relief bills were introduced, and in spite of continuing opposition from Hoover and his surrogates in Congress, one was agreed upon and passed. The president vetoed it on grounds that its proposed $2.2 billion public works program was a pork-barrel enterprise that would bankrupt the nation. Congress went back to work and came up with another version, the Emergency Relief and Construction Act. In this one, the public works program was reduced to $322.2 million (though another $1.5 billion in RFC loans was approved); although the bill authorized up to $300 million in RFC relief loans to those states that could prove their need beyond all reasonable doubt, Hoover gritted his philosophical teeth and signed it on July 21.[80]

The bill, *Fortune*'s editors wrote, "is neither an adequate nor an impressive piece of legislation."[81] Too little, too late, they might have added. Too little and too late to bring much real help, certainly, but also too little and too late to relieve an emotion simmering almost unacknowledged during all the months of shock, struggle, and adjustment, while sublimely high-minded experiments in self-reliance and commu-

77. Quoted in William W. Bremer, *Depression Winters: New York Social Workers and the New Deal*, p. 73.
78. Gifford Pinchot, "The Case for Federal Relief," *The Survey* (January 1, 1932).
79. Quoted in Ellis, op. cit., p. 197.
80. For progress of relief legislation, see Warren, op. cit, pp. 197–208.
81. "'No One Has Starved,'" *Fortune* (September 1932).

nity cooperation joined with inspirational bulletins from the White House to obscure the hard edges of reality. It was a feeling shared by millions of the newly poor and the always poor alike, by the respectable and the unrespectable, the thoughtful and the impulsive—and it would do more to change the nature of the national response to the Great Depression than all the self-help projects that the most imaginative leader could design.

Call it anger.

4

---◆---

"The Long Slow-Match
of Destiny"

In the crucible years of the Great Depression, the natural anger of whole groups of people would be given expression—some of it political, some of it more direct and even violent, some of it nearly spontaneous, some of it carefully manipulated by those willing to help it along for their own purposes. The manipulators were given a great deal of ammunition with which to exploit fear and resentment. If nearly 25 percent of the labor force was unemployed, after all, that left 75 percent making some kind of living—and some of the living was reasonably comfortable. If 300,000 businesses had gone under, there were still 1.9 million providing some kind of service or product—and some of those surviving businesses flourished. Though they found their fondest certitudes sorely tested, those in the upper levels of the middle class who had weathered the worst buffetings of the depression did not vanish into the unforgiving maw of history. They lowered their expectations, certainly, and were hardly immune to the chill of fear that came over anyone who saw others of his class brought down to absolute ruin, but the great majority simply refused to abandon the values by which they defined themselves. One Park Avenue matron celebrated the ingenuity with which she and her compatriots managed to keep up appearances. "This new standard of acceptances has given a rebirth to the salvage shops of our grandmother's day," she wrote. "Only the modern counterpart is up to the minute in smartness and style. These new deluxe salvage shops are a product of the hard times, made known through whispering campaigns. Thus, the secrets of their treasures are guarded for those in the know." Everywhere, she noted proudly, her friends had made adjustments:

> Who would have expected . . . ten years ago to hear conversations in the smart circles along this order: "I just rode up in the subway and walked over. . . . [Y]es, I cut my finger opening a tin can last night. . . ."
>
> And off in the smoking room, the men: "Yes, the wife and kiddies are in Europe. Some difference, though. They're living on twenty-five dollars a week this trip. . . . These new three-for-a-dime cigars aren't so bad once you get used to them. . . . My wife's turned out to be a good cook!"[1]

If the upper middle class did not go away, neither did many of the very rich, particularly those whose financial roots lay not in the delicate bubble of twenties speculation but deep in the industrial machinery of the nineteenth century. Some of them grew a little nervous, perhaps, in the face of a destitution that only the most profoundly self-centered upper-crust sociopath could pretend did not exist. John P. Morgan Jr., for instance, had brushed off reporters who accosted him upon his return from a European trip in May 1931. "I don't know anything about any depression," he said. "What depression is this? You know I can't discuss anything."[2] By the spring of 1932, his consciousness had somehow been raised and he decided not to sail his yacht, the *Corsair*, for a while. "It seems very unwise," he wrote his friend, the Archbishop of Canterbury, "to let the 'Corsair' come out this summer. There are so many suffering from lack of work, and even from actual hunger, that it

1. Beatrix Fenton, "The Rich Can Take It," *Mademoiselle* (February 1935).
2. Quoted in "What Killed Cock Robin?" *Fortune* (August 1931).

is both wiser and kinder not to flaunt such luxurious amusement in the face of the public."[3] And, speaking in June 1931 at the University of Pennsylvania, where he had just been conferred an honorary degree, Daniel Willard, president of the Baltimore & Ohio Railroad, warned against complacency: "A system—call it what you will—under which it is possible for 5,000,000 or 6,000,000 of willing and able-bodied men to be out of work and unable to secure work for months at a time, and with no other source of income, cannot be said to be perfect or even satisfactory. . . . While I do not like to say so, I would be less than candid if I did not say in such circumstances I would steal before I would starve."[4]

Not all the well-to-do were so sensitive. Some could even find true value glittering in the depression's dark rubble: a solution to the servant problem, for instance. Ever since the end of World War I, the pool of men and women willing to suffer the serflike wages, hours, and working conditions of most domestic servants had steadily declined. "Capitalism," the editors of *Fortune* complained in December 1931, "is supposed to provide wealth and make it easily convertible into human satisfactions. As a group, the well-to-do of America find that wealth . . . procures very little in the kind of basic comforts which arise from good domestic service."[5] A year later, after the depression had reached its lowest point, the news was better, the magazine noted with little visible irony: "For the first time, the bargaining power is on the side of the housekeeper. . . . You can have your garden taken care of in Los Angeles for $1 a week. You can get a dignified couple to run your Commonwealth Avenue house in Boston for $80 a month. A shuffle-footed but affable Negro will fry your chicken and do your washing for $8 a month in Virginia."[6]

With or without a proper supply of servants, many of the very rich were even less willing to abandon that which made them *feel* rich than those of the upper middle class were to give up the pitiful vestiges of what separated them from the lower classes. The Vanderbilts,

3. Quoted in Chernow, *The House of Morgan*, p. 348.
4. Quoted in "What Killed Cock Robin?" *Fortune* (August 1931).
5. "The Servant in the Home," *Fortune* (December 1931).
6. "A Note on the Servant Problem," *Fortune* (December 1932).

Twomblys, Belmonts, Fishes, Harrimans, and most of the rest of what remained of New York's empyrean "400," for example, still cavorted stylishly every summer up in Newport, Rhode Island, as they had done for decades, playing croquet or sipping cocktails on the lawns of their ornate Victorian mansions, changing into their swimsuits in the elegant bathhouses that bracketed the Golden Cupola on the white-sanded curve of Bailey's Beach, competing on the grass-covered tennis courts at the Casino, tacking their sloops and ketches up and down Narragansett Bay, oblivious, at least for a season, to the world beyond the colony's manicured hedges and towering, house-hiding trees.

Then there were the debutante balls, those annual extravaganzas at which the virginal daughters of the socially prominent were introduced to the marriage market. The December 1930 issue of *Fortune* laid out the details of what even a modest event might run to if held, say, in the Ritz Tower Hotel in New York for one thousand guests. The cost of the ballroom, with food, entertainment, champagne, flowers, and other necessities, should come to no more than $11,500, the editors decided, although one had to take into account the debutante's obligation to throw a few ancillary teas, luncheons, and theater parties for friends and relatives, as well as her need for a rack of new clothes that could add at least another $10,500 to the total cost (which, in modern dollars, would come to about $100,000). "The whole purpose, on the parents' part," the magazine noted primly, "is to tell the world that their daughter, having reached a certain age, is prepared to marry. Of a certainty it is a lavish way of making the announcement for, when you think of it, a notice on the society pages of the newspapers would serve the purpose just as well."[7]

Whether an unemployed steamfitter in Pittsburgh or a destitute housewife in Denver knew much in the way of detail about the life of the very rich—though in fact the newspapers were diligent in their coverage, as Americans have always enjoyed watching the wealthy at play even when amusement is underlain with envy or anger—neither would likely have been surprised by what they could have read in the June 1931 issue of *Reader's Digest*. "Do the Rich Give to Charity?" asked

7. "The $3,000,000 Machine," *Fortune* (December 1930).

social security advocate Abraham Epstein in an article condensed from its first appearance in *The American Mercury* earlier that year. The answer was no, most of them did not, Epstein said, and while his long crusade for state and federal old-age relief programs might have put his objectivity in question, he had little trouble citing plenty of evidence, including a complaint from Harry A. Mackey, the mayor of Philadelphia: "Up to the present a great proportion of the relief funds has been contributed by the working class. It is a lamentable fact that many of our wealthy men and women have failed to respond, while many others who are rich have sent contributions for insignificant sums. I say to you it is the poor man who has saved the situation up to this time."[8] Epstein also could have cited the efforts of Michigan Senator James Couzens, who offered to contribute a million dollars of his own toward the creation of a $10 million relief fund for Detroit if other Detroit millionaires would come up with the remaining $9 million; they refused.[9]

The most truly deprived of Americans may not have known all this precisely, but the knowledge was in their bones, and it helped to inspire public eruptions that many—including many of the guilty rich—interpreted as the beginning of a violent American revolution, one that would see the mighty brought low and the lowly raised up with a good deal of bloodshed along the way. "What's the meaning of this queue, / Tailing down the avenue," asked Florence Converse in "Bread Line," a poem that appeared in the January 1932 issue of the numbingly respectable *Atlantic Monthly*. She then went on to suggest an answer that would not have brought comfort to the secure:

> If by fasting visions come,
> Why not to a hungry bum?
> Idle, shamed, and underfed,
> Waiting for his dole of bread,
> What if he should find his head
> A candle of the Holy Ghost?
> A dim and starveling spark at most,
> But yet a spark? It needs but one.

8. Abraham Epstein, "Do the Rich Give to Charity?" *Reader's Digest* (June 1931).
9. See Conot, op. cit., pp. 274–76.

A spark can creep, a spark can run;
Suddenly a spark can wink
And send us down destruction's brink.
It needs but one to make a star,
Or light a Russian samovar.
One to start a funeral pyre,
One to cleanse a world by fire.
What if our bread line should be
The long slow-match of Destiny?

"I am just seething within like a volcano, sending forth a rumbling sound ere it goes into eruption," a clearly well read textile worker wrote to columnist Mildred Seydell of the *Atlanta Georgian* in 1931. The letter-writer had married young and badly, and now found herself trying to raise two children alone at wages her mill was willing to pay. "I am bursting with red hot revolt. I want to snatch things up and tear them to shreds."[10] The young woman may or may not have translated anger to action. Others certainly did. When Red Cross aid faltered outside the drought hamlet of England, Arkansas, on January 1, 1931, a farmer shouted, "All you that hain't yeller climb on my truck. We're a-goin' into England to get some grub," and led a contingent of several hundred sharecroppers and tenant farmers into the town, where the men—some of them armed and some accompanied by wives and children—agitated until Red Cross officials handed out enough food to satisfy them.[11] "Our children are crying for food," one of them told a stringer for the *New York Times*, "and we are going to get it. We are not going to let our children starve."[12]

In Minneapolis one afternoon in 1930, Meridel LeSueur watched a crowd of women surge against the windows of a grocery store in the working-class district of Gateway Park. "The windows seemed to break," she remembered, after which, the women clambered through the opening and began raiding the shelves inside. The women made a

10. Quoted in Julia Kirk Blackwelder, "Letters from the Great Depression," *Southern Exposure* (Fall 1978).
11. Quoted in Woodruff, op. cit., p. 57.
12. Quoted in the *New York Times* (January 4, 1931).

list of the purloined food and assured the owner that he would be paid
for everything. "Who has the most children here?" a black woman
shouted, then handed out slabs of stolen bacon to those who stepped
forward.[13] Another Minneapolis grocery store raid in February 1931
was less benign; the owner was jumped by the crowd when he tried to
resist and had his arm broken for his trouble. The police had to be called
in, and seven of the raiders were arrested.[14]

Radical writer Joseph North watched two hundred men, women,
and children marching down the main street in Van Dyke, Michigan.
They piled into an A&P market and "dismantled it in a matter of minutes," North remembered. "I spoke to a large, round-faced woman who
stuffed a bologna, five loaves of bread, and half a dozen cans of soup into
a big sack. 'Mr. Licht at the Welfare said he couldn't help us, mister.
Well, we're helping ourselves. You expect us to starve while there's food
on the shelves?'"[15]

Similar "food riots" erupted in San Francisco, Oklahoma City, St.
Paul, and other cities. Will Rogers thought that the rioters were trying
to tell the country something. "Paul Revere just woke up Concord,
these birds woke up America," he wrote of the Arkansas farmers in his
column. "I don't want to discourage Mr. Mellon [Hoover's Secretary of
the Treasury] and his carefully balanced budget, but you let this country get hungry and they are going to eat, no matter what happens to
Budgets, Income Taxes or Wall Street Values."[16]

Others turned their anger to longer-range goals. In Chicago, Mrs.
Willye Jeffries found herself in a state of almost constant fury when her
husband, a packinghouse worker, dropped dead and left her with a little
girl to raise alone. "I was very mean. Very mean," she remembered. She
heard about an apartment building in her South Side neighborhood
that the landlord had refused to keep in repair. "I moved in there to get
into a fight," she said. "And I got a good fight." She started to organize
the building's tenants, encouraging them to stand up for their rights.
The landlord offered her a bribe to shut her up. She refused his five hun-

13. Story and quotes in Elizabeth Faue, *Community of Suffering and Struggle: Women,
Men, and the Labor Movement in Minneapolis, 1915–1945*, p. 65.
14. See the *New York Times* (February 25, 1931).
15. Joseph North, *No Men Are Strangers*, pp. 66–67.
16. Quoted in Ellis, op. cit., p. 147.

dred dollars. He then paid a policeman to attempt to catch her with a man so that her relief payments would be cut off on moral grounds. She did have a man playing cards with her when the policeman came to call, but the officer made the mistake of breaking down her door without a warrant. She was a good-sized woman and still feeling mean, and while her card-playing friend cheered her on, she beat the invader upside the head with a broom handle for quite a while before she was subdued, and both she and the friend were taken off to jail. At her trial, the charges were dismissed. She had refused a plea bargain. "I was a free woman when I came in here," she said. "And when I walk out I'm gonna be free." Her landlord ultimately capitulated to her demands to fix his building, and she went on to become one of the South Side's most effective activists.[17]

EVEN WHEN INCHOATE and unstructured, anger could briefly light some of the darkest corners of the depression. Properly organized and more precisely focused, it might produce a glare of incandescence that would illuminate the failures of the entire capitalist system—and even bring it down. Such was the hope of the American Communist Party (CP/USA), at any rate—though to look at the party in 1930 was to wonder how it could hope to organize a Lenin's birthday picnic, much less the overthrow of American capitalism.

Among other things, the American party was still suffering severe growing pains, complicated by the residual effects of the antiradical and antiforeign sentiments that had flowered during and immediately after World War I. It had been only a little more than a decade since the Communists had split off from the Socialist movement, itself a fragile and often contentious—and singularly American—agglomeration. Since the Civil War, this movement had at one time or another included traditional American Utopianists and communalists, German American and other foreign-born acolytes of the political and economic philosophy of Karl Marx and Friedrich Engels, radical offshoots of Populism, Single-Taxers, militant syndicalists like the Industrial Workers of the World (IWW), and other leftist splinter groups. Already

17. Mrs. Jeffries told her story in Terkel, op. cit., pp. 453–59.

loosely organized to accommodate this variety, socialism was further weakened when its principal standard-bearer, labor leader Eugene Debs, was imprisoned in 1919 for protesting sedition laws (though he managed to garner some two million votes during the 1920 presidential elections). The party was maimed again when the Communists left its fold in September of 1919. It would not be significantly revived until the latter part of the decade, when Norman Thomas, a former Presbyterian minister and zealous civil libertarian, helped revive it and mold it into the viable, if minor, political entity that he would lead for the next forty years.[18]

If American socialism had been left weakened by the radical split of September 1919, the Communists themselves were hardly better off. Even at the moment of the split they were divided into two rival bodies: the Communist Party, a largely Russian-speaking, "right-wing" element that distrusted the liberal cast of much of the Socialist movement; and the Communist Labor Party, which emerged from socialism's traditional leftist labor elements. In Moscow, the Communist International (Comintern), formed in March 1919 to promote and govern the effort to establish a soviet world, ordered the two groups to merge in 1921, but the uneasy partnership, with anywhere from 25,000 to 30,000 members, was plagued by constant internal bickering.[19]

What was more, the Communists had found themselves under almost immediate attack from mainstream America, whose sporadic instincts for political repression had been aroused by war. A mindless bellicosity had tolerated federal censorship of the mails and passage of the Espionage Act of 1917 and the Sedition Act of 1918, all of which curtailed or violated the most basic of civil liberties. Millions of people had smiled upon and supported the American Protective League, a band of citizen vigilantes not only sanctioned by the U.S. Department of Justice but supervised, unofficially but most energetically, by an

18. My discussion of socialism and the early years of the CP/USA is based largely on that of Theodore Draper in *The Roots of American Communism*; Edward P. Johannigsmeier in *Forging American Communism: The Life of William Foster*; Harvey Klehr in *The Heyday of American Communism: The Depression Decade*, pp. 3–27; and Fraser M. Ottanelli in *The Communist Party of the United States: From the Depression to World War II*, pp. 9–16.
19. Figures from Klehr, op. cit., p. 4.

ambitious young FBI agent named J. Edgar Hoover. The league's accomplishments included the violent, systematic destruction of the troublesome (hence seditious) IWW in 1917 and the wholesale roundup of 50,000 suspected "draft dodgers" in 1918.[20] Further, the war spirit inspired a feast of hatred for things German that at its most innocuous dictated that sauerkraut should be renamed "Liberty Cabbage," and at its most reprehensible encouraged violence against Americans of German birth or extraction.

After the war, when the Germans no longer provided targets of opportunity, public and private antipathy turned toward the perceived Red Menace. Conservative Americans, who had always viewed radicals of whatever stripe with a jaundiced eye, had been extremely nervous about Bolsheviks ever since the Russian Revolution in November 1917. Now, it seemed, internal subversion might be joined to international communism to bring down the Republic with violence. No one could gainsay the violence (though it was impossible to fix provable blame on specific individuals and specific groups). Bombs, for instance. The first one appeared on the desk of Seattle Mayor Ole Hanson on April 28, 1919; it did not explode, but it did leak acid onto his papers. The next day, a maid for Georgia Senator Thomas W. Hardwick lost both hands when she opened an exploding package. On May 1—May Day, a traditional day of celebration for labor—sixteen similar bombs were discovered in the central post office in Manhattan, and eight more were found in post offices scattered around the country. None of these exploded, but on June 2 eight bombs went off at the same hour in eight different cities, including Washington, D.C., where the luckless perpetrator stumbled immediately after placing his offering at the front stoop of Attorney General A. Mitchell Palmer's house near Dupont Circle. Palmer and his family were not harmed, though bits of both their front stoop and the bomber himself rained down on the neighborhood for a while. They also landed on the sidewalk in front of the home of Assistant Secretary of the Navy Franklin D. Roosevelt, which provided for some interesting breakfast conversation the next day with his son James. "Examining the debris in the morning," James remembered, "I

20. For Hoover and the APL, see Curt Gentry, *J. Edgar Hoover: The Man and the Secrets*, pp. 70–74.

discovered an unusual object, which I showed to my father. He paled, placed it in a napkin and took it to the police. It turned out to be a piece of the assassin's collarbone."[21]

Enough was enough, Palmer had decided, and on November 7, after five months of investigation, he ordered raids on the homes and offices of presumed radical aliens in twelve different cities. Even more ambitious raids were launched in thirty-two cities on January 2, 1920. All together, more than four thousand aliens suspected of being members of the Communist Party or of organizations sympathetic to communism were rounded up and held for possible deportation. Not enough, apparently: On September 16, 1920, a huge bomb exploded at the noon hour in New York City's crowded Wall Street; this time, thirty people died.

The perpetrator of the Wall Street bombing was never discovered, and to his everlasting sorrow, Attorney General Palmer found that his evidence against most of the 4,000 aliens he had seized was so puny that he was able to deport only 591. Still, both these raids and the raids against the IWW in 1917 had accomplished much of what they had been intended to do. Radicalism had been effectively stifled and the Communist Party itself forced underground, leaving behind an ostensibly harmless "Workers Party" as its only official political expression. It was not until 1924, after antiradical emotions had somewhat abated with the arrival of good times, that the Workers Party was disbanded and the Communist Party reemerged as a registered political body. Still, for the rest of the decade (and the decades to come), the party was riven by intense squabbling among various contending factions that was at times almost comic. By 1930, the two most virulent contenders for the soul of American communism were the "Lovestoneites" and the "Trotskyites." The first group was led—insofar as any such group *could* be led—by Jay Lovestone. He was a Lithuanian-born labor leader from the textile industry, who gave his allegiance to the "right-wing" element of the Comintern headed up by Nikolai Bukharin, a supporter of the soviet vision as proclaimed by the late V. I. Lenin as head of the all-powerful Communist Politburo, and practiced by his successor, Joseph Stalin. The Trotskyites, led by James P. Cannon, a former IWW orga-

21. James Roosevelt, *My Parents: A Differing View*, p. 44.

nizer, on the other hand, took their doctrine from Stalin's chief rival (officially expelled from the Communist Party and exiled in 1929), and vociferously criticized the "Marxist-Leninist" bureaucracy that the USSR had become under Stalin.

By the end of 1930, both Lovestone and Cannon, among others, had been officially expelled from the CP/USA by the Comintern, but the sentiments they represented continued to simmer within the ranks. Membership had fallen to only a little over 7,500, and in an effort to promote enrollment and subdue internal dissensions, the Comintern had established a three-person "secretariat" to govern the party's American operations. Of the three members of the secretariat, the two most important were Earl Browder, the general secretary, and William Z. Foster, the trade union secretary, both of whose proletarian credentials were impeccable.

Browder, a somewhat deferential, almost mousy man, had been one of ten children born to a farm family outside Wichita, Kansas, in 1891. He had turned to socialism in 1907 and had resisted American entry into World War I with such uncharacteristic vehemence that he went to jail for it. After his release in 1919, he turned to communism. A book-keeper by trade and gifted with a certain genius for the Byzantine world of Communist bureaucracy, he worked his way up through the ranks industriously, editing *Labor Herald*, the official newspaper of the party's labor entity, the Trade Union Educational League (TUEL, founded by Foster), serving as an organizer in China, and otherwise making himself useful (and increasingly visible) to the Comintern until his appointment to the secretariat in 1930.

Unlike Browder, there was little that was retiring or deferential about Foster, and visibility was not a problem; by 1930, he was probably the most notorious Communist in America, though one whose maverick instincts regularly got him into trouble with the Comintern. Born in Taunton, Massachusetts, in 1881 but raised in the slums of Philadelphia, Foster had made a living as a deepwater sailor, lumberjack, streetcar conductor, fruit-picker, and miner, among other jobs. He became a Socialist, then an IWW activist, then an AFL organizer, where he distinguished himself particularly during a nationwide steel strike in 1919. While he did not become a party member until 1921, he had loosely allied himself with the Communists as early as 1919, and in

1920 had created the Trade Union Educational League as a radical body designed to transform the AFL. It was time, he had written to Socialist muckraker Upton Sinclair, "that the left wing of the great labor movement develop an industrial program. It had one fifteen years ago, but that led to the IWW and all these years of impotency. The time is ripe for another, and the new one, if it is to fare better than the last, must call for the development of the inevitable industrial unionism through the old trade unions."[22] After he joined the CP/USA, the TUEL came with him, while Foster himself became the official Communist Party candidate during the presidential elections of 1924 and 1928. In 1929, over Foster's opposition, the Red International of Labor Unions, or Profintern, the Comintern's labor committee, declared that henceforth the CP/USA should no longer waste its time trying to infiltrate AFL unions but must form its own, and to that end it restructured the TUEL and renamed it the Trade Union Unity League (TUUL). The next year, in recognition of Foster's continuing power, the Comintern named him to the secretariat, with responsibility for all trade union activity. To many in the lower ranks, Foster was the de facto leader of the party. "In our eyes he remained the authoritative public spokesman on issues confronting the labor movement," California field organizer Dorothy Healey recalled. "It is an over-simplification to assume that just because Browder was general secretary and he said or did something, that's what filtered down to us in the rank and file as the last word on Party policy."[23]

While the two men cordially despised each other and often disagreed noisily over questions of doctrine and program, Foster and Browder were thoroughly dedicated zealots and would steer the CP/USA through its most fruitful decade, using such subordinate entities as the TUUL, the Young Communist League (YCL), and a legal arm, the International Defense League (IDL), to infiltrate and agitate on myriad fronts. And if the party never acquired the power it dreamed of and its enemies always claimed it had, it still exerted far more influence on public policy and struck greater terror in the hearts of the comfort-

22. Quoted in Johanningsmeier, op. cit., p. 157.
23. Dorothy Healey and Maurice Isserman, *Dorothy Healey Remembers: A Life in the Communist Party*, p. 75.

able than its numbers would have suggested possible.[24] The party's effectiveness probably stemmed less from inspired leadership at the top, however, than from the intensely devoted and often courageous acolytes who ran its street-level cells, or "cadres," whose fidelity was matched only by an almost lunatic energy. "The most fully employed persons I met during the depression," one labor leader remembered,

> were the Communists. They worked 10 or 12 hours a day—maybe 16, if you counted yakking time. Most got no pay. . . . They were in on every protest I saw or heard of. If they didn't start things them-selves, they were Johnnies-on-the-spot. . . .
>
> The Communists brought misery out of hiding in the workers' neighborhoods. They paraded it with angry demands through the main streets to the Public Square, and on to City Hall. They raised particular hell.[25]

Parading misery and raising particular hell, in fact, became the first and in some respects the most successful work the party ever did, cer-tainly in the early years of the depression. First, it organized. Late in 1929, the Comintern directed that "a broad unemployment movement

24. Some recent history—chiefly, Maurice Isserman in *Which Side Were You On? The American Communist Party During the Second World War* and Ottanelli, op. cit.—argues that the connection between the Comintern and the CP/USA was largely pro forma and that the domestic Communists were nearly autonomous. Moreover, this theory has held that the charges of financial support from the Comintern, the existence of elabo-rate clandestine operations, and the infiltration of government agencies and liberal institutions, including the labor movement, have been grossly exaggerated, especially for the period of the 1930s. But in *The Secret World of American Communism* (1995), Har-vey Klehr, John Earl Haynes, and Fridrikh Firsov use newly available materials in Moscow's Russian Center for the Preservation and Study of Documents of Recent His-tory to argue that the Comintern's control over the activities of the CP/USA was far more rigid than has been supposed, that operations in the United States were financed at least in large part from Moscow (some of the money in the 1920s being laundered through the commercial operations of the American entrepreneur Armand Hammer), and that clandestine operations and infiltration were more widespread than previously imagined. In short, they suggest, if the Comintern had failed to subvert both the gov-ernment and most of the nation's social institutions by the end of the 1930s, it cer-tainly was not for lack of trying.
25. Quoted in Franklin Folsom, *Impatient Armies of the Poor: The Story of Collective Action of the Unemployed, 1808–1942*, p. 232.

on a national scale shall be organized, guided and led by the TUUL."
The TUUL responded with its own order that each of its local and district bodies "must take immediate initiative in organizing Unemployed
Councils. Into these Councils shall be drawn representatives of the revolutionary unions, shop committees and reformist unions, as well as
unorganized workers."[26]

In city after city, cadre organizers moved among clots of unemployed men who gathered outside closed factory gates and relief offices,
assembled in abandoned lofts for union meetings, stood around on
street corners or in breadlines, huddled around oil drum fires in
Hoovervilles, or, when they had some loose change, clustered in "blind
petes" to toss back whiskey raw enough to destroy their sight or
kill them. In all these grim, dimly lit corners of society, "hatless young
men in imitation leather jackets," as historian Arthur Schlesinger Jr.
described them, could be found handing out literature, giving short,
rapid, intense speeches, providing advice on how to organize a council,
encouraging anger, manipulating frustration, sliding away at the
approach of a cop, relentless, persuasive, effective.[27] The first council
was formed in Detroit in December and immediately marched on the
mayor's office to lodge its complaints. In Buffalo in January, an Unemployed Council led 3,000 people on a parade through the winter streets.
In February, council demonstrations in New York, Philadelphia, Chicago, Cleveland, and Los Angeles brought the police down on them.

By then, the Comintern had called for an International Unemployment Day to dramatize the problem, and the CP/USA turned to the
new Unemployed Councils to organize and lead demonstrations around
the country on the chosen day of March 6, 1930. In most cities, the
authorities responded to this news with paranoia. In Manhattan, for
example, Police Commissioner Grover Whalen made public an unsigned
letter ostensibly sent by the U.S. Department of Justice. The letter
claimed that the Communists were going to march on City Hall,
destroy it, then move on to obliterate the New York Stock Exchange,
the Woolworth Building, and other temples of capitalism, while teams
of assassins were ready to murder Mayor Jimmy Walker and other offi-

26. Quotes in Klehr, op. cit., p. 50.
27. Arthur M. Schlesinger Jr., *The Crisis of the Old Order*, p. 219.

cials. The city refused the Unemployed Council a permit to march anywhere outside Union Square, where a rally was scheduled to take place,
and Whalen beefed up his police force, surrounded City Hall with 250
men, assigned extra guards to both Mayor Walker and Governor
Franklin Roosevelt, who was in town to attend a conference, and laid in
a supply of tear gas to help put down the coming Armageddon.

In Chicago on the eve of the national demonstration, an Unemployed Council meeting in Mechanics Hall was invaded by Chicago
police, who arrested thirteen of the leaders for sedition and hauled them
downtown, where several were systematically beaten. Among them was
party member Steve Nelson, who said he was strapped to a chair and
hammered with a blackjack until he managed to overturn the chair
with a violent movement. He lay on the floor and feigned unconscious-
ness—until one of the detectives kicked him in the ribs so hard that he
did pass out. "When I regained consciousness," he remembered, "I
cleaned my bloody face in the washroom. . . . An hour later I found my
friends sitting on a cement floor in front of the elevator. Harold
Williams was stretched out, his torn pants revealing an enormous rup-
ture, and B. D. Amos had had his front teeth knocked out. Joe Dallet
was bleeding from the mouth and had a gash on his cheek, and Rod-
man's thick black hair was caked with blood."[28]

Similar incidents of overreaction were common, while the newspaper press cheerfully fanned the flames of official trepidation. The results
were predictable and, for the Communists, eminently exploitable.
"March 6, 1930," Foster remembered, "was a memorable day of struggle."[29] It was indeed. While his claim that a million and a quarter
people took part in rallies and marches that day was inflated by about
three-quarters of a million, 500,000 Americans making rather a lot of
noise on the same day for the same purpose all over the country was a
legitimately awesome phenomenon. In some cities, peace reigned in
spite of all the premarch agitation. In San Francisco, Mayor James J.
("Sunny Jim") Rolph, a conservative Republican who would go on
to become governor, ordered his chief of police to march right along
with the 2,000 council demonstrators to City Hall, after which Rolph

28. Quoted in Folsom, op. cit., p. 249.
29. William Z. Foster, *Pages from a Worker's Life*, p. 184.

listened to what they had to say, then responded with a friendly, if non-committal, speech. In Chicago, despite the previous night's brutality, some 5,000 council members marched without incident, while Mayor William ("Big Bill") Thompson cheerfully accepted a petition from a delegation of fifteen. In Baltimore, the mayor greeted the marchers to his own city hall, wearing a bright red tie and a red carnation in his lapel, and in Trenton, the city's director of public safety not only allowed the council to demonstrate but asked speechifiers to "speak up louder."[30]

Such incidents of tolerance were more than countered by head-breaking elsewhere. In Washington, D.C., tear gas was used to disperse a rally in front of the White House. In Detroit, an armored car and 3,600 police battled with demonstrators for two hours. In Los Angeles, possibly the most rigidly conservative city in America, the police force was turned loose on city hall marchers with particular vehemence; on foot and horseback, club-wielding patrolmen beat hundreds of people, while others were chased down by patrol cars. Seattle, Boston, Cleveland, and Milwaukee all experienced similar clashes.[31]

Nowhere was the violence more pronounced and exploitable than in New York, where an estimated 35,000 people gathered at noon in Union Square to hear Foster and others speak from five platforms arranged around the square. The crowd was ringed by at least three hundred policemen, who at first made no move to interfere. When Foster finished his official address, he met with Police Commissioner Whalen at the temporary police headquarters set up in a nearby building to ask again for a permit for the crowd to march to City Hall. Whalen refused. Foster moved back through the crowd to the central platform, where he stood and shouted: "Whalen and the city officials have handed Broadway and other streets over to every monarchist and militarist exploiter of Europe and Asia to parade on, but now when the workers and the unemployed workers of New York demand the use of

30. Quoted in Daniel J. Leab, "'United We Eat': The Creation and Organization of the Unemployed Councils in 1930," *Labor History* (Fall 1967). This also is my source for International Unemployment Day events in San Francisco, Chicago, Baltimore, and Trenton.
31. See Ottanelli, op. cit., p. 31.

the streets, Whalen's answer is that they cannot have them. Will you take that for an answer?"

"No!" the crowd roared.[32]

Foster waved toward City Hall, and about two thousand of the 35,000 gathered began oozing into Broadway and heading south. They were met by the police, mounted and on foot and motorcycle and supported by a squad of detectives. "Thousands of terrified people scattered," the *New York Times* reported the next day,

> rushing for safety from the flailing police, shouting, stumbling, stepping over one another in their fear and haste to get away. Hundreds of policemen and detectives, swinging nightsticks, blackjacks, and bare fists, rushed into the crowd, hitting out at all with whom they came in contact, chasing many across the street and adjacent thoroughfares. . . . A score of men with bloody heads and faces sprawled over the Square with policemen pummeling them. The pounding continued as the men, and some women, sought refuge in flight.[33]

"Cossacks!" a woman shouted, reverberating to the memory of another kind of violence in another kind of land. "Bloody Cossacks!"[34]

Foster, after escaping the riot area, met with other leaders outside the square. They walked down to City Hall Plaza and attempted to deliver a petition to Mayor Walker; they were arrested before they could get anywhere near him, charged with felonious assault, and carried off to jail.

The conflicts in Union Square and elsewhere on March 6 became headline news all over the country—not, Louis Adamic would insist in *Dynamite*, his lively 1935 history of militant radicalism, "because they were demonstrations of the unemployed, or because the Communists had organized them, but because they produced bloody heads."[35] That may have been true, but the Communists were ready to take

---

32. Quote and account of Foster's actions in Johanningsmeier, op. cit., pp. 251–52.
33. Quoted in Leab, op. cit.
34. Quoted in Edward Robb Ellis, op. cit., p. 138. My account of the Union Square riot is from this source, pp. 135–38, and Johanningsmeier, op. cit., pp. 251–52.
35. Quoted in Leab, op. cit.

full credit. The riot, Herbert Benjamin, the party's New York district organizer, crowed, "was a great success,"[36] while *The Daily Worker*, the party's official newspaper, announced that "a great movement is under way."[37] Energized party officials met at the end of March to plan for a meeting in Chicago in July to cultivate with further organization what they saw as a massive nationwide sentiment for upheaval. At the Chicago meeting, 1,320 council delegates from around the country voted to establish the Unemployed Councils of the U.S.A. as the umbrella organization to oversee the "immediate organization of all unemployed," in the words of Nels Kjar, the meeting's chairman, and appointed a thirty-eight-member National Committee for such purposes, including William Z. Foster, who by then was serving time for his activities on March 6.[38] A month later, party leaders unveiled a "Workers' Unemployment Insurance Bill," which would pay a minimum of $25 a week to unemployed workers, with an additional $3 for each dependent; corporate and income taxes were to furnish the money. This cause, the party felt, was something around which a national movement could be built, even among those with no particular interest in communism itself.[39]

Like most American zealots, however, the Communists badly overestimated the dimensions of their support from ordinary citizens. Many working people genuinely admired the party and applauded the fortitude of men and women who were willing to take on the issues of hunger and government failure directly, as virtually no one else was doing. When sufficiently angered or frustrated, many were willing to join the occasional council demonstration or street march, and even risk the odd riot, but—unlike the most dedicated Communists themselves—they were not quite ready to give over their lives to constant violent activism, even in the cause of something as appealing as unemployment insurance. Membership in local councils declined over the

36. Quoted in Ellis, op. cit.
37. Quoted in Johanningsmeier, op. cit., p. 252.
38. Quoted in Leab, op. cit.
39. See Harvey Klehr, op. cit., pp. 51–52; and Fraser M. Ottanelli, op. cit., p. 33. Klehr says that the dependency stipend was $5, but Ottanelli's source is the text of the proposed bill itself, so I have gone with his figure of $3.

next several months, and while the Unemployed Councils of the U.S.A. continued as an organization well into the decade, its work fell far short of what the party had hoped.

Not that the marching and the violence stopped. The number of participants in any given event may have declined sharply, but the level of agitation remained high. The Comintern became a constant scold, demanding more activism from the CP/USA in support of the unemployment insurance bill. There must be, it said, "mass actions, demonstrations, strikes, and the whole struggle directed towards mass political strikes."[40] Like overdrawn and exhausted cities trying to live up to Hoover's call for self-reliance in the matter of relief, the CP/USA did its best to obey the dicta of the Comintern, though hamstrung constantly by lack of funds and staff. In New York in October, a crowd battled with police in front of City Hall and dodged paper bags full of water dropped from the windows above by amused spectators. Inside, meanwhile, the secretary of the New York Unemployed Council was jumped by police when it appeared that he and Mayor Jimmy Walker were going to get into a fistfight after the Communist called the mayor "a grafting Tammany politician and a crook" and Walker countered with "You dirty red!"[41] Over the next several months, the councils engaged in rent strikes, eviction resistance, and other actions, while in February 1931 the newly formed National Campaign Committee for Unemployment Insurance brought a petition with a claimed 1.4 million signatures to Washington, where three of its delegates were ejected from the Senate gallery for creating a disturbance.

Throughout the spring and summer of 1931, unemployment and hunger marches erupted from Columbus, Ohio, to Sacramento, California; Albany, New York, to Jefferson City, Missouri. There were so many, in fact, that in August 1931, the Central Committee decided that what was required was another committee: the National Hunger March Committee of the Unemployed Councils. This body would supervise the preparations for a nationwide demonstration against hunger that would culminate in Washington, D.C.—a deliberate attempt to

40. Quoted in Klehr, op. cit., p. 52.
41. Ibid.

replicate the great march on Washington by the "army" of Jacob S. Coxey in 1894 during another age of economic crisis. The date chosen was December 6, and that evening 1,620 delegates, trucked in from Buffalo, Boston, Chicago, St. Louis, and several Pacific Coast cities, met at the Washington Auditorium to hear speeches by Herbert Benjamin and other party luminaries and some uplifting revolutionary music provided by the Unemployed Workers Club Martini Horn Band.

The next morning, as Vice President Charles Curtis was getting ready to call the Senate to order on the first day of the Seventy-second Congress, the demonstrators began a long march down a route laid out by the new Washington, D.C., Superintendent of Police, Pelham G. Glassford, a West Point graduate who had earned the field rank of brigadier general during World War I. The length of the route, it was rumored, was designed to wear the marchers out, and there was no question that Glassford was determined not to have his first few months on the job marred by a repetition of the violence that had occurred during the demonstrations of March 6, 1930. A few days before, he had met with Benjamin, the march leader, offering to provide cots and tents for the men and rooms for the women, rations supplied by the Salvation Army, and the promise of fair treatment. Somewhat startled at being received in a friendly manner, Benjamin had concurred. Just to be on the safe side, however, Glassford had lined the parade route with at least a thousand policemen, and as the marchers shuffled toward the Capitol Building, the superintendent himself could be seen speeding from one point to another along the route on a motorcycle, keeping an eye on things, a pipe jutting sternly from his mouth. "The city was very apprehensive about [the marchers]," Glassford later explained, "and the preparations I made for police control were as much to allay public alarm as to handle the actual situation."[42]

Whether from exhaustion or fear, the marchers did not force the issue when their delegation was not allowed to enter the Capitol to present their demands for unemployment insurance. The fear would have been understandable. "On the huge ramps of the steps that lead to the central portico," John Dos Passos reported in *The New Republic*, "the metropolitan police have placed some additional statuary; tastefully

42. Quoted in Folsom, op. cit., p. 292.

arranged groups of cops with rifles, riot guns and brand-new tear-gas pistols that look as if they'd just come from Sears, Roebuck."[43] Accompanied by the New York Council's German Red Front Band, the marchers sang a verse or two from "The Internationale," then moved on to the White House, where they were again rejected, and from there to the headquarters of the AFL to demand its support. AFL president William Green accepted a delegation from the marchers, but spent the few minutes he allowed for the meeting lecturing them on their sundry excesses and stupidities. On that sour note, the demonstration ended and the marchers drifted away.[44]

Jacob Coxey, now the mayor-elect of Massillon, Ohio, generally approved of this echo of his 1894 event. "As I expected," he wrote in a story for the United Press, "it was an orderly as well as an impressive demonstration."[45] On the other hand, Father James R. Cox, known as the "Mayor of Shantytown" for his work among the homeless and unemployed in Pittsburgh, found the actions of the Communists "repugnant" and believed "a body of real American citizens should go to Washington and protest against unemployment conditions."[46] The priest forthwith led a troop of 12,000 of his own hunger marchers to the city on January 6, 1932, where he was allowed an audience with Hoover himself. After listening for a few minutes to Cox's plea for direct federal relief, a $5 billion public works program, farm loans, and increased income taxes on the rich, the president politely assured the priest that his administration's recovery plan was humming right along and that "we are giving this question our undivided attention."[47]

Both of the Washington hunger marches got the requisite ink in the national press, but since both were essentially peaceful affairs, neither did much to generate lurid conservative alarums or validate Communist claims of capitalist repression. In both regards, the March 7,

---

43. John Dos Passos, "The Hunger Marchers," *The New Republic* (December 31, 1931).
44. For the Washington hunger march, see Klehr, op. cit., pp. 56–58; Folsom, op. cit., pp. 284–97; Ottanelli, op. cit., p. 33; and Donald J. Lisio, *The President and Protest*, pp. 59–61. In *Pages from a Worker's Life*, William Z. Foster gives his own, considerably overblown, version, pp. 187–91.
45. Quoted in Folsom, op. cit., p. 298.
46. Quoted in ibid., p. 299.
47. Ibid.

1932, Hunger March on Ford's River Rouge complex was infinitely more successful. The target of what became the most notorious of all the hunger marches of the early thirties was natural enough. Back in 1927, a public poll had declared Henry Ford the third greatest man in history, surpassed only by Napoleon Bonaparte and Jesus Christ. Five years later, at least among workers in Detroit, Ford was by far the most hated man in America. "These are really good times," he had announced obscurely in March 1931, "but only if you know it. . . . The average man won't really do a day's work unless he is caught and cannot get out of it."[48] Five months later, when sales of the Model A had dropped from 1.4 million to 620,000 and the company had lost $37 million, the "good times" he had somehow discerned in March had clearly vanished. In reaction, he simply shut down most operations entirely, laying off tens of thousands of workers who may or may not have been willing to do a day's work, but certainly would not be doing it for the Ford Motor Company.[49] The company would not resume full production, Ford said, until it had developed a new model.

That new car was the Ford V-8, which did not begin preliminary production until December. Ford began hiring once again, but there was no talk now of seven dollars a day—or even the magical (indeed, illusory) five dollars instituted in 1914. Pay now was four dollars a day for ten hours a day, five days a week. That came to a little over one thousand dollars a year, less than half what it took to keep a family anywhere near subsistence levels, even assuming that the worker got a full week's work in any given week and never got sick. The latter was increasingly unlikely, since in addition to cutting wages, Ford, like the rest of the industry, had instituted the "speedup" on the theory that greater efficiency in production would make up for declining sales. This was an old tradition at Ford by then. In the mid-twenties, when sales of the Model T had started to slide, production schedules had been increased in order to reduce per-unit costs and lower the purchase price. "We were driving them, of course," one supervisor remembered. "Ford was one of the

48. Quoted in Lacey, op. cit., p. 305.
49. Figures from Conot, op. cit., p. 284.
50. Quoted in Lacey, op. cit., p. 351.

worst shops for driving men."[50] Already famously speedy production lines were speeded up even more, leaving men shaking with exhaustion at the end of every day, their innards knotted in a condition of stress dubbed "Ford stomach." Day after day, they endured, hanging on as best they could; anything less and they were gone. "The workers were being fired if they slowed down and were unable to make production," recalled one autoworker. "They were dismissed in lieu of getting younger blood into the plants, someone who could produce more and accumulate more wealth for the companies."[51]

Under Harry Bennett, Ford's security force—which was euphemistically called the Service Department—used an elaborate spy system that monitored everything from production performance to bathroom breaks, with an especially close watch out for anything that might smack of union agitation. Troublemakers were summarily fired, and if they objected too strenuously, were seized and escorted from the premises by Bennett's gang of ubiquitous strong-arm men.[52] "Unions," Ford declaimed, "are organized by Jewish financiers, not labor. A union is a neat thing for a Jew to have on hand when he comes around to get his clutches on industry."[53] There were no unions at Ford, and while there probably were a few Jews, it is not likely that any of them was a financier.

Unlike most of the other hunger marches, then, which merely tended to sloganize about the generic failures of capitalism, the protest sponsored by the Detroit Unemployed Council on March 7, 1932, had some relatively specific complaints to air and some specific demands to make, including the abolition of the spy system, a reduction in the

51. Quoted in Joyce Shaw Peterson, *American Automobile Workers, 1900–1933*, p. 133.
52. On Ford working conditions and Harry Bennett's Service Department, see Lacey, op. cit., pp. 350–51; Conot, op. cit., pp. 274–75; Peterson, op. cit., p. 59; and Peter Collier and David Horowitz, *The Fords: An American Epic*, pp. 152–56.
53. Quoted in Collier and Horowitz, op. cit., p. 156. It was Henry Ford, it will be remembered, who had shared with the nation other aspects of his anti-Semitism when he published a series of no fewer than ninety-one successive articles on the subject of "The International Jew: The World's Problem" in his newspaper, *The Dearborn Independent,* in 1920. When asked why, Ford explained that he was "only trying to awake the Gentile world to an understanding of what is going on. The Jew is a mere huckster, a trader who doesn't want to produce, but to make something out of what somebody else

speed of production, a seven-hour day, and the right to organize. The temperature stood at zero, and a stiff wind brought it well below that, when about three thousand marchers assembled on Detroit's west side to get their instructions from Al Goetz, leader of the Detroit council. "We don't want any violence!" he emphasized.[54] On the other hand, he added, "If we are attacked, we will know how to defend ourselves."[55] That said, the frozen-faced marchers, men and women, black, white, and brown, set off on a pace whose briskness may have had as much to do with the weather as it did with their determination to get where they were going.

That destination was Gate No. 3, the employment gate, of the River Rouge plant, but they would have to pass through a section of Dearborn along Miller Road to get to it. Detroit's mayor, the slightly radical Frank Murphy, had issued the council a march permit, but Dearborn's mayor, Clyde Ford (a distant relative of Ford and a Ford dealer himself), had not. What he had provided was about forty policemen, reinforced with a group of Ford's own security police. They stopped the marchers at the Dearborn city line. "Where are your leaders?" Dearborn's acting chief of police asked.

"We are all leaders!" many in the crowd shouted back.

"Where is your permit?" the chief asked.

"We don't need one," someone answered, and the crowd began to cross the line and move down Miller Road to Gate No. 3 a few hundred yards away.[56]

Tear gas was fired, but the wind swirled it around in ragged clouds that enveloped marchers and policemen alike. The marchers answered by pelting the police with rocks and pieces of frozen mud. A number of

---

produces." (In Leonard Dinnerstein, *Antisemitism in America*, p. 81.) In 1925, he was sued for libel because of the series; when it appeared that he might lose the million-dollar claim, he settled out of court for $140,000 and a public apology "for the wrong done to the Jews as fellow-men and brothers." (In Albert Lee, *Henry Ford and the Jews*, page 81.) Jewish showman Billy Rose wrote a song to commemorate the moment: "I was sad and I was blue, / But now I'm just as good as you, / Since Henry Ford a-pol-o-gized to me." (Ibid., p. 83.)

54. Quoted in Alex Baskin, "The Ford Hunger March—1932," *Labor History* (Summer 1972).

55. Quoted in Klehr, op. cit., p. 59.

56. Dialogue from Bird, op. cit., p. 171.

policemen, including the chief, were dropped, but the police held their fire even as the marchers ran toward Gate No. 3, where they began to mill and teem. On the overpass that crossed over Miller Road from the car park to the plant, firemen began spraying the crowd with water from fire hoses. Given the weather, that might have been enough to put an end to the march, had not Harry Bennett himself raced out of the Ford plant, where he had been giving Michigan Governor Fred Green a private showing of the latest Ford movie. Bennett jumped out of his automobile and confronted the nearest man who appeared to be a leader of the increasingly wet and swiftly freezing marchers. Bennett was almost immediately struck on the head by a large piece of slag that had been thrown. As he fell, bleeding copiously, he dragged the marcher, YCL leader Joseph York, down with him. When York managed to disentangle himself from Bennett and stand up, machine-gun fire broke out from the overpass and cut him down, then rippled through the rest of the crowd, sending it scattering. Four men, including the twenty-two-year-old York and a sixteen-year-old boy, were killed, and more than sixty marchers wounded and otherwise injured. Dearborn police, with the cooperation of Ford's men, began rounding up everyone they could lay hands on, arresting them on various charges. Some of the wounded and injured were thrown into jail cells and chained to their cots without treatment.

"Responsibility is not difficult to fix," the *Detroit Free Press* editorialized. "The inciters were William Z. Foster and the other Red agitators [Foster, since released from jail, had given a speech the night before the march, then had gone on to Milwaukee]."[57] The *New York Herald Tribune* was not so sure: "The Dearborn police are to be condemned for using guns on an unarmed crowd, for viciously bad judgment and for the killing of four men," it reported, and national sentiment tended to agree.[58]

Five days later, there was another march. This one included at least 15,000 mourners (some accounts say there were as many as 30,000) who followed the shoulder-borne coffins of York and the other slain workers

57. Quoted in ibid., p. 173.
58. Quoted in Lacey, op. cit., p. 344.

through the streets of Detroit. There was no mistaking its leadership. The coffins were draped in red; many of the marchers wore red arm-bands, and carried red flags and Communist banners, while a band played "The Internationale," as well as a funeral march that had played when slain Russian revolutionaries were carried to their graves in 1905. Upon his release from the hospital, Harry Bennett, with the approval of Ford, stockpiled tear gas at the River Rouge plant and installed machine-gun nests at Ford's estate.[59]

Bennett could not know any more than the demonstrators them-selves that the Communist Party/USA would never again march in such numbers or be given quite so large a measure of public sympathy as on that funeral day—nor could anyone know that even the violence of March 7 would soon pale when the saddest and most unnerving pop-ulist uprising in the nation's history resulted in a conflict in which the Communists, to their regret, played virtually no part.

59. My account of the Ford Hunger March and its aftermath is drawn from Collier and Horowitz, op cit., pp. 156–57; Lacey, op. cit., pp. 342–44; Conot, op. cit., pp. 284–85; Peterson, op. cit., pp. 138–39; Bird, op. cit., pp. 169–74; Baskin, op. cit.; Klehr, op. cit., pp. 58–60; and Folsom, op. cit., pp. 304–9. Folsom includes the intriguing, if possibly apocryphal, story that a fifth man, an African American named Curtis Williams, died later in the year from complications resulting from the tear gas he had inhaled. When Detroit officials refused to let him be buried next to the four white victims, Folsom writes, "The funeral committee answered with a threat to scat-ter Williams's ashes from a plane flying over the Ford plant. Ford sent up a plane to avert this danger, but when it returned to the ground to refuel, another plane hired by the committee took to the air. Ashes of the Jim Crowed man were then scattered where he had once worked" (p. 309).

5

Making Ashes of Loyalty

Less than five months after the killings at River Rouge Gate No. 3, thousands of refugees from another demonstration, hot, fatigued, many of them bruised and battered, straggled wearily along the roads of southern Pennsylvania under a killing summer sun, their faces bearing the numbed, haggard look of refugees everywhere. They sprawled to nap on the road banks next to fields of grain that had been cut and stacked for the threshers, or under the shade of second-growth woodlots in the hills.[1]

Slowly, individually and in tiny groups, they shuffled into a makeshift encampment in a slightly swampy clearing near an amusement complex called Ideal Park in Johnstown, Pennsylvania. Many of the town's citizens had wanted them sent on their way, but Mayor Eddie McClosky refused, noting the presence of many women and children.

---

1. My description of the scene on the road to Johnstown and at Ideal Park is based on that given by Malcolm Cowley in "The Flight of the Bonus Army," *The New Republic* (August 17, 1932). See also Jack Douglas, *Veterans on the March* (1934), pp. 251–66; and Jellison, op. cit., pp. 84–86.

"To hell with everybody!" he said. "Let them come!"[2] And so they did, anywhere from 4,000 to 7,000 of them, and here they would remain for the better part of two weeks, tattered remnants of a once-hopeful crusade whose desperate intensity was perhaps the single most dramatic illustration of the misery of the Great Depression.

They were not Reds, most of them; they were farm people, labor people, working men and women, ordinary middle-aged Americans who had been brought to this sorry condition not by local police or by gangs of industrial thugs or even by National Guard troops but by the regular army of the United States under the command of the chief of staff, who had driven them at bayonet point from the capital of the United States at the direct order (they would forever believe) of the president of the United States. Most of the men in the encampment (there were numerous families, too) had served in the very army that had sent them reeling across the Eleventh Street Bridge in Washington, D.C.

They had come to Washington from all over the country that spring and summer of 1932 to persuade the Congress of the United States to give them their money—now. The money in question had been authorized by the "bonus bill," passed by Congress in 1924 as an aid to World War I veterans. Those who had served overseas were to be paid $1.25 for each day of service; those who had remained in the United States, $1. With interest, the payments in 1932 would have averaged about $1,000 per man, just about what a full-time worker at the Ford Motor Company might expect to make in a year; unfortunately, payments were not to begin until 1945.

And so things remained until 1929, when Representative Wright Patman of Texas, an ambitious if otherwise unremarkable politician looking for a horse he might ride to national prominence, seized on the bonus bill issue and introduced legislation that would authorize payment immediately. When that bill died in committee, he introduced another. Throughout much of April 1932, the House Ways and Means Committee spent most of its time listening to testimony for and against the Patman bill. The Hoover administration, insisting that its passage would cost as much as $4 billion—more than the entire income of the

2. Quoted in Donald J. Lisio, *The President and Protest: Hoover, Conspiracy, and the Bonus Riot*, p. 225.

United States government that year—opposed it vehemently. Those testifying just as vigorously in favor of it included the American Legion and the Workers Ex-Servicemen's League, another committee of the CP/USA—perhaps the only time in history that the American Legion and the Communists ever agreed about anything.

To no one's real surprise, the House Ways and Means Committee reported the bill with an adverse recommendation in May. The Communists, who during the Hunger March on Washington in December 1931 had conceived the idea of organizing "a march of delegates of war veterans on Congress before it adjourned its seventy-second session," began laying plans for such a gathering to persuade the Congress to pass the Patman bill in spite of the committee recommendation.[3] For once, they were too late. Out in Portland, Oregon, a group of about 300 unemployed men blocked the tracks of an eastbound Union Pacific freight on May 11, seized a few boxcars, and set off for Washington, D.C., on their own. By the time they reached Pocatello, Idaho, the men had taken on a quasi-military form and were calling themselves the Bonus Expeditionary Force (BEF). Choosing as "regimental commander" a forty-four-year-old former medic with the 146th Field Artillery named Walter Waters, they had broadcast the BEF's intentions at every stop along the way. By the time the Portland contingent arrived in Washington, eighteen days after it started, met with Superintendent of Police Pelham G. Glassford, who assured Waters and his men of fair treatment, and began settling into the abandoned government buildings that Glassford had provided, the "march" of the BEF had become a major national phenomenon.

Over the next several weeks, thousands of people made their way to Washington by boxcar, truck, automobile, and foot, responding to the publicity that the Portland group had engendered. In groups ranging from the handful to the hundreds, they came throughout the spring and early summer. Seven hundred came down from Philadelphia, twenty-five from Des Moines. The National Soldiers Home in Johnson City, Tennessee, rented four boxcars and sent a contingent of two hundred men and a goat named Hoover. From Los Angeles came a cross-country caravan of 131 automobiles. Some brought their families with them,

3. Quoted in Klehr, op. cit., p. 60.

even on the boxcars. "Families were there galore, just couples and families with strings of kids," march organizer Jack Douglas remembered:

> Mr. and Mrs. Clayton Witmer arrived from Lancaster, Pa., with five children, the youngest thirteen months and the oldest eleven years. . . . Mr. and Mrs. O. J. Hornbeck and their five-month infant came from Goodrick, Colorado, in boxcars. They said the trip was not trying because they were used to privation. He was a concrete worker when he last worked, two years back. . . . Mr. and Mrs. J. D. Hogan hitchhiked from Birmingham, Alabama, with two small children. The trip took six weeks. Mr. Hogan, a barber, had been out of work two years.[4]

The number of "marchers" who filtered into Washington from all directions soon began to approach 20,000. "We had two alternatives," Glassford remembered—"feed them or fight them," and even though his city already was burdened with 19,000 resident unemployed for whom it could not adequately care, he was still determined to avoid violence.[5] Somehow, he would feed them. He turned to Secretary of War Patrick J. Hurley, who told him that the federal government could not officially recognize the marchers; Hoover had decided that the best way to deal with the BEF was to ignore it in the hope it would go away. It did not, and after determined lobbying on Glassford's part, the president secretly agreed to let the marchers be housed in all the available abandoned government buildings just northwest of the Mall. He also approved the loan of enough matériel to help Glassford and the marchers establish a number of quasi-military encampments, some complete with field kitchens and medical dispensaries. Glassford became the de facto treasurer of the BEF, taking responsibility for the disposal of donations that came in from various fund-raising events, local merchants, and a largely sympathetic public. "Dangerous?" Glassford repeated after a reporter's question. "No, except the danger of

4. Douglas, op. cit., p. 132.
5. Quoted in John D. Weaver, "Bonus March," *American Heritage* (June 1963).

gradual rust and rot which attacks those with no occupation and no incentive. They are just middle-aged men out of a job."[6]

The most ambitious of what would come to be twenty-seven individual encampments was set up on the Anacostia Flats just beyond the Eleventh Street Bridge, which led across the Anacostia River from the city proper. At its height, the complex of about 15,000 people, John Dos Passos reported, was

> a ghost of a camp from the big parade [World War I], with its bugle calls, its mess lines, greasy K.P.'s, M.P.'s headquarters, liaison officers, a medical officer. Instead of the tents and the long tarpaper barracks of those days, the men are sleeping in little lean-tos built out of old newspapers, cardboard boxes, packing crates, bits of tin or tarpaper roofing, every kind of cockeyed makeshift shelter from the rain, scraped together out of the city dump.[7]

Periodic rain turned the flats into an enormous, bug-ridden quagmire. Water for drinking and bathing remained scarce and sanitary conditions were abysmal. Dysentery, common colds, trench mouth, and skin eruptions were common, although there was no major outbreak of serious disease. In the beginning, in spite of such conditions, good feeling ran high. Among many, the event was a kind of reunion. "Again and again," Jack Douglas recalled, "vets met wartime buddies after not having seen them since being demobilized, in some cases, friends they had thought killed in action."[8] Humor was common, though of a somewhat mordant stripe. One man set up housekeeping in a big piano box he labeled an "Academy of Music," while outside a small tent a pair of children sat guarding a Mason jar into which passersby could deposit change for "Hoover's Poor Farm Tobacco Fund." "HARD TIMES," a sign propped against the jar explained, "ARE STILL 'HOOVERING' OVER US." Elsewhere, a patch of ground blossomed with little white crosses, each of which carried the name of a politician unfriendly to the bonus; two

6. Quoted in ibid.
7. Quoted in Winslow, op. cit., p. 31.
8. Douglas, op. cit.

were reserved for Hoover and his secretary of the Treasury, Andrew Mellon.

In the House of Representatives, the once-hopeless Patman bill suddenly found new life, as nervous congressmen contemplated the implications of the BEF's presence in Washington. On June 15, the House passed the bill by a vote of 211 to 176, then sent it over to the Senate for consideration. Rejoicing among the veterans became more subdued the morning after, when the Senate Finance Committee reported the bill out with an adverse recommendation. The next day, June 17, the Senate prepared to debate and then vote on the proposal.

As the discussion on the floor of the Senate continued into the evening of June 17, the crowd of veterans outside in the Capitol Plaza slowly grew, until there were perhaps twelve thousand present. Inside, even those senators who fully sympathized with the plight of the veterans nevertheless argued that the $2.3 billion in immediate payments that the bonus bill authorized would effectively kill federal relief legislation then under consideration, with its own price tag of $3.8 billion. The bonus bill was defeated. Walter Waters, who by then was accepted by most of the BEF men as their leader, was called inside and told the news. He returned to the steps of the Capitol. "Comrades," he shouted to the men, "we have just sustained a temporary setback. The Senate has rejected the bill." At this point, one account has it, a Hearst reporter whispered a suggestion in Waters's ear: "Tell them to sing 'America,'" he said. Waters took the advice. "Let us show them that we can take it on the chin," he continued. "Let us show them that we are patriotic Americans. I call on you to sing 'America.'"[9] Slowly, the men complied, and after the last ragged note was lost in the summer night, a few of them booed the name of Hoover, then all drifted back to their encampments.

THE CITY'S COMMISSIONERS had announced that on June 9 all official support of the BEF would end, that the government buildings under construction would be cleared of veterans, and that trucks would be

9. The story and quotes appear in Jellison, op. cit., p. 72.

provided to get the men and their families out of town. City officials did cut off aid, but let the deadline for eviction go by, probably because no one was ready yet to use the level of force that might be necessary. As a substitute measure, Hoover persuaded Congress to pass a transportation loan bill that provided $100,000 to help the men and their families return home.

As summer continued and almost unbearable heat and humidity oozed through the city, the ranks of the BEF thinned, even though Walter Waters vowed that the veterans would stay to press their case until 1945, if need be. Those who remained in the camps grew a little less disciplined with every day. Drinking increased, as did panhandling and general rowdiness, particularly after all city rations ceased. Waters surrounded himself with bodyguards, expanded the powers of the BEF's "military police," said that he was restructuring the entire movement into something he called the "Khaki Shirts," and began to strut and pontificate in a manner reminiscent of Mussolini in Italy and Hitler in Germany; he accepted the comparisons as praise, writing in the poorly composed *B.E.F. News* that "for five years Hilter [sic] was lampooned and dirided [sic]," and that "Mussolini before the war was a tramp priner [printer], driven from Italy because of his political views."[10] Opposition to his leadership developed among the ranks, and some men moved out of the Anacostia Flats encampment to seize several more unoccupied government buildings. Communists, though numbering probably no more than a couple of hundred, stirred up whatever fuss they could.

On July 28, the federal and district governments finally decided to remove all those still occupying government buildings. That morning, Glassford and a contingent of about one hundred police began evicting the occupants of the old National Guard Armory, carrying them out when necessary. The action went smoothly enough during the morning, but by the afternoon several truckloads of veterans from the Anacostia Flats camp had arrived on the scene under Waters's "orders." Others had seized the Eleventh Street Bridge so that it could not be raised to prevent marchers from crossing back and forth into the city. A group of the

10. Quoted in Lisio, op. cit., p. 122.

new arrivals attempted to reoccupy the armory. When Glassford's men resisted, the marchers started throwing bricks, one of which dropped Glassford himself temporarily. That assault was beaten back without gunfire, but fighting soon broke out around another building down the street. This time an officer panicked and shot one man, killing him, and wounded several others, one of whom soon died.

Over Glassford's objections that it might cause a bloodbath, the district commissioners officially requested that President Hoover send in the army. Hoover complied, and through Secretary of War Patrick Hurley ordered General Douglas MacArthur, Chief of Staff, to

> have United States troops proceed immediately to the scene of disorder. Cooperate fully with the District of Columbia police force which is now in charge. Surround the affected area and clear it without delay.
>
> Turn over all prisoners to the civil authorities.
>
> In your orders insist that any women or children who may be in the affected area be afforded every consideration and kindness. Use all humanity consistent with the due execution of the order.[11]

MacArthur, never one to shun the limelight, took command personally, against the advice of his aide, Major Dwight D. Eisenhower, who thought it unseemly for the chief of staff to get himself involved in anything resembling a "street corner embroilment."[12] But MacArthur was utterly persuaded that the fighting at the government buildings was just the beginning of a communist-planned revolutionary movement. "We are going to break the back of the BEF," he told Glassford just before sending a force of infantry down Pennsylvania Avenue with a troop of cavalry and six tiny tanks at their head. "It will be done tonight."[13]

11. Quoted in Winslow, op. cit., p. 41.
12. Quoted in Lisio, op. cit., p. 192.
13. Quoted in ibid., p. 204. More than thirty years later, MacArthur was still claiming that the uprising of July 28 was inspired and led by Communists. "Red organizers infiltrated the veterans groups and presently took command from their unwitting leaders," he wrote in his *Reminiscences* (p. 93).

It was. As the infantry approached an occupied building, at Third Street and Pennsylvania Avenue at about 5:30 P.M., some veterans began to throw bricks. Instead of surrounding the rioters, as their orders directed, MacArthur's infantrymen put on their gas masks and began firing tear-gas bombs into the crowd, driving the veterans at bayonet point into the street along with hundreds of spectators. Relentlessly, the tanks, infantrymen, and cavalry pushed the crowds in a southeasterly direction. Major George S. Patton, furious over brick-throwing and taunts, ordered his cavalry to ride into the mass of people with unsheathed swords. "Into the crowds they ruthlessly drove," one erstwhile spectator, former Postmaster General John Henry Bartlett remembered, "scattering us like sheep, knocking down many pedestrians. I backed double quick or a horse would have hit me."[14] One man less nimble than Bartlett lost his ear to a flashing sword; another was stabbed. Gas was everywhere. Paul Y. Anderson of the *St. Louis Post-Dispatch* watched as a company of infantrymen lobbed tear-gas canisters into a neighborhood removed from the center of action. "Some fell in front yards jammed with Negro women and children," he wrote. "One appeared to land on the front porch of a residence. Two small girls fell to the sidewalk, choking and screaming. But the veterans were beyond the street intersection more than fifty yards away. This gas was intended for the spectators."[15]

By six-thirty, the troops were at the Eleventh Street Bridge, over which the bulk of the veterans had retreated. MacArthur gave his men a brief rest. Hoover and Secretary of War Hurley, meanwhile, distressed that the evacuation had turned into a matter of blood and gas, sent direct orders to MacArthur forbidding him and his men to cross over the bridge to rout the rest of the BEF. For reasons still unknown, MacArthur apparently did not get the message, sending tanks, cavalry, and infantry across the river at about 10:00 P.M. By midnight, the Anacostia Flats camp was in flames. Some of the fires had been set by

14. John Henry Bartlett, *The Bonus March and the New Deal*, p. 33. Bartlett had donated a portion of his own land outside the city for the construction of a B.E.F. encampment called "Camp Bartlett," a small affair but by all accounts the best kept and most pleasant of all the camps.
15. Quoted in Weaver, op. cit.

retreating marchers, Major Eisenhower remembered, "these ragged, discouraged people burning their own little things," but the rest of the job was done by the soldiers.[16]

Hoover chose not to reprimand MacArthur. "A challenge to the authority of the United States Government has been met, swiftly and firmly," he told the press the next day as the thousands of defeated marchers drifted into the countryside of Maryland and Pennsylvania.[17] "It was a great victory," Secretary of War Hurley reportedly boasted. "MacArthur is the Man of the Hour." Hurley later denied having said any such thing. "There is no glory in this terrible episode—no hero," he insisted.[18] But there were plenty of victims—and those hours of violence in the nation's capital, most felt, were nothing less than a betrayal. "The camp at Anacostia now / Is a waste of ashes black," one angry verse sang.

> For they put the torch to the tattered tent
>   And the flame to the crazy shack.
> But there's a wasteland in many a heart
>   That the rulers do not see:
> For the searing flame of betrayal
>   Makes ashes of loyalty.[19]

"At the worst," contemporary journalist Edwin C. Hill mused, "it was only a discouraged, half-despairing assemblage; men who, even at the bitter end, maintained remarkable control of themselves, men whose fingers snapped automatically to their old army caps as the Flag came slowly down at dusk."[20] And if many of the marchers would carry anger with them for the rest of their lives, most were left in a state of shock—that, and a sense of shame and sorrow, though whether it was for themselves or their country they probably could not have said. A few days after the rout, a number of BEF refugees made their way back to New York City, where they scratched around until they had found

16. Quoted in Lisio, op. cit., p 213.
17. Quoted in Winslow, op. cit., p. 43.
18. Both quotes from Weaver, op. cit.
19. Anonymous, "The Ashes of Anacostia," in *Ballads of the B.E.F.* (1932), p. 5.
20. Edwin C. Hill, *The American Scene* (1933), p. 143.

enough lumber and used bricks to build an uncommonly sturdy little community—a kind of late-blooming Hooverville—in Central Park. "Will Hoover drive me out of here?" one of them asked a reporter. The newspaperman replied that he thought it was unlikely. "Well," the man said uncertainly, "he drove me out of Washington." Nearby, another man sat curled in on himself with his face in his hands, refusing to talk or to look at the curious people who had wandered in from Central Park West or Fifth Avenue to gape at the tiny settlement and its defeated veterans. Perhaps he had found refuge in the old children's game: If I close my eyes, you can't see me.[21]

21. The story is told in Seldes, op. cit.; footnote, p. 192.

11

---◆---

HOLDING UP
THE WALLS

At last the day was over. I looked over the forty-odd application slips I
had made out, and sorted them out into four neat little piles for the case-
workers. It seemed somehow a great moment, for me, the first time the
four case-workers gathered about my desk to get their assignments. . . .
I believe that moment was a thrill for all of us. We were off. The
big adventure had begun. We were part of the great machinery of the
New Deal.

—Federal Emergency Relief Administration
worker Louise W. Armstrong in
We Too Are the People (1941)

6

The Present Instrument
of Their Wishes

Y ou know what this means?" a hollow-eyed veteran had shouted to
reporter Malcolm Cowley at the shabby BEF camp in Johnstown
in August 1932. "This means revolution!"[1] He was right, though the
political revolution that emerged in November and would help shape
the character and quality of the national life for the next seven decades
probably disappointed him. If so, he would not have been alone. The
Communists, of course, had used every limited resource at their command to bring down capitalism and raise up a new soviet of American
states, looking upon every moment of confrontation—including the
Bonus Army riot—as the spark to start a conflagration as fierce as that
which had swept over Russia in 1917. As it happened, there had been a
good deal more smoke than fire—so far, at least. What, then, of fascism,
another kind of revolution? Cries for a "strong man" not unlike "Il
Duce," Benito Mussolini, whose Fascist "Blackshirts" had been ruling
Italy since 1923, were common enough. Magazine publisher and health

1. Quoted in Cowley, op. cit.

faddist Bernarr McFadden, for instance, made no bones about it: "What we need now," he instructed the readers of *Liberty*, "is martial law; this is no time for civil law. The President should have dictatorial powers. The edicts of the Constitution do not interfere with a general when he is fighting a battle and the Constitution should not interfere with the remedies which are essential to get us out of this appalling depression."[2]

If the country's leaders did not do *something,* the members of the President's Committee on Social Trends reported at the end of 1932 (the body had been appointed by Hoover in 1929), one extreme or the other was nearly inevitable. Deploring such "astonishing contrasts" in American life as that between "the splendid technical efficiency in some incredible skyscraper and monstrous backwardness in some equally incredible slum," the committee concluded that the nation must demonstrate

> Willingness and determination to undertake important integral changes in the reorganization of social life, including the economic and political orders, rather than the pursuance of a policy of drift. . . .
>
> Unless there can be a more impressive integration of social skills and fusing of social purposes than is revealed by present trends . . . there can be no assurances that these alternatives with their accompaniments of violent revolution . . . can be averted. . . . The Committee does not wish to assume an attitude of alarmist irresponsibility, but on the other hand it would be highly negligent to gloss over the stark and bitter realities of the social situation. . . . There are times when silence is not neutrality but assent.[3]

The electorate certainly had not been silent on November 8, 1932. They had not known the shape and dimensions of change that might result, but voters had demanded it themselves when they had gone to the polls in greater numbers than at any other time in history and had elected the governor of New York, Franklin Delano Roosevelt, president over Herbert Hoover by a margin of more than seven million votes.

2. Quoted in George Soule, *The Coming American Revolution*, pp. 194–97.
3. Ibid.

Roosevelt had promised the people of the nation a "new deal" in his acceptance speech at the Democratic National Convention that summer and declared that he was "the present instrument of their wishes" in his first inaugural address on March 4, 1933. But at first blush, he seemed an unlikely rock upon which to base truly radical change. A cousin of Theodore Roosevelt (whose niece, Eleanor, was also FDR's wife), he had been reared in the Hudson River Valley of New York as the well-cared-for son of a gentleman farmer, whose dedication to the Democratic Party was as deeply rooted as was the love of Republicanism among the other branch of the Roosevelts in and around Oyster Bay. Part of him would always yearn for the pastoral gentility of life on Springwood, the family estate at Hyde Park (in later years he would be fond of listing "tree farmer" as his occupation), but a nearly unfathomable mix of raw ambition and old-fashioned noblesse oblige had moved him to exchange that life as well as the relatively serene career of a gentleman lawyer for the grubby possibilities of politics.

Armed with a natural charm and an opportunistic eye, he had made enough of a name for himself during two terms in the New York State Assembly to be appointed assistant secretary of the navy in 1915, then parlayed that into becoming James W. Cox's running mate in the 1920 presidential election—only to be buried with the ineffectual Cox beneath Warren Harding's landslide. Defeat had been followed by an attack of poliomyelitis in 1921 that nearly killed him and left his legs permanently useless—though he never fully abandoned the hope that constant therapy would someday bring them back to life. "When he wants something a lot," Roosevelt adviser Raymond Moley would write in later years, "he is hard, stubborn, resourceful, relentless."[4] That willfulness had brought him through the worst months of his illness, and it underlay his refusal to let his disability end or even significantly hamper his political career. In 1928, he captured the governorship of New York.

Governing New York during the first years of the depression had been a tempering experience, too. At heart, he was (and would largely remain) a fiscal conservative, but the somewhat flaccid political instincts of his youth had long since settled into a kind of pragmatic Jacksonianism; he always enjoyed being likened to Jackson, and on

4. Quoted in Nathan Miller, *FDR: An Intimate History*, p. 245.

more than one occasion was not above comparing his efforts against those he called "economic royalists" to Jackson's feisty struggle with the Second United States Bank in the 1830s. Shortly after taking office in 1929, Roosevelt had challenged the state legislature over the control of the budget and had won. His administration had gone on to institute a number of reforms, including tax relief for farmers, increased state aid to rural education, the public ownership of state water power sites, and an eight-hour day for state workers, and, under the leadership of Frances Perkins as director of the state Industrial Commission, he had consistently supported labor's right to organize. Roosevelt also had been the first governor to call for old-age pensions funded by "contributions from public resources, employers, and the workers themselves."[5]

In his reelection bid in 1930, the governor had trounced his opponent by more than 725,000 votes, and with this mandate turned to the question of unemployment relief. By then, New York City's Social Service Exchange was taking five thousand relief applications a day, far more than private charity could possibly handle. A mass gathering of social workers on February 27 had resolved that "charitable relief can never be expected to fill the tremendous void in the purchasing power that is created when payrolls stop" and demanded that the city institute a $10 million public works and work relief program.[6] But state law prohibited the use of city funds for relief purposes, so on March 30 Roosevelt had sent an emergency message to the state legislature, which promptly passed enabling legislation. Even that had not been enough, of course, and on August 28 Roosevelt called an extraordinary session of the legislature. "What is the state?" he asked the assembled lawmakers.

It is the duly constituted representative of an organized society of human beings, created by them for their mutual protection and well-being. . . . The duty of the State toward the citizens is the duty of the servant to its master. . . . One of these duties of the State is that of car-

5. Quoted in Frank Annunziata, "Governor of New York," in Otis L. Graham Jr. and Meghan Robinson Wander, eds., *Franklin Roosevelt: His Life and Times, An Encyclopedic View*, p. 160.
6. Quoted in William W. Bremer, *Depression Winters: New York Social Workers and the New Deal*, p. 35.

ing for those of its citizens who find themselves the victims of such adverse circumstance as makes them unable to obtain even the necessities for mere existence without the aid of others.[7]

He then proposed the creation of a Temporary Emergency Relief Administration (TERA), funded by an appropriation of $20 million to be raised by a personal income tax and designed to provide four state dollars for every six dollars spent by any city for relief. The legislature had complied, and if the TERA, like all other private, city, county, and state efforts in the nation, had fallen far short of meeting the crisis, it had established Roosevelt's credentials as a man willing to challenge conventional wisdom, a man who demonstrated compassion for individual human beings.

If Roosevelt's strategies were vague and his tactics often devious, impulsive, and sometimes extravagantly tempered by political considerations, his instincts were superb, and in his own peripatetic fashion he would hold firmly to his belief in the government's solemn compact of responsibility to the people. This was a commitment that would make Roosevelt the most mythologized president since Abraham Lincoln—beloved and hated, castigated and deified, satisfying the need of tens of millions for a Moses and the equally profound need of some fewer millions for a Satan. What those who opposed him never fully understood, but Roosevelt himself somehow knew with instinctive certainty, was the fact that the majority of ordinary Americans would always be with him.

Their response was immediate and a little overwhelming. By the spring of 1934, the old Post Office Building on Pennsylvania Avenue was swimming in mail. More than 45,000 letters were being sent to Roosevelt every week, and the staff under I. R. T. Smith, who had served as the executive mail clerk for the White House since 1897, had been increased from three to twenty-two and could still barely keep ahead of the flow. There were letters of sympathy, complaint, outrage; letters asking for jobs, for money, for help with a government agency; letters wanting nothing other than to say hello; poetry, original musical compositions, pack-

7. Quoted in Samuel I. Rosenman, ed., *The Public Papers and Addresses of Franklin D. Roosevelt*, 1: pp. 457–58.

ages containing food, ships in bottles, wood carvings. No other president
in our history had received such an outpouring from the public, and it
would continue unabated until Roosevelt's death. Louis McHenry Howe,
Roosevelt's assistant, saw in this flood of letters nothing less than a
national declaration of faith in Roosevelt the man. "So many of [the let-
ters]," he told the readers of *American Magazine*, "reflect an eagerness to
help, a newly aroused consciousness of United States citizens of their own
part in the Government and of an actual, intimate bond between themselves and the man in the mansion on Pennsylvania Avenue."[8]

Born to great wealth, educated as few of them could ever hope to
be, Franklin Roosevelt was not one with the great mass of Americans,
but he touched them as they had not been touched by any president
they had ever known, and they would give him more than twelve years
of their devotion.

FROM THE BEGINNING, the new administration brought with it an
uncommon sense of urgency. In the predawn hours of Sunday, March 5,
1933, with almost no one visible on dark downtown streets still littered
from the inaugural parade, Morris Markey wrote that "the windows in
the Executive Offices were all bright, and upstairs in the White House
the lights were burning in four or five rooms. The radiance they cast fell
across the lawn, through the bare trees, and struck wanly against the
great wooden stands built for the parade."[9] It is a fair assumption that
most of the people behind most of those bright windows were talking
money, for it was over that inaugural weekend that the president and
his economic advisers decided to close all the banks in the country on
Monday, March 6. Given that more than four thousand banks had gone
under during the first two months of 1933, the governors of forty-seven
states had already declared bank holidays for all their state banks in
order to stop frantic withdrawals. But Roosevelt's proclamation of
March 6 went beyond state actions by putting a halt to all banking
transactions everywhere not specifically authorized by the secretary of

8. Louis McHenry Howe, "The President's Mail Bag!" *American Magazine* (June 1934).
9. Morris Markey, "Washington Weekend," in Milton Crane, ed. *The Roosevelt Era*,
pp. 8–9.

the treasury and the president. The order also prohibited the export of gold, a move designed to keep reserves in this country from being depleted any further than they already had been during more than three years of economic crisis (on March 3 alone, more than $109 million in gold had been "earmarked" for European investment).

Roosevelt's executive order was a temporary device to remain in effect only until Congress acted—with unprecedented speed, as it happened. Still floundering in a bog of uncertainty and grateful for any kind of firm direction, legislators gathered at Roosevelt's order for a special session on Thursday, March 9. In a matter of hours, both houses approved an administration-drafted Emergency Banking Act—the first piece of legislation in what was to be the busiest three months in Congressional history. This was the period that would come to be called "The Hundred Days" and see the passage of legislation embracing everything from regional development (the Tennessee Valley Authority) to frugality in government (the Economy Act), from the regulation of stocks (the Securities Act) to the purchase of homes and farms (the Home Owners Loan Act and the Emergency Farm Mortgage Act), all of it calculated to bring a sense of order and all of it profoundly enlarging the role of the federal government in the affairs of institutions and individuals.

The Emergency Banking Act of 1933 was the first in this spectacular cascade of laws and arguably one of the most effective. The act not only authorized the president to do what he already had done—close the banks and embargo gold—but stipulated that no bank could be reopened until approved by the secretary of the treasury, permitted the comptroller of the currency to install conservators over insolvent banks and gave such conservators the power to reorganize them, authorized the purchase of bank stocks and notes by the Reconstruction Finance Corporation to provide qualified banks with long-term investment funds, gave the president greater control over credit, currency, foreign exchange, and the setting of the price for gold and silver, and allowed the Department of the Treasury to call in all privately held gold and gold certificates to be exchanged for paper currency.

The following Sunday night, in the first of his "Fireside Chats," the president went on the radio to explain to the American people some part of what he had done so far with the gift of election they had given him. The banking system, he explained, had been so undermined by panic that by the time of his inauguration he had no other choice but to suspend transactions as the "first step in the government's reconstruction of our financial and economic fabric." Congress, showing "a devotion to public welfare and a realization of the emergency and the necessity for speed that is difficult to match in all our history," had complemented his action with passage of the Emergency Banking Act and so, beginning on Monday, March 13, the banks would be reopened on a carefully controlled basis. Why not all at once? "The answer is simple, and I know you will understand it," the president intoned soothingly.

> Your government does not intend that the history of the past few years shall be repeated. We do not want and will not have another epidemic of bank failures. . . .
>
> I can assure you, my friends, that it is safer to keep your money in a reopened bank than it is to keep it under the mattress. . . .
>
> You people must have faith; you must not be stampeded by rumors or guesses. Let us unite in banishing fear. We have provided the machinery to restore our financial system; and it is up to you to support and make it work.[10]

No president had ever gone to so much trouble to explain to the public in simple language just what was happening and what he and his people were doing. He appeared to take all citizens into his confidence as equal partners in the great task of recovery, a tactic he would use thirty more times in his presidency. If it was an illusion, the magician himself sometimes seemed caught up in it. "I often was at the White House when he broadcast," FDR's labor secretary Frances Perkins remembered,

> and I realized how unconscious he was of the twenty or thirty of us in that room and how clearly his mind was focused on the people listen-

10. This version of FDR's speech is the first of the thirty-one radio addresses included in *FDR's Fireside Chats*, edited by Russell D. Buhite and David W. Levy (pp. 13–17). For their text, Buhite and Levy transcribed the actual broadcasts as rendered in tape recordings produced by Mass Communications, Inc., in 1973. All future quotations from Fireside Chats in this book will be from this source.

ing at the other end. As he talked his head would nod and his hands would move in simple, natural, comfortable gestures. His face would smile and light up as though he were actually sitting on the front porch or in the parlor with them. People felt this, and it bound them to him in affection.[11]

Illusory or not, this first Fireside Chat was extraordinarily effective—particularly when it was followed by swift and visible action. By March 15, 1933, 12,756 banks—out of a total of 18,290—had reopened. Some did so with a flourish. In Tucson, Arizona, the Consolidated National Bank got word from the Treasury Department at 3:45 A.M. on March 15 that it had been approved; it opened its doors a few hours later to more than 5,000 waiting customers, who found the lobby banked with flowers, while a full orchestra played a bouncy rendition of "Happy Days Are Here Again." Happy indeed they were at the Consolidated: by day's end, more than $640,000 had been deposited and only $32,000 had been withdrawn, most foot-tapping customers taking out only enough money to pay current or overdue bills.[12] In Boston, where deposits also exceeded withdrawals by a comfortable margin, the city council issued a resolution celebrating "the summary, intelligent, and courageous action taken by President Roosevelt and Governor Ely," while in Phoenix a real estate man declared that "the new public feeling is general enough to convince the most skeptical that the psychology of depression is past, and the psychology of better times is here."[13]

Optimism might have been expected from a real estate agent, since it is a condition natural to the breed, but this one was not far off the mark. All over America, mattresses were lifted up, literally or figuratively, and their contents stuffed into sacks and briefcases and carried downtown. There was so much cash, raw gold, and gold certificates being hauled in by hand that many banks posted extra guards to prevent robberies at their thresholds. Deposits exceeded withdrawals everywhere. By the end of March, most of the reopened banks had been

11. Frances Perkins, *The Roosevelt I Knew*, p. 72.
12. See William H. Jervey, "When the Banks Closed: Arizona's Bank Holiday of 1933," *Arizona and the West* (Summer 1968).
13. Boston city council quoted in Trout, op. cit., p. 125; Phoenix real estate man quoted in Jervey, op. cit.

declared solvent, and over the next two months, most of the remainder would be shored up with RFC loans totaling $1.17 billion, as government auditors were dispatched from Washington to paw through the records of banks all over the country, owners and managers hovering nervously behind them. In one bank in the Democratic South, a manager offered auditors from the RFC twenty-dollar bribes if they would speed things up. "We said that was typical of the Democrats to offer little people $20 bribes," one of the auditors remembered, "whereas the Republicans would have offered large bribes to big people."[14] In the end, more than 3,000 banks would be completely reorganized and 1,100 dissolved.

In June, the New Deal Congress would climax banking reform efforts by passing another Banking Act, this one establishing the Federal Deposit Insurance Corporation (FDIC) to guarantee most bank deposits. Ironically, Roosevelt had not wanted the FDIC, fearing so large a commitment, but the program was an immediate success; between 1921 and 1933, depositors had lost some $156 million in savings every year, but after the FDIC program officially started on January 1, 1934, average yearly losses over the next quarter century dropped to only $706,000. And in 1936 not a single bank in the United States failed—a stability unheard of since the 1870s.[15]

Virtually everyone within and without the administration applauded the results of the attack on the banking crisis. Monetary policy was another matter. The provisions of the Emergency Banking Act regarding gold did not, the administration wanted everyone to know, mean that the United States was abandoning the gold standard. "It is ridiculous and misleading to say we have gone off the gold standard," Treasury Secretary William H. Woodin told the *Commercial and Financial Chronicle* on March 11. "We are definitely on the gold standard. Gold merely cannot be obtained for several days."[16] That was one way of looking at it, but the fact of the matter was that the president was determined to bring prices back up to pre-depression levels by any

14. Quoted in Michael E. Parrish, *Anxious Decades: America in Prosperity and Depression, 1920–1941*, p. 291.
15. See Anthony J. Badger, *The New Deal: The Depression Years, 1933–40*, p. 73.
16. Quoted in Eichengreen, op. cit., footnote, p. 329.

means necessary. This was true even if it meant a steady depreciation of the dollar, a deliberately inflationary policy that he insisted on following in spite of the vigorous objections of some of his own economic advisers.

To that end, the president announced on April 19 that the United States was indeed abandoning gold. Two weeks later, he cheerfully signed the Agricultural Adjustment Act, which gave him the power to induce inflation by several means, including the issuance of as much as $3 billion in "fiat" money, or "greenbacks." Two months after that, he capped his inflationary crusade when he rejected an agreement designed to stabilize world prices that had been reached during an international monetary conference in London. For a while, FDR's strategy seemed to work. Commodity prices rose by more than 70 percent between April 1 and the middle of July, stock prices rose by 53 percent by December, and industrial production for the rest of the year stayed about 15 percent higher than in the previous year.[17]

None of this growth came anywhere near the levels of the pre-Crash years and it would not remain even at these levels for very long, but in the meantime the president could bask in the glow of temporary accomplishment, knowing that his level of public support remained high. No one, he had remarked archly at his first press conference on March 8, "knows what the gold basis or gold standard really is," and while he was perfectly aware that the statement was as false as it was glib, he also knew that ordinary citizens were no more inclined to study the singularly arcane world of international monetary policy in the 1930s than at any other time in history.[18] Their understanding remained at about the level of that of librettist Moss Hart and songwriter Irving Berlin in producer Sam Harris's *As Thousands Cheer*, a musical that opened on Broadway in September 1933 (it became the only significantly profitable show of the entire 1933–1934 season). Among the show's several satirical "headline" vignettes was one that depicted a meeting of foreign economic ministers who had come to Washington to discuss paying their war debts. When they were informed that the United States had gone off the gold standard, the ministers

---

17. Ibid., pp. 340–43.
18. Quoted in Arthur M. Schlesinger Jr., *The Coming of the New Deal*, p. 195.

cheerfully sang that they would be happy to repay their debts in silver, zinc, tin, or, for that matter, wood. Afterward, singer Helen Broderick, gotten up as the Statue of Liberty, warbled "Uncle Sam will be in Heaven / When the dollar goes to Hell!"[19]

Whatever the international permutations might have been, what most Americans understood with clarity was that they now could go down to their neighborhood banks and deposit their money with confidence that it would still be there when they needed it back, while the business community could look at rising prices and begin at least to think about such things as restocking the inventory. Roosevelt would cheerfully balance that renewed confidence against any discombobulation he might have caused the international world of finance or his own subordinates.

19. For *As Thousands Cheer*, see Stanley Green, *Ring Bells! Sing Songs! Broadway Musicals of the 1930s*, pp. 83–85. American confusion aside, in Europe the impact of Roosevelt's abandonment of the gold standard and his rejection of currency stabilization, while varied in intensity, was uniformly great. While France held on until 1936, most of those few countries that had not already given up the gold standard would soon do so. "Until then [the spring of 1933]," Netherlands economic minister G. M. Verjinn Stuart wrote in 1937, "I still hoped that some form of international understanding might lead to putting into effect a policy of 'reflation within gold.' The deplorable results shown by the London Economic and Financial Conference in the first month convinced me that the only way for the Netherlands to escape from the difficulties was to give up the gold base of the guilder and devalue." (Quoted in Charles P. Kindleberger, *The World in Depression, 1929–1939*, footnote, p. 246.) Most countries adopted similar policies of devaluation, and while price and industrial production indexes subsequently rose in many areas, currencies remained in a state of chaos and economic growth continued as sporadically in Europe as in the United States. This country would not reenter the European currency sphere in any significant manner until 1936, when it signed a Tripartite Monetary Agreement with France and Great Britain that brought a measure of stability to exchange rates among the franc, the pound, and the dollar (see Eichengreen, op. cit., pp. 378–81).

7

A Scuffling Pageant of Relief

Confidence, of course, could not buy food, clothing, and shelter for the millions who still needed it, and the administration, in partnership with a still somber and cooperative Congress, moved to meet this grim challenge almost as swiftly and decisively as it had met the banking crisis. There was plenty to be done. Back in November 1932, a Harvard economist had cited expectations in New York City that the number of people on relief would jump from about 46,000 to more than 90,000 in the coming winter; the prediction proved entirely correct, as did similar predictions for other cities around the country, where the number of relief cases would on average double in the winter months. By February 1933, there were 4.7 million families representing 18.6 million people who were receiving some form of relief— almost 15 percent of all Americans. The number of unemployed was estimated at anywhere from a little over 12 million to as many as 14.6 million.[1] Nowhere was there enough state or local money to take care of

---

1. For statistics on relief cases and unemployment, see Sumner Slichter, "The Immediate Unemployment Problem," an address delivered on November 11, 1932, in *History*

such numbers. Scores of cities were nearing bankruptcy, their tax revenues down and their bonds unmarketable; municipal welfare agencies were depleted, local and even national charities exhausted, and state agencies had already gone through most of the $300 million that Congress had appropriated for relief in the summer of 1932. "We have substituted to a considerable extent a relief economy for an industrial economy," William Hodson of the New York Welfare Council said, "with the result that standards of living have fallen and we find ourselves struggling at every point to meet the creature necessities of life."[2]

On March 21, the president asked Congress for two specific items to address the problem of relief immediately. First, he said, the 1932 federal appropriation of $300 million in relief funds was going to last only until May: "Therefore, and because a continuance of Federal aid is still a definite necessity for many States, a further appropriation must be made before the end of this special session. I find a clear need for some simple Federal machinery to coordinate and check these grants of aid," he went on. "I am, therefore, asking that you establish the office of Federal Relief Administrator." Second, he said,

> I propose to create a civilian conservation corps to be used in simple work, not interfering with normal employment, and confining itself to forestry, the prevention of soil erosion, flood control and similar projects. . . .
>
> The vast majority of unemployed Americans, who are now walking the streets and receiving private or public relief, would infinitely prefer to work. We can take a vast army of these unemployed out into healthful surroundings. We can eliminate to some extent at least the threat that enforced idleness brings to spiritual and moral stability. It is not a panacea for all the unemployment but it is an essential step in this emergency.[3]

---

of *Employment and Manpower Policy in the United States. Parts I and II: Depression Experience, Proposals, and Programs*, pp. 1787–1799. See also Social Security Board, *Social Security Bulletin* (February 1941), pp. 68–70; and Harry Hopkins, *Spending to Save: The Complete Story of Relief* (1936), p. 95.

2. Quoted in Bremer, op. cit., p. 119.

3. Samuel I. Rosenman, ed., *The Public Papers and Addresses of Franklin D. Roosevelt, 2:* pp. 80–81.

He also warned the legislators that he would be asking for another item soon, the details of which he was still studying (this would be the National Industrial Recovery Act, the legislation for which would be introduced on May 17). In the meantime, these two proposals were crucial, and while neither sailed through the Congress in hours, as did the Emergency Banking Act, serious opposition was minimal. On March 31, an act authorizing the Civilian Conservation Corps was passed, and on April 5 Roosevelt signed the executive order that established the agency. It took another six weeks for an Emergency Unemployment Relief Act to get through Congress, but that, too, was on Roosevelt's desk by May 12, complete with an appropriation of $500 million.

While Senators La Follette of Wisconsin, Wagner of New York, and Costigan of Colorado had consulted with White House emissaries before introducing the relief bill, Congress otherwise played little part in the actual structuring of either bill. Each was predominantly the child of the White House New Dealers; consequently, the implementation of each would go a long way to illuminate the character and depth of the relationship that was beginning to sprout between the government, as represented by the sitting president, and the people, as represented by those whose pain he had declared it to be the nation's responsibility to relieve.

"I'M ON A GREAT TEAM," young Lennie Mallory wrote his girl from the rolling foothills of the Blue Ridge Mountains in the summer of 1933. "We live in camp, army style. Each camp has two faces—civilian and military. . . . The military being the one we live in, our home. . . . The civilian face is the day of work. The engineers and the technicians teach us to be soil soldiers, a name they call us here, because we are the army who are training to repel the enemies of the land."[4] Lennie was from Dorchester, Massachusetts, a suburb of Boston, and he had escaped a home being ripped to tatters by the pressures of the depression—his father out of work for four years, sick, constantly fighting with Lennie's

4. Quoted in Leslie Alexander Lacy, *The Soil Soldiers: The Civilian Conservation Corps in the Great Depression*, p. 30.

mother. His sanctuary was the Civilian Conservation Corps, and before his service was done (he would reenlist twice), Lennie would come to believe that his experience as a member of Mr. Roosevelt's "soil soldiers" had transformed his life, bringing him both self-respect and security.

That would have pleased the president. No single piece of legislation passed in the Hundred Days—or in the years to follow, for that matter—was as close to Roosevelt's heart as that which created the CCC. He was a practical, utilitarian conservationist whose own devotion to rational forestry practices had made the groves of the Roosevelt estate in Hyde Park, New York, among the healthiest private forest land in the country. He saw no reason why the same kind of intelligent stewardship could not be applied to the overcut forests and overfarmed agricultural land of the whole country, restoring a national landscape that had been poorly used for more than a century. The CCC was his instrument.

If Roosevelt's vision was simple (or at least simply stated), the agency's structure was fashioned by an interagency committee headed up by Interior Secretary Harold Ickes, with contributions from the departments of agriculture, labor, and war, and the result was quite as complicated as one would expect. The Labor Department would have responsibility for recruiting the enrollees, who had to be unemployed males no longer in school, no younger than 18, and no older than 25, in good health, at least 107 pounds in weight, no shorter than 60 inches and no taller than 78 inches, and should have in their mouths no fewer than three working teeth above and below. The War Department would clothe, house, and feed the men, tend to their medical and dental needs, and pay them—$30 a month for regular recruits, $36 for assistant leaders, and $45 for "local experienced men" (LEMs, as they would come to be known); those recruits with dependent families were required to send home anywhere from $23 to $25 of their monthly pay. The Interior Department would provide vocational and academic education through the U.S. Office of Education and supervise CCC work in national parks through the National Park Service, while the Department of Agriculture would oversee all work done on the 171 million acres of national forests, wildlife refuges, and other Department of Agriculture lands.

The involvement of the military was a matter of concern to many, including the Socialist Party's Norman Thomas, who said that such "work camps fit into the psychology of a Fascist, not a Socialist state," as well as the New Deal's most unreconstructed liberal, Harold Ickes, who had earned his political stripes as one of Chicago's most persistent reformers.[5] "So this will be a military training proposition, will it?" Frances Perkins remembered Ickes sputtering when Roosevelt first proposed that the camps be supervised by the army. "This will be forced military training. Take the poor fellows off the streets and put them into the military."

"Oh, no!" Roosevelt replied. "That must never be. That must never be!"[6] He was even more forceful during a press conference on March 22. Talk about military control and militarization, he insisted, was "just utter rubbish. . . . Obviously, you have to have some form of policing. In other words, you cannot allow a man in a dormitory to get up in the middle of the night and blow a bugle. You have got to have order—just perfectly normal order. . . . [So] much for the military end."[7]

Ickes aside, the committee as a whole had been more worried about reaction from the labor movement, and for better reason. From the first, AFL president William Green had complained that low government wages would undercut those being demanded by organized labor. In an effort to take the steam out of Green's argument, the committee's report to the president on organization had suggested specifically that the CCC confine itself to those land-based projects that would not compete with more ambitious public works and alienate "those who fear the depressing effect on the wage levels of free labor, due to the wide use of this recruited army, and also those who feel that works which should be done by contract by free labor will be progressively urged as suitable for the Conservation Corps."[8] The president had agreed and revised his legislative message to Congress accordingly, then went one step further in offering the olive branch of conciliation to Green when he appointed Robert Fechner, a vice president of the International Association of Machinists, overall director of the corps.

5. Norman Thomas quoted in Frank Freidel, *Launching the New Deal*, p. 261.
6. Frances Perkins told this story in her oral memoirs, Columbia University, 4: p. 485.
7. Quoted in Freidel, op. cit., p. 261.
8. Cabinet committee to FDR, in Edgar B. Nixon, ed., *Franklin D. Roosevelt and Conservation, 1911–1945*, pp. 141–42.

Low pay and a quasi-military atmosphere notwithstanding, the rush to join the CCC was phenomenal. The first man—Fiore Rizzo of Manhattan—was enrolled on April 7, and the first camp—in George Washington National Forest near Luray, Virginia—was established on April 17. By the last week of July, there were 1,500 camps in place, some on private lands but most in state and national forests and other federal public lands, and 250,000 of the full authorization of 274,374 "junior" enrollees had been filled, together with a major portion of the 32,250 "local experienced men" who had been authorized. A further contingent was added in early May, after about 3,000 veterans of 1932's Bonus Expeditionary Force had returned to Washington to demand their money again. Roosevelt was no more inclined to approve the bonus than Hoover had been (nor was the new Congress), but there the resemblance between the two men ended, so far as the BEF was concerned.

Louis Howe was ordered to take care of the veterans. They were given shelter, coffee, three meals a day, and medical service at Fort Hunt across the Potomac. The navy band provided music, and on one notable rainy afternoon Eleanor Roosevelt herself came to call, slogging through ankle-deep mud to have a cup of coffee, take a tour, share some stories and a great deal of sympathy, and lead the men in a heartfelt rendition of "There's a Long, Long Trail" and other popular songs from the war years. Hoover, one veteran marveled, "sent the army; Roosevelt sent his wife."[9] He did more than that: on May 11 he sent an executive order that authorized the creation of a special enrollment in the CCC to be filled by a maximum of 25,000 veterans. Most of this quota, too, was met almost immediately, and among the new recruits were 2,600 of the 3,000 veterans who had sung along with Eleanor Roosevelt.

By the end of July, then, the CCC's ranks contained more than 300,000 out of a total authorized enrollment of 352,711 men. During the remaining nine years of the CCC, even after higher quotas had been authorized, that number would be exceeded only once, enrollment soaring to a little over half a million in August 1935; most years, the average was about 250,000 for a total of more than 2.75 million participants over the life of the program. The majority joined in order to help

9. Quoted in Freidel, op. cit., p. 264.

their families, though in one survey of 374 young men, more than half said that the main reason for signing up was the fact that they were "tired of having nothing to do," while a fifth admitted that they joined mainly because their friends had, and 15 percent because they had wanted, like Lennie Mallory, "to get away from home."[10]

What they found in the CCC camps was a regimen that managed to combine aspects of a military operation with those of an urban construction gang, a YMCA summer camp, and a Chautauqua session. Each camp housed anywhere from 150 to 200 men. They slept in barracks, as in the army; were wakened with a bugle blowing reveille, as in the army; were fed in a mess hall, as in the army; endured calisthenics, as in the army; policed their barracks and the grounds outside, as in the army; and assembled at the end of the day for dismissal, as in the army. Generally speaking, however, the relationship between the men and the officers who ran the camps was a good deal less formal than that in a genuine military outpost, and discipline more a matter of moral persuasion than force—a policy emphasized by Secretary of War George Dern, who said that camp commanders "had to learn to govern men by leadership, explanation, and diplomacy."[11] The workday typically began at 7:00 A.M., with the men getting their tools together and climbing into trucks for delivery to work sites, was interrupted at 11:45 for an hourlong lunch, and ended at 4:00 P.M., when the men were trucked back to camp. After dismissal and the evening meal, the recruits could engage in sports or take any one of several classes offered in everything from simple literacy training to high school courses in academic or vocational subjects. The lights were turned out at 10:00 P.M.

Viewed purely as a relief measure, the creation of the CCC was insignificant, since even at its highest enrollment it helped only a fraction of those in need. But there was no denying the utilitarian value of a small army of generally healthy and energetic young men, most of whom were willing to do what they were told and grateful to be doing it, and the departments of Interior and Agriculture found plenty to occupy them. The men built picnic tables, outdoor toilets, roads, thousands of miles of hiking trails, and other recreation facilities in the

10. See Kenneth Holland and Frank Ernest Hill, *Youth in the CCC*, p. 47.
11. Quoted in Ellis, op. cit., p. 299.

national parks, and restored long-neglected national battlefields and other historical monuments. They planted millions of hatchery fish in lakes and streams all over the country, built stock-watering facilities on public rangelands, improved the habitat in hundreds of federal wildlife refuges and state wildlife sanctuaries, and helped to improve state and county park systems with new campgrounds, museums, trailside shelters, swimming holes, and other facilities. The most spectacular of these may well have been Denver's Red Rocks Amphitheater, an amazing place carved out of natural stone in the foothills of the Rocky Mountains. They helped to feed western sheep with seedcakes during the terrible Rocky Mountain storms of 1936 and 1937, drained mosquito-breeding bogs and wetlands, joined in to help build sandbag levees and rescue victims when the Mississippi River flooded in 1937, and poisoned billions of grasshoppers during infestations on the Great Plains.

When the Soil Erosion Service was established in the Department of the Interior in 1933, and when it was transferred later to the Department of Agriculture and renamed the Soil Conservation Service, teams of CCC workers in some five hundred "soil camps" were put to work helping to restore millions of acres of farmland ravaged by the twin plagues of drought and human abuse. In the national forests, CCC workers built or rebuilt even more thousands of miles of trails than in the national parks, fought pine bark beetle, Dutch elm disease, and white pine blister rust epidemics, constructed 3,475 fire towers and tied them together with 65,100 miles of telephone line, built firebreaks, and put in no fewer than 4.1 million man-hours extinguishing forest fires from the northern Rockies of Montana to the San Bernardinos of southern California, from the Bitterroots of Montana to the Appalachians of Georgia. And they planted trees—1.3 billion new trees were tucked into the clear-cut soils of the national forests in the corps' first five years alone, hundreds of millions of them seedlings grown in its own tree nurseries. Another 220 million trees went into Roosevelt's vaunted "Shelterbelt" program, and many of these millions were planted by the CCC.[12]

12. For the Soil Erosion Service and the Shelterbelt Program, see chapter 17. Sadly, some of the CCC's programs, like others in the New Deal years, had unintended conse-

In 1942, the regional forester for Region 9 of the U.S. Forest Service summarized his view of the CCC experience. "The history of these nine years," he said with understandable pride, "is a saga of service in which the largest body of men in the country, working as a single unit, have labored with tractor, pick, shovel, and planting tools in rebuilding the resources of a nation."[13] The experience was not always benign and the record was not an unmixed triumph, of course. At the height of the program, there were more than 35,000 administrative employees of the CCC, but only about 1,500 were teachers—or "educational advisers," as they were mysteriously called. That was an average of one teacher per camp, clearly too few even if only half of the 150 to 200 men in each wanted to learn something (in fact, the CCC estimated that 52 percent of the enrollees ultimately did take part in some kind of educational activity during their terms of enlistment). Most teachers also were expected to be athletic coaches, social directors, and personal counselors to the boys, many of whom were nearly strangers to formal education and apathetic, ignorant, and often resistant. "Most of these kids," one teacher complained, "have a 'Now don't try to get *me* interested in anything' sort of attitude. Also, a rule is just something to be broken. You have to pull them out of these attitudes before you can get results."[14] Many teachers could not deal with the consequent pressure; the turnover rate for educational advisers was about 30 percent. Furthermore, CCC director Robert Fechner had little sympathy for the educational aspects of the program, fearing that class time would compete with work time, and C. S. Marsh, the Office of Education official placed in charge of the CCC's teaching program, often found it difficult to pry

---

quences. The draining of mosquito-breeding areas, for instance, contributed significantly to the loss of wetlands, whose importance to the preservation of biological diversity and the ecological health of natural systems on which all life, including human life, depends is now common knowledge. And the kind of diligent fire suppression practiced on so wide a scale by the CCC ultimately helped to produce so much natural fuel—unburned understory growth and dead and dying trees—that disaster was inevitable: after several years of intermittent drought in the West, the fires that erupted in the late 1980s and early 1990s were of an unprecedented scale, sweeping through millions of acres of national forest and national parklands with implacable ferocity.

13. Quoted in Lacy, op. cit., pp. 149–51.
14. Quoted in Holland and Hill, op. cit., p. 126.

money out of Fechner's office to buy enough textbooks, stationery, and library books to support a decent effort. After Marsh resigned in embarrassingly public disgust in 1935, the situation improved somewhat, but in scores of camps educational materials remained in short supply. So did balls, bats, gloves, and other athletic equipment, and in many camps educational advisers and camp commanders spent a good deal of their time scavenging for materials from nearby communities or raising funds from individual donors.

Nor were the individual camps adequately monitored by Fechner's office or even the War Department. Fechner had only one inspector in each of the nine corps areas, and some critics maintained that the director—a militant union man, after all—had most of his inspectors spending the majority of their time making sure that the construction of the camps themselves was being done by union labor. The only other means of oversight—aside from regular visits by Fechner himself, which was a large order, given the number of camps—was through the commanders of the nine army corps areas that matched the CCC areas, but most of these officers took little interest in the conditions of the camps and some even resented the responsibility (one notable exception was future Chief of Staff George C. Marshall, a CCC enthusiast, who worked hard at maintaining standards in the twenty-seven camps in his jurisdiction in the Pacific Northwest). For the most part, then, the individual camp commanders were on their own, and since their abilities and commitment to the program varied, problems of administration, morale, and discipline erupted in a substantial minority of camps. Food riots were fairly common (whether in a CCC camp or a regular army outpost, mess hall food was nothing to celebrate, then or ever), the desertion rate remained close to 20 percent, and in some instances the frustration expressed went beyond mere postadolescent high spirits. At the Pine Valley camp in Oklahoma, an officer was killed, and at another an assistant commander was beaten badly enough to be sent to the infirmary, leaving the camp in a condition succinctly described by a reporter for *The New Republic* (though without naming names): "The camp resembles a jail, and social behavior appropriate to a jail, toadying, malingering, wreaking petty revenges, is being inculcated in the boys. . . . The company commander is bitter . . . but does not dare relieve his bitterness by discharging the leaders, since he fears an investigation by the corps area headquarters."[15]

It was not always the boys who caused the trouble. The commander of a camp near Lexington, Indiana, encouraged the use of alcohol and had prostitutes brought in to entertain the boys; he was discharged from the army, as was a camp commander who actually sold the boys liquor and another who embezzled $20,000 in funds from his camp.

Incidents of violence and official malfeasance, though relatively rare, were widely reported by the press. Another endemic problem was not. Even though the act authorizing the creation of the CCC had stipulated that "no discrimination shall be made on account of race, color, or creed," racism in the CCC, as elsewhere in and out of even this liberalized New Deal government, was a fact of life. For one thing, Robert Fechner was a son of the South and no more inclined to challenge common prejudice in the CCC than he would have been back in his native Tennessee. Only about 200,000 African Americans ever joined the CCC, representing about 7 percent of the total, substantially below the 10 percent goal that the CCC had established for black participation. A large part of the problem was the fact that many recruiters in the South systematically rejected most black applicants. In Georgia, for instance, where African Americans made up 36 percent of the population, there were only 143 black men enrolled by the end of June 1933—just 1.9 percent of the state's total CCC enrollment. Pressure from Labor Secretary Perkins eventually got the number raised to 1,733, but at no time did it reach an appropriate percentage. "The benefits of the Civilian Conservation Corps," sociologist Arthur Raper wrote of the South in *Preface to Peasantry* (1936), "have been limited almost wholly to whites. . . . The CCC has remained a white institution, with no more coloring than landownership, which tolerates the possession of one acre in twenty by Negroes."[16]

North or south, most of those black men who managed to get into the CCC found themselves segregated, like the army itself, into separate camps. That worried a number of local communities, many in the

15. Jonathan Mitchell, "Roosevelt's Tree Army," *The New Republic* (May 29, 1935).
16. Arthur S. Raper, *Preface to Peasantry*, p. 263.

northern states, who entertained ludicrous visions of impending rape and pillage from such large contingents of young black men, and many petitioned Fechner to have the camps removed out of sight and mind of peaceable white citizens. Fechner complied more often than not. Only two of the black camps were commanded by black officers, and few had any other black officials of any kind. As late as 1940, Judge William Hastie, the War Department's Aide on Negro Affairs, reported that in the 150 black CCC camps then in existence, there were only nine black doctors and four black chaplains on duty. The same disparity existed with regard to educational advisers.[17]

At its best, however, which it was more often than not, the CCC was an experience that could illuminate lives, even for black recruits. "I git to go more, git to see more," one black enrollee who had been lucky enough to work in one of the few integrated camps told a social researcher in 1936.

> I'm learning, too. I watch the others. . . . I don't work nearly as hard in this as I do in the field at home. I git to be with lots of boys that I wouldn't at home. They help me lots, show me how to do things I wouldn't have never knowed about. I like all my bosses and I like all the fellers. They tease me sometimes, but they like me, too.[18]

Even allowing for the likelihood that the young man was telling his listener pretty much what he thought his listener wanted to hear, this being the time-honored survival tactic of most southern blacks (one has to wonder what form the "teasing" took), there was a discernible level of satisfaction in his statement, and it is not at all impossible that he would have echoed the sentiments of a white enrollee who penned an ornate but heartfelt valedictory in *Happy Days*, the CCC's national newspaper: "We shall all cherish the memory of this brief adventure. We shall be proud to have been members of this army of pio-

17. For the black CCC experience, see Charles Johnson, "The Army, the Negro and the Civilian Conservation Corps," *Military Affairs* (October 1972); Allen Francis Kifer, "The Negro Under the New Deal, 1933–1941," pp. 2–76; and Howard Sitkoff, *A New Deal for Blacks*, pp. 50–51, 74–75.
18. Quoted in Federal Writers Project, *These Are Our Lives*, pp. 411–15.

neers, as our forefathers were proud of being the forerunners of a great nation."[19]

"Discipline, that was the key," one CCC boy remembered in later life. "You agreed to do something and you did it. I learned a work ethic, how to do things safely and right. . . . There was pride in the work. We built something, and I knew I helped and I saw the result. It was something you could take pride in, and there wasn't a lot of pride available in those days."[20] A Colorado circuit court judge would have agreed. "It had all kinds of intangible values," he said of his own experience. "It helped you grow up."[21]

WHILE THE CIVILIAN Conservation Corps was beginning to help about 2.75 million young men grow up, the Federal Emergency Relief Administration (FERA), the New Deal's first direct answer to the question of absolute need, launched an effort to keep the walls of destitution from collapsing on 18 million people of both sexes and all ages. After Congress authorized the creation of the office of Federal Relief Administrator, as Roosevelt had asked them to do on March 21, Harry Lloyd Hopkins was brought down from Albany, New York, to take the job. It was Hopkins who had headed up Roosevelt's Temporary Emergency Relief Administration during the president's second New York gubernatorial term. Roosevelt had drawn on that experience even before the federal appointment, making Hopkins part of a working group whose other members included Labor Secretary Frances Perkins and Senators Robert Wagner, Edward Costigan, and Robert M. La Follette Jr., and whose responsibility was to meet among themselves and with such other groups as the American Association of Social Workers to come up with a functional relief plan. By the time the informal committee had done its work, Hopkins was "fully understood to be slated for Administrator of Federal Relief," as one of them remembered it, and the structure of

19. Quoted in Lacy, op. cit., p, 138.
20. Quoted in "They Were Poor, Hungry, and They Built to Last," by Donald Dale Jackson, *Smithsonian* (December 1994).
21. Quoted in Leonard, op. cit., p. 61.

the FERA program that was developed and then authorized by Congress on May 9 was nearly identical to the New York model.[22]

The FERA would distribute half of its appropriation of $500 million in relief funds (provided by the RFC) to the states on a matching-grant basis, with one dollar of federal money for every three dollars of state money. The remaining $250 million would go into a discretionary fund from which relief payments could be made to those states that simply could not meet the matching requirements. State relief agencies already in place or to be formed would handle the actual interviewing of applicants and the distribution of relief—at least some of which was to be in the form of cash. "This is by all odds the best form of relief except work," Hopkins would later insist. "Although the amount may be small, it is a man's own business how he spends it. It is a matter of opinion whether more damage is done to the human spirit by a lack of vitamins or complete surrender of choice."[23]

Hopkins had run New York's TERA with a combination of pragmatic flexibility, honest compassion, and terrific energy, and it was these qualities that the chain-smoking, cocktail-drinking, horse-playing, and generally flamboyant social worker brought with him to a task that would require all of these and more—and along the way make him perhaps the best-known New Dealer other than the president.

He set the tone immediately, going to work on May 22 even before a desk had been moved into his office, approving $5 million in grants to Colorado, Illinois, Iowa, Michigan, Mississippi, and Texas within a matter of hours and sending out telegrams to governors all over the nation, informing them that there was a new game in town and that he was the dealer. "MONEY FLIES," read the headline over a *Washington Post* story the next morning. "The half-billion dollars for direct relief of States won't last a month if Harry L. Hopkins, new relief administrator, maintains the pace he set yesterday in disbursing more than $5,000,000 during his first two hours in office."[24]

The pace slowed, but Hopkins never hesitated to use his considerable power with similar dispatch whenever he felt it was in the best

22. AASW, "Notes on Meeting," March 17, 1933; in Bremer, op. cit., p. 129.
23. Harry L. Hopkins, *Spending to Save*, p. 105.
24. Quoted in Henry H. Adams, *Harry Hopkins: A Biography*, p. 49.

interests of his "clients," the needy, often seeming to make up policy as he went along. "The whole business of experimentation is very broad," he admitted in an address given to the National Conference of Social Work. "I am for experimenting with this fund in various parts of the country, trying out schemes which are supported by reasonable people and see if [the schemes] work."[25] Sometimes, circumstances led him to "experiment" with a certain drama. "Every department of government that has any taxing power left," he said, "has direct responsibility to help those in distress." And when states did not meet that responsibility to his satisfaction, he was entirely capable of withholding federal money until they did, as officials in Kentucky, West Virginia, Ohio, and New York learned at various junctures. He could and did go further. When Oklahoma's state government refused to raise oil taxes to pay for relief, Hopkins "federalized" the state's relief system by cutting off funds to the state and setting up new FERA offices controlled by his people and financed entirely by the federal government. He did the same for Georgia, when Governor Eugene Talmadge, calling the New Deal "a combination of wet-nursin', frenzied finance, downright communism, and plain damn-foolishness," declared that relief applicants should be lined up and given "a dose of castor oil" and encouraged his appointees in the local FERA office to make minimal payments.[26] Louisiana got federalized by Hopkins when Senator Huey Long started using the relief system to reinforce his already powerful political machine.

The director's attitude toward the "clients" themselves was a good deal more benign, informed by the decent progressivism that characterized the best of social workers. He deplored the necessity of investigation, of relief workers prying into the private affairs of applicants before assigning funds; he was, he implied in *Spending to Save*, his 1936 history of the administration's relief programs, saddened by the kinds of "questions to which decent citizens, with as much longing for privacy as you or I, have had to submit."[27] He disliked even more, however, the traditions of poor relief that typified most local welfare programs, in which

25. Quoted in George McJimsey, *Harry Hopkins*, p. 55.
26. Quoted in Roger Biles, *A New Deal for the American People*, p. 101.
27. Hopkins, op. cit., p. 101.

applicants for aid were made to feel like mendicants who should fall to their knees in gratitude. In the state FERA offices, he said, "We tried to have the applicant received by an intelligent and sympathetic human being who did not, in his own mind, put a stigma upon the unfortunate person before him. We tried to see that relief officials were people who understood that the predicament of the worker without a job is an economic predicament not of his own making; that his religion, race or party is irrelevant."[28]

One of those officials was Louise Armstrong, whose remarkable 1938 memoir, *We Too Are the People*, provides an enduring portrait of how it was for administrator and recipient alike to be part of the machinery of relief in this new age of federal beneficence. Armstrong was a Chicago social worker who, with her husband, a commercial artist, had moved to northern Michigan in 1932 when the depression made it impossible for them to remain in the city. In earlier flush times, they had bought a summer place in the Upper Peninsula on the shores of Lake Huron; that had now become their permanent home. She was one of only two experienced social workers in the area, and in September 1933 the newly appointed three-man county relief commission called her out of bed just before midnight to meet with the state relief director in a downtown hotel. In less than an hour, she had been appointed director of the county's first FERA office and told to start work at nine the next morning. Her salary would be $100 a month (later raised to $125).

The county seat (unnamed) in which she lived and worked was a town that for decades had depended on the white pine timber industry for economic sustenance, but the last of the merchantable trees had been stripped off the hillsides more than fifteen years before. Both town and county had been suffering their own private recession ever since and were even more poorly equipped than most communities to deal with the added burden of a national depression. "I don't believe you realize how bad things were getting," one young man told Armstrong early on. "I used to hear the men talking. . . . They all said if things got any worse and something didn't happen pretty soon, they'd go down Main

28. Ibid., pp. 100–101.

Street and crash the windows and take what they needed. They would-n't pick on the little stores. They'd go after the big stores first."[29]

In spite of so clearly defined a need, Armstrong's tenure began in the shadow of considerable resentment on the part of county leaders, which mystified her. "Thousands of dollars of Government money were going to be poured into this half-populated and half-starved county," she complained a little imperiously. "Not only would the poor be made less miserable, but every merchant in the county would benefit. . . . Why didn't they have flags waving on Main Street, and the town band out?" They wanted the money, right enough, she finally decided, "but they did not want any outsider telling them how to spend it. As nearly as I could figure out, that was where the shoe pinched."[30]

The resentment continued throughout her three years of service, but by the time she had hired three caseworkers, chosen and furnished a downtown office (no, she was told, she could not have a picture of Presi-dent Roosevelt on her office wall; this was *nonpartisan* relief), and got her first monthly allotment of $20,000 from state and federal funds, she was too busy to worry about it. On the first day, the office filled imme-diately with applicants, most of them people who had been getting their mites from the County Poor Commission, which, as Harry Hop-kins would not have been surprised to learn, apparently had treated them with the thinly veiled contempt that often accompanies righteous charity. "I interviewed over forty applicants that day," Armstrong remembered. "There was something strange about these poor people: Nearly all of them, especially the old people, came in apparently terri-bly frightened. Some of them were trembling so that I could actually see them shake, and at first they could hardly speak."[31]

It was not just old people who were frightened, she soon learned. One of her earliest clients was a young woman who came up to Arm-strong's desk, sat down in the chair provided for her, and, when Arm-strong smiled and asked what she could do for her, promptly burst into tears.

29. Quoted in Armstrong, op. cit., p. 30.
30. Ibid., pp. 79–80.
31. Ibid., p. 84.

"I've been up here five times before, but I couldn't get up my nerve to come in," the woman said between sobs. "If I'd only known! If I'd only known!"

"Known what?" Armstrong asked.

"That you weren't going to be mean to me!"[32]

Armstrong and her staff—which at one point reached seven people—spent most of the next three years trying not to be mean to people, interviewing hundreds of applicants, digging into the details of their lives and filling out the necessary forms with an initial embarrassment that soon gave way to the numbness of procedure. She was trying especially to treat everyone with democratic impartiality (though neither Armstrong nor her fellow workers were ever entirely free of the class and racial prejudices of the fairly well educated, and her memoir is pocked with archly humorous tales about the antics and ignorance of blacks, Polish Americans, and others outside the middle-class fold). They investigated suspected fraud and fought with township commissioners who stubbornly underreported the number of needy in their region and with local politicians who wanted to use the system to enhance their power. They doled out cash, dispensed purchase slips for groceries, fuel, medicine, tried to deal with child abuse and violent husbands, helped old people without families find places to live, counseled against despair, and if there never was enough money to do everything that needed to be done, conscientiously tended to the perpetual needs of their clients in what Armstrong remembered as a "thrilling, inspiring, sinister, pathetic, touching, amusing, comic and tragic pageant of human life. Men, women, children, babies, white men, black men, red men, old men, young men, girls, boys, officials, laborers, husbands and mothers. In they come and out they go to the never-ending sound of . . . tramping, scuffling feet."[33]

It was a scene duplicated in character (if often greatly exceeded in numbers) in FERA offices throughout the country as understaffed and underfunded FERA workers struggled not merely to handle caseloads that ran into the hundreds for each worker—"You never knew if you were going to be able to go home to get dinner," one Atlanta FERA employee remembered—but to keep grafting politicians and resentful

32. Ibid., p. 91.
33. Ibid., pp. 3–4.

local bureaucrats and sometimes their own colleagues from either corrupting or gumming up an already imperfect and difficult system.[34] In Grand Junction, Colorado, FERA officials were forced to move a transient camp set up in the town because local Congressman Edward J. Taylor insisted that its occupants—"a nuisance and a flagrant lot"—had offered "an awful spectacle of debauchery adjoining the homes of a great many respectable people and women and children."[35] In Massachusetts, FERA commissioner Joseph A. Bartlett did his best to funnel relief money out into the suburbs, where his friends were, and away from Boston, where it was most desperately needed. A FERA worker said that Bartlett believed that the "money belongs to Massachusetts, and how they spend it does not concern the Federal Administration."[36] In Toledo, Ohio, the county relief commission uncovered spectacular levels of graft, bid-splitting, and favoritism in the city-run Relief Center.[37] In Dade County, Florida, it took the county FERA administrator two months to persuade local politicians that he "wouldn't stand for any monkey business."[38]

In the South there were inequities that had less to do with politics than with race. While administrators in the major urban areas like Memphis, Atlanta, and New Orleans were generally nondiscriminatory, less enlightened local FERA people in rural areas operated according to ancient principles. Many southern blacks consistently were refused relief or received less than their white counterparts, the theory appearing to be that since black people did not really expect anything from any white agency and were used to getting along on next to nothing anyway, they simply did not need it. One relief officer told sociologist Arthur S. Raper that "most any nigger who wants to work can get something to do."[39]

---

34. Quote in Cliff Kuhn, "Reminiscences: Interviews with Atlanta New Deal Social Workers," *Atlanta Historical Journal* (Spring 1986).
35. Quoted in Leonard, op. cit., p. 53.
36. Quoted in Trout, op. cit., p. 148.
37. See John N. Sobczak, "The Politics of Relief: Public Aid in Toledo," *Northwest Ohio Quarterly* (Fall 1976).
38. Lorena Hickok to Harry Hopkins, January 28, 1934; quoted in John F. Bauman and Thomas H. Coode, *In the Eye of the Great Depression: New Deal Reporters and the Agony of the American People*, p. 159.
39. Quoted in Raper, op. cit., p. 258.

Hopkins learned about racism and much else from the regular reports he received from the state offices, but he learned even more from a corps of journalists and writers, led by Lorena Hickok, a former reporter for the Associated Press and a good friend of Eleanor Roosevelt, whom he sent out into the field to travel the country and tell him how it looked to her. "I don't want statistics from you," he told Hickok before sending her to Pennsylvania in July 1933. "1 don't want the social worker angle. I want your own reactions, as an ordinary citizen. Go talk with preachers and teachers, businessmen, workers, farmers. Go talk with the unemployed, those who are on relief and those who aren't. . . . Tell me what you see and hear. All of it. Don't ever pull your punches."[40]

Most of the time, the reporters did not, and the most honest of them all was Hickok, who did the bulk of the FERA investigative work for 1933. In her first report, an account of her wanderings in Pennsylvania that summer, she wrote that "on the whole, I have encountered little dissatisfaction with the way the relief is administered or with its adequacy—which is rather surprising considering the fact that in some cases it is pitiably small." In the town of Media she met an FERA supervisor who, "with one assistant, has had as many as 800 families to look after at one time, and who has spent days and nights trying to figure out how to get relief to people who need it and won't ask for it." On the negative side, she found that many people thought that grocery and fuel slips demeaned the recipients, who sometimes were treated as if they would run to the nearest saloon or beauty parlor or racetrack and throw it away if given money. "'These people aren't children,' you hear over and over again. 'They're honest, self-respecting citizens who, through no fault of their own, are temporarily on relief. The vast majority of them have always managed their own affairs, can be trusted with cash—however little they're going to get to live on—and should be.'"[41]

Hickok was a good deal gloomier a few weeks later in Harlan County, Kentucky, writing that she had "heard of a miner's widow with

40. Quoted in Bauman and Coode, op. cit., p. 1. The fifteen Hopkins correspondents included four other women reporters—future novelist Martha Gellhorn, who joined the crew in 1934, among them. Male or female, almost all had some degree of newspaper experience.
41. Ibid., p. 67.

six children who had nothing at all to eat that day and no prospects of getting anything the next day either. At the Continental Hotel in Pineville I was told that five babies up one of those creeks had died of starvation in the last ten days."[42]

In Bottineau County, North Dakota, in November, she found people who had not had a crop of any significance for "something like four years," and in "what was once a house," she found two children "without a stitch on save some ragged overalls." Their feet, she wrote, were "purple with cold." She had heard of women having given birth in their ragged beds "with only coats thrown over them." There were some eight hundred families on relief in the county, with anywhere from twelve to fifteen coming into the FERA office every day.[43] In upstate New York, a dairy farmer told her that he and others doubted that they would be able to feed their animals over the winter. "Well, I know what we'll do," he said. "We'll have to shoot our cows." This, in spite of Hickok's report that the FERA operation in New York State was "so far ahead of what I had seen in other states that there just isn't any basis for comparison at all."[44]

As former administrator of New York's TERA, Hopkins would have been glad to hear that. Nevertheless, the thrust of what he was learning from Hickok and from his other sources by the late fall of 1933 was that the present FERA program was not going to be sufficient to get people through the coming winter, even with the aid of the Federal Surplus Relief Corporation, a quasi-public agency created by executive order by Roosevelt on October 1 and directed to purchase surplus commodities—hogs, corn, rice, dairy products, and other foodstuffs—for distribution to the needy through the FERA. Unemployment remained high, hunger and general privation were still common, and the possibility of a genuine disaster was real. In October, Hopkins ordered his state administrators to prepare for even higher unemployment in the winter months by winnowing out as many undeserving FERA recipients as possible before the new applicants shuffled through the door.

42. Ibid., p. 98.
43. Quoted in Richard Lowitt, *The New Deal and the West*, pp. 10–11.
44. Quoted in Bauman and Coode, op. cit., p. 120.

Meanwhile, he took another idea to Roosevelt. One of the most stubborn litanies in what Lorena Hickok had been hearing from people was that they wanted work, not handouts. "These people don't want to be on relief," she reported from Pennsylvania. "They loathe it. The percentage of those who call up and announce that they have jobs and won't want any more food orders is truly impressive."[45] Louise Armstrong would have seconded that conclusion. "Maybe you think I like to come up here beggin'!" one client had exclaimed in frustration. "I don't want no God-damn relief orders! I want work, I tell you! Work! Work! I got to have a job!"[46]

Work was what Hopkins had in mind. There already were about 1.9 million people on work-relief jobs in the FERA, but most of these jobs were crude, low-paying state and county make-work holdovers from the programs of the Hoover administration. In the summer, Hopkins had brought in Jacob Baker, who had helped to run a cooperative in New York State, to improve the FERA Works Division, but by the fall of 1933 Baker had not yet been able to do much to strengthen and streamline the system. Nevertheless, urged on by his assistant, Aubrey Williams, who stated outright on October 30 that "relief as such should be abolished" and that the FERA should "lift the status of relief to the employment level," this was the somewhat shaky platform from which Hopkins proposed that the administration launch a winter-long program of government employment for more than four million people.[47]

Hopkins took the idea to Roosevelt on November 2. "Let's see," the president said, doubtlessly taking a drag on his cigarette through its stylish holder and looking up at the ceiling. "Four million people—that means roughly $400 million."[48] Yes, it did, Hopkins agreed. Seven days later, having ordered the $400 million transferred from other government programs, Roosevelt created the Civil Works Administration (CWA) by executive order, and Hopkins—who had already met with

45. Ibid., p. 138.
46. Quoted in Armstrong, op. cit., pp. 120–22.
47. Aubrey Williams to Hopkins, October 30, 1933; in Bonnie Fox Schwartz, *The Civil Works Administration, 1933–1934: The Business of Emergency Employment in the New Deal*, p. 36.
48. Ibid., p. 38.

his people to start drawing up rules, regulations, and procedures—went to work.

By all measures, it was an astonishing performance. To streamline the operation, Hopkins made it a federal program from top to bottom; there would be no state or county commissions to muck up things with the CWA. Two million FERA work-relief recipients suddenly found themselves on the CWA payroll as employees. A National Re-Employment Service was put together to solicit and screen another two million employees by Christmas. There was no shortage of applicants. About 15,000 people applied in the five boroughs of New York City alone on November 28, though Chicago did New York one better with a crowd of 70,000, and in North Carolina about 150,000 showed up at CWA offices in the first week.[49] Hopkins promised that the first paychecks would be issued within two weeks of the program's beginning, and to get the necessary one million checks out, the Bureau of Printing and Engraving ran three shifts a day, the finished forms then being shipped by air and other means to arrive at CWA offices on time. That first payroll amounted to almost $7.9 million.

To correct the casual, make-work character of so many of the original FERA jobs, Hopkins established an engineering division to oversee the development and completion of public works projects and appointed Jacob Baker to head it up. Baker, in turn, hired John Michael Carmody, a former president of the Society of American Engineers and long an advocate of technical solutions to economic problems, including unemployment, and Carmody hired engineers from all over the country to head state and local projects. "They were glad to work," he remembered. "They enjoyed it. They were enthusiastic. All of us were. I recall nothing that approached it."[50]

By December 7, 1933—less than one month after the CWA was created—there were a little over two million people working for the new agency; by the middle of January 1934, the figure had risen to more than 4.2 million, and the program was so popular that in February

49. Figures from Schwartz, op. cit., p. 42. Most of my account of the CWA's brief life is from this source.
50. Ibid., p. 56.

Congress appropriated another $950 million for relief, $450 million of it to keep the CWA going. The work those four million new government employees accomplished—however much conservatives still like to invoke the specter of lines of men sweeping streets that needed no broom work—made a genuine impact on the physical well-being of the national estate. Half a million miles of highways in every state and territory in the United States were improved, with hundreds of bridges built, tunnels excavated, and culverts laid. Thousands of schools, courthouses, city halls, library buildings, zoos, sewerage plants, heating plants, police stations, hospitals, jails, and community housing projects were rehabilitated, as were many state capitols. Hundreds of other buildings were torn down and replaced. There were 529 airports improved, and 489 new ones built; scores of flood control projects completed; 250,000 outdoor privies constructed. Municipal recreational facilities were built and rehabilitated in most cities, but none more than those in New York, where park commissioner Robert Moses put no fewer than 52,000 CWA employees to work all by himself.

Roughly 10 percent of CWA jobs were for white-collar workers, including some 50,000 teachers in the Emergency Educational Program who instructed more than 1.1 million grade school, high school, college, and adult education students who otherwise would have learned nothing. Artists were put to work in the Public Works of Art Program, musicians and singers were supported in the formation of orchestras and choruses, clerks and draftsmen and display specialists were placed in museums, architects and historians were assigned the task of beginning the Historical American Buildings Survey, and archeologists were put to digging at prehistoric sites from the San Joaquin Valley of California to the mountains of Georgia.

There were women's programs, the CWA was proud to announce, though without adding that these were in place mainly because Eleanor Roosevelt had persuaded Hopkins to establish a women's division in the FERA back in August and then had gone on—together with Ellen Woodward, chief of the women's division—to insist that Hopkins expand his efforts to find work for women in the CWA program. For all their efforts, however, there were never more than 300,000 women in the CWA workforce, most of them in sewing projects or nursing, secretarial, and home economics programs, and at no point did their salaries match those of male employees.

While the standard disclaimer as to race, creed, and color was included in CWA hiring practices, another major failing of the program was its inability to control bigotry at the local level; in some areas of the South, blacks got a minority of CWA jobs even where they constituted the great majority of the population, and they were more likely to receive the minimum wage of thirty cents an hour when they did work. The mayor of Jackson, Mississippi, may not have been typical, but he was emblematic. When black ministers and others petitioned the city to use CWA funds to hire unemployed blacks to build a park, pave some streets, and put in sewer lines in the black section of town, the mayor told them he "would not grant them a damned thing" and that if they disapproved of the way things were being run, they should get out of town.[51] A Southern CWA relief worker told Lorena Hickok that blacks "regard the President as a Messiah, and they think that, if only they can get on CWA jobs, they'll all be getting $12 a week for the rest of their lives."[52]

Like any other New Deal program, the CWA was less than all it had hoped to be. But it had helped keep more than four million people working and their families eating through the winter of 1933–1934, and along the way had instilled some measure of pride in those who were lucky enough to have been part of it. "Three loud cheers for CWA!" Hickok had written Hopkins early in the program. "I may be wrong, but I think it may be the smartest thing that has been tried since we went into the relief business." In Iowa, she watched 5,000 men line up for their first CWA paycheck. "They took it with wide grins and made beelines for the grocery stores, NOT to shove a grocery order across the counter, but to go where they please [sic] and buy what they pleased for cash."[53] During the Christmas season of 1933, Louise Armstrong remembered,

we saw a little less of sorrow and discontent and a little more of happiness in the faces in the office. Christmas during CWA was a cheerful

---

51. Quoted in Kifer, op. cit., p. 216.
52. Quoted in Bauman and Coode, op. cit., p. 168.
53. Quoted in Schwartz, op. cit., p. 188.

episode. . . . Christmas eve as I went about doing a bit of last minute shopping, I saw our men in boots everywhere along Main Street. Some had their wives with them, and some were leading their children by the hand. "Merry Christmas! Merry Christmas!" greeted me, as I passed some of them grouped around a window full of toys. Meager little displays there were in the windows of these small town stores, but how much they meant! As I neared the Ten Cent Store several of the men came out, grinning, with their arms full of bundles.[54]

And then it was done. It had never been seen as a permanent program, for all its popularity. Roosevelt, who worried almost as much as Hoover about the moral fiber of the people, was concerned that it "might become a habit with the country."[55] While they were still floating high on the adrenaline of accomplishment early in December, Hopkins warned his staff that "it must be assumed in this office and everywhere else that Civil Works was set up purely as an emergency measure; that there is no implication in this of any permanent policy in the government." At most, he said, there might be "a continuance of this thing through the middle of March, on a descending scale after that and out by the middle of May or the 1st of June."[56]

In fact, the program officially closed down at the end of March, its remaining projects folded back into the Works Division of the FERA, which now administered them under an emergency work program that was employing more than two million people by the end of winter 1934–1935. And in the happy memory of the CWA experience perhaps there was a lesson to be learned, the assistant FERA administrator told the American Economic Association in March 1935, hinting at the possibility that additional Hopkins-like "experiments" might be coming down the line:

> The total cost of the CWA was approximately $1 billion, of which the Federal Government furnished $825 million and States and localities $175 million. About $750 million was expended directly for wages

54. Armstrong, op. cit., pp. 175–76.
55. Quoted in William E. Leuchtenberg, *Franklin Roosevelt and the New Deal*, p. 122.
56. Quoted in Bremer, op. cit.

and $250 went into other expenditures, including materials. The immediate purpose of the civil works program was to meet the crisis during the winter of 1933 and there is no question but that it accomplished this purpose. From a long-term standpoint, however, the chief value of the civil works program may very well prove to be that of effectively demonstrating the possibilities of public work as a means of meeting the needs of millions of destitute unemployed.[57]

57. Corrington Gill, "Unemployment Relief," *Proceedings of the American Economic Association*, March 1935.

8

The Scream of the Eagle

ate one evening in 1933, a presidential adviser heard the sound of whole-souled laughter issuing from the Oval Room of the White House. As the man came into the room, the president waved a copy of the *New York Times* at him, explaining that he was reading a story regarding a group of financial wizards in New York who had been trying to unravel the intricacies of one New Deal economic policy or another. The president pointed to the headline over the story—"EXPERTS CONFUSED," it read—then burst into laughter again.[1]

However refreshing Roosevelt's delight in boggling the minds of pundits, there was in fact plenty of confusion to go around—not least (and not last) in the National Recovery Administration (NRA), which was supposed to be the great foundation stone on which full economic recovery would be built. Propping up and restructuring the banking system had brought some measure of stability to the nation's financial edifice, and relief and work-relief programs would go a long way toward keeping millions of people from tottering across the line that separated hardship from starvation. But both efforts were not enough to meet what columnist Walter Lippmann described as the "long and difficult

1. As told by Henry F. Pringle in *The New Yorker* (June 30, 1934).

task of making the modern economic system work with enough efficiency to give security and with sufficient justice to command the loyalty of the people."[2]

In his inaugural address, Roosevelt had warned that he might be
forced to ask Congress to give him power comparable to that exercised
by a wartime president. He never went so far as that, but on June 16,
1933, he did sign the National Industrial Recovery Act (NIRA),
which, he said, history probably would record as "the most important
and far-reaching legislation ever enacted by the American Congress."[3]
The act was indisputably important and in some of its parts even more
far-reaching than the president had imagined (or wanted). But it may
also have been one of the most complicated and least understood laws in
history, a bundle of expedience that demonstrated Lippmann's added
comment regarding the "hastily contrived schemes" the administration
had produced in its first hundred days. "It would be unreasonable," he
noted, "to regard them as perfected revelation of the New Deal when
every man who knows anything knows they were put together in a
hurry by harassed men and are being administered by men who are too
busy to think about them."[4]

The NIRA was conceived in desperation and shaped into its final
confusion by a multitude of pressures—some of them coming from the
business community itself, most of which had been left wallowing in as
much uncertainty as the Congress. From respected quarters came
charges that if the survival of the capitalist system were threatened,
business and industry had no one to blame but themselves and their
mindless dedication to the principles of feral competition, not to mention their infatuation with the bubble of Coolidge prosperity in the
twenties. The crisis, said Alexander Sachs of the Lehman Corporation,
the investment trust subsidiary of the Lehman Brothers on Wall Street,
was "a spontaneous disintegration from within," the result of *economic
nihilism, which, from a national point of view, cannot be permitted to go on.*"[5]

---

2. Walter Lippmann, *Interpretations, 1933–1935*; in Milton Crane, ed., *The Roosevelt
Era*, p. 13.
3. Franklin D. Roosevelt, "The Goal of the National Industrial Recovery Act," in *The
Public Papers and Addresses of Franklin D. Roosevelt*, 2: p. 246.
4. Lippmann, op. cit.
5. Quoted in Schlesinger, op. cit., p. 95. Italics in original.

If not nihilism, then control—but how much, and by whom? Surely not from the government, said "Sunshine Charlie" Mitchell, whose National City Bank stock had sunk from $585 to $59 a share within two years of the crash. In spite of his own disaster, Mitchell viewed with deep suspicion any such notion as government control. "I cannot help feeling . . . that business will be governed best by the natural laws of supply and demand," he had told a Senate committee looking into such questions in 1932, "which will control the situation more effectively than the best-intentioned regulatory or advisory body imposed from above could possibly do."[6]

R. E. Flanders of the American Engineering Council could not have disagreed more. "I think it is dangerous for industry to put itself in the position that if given power it can produce the results," he told the same committee. "I think it cannot because the primary elements of the thing seem to me to be in the control of the government and in the field of government rather than in the field of industry."[7]

Just so, said Sidney Hillman of the Amalgamated Clothing Workers of America, insisting that all history argued that industry's leaders were incapable of regulating themselves. "They won't do it," he insisted, "they have not done it, and they will not do it. The only power that can put it into effect is governmental action."[8]

While both sides of the argument—and variations on both sides—found a home somewhere in the Roosevelt administration, sentiment leaned heavily in the direction of government action of some kind, and soon. Within days of the inauguration, everyone from brain truster Raymond Moley to Assistant Secretary of Commerce John Dickinson was tinkering with compendious legislative proposals designed to stimulate the economy, stabilize prices, control competitive excess, and regularize wages, hours, and working conditions. They got plenty of advice and suggestions from such nongovernment types as Felix Frankfurter at Harvard and Harold Moulton at the Brookings Institution, while

6. Quoted in Isador Rubin, "The New Lead from Capitol Hill," *The Survey* (March 1, 1932).
7. Ibid.
8. Ibid.

even farther outside the New Deal ring others exchanged ideas—most notably, Alexander Sachs and his good friend Hugh S. Johnson, who as a brigadier general and head of the U.S. Army's Purchase and Supplies Division during World War I had served on the War Industries Board (WIB) chaired by financier Bernard M. Baruch (Johnson was now one of Baruch's principal assistants). In the Congress, meanwhile, Senators Robert Wagner and Robert M. La Follette put their own people to work on the subject—and Senator Hugo Black of Alabama took matters into his own hands by fashioning legislation that would establish a thirty-hour workweek in an effort to spread employment around.

Black's bill, popular enough to be supported by both the American Federation of Labor and the American Legion, passed the Senate on April 4, but it went too far too soon for Roosevelt's tastes. He began to nag Raymond Moley to see what he could do to get a single piece of acceptable legislation into shape in time to head off House passage of Black's bill. It was at this juncture that Moley encountered Hugh Johnson in the lobby of the Carlton Hotel in Washington on April 25. Johnson, Moley decided on the spot, was just the man to whip such a document into shape. "Nobody can do it better than you," he told Johnson. "You're familiar with the only comparable thing that's ever been done—the work of the War Industries Board."[9]

Never a man to argue with raw flattery, Johnson accepted the task. Moley found him a vacant office in the State, War, and Navy Building that afternoon and on its desk placed a bewildering pile of legislative proposals. Johnson took off his jacket, rolled up his sleeves (literally), went to work, and in twenty-four hours delivered up a proposal that covered, he remembered, only "a couple of sheets of legal cap paper."[10] Brief, but pungent: Johnson proposed that the president be given near-dictatorial licensing authority to enforce codes of competition and labor practices on business and industry. His experience with industrial "slackers" during his years on the WIB had persuaded him that nothing less than absolute authority was necessary. "This is just like a war," he

9. Quoted in Schlesinger, op. cit., p. 97.
10. Hugh S. Johnson, *The Blue Eagle from Egg to Earth*, p. 196.

later told Labor Secretary Frances Perkins. "The individual who has the power to apply and enforce these regulations is the President. There is nothing that the President can't do if he wishes to! The President's powers are unlimited. The President can do anything."[11]

This was a good deal more power than Roosevelt had in mind. Moley rejected Johnson's two-page effort, and the general was soon back to work on another draft. He was not alone, now. To help out, Moley had brought in Donald Richberg, a Chicago labor lawyer and former law partner of Interior Secretary Harold L. Ickes, and on May 10, Roosevelt himself ordered Johnson, Richberg, Senator Robert Wagner, Assistant Secretary of Commerce John Dickinson, Assistant Secretary of Agriculture Rexford Tugwell, Labor Secretary Perkins, and budget director Lewis Douglas "to shut themselves up in a room" until they had patched together a bill.[12]

What emerged five days later was not brief, but it did meet with Roosevelt's approval, and on May 17 he sent it to Congress. The House passed it on May 26, the Senate on June 13, and with Roosevelt's signature on June 16, the National Industrial Recovery Act became law.

THE NIRA PROVIDED a little something for everyone, as might have been expected, given the conditions of its birth. Title I of the act established a National Recovery Administration (NRA) and gave that agency the power to work with business and industry to develop codes by which they would be asked to live as a means to end cutthroat competition and ensure shorter hours, better wages, and fair labor standards. While the law made no specific recommendations, in practice the entities that would represent business and industry in these negotiations would be the great trade associations. The National Automobile Chamber of Commerce might be one example, or the Edison Electric Institute, the Drug Institute of America, the National Coal Association, and the Silk Association of America, among about 15,000 such organizations—a situation in which *Fortune* magazine, for one, discovered some delicious

11. Quoted in Perkins, oral memoirs, 5: pp. 50–51.
12. Quoted in John Kennedy Ohl, *Hugh S. Johnson and the New Deal*, p. 100.

irony. "[If] there is one corporate personality in these United States more like Mr. George Follansbee Babbitt [satirist Sinclair Lewis's fictional creation] than another, it is the great American Trade Association," one of its anonymous writers proclaimed. "The consequence is that the world is presented with as pretty a paradox as it has recently beheld. A Democratic President appoints to the direction of a socialistic plan a rock-ribbed, old-guard institution. . . . And the institution accepts. Fiction itself, even the fiction of Mr. Sinclair Lewis, has nothing half so odd!"[13]

As an inducement, each firm that agreed to abide by the codes that were expected to emerge from this ironic partnership would be exempt from federal antitrust laws. Labor's carrot was embodied in Section 7(a) of Title I, which mandated that participating employers had to abide by hours and wages established by the codes and that employees would "have the right to organize and bargain collectively through representatives of their own choosing," while no "employee and no one seeking employment" would "be required as a condition of employment to join any organization or to refrain from joining a labor organization of his own choosing." Title I also established an Industrial Advisory Board, a Labor Advisory Board, and a Consumers' Advisory Board, bodies by which all codes were to be passed for review before being put into final form by the NRA staff and sent on to the president for final action (though the boards had no statutory power).

If Title I of the NIRA was designed to stabilize the conditions under which business was to be done in America, Title II was conceived to prime the pump of recovery by establishing a Public Works Administration and injecting $3.3 billion of federal money into the most ambitious public works program in the nation's history. "We regarded these two plans, NRA and PWA," Johnson later wrote, "as complementary and necessary to each other. We thought that if we could not get the construction and heavy goods industries into operation along with consumers' goods, there would not be enough balanced buying power to sustain the reemployment in commerce, the lighter manufactures, and auxiliary services."[14] A final provision, Title III, put in place new

13. "The Trade Association Emerges," *Fortune* (August 1933).
14. Quoted in Johnson, op. cit., p. 200.

taxes on capital stocks and excess profits as a means of paying for the implementation of the act.

Early on, Roosevelt had his eye on Johnson to be the mahout for this legislative elephant. "Hugh," he said at one point while poring over the complex organizational charts of the act, "you've got to *do* this job." Johnson agreed immediately, though when the story of his selection broke the next day, he waved off congratulations from his friends. "It will be red fire [enthusiasm] at first," he said, "and dead cats [criticism] afterward. This is just like mounting the guillotine on the infinitesimal gamble that the ax won't work."[15]

In fact, the dead cats began to be thrown fairly early. Johnson, for all his brilliance, was not the stablest man in Washington, a fact that had not escaped the attention of the New Dealers. Burly, blunt, often tactless and profane, with a face that seemed designed to fit the description of "forty miles of bad road," he chain-smoked Old Golds, drank too much and too often, and sometimes vanished into an alcoholic void. He flaunted a relationship with his assistant, Frances ("Robbie") Robinson, that many then and later assumed was sexual (Johnson was married, Robinson was not).[16] Jerome Frank, a Department of Agriculture lawyer who had known Johnson during the general's days as head of the now-defunct Moline Plow Company, warned Senator Robert Wagner that Johnson "will not think things through. He's impulsive and you don't want to trust legislation of this kind to him."[17] Even Bernard Baruch, Johnson's mentor and employer, was appalled when he learned of Roosevelt's decision. "He isn't fit for that," Baruch told Frances Perkins. "He's dangerous and unstable. He gets nervous and sometimes goes away without notice. I'm fond of him, but do tell the President to be careful. Hugh needs a firm hand."[18] For his part, Johnson was not bashful about expressing his contempt for the bureaucrats and politicos of Washington. He would rather, he once told reporters in a typically colorful, if obscure, colloquialism, be "down between Brownsville and Matamoras where the owls fucked the chickens."[19]

15. Both quotes in ibid., p. 208.
16. For the relationship with Frances Robinson, see Ohl, op. cit., pp. 152–57.
17. Quoted in ibid., p. 105.
18. Quoted in Perkins, *The Roosevelt I Knew*, pp. 200–201.
19. Quoted in Jordan A. Schwarz, *The New Dealers: Power Politics in the Age of Roosevelt*, p. 103.

Still, Roosevelt found Johnson's energy compelling and his antics at worst amusing and could not be dissuaded from naming the general NRA administrator. He did decide, however, to separate responsibility for the NRA from that of the PWA, giving administration of public works to Interior Secretary Harold L. Ickes. Johnson did not learn of this decision until his own formal appointment to head up the NRA was announced at a cabinet meeting to which he was invited on June 16, the same day Roosevelt had signed the NIRA. He was put in a state of rage by the news, but managed to keep his silence—though Perkins remembered that his face turned "red, then dark red, then purplish" as the meeting wore on.[20] Afterward, only some relentless persuasion on Perkins's part kept Johnson from resigning.

Having swallowed his fury, Johnson returned to duty like a good, if somewhat erratic, soldier. Even before Congress had given its approval of the NIRA and he had officially been appointed, he had pinpointed the six industries he believed most likely to develop workable codes first—those producing steel, textiles, coal, petroleum, automobiles, and lumber—and concentrated his efforts there. At the time of the NIRA's passage, the textile industry appeared closest to agreement, and as a kind of public demonstration project, Johnson brought negotiators from the Cotton Textile Institute to the auditorium of the Commerce Building on June 27 and sat them down at a big table with NRA officials and advisers from business, government, and labor. Here, before an audience of more than eight hundred, final revisions were to be made on the first set of codes produced under the aegis of the NIRA. "It took England 120 years to arrive at the 'Law Merchant,' which was codification of commercial practice, thereafter accepted as a part of the common law," Johnson said at a press conference before the gathering. "We are trying to do that in America in an hour and a half, by agreement. It is no easy thing to reorient the universe."[21]

He could hardly have picked a universe more in need of reorienting than that of the cotton textile industry—or one that would generate more good publicity for the brilliance of the NRA and its general if the industry's problems could be resolved. It was one of the largest in the

20. Perkins, oral memoirs, 5: p. 171.
21. Quoted in Johnson, op. cit., p. 223.

country, with 1,057 mills and 379,445 workers, most located in New England and the South.[22] As they had been for many, the wartime years had been good ones for cotton mill owners and workers alike; foreign and domestic demand for cotton cloth products had been insatiable, and if the hours were long, wages were high. Not as much could be said for the twenties, when demand was gutted because of overseas competition and a simultaneous rise in the hemline of the average skirt from midcalf all the way up to the top of the knee—a development that had given far more satisfaction to clothing designers and lubricious males than to textile manufacturers.

Mill owners had reacted as most industrialists did when faced with a cut in profits: they immediately lowered wages. They went on to adopt a multi-loom system that forced weavers, the most skilled and highest paid of the mill workers, to handle two or more looms simultaneously, then passionately embraced the scientific management principles of economic theorist Frederick W. Taylor, much in fashion in the twenties. "They got a stopwatch," a weaver remembered of those days, "and they followed [you] around. They figured out exactly how long it took you to tie that thread and start the loom up. They figured right down to the tick of that stopwatch. Then they expected you to stretch it out a little bit, to do a little more. You couldn't please them. The more you done, the more they wanted done."[23] Moreover, if it was good enough for the weavers, owners felt, it was good enough for all workers, and production all down the line in the mills was speeded up with no parallel increase in wages. The system was called a "stretch-out," with no visible affection by the workers, and nowhere was its impact greater than in the mills of the South, where its effects have been described by one South Carolina textile worker:

> My husband and I go to the mill at seven. He's a stripper in the cardin' room and gets $12.85 a week. . . . They put this stetch-out system on

---

22. For figures, see James A. Hodges, *New Deal Labor Policy and the Southern Cotton Textile Industry, 1933–1941*, p. 9.
23. Quoted in Jacquelyn Rowd Hall, Robert Korstad, and James Leloudis, "Cotton Mill People: Work, Community, and Protest in the Textile South, 1880–1940," *The American Historical Review* (April 1986).

him shore enough. You know he's runnin' four jobs ever since they put
this stretch-out system on him and he ain't gettin' any more than he
used to get for one. Where'd they put the other three men?—why,
they laid 'em off and they give him the same $12.85 he got before.[24]

In 1929, the combination of lower wages and the stretch-out had
helped the National Textile Workers Union, a Communist-controlled
rival of the AFL's more conservative United Textile Workers Union, to
engineer strikes in Gastonia and Marion, North Carolina. This was a
singularly bloody business during which the Gastonia sheriff, three of
his deputies, and eight strikers had been killed, including a rawboned,
twenty-six-year-old loom tender named Ella May Wiggins, an appealing figure whose death came to symbolize all that was perceived to be
noble in the labor movement and pernicious in the textile industry.

Wiggins had lost four of her five children to whooping cough
because there had been no time for her to care for them and no money
for medicine or doctors: "I asked the super to put me on day shift so's I
could tend them," she said during a union demonstration, "but he
wouldn't. I don't know why. So I had to quit my job and then there
wasn't any money for medicine, so they just died. I never could do anything for my children, not even to keep 'em alive, it seems. That's why
I'm for the union, so's I can do better for them."[25] Like many of her
people, Ella May had deep roots in the musical traditions of the mountains, and had written many labor songs, among them a rousing ballad
almost certainly inspired by the deaths of her own children:

> We leave our home in the morning,
> We kiss our children good-bye,
> While we slave for the bosses
> Our children scream and cry.
>
> It is for our little children
> That seem to us so dear,

24. Quoted in Paul Blanchard, "How to Live on Forty-six Cents a Day," *The Nation*
(May 15, 1929).
25. Quoted in Klingaman, op. cit., p. 200.

But for us nor them, dear workers,
The bosses do not care.

But understand, all workers,
Our union they do fear,
Let's stand together, workers,
And have a union here.[26]

On September 14, 1929, Ella May and a truckload of workers were ambushed outside Gastonia by men who jumped out of a car and began firing shotguns and rifles at the people huddled in the truck bed. "Lord," Ella May cried, "they done shot and killed me."[27] A bullet had pierced her in the left breast and she was soon dead.

The balladeer's death had received nationwide attention, with public demonstrations and newspaper editorials decrying the savagery of the backward South. These outbursts only intensified when no one was indicted for her murder or for those of the other strikers—while seven union men were summarily tried and convicted of the murders of the Gastonia sheriff and his men. The conviction, defense attorneys supplied by the Communist Party claimed, was a "class verdict," and *The New Republic*, no revolutionary forum, seemed to agree.[28] "What can those who do not believe that the class struggle is as fundamental and determining as do the Communists say about this situation?" editor Bruce Bliven asked in his editorial for September 29, 1929. "They must admit that in this case and in this locality the class war has been real."[29]

In the symbolically weighted shadow of Ella Wiggins's death and the Gastonia verdicts, then, the textile industry had staggered through the early years of the depression in a condition that grew increasingly desperate, marked by frenzied competition among hundreds of mills, numerous failures, and sporadic and often violent local walkouts and

26. Quoted in Shachtman, op. cit., pp. 183–84.
27. Quoted in ibid., p. 236. Most of my account of the Wiggins incident is from this source.
28. Quoted in ibid, p. 258.
29. Bruce Bliven, "Class War in North Carolina," *The New Republic* (September 25, 1929).

strikes. Some of these were led by the NTWU, but many were organized and controlled only by the workers themselves. If the NRA could
bring peace and a measure of prosperity to this chaotic, bloody industry,
Johnson and his people reckoned, it could be done anywhere.

On the face of it, at least, they succeeded. After four days of public
hearings and after-hours backroom maneuvering, Johnson himself presiding at both more often than not, the Cotton Textile Institute's negotiators and NRA officials had hammered out an agreement. The finished
code called for the industry to operate on the "40-40" system—two
forty-hour shifts per five-day week—and for the regulation of how
much new milling machinery any mill could install, both stipulations
designed to control overproduction and maintain prices. It recognized
the provisions of Section 7(a) of the NIRA and established a minimum wage that would range from $12 to $13 per forty-hour week,
a significant increase over wages that had often fallen as low as $5.
The use of child labor would be prohibited (a longtime goal of reformers, though by the time the industry agreed to ban the practice, economic considerations already had eliminated most of it). Finally, the
code established a Cotton Textile Industry Committee whose industry-
appointed members would largely oversee compliance with the code's
various stipulations.

"You men of the textile industry have done a very remarkable
thing," Johnson said when announcing his willingness to present the
code for the president's approval on June 30. "Never in economic history have labor, industry, government and consumers' representatives
sat together in the presence of the public to work out by mutual agreement a 'law merchant' for an entire industry. . . . The textile industry is
to be congratulated on its courage and spirit in being first to assume
this patriotic duty and on the generosity of its proposals."[30] Even
though Roosevelt later insisted on some minor amendments (among
other things, he extended the code to embrace office workers as well as
mill floor laborers), the industry as a whole welcomed the agreement,
and over the next few months textiles appeared to have entered a new
age of prosperity. Prices rose, inventories declined, dividends in 230

30. Quoted in Ohl, op. cit., page 118.

selected southern mills rose from 6.8 percent a share in May to 13.82 percent in December, while employment increased by more than 145,000 workers and the number of walkouts and other worker protests diminished.[31]

Circumstances eventually would demonstrate all too precisely the fragile character of this new era of peace and prosperity in the textile industry. In the meantime, however, fresh from an apparent and relatively easy victory, Johnson turned to the other big industries from which he hoped to pry similarly triumphant agreements. The codes did emerge one by one, but only after weeks of protracted and sometimes agonizingly difficult and contentious negotiations that often had Johnson hopping on airplanes and flying from one participant to another in his struggle to stitch together compromises.

Disagreement between industry negotiators and government foresters over timber-cutting practices on private lands stalled a code for the lumber industry until the middle of August. The steel industry's code took even longer, and it was not until Roosevelt himself stepped in that industry leaders finally agreed to raise wages to an average of forty-five cents an hour and accept the eventual phasing in of an eight-hour day. Getting a petroleum code was even more difficult, eventually involving not just the usual run of industry and NRA negotiators but Interior Secretary Harold L. Ickes, whose department had a long-standing history with the industry; the powerful Texas Railroad Commission, which controlled production levels in the oil-rich state; and the Association Opposed to Monopoly, a collection of small independent producers—who eventually refused to sign what even Johnson called a "hermaphroditic compromise" that pleased almost no one.[32] The National Automobile Chamber of Commerce did its best to make its open shop (essentially nonunion) policy part of the auto industry code; when that failed, its negotiators forced acceptance of code language that effectively diluted Section 7(a): "The selection, retention and advancement of employees will be on the basis of individual merit without regard to their affiliation or non-affiliation with any labor or

31. For figures, see Hodges, op. cit., p. 56.
32. Johnson, op. cit., p. 246.

other organization."[33] Even this concession was not enough for Henry Ford, who refused to sign the automobile code or otherwise have any truck with what he saw as government interference with private enterprise, remarking that "I was always under the impression that to manage a business properly you ought to know something about it"; as a gesture of crotchety independence, however, he accompanied this rejection with a promise to meet or better the maximum hour and minimum wage provisions of the code (and did).[34] Coal industry negotiations took longer than those for any of the other major codes, requiring presidential intervention on two occasions, and while the operators finally did agree to recognize Section 7(a) and adopted stipulations prohibiting child labor, payment in scrip, and the much-hated company store, the cost to NRA principles was high: operators were allowed to structure the industry into nineteen independent divisions and subdivisions, creating a regulatory nightmare.

To charges from labor and other reformers that on several points— such as the creation of the Cotton Textile Industry Committee in the textile code or the adoption of language in the automobile code that subverted the intent of Section 7(a)—Johnson and the president had caved in to industry pressure, the former took characteristic umbrage. "NRA did the job," he wrote in 1935. "It did it from one end of this country to the other, and it did it in a few months. . . . We did not favor industry, and we did not favor labor."[35]

Nevertheless, even conservatives were forced to admit that so far industry had gotten a good deal more out of the NRA than labor or consumers (whose needs, in spite of the presence of the Consumers' Advisory Board, had been generally ignored during the negotiation process). Price and production stipulations in the codes gave each industry a substantial degree of control over its market. The forty-hour week had been institutionalized, and while industry would have been happier with fifty hours, labor would have preferred thirty-five or even thirty in order to spread work around, and the minimum wages that

33. Quoted in Ohl, op. cit., p. 128.
34. Quoted in Lacey, op. cit., p. 403.
35. Johnson, op. cit., pp. 246–47.

had been established by most of the codes still remained below levels
that labor considered decent. As a final genuflection to the influence of
industry, it seemed obvious that for the most part it was going to be the
fox watching the chicken coop; industry would be allowed to police
itself. "The regulations . . . so far imposed are not oppressive," William
Allen White editorialized in the *Emporia* [Kansas] *Gazette*, echoing
much general middle-class opinion. "So three long cheers for NIRA,
cock-eyed, pug-nosed, hump-backed, slather-mouthed and epileptic as
she may seem at the first casual glance. She is no beauty, but, gentlemen, she has a heart of gold and good intentions, which should count
for something in this wicked world."[36]

But it had all taken so long, and Johnson became convinced that if
the NRA was going to be the engine driving a rebuilt economy, it could
not wait around for the completion of each one of the hundreds of codes
that ultimately would be necessary. Early in the negotiations with the
six targeted industries, he had proposed the creation of a "blanket code"
that businesses and industries could sign as an interim measure until
their individual codes were completed. Called the President's Reemployment Agreement, this code would grant the antitrust benefits of the
NRA to any business that agreed to provisions abolishing child labor,
instituted a minimum wage of $12 to $15 a week, and established a
thirty-five-hour week for blue-collar workers and a forty-four-hour
week for white-collar workers. The agreement would remain in effect
until December 31, 1933, or until final codes for the relevant industries
were developed and approved by FDR.

By mid-July, Johnson was ready to launch a nationwide sign-up
campaign, utilizing every advertising and promotional gimmick his
publicity team could dream up. He had even seen to the development of
a symbol "designed for visibility and uniqueness," as he put it.[37] The
result was the image of a Blue Eagle patterned after the thunderbird
ideograph common in the ritual art of the Navajo Indians. The bird's
wings were outspread, its head and beak facing left (naturally, some suspected). In its left talon it held the cog from a factory wheel and in its
right, a clutch of lightning bolts. At the bottom of the image appeared

36. William Allen White, "NIRA," the *Emporia Gazette*, July 24, 1933.
37. Johnson, op. cit., p. 256.

the words, "We Do Our Part." Any business that signed a blanket agreement was entitled to display the birdly symbol with pride, and as poster, flag, banner, window sign, windshield sticker, lapel badge, billboard, magazine cover, and editorial cartoon, the Blue Eagle of the NRA was destined to become as enduring a symbol of the times as the swastika of the German National Socialist Party (indeed, the Communist party organ, *The Daily Worker*, smelling fascism at the heart of the NRA program, would publish an editorial cartoon in which the bird spun itself into the actual shape of the grim Nazi emblem).[38]

What Johnson did not have was unanimity on the need to get the campaign under way. "I am just scared to death," worried Rexford Tugwell, resident intellectual light in the Department of Agriculture. "I am afraid of the commitment and of getting the President into this. If we strike what a number of us anticipate, which is a flattening out of markets and maybe a precipitous drop right in the midst of a ballyhoo campaign, we will look like ten cents."[39] Others agreed, but Roosevelt was enamored of the boldness and sweep of Johnson's scheme—which the general deliberately likened now to the great bond drives of World War I—and his inclinations got reinforcement when stock market prices took a bad slide on July 19. Something had to be done to energize the economy, Roosevelt was convinced, and maybe the Blue Eagle was just the bird for the job. He gave Johnson his permission.

THERE WAS NO escaping the eagle that summer and fall of 1933. In one form or another, it fluttered and screamed its way into nearly every cranny of the American social landscape. On July 21, Johnson sent telegrams to the presidents of the chambers of commerce in every city with 10,000 people or more, asking them to

> take the initiative immediately in organizing a campaign committee
> in your community to be composed of the Mayor, the official heads of
> the Chamber of Commerce, Clearing House Association, Rotary,
> Kiwanis, Lions, Retail Merchants, Federation of Labor, Advertising

38. See Ellis, op. cit., p. 344.
39. Quoted in Schlesinger, op. cit., p. 113.

Club, Federation of Women's Clubs, Welfare societies, Ministerial Association, Real Estate Association, and any other civic organization which in your judgement is representative of an important element in the economic life of your community.[40]

The mission of these platoons of middle-class institutions, Johnson said, was "to direct a campaign of education and organization which is to be part of a national movement to speed the return of prosperity through the expansion of consumer purchasing power in accordance with the principles set forth in the National Recovery Act."[41] Three days later, Roosevelt went on the air for his third Fireside Chat, summing up his administration's accomplishments so far and pitching the virtues of the NRA. "On the basis of this simple principle of everybody doing things together," he said, "we are starting out on this nationwide attack on unemployment. . . . When Andrew Jackson, 'Old Hickory,' died, someone asked, 'Will he go to heaven?' And the answer was, 'He will if he wants to.' If I am asked whether the American people will pull themselves out of this depression, I answer, 'They will if they want to.'"[42]

They wanted to, clearly enough, and communities did respond. Boosterism, after all, had been a kind of ideology in the American middle class for decades, and ornate celebrations of civic pride—usually having to do with ever-higher levels of economic and physical growth—had punctuated the daily life of any community worthy of the name during much of the pixilated twenties. But it had been a long time since the cities and towns of the nation had found anything to boost, and most seized upon the opportunity now with enthusiasm and energy.

In Boston, the president of the chamber of commerce allowed as to how the American people were "in a state of mind to play the game," and helped organize a sixty-member Boston Recovery Committee; on the Boston Common, some 100,000 schoolchildren clustered, put their hands over their hearts, and were led in an oath administered by Mayor James M. Curley: "I promise as a good American citizen to do my part

40. Quoted in Johnson, op. cit., p. 257.
41. Quotes in ibid., pp. 258–59.
42. Quoted in Buhite and Levy, eds., op. cit, p. 36.

for the NRA. I will buy only where the Blue Eagle flies."[43] In San Francisco, 8,000 schoolchildren showed their own allegiance to the NRA by forming themselves into a human Blue Eagle on the outfield in Seals Stadium. In Cleveland, 35,000 people watched a two-hour military parade, then gathered in the public square to cheer the unveiling of the Blue Eagle flag while city officials proclaimed "the end of the depression."[44] Muncie, Indiana, in spite of an official endorsement of the NRA that fell a little short of exuberance ("Get behind the NRA until something better comes along"), staged what one of its newspapers called "the greatest peacetime parade" in the city's history—"distinctly big-town stuff!"[45] In Memphis, 125,000 people watched another 50,000 march in the city's traditional Christmas parade on the Thursday before Thanksgiving, "the largest single procession within the memory of the present generation," the *Commercial Appeal* exulted; on the final float was Santa Claus resplendent upon a big Blue Eagle, from which perch he threw candy to the children along the way.[46] In a New Orleans park, NRA celebrants erected an enormous pyramid on which had been inscribed the names of 7,000 individuals and businesses who had taken the pledge; on the top of the pyramid was a nine-foot eagle made of blue lights, while red and white bulbs spelled out, "WE DO OUR PART."[47]

In Tulsa, Hugh Johnson's mother stood up and admonished a rally: "People had better obey the NRA because my son will enforce it like lightning, and you can never tell where lightning will strike."[48] In Philadelphia, citizens not only turned out for rallies but would be cheering for a brand-new team soon to be cracking helmets with the Chicago Bears, the Chicago Cardinals, the Milwaukee Badgers, the Detroit Lions, and other species in the National Football League's pigskin menagerie: given all the hoopla regarding the NRA's bird, the young team's owner decided, what name could possibly be better than

---

43. "[I]n a state of mind" in Trout, op. cit., p. 131; "I promise as a good American citizen" in Cabell Phillips, *From the Crash to the Blitz*, pp. 220–21.
44. Quoted in B. P. Adams, "Marching as to War Under the Blue Eagle," *The Literary Digest* (August 12, 1933).
45. Quoted in Lynd and Lynd, op. cit., p. 23.
46. Quoted in Douglas L. Smith, *The New Deal in the Urban South*, p. 45.
47. See ibid., p. 46.
48. Quoted in Phillips, op. cit., p. 220.

the Philadelphia Eagles? In Richmond and other Virginia cities, torch-light parades were common, while in Roanoke, "Shanghai Mickey" offered Blue Eagle and "We Do Our Part" tattoos for a mere fifty cents.[49] In Atlantic City, beauty contestants had the Blue Eagle stamped on their thighs. In Upper Derby, Pennsylvania, a woman chris-tened her newborn daughter with the name of "Nira" in honor of the Blue Eagle's programs; FDR wrote to congratulate her on her choice, since, he said, the name signified "the faith, confidence, and cooperation necessary in any great human endeavor."[50]

No demonstration of institutional or individual support came even close to matching that of New York City on September 13. A parade of 250,000 people—with an estimated two million watching—started up Fifth Avenue at one-thirty in the afternoon and continued until well after midnight. It was, wrote a breathless reporter for *The Literary Digest*, "a surge of optimism. Those thousands of plain, ordinary, every-day citizens, mostly in ordinary garb, no 'black shirts' or 'blue shirts'! The coming together of workers in every kind of business, portly bankers and slim office boys, thousands of women workers making probably the largest parade of women ever to march in this country, all voluntarily assembled, without threats or coercion."[51] Above all the floats and marching bands and ranks of working men and women floated a navy blimp with a hundred-foot banner rippling behind it— "WE DO OUR PART"—while Hugh Johnson and other NRA officials stood on a reviewing stand and beamed in delight. And for good reason, according to columnist Heywood Broun the next day: "When 250,000 people begin to march, they are going to get somewhere. Pressing eco-nomic problems are not solved the instant fifes and drums set dancing the dust which was John Philip Sousa. But when a line forms and your shoulder touches that of a fellow and a comrade, solidarity is about to be born."[52]

49. See Heinemann, op. cit., p. 51.
50. Quote and Atlantic City and Upper Derby stories from Kenneth Davis, *FDR: The New Deal Years*, p. 252.
51. "Parades and Paradoxes in the Life of the NRA," *The Literary Digest* (September 23, 1933).
52. Heywood Broun, "It Seems to Me," *New York World-Telegram* (September 14, 1933).

Stentorian reports of the New York parade appeared during the next week in every newsreel from the Pathé News to William Randolph Hearst's Monotone News, but this was by no means the Blue Eagle's only cinematic appearance. During a nationally distributed ten-minute short called *New Deal Rhythm* commissioned by Charles Horner, the Blue Eagle campaign's publicity manager, ersatz politicians pranced and sang, while Charles ("Buddy") Rogers trilled the lyrics to a ditty not heard before and seldom (mercifully) since:

> New-Deal-rhythm,
>
> Get up, get up, get out, and get into it,
>
> Put all your steam and spin to it—say!
>
> Get into the New-Deal-rhythm,
>
> We're on the up and up and yellin' it,
>
> From coast to coast they're spellin' it—
>
> N-R-A![53]

In a big finish, the obligatory gaggle of chorus girls tap-danced energetically, lining up to spell out "NRA" in a ragged imitation of Busby Berkeley's renowned choreography in films like *Forty-second Street* or *Gold Diggers of 1933*; above all the frenetic tap dancing, a big Blue Eagle descended shakily from the ceiling.

Hollywood did not confine itself to newsreels and selected short subjects when it came to offering up the New Deal's bird. After all, the movie capital had as much reason as any other industry to look to Washington for salvation. The effects of the depression had come fairly late to "fairyland on a production line," as Otis Fergusson, movie critic for *The New Republic*, called the studio system that had been established beneath the San Gabriel Mountains of southern California, but by 1933 disaster had struck here, too.[54] Attendance had dropped from 110 million people a week in 1930 to about 60 million.[55] Still, given the fact

---

53. As transcribed by author from original film.
54. Quoted in McWilliams, *Southern California Country*, p. 337.
55. Attendance figures from Andrew Bergman, *We're in the Money: Depression America and Its Films*, p. ii.

that even the few cents it took to gain admission to the most shabby neighborhood theater was for many an extravagance, 60 million people a week is a figure that demonstrates the power of the movies as a cultural institution. No other form of entertainment—not even radio, as pervasive as it was in daily life by the thirties—so perfectly mirrored the world of fantasy that flourishes in the human mind, and the movies had become necessities, even when the cost was painful. During all the upheaval and economic vicissitudes of the thirties, in the dark anonymous comfort of neighborhood movie houses, with their reassuringly predictable Friday-night marquee changes, their Saturday matinees for the children (where Tarzan, Tom Mix, Flash Gordon, and Buck Rogers reigned), their Dish Nights, Bingo Nights, Keno Nights, Double Feature Nights, and other inducements to which hard-pressed exhibitors resorted, tens of millions of people would continue to seek escape in the glimmering unreality of film, sharing in a weekly communal experience while embracing the democratic therapy of fantasy.

That faithfulness ultimately would save the industry. In the meantime, since, like most of the nation's business leaders, those in the fairyland trade had laid their plans and made their commitments on the assumption that prosperity would last forever, it was hurting. Between 1930 and 1933, the combined stock value of the five "majors"—RKO, Paramount, Metro-Goldwyn-Mayer, 20th Century-Fox, and Warner Brothers—had gone from about a billion dollars to less than $200 million. Warner Brothers had to sell $60 million in assets to stay in business. Paramount filed a profit of $25 million in 1930, and bankruptcy papers in 1933. Of all the five majors, only MGM was able to stay in the black—and its profits had sunk from $14.6 million in 1930 to $4.3 million in 1933.[56]

What was more, vulgarity, scanty clothing, suggestive dialogue, seduction scenes, and other lewd threats to the public's moral safety had brought on the wrath not merely of Will Hays—former postmaster general, now president of the Motion Picture Producers and Distributors of America, chief enforcer of the puritanical Motion Picture Production Code, and the "highest salaried nitwit in America," according

56. Statistics from Thomas Schatz, *The Genius of the System: Hollywood Filmmaking in the Studio Era*, p. 159.

to one observer[57]—but of the Catholic Church. In 1933, the church established the Catholic Bishops' Committee on Motion Pictures to head up what it called a "Legion of Decency" campaign to identify and order all good Catholics to avoid on pain of eternal damnation, any movie that violated the dicta of purity. Nor was the legion exclusively Roman; in an early instance of ecumenism, the Catholic bishops welcomed into the fold of their campaign both the powerful Protestant Council of Churches in America and the Central Conference of Jewish Rabbis, the strongest rabbinical organization in the world.

Under pressure from its bankers and sniped at from various moral heights, then, the industry was all too happy to embrace and promote General Johnson's program of redemption. The big studios were among the first to sign reemployment agreements, and the Blue Eagle soon could be seen at a theater near you, often right up there in the opening credits and sometimes in the body of the film itself. In "Shanghai Lil," for example, the big production number in the Warner Brothers musical *Footlight Parade*, singer Ruby Keeler was backed by a chorus line holding flash cards that the girls flipped up and down in a kind of musical semaphore; one of the cards flashed the Blue Eagle; another, a grinning Franklin D. Roosevelt. The message was equally blatant in another Warner Brothers film that fall, *Wild Boys of the Road*, an earnest if badly overheated attempt to depict the problems of America's transient youth. At the film's conclusion, the hero was brought before a judge who bore a marked resemblance to FDR. "Things are going to get better all over the country," the kindly judge told the boy. "I know your father will be going back to work soon." Prominent on the wall behind him was a large Blue Eagle poster.[58]

If subtlety was not Hollywood's strong suit, it did not bother Hugh Johnson, whose distinctly unsubtle presence could be seen and heard almost as frequently as that of his bird. In Washington, he opened his office to any reporter or collection of reporters who might want to see him, issued showers of press releases, scowled authoritatively in newsreel segments, and went on the radio frequently to growl about the need

57. Quote in William E. Berchtold, "The Hollywood Purge," *North American Review* (December 1934).
58. See Bergman, op. cit., pp. 100–103.

for America to sign up. Much of the time, however, he was sitting at a desk that the Army Air Service had installed in the cabin of a big Condor airplane, writing speeches while he was bounced through the air from city to city to deliver himself of inspired bombast, like this appeal in St. Louis: "When every American housewife understands that the Blue Eagle on everything that she permits to come into her home is a symbol of its restoration to security, may God have mercy on the man or group of men who attempt to trifle with this bird."[59] Roosevelt got on no airplanes to promote the Blue Eagle, but he did issue an executive order on August 10 that required all government purchases to be made only from those private contractors who complied "with all provisions of the applicable approved code of fair competition for the trade or industry or subdivision thereof concerned . . . or with the provisions of the President's Reemployment Agreement."[60] The combination of bombast and presidential coercion had the desired effect. By the beginning of September, more than two million businesses had signed blanket codes and collected their Blue Eagles, while industry groups worked up draft codes and sent them to Washington for consideration. At the end of July, 144 such codes had been submitted; another 546 arrived in August, and by the end of the year more than 500 more would arrive.[61] In an extemporaneous speech at Vassar College on August 26, Roosevelt said he discerned "a unity in this country which I have not seen and you have not seen since April 1917, by which the American people are getting together behind the spirit of the NRA and deciding in every community in every State, that they are going to live by these principles, and that through its operation and through the operation of other great agencies of the Government which we have started, we are going to bring this country back to better times."[62]

Enthusiasm was running high in August 1933, and the president could be forgiven the hyperbole. He would find it difficult to wax quite so ardent by the end of 1934, however, and in spite of his love of a good

59. Quoted in Johnson, op. cit., p. 263.
60. In Rosenman, ed., *The Public Papers and Addresses of Franklin D. Roosevelt,* 2: p. 321.
61. Figures from Davis, op. cit., p. 253.
62. In Rosenman, op. cit., p. 345.

laugh probably would have found little humor in novelist William Saroyan's bit of NRA whimsy. "A few evenings ago I was listening to the radio, out here in San Francisco," Saroyan wrote in the iconoclastic (and largely anti–New Deal) *American Mercury*:

> I was listening to a very good program, sponsored by one of America's most prosperous manufacturers of aspirin. You know the name. . . . Then the announcer said, Aspirin is a member of the N.R.A.
>
> It made me laugh to hear that. But it is the truth. Aspirin is a member of the N.R.A. It *is* helping everyone to evade fundamentals. . . . It *is* deadening pain everywhere. It *isn't* preventing anything, but it is deadening pain. . . .
>
> Maybe the N.R.A. is a member of aspirin. Anyhow together they make a pretty slick team. They are deadening a lot of pain, but they aren't preventing any pain. . . .
>
> All I know is this: that if you keep on taking aspirin long enough it will cease to deaden pain.
>
> And that is when the fun begins.[63]

The peripatetic author of *The Daring Young Man on the Flying Trapeze* perhaps was not the most reliable of economic analysts, but he had cut close to the truth here. In spite of all the codes spilling in from all quarters of the nation, and in spite of all the public hoopla surrounding "We Do Our Part" campaigns, the NRA bird was in trouble. Part of the problem was Hugh Johnson. In 1933, when newspaper reporters had questioned him about his relationship with Frances Robinson, Johnson replied that she was "no mere stenographer." The next day, this information was translated in print to "more than a secretary." "Boys," Johnson then complained, doing himself no good at all in the process, "you're hitting below the belt."[64] His erratic behavior had created a bureaucratic shambles at the agency, according to presidential adviser A. A. Berle, who confided to his diary in August 1934 that the NRA was "practically over," with "about half the men resigning, largely

---

63. William Saroyan, "Aspirin Is a Member of the N.R.A.," *The American Mercury* (May 1934).
64. Quoted in John Franklin Carter (The Unofficial Observer), *The New Dealers*, p. 36.

208THE HUNGRY YEARS

because of the affair between Johnson and 'Robbie' . . . which has now reached an acute stage."[65]

Publicity over Johnson's lurid personal life was bad enough. But increasingly strident criticisms regarding the domination of the NRA process by big business to the detriment of small businesses and labor also served to undermine the general's position. "The NRA has given the sanction of government to self-governing combinations in the different industries," Clarence Darrow and W. O. Thompson, members of the presidentially appointed National Recovery Review Board, complained as early as April 1934. "Inevitably, this means control by the largest producers."[66] In June, Thompson resigned in protest, claiming that the NRA "reflects its class character as an attempt of the capitalists to find 'a way out of the crisis' by passing the burdens on to the shoulders of the masses of workers and farmers."[67]

By September 1934, Johnson himself had already offered to resign three times and been talked out of it by Roosevelt; the fourth resignation, tendered on September 25, was accepted. The next day, Roosevelt reorganized the agency and created an Industrial Recovery Board to administer it. He then explained his actions in a Fireside Chat on September 30, expressing some irritation himself about the high-handed and self-serving attitudes of big business—as well as labor's own failings. After celebrating what the NRA had managed to accomplish in its first fourteen months—the abolition of child labor, the establishment of minimum wages and maximum hours, the reemployment of millions, a rise in industrial profits—he went on to call the attention of his listeners

> to the fact that the National Industrial Recovery Act gave businessmen the opportunity they had sought for years to improve business conditions through what has been called self-government. . . . It is now time to review these actions as a whole. . . . The employer who turns away from impartial agencies of peace, who denies freedom of

65. Quoted in Davis, op. cit., p. 413.
66. Quoted in Rhonda F. Levine, *Class Struggle and the New Deal: Industrial Labor, Industrial Capital, and the State*, p. 92.
67. Ibid.

organization to his employees, or fails to make every reasonable effort
at a peaceful solution of their differences, that employer is not fully
supporting the recovery effort of his government. And the workers
who turn away from these same impartial agencies and decline to use
their good offices to gain their ends, those workers likewise are not
fully cooperating with their government.[68]

Roosevelt and his newly created NRA board never would get the
chance to fully restructure its operations. The agency was still floundering when the Supreme Court stepped in to trifle with the Blue Eagle in
no uncertain terms. On May 27, 1935, in a decision in the case of
Schechter v. United States, the court declared that the NIRA's code system
was an unconstitutional delegation of legislative power to the executive
branch of government. Title II of the act—by which the Public Works
Administration had been established—and Title III—putting in place
excess profits taxes—were untouched by the decision, but while many
of the provisions of Title I would show up in somewhat different form
in future legislation (which the Supreme Court would uphold), as of
May 27, 1935, it was invalidated and the Blue Eagle, like its equally
colorful creator, was permanently grounded.

But even before the Supreme Court's decision, the National Industrial Recovery Act had loosed consequences so troubling that the president had not been able to bring himself to do anything more than hint
at them in his September 30 Fireside Chat. Peace had not broken out
between capital and labor as a result of the NIRA; domestic war had,
and in this terrible failing, death became a commonplace.

68. Quoted in Buhite and Levy, eds., op. cit., pp. 58–60.

9

"The President Wants *You* to Organize!"

The Blue Eagle of the NRA had flown for less than two years before the Supreme Court put an effective end to the program. In those two years the agency came nowhere near achieving the national cohesion that Roosevelt had dreamed of when he said he detected "a unity in this country which I have not seen . . . since April, 1917."[1] There was little unity to be found anywhere after passage of the NIRA, except perhaps where the New Dealers had not really expected (or particularly wanted) to find it: among the working people. Section 7(a) of the NIRA, with its stipulation that employees had "the right to organize and bargain collectively through representatives of their own choosing," was seen by most of the New Dealers as a necessary recognition of labor's right to be considered a partner with industry (though in practice never quite an equal partner) in the process of recovery. To working men and women, however, Section 7(a) was "like the realization of a dream," as Sidney Hillman, president of the Amalgamated Clothing Workers of America, described it, and it would inspire perhaps the

1. Quoted in Davis, op. cit., p. 345.

largest—and certainly the most rapid—rank-and-file movement in American history.[2] It got workers "moving and fighting and stirring," Chicago packinghouse organizer Herbert March said. "People by that time had had it up to here—up to their ears. They had come through a real period of suffering and oppression and they were ready to revolt."[3]

The suffering and oppression had been real enough. While the production demands of World War I had encouraged an uneasy (and sometimes violated) truce between industry and labor that had seen union membership rise to an all-time high of more than five million, the postwar years were marked by a virulent anti-union campaign on the part of both industry and the federal government that had left the labor movement reeling by the end of the twenties. The campaign was called "The American Plan," and the association of industries and businesses that came up with it issued a proclamation declaring it their determination to see that every working man would be allowed "to work out his own salvation and not to be bound by the shackles of organization to his own detriment."[4] This crusade to free the worker from the chains of unionism had systematically used court injunctions, infiltration, battalions of professional strikebreakers, and simple brutality to achieve its ends. To a large extent, it had succeeded.

Even if the labor movement had been able to call upon true solidarity to resist such a campaign, it probably could have done little to dull its effects—and in the twenties solidarity forever eluded it. The American Federation of Labor, founded in 1886 and the largest labor body in the country, was led by the relatively conservative Samuel Gompers, who refused to taint the AFL's traditional craft-oriented character by opening it to a wider band of workers, including semi-skilled and unskilled labor, even when challenged vigorously from within by such influential dissidents as William Z. Foster, president of the Trade Union Educational League, and John L. Lewis, president of the United Mine Workers. Only by the inclusion of the great mass of unorganized workers, Foster, Lewis, and a few others believed, could the labor movement ever hope to meet power with power. Gompers refused to corrupt

2. Quoted in Matthew Josephson, *Sidney Hillman: Statesman of American Labor*, p. 362.
3. Quoted in Elizabeth Cohen, *Making a New Deal: Industrial Workers in Chicago, 1919–1939*, p. 304.
4. Quoted in Philip Taft, *The A. F. of L. in the Time of Gompers*, p. 246.

the AFL with the great unwashed. So did William Green, who succeeded Gompers after the old labor leader's death in 1924 and remained
locked in a struggle with the "industrial unionists" for the rest of the
decade while union membership steadily declined. By 1933, the number of union members had shrunk by two million from its high in 1920;
there now were only a shade over three million union members in the
United States out of a total of 31.3 million nonfarm employees. From
an Illinois coal field, one representative of the United Mine Workers
reported to headquarters in early 1933 that "things are in a bad way. . . .
The future does not look bright," while another in western Kentucky
complained that he "could not organize a *baseball team*."[5]

IN PROBABLY NO other major industry, in fact, had the future seemed less
bright for unionism than in coal mining, and nowhere did the outlook seem so bleak as in Harlan County in eastern Kentucky—"Bloody
Harlan"—where the divisions between capital and labor were drawn
with especially bold strokes. In both its dark history and in the hope
of redemption that the New Deal inspired, Harlan's experience was
emblematic of the entire industry.

Here, in the timber-stripped and mine-riddled old hills of the
Appalachians, the members of the Harlan County Coal Operators Association—in thrall to the U.S. Coal and Coke Company—had fought
attempts to unionize the industry for years, using every device, legal or
illegal, at their command. There was plenty of reason to organize, for
Harlan County may have been the most oppressed industrial region in
the country, and its workers and their families the most profoundly
abused and deprived. Some of the deprivation was unavoidable. The
industry had been staggering through levels of economic stress that
were unmatched anywhere but in Detroit. Mine after mine had shut
down completely during the early depression years, as they had done
throughout the whole of the Appalachian coal region. Unemployment
figures were the worst in the country. Neither the federal government,

5. Quotes in Melvin Dubofsky and Warren Van Tine, *John L. Lewis: A Biography*, p. 185.
Italics in original.

the states, nor the cities in the region could come anywhere near providing enough relief.

The miners and their families lived in the ugly black piles of company towns that wormed their way through the hollows and narrow river valleys of the region—electricity rare, sanitation primitive at best, coal tipples and breakers the tallest structures in sight, the air polluted with coal dust and stinking almost constantly from slag fires that never seemed to die. The workers endured a life whose quality had less to do with the Great Depression than with the cultural climate of a region that had been dominated by its powerful industry so long and so absolutely that it could easily be mistaken for eighteenth-century Wales. Those lucky enough to have jobs earned a maximum of one dollar a day for twelve- and fourteen-hour days. "In the morning when they'd go to work before daylight," Florence Reese, a miner's wife and union balladeer, remembered, "you could see the kerosene lamps they wore on their hats. It was just like fireflies all around the mountain."[6] For six days a week they clawed out the coal and loaded the cars under conditions that included little or no ventilation, poor drainage, inadequate timbering, and constant danger from fire, coal gas explosions, and cave-ins.

Wages and piece-rates (sometimes falling as low as thirteen cents for each sixteen-ton car of coal loaded) were regulated and paid entirely at the discretion of the companies, and mostly in company scrip whose value ranged anywhere from forty to eighty cents on the dollar. The shacks the miners lived in were owned by the companies, which deducted the weekly rent from the worker's pay. Company stores, or commissaries, often conveniently located near the pay shack, provided the only place to buy groceries and other necessities. The prices were usually inflated, but a miner who bought from any other source would be warned no more than once or twice before being fired and thrown out of his home.

The law, such as it was, resided in the pockets of the companies under the direction of County Sheriff John Henry Blair, while the local

6. Quoted in Kathy Kahn, *Hillbilly Women: Mountain Women Speak of Struggle and Joy in Southern Appalachia*, p. 29.

press parroted the company line. Radical literature was forbidden; homes were regularly entered and searched without warrants, and miners discovered to belong to Lewis's United Mine Workers or to the smaller Communist-controlled National Miners Union were fired and blacklisted. Union organizers from any branch of the labor movement were frequently beaten and run out of the county, occasionally shot, and sometimes killed by gangs of armed and deputized hooligans who had been supplied from as far away as Chicago. The law, one woman said, "is a gun thug in a big automobile."[7]

In spite of grotesque odds, workers still tried to strike for decent wages and working conditions. In March of 1931, when two hundred men were fired after a mass meeting held by the United Mine Workers, more than 11,000 workers had gone on strike. On May 4, when a group of miners stopped several carloads of deputies who were threatening to "shoot up the town of Evarts," where many striking miners lived, the ensuing "Battle of Evarts" resulted in the deaths of three deputies and one miner.[8] The owners and their deputies retaliated in kind, arresting twenty-eight miners for the death of the deputies and raiding and breaking up UMW offices. Under such pressure, the AFL-affiliated union called it quits, but the National Miners Union stepped in to take its place and Harlan County continued in the grip of violence, with shootings and bombings and arson on all sides. The National Guard did little or nothing about the situation, and the federal government barely looked in the direction of Cumberland Gap.

The government's calculated disinterest did not alter noticeably, even when a group of radical New York writers acted to bring the situation in Harlan County to national attention. Novelist Theodore Dreiser and a troop from his National Committee for the Defense of Political Prisoners came down to the mountains in November 1931 to investigate the situation. Although the investigatory radicals were under constant threat and followed at all times during their stay, they did a pretty fair job of gathering testimony and evidence before escaping back to the liberal warrens of New York without serious incident. Another group

7. Quoted in George B. Tindall, *The Emergence of the New South, 1913–1945*, p. 384.
8. Quote in Melvin P. Levy, "Class War in Kentucky." In Theodore Dreiser, ed., *Harlan Miners Speak*, p. 44.

was not so lucky. In the second week of February 1932, Waldo Frank, Malcolm Cowley, Mary Heaton Vorse, and a few other sympathizers from New York set off to deliver three truckloads of food to striking miners and their families. "This is another war," a coal operator warned Cowley. "I admire your nerve in coming here where you don't know anything about the conditions or the feeling of the people. If you don't watch out, you'll find out how ugly we can be."[9] The writers found out almost immediately. On the night of their arrival, after being arrested and then released by officials, they were seized in their hotel by a mob, pushed into cars, and driven up to the top of Cumberland Gap on the Tennessee state line. Two were beaten and tossed out on the highway. The rest merely had their luggage ransacked before the kidnappers piled into cars and sped off into the night, leaving their victims standing in the cold. "Never come across that border again, sister," one of the men called out to Vorse, "or worse will happen."[10]

Formal complaints to a congressional committee were made shortly after the group returned to New York. Their stories were listened to with respect and interest. The liberal press publicized the outrage. Later in the year, Theodore Dreiser published the findings of his own group under the title of *Harlan Miners Speak*. It, too, was received with interest and a good deal of publicity. But in Harlan County, Kentucky, the repression and hunger continued, and with it the bitter dichotomy described in one of Florence Reese's most enduring union songs: "If you go to Harlan County, / There is no neutral there, / You'll either be a union man / Or a thug for J. H. Blair."[11]

As it was in Harlan County, so it was in most of the rest of the coal mining regions, where a rigid social structure erected walls against hope. It was to assault such bastions that John L. Lewis invoked Section 7(a) of the National Industrial Recovery Act and began an industry-wide organizing drive even before the ink had dried on the president's signature converting the act to law. Lewis already was becoming the

9. Quoted in Page Smith, op, cit., p. 519.
10. Quoted in Dee Garrison, *Mary Heaton Vorse: The Life of an American Insurgent*, p. 247. Most of my account of the Pineville incident is from this source, pp. 241–48, and from testimony by Waldo Frank and others reprinted in Theodore Dreiser, ed., *Harlan Miners Speak*, pp. 318–22.
11. As reprinted in Kahn, op. cit., pp. 35–36.

best-known labor leader in the nation. With the face of an angry bulldog and the most prominent eyebrows in America, his physical presence alone was impressive, and when it was combined with a megaphone voice that rang with biblical power and the cadences of nineteenth-century elocution, his appeal was powerful. Indeed, it was Lewis who had helped to win inclusion of Section 7(a) in the first place—"Let there be no 'moaning at the bar' when we put out to sea on this great adventure," he had told the members of the Senate Finance Committee—and in consequence, he gained a seat on the NRA's Labor Advisory Board (his friend and ally, Sidney Hillman, was named chairman).[12] The passage of the NIRA, Lewis was convinced, had "given labor the greatest opportunity it has ever had to work out its own destiny," and he sent organizers out into the coal mining towns to broadcast the message of Section 7(a) like a new version of the Gospel.[13] "THE PRESIDENT WANTS *YOU* TO ORGANIZE!" said signs plastered to the sides of sound trucks that rattled and backfired their way along the twisting roads of the mountains and into all the gray company towns, where they would stop just long enough to boom out the good news, hand out a few leaflets, then get out before the law took action against them. (When accused of distorting Roosevelt's approval of Section 7(a), organizers glibly insisted that the term "president" in such signs referred to Lewis, not FDR.)[14]

The response probably startled even Lewis. "We expect to be practically through with every mine in the state and have every miner under [the] jurisdiction of our union by the first of next week," an organizer reported from West Virginia on June 23—just one week after passage of the NIRA. In the southern part of the state, he added, the "field is completely organized, and unbounded enthusiasm prevails among the miners and their people."[15] Within the next several weeks, the UMW's drive not only reclaimed tens of thousands who had abandoned unionism entirely during the previous twelve years but won back many of

12. Quoted in Dubofsky and Van Tine, op. cit., p. 184.
13. Quoted in Thomas R. Brooks, *Picket Lines and Bargaining Tables: Organized Labor Comes of Age, 1935–1955*, p. 62. The statement appeared unsigned in the *United Mine Workers Journal*, but almost certainly came from Lewis.
14. See Jeremy Brecher, *Strike!* p. 150.
15. Quoted in Dubofsky and Van Tine, op. cit., p. 185.

those who had defected to the Communist National Miners Union, and by the end of the summer UMW membership stood at more than 400,000.

"[Lewis] sent sound trucks with fiery speakers and free beer lumbering into the very citadels of the open shop," marveled *Fortune* magazine in December 1933. "The results were spectacular. . . . By the time the operators sat down with Lewis to write a code [in September], they found their mines had been unionized right out from under their feet."[16] The presence of those hundreds of thousands of suddenly unionized miners stood like an invisible army behind the negotiators as they squabbled over the details of the coal industry's NRA code. And though the government's powers to regulate the industry were severely diminished by a complex restructuring formula that had been agreed upon when the code finally was completed and signed on March 31, 1934, Lewis and the UMW won something close to a complete victory: a seven-hour workday, a five-day workweek, base wages of $5 a day in northern districts and $4.60 in southern districts, and the acceptance of the UMW as virtually the only union in the industry—even in "Bloody Harlan." Only the mine operators of Alabama refused to accept the $4.60 minimum, and even these finally capitulated when Lewis neatly marshaled evidence to disprove their contention that black miners did not need as much money as white miners, then combined fact with fire in the best Lewisian manner. Did the Alabama operators think they were in a position to declare war on the United States government? he thundered. "If they think they are . . . the United Mine Workers of America is ready . . . to furnish the President . . . with twenty army divisions to help make the Alabama operators comply with the law of the United States."[17]

THE EXPLOSION IN union membership that had so suddenly transformed the relationship between labor and capital in the coal mines of Appalachia was echoed throughout much of industrial America. Many union leaders were perfectly happy to take credit for this organizational

16. "The American Federation of Labor," *Fortune* (December 1933).
17. Quoted in Dubofsky and Van Tine, op. cit., p. 199.

outburst and most industry leaders were just as happy to blame them for it, but in most of the union drives, Lewis and the other union bosses—certainly including the AFL's William Green, who had neither expected nor knew quite what to do about such a development—were minor players at best. "When we first received word about the textile code, the Blue Eagle, and our right to organize," a southern textile worker remembered, "it seemed too good to be true. It was a real New Deal for us."[18] So it was the country over. "There was a virtual uprising of workers for union membership," the executive council of the AFL reported in some amazement during the organization's 1934 convention. "Workers held mass meetings and sent word they wanted to be organized."[19] Thomas Burke, general secretary of the United Association of Journeyman Plumbers and Steam Fitters, was driven to flights of rhetoric not ordinarily associated with his trade. "Men who have never dared consider joining a union now come forward openly, eagerly and joyously, to join with their fellows in a great humanitarian movement of labor for the betterment of its conditions and for the enlargement of the whole scheme and sphere of human life," he wrote in the United Association's *Journal*. "This great influx of workers into the unions of America is one of the great inspirations of our time. It is a picture of the opening of the gates of freedom. It is emancipation before our eyes."[20]

Emancipation brought flights of enthusiasm and nerve. When James B. Carey, a young worker in the Philco Radio Company plant in Philadelphia, organized a union, company officials said they would not recognize it until they had authorization from NRA director Hugh Johnson himself. Carey and a few others hopped into their cars and raced off to Washington, D.C., armed only with a newspaper photograph of the general. With that in hand, they wandered from office to office in the Commerce Building until they found the face to match the picture. Frances Robinson, Johnson's militant "gatekeeper," must have been away from her desk, for the men resolutely marched straight into

18. Quoted in James A. Hodges, *New Deal Labor Policy and the Southern Cotton Textile Industry, 1933–1941*, p. 90.
19. Quoted in Thomas R. Brooks, op. cit., p. 63.
20. Quoted in Samuel G. Freedman, *The Inheritance: How Three Families and America Moved from Roosevelt to Reagan and Beyond*, p. 103.

Johnson's office. "Haven't we got law on our side?" Carey asked the general, who agreed that they did. "Well, then," Carey went on, "sign your name. Management won't take our word for it." Johnson, who probably admired their gumption, did as they demanded, and back in Philadelphia his signature apparently was enough for the union to win an agreement for a closed shop, a 36-hour week, and significant pay increases.[21]

Some people surprised even themselves. In his regular syndicated feature for the *New York World-Telegram* on August 7, 1933, columnist Heywood Broun indulged himself in a jest. "[The] fact that newspaper editors and owners are genial folk," he wrote,

> should hardly stand in the way of the organization of a newspaper writers' union. There should be one. Beginning at nine o'clock on the morning of October 1, I am going to do the best I can to help in getting one up. I think I could die happy on the opening day of the general strike if I had the privilege of watching Walter Lippmann heave half a brick through a *Tribune* window at a non-union operative who had been called in to write the Today and Tomorrow column on the gold standard.[22]

But many of Broun's fellow journalists were not willing to let the idea stand as a joke—nor were they about to wait until October 1. The columnist got so many telephone calls and letters that he soon found himself chairing a serious discussion among a dozen or more working journalists. Roy Howard, president of the Scripps-Howard newspaper chain and Broun's boss, was not pleased. "You're doing a very silly and evil thing in trying to get reporters into a union," he wrote Broun. "That would rob them of their initiative and take the romance and glamour [sic] out of the newspaper business."[23] Romance and glamour did not put bread on a reporter's table, and the initial penthouse gathering was followed by a mass meeting of several hundred at the City Club

---

21. The story of Carey and the Philco union is told in Thomas R. Brooks, op. cit., pp. 61–62.
22. Quoted in Dale Kramer, *Heywood Broun: A Biographical Portrait*, p. 244.
23. Quoted in Bruce Minton and John Stuart, *Men Who Lead Labor*, p. 115.

on September 17, during which occasion the Guild of New York News-paper Men and Women—the core of what soon became the American Newspaper Guild—was formally established.

By the spring of 1934, membership in the International Ladies' Garment Workers' Union increased from 40,000 to over 200,000. By August 1934, NRA analysts estimated that the United Textile Workers Union had blossomed from 20,000 to more than 340,000 members. The Amalgamated Clothing Workers of America doubled its member-ship to 120,000, with Sidney Hillman and his organizers taking a page from John L. Lewis's book: "The Law is behind you," one of the union's leaflets declared. "The NRA protects your right to have a union and will punish the boss if he tries to stop you. . . . The President is behind you."[24] In city after city, workers proceeded to organize everything in sight. In Akron, Ohio, where "rubber workers believed, blindly, pas-sionately, fiercely, that the union would cure all their troubles," as Ruth McKenney put it in her radical novel *Industrial Valley*, membership in the various unions involved in the production of tires and other rubber products increased by 23,000, and membership in unions outside the industry jumped to 7,000.[25] Nationwide, membership in the AFL grew by some 900,000 people over the course of a few months. New unions and new locals for old unions erupted everywhere, so many that existing unions simply could not deal with the numbers. "I have so many calls for organizers," the president of the Pulp and Paper Workers' Union complained in July 1933, "that I have neither the men nor the money to take care of all of them."[26]

Neither did the AFL, which was forced into some agonizing contor-tions over the question of what to do with the new unions—3,537 of them between June and October. Many of the new groups had no direct connection with the traditional craft unions that made up the AFL; indeed, many were populated by unskilled laborers, a class of worker the AFL had studiously disregarded for decades. But to continue to

24. Quoted in Steven Fraser, *Labor Will Rule*, p. 292.
25. Ruth McKenney, *Industrial Valley*, p. 101. The book might be described as an early version of the "nonfiction novel," and its communist slant is undisguised. For figures, see Daniel Nelson, *American Rubber Workers and Organized Labor, 1900–1941*, p. 122.
26. Quoted in Robert H. Zieger, *American Workers, American Unions, 1920–1985*, p. 31.

ignore these suddenly organized and militant unionists would be to chance losing the strength they could bring to the movement—and to risk even losing them to the much-despised and greatly feared clutches of the Communist TUUL. Compromise, then: the new unions could petition for membership in the AFL as "federal labor unions," a category that gave them the privilege of paying dues to the AFL while they waited until such time as the leadership of the big union might choose to give them equal rights. Most accepted this second-class position—for the time being.

Organization was well and good, Sidney Hillman and others pointed out, but organization alone was not going to get labor its goals. "You don't transfer power by statute," Hillman told one of his lieutenants. "Section 7(a) can be enforced through strikes. You don't expect the Government to send the American working class to Labor Unions. That is the union's job."[27] So saying, he sent his organizers into sweatshop shirt and hosiery factories scattered through New England, New York, New Jersey, Pennsylvania, and Ohio, where they helped birth new union locals and initiate strikes, winning a number of satisfying victories.

Overall, by the end of 1933, more than 1.1 million workers (more than one-fourth of them women, the highest percentage in history) had been involved in 1,672 strikes in nearly every venue from steel plants to hotel kitchens—and nearly two-thirds of the strikes had ended with partial or substantial gains for workers in the matter of wages, hours, and union recognition.[28] "Industrial centers like New York and Chicago are jammed, packed with pickets warring against sweatshops, unwilling employers," a breathless caption-writer for *Fortune* announced in December 1933. "Traditional sore spots like Pennsylvania and Illinois are erupting with recognition strikes, jurisdictional warfare. . . . NRA has restored fighting guts to labor, taken the lid off many a boiling industrial pot."[29]

27. Quoted in Fraser, op. cit., p. 290.

28. For statistics, see Bureau of Labor Statistics report *Strikes in the United States, 1880–1936*, pp. 41–70.

29. "The American Federation of Labor," *Fortune* (December 1933).

The proliferation of strikes, of course, was not what Roosevelt and the several authors of the NIRA had in mind when they included Section 7(a) in the act. On the contrary: the act was supposed to provide the atmosphere and the machinery for compromise, and to that end Roosevelt had established a National Labor Board (not to be confused with the National Labor *Advisory* Board) with Senator Robert Wagner at its head and regional boards appointed to facilitate its work. Hugh Johnson described the ordained function of these boards succinctly: there is, he said, "always a short breathing space where frequently a quiet conference between leaders on both sides, in the presence of someone with power and authority to help (so far as government can help) . . . can bring not only composition and peace but a new feeling of helpful cooperation."[30]

In June 1934, Roosevelt would replace the National Labor Board with a National Labor Relations Board. The trouble with these bodies, by whatever name, was the fact that they possessed no real power. They could investigate, advise, and recommend, but they could not impose. That powerlessness tended to foster contempt among industrialists and distrust among labor leaders, and when representatives of either management or labor felt that any given board's conclusions were unacceptable, they were prone to ignore these findings. With some justification, labor viewed the boards with special skepticism, since decisions often seemed weighted toward management—and even when they were not, labor could not often count on the officials of the NRA to impose what sanctions were open to them. In the spring of 1934, for example, the regional labor board in Chicago ruled that the Chicago Motor Coach Company should reinstate fifteen members of the Amalgamated Association of Street and Railway Employees Union whom the company had fired. The company refused. The board then recommended to Hugh Johnson that the company's Blue Eagle be stripped from its corporate shoulders. Johnson rejected the advice, insisting that 95 percent of the company's workers were against the union. He said the board should do some more investigating. The union promptly went on strike, and by the end of the year had won reinstatement for the workers and recogni-

30. Johnson, op. cit., p. 313.

tion of the union (though nothing in the way of better wages or work-ing conditions).[31]

If labor's strength grew after passage of the NIRA, then it was not because the New Deal was willing to throw the weight of government behind the movement; it was because millions of workers—many of them unionized for the first time in their lives—were willing to take to the picket lines, in spite of the National Labor Relations Board chair-man Wagner's belief that "strikes should be abandoned as an instru-ment of first resort."[32] The workers had already done so in the last six months of 1933, but in 1934 they eclipsed even that experience, turn-ing out in such numbers, over so wide a territory, among so various a collection of businesses and industries, and with such ferocious energy, that commentators could be forgiven their weakness for describing it in apocalyptic tones.

31. See Barbara Warne Newell, *Chicago and the Labor Movement: Metropolitan Unionism in the 1930s*, pp. 50–51.
32. Quoted in Christopher L. Tomlins, *The State and the Unions: Labor Relations, Law, and the Organized Labor Movement, 1880–1960*, p. 109.

10

Freedom's Fire

Nowhere did all the industrial pots boil more violently than in Toledo, Minneapolis, San Francisco, and the mill towns of the textile industry from New England to the southern Appalachians, where throughout the spring and summer of 1934 workers defied employers, civic authorities, the federal government, and sometimes their own national leadership in pursuing their goals. If ever the eternal conflict between labor and capital earned its common description as warfare, it was in these clashes, whose levels of fury had not been witnessed over so much of the country since the labor riots of 1877 and would help to slather the entire era of the thirties with the gloss of class struggle.

As usual, most conservatives blamed the turmoil on the Communist Party. But if the TUUL unions and other formal party groups were eager and sometimes important participants, each of these big strikes was orchestrated and controlled from beginning to end almost entirely by nonparty leaders. "In 1934," Earl Browder admitted a year later, "the

Red Unions definitely passed into the background in the basic industries, and to some extent also in light industry. The main mass of workers had definitely chosen to try and organize and fight through the A. F.
of L. organizations."[1] Ironically, in many instances the Executive Council of the AFL, naturally conservative itself and fearful of being spat-
tered by accusations of irresponsibility and communism, went out of its
way to discourage strikes. In March 1934, for example, the AFL's willingness to negotiate with the major auto manufacturers (not including
the still-recalcitrant Ford), coupled with the direct intercession of Roosevelt, had averted a strike of potentially monstrous dimensions on the
part of newly organized "federal unions," and, according to AFL president William Green, stood as "a great step forward for the automobile
workers. For the first time in the history of the automobile industry,
the right to organize has been conceded, and collective bargaining is
assured through representatives chosen by the employees."[2] That may
have seemed true in Detroit (though the agreement would prove both
fragile and temporary), but in Toledo, Ohio, where many automobile
parts for the industry were manufactured, 4,000 workers in a new federal union did not find the atmosphere quite so congenial. Early in February, the union had struck several parts plants, and the strike had been
settled after just six days with some wage increases and, more important, a willingness on the part of the companies to negotiate other
points of disagreement, including the matter of union recognition and
jurisdiction. But the biggest plant in town, Electric Auto-Lite, went
back on its word and refused to discuss the issues. On April 12, the
union struck Auto-Lite again. Only about half the workers joined the
walkout this time, and the company swiftly brought in strikebreakers.
The union, unsupported in any real fashion by the AFL, seemed doomed
to fail until the Lucas County Unemployed League and the American
Workers Party—founded by the Reverend A. J. Muste, one of several
dissidents then helping to rip the Socialist Party to tatters—brought in
hundreds of the unemployed to help man the picket lines around the
Auto-Lite plant. "The point about Toledo," newspaper owner Roy W.

1. Quoted in Klehr, op. cit., p. 124.
2. Quoted in the *New York Times*, March 26, 1934.

Howard, whose chain included the *Toledo Blade*, later wrote FDR's assistant, Louis Howe,

> was this: that it is nothing new to see organized unemployed appear in the streets, fight police, and raise hell in general. But usually they do this for their own ends, to protest against unemployment or relief conditions. At Toledo they appeared on the picket lines to help striking employees win a strike, though you would expect their interest would lie the other way—that is, in going down and getting the jobs the other men had laid down.[3]

That, a union member doubtless would have been happy to remind Howard, was what was meant by the term "solidarity." In any case, Auto-Lite soon exercised its own version of solidarity: its lawyers asked for and received an injunction against the union that barred the presence of more than twenty-five pickets at each of the company's gates. The picketers ignored the injunction, and police started arresting strike leaders. Every day, while the union men were being tried on contempt of court charges, the numbers of picketers at the factory increased, and mass rallies of union supporters were held every noon. On May 23, when the daily numbers had grown to nearly 10,000, Lucas County Sheriff David Kreiger deputized a special force and started arresting the picketers themselves. During the course of one such arrest, a deputy beat an old man senseless, enraging the crowd. It boiled through the gates of Auto-Lite and surrounded the plant, trapping 1,500 workers inside. Tear gas, fire hoses, and even guns were brought into play by the police and the deputies. The crowd responded by throwing brickbats and paving stones through the windows of the plant ("*Now* you have your open shop," one of them reportedly shouted as a rock burst through a window).[4]

The fighting went on into the post-midnight hours, and at dawn Governor George White sent seven hundred National Guard troops into the city. The troops, bayonets fixed, managed to drive the crowd away from the plant briefly, only to be pushed back themselves. At

3. Quoted in Brecher, op. cit., p. 158.
4. Quoted in Schlesinger, op. cit., p. 393.

some point in the melee, orders to fire were given, and two strikers were killed and fifteen others wounded. Still, the fighting continued, even when another 200 troops were called in.

One of those caught in the mess was the newborn union organizer Heywood Broun, who provided a moment of humor in an otherwise humorless set of events. While covering the strike violence, Broun had escaped being gassed only by climbing a fence and losing the seat of his pants, including his wallet. Later, when a trooper overheard someone describing Broun as a columnist from New York, he arrested the writer and took him to his superior. "He's a big Communist from New York," the trooper told his officer.

"Columnist," Broun corrected, producing his downtown hotel key as the only means of identification left in his torn trousers.

"Oh," the officer said, "one of those *rich* New York Communists."[5]

Broun was released after other newspapermen vouched for him. But not until the company was persuaded to shut down operations entirely was a shaky truce established. Two weeks of negotiation under the direction of federal mediator Charles P. Taft finally gave the union recognition, jurisdiction, and an hourly wage increase of 22 percent. Simultaneously, mediation prevented a threatened citywide general strike over union recognition for workers in the Toledo Edison Company electric plant.

Peace did not come quite so easily to Minneapolis that violent spring and summer of 1934. In few cities in the country had the labor movement been more successfully stifled, even though the state itself was firmly in the hands of the supremely radical Farmer-Labor Party, an entity that had evolved out of rural discontent and, in 1930, had seen its candidate for governor, Floyd B. Olson, elected. Olson supported FDR in 1932 and had instituted a state-level "Little New Deal." But by the end of 1933, both he and his party were beginning to move farther to the left than Roosevelt had any intention of drifting—encouraged in that direction by the CP/USA, with whom the Olson administration maintained an on-again, off-again alliance until Olson's death from cancer in 1936. Minnesota consequently had become the most thoroughly radicalized government entity in the nation. Before internal friction

5. Broun's story is told in Kramer, op. cit., p. 254.

began to dismember it in the latter half of the decade, the Farmer-Labor Association, the party's membership body, grew to somewhere between 20,000 and 30,000. This was not far below the national membership of the Communist Party, and the association became the state's dominant political machine, doling out patronage and controlling work-relief disbursements in an atmosphere of benevolent paternalism with which traditional Republican or Democratic machines might have felt perfectly comfortable.[6]

Little of this radicalism had managed to shake the hold of raw capitalism in Minneapolis, however. The Citizens Alliance, a powerful group of Minneapolis and St. Paul businessmen who had joined together as long ago as 1903 for the expressed purpose of beating back unionism, still held the reins of power. Described by a reporter for *The Nation* in 1934 as "a mysterious organization with no known membership but immense power and resources," the alliance had put in place its own employment agency, established its own trade schools, and, so it was said, created a network of labor spies as effective as any in the nation. The result, in union terminology, made Minneapolis "the worst scab town in the Northwest."[7] While wages rose by about 11 percent nationwide during the decade of the twenties, in Minneapolis the increase was held to 2 percent.

On the other side was a local collection of AFL unions infinitely more radical than the national body. None was more openly leftist than Local 574 of the Teamsters' Union affiliate, the General Drivers and Helpers Union, which had become dominated by a clutch of Trotskyist dissidents, former Communists, Socialists, Farmer-Labor Party members, and Wobblies, all of whom had gathered under the banner of a tiny splinter group, the Communist League of Struggle. In February 1934, Local 574 went on strike against the city's sixty-seven coal yards. It was one of the coldest winters in memory, and while the coal yard owners refused to deal directly with the union, the loss of income from coal sales persuaded them at least to bargain through the regional office

6. The story of Minnesota's Farmer-Labor Party is extensively treated in Richard M. Valelly, *Radicalism in the States: The Minnesota Farmer-Labor Party and the American Political Economy.*
7. Quotes in Thomas E. Blantz, "Father Haas and the Minneapolis Truckers' Strike of 1934," *Minnesota History* (Spring 1970).

of the National Labor Board. Within a few days, the board had negotiated an agreement for wage increases and overtime pay. The rank and
file voted to go back to work, even though their leaders pointed out that
they had not won the key point—union recognition.

Success, however limited, bred success. A subsequent organizing
drive raised Local 574's membership to about 3,000. This was enough,
the union's leadership decided, to seek recognition and wage and hour
concessions from every major employer in the city—from taxi companies to furniture companies—who used or owned commercial transport
systems. They presented their demands to the employers' bargaining
committee on April 1. The employers rejected them out of hand, and
while the officers of the regional Labor Board in St. Paul fruitlessly
tried to negotiate a settlement, both sides prepared for urban warfare.
The Citizens Alliance, through its front group, the Employers' Advisory Committee, set up headquarters in a downtown hotel, while Local
574 took over a huge garage on Chicago Avenue. "The garage offices
have been converted into the strike office, with desks, typewriters, and
stenographers," a reporter for the *Minneapolis Tribune* wrote. "Much of
the garage space will be needed for the fleet of cars that the union is
mobilizing to carry officials and members about the city on strike
business."[8]

On the evening of May 15, the rank and file gathered in the big
union meeting hall and voted to go out on strike the next day, and for
the next eleven days Minneapolis was closed "as tight as a bull's eye in
flytime," as strikers described it. The sheriff agreed: "They had the town
tied up tight. Not a truck could move in Minneapolis."[9]

If it was as carefully organized and directed a strike as any in American history up to that time, it also was one of the bloodiest. Platoons of
union pickets armed with ax handles and baseball bats prowled the
streets, clashing with their counterparts among police and Citizen
Alliance groups. The worst fight was the so-called Battle of Deputies
Run, which took place on the morning of May 22, when about a thousand deputized members of the Citizens Alliance were surrounded
and beaten by several thousand pickets and union sympathizers. Two

8. Quoted in Valelly, op, cit., p. 108.
9. Quotes in Blantz, op. cit.

deputies, including Arthur Lyman, a member of the alliance's executive board, were clubbed to death.

The Battle of Deputies Run brought in a federal mediator from Washington, and after five days of negotiation, an agreement was reached that established Local 574 as the bargaining agent among those companies whose truckers and truckers' helpers might vote to have it so. The strike consequently was called off on May 26. But the agreement did not include the "inside" workers, those warehousemen, dock workers, and others who did not work on the trucks directly but over whom the union nevertheless claimed jurisdiction. The union wanted these workers included. The employers refused, and the union voted to strike again on July 16.

To engineer a quick settlement, Lloyd Garrison, chairman of the newly formed National Labor Relations Board, sent Father Francis J. Haas to Minneapolis. Haas, director of the National Catholic School of Social Service and a member of the original National Labor Board, was one of the New Deal's best mediators, and on the morning of Friday, July 20, he told the press that "I am sanguine that we are going to settle this strike without much more delay."[10] That hope was blasted the same day when a truck full of picketers rammed a produce truck manned by strikebreakers and accompanied by a police convoy armed with shotguns. The police opened fire on the picketers and on the surrounding crowds as well. As strikers ran to help the wounded, an eyewitness said, "They flowed directly into the buckshot fire. . . . And the cops let them have it as they picked up their wounded. Lines of living, solid men fell, broke, wavering." One of the wounded, the witness said, was "stepping on his own intestines, bright and bursting in the street," and another was seen "holding his severed arm in his right hand."[11]

Two men died, and sixty-seven were wounded in the grisly "Battle of Bloody Friday." Governor Olson immediately sent in National Guard troops to help patrol the city's streets, and while Father Haas and the other negotiators continued to work day and night on a possible agreement, both sides remained intransigent until July 26, when the union voted to accept a compromise. The employers, however, goaded and

10. Ibid.
11. Quoted in Zieger, op. cit., p. 34.

threatened by the Citizens Alliance, refused to settle. Olson put the city under martial law and on August 8 played his trump card. President Roosevelt had come to Minnesota to take part in a ceremony honoring William and Charles Mayo, founders of the Mayo Clinic in Rochester, and during a meeting with the president, Olson let it be known, first, that it was the Twin Cities bankers who held the control over the Citizens Alliance and, second, that the Reconstruction Finance Corporation had made $25 million in loans to the local banking community. FDR did not need to know much more. He placed a call to Jesse Jones, director of the RFC. Jones made calls of his own over the next ten days, during which time the possibility that the RFC might just call in its $25 million came up for discussion. On August 19 the Employers Advisory Committee, speaking for 166 employers, accepted another proposal fashioned by Father Haas. The next day, the union voted to endorse the same agreement—and for good reason. Local 574 had won recognition as the workers' bargaining agent, jurisdiction over "inside" workers, rehiring without discrimination against union members, and the binding arbitration of wage increases, overtime, and other matters of dispute. The agreement, union leader Vincent Dunne said, gave the truckers of Minneapolis "substantially what we have fought for and bled for since the beginning of the strike."[12]

Even as the Minneapolis strike was settled, events in San Francisco had pushed the Midwestern city off the front pages. Here, a militant wing of the newly organized local of the International Longshoremen's Association (ILA), an AFL affiliate, had been formed by a group of radical dissidents led by a young and militant Australian-born dockworker named Harry Bridges. As early as September 1933, the radical group had shown its muscle by persuading some 400 dockworkers to walk off the job in a five-day wildcat strike to demonstrate their contempt for the so-called Blue Book union, which was sponsored and controlled by the Waterfront Employers Association.[13]

But in San Francisco, as in the other West Coast ports of Seattle, Tacoma, Los Angeles, and San Pedro, the major issue at hand was the

12. Quoted in Blantz, op. cit.
13. The union got its nickname from the color of the little membership books each worker was required to carry.

"shape-up," a hiring system that forced longshoremen to show up on the docks every morning, hoping to be selected by employer-controlled crew bosses. It was not unlike a slave market, and "a more cruel, graft-ridden and senseless system of hiring could not be devised," declared an ILA publication. "Thousands of men seeking employment were forced to hang around the piers at all hours, exposed to every kind of weather. Often, hundreds would report at a single pier at dawn, stand around for hours, only to be told, 'No work today,' long after there was any chance of obtaining work elsewhere."[14]

Citing the Blue Book union and the shape-up as demonstrable evils, Bridges and his fellow dissidents deposed the San Francisco local's timid president early in 1934. Then, after the Waterfront Employers Association refused to negotiate, they ignored orders from Joseph P. Ryan, the ILA's reactionary and self-indulgent national president in New York ("Next to myself," he was known to remark, "I like silk underwear best"[15]), and on May 9 called some 12,000 dockworkers off the job in every port but Los Angeles (in matters of labor, at least, that city remained far behind the rest). The Maritime Union of the Pacific and the Maritime Workers Industrial Union (MWIU), a TUUL union, joined the strike within hours, while the Teamsters Union vowed not to allow its truckers and wagon drivers to go anywhere near the docks.

Employers took to the courts for the usual rash of injunctions, brought in carloads of strikebreakers, and enlisted the aid of local police to break up picket lines and presumed union meetings wherever they might be found ("Clubs are trumps," it was said, became a motto among San Francisco police—it was an age in which *everybody* played bridge).[16] Workers responded in kind. In Oakland, hundreds of strikers broke through police lines and drove off scores of strikebreakers. In Seattle, a policeman was thrown into Puget Sound when strikers attacked a barge that housed scabs. In Tacoma, 2,000 workers rampaged along the docks, ripped off dock gates and pier doors, and stopped work on eleven ships.

14. Quoted in Bruce Nelson, *Workers on the Waterfront: Seamen, Longshoremen, and Unionism in the 1930s*, p. 106.
15. Quoted in ibid., p. 142.
16. As reported by Mike Quinn in *The Big Strike*, p. 63.

On July 3, after more than six weeks during which time the shipping industry on the entire West Coast had been effectively shut down and the union had rejected settlements offered by negotiators from the National Labor Board, the Waterfront Employers Association in San Francisco moved five cargo trucks onto the Embarcadero with an escort of seven hundred municipal police. "The port is open!" one of them shouted. No, it was not. Thousands of strikers attacked the convoy. "Mounted and foot police swung their clubs and hurled tear-gas bombs," the *New York Times* reported, "strikers hurled bricks and rocks, battered heads with clubs and railroad spikes and smashed windows. . . . Mounted and foot police relentlessly drove the pickets behind . . . freight car barriers. The safety line remained intact but on its fringes pandemonium raged."[17] Twenty-five people, half of them policemen, were hospitalized at the end of the battle.

July 4, the holiday, was quiet, but the struggle intensified the next day, when police used guns, gas, and clubs to disperse clots and bands of strikers and spectators alike, the fighting surging up and down streets and into lanes and alleys all along the waterfront from Pier 38 to the shadow of Telegraph Hill. Here were dozens of square blocks in which the stink of tear gas and vomit gas seeped into nearby warehouses and office buildings and the sound of gunfire, of hoofbeats on cobblestones, of sirens, shouts, and screams rang until nightfall, when eighty-five people were counted among the seriously injured and two were pronounced dead, both of them strikers. Governor Frank Merriam sent in 1,700 National Guard troops that night. "In view of the fact that we are equipped with rifles, bayonets, automatic rifles and machine guns, all high-powered weapons," Colonel R. E. Mittelstaedt explained, "the Embarcadero will not be a safe place for persons whose reasons for being there are not worth the risk of serious injury."[18]

Bridges agreed that there was nothing to be gained by taking on "police, machine guns, and National Guard bayonets," and violence diminished over the next several days.[19] But the unions were not done. On July 14, a mass meeting of representatives from 115 local unions

17. Both quotes in Brecher, op. cit, p. 152.
18. Quoted in "On the Embarcadero," *Time* magazine (July 16, 1934).
19. Quoted in Brecher, op. cit., p. 153.

voted to declare a general strike, and on the following Monday 127,000 Bay Area workers either walked off or did not show up for their jobs. "If you had walked down Market Street in San Francisco last Monday morning," *Time* magazine reported on July 23, "you would have had the uncanny impression that it was still Sunday." For the next four days, no cabs or streetcars were running. Only hotels and hospitals were allowed to stay open. Most offices were closed. All but nineteen restaurants— those "accredited" by the General Strike Committee, like the Eagle Café on the waterfront—were closed down. Most gas stations were closed, only a few being accredited by the committee—and allowed to sell only to those with committee-approved permits, such as doctors. Grocery stores and butchers were closed, and milk and bread deliveries limited, though medical supplies were allowed to be sold and transported. "A private family in San Francisco," *Time* said, "stood a good chance of going hungry if it had not laid in plenty of supplies. Visitors had left the city in droves, for the ferries were still running if you could get to them. . . . The electric supply, telegraph and telephone services were still functioning. The city could talk to itself and to the world, and when night fell there was still light."[20]

The general strike was not well received in the warrens of the New Deal, none of whose social and economic planners had foreseen any such inconvenience. Hugh Johnson, who had come to the Bay Area in the middle of the strike to give one of his standard NRA pep talks at the University of California at Berkeley, was even more livid than usual. He scrapped his prepared remarks and proceeded to savage the general strike. It was, he said, "a threat to the community. It is a menace to government. It is civil war. . . . I am for organized labor . . . but this ugly thing is a blow at the flag of our common country and it has got to stop."[21]

And so it did. After threats of federal intervention and pressure from AFL officials, the General Strike Committee voted by a narrow margin to end the shutdown on July 19, much to the anger of Bridges and other radicals. A week later, ILA members voted by more than four to one to accept federal arbitration on all points in dispute, and in Octo-

20. "Paralysis on the Pacific," *Time* (July 23, 1934).
21. Quoted in Johnson, op cit., p. 323.

ber, when an agreement gave the ILA recognition over the Blue Book union, as well as higher wages, overtime, a five-day, thirty-hour work-week, shared responsibility for hiring, and an end to the hated "shape-up," they accepted it.[22]

SUBSTANTIAL, IF INCOMPLETE, victories in Toledo, Minneapolis, and San Francisco were more than countered that summer by the largest single union failure of the decade, a miscarriage that revealed not only the lev-els of stubbornness that remained among many if not most industry leaders but the inability of the New Deal to do much about it and, per-haps most tellingly, its ambivalent attitude toward organized labor. Caught in the middle were the nearly 350,000 members of the Union of Textile Workers (UTW), and if they were among those most tempted to call the NRA the "National Run-Around," they had their reasons.

So did the industry, for that matter. The blush of success that had followed the signing of the Cotton Textile Code in June 1933 had paled by the spring of 1934. Demand had declined, and prices for finished goods had leveled off, then started falling. At the same time, produc-tion limits and cost increases imposed by the NRA code had driven many mills against the wall again. One estimate had it that between October 1933 and March 1934, hourly earnings increased by 67 per-cent while the number of hours worked dropped by 25 percent; mills were paying more for workers to produce less. Even so, inventories con-tinued to climb as demand fell. In December 1933, in an attempt to lower inventories and, he hoped, encourage a price rise, Hugh Johnson approved an NRA Code Authority recommendation that, for a period of

22. The seamen's unions did not fare so well. Left in the lurch by the ILA's acceptance of the strike agreement, both the conservative Maritime Union of the Pacific and the TUUL's Maritime Workers Industrial Union were forced to return to work with noth-ing gained but the preservation of their jobs. Ironically, Harry Bridges had accepted the help of the Communist union cheerfully and never disavowed the relationship. This, together with his own radical bent, left him open to the charge that he was a card-carrying member of the CP/USA. He denied it and would go on denying it, but the charge was revived on a regular basis until the 1970s, when, after he joined the board of the San Francisco Port Authority as an equal to Cyril Magnin and other noted capitalists (some of whom had been around during the days of the big strike), it no longer seemed to matter all that much.

at least ninety days, mill hours should be cut from eighty to sixty hours per week in two thirty-hour shifts. There would be no increase in wages to compensate the workers for the fact that their freshly won weekly pay increases would be reduced by 25 percent.[23]

The curtailment, imposed once again in May 1934, did no good for the industry, where prices continued to fall and the profits it had enjoyed in the summer months of 1933 dropped as fast as they had risen. While many in the industry still believed that the code remained "an absolutely indispensable part" of manufacturing, as the editor of *Textile World* put it, most southern mill owners grew increasingly disenchanted.[24] They had accepted the notion of government interference reluctantly at best, and now they began to resent it actively. In most mills, the "stretch-out" continued, as did antiunion activities. Workers were fired for attempting to organize their mills, and company officials either refused to recognize the UTW out of hand or dismissed its membership claims as fabrications. Meanwhile the NRA, through a special three-member body called the Cotton Textile National Industrial Relations Board, which met infrequently and was stacked against organized labor, adjudicated complaints slowly, inconsistently, and without muscle and, finally—to the growing anger of the rank and file—refused to actively back the UTW as the collective bargaining agent for the industry.

Most mill workers had invested considerable hope in the Textile Code. "The laboring people here are trying to uphold our President and also the code," one woman wrote Frances Perkins from Charlotte, North Carolina. "We believe in it—We talk it—And we would so love to live it."[25] But for her and many others, it became increasingly clear that they could expect nothing substantial from either the board or Washington. For a time, union officials tried to walk the thin line between direct action and negotiation through the NRA, but beginning in July a rash of wildcat strikes spread across Alabama, involving perhaps 20,000 mill workers, many of them union members who refused all requests from their national leaders to go back to work. Finally, more

23. For all figures, and background, see Hodges, op. cit., pp. 56–57.
24. Quoted in ibid., p. 78.
25. Quoted in Hall, Korstad, and Leloudis, op. cit.

than 500 delegates met in New York City for a special union convention in mid-August 1934. "Unless we arouse ourselves from the
lethargy now prevailing," UTW president Thomas McMahon told them,
"the NRA, if allowed to function in the future, will become a plaything
for the manufacturers."[26] But it was from the floor, not the dais, that the
demand for an industry-wide strike came, and it was the delegates on
the floor who voted for such a resolution with only ten dissenting votes
on August 16. Now, McMahon declared, "President Roosevelt is the
only man on God's green earth who can stop the strike."[27]

On the advice of Perkins, who insisted that the National Labor
Relations Board could quickly adjudicate a settlement, Roosevelt did
not intervene directly. Perkins was wrong. On September 1 the strike
was launched. Within two weeks, somewhere between 350,000 and
400,000 cotton, woolen, and silk textile workers were on strike in
scores of mill towns scattered from the Deep South to New England. It
was the largest single-industry strike in American history up to that
time, and one of the most violent—not merely because of single vicious
encounters similar to those in Toledo, Minneapolis, and San Francisco
but because of the widespread character of the conflict.

The strike ostensibly was directed by Francis Gorman, a vice president of the UTW, who instructed locals to hold firm to the union's
goals—"Shorter hours! Higher wages! Reduce the working load! Recognize the union!"[28]—and recommended that strikers organize themselves
into "flying squadrons," wonderfully effective phenomena described by
the New York Times on September 5:

> Moving with the speed and force of a mechanized army, thousands
> of pickets in trucks and automobiles scurried about the countryside
> in the Carolinas, visiting mill towns and villages and compelling
> the closing of the plants. . . . strikers in groups ranging from 200 to
> 1,000 assembled about mills and demanded that they be closed. . . .
>
> The speed of the pickets in their motor cavalcades and their sur-
> prise descent on point after point makes it difficult to follow their

26. Quoted in ibid., p. 98.
27. Quoted in ibid., p. 99.
28. Quoted in Hodges, op. cit., p. 105.

movements and makes impossible any adequate preparation by mill owners or local authorities to meet them.

To mill owners and the local authorities, historian Jonathan Daniels remembered four years later, "Those cars and lines of cars were something new and strange, wicked and terrifying." But for the workers, the flying squadrons evoked a kind of freedom. "It was good to be young then," he wrote, "good to go in tumultuous crowds and shout at the fence of the Old Man's House, good to climb into Fords and rush across counties to join other familiar-unfamiliar young people in clamoring at the mesh wire of mill gates"—even though, as he added, "governors and mill owners played at the equally dangerous and exciting business of exerting simple force."[29]

The resulting violence was notable, a destructive, unpredictable, and bloody eruption of rage over which the union exercised virtually no control, even though Gorman and other union leaders tried manfully to persuade picketers to slow things down and at one point even repudiated the flying squadrons, claiming that the union had had nothing to do with them. Nothing worked. Skirmishes broke out up and down the eastern seaboard like firecrackers on a string. In dozens of towns, localized strikes became citywide riots, and riots became full-scale battles between police and National Guard troops and strikers wielding the usual assortment of clubs, brickbats, and cobblestones (though some strikers used guns, and women strikers in Lancaster, Pennsylvania, were said to have employed hatpins), seizing mill buildings, destroying machinery, beating scabs, looting and burning. Meanwhile the authorities responded with bayonets, tear gas, vomit gas, buckshot, and bullets, declared martial law here, and initiated mass arrests there. Overall, at least thirteen people were killed in Georgia and the Carolinas, and scores seriously injured throughout the textile states (in Hosea Path, South Carolina, alone, seven strikers were killed by deputies and armed strikebreakers).[30]

The strikers put on a good show, but as on the waterfront of San Francisco, it was no contest, and by the middle of September, National

29. Jonathan Daniels, *A Southerner Discovers the South*, p. 26.
30. For an especially good account of strike violence, see Brecher, op. cit., pp. 168–76.

Guard units had been able to suppress most of the turbulence. Mills that had closed when the strikes began (in South Carolina, at least 100 mills had been shut down) reopened with nonunion labor, much of it made up of workers who had joined the strike but not the union. The industry, led by George Sloan, president of the Cotton Textile Institute, refused to bargain with anyone, and while Gorman and the UTW continued to issue brave pronouncements, union membership began to slide and the strike to disintegrate.

Public support for the strike, at first fairly strong, had been severely undercut by the level of violence, which had especially appalled the Roosevelt administration. Hugh Johnson, for one, never silent on such matters, declared that the strike "was pulled in contravention of the solemn arrangements" that had led to the code agreement of June 1933 and went on to lay responsibility on the Socialists.[31] Roosevelt himself made no such claim, but on September 5, not long after the strike began, he had appointed a special commission to investigate the industry's labor problems. On September 20 the commission made its recommendations. Mainly, it called for a lot of study: a newly created Textile Labor Relations Board would initiate a study of workloads and working conditions, the Federal Trade Commission would study production capacity, and the Department of Labor would study wage practices and differentials. On the strength of this, Roosevelt asked the UTW to call off the strike. On September 22, the union complied, its executive council sturdily claiming that "the union has won an overwhelming victory" and that "we now go forth in a triumphant campaign of organization."[32]

This was face-saving nonsense. The union had won nothing, and the industry had been forced to concede nothing. The stretch-out continued, mills refused to deal with union locals, those suspected of union activity were systematically fired and blacklisted, union membership declined, and the government did nothing. "When the people here went back into their jobs," Ruby Brown wrote FDR from Greenwood, South Carolina, on November 5, 1934, "many of them were discharge [sic] . . . because they joined a union. . . . [The] managers by discharging

31. Quoted in Hodges, p. 114.
32. Quoted in ibid., p. 115.

our strongest union members therefore broke up our local union, caus-
ing the rest of us to submit to them to hold a job."[33]

From the White House in response came little more than the sound
of paper being shuffled.

MORE THAN A year of organization and sometimes murderous confrontation after passage of the NIRA had swelled labor union membership,
created new unions, and won at least a few notable victories—all of
which had given the movement an almost mystical character for many
people. Meridel LeSueur walked into union headquarters in the middle
of the Minneapolis strike as a witness and reporter for the *New Masses*.
Unwilling to maintain the role of dispassionate observer, the unabashedly
radical LeSueur immediately began working with other women in the
big kitchen—washing dishes, handing out cups of coffee, and, finally,
"dabbing alcohol on the gaping wounds that buckshot makes, hanging
open like crying mouths," finding herself part of something she celebrated as "a strange powerful trance of movement *together*," a silent
bonding that drew the workers "into a close and glowing cohesion like a
powerful conflagration in the midst of the city. And it filled me with
fear and awe and at the same time hope."[34]

While few of them shared LeSueur's Communist leanings, much
less her delicate literary sensibilities, the movement's rank and file
would have understood her words precisely. Like soldiers in any war,
most remembered these months of solidarity and hope for the rest of
their lives with a mixture of sorrow, anger, and pride, passing the stories
down the years and investing everything with a Pentecostal zeal that
would color labor's memory of the era with a kind of joy. "The very air
was tonic," labor historians Richard O. Boyer and Herbert M. Morais
would write twenty years later of the passion common to these times—
and still powerful in recollection: "Courage was contagious. It multi-
plied by the industry and city, by the shop, by the county and the
state. . . . It was good to be alive. . . . It was good to release in triumphant

33. Quoted in Hall, Korstad, and Leloudis, op. cit.
34. Meridel LeSueur, "I Was Marching," *New Masses* (September 18, 1934).

mass action the long-pent-up bitterness, the helplessness, the defeats, the humiliations, not only of the depression but of the generations."[35]

Passion was not enough, however. Labor's day would arrive, but it was clear by the end of 1934 that it had not come with passage of the National Industrial Recovery Act. Perhaps the most difficult obstacles lay in the Roosevelt administration. For all their liberal credentials, most of the New Dealers were informed by middle-class certitudes that showed little sympathy for the working class. Like the Progressives who preceded them, who largely disavowed militant labor as just one side of an extremist coin on the other side of which resided equally reprehensible industrial plutocrats, the New Dealers demonstrated little real understanding of what motivated working men and women. "It is hard to find anybody in [the New Deal]," Edmund Wilson insisted, "who, even from a journalist's experience, knows anything of the way that the American world looks and feels to labor. . . . [The] point of view of human beings who want to eat, keep dry and warm, give their children some education and have some chance to enjoy their lives—in a word, of American citizens who want ordinary American rights."[36]

Unionism was a right, industry could be stubborn and oppressive, and strikes were sometimes necessary—all of this most of the New Dealers were ready to admit. Still, as the sad ending to the textile strikes of 1934 demonstrated with particular force, the Roosevelt administration would never quite be ready to grant unionized workers a genuinely equal place at the table of democracy. The administration was a good deal more comfortable with the idea of the working man and woman finding a place at the table of government jobs, where the hated dole could be avoided and the simple dignity of work might provide both self-esteem and at least a margin of security.

35. Richard O. Boyer and Herbert M. Morais, *Labor's Untold Story*, p. 291.
36. Wilson, op. cit., p. 561.

11

The Machinery of Pride

When his mother told him she was going to take some of the money she made at her part-time job as a cigar-roller to buy him a suit, eighteen-year-old Steve Hatalla Jr. put his head down on the kitchen table and cried. "I'm no good," he said. "I make no money. I got nothing—and you go without so I have a suit."[1] It was early 1935 in Harrisburg, Pennsylvania, and the family had been going without for a long time by then. Counting all income from all sources, the six Hatallas had been living on an average of fifty dollars a month for four years. The golden dream of possibility that had brought his father, Steve Sr., to America from Zagreb, Croatia, in 1909 and his mother, Mary, from Romania in 1911 had been dimmed to the point of extinction.

When the couple met and married in 1916, Steve was working as a boilermaker in the shops of the Pennsylvania Railroad, a job he held for more than five years. In 1919, he went to work as a stonemason for the city's largest construction company. He was a hard worker and learned

1. The Hatalla family's story was told in "Family on Relief," *Fortune* (February 1936).

his trade well, and was soon placed in charge of work crews. In his best years, he made anywhere from forty to sixty dollars a week, extraordinarily good money for a working man in those days. By 1923, Steve and his wife had saved up enough to take out a mortgage on half of a good double house, with schools, shops, and a streetcar line all nearby. Taking full advantage of installment buying, they purchased such luxuries as a console radio, a player piano, a gas stove, and a washing machine. In 1925—just a year after the anti-alien Johnson-Reed Act all but eliminated further immigration from his homeland (by then a part of Hungary)—Steve Hatalla became an American citizen.

Then on November 12, 1931, Steve was called into the office of the construction company and told he was being laid off—not fired, just laid off. There was not enough work. When things got better, he would be rehired in a minute, he was told. Things never did get better, and Hatalla and his family entered a labyrinth of survival that was no less agonizing for the fact that the journey was shared by so many millions. Steve cashed in his insurance policies, took out a small personal loan, looked for whatever work he could find. Mary went back to her own old trade, cigar-making, whenever part-time work was available, and was hired to clean the Magyar Baptist Church once a week. It was not enough. In October 1932, Steve applied for relief and got a five-dollar weekly food order redeemable at the corner grocery store.

For nine weeks in the summer of 1933, Steve was hired as a construction worker for $24.75 a week and was able to pay off some of his mounting debts. Then, it was back on the relief rolls, this time those of the state office of the Federal Emergency Relief Administration. In February 1934, he dropped off the FERA rolls and went to work as foreman of a highway grading crew in the Civil Works Administration. When the CWA was discontinued, he was back on relief, a situation that would be alleviated by intermittent periods of employment with those few FERA work relief programs that continued after the CWA's demise. Earlier in 1934, the mortgage company had foreclosed on the house but allowed the family to stay on for twenty dollars a month. When Steve fell behind on the rent, the company carried the Hatallas until the beginning of March 1935, then forcibly evicted them. The family moved into a tiny frame cottage without an indoor bathroom. The older daughter, Margaret, went to work as a live-in domestic for five dollars a week. Young Steve dropped out of high school and looked for a job. When he could find nothing, he applied to the Civilian Conservation Corps, but the CCC turned him down because of a recurring ear infection.

It was at this juncture in the family's life that the boy burst into tears at his mother's offer to buy him a suit. Then, on October 22, 1935, Steve's father once again became a working ward of the federal government as Works Progress Administration case no. 4422-2755, assigned to WPA project no. 1991—the construction of an underground tunnel between two buildings at the state insane hospital. The pay was eighty-five dollars a month. It was not even half as much as he had made during his best years, and when a reporter for *Fortune* magazine found him in November, Steve could still speak with bitterness about the rich people he believed had brought him and his kind so low. "And where do the rich men get their money?" he asked the room at large, slapping his knee in what was obviously an old angry ritual. "From the poor people," his younger son Lewis answered dutifully while lying on his stomach, idly turning the pages of a magazine. Still, the government job gave Steve back at least some measure of pride; the eighty-five dollars a month would put food on his family's table and keep a roof over their heads, and Steve was not even tempted to return to the old country—"Worse times here is better than best times there, you bet," he said firmly.

IF THERE WAS one thing the New Dealers knew how to do by the middle of the decade, for all the frailties, inconsistencies, and overwrought ambition of many of their schemes, it was how to put people on the government payroll. Interior Secretary Harold L. Ickes had been doing it since the summer of 1933 as administrator of the Public Works Administration and would continue to do so until the PWA was phased out in 1939. In all but three of the nation's 3,073 counties, there would be at least one PWA construction project—583 municipal water systems, 368 street and highway projects, 622 sewage systems, 263 hospitals, and 522 schools, including replacements for those destroyed in the great earthquake of 1933 in Long Beach, California. The PWA loaned $200 million to railroads for improvements to roadbeds and the construction of yard facilities, including $80 million to electrify the Pennsylvania Railroad on its New York–Washington route. Atlantic Beach, Florida, got a seawall; Port Heuneme, California, got massive new dock facilities; the Chicago Sanitary District got a $42 million waste treatment complex; Virginia State College for Negroes got a $2 million expansion; Santa Fe, New Mexico, got a new courthouse and so did Kalamazoo, Michigan; and slums were torn down in Atlanta and Indianapolis and low-rent housing erected in their place. In New York City, the Queens-Midtown Tunnel would cross under the East River and the Lincoln Tunnel would cross under the Hudson, both financed with PWA money, while the Harlem Houses and the Williamsburg Houses would rise as the largest black housing projects in the country. PWA bridges crossed the Mississippi River at Baton Rouge, Louisiana, and Davenport, Iowa, and the concrete piers for the Oakland–San Francisco Bay Bridge were poured with PWA money. Elsewhere in the West, tens of millions of dollars were helping to finance huge river basin projects on the Colorado, Columbia, Missouri, and Sacramento Rivers. By 1935, the PWA claimed to be providing an average of 500,000 jobs per year—and, if one looked at it correctly, Ickes said, the real numbers were even higher. "If we use the very conservative average figure of three indirect for every one on direct employment," he wrote, "the reckoning is that PWA has kept approximately two million persons at normal productive work."[2]

The secretary was publicizing such figures with so much vigor because by then he and his PWA were locked in sweaty bureaucratic combat over work relief funds with Harry Hopkins at the Works Progress Administration, the oddly named federal relief agency that had come to the rescue of Steve Hatalla and his family in October 1935.[3] The new agency's creation in the spring of that year lay at the heart of what came to be called the Second New Deal, when a spate of economic and social legislation to rival that of the Hundred Days of 1933 erupted from the administration and Congress, both of which

2. Harold L. Ickes, *Back to Work: The Story of the PWA*, p. 200. This is the source for my PWA figures.
3. The WPA's name, which Hopkins hated, had been suggested by FDR, though to the day of his death Ickes believed that Hopkins had come up with it so that the public would confuse its initials with those of his own—presumably superior—agency.

believed that they had been given marching orders by the voters in the midterm congressional elections of November 1934.

Ordinarily, the party in power tends to lose congressional seats during midterm elections. Not in 1934: more than 32 million Americans went to the polls that November—more than in any previous midterm election in American history—and the 17.4 million votes for Democratic congressional candidates over 13.5 million for Republicans, constituted the widest midterm margin ever recorded. In the House, the Republicans lost fourteen seats and the Democrats gained nine, giving them a majority of 322 to 103—as well as a few on-again, off-again allies among the handful of Progressives and Farmer-Laborites who also had gained seats. In the Senate, the Democrats increased their number to sixty-nine seats, giving them a three-quarters majority, never achieved before and never equaled since by either party. Meanwhile, state elections gave the Democrats thirty-nine governorships and the Republicans only seven. "There has been no such popular endorsement since the days of Thomas Jefferson and Andrew Jackson," William Randolph Hearst wrote.[4] He was wrong. There had never been such a popular endorsement—period.

Time would prove this legislative majority to be something less than cohesive when it came to matters of policy and legislation, but for the moment the New Dealers would operate as if they owned the 74th Congress. "Boys—this is our hour," Hopkins reportedly told a carful of colleagues while they were on the way to a racetrack outside Laurel, Maryland, shortly after the election. "We've got to get everything we want—a works program, social security, wages and hours, everything—now or never. Get your minds to work on developing a complete ticket to provide security for all the folks of this country up and down and across the board."[5] Still, Hopkins and his companions were inspired by more than just their belief that they had been beatified by the elections of 1934. An increasingly radical and often confusing grassroots political climate that almost certainly had helped to swell the number of voters that November was giving the New Dealers a sense of urgency not unlike that which haunted them during the early months of 1933. There were,

4. Quoted in Davis, op. cit., p. 422.
5. Quoted in Robert E. Sherwood, *Roosevelt and Hopkins: An Intimate History*, p. 65.

for example, the fulminations of a quartet of political messiahs whose colorful agitations were as easy to ridicule as they proved impossible for millions of Americans, including the New Dealers, to ignore.

FRANCIS TOWNSEND WAS a neurasthenic sixty-six-year-old Long Beach doctor who found himself especially affected by the plight of old people during the first years of the depression. "I discussed the situation with my medical confreres," he remembered, "and gave it as my opinion that unless we could do something to raise the morale of the hopeless old ones of the community and relight their extinguished candles of hope, there would soon be no old folks left, and no young folks would ever want to grow old."[6] The doctor spent some time thinking about what could be done, then put together a solution "with all the self-confidence of a country doctor preparing to remove an appendix on the kitchen table of a South Dakota shanty," as John Franklin Carter put it in 1935.[7] What the doctor came up with was the Old-Age Revolving Pension Plan, soon known simply as the Townsend Plan. He had calculated that the gross sales receipts of business and industry in the United States amounted to $935 billion annually. A sales tax of only a little over 2 percent on that amount would provide some $20 billion, which would be enough to give every person in the country who was sixty years old or older the sum of $200 a month. Those receiving the $200 pension would be required to spend it all each month on goods and services, thus initiating a perpetual cycle of getting and spending that would prime the pump of prosperity as it had never been primed before.

Like most such magical schemes, the Townsend Plan was simple enough to be understood by anyone, particularly those who did not want to bother their minds with the facts that, for several reasons, the sales tax could never garner as much as predicted, or that it could reduce actual individual income by as much as 40 percent, or that administrative costs would be grotesque.[8] The popularity of the plan—which

6. Francis Townsend, *New Horizons (An Autobiography)*, edited by Jesse George Murray, p. 135.
7. John Franklin Carter (The Unofficial Observer), *American Messiahs*, p. 79.
8. A good analysis of the plan can be found in David H. Bennett, *Demagogues in the Depression: American Radicals and the Union Party, 1932–1936*, pp. 156–62.

Townsend first offered in a letter to the "People's Forum" column of the *Long Beach Press-Telegram* on September 30, 1933—was immediate and only grew when the inexperienced and uncharismatic doctor, who was thin to the point of emaciation and looked more like a victim than a savior, had the wits to hire a masterful real estate promoter—that definitive California profession—to boost the program. The promoter, Earl Clements, incorporated the cause as Old-Age Revolving Pensions, Ltd., in January 1934, then organized a series of open-air meetings, beginning in San Diego, one of the most popular destinations for elderly middle-class refugees from the travails of midwestern winters. The city's old people "flocked to the doctor's movement like pilgrims entering a holy city," according to a not entirely sympathetic 1936 study, and by doing so revealed that "the Townsend Plan was not a cause but a religion."[9] Clements also sent out hundreds of thousands of leaflets, planted magazine articles, generated national newspaper coverage, and started *The Townsend National Weekly*, the whole promotion financed by twenty-five-cent membership dues collected in "Townsend Clubs" that began popping up everywhere. By the end of 1934, the Townsend pension-plan movement had grown to more than 5,000 clubs with about 2 million members and had become a national political force.

Then there was Upton Sinclair, who managed to scare the daylights out of mainstream Democrats and conservative Republicans alike in 1934. In September 1933, the widely read novelist and Socialist reformer—best known for *The Jungle*, a novel about the Chicago meatpacking industry—had changed his registration from Socialist to Democratic and announced his candidacy for the Democratic nomination for governor of California. In a self-published fantasy called *I, Governor of California, and How I Ended Poverty: A True Story of the Future*, he outlined what he called EPIC—End Poverty in California. Its motto was "Production for Use," and it called for the state to establish a graduated income tax. With that funding, it was to rent or purchase idle factories and other industrial concerns that had been shut down by the depression. These resuscitated businesses would be put into the hands

9. Quoted in Jackson K. Putnam, *Old-Age Politics in California: From Richardson to Reagan*, p. 59.

of the unemployed, who would use them to manufacture the goods they needed to provide a decent life. Furthermore, the state would buy, warehouse, and distribute all agricultural products, which would then be traded to the factory workers for the goods they produced. The state would also impose a 10 percent tax on undeveloped vacant land to finance the creation of cooperative "land colonies," where workers would manufacture goods and grow their own food (an echo of Henry George's "Single Tax" proposal in the nineteenth century). The whole system would be tied together by money issued in the form of scrip, and in time the cooperative businesses operated by the state and the workers would prove so superior to all for-profit concerns that capitalism would die a natural death.

Sinclair's ideas were as swiftly seized upon as those of Francis Townsend, and his book sold more than 100,000 copies within weeks. Unlike Townsend, Sinclair may have been his own best publicist; as a speaker and a promoter, he was charming, witty, capable, and knew the arts of promotion. He started up a newspaper called *EPIC News*, and it soon reached a circulation of 1.4 million. He encouraged the formation of EPIC clubs, many of them originating in the self-help cooperative associations that had proliferated in the early years of the decade, and within months there were 2,000 of them. He traveled up and down the state, giving speeches, inviting interviews, holding rallies, while cheerfully exploiting his many friendships in the literary and film worlds; Theodore Dreiser became an outspoken supporter; so did John Dos Passos, Charlie Chaplin, James Cagney, and Dorothy Parker. And in August 1934, Sinclair walked away from the state convention in Sacramento with the Democratic nomination in the pocket of one of the white suits he habitually wore, beginning one of the most closely followed political campaigns in American history.

Many Roosevelt Democrats found the candidate's ideas horrifying and urged the president to repudiate Sinclair, but Roosevelt refused. "Perhaps they'll get EPIC in California," he said to Labor Secretary Frances Perkins at one point. "What difference, I ask you, would that make in Dutchess County, New York, or Lincoln County, Maine? The beauty of our state-federal system is that the people can experiment. If it has fatal consequences in one place, it has little effect upon the rest of the country. If a new, apparently fanatical program works well, it will be copied. If it doesn't, you won't hear of it again."[10] At the same time, FDR could not openly support Sinclair without getting tarred by the brush of his ideas. The candidate courted Roosevelt for his endorsement assiduously during a visit to Hyde Park in September, but the president dipped into his bottomless well of charm, managing to placate Sinclair without actually saying anything one way or the other. The endorsement never would come, though Sinclair persuaded himself that it was imminent right up to the eve of the election.

There was no ambivalence at all among conservatives, of course. In their view, Sinclair was just a Socialist wolf hiding in the sheep's clothing of a Democrat, and it would be difficult to find anything short of communism itself that could infuriate Republicans—particularly California Republicans—more thoroughly than the protocols of the EPIC plan. They seized every resource that money could buy to defeat it. The campaign, brilliantly orchestrated by Clem Whitaker, founder of the pioneering political firm of Campaigns, Inc., and Don Francisco, head of the West Coast office of the Lord & Thomas advertising company, was designed less to raise up the Republican candidate, incumbent Frank Merriam, than to bury Sinclair, and it set standards of slander, deceit, and calumny not equaled until the age of television politics. Louis B. Mayer and Irving Thalberg donated the services of MGM to produce a series of fraudulent "newsreels" showing California inundated by freight-riding bums seeking EPIC handouts and scraggly-bearded Bolsheviks spouting praise for Sinclair. Every newspaper of note in the state saturated its pages with anti-Sinclair material. Virtually every radio station blared misinformation regularly, while billboards all over the state were slathered with ridicule and artful lies.

However efficiently run, this profoundly negative media campaign almost failed. In spite of abdication on the part of the Roosevelt Democrats and the splenetic efforts of the California Republicans, Sinclair might still have won had it not been for the candidacy of Raymond

10. Quoted in Greg Mitchell, *The Campaign of the Century: Upton Sinclair's Race for Governor of California and the Birth of Media Politics*, p. 258. This authoritative and rollicking account is my main source for the Sinclair campaign.

Haight, a Progressive, whose 302,000 votes may well have concealed enough to offset Sinclair's margin of defeat—260,000 votes. Sinclair, not without humor, soon explained all in yet another book, *I, Candidate for Governor, and How I Got Licked*, while Republicans congratulated themselves and most Democrats outside California heaved sighs of relief.

If nothing else, the EPIC campaign had provided the public with a political entertainment in the grand manner. So did Huey Long, another loose cannon who was giving the Roosevelt Democrats cause for worry in 1934 and 1935. Bumptious, crafty, ambitious, and more than a little corrupt, the down-home Populist senator from Louisiana was not satisfied with running his state as if it were an island kingdom and he the political monarch; he wanted to be president of the United States and unabashedly let the world know it. He may have been a demagogue, but like most successful demagogues, his political genius derived from a deep understanding of the fears and desires of ordinary people; unlike most demagogues, however, Long truly sympathized with his people and harbored an erratic but probably genuine determination to help them—though not without making sure he was helping himself as well (in his mind, the two goals probably were inseparable).

Long, too, had a plan. His was called Share Our Wealth, and its motto was "Every Man a King" (also the title of Long's 1933 autobiography). It was an income tax plan designed to redistribute wealth, and he outlined its essentials in a Senate speech on March 14, 1934: "Every man a king,"

> so there would be no such thing as a man or woman who did not have the necessities of life. . . .
>
> We have to limit fortunes. Our present plan is that we will allow no one man to own more than $50 million. . . . It may be necessary that we limit it to less than $50 million. . . . Be that as it may, it will still be more than any one man, or any one man and his children and their children, will be able to spend in their lifetimes.[11]

11. Quoted in Henry M. Christman, ed., *Kingfish to America: Share Our Wealth: Selected Senatorial Papers of Huey P. Long*, p. 42.

Ten months later, Long refined his plan, recommending a graduated tax structure that would become more punitive with every million dollars of income an individual might have, until everyone would be limited to about three million dollars in total liquid wealth (and no more than one million dollars could be earned in a single year). The taxes collected through this system would be distributed, after government expenses were met, in outright grants to the unemployed in order to keep them living in a decent manner until jobs became available; in guaranteed wages for the working class to enable them to own their own homes and buy all the conveniences; in educational grants to build new schools and hire new teachers; and in old-age pensions for anyone over sixty. In a final bit of manna, he promised that "until we could straighten things out—and we can straighten things out in two months under our program—we would grant a moratorium on all debts which people owe that they cannot pay."[12]

Two months to salvation were an appealing prospect, and by the time this statement appeared in *The Congressional Record*, the Share Our Wealth movement had already become a phenomenon, spreading through most of the southern states and even into such distant areas as California, Minnesota, and New York, thanks to the magic of radio, on which the senator's raspy holler could be heard on a regular basis. Long's supporters were claiming that by April 1935 the senator's office was getting 60,000 letters a week and that more than 27,000 Share Our Wealth clubs had been formed with at least 4.6 million members, with much of the growth the work of Share Our Wealth advocate Gerald L. K. Smith, an itinerant Disciples of Christ minister whose oratorical skills were nearly a match for those of Long himself. "Let's pull down these huge piles of gold until there should be a real job," he would shout in evangelical fervor before crowds of country folk, "not a little old sow-belly, black-eyed pea job but a real spending money, beefsteak and gravy, Chevrolet, Ford in the garage, new suit, Thomas Jefferson, Jesus Christ, red, white, and blue job for every man!"[13]

12. Quoted in ibid., p. 53.
13. Quoted in T. Harry Williams, *Huey Long: A Biography*, p. 700. This is the source for most of my treatment of the Long story.

While the numbers Long's people claimed probably were exaggerated and while most of Share Our Wealth's membership was confined to the South, the movement was yet another political threat with which the New Dealers would have to deal. If Long's chances of ever attaining the Democratic nomination in 1936—much less winning the election—were slim to none, many feared that the three or four million votes he probably could command as an independent candidate might prevent Roosevelt from getting the majority needed to beat a strong Republican opponent. Long might also use those potential votes to broker himself a vice presidency. Neither possibility pleased the president, who may have held to a hands-off policy with regard to Upton Sinclair but was not about to do the same with Long. FDR wrote a friend early in 1935 that Americans were "jumpy and ready to run after strange gods," and warned his people in the Cabinet: "Don't put anybody in and don't help anybody that is working for Huey Long or his crowd: that is a hundred per cent!"[14]

Long enjoyed himself immensely through all of this, not least when he sat down in the spring of 1935 and started dictating a Sinclair-like fantasy, entitled *My First Days in the White House.* Among other gleeful tidbits, he pictured himself appointing Franklin Roosevelt secretary of the navy and Alfred E. Smith director of the budget shortly after his inauguration, both of which appointments were swiftly confirmed by the Senate. "I then retired to the second floor of the White House proper and went to a study overlooking the avenue," Long wrote. "I could see the marching throngs parading happily up and down that historic street."[15]

The senator would never see those imagined throngs—or even the published book in which he had imagined them. On September 8, 1935, a doctor, for reasons and under circumstances still not fully understood, shot Long in the abdomen while the senator was striding with his bodyguards through the rotunda of the state capitol in Baton Rouge. The doctor was immediately shot to ribbons by Long's bodyguards; the senator died two days later from internal bleeding.[16]

14. Ibid., p. 795.
15. Huey Pierce Long, *My First Days in the White House,* p. 8.
16. For differing accounts of Long's death, see David Zinman, *The Day Huey Long Was Shot: September 8, 1935* and T. Harry Williams, op. cit., pp. 848–76. Williams believes

Even before Long had refined his Share Our Wealth scheme into a potential run at the presidency, one of the most popular and least likely political demagogues in American history had come up with his own redistribution plan. His name was Charles Edward Coughlin, and he was a Catholic priest from an obscure parish in suburban Detroit who between 1926 and 1935 had transformed a modest weekly broadcast of the mass on Detroit's WJR into a pulpit from which he preached to millions of listeners through his own national network. Most Americans did not like Catholics much. Anti-Catholic feelings had run strong in this country for generations, rising up most recently during the brief reign of the Ku Klux Klan in the Midwest during the 1920s, and voters had rejected Alfred E. Smith in 1928 not least because of vague fears among many that if Smith were elected president, the pope would become an invisible power behind the presidency. But millions of otherwise solidly Protestant Americans venerated Father Coughlin. Broadcast pioneer Frank Stanton, who said that Coughlin had "the greatest voice of the twentieth century," remembered growing up in a Dayton, Ohio, neighborhood that was "probably anti-Catholic. Very white, Anglo-Saxon Protestant." But his family and most of their neighbors listened to Coughlin avidly. No one that he knew, Stanton remembered, brought up "the Church issue at all with Coughlin. . . . He seemed to reach out and break that barrier down. Radio broke it down."[17]

The popularity of his broadcasts had inspired Coughlin to create the Radio League of the Little Flower, after the name of his Royal Oaks church, the Shrine of the Little Flower. Coughlin was soon receiving at least 80,000 letters a week—and in some weeks hundreds of thousands—many of them containing donations that ultimately amounted to $5 million a year, making his little church one of the richest parishes in the nation. Coughlin therefore was a force to be reckoned with as early as 1932, and Roosevelt was gratified that the "radio priest" had

---

his death was a deliberate assassination by a disaffected Louisianan involved in a conspiracy; Zinman discounts the conspiracy theory and thinks it could just as well have been a spur-of-the-moment act following an argument—or even a possibility that one of Long's bodyguards, in his frenzy to gun the young man down, might have fired the bullet that killed the "Kingfish."

17. Quoted in Donald Warren, *Radio Priest: Charles Coughlin, the Father of Hate Radio,* p. 26.

thrown his considerable weight behind FDR's campaign and continued
to support him during the early months of the New Deal, calling it
"Christ's Deal," and at one point writing the president to say "that
unless you are a success, I can never be considered one."[18]

But Coughlin had a few prejudices of his own. One of these was a
lurid hatred of Wall Street as an institution and financiers as individuals—particularly bankers, most of whom, he hinted darkly and regularly, were Jews or in the control of Jews. "Oh rob, steal, exploit
and break your fellow citizens," he shouted to these imagined villains
in one radio jeremiad. "Every time you lift a lash of oppression you
are lashing Christ!"[19] The key to getting America out of the clutches of
the bankers, he believed, was to make more money and make it more
available to everyone. And the best way to do this, he had decided,
was to remonetize silver, a policy that Secretary of the Treasury
Henry Morgenthau thoroughly opposed, although Coughlin apparently
believed that FDR himself supported the idea. Legislation to remonetize silver was under consideration in Congress by early 1934, and
Coughlin, blindly confident of the president's sentiments, boomed out
his support of it. "Why restore silver as an auxiliary basic money?"
he asked during a broadcast on March 11 that was reminiscent of
William Jennings Bryan's famous "Cross of Gold" speech in 1896. "The
answer is simple. It is this: It will help the manufacturers of this country. It will help the laboring man of this country. . . . And, finally,
it will be the next logical step towards freeing the human race from
the curse of gold."[20] What Coughlin did not tell his listeners was the
fact that the treasurer of the Shrine of the Little Flower had begun
using church funds to buy silver certificates, a development that came
to light only when Secretary of the Treasury Henry Morgenthau published a list of major silver certificate holders in April in an attempt to
expose the self-interest of the silver bill's advocates. The church treasurer's name was on Morgenthau's list, and the connection to Coughlin
was swiftly unearthed by the press, giving his support of remonetiza-
tion a distinct taint.

18. Quoted in Bennett, op. cit., p. 38.
19. Quoted in ibid., p. 49.
20. Charles E. Coughlin, *Eight Lectures on Labor, Capital and Justice*, p. 113.

Coughlin was infuriated by what he considered a direct attack on him by the administration. "Mr. Henry Morgenthau Jr. has completed his clumsy effort to protect the gold advocates," he bellowed, going on to claim that the secretary's actions had been "for the benefit of the one billion Orientals who from time immemorial have identified their trade and commerce with Gentile silver" (the term "Orientals," of course, was a commonly used code word for "Jews" among anti-Semites who pretended to respectability).[21] From that point on, Coughlin's support of the president grew thinner, and by the end of 1934 the priest was openly criticizing Roosevelt and his people as often as he was praising them.

LONG MAY HAVE been shot and Sinclair defeated, but Townsend and Coughlin were both alive and flourishing, and the levels of radical discontent their millions of supporters illustrated lay like a shadow over the New Dealers as they began the second stage of the legislative revolution they still hoped to achieve. In spite of Hopkins's pep talk in the crowded automobile after the 1934 elections, the New Dealers would not get everything, but by the summer of 1935 they would get a lot. They would get, as we shall see, the National Labor Relations Act to carry on the intent of the National Industrial Recovery Act's Section 7(a), struck down by the Supreme Court in January 1935 along with the rest of Title I of the act. They would get the Public Utility Holding Company Act, in spite of a million-dollar lobbying campaign against it, and in time this law would dissolve most of the investment trusts that dominated private power production in the United States (in 1935, just thirteen holding companies controlled three-quarters of all private power companies). They would get the Revenue Act, which imposed heavy income taxes on the very *very* rich but fell far short of the across-the-board "wealth tax" that many liberals had called for as a means of redistribution—and came nowhere near Huey Long's "Share Our Wealth" proposals. They would get the Banking Act, which replaced the Federal Reserve Board with a board of governors of the Federal Reserve System and gave it greatly enhanced powers over the nation's

21. Quoted in Warren, op. cit., p. 60.

bankers. They would get the Rural Electrification Administration, whose loans to rural electrical cooperatives—financed by Hoover's old creation, the RFC—would assure affordable power to 773 rural communities by the end of 1941 (and to more than a thousand by the 1970s).

They would get, thanks in no small part to the agitations of the Townsendites, Social Security. "We have to have it," Roosevelt told Labor Secretary Frances Perkins. "The Congress can't stand the pressure of the Townsend Plan unless we have a real old-age insurance program, nor can I face the country."[22] In June 1934, in an attempt to head off legislation being carpentered by Townsend enthusiasts in Congress, Roosevelt appointed Perkins to chair yet another presidential study group, the Committee on Economic Security. Its tasks would be to develop a comprehensive old-age pension system, an unemployment insurance program, and a national health insurance program, the package to be ready for delivery to Congress in January 1935.

After months of haggling over questions of eligibility, financing, and the relative shares of federal-state responsibility—extraordinarily lively discussions even by New Deal standards—the committee and its staff came up with a program and sent it along to the president on January 15. He incorporated these recommendations into draft legislation presented to Congress two days later. The proposal was already a nest of compromises when it arrived on Capitol Hill, and by the time it survived the legislative process—as well as some last-minute meddling on the part of FDR and his ever-worried Secretary of the Treasury Henry Morgenthau—and came to the president's desk for signature on August 14, it was encumbered by even more changes.

The bill did establish an unemployment and disability insurance program financed by a tax on employers—to be collected by the states, then distributed as unemployment or disability payments to those who qualified under state-established standards. Old-age payments would be the province of the federal government, financed by mandatory contributions made by both employers and employees; benefits would begin at age sixty-five. Finally, the act established a system of payments to the states for the blind, for disabled children, and for aid to dependent children.

22. Quoted in Davis, op. cit., p. 456.

Among the most important ideas lost between the committee's first session and the final bill was national health insurance; neither FDR nor the Congress wanted to challenge the political power of the American Medical Association and its allies, who despised even the hint of "socialized medicine." Gone, too, was any sort of coverage for migrant farm workers, other transient laborers, and domestics, the argument being that it would be too difficult to collect payments from and for them. Amendments in future years would broaden the coverage to include many such people, but national health insurance would remain beyond the pale for the rest of the twentieth century.

The Social Security Act was imperfect, to say the least, but it became the single most venerated piece of legislation the New Dealers ever contrived, which Roosevelt probably would have said was only as it should have been. "I guess you're right on the economics," he responded when a critic pointed out that the payroll deductions would never be enough to finance the Social Security system alone, "but those taxes were never a problem of economics. They are politics all the way through. We put those payroll contributions there so as to give the contributors a legal, moral, and political right to collect their pensions and the unemployment benefits. With those taxes in there, no damn politician can ever scrap my social security program."[23] And no politician ever has.

SOCIAL SECURITY WAS more important as a demonstration of the New Deal's commitment to a principle—however limited—than as a means of providing any immediate help to offset the continued problem of unemployment, which at the beginning of 1935 still stood at 11.3 million, nearly 22 percent of the civilian labor force. It would take another two years before all the states had developed the legislation required to implement their participation in Social Security, so it was not until the end of 1937 that the first 32.9 million workers were enrolled. By the end of June 1937, only $45 million had been paid out in unemploy-

23. Quoted in Mark H. Leff, "Taxing the 'Forgotten Man': The Politics of Social Security Finance in the New Deal," *The Journal of American History* (September 1983). See also W. Andrew Achenbaum, *Social Security: Visions and Revisions*, pp. 22–23.

ment benefits and $20 million in retirement benefits. By June of 1938 those figures would swell to $436 million and $26 million respectively, but overall, Social Security played a relatively minor role in the government's recovery programs for the rest of the decade.

Of much greater immediate importance was the Emergency Relief Appropriation Act. During his State of the Union Message of January 1935, Roosevelt had announced his intent to get rid of the Federal Emergency Relief Administration and reorganize "all emergency public works . . . in a single new and greatly enlarged plan." It was time, he said, that the government got out of the business of doling out relief money and food chits, or, at best, work without pride. "I am not willing that the vitality of our people be further sapped by the giving of cash, of market baskets, of a few hours of weekly work cutting grass, raking leaves, or picking up papers in public parks. We must preserve not only the bodies of the unemployed from destruction but also their self-respect, their self-reliance and courage and determination."[24]

He did not spell out in much detail just how he intended to achieve this goal, but nevertheless asked for $4 billion in new money to get things going, to which would be added $880 million in relief money still unspent. The House went along with his proposal with some enthusiasm, passing a version of the new appropriations act almost immediately. It took a few weeks more in the Senate, but on April 8, 1935, Roosevelt signed the bill, and on May 6 issued an executive order establishing the Works Progress Administration and charged Harry Hopkins with "the honest, efficient, speedy, and coordinated execution" of a program to move from the relief rolls to WPA projects or private employment "the maximum number of persons in the shortest time possible."[25]

Within weeks, Hopkins had transferred the works division of the FERA to the WPA and set up regional and state administrative offices, most of them manned by former FERA staffers. Unlike the FERA programs, however, whose local offices had been administered by the states, with problems ranging from corruption to gross ineptitude, the WPA was to be a federal operation from top to bottom, and everybody in it

24. Quoted in Samuel Rosenman, ed., op. cit., 5: pp. 21–22.
25. Quoted in ibid., p. 164.

was to be a federal employee (at its height, the WPA would have more than 30,000 administrative workers).[26] The administrative and policy confusion at the beginning was harrowing. Out of a bewildering welter of candidate projects submitted by states, counties, and cities, final selections were made through a complex and time-consuming process involving Hopkins, Ickes, and a platoon of officials from such diverse agencies as the Bureau of Reclamation, the U.S. Forest Service, and the Division of Grade Crossing Elimination. These sat through round after round of committee meetings during which the PWA administrator and the WPA administrator were almost constantly bickering. "All day planning the work program," Hopkins complained to his diary at one point, "which would be a good deal easier if Ickes would play ball— but he is stubborn and righteous which is a hard combination. . . . He bores me."[27] Money was slow coming in through the appropriations process—the procedures for establishing regional hiring needs and eligibility, as well as the local certification of work projects, were cumbersome and exhausting—and Hopkins was soon on his way to stomach problems that would plague him for the rest of his life. "It has been a tough job," he wrote his brother, "loaded down with government red tape of an almost unbelievable variety."[28]

But even as Hopkins and his staff struggled to set up the very skeleton of the agency, job applications were flooding state offices, putting terrible pressure on local administrators like Atlanta's Robert Mac-Dougall, in charge of construction projects for the state of Georgia. "They had to put hundreds of people to work just overnight," his wife Margaret remembered. "And it was like a war." Her husband often did not get home until midnight, and sometimes he worked the night through—when Margaret would get a share of the pressure herself. "People would call Bob over the phone, trying to get jobs," she recalled. "And they would talk on and on and on. And he told me that I should listen as long as people wanted to talk, those people were starving. And I remember, too, that he couldn't sleep at night. I've heard him scream

---

26. For figures, see Donald S. Howard, *The W.P.A. and Federal Relief Policy*, pp. 115–16.
27. Quoted in Henry H. Adams, *Harry Hopkins: A Biography*, p. 61.
28. Quoted in George McJimsey, *Harry Hopkins: Ally of the Poor and Defender of Democracy*, p. 87.

out in a nightmare, 'I'm so sorry! I'm so sorry!' And I'd wake him up, and he would have been talking to starving people."[29]

On the face of it, there seemed to be little in the WPA program attractive enough to inspire such frantic appeals. The pay was minimal. Radical observers like *The New Republic*'s Jonathan Mitchell believed this to be a sign of "the administration's surrender to big business. Where real public works, paying union wages, would compete with private employers, the new program has been framed deliberately not to restrict, even potentially, the supply of cheap labor available to industry."[30] The WPA was not the union-busting tool that Mitchell implied, but its wages were nowhere near those of union employees—or at least wage levels that unions hoped to achieve—and it took some artful persuasion on the part of Hopkins to prevent a threatened strike against WPA projects by the AFL Council. In fact, low wage scales were dictated mainly by FDR's desire not to subvert the moral character of American workers by making employment in the WPA more attractive than that in the private sector. If wages were kept low, it was theorized, workers would be driven to get off the WPA rolls just as soon as better-paying private employment became available.

Wages were calculated by a tortured process involving the region of the country where participants lived, the population of the nearest urban center, and the skill level of the individual worker, resulting in a maddeningly complicated wage schedule that could include dozens of figures—none exorbitant. For unskilled labor, which included the majority of those who qualified to take part, wages ranged from a high of $44 a month (about $524 in 1998 dollars) to a low of $19; for skilled labor, the range was from $94 to $55. In some regions, WPA payments for a significant minority of participants actually fell *below* what they had been receiving under the old Federal Emergency Relief program—though in most regions people could receive supplementary relief payments that raised the level of income closer, but rarely equal to, the minimum for secure family living.[31]

29. Margaret MacDougall told her story in Clifford M. Kuhn, Harlan E. Joye, and E. Bernard West, *Living Atlanta: An Oral History of the City, 1914–1948*, p. 224.

30. Jonathan Mitchell, "Jobs for All," *The New Republic* (July 10, 1935).

31. For figures, see Howard, op. cit., pp. 160–61, 191–93. See also Nancy E. Rose, *Put to Work: Relief Programs in the Great Depression*, pp. 96–98.

No matter how incomprehensible the schedules or low the wages, most of those who participated in the WPA work relief program considered it a godsend. Many, as Atlanta's Robert MacDougall had said, were indeed starving—or were close enough to it to justify desperation. "My husband and daughter were employed by the WPA," an East Texas woman remembered. "Without the little money they brought in, we wouldn't have been able to survive. Many times I thought that some days we would have to go downtown to those soup lines, but with the help of God, we never did."[32] But the benefits of the WPA, again like those of the CWA, may have been as psychological as they were financial. So concluded two sociologists in St. Paul, at any rate. Like most social scientists of the era, this pair believed there was little under the sun that could not be rendered into a statistic, and armed with that confidence they proceeded to quantify the impact the WPA had on the psychological well-being of its participants. "The morale of eighty WPA workers," they reported after their study, "was found to be 5.46 per cent higher than the morale of a matched group of forty-two direct-relief clients." Not only that, they went on, when it came to such matters as "social adjustment, social participation, and social status," the WPA workers achieved 5.67 percent higher scores than direct-relief clients.[33] These peculiar statistics, doubtless, would have gratified FDR, though he probably would have found even greater pleasure in what one WPA enrollee said after just three weeks on the job. "Now I can look my children straight in the eyes," he told a relief official. "I've gained my self-respect. Relief is all right to keep one from starving . . . but, well, it takes something from you. Sitting around and waiting for your case worker to bring you a check, and the kids in the house find that you contribute nothing toward their support, very soon they begin to lose respect for you. It's different now."[34]

The difference extended to 2.6 million workers by the end of 1935. From then until the end of the decade, the WPA employed an average of 2.3 million people every year, spending $11.4 billion by the end of

32. Quoted in Bill O'Neal, "The Personal Side of the Great Depression in East Texas," *East Texas Historical Association* (Spring 1980).
33. The study is discussed in Howard, op. cit., p. 814.
34. Quoted in ibid., p. 812.

fiscal 1940, far surpassing the figures claimed by Ickes for his PWA (the PWA would spend about $6 billion before it was done).[35] There was another difference between the two: while the PWA contracted with outside companies for its construction work and the labor force needed to complete it, the WPA's regional offices either did the work themselves and paid their workers directly or assigned the work to city, county, and state governments, which supervised the construction and paid the workers with WPA grants (in some cases sharing the cost).

Most of the WPA money, and more than 75 percent of its workforce, went to engineering and construction projects that made up in sheer numbers what they may have lacked in individual bulk when compared to the projects of the PWA. The WPA built or repaired 1.2 million miles of culverts and nearly 600,000 miles of highways, streets, and roads, and laid 24,000 miles of sidewalks. It constructed or restored more than 110,000 public libraries, schools, auditoriums, stadiums, and other public buildings. It constructed 5,898 playgrounds and athletic fields and 1,667 parks, fairgrounds, and rodeo grounds. It built 256 new airports and fixed 385 more, built 880 sewage treatment plants and repaired 395, spanned rivers and creeks and gullies with 75,266 bridges and viaducts, laid 22,790 miles of sewerage lines, and dug 770 municipal swimming pools. "Why, it sounds almost like the accomplishments of King Solomon," marveled a congressman in 1940.[36]

There was not a city or county in America that was not touched by the WPA in one way or another. Consider Otter Tail County, an agricultural region in west-central Minnesota with a 1930 population of a little over 51,000, most of whom lived on 6,702 farms, the rest in the town of Fergus Falls (1930 population: 9,389) or in one of seventeen farm hamlets. The 1,962-square-mile county was part of the seventh district of the WPA, and, during the life of the work relief program, the agency spent $4.8 million here, employing an average of 500 to 750 people during peak years at wages ranging from $48 to $75.90 per month. With the county and the towns furnishing materials, as required by WPA regulations, and the government supplying the labor, classrooms

35. Figures from ibid., appendix, pp. 854–57.
36. Figures in ibid., pp. 125–28; quote, p. 129. Itemization of WPA projects also is from Howard.

in the town of Battle Lake got painted and the Fergus Falls State Hospital was refurbished. The town of New York Mills built a new municipal building and an up-to-date sewage system, as did Henning, Underwood, Perham, and Parkers Prairie, while Fergus Falls laid out a golf course, paved its streets, and improved its own sewage system. When drought conditions threatened to dry up the county's lakes, WPA money helped build new dams and raise old ones to hold more water, restoring sixty-three lakes to levels that would assure local water supplies. WPA money also helped to clean up the polluted Pelican and Otter Tail Rivers and plant trees. Almost a million dollars of the WPA's $4.8 million went for road construction and repair, particularly during 1936. The county was declared a drought-stricken area that year, which allowed 1,500 farmers to engage in WPA work (without the drought classification, farm workers were not allowed to participate in WPA programs on the theory that those who could still farm were better off than most others). More than 1,300 laborers armed with shovels could be seen working the roads that year, together with 475 teams of horses dragging Fresno scrapers and twenty-seven trucks spreading gravel and asphalt, and the whole scene suggested an air of dynamic industriousness that Otter Tail County had not enjoyed for years.[37]

Buildings, roads, dams, and other construction projects in Otter Tail County and the rest of the country, of course, were considered men's work, and what to do about women in the program remained a conundrum among the male-dominated leadership of the WPA. The first problem was eligibility. Most women on relief were without a work history and therefore not considered part of the "labor market," the pool of unemployed from which the WPA was supposed to draw its workers. Many women had dependent children at home and thus were not available for full-time employment—and the concept of federally supported day-care centers was six decades away. Many could not qualify as "economic heads" of households, a position ordinarily reserved for males in the bureaucratic protocols of the WPA. The second problem was the availability of WPA-appropriate jobs. Ellen Woodward, who had headed

37. My summary of the role of the WPA in Otter Tail County is taken from D. Jerome Tweton's study, *The New Deal at the Grass Roots: Programs for the People in Otter Tail County, Minnesota*, pp. 70–87.

up the women's divisions of both the FERA and the CWA and had taken on the same responsibility in the new agency, complained to her friend Eleanor Roosevelt that in its rush "to put men to work first," the WPA had disqualified most of the 250 job categories that Woodward had established as appropriate for women.[38] There wasn't much left but sewing, and while Woodward was able to institute training and employment programs in mattress-making, bookbinding, domestic service, canning of relief foods, school lunch preparation, and supplemental child care, most of the WPA women ended up in one of the 9,000 sewing centers scattered around the country. Some centers employed as many as 1,500 women; some, only a handful. But by February 1936, Woodward had 294,532 women turning out clothing, sheets, blankets, pillows, and professional uniforms for free distribution through public agencies; by October 1937 more than 122 million items had been created and distributed.

For the women, as much as for the men, the psychological benefits of a WPA job were enormous. "The social benefits of this work cannot be reckoned in terms of silver or gold," one WPA official wrote to his district supervisor.

> No word picture can adequately portray the rehabilitation and transformation taking place in some of these women, after a few months association and contact with other people, coupled with the sense of achievement of being able to procure a few of the things in life so essential to their happiness. Not frivolities but necessities, which cannot be obtained without money. One woman bought a comb, a broom, scouring powder and disinfectant, when she received her *first* check. The food order she had been getting her groceries with, simply could not be stretched to include these items.[39]

The sewing-room system, however, was not much help in meeting the WPA's goal of getting women off work relief rolls and into private industry as soon as possible. Sewing jobs simply were not available

38. Quoted in Martha H. Swain, "'The Forgotten Woman': Ellen S. Woodward and Women's Relief in the New Deal," *Prologue* (Winter 1983).
39. Quoted in Freedman, op. cit., pp. 77–78.

everywhere. Not in Washington, D.C., for example. "Although these women have learned to do excellent work as seamstresses," a WPA economist for the district reported in 1938, "the commercial possibilities of their acquired skills are not great. Washington has no large garment industry to absorb them." Moreover, the economist went on, a lot of the women were simply not employable. "Many are too old, and a large number have physical disabilities, such as cardiac conditions, orthopedic troubles, etc."[40]

In its best year—1938—the women's division of the WPA kept nearly 400,000 women employed, but to Woodward's frustration, it never managed to include the full complement of women who qualified. The WPA did a somewhat better job when it came to the employment of black Americans (or at least black *male* Americans). Hopkins and the WPA took with absolute seriousness the stipulation in Roosevelt's executive order creating the agency that all individuals who "qualified by training and experience to be assigned to work projects shall not be discriminated against on any grounds whatsoever."[41] The rule did not go unappreciated. Of all the programs of the New Deal that affected them, the WPA was one of the few that earned consistent praise from African Americans. This was true in spite of the fact that black WPA applicants in the rural and small-town South often were subjected to the same kinds of bureaucratic "Jim Crowism," as one observer put it, that they had endured under the FERA and the CWA: different standards of eligibility were imposed, applications were processed with all deliberate leisure, and unofficial quotas were maintained.[42] Conditions were measurably different in the urban part of the South, however—at least according to numbers calculated in 1940. In 14 out of 22 southern cities with a population of 100,000 or more, the percentage of

---

40. Quoted in Howard, op. cit., p. 285, footnote.
41. Quoted in Sitkoff, op. cit., p. 69.
42. "Jim Crowism" quote from Ruth Durant, "Home Rule in the WPA," *Survey Mid-monthly* (September 1939). The situation was particularly hard on women, according to Richard Sterner in *The Negro's Share: A Study of Income, Consumption, Housing and Public Assistance*. In the thirteen southern states and the District of Columbia, he reported in 1943, black men comprised 26.2 percent of the WPA workforce, but the figure for women was only 15.9 percent. "This difference," Sterner wrote, "was largely due to the regulations concerning local sponsorship of projects. While Negro and white males

blacks on the WPA rolls by then was significantly greater than their percentage within the whole population. In three other cities, the percentage of WPA employment was roughly the same as that for whites, and in only five cities were blacks underrepresented. Nationwide, the percentage of blacks employed on WPA projects ranged anywhere from 15 percent to 20 percent for the rest of the decade—and in all nonsouthern states the percentages actually exceeded those for blacks in the general population.[43]

Such numbers represented a great deal of money being pumped into black American neighborhoods for the first time, and if it was just as hard for African American workers to get by on the WPA pittance as it was for whites, it was more money than they had seen for years. Reason enough, then, for one black worker in North Carolina to declare that "the government is the best boss I ever had," and for *Opportunity*, the Urban League's journal, to say that it was "to the eternal credit of the administrative officers of the WPA that discrimination on various projects because of race has been kept to a minimum and that in almost every community Negroes have been given a chance to participate in the work program."[44]

FOR THOSE WHO were too young or otherwise unqualified to take part in the WPA's work programs, the New Dealers offered up a WPA subsidiary called the National Youth Administration. The Civilian Conservation Corps had established itself as the New Deal's preeminent youth program by 1935, but the CCC did not admit women, had at best a mixed record with regard to the treatment of black participants, and

---

may work on the same outdoor projects in the South, women's projects, which are carried on indoors, are entirely segregated. Therefore, sponsorship of work projects on which Negro women can be employed is frequently difficult to obtain as most sponsoring agencies in the South have little interest in creating work-relief jobs for Negro women. At the same time public opinion is opposed to WPA employment for Negro women which competes with domestic service. It is evident that the situation works considerable hardship on Negro women, since they more often than white women are the main supporters of their familes" (pp. 245–46).

43. See Sterner, op. cit., pp. 239–53. See also Sitkoff, op. cit., pp. 69–72.

44. Worker quote in Howard, op. cit., p. 295; editorial in *Opportunity* (February 1939).

above all had barely tapped into the well of those between the ages of sixteen and twenty-four who were still on relief—a number estimated at 2.8 million, more than 1.25 million of whom were looking for work but could not find it.[45] In families that often depended upon multiple incomes to survive, the lack of jobs for young people was no small matter. "Maybe you don't know what it's like to come home and have everyone looking at you," one teenager lamented, "and you know they're thinking, even if they don't say it, 'He didn't find a job.' It gets terrible. You just don't want to come home."[46]

Idle hands, it was commonly believed, made for the devil's work. Young people deserved the government's compassion as much as any other group, Mrs. Roosevelt said in her "My Day" column, and went on to warn that the nation's own self-interest demanded action. If they were not given employment, she said, "we are going to have a generation of people who do not know how to work . . . and who ignore our old standards of morals and ethics because they cannot live up to them. Economic conditions are different but human nature remains the same and an embittered, unfulfilled and disappointed generation will be more dangerous to our future happiness than any loss in material possessions."[47]

For evidence to support her apprehensions, Mrs. Roosevelt would not have had to look beyond the average urban college campus, where leftists of all stripes were doing the devil's work by organizing the despair of students who had little hope for employment even if they managed to stay in school long enough to graduate. The Young Communist League, the Young People's Socialist League, the National Student League, the Student League for Industrial Democracy, the Young Communist International, and other covens of college radicalism had been alarming their middle-class elders for years with a mixture of Marxist-Leninist-Trotskyist-Stalinist-Socialist rhetoric and agitation. Their members constituted a minority among the national college pop-

45. Figures from Betty and Ernest K. Lindley, *A New Deal for Youth: The Story of the National Youth Administration*, p. 12.
46. Quoted in ibid., p. 21.
47. Quoted in Carol A. Weisberger, *Dollars and Dreams: The National Youth Administration in Texas*, p. 18.

ulation, but they were noisy, supernaturally energetic, and not afraid to challenge teachers and administrators alike with campus demonstrations—particularly with regard to college ROTC programs. Most student radicals, citing the fruitless slaughter of World War I, embraced the antiwar tenets of the British-born Oxford Pledge movement, which, by 1933, had crossed the Atlantic to American campuses. While many church and student organizations took part, the radicals were the dominant force behind student strikes and antiwar demonstrations that had erupted at many colleges between 1933 and 1935, some of them attended by the kind of violence that would become commonplace a little over thirty years later. One such demonstration, the Student Strike Against War in April 1935, involved about 175,000 students on 130 campuses scattered from the City College of New York to UCLA, and even to Texas Christian University in the heart of fundamentalist Texas. Most college officials responded to such agitation by banning or severely restricting demonstrations and rallies and by expelling students who violated the rules; as usual, repressive measures only served to further fuel the movement, and many campuses would continue to simmer with antiwar and antigovernment fulminations regularly until the beginning of World War II.[48]

These were the kinds of young people who worried Mrs. Roosevelt—and many others—and they probably were prominent among those in FDR's mind when he issued Executive Order 7086 establishing the National Youth Administration on June 26, 1935, appropriating $50 million out of the WPA relief fund as start-up money, placing the agency under the wing of the WPA, and naming as its administrator Aubrey Williams, Harry Hopkins's principal assistant. "[We] can ill afford to lose the skill and energy of these young men and women," Roosevelt said in a public statement. "They must have their chance in school, their turn as apprentices and their opportunity for jobs—a chance to work and earn for themselves."[49]

48. For a good discussion of the college antiwar movement and other aspects of student radicalism, seeee Robert Cohen, *When the Old Left Was Young: Student Radicals and America's First Mass Student Movement, 1929–1941*, pp. 73–133.
49. Quoted in Rosenman, op. cit., p. 281.

Under the NYA's programs, those between the ages of eighteen and twenty-five who were out of school and on relief could work no more than seventy hours a month on an NYA job, for a maximum of twenty-five dollars a month. Roughly 90 percent of the out-of-school participants—who would number nearly 155,000 by March 1938—worked out of their own homes, but many of those in rural areas were assigned to live in resident centers, where they not only received job placement in nearby businesses and municipal and county offices but were trained in masonry, welding, baking, barbering, carpentry, plumbing, and other trade skills. Among younger participants, a qualified high school student was allowed to work a maximum of three hours a day during the school week and seven hours on Saturday; he or she could earn no more than six dollars a month. Undergraduate and graduate college students could work as much as eight hours a day—undergraduates for a maximum of twenty dollars a month, graduate students for a maximum of forty dollars.[50]

Most out-of-school workers performed tasks similar to those of the WPA at large, building roads and highways, laying sidewalks, building and refurbishing schools and other public buildings, constructing recreational facilities, landscaping parks. Student projects tended to be more sedentary, with nearly 20 percent of the participants engaging in clerical work for government and nongovernment agencies and businesses, the rest scattered through a plethora of jobs, with students serving as nurse's aides, teacher's aides, researchers, assistant librarians, recreation supervisors, school cafeteria workers, museum docents, and dozens of other positions. Whether their jobs were physical or sedentary, by March 1938, more than 480,000 young people were employed in NYA programs—far more than would ever participate in even the best year in the CCC. Unlike the rest of the WPA, the jobs were more equally divided between men and women, even in the out-of-school programs, where in March 1938, 73,731 young women and 81,119 young men participated. In student programs, the difference was even closer, with 165,466 male participants and 162,018 female partici-

50. Figures from Broadus Mitchell, *Depression Decade: From New Era Through the New Deal, 1929–1941*, p. 330; and Betty and Ernest Lindley, op. cit., pp. 20 (footnote) and 159.

pants, and for many of these young women, an NYA job made the difference between continuing school or dropping out.[51] "My father had
deserted and my mother was seriously ill and we had been living on
welfare," Sophia Poster remembered of her freshman year at UCLA,
where she got an NYA job reading to a blind student. "Without NYA I
do not know how I would have been able to begin university."[52] The
fact that between 1930 and 1938 college enrollment increased by more
than 400,000 and that the largest period of growth was between 1935
and 1938 may well be attributed at least in part to the financial aid provided to thousands of these students by the NYA.[53]

Just as much to the program's credit was the opportunity it provided black youth. This was no accident, for in 1936 an NYA Division
of Negro Affairs was created. Appointed to head it up was Mary
McLeod Bethune, once one of Washington's leading middle-class black
club women and now the city's most vigorous advocate for African
American rights. She was reassuringly nonmilitant, but she had her
moments: while crossing the White House lawn for her first visit with
the president, one story has it, Bethune was hailed by a gardener. "Hey,
there, Auntie," he asked, "where y'all think you're goin'?" The big, very
black Bethune turned around, walked up to the man, and looked him
straight in the eye. "For a moment, I didn't recognize you," she said.
"Which one of my sister's children are you?" The gardener fled.[54]

Bethune was "Mother Superior" to the more than forty black men
and women who had found administrative positions in Cabinet offices
and federal agencies and who, in 1936, would form an unofficial arm of
the New Deal. They called themselves the Federal Council on Negro
Affairs—though to most people they became known as the Black Cabinet. Their influence in the administration would be limited, but Harold
Ickes in the Department of the Interior and Harry Hopkins and Aubrey
Williams in the WPA were particularly outspoken in their support of

51. Figures in Betty and Ernest Lindley, op. cit., p. 256. In high school programs,
young women outnumbered young men by 121,027 to 105,139, while in college programs men had it over women by 98,705 to 58,395—roughly equivalent to the ratio
of men to women in the college population.
52. Letter to the author, May 22, 1992.
53. Figures from Cabell Phillips, op. cit., p. 280 (footnote).
54. The story is told in Sitkoff, op. cit., pp. 80–81.

racial justice in and out of their agencies, and Bethune herself had become close to Eleanor Roosevelt, a friendship she would nurture diligently over the years. With her appointment as head of the NYA's Division of Negro Affairs, Bethune became the highest-ranking black person in the New Deal, and she used that position not only to promote the cause of black people generally but to ensure that young blacks would get their share of the NYA's opportunity. As usual, in spite of Bethune's efforts, that share turned out to be proportionately smaller in the South than in the North, but during the life of the program (like the CCC, the NYA would be discontinued in 1943), the agency still managed to employ some 300,000 black men and women, somewhere between 10 and 12 percent of all those who participated. They were paid precisely the same as whites, were given the same chance at training in trades and professions, and further were given access to a special fund created to help keep in school those who could not take part in the NYA program for various reasons—an early version of affirmative action. There was some justification then for Bethune's slightly evangelical declaration during a speech before the Kentucky Negro Educational Association at Louisville in April 1937. "Above all," she said, in summing up what her division had been able to accomplish, "the NYA has dispelled the thick and oppressive clouds of despair under which Negro youth has long struggled until they now see through the rift the blue sky of hope and promise."[55]

55. Quoted in Weisberger, op. cit., p. 130.

12

*

Another Form of Hunger

For its physical work projects alone, the WPA may well have qualified as the most ubiquitous federal agency in the country, familiar to
millions, most of whom admired it greatly even when poking fun at it.
Jokes about WPA workers leaning on shovels were especially popular,
and at one point Postmaster General James Farley sent Hopkins a newspaper clipping about a WPA worker who had fallen and broken his
wrist when he lost his grip while leaning on his shovel. Perhaps, Farley
suggested, the agency should develop a "non-skid shovel handle." On
the other side of the question, some anonymous worker got his own
licks in with a bit of inspired doggerel:

> We've made a lot of lovely things,
> Just "leaning" on a shovel;
> Parks with flowers and sparkling springs,
> Just "leaning" on a shovel.
> The winding roads and the highways straight,
> The wonderful buildings that house the great,

We built them all at our "lazy" gait,
Just "leaning" on a shovel.[1]

But the ubiquity of the WPA cannot be measured solely by the number and magnitude of its buildings, airports, sewers, or road-building projects, or even by the fact that tens of millions of Americans in hundreds of American cities would find themselves walking on WPA sidewalks for the next sixty-five years. Not all the unemployed, after all, were laborers, skilled or not. There were nearly five million people unemployed in 1935, and more than 11 percent—558,429—were white-collar workers.[2] Both the FERA and the CWA had embraced the needs of such workers, and in spite of criticisms from those who ridiculed white-collar programs as effete and useless, Hopkins held firm. "They are damn good projects—excellent projects," he exploded during a press conference on April 4, 1935, when a reporter asked if he was going to investigate a project in New York for its alleged pointlessness. "You know . . . dumb people criticize something they do not understand, and that is what is going on. . . . God damn it! Here are a lot of people broke and we are putting them to work. . . . I have no apologies to make. As a matter of fact, we have not done enough."[3] Hopkins's remark about "dumb people" was promptly misinterpreted, deliberately or otherwise, by much of the anti–New Deal press, which said he had meant that all Americans were stupid, but Hopkins still had no apologies to make when the WPA greatly expanded white-collar programs. It did so across an extraordinarily wide range of fields and professional disciplines, particularly when Ellen Woodward persuaded Hopkins to combine her women's division with the professional projects division in July 1935, a scheme aimed at broadening her ability to make sure that as many women as possible were being funneled into available WPA jobs.

Clerks and stenographic workers from the WPA's records and clerical department were assigned to supplement regular staffs in city, county, and state government offices. Investigators and analysts in the

1. The Farley story and the poem are both quoted in Adams, op. cit., p. 92.
2. Figures from William F. McDonald, *Federal Relief Administration and the Arts*, p. 94.
3. Quoted in Robert E. Sherwood, *Roosevelt and Hopkins: An Intimate History*, p. 60.

research and statistical department compiled and massaged statistics, conducted surveys, and kept the records for government and university research programs. Orderlies, laboratory technicians, nurses, and even doctors and dentists from the WPA's department of hospitals and health went to work in city and county hospitals and clinics. Teachers from the education department enhanced local programs in literacy, remedial reading, nursery school education, extracurricular activities, and adult education. In the Workers' Service Program, a thousand instructors taught working men and women the rudiments of current events, labor law, labor history, and consumer rights; by 1936, the program had an enrollment of 65,000 and had become a favorite of Eleanor Roosevelt, who said in her "My Day" column that "this particular phase of adult education is important to democracy. It develops an ability to read and to reason, to listen to other people's viewpoints, and to discuss questions before making decisions. This is valuable enough in relations between individuals, but in employer and employee relations . . . it will mean a great step towards reasonable and peaceful settlement of many disputes."[4]

Either directly or indirectly, then, as participants or as those being served by participants, millions of Americans were being touched by the generally mundane, if often useful, white-collar programs of the WPA every day, as the agency demonstrated Hopkins's credo that in the crusade to help the needy, the government should be willing at all times to try out "various schemes which are supported by reasonable people."[5] But probably no aspect of the WPA program demonstrated the New Deal's willingness to improvise in the name of need more precisely than its commitment to the arts—or at least to artists, whose dilemma Hopkins had earlier acknowledged by including a few limited FERA and CWA programs designed for writers, artists, theater people, and musicians. "Hell, they've got to eat just like other people," he had said when criticized for his generosity in 1934.[6]

4. Quoted in Joyce L Kornbluh, *A New Deal for Workers' Education: The Workers' Service Program, 1933–1942*, p. 102.
5. Quoted in McJimsey, op. cit., p. 55.
6. Quoted in Jerre Mangione, *The Dream and the Deal: The Federal Writers' Project, 1935–1943*, p. 4.

Their needs had not appreciably diminished by 1935. Thousands of musicians, for example—particularly those who performed before audiences in dance bands, concerts, and orchestras, or taught others how to do so—had lost work, many of them even before the onset of the depression. The rise of the record industry and radio in the twenties had combined to reduce the demand for live performances, and the film industry's almost universal conversion to sound by the beginning of the thirties had eliminated most of the live musical accompaniment that had been a regular part of the movies in all but the poorest theaters; by 1930, it was estimated, as many as 22,000 professional theater musicians were out of work. During the early depression years, the situation only grew worse; philharmonic orchestras closed, dance bands folded, and music teachers found themselves without clients among a population that had more pressing needs to worry about than having their children learn the scales. The American Federation of Musicians claimed that more than two-thirds of the professional musicians in the United States had been rendered unemployed between 1929 and 1934 and that most of the rest were not earning even subsistence wages.[7]

Theater folk had suffered similarly hard times, and the growth of the motion picture industry had played a role here, too, as thousands of theaters across the country had eliminated live vaudeville performances in favor of the cheaper and increasingly popular movies. In 1930, for instance, the Loew's theater chain had featured regular vaudeville shows in thirty-six of its theaters, offering anywhere from fifty to sixty weeks of full-time employment; in the 1933–34 season, only three of its theaters included any kind of stage show.[8] In the legitimate theater generally, fewer and fewer people found themselves able to pay the one or two dollars most performances required even outside the ring of New York's Broadway and Off-Broadway productions. On Broadway itself, the doldrums that James Thurber had witnessed during the first year of the depression had continued. The League of New York Theaters estimated that between 1928 and 1933, the number of productions on Broadway had dropped by half and the number of working employees had fallen from 25,000 to only 4,000. Nationwide, traveling stock companies and

7. Figures from William F. McDonald, op. cit., pp. 586–87.
8. Figures in Hallie Flanagan, *Arena*, p. 13.

local repertory groups folded by the dozens. By the summer of 1933, the International Alliance of Theatrical Stage Employees said, there were only 6,010 stagehands at work in the entire country, and they were averaging only $681 a year.[9]

The overall impact of the depression on professional painters, sculptors, and others who worked in the graphic and plastic arts is more difficult to measure, because most were poorly organized and often unemployed under the best of circumstances. (In the depression, one painter remembered, "Everybody was unemployed and the artist didn't seem strange anymore."[10]) A March 1935 government study listed 2,900 artists, sculptors, and teachers of art on the FERA relief rolls, but the true number almost certainly was higher. A measure of their plight is suggested by the fact that early in 1931 Manhattan art galleries already were putting on "unemployment fund" exhibitions to raise money for destitute artists.[11] The situation with regard to writers is even harder to pin down (the 1935 study did not even include them), but the book, magazine, and newspaper publishing industries had been quite as devastated by the depression as any others. The sales of trade books had fallen from an estimated $42 million in 1929 to about half that by the end of 1933, and royalties to even established authors declined proportionately.[12] Magazine advertising linage plummeted by more than 30 percent in the same period, and even the biggest publications lowered their rates for freelance work and drastically reduced their purchases and assignments. Even the pulps, where such as Raymond Chandler and Dashiell Hammett still earned the bread on their tables (or the gin or scotch in their tumblers), dropped from two cents to a penny a word. Almost half of all daily newspaper editions were canceled between 1930 and 1935, throwing thousands of reporters out of work.[13] Whatever the precise number of writers affected, the situation was bad enough for the Communist-led Writers Union of New York City to sponsor a picket line at the Port Authority building on Eighth

9. Figures from William F. McDonald, op., cit., p. 486.
10. Robert Gwathmey in Terkel, op. cit., p. 373.
11. Figure from William F. McDonald, op. cit., p. 85.
12. Figures in Monty Noam Penkower, *The Federal Writers' Project: A Study in Government Patronage of the Arts*, pp. 4–5.
13. Ibid., pp. 5–6.

Avenue (the building contained the WPA's New York offices) in late February 1935; among the more prominent writers present was Maxwell Bodenheim, and among the more effective signs displayed was one hanging from the neck of Earl Conrad: "CHILDREN NEED BOOKS. WRITERS NEED A BREAK. WE DEMAND PROJECTS."[14]

The projects they had in mind were federal projects, and the government was ready to listen—to writers, artists, musicians, and theater people alike. When the Professional Projects Division was organized in July, it stipulated that "persons now on relief who are qualified in fields of Art, Music, Drama, and Writing" would be considered for the WPA work program in the areas of their expertise, and to that end a subdivision called Federal Project Number One—Federal One for short—was established.[15] Under its aegis a federal music program, a federal arts program, a federal writers program, and a federal theater program were instituted.

Federal One would earn its description as the New Deal's greatest claim to intellectual respectability, but it can hardly be described as the most sweeping of its programs. The number of unemployed artists was infinitesimal when compared to those of the larger pool of the unemployed, and the amount of money Federal One would spend to support them came to only about 1 percent of the WPA's entire budget. But, as with many New Deal institutions, there was something more than the satisfaction of simple survival needs at work in Federal One. The American public, it was commonly believed among the intelligentsia in and out of government, was avid for enlightenment. Hallie Flanagan, for instance, director of the Vassar Experimental Theater, conceded that hungry artists must be fed. But, she asked, "was there not another form of hunger with which we could rightly be concerned, the hunger of millions of Americans for music, plays, pictures, and books? Were not these two aspects of hunger a part of the same equation?"[16] This sentiment was entirely in keeping with modernism, the twentieth-century intellectual response to the Victorian age, which held, among other

14. Picket line described in Mangione, op. cit., p. 37.
15. Quoted in William F. McDonald, op. cit., p. 129.
16. Flanagan, op. cit., p. 19.

things, that while the individual artist—whether in literature, theater, music, or the graphic or plastic arts—was an elite being subject to few, if any, social or moral restraints, his or her work must be made accessible to the great mass of the people, because it was through the arts, far more than religion or ethics, that humanity would find the way to perfection.[17] Americans, presumably, yearned for the path.

The first federal program to reflect that conviction had emerged even earlier than Federal One. In December 1933, FDR had established the Public Works of Art Project (PWAP), supported by a grant from the CWA and placed in the Treasury Department. The agency was instructed to commission murals and other works of art to ornament post offices and other public buildings around the country. While the relief needs of professional artists had inspired its creation, the PWAP was less interested in feeding its employees than in fulfilling modernist instincts. "Before 1933," Forbes Watson, the program's assistant director, said, "we had a large, groping, hungry public which looked to art as a means whereby its cultivation and outlook on life could be broadened"—a mute desire that Watson believed the PWAP was born to satisfy.[18] PWAP director Edward Bruce had even more elegant visions. Up to now, he told Eleanor Roosevelt, America had spent its energies on the conquering of the frontier and the nurturing of material progress; now it was time to join the great civilizations whose commitment to art had "left the world richer because they lived."[19] The desire for quality was consequently high, and while the project did feed many struggling artists among the 3,600 or so who participated, it also gave work to a number of artists who had no particular need of it, including John Sloan, Thomas Hart Benton, and Grant Wood. The PWAP died with the demise of the CWA in March 1934, but it was swiftly revived as the Treasury Department's Section of Fine Arts. And for the rest of the decade it sought "art of the best quality available for the embellishment

17. For a good discussion of modernism's airy tenets, see Norman F. Cantor, with Mindy Cantor, *The American Century: Varieties of Culture in Modern Times*, pp. 43–51.
18. Quoted in William F. McDonald, op. cit., p. 368.
19. Quoted in Karal Ann Marling, *Wall-to-Wall America: A Cultural History of Post-Office Murals in the Great Depression*, p. 44.

of public buildings" and ultimately commissioned more than a thousand murals, most of them in post offices.[20]

Federal One's own arts project was not indifferent to artistic quality and certainly not to the importance of mass education and uplift, but the FAP's director, Holger Cahill, entertained no Bruce-like ambitions of leaving behind a legacy comparable to that of ancient Greece or Renaissance Italy. Nor did he share modernism's reverence for the individual artist, at least not when it came to publicly supported art. To him, it was not "the solitary genius but a sound general movement which maintains art as a vital, functioning part of any cultural scheme."[21] To foster that kind of movement, the FAP's art commissions leaned heavily on local "easel painters"—those who worked directly on canvas, either in supervised FAP workshops or in their own homes and studios—to produce in eight years probably more public art than had been committed in the entire previous history of the Republic. By the end of 1938, these artists, whose work varied wildly in quality (even bad artists, Harry Hopkins might have said, need to eat), had produced no fewer than 27,000 watercolors and 15,000 oils, depicting local city scenes and landscapes, regional history and folkways, official portraits, and other items designed to illuminate the past and present of American life. Most had been distributed to adorn the walls of schools, museums, hospitals, and city, state, and federal government offices and agencies, where many continued to hang for decades. Sometimes, however, the art was so bad that it could not be displayed, and Cahill was forced to come up with bureaucratic procedures for the proper method of destroying such failures.

If "easel art" had been the only form of FAP expression, the agency's work still would have been noteworthy, if nothing else, for the sheer number of works produced. But there was more. Some five hundred sculptors turned out thousands of busts and frescoes and commemorative statues for parks and other public places, including a twenty-four-foot tribute to Chinese philosopher Sun Yat-sen in San Francisco,

20. Quote in ibid., p. 30. Marling points out that depression-era post office murals are frequently misidentified as "WPA" art; the vast majority, however, were commissioned by either the PWAP or the Section of Fine Arts.
21. Quote in ibid., p. 44.

life-sized busts of Civil War generals for Grant's Tomb in New York, and "The Muse of Music" for the Hollywood Bowl in Los Angeles. Two hundred and fifty graphic artists produced more than 95,000 prints, which were donated to public institutions, and 1.6 million posters, most in striking Art Deco style. These were used to promote everything from dental health to mental health, workplace safety to child care, as well as to issue warnings against the dangers of venereal disease, drunk driving, shoplifting, juvenile delinquency, among other social problems. "By Pearl Harbor time," social historian J. C. Furnas remembered, "one could hardly buy a postage stamp or visit a federal office without encountering in the lobby or stairway a well-meaning example of Federal Art."[22] Meanwhile, FAP researchers, artists, and photographers relentlessly collected or recorded the millions of items that would go into its Index of American Design, an attempt to document the design history of everything from kitchen utensils to window casings, while FAP art teachers established more than 600 community art centers in settlement houses, schools, and church basements, where local people, including thousands of children, were encouraged to develop their own talents, if any, and were exposed to art history and appreciation for the first time in their lives through ongoing shows and traveling exhibits.

In all, the FAP put about 4,000 artists to work, together with some 2,000 other teachers and researchers. The overall quality of much of the work they produced may have been low, even among those pieces that were not destroyed, but President Roosevelt, like FAP director Cahill, saw in the programs of both the PWAP and the FAP a democratization of the arts that Americans would surely appreciate. "Some of it good, some of it not so good," he said of the mural art produced by the PWAP, "but all of it native, human, eager and alive—all of it painted by their own kind in their own country, and painted about things that they know and look at often and have touched and loved."[23] Ben Shahn, who was on the FAP payroll for a time, admitted that most FAP art was not going to win any prizes, but gave the program credit for providing "an

22. Furnas, op. cit., p. 424.
23. Quoted in William E. Leuchtenberg, *Franklin D. Roosevelt and the New Deal*, pp. 127–28.

un-judged, un-censored fellowship" to artists. In doing so, he believed, it "begot an enlightened public art . . . the first widespread indigenous art movement that the country has known."[24]

Nikolai Sokoloff, director of the Federal Music Project (previously, conductor of the Cleveland Symphony Orchestra), did not have much interest in nurturing a widespread indigenous musical movement comparable to what Shahn claimed for American art in the FAP, but he was indisputably committed to the FMP's educational role, particularly with regard to pre–twentieth century classical music. There were only eleven symphony orchestras in the United States at the beginning of 1935; by the end of 1936, the FMP had established another thirty-four, including orchestras in such unlikely venues as San Bernardino, California, and Omaha, Nebraska. Chamber orchestras, choral groups, and string quartets and trios also had begun to proliferate. Many groups took their performances into the hinterlands of their regions on a regular basis, and within a little over a year after the program's inception, the FMP estimated that some 32 million people had attended 36,000 concerts.[25] Classical music also became a mainstay of the FMP's sponsorship of regular radio concerts on all the major networks, and it was training in the classical instruments and compositions that dominated the program's ambitious educational effort; at its height, the FMP employed more than 6,000 music teachers, and by the end of June 1939 it had sponsored more than a million classes with a total of 13.8 million pupils.[26]

Sokoloff, the supreme classicist, had little fondness for modern composers of any kind, and FMP composers or artists, he said, "will get no place playing stupid things."[27] Nor did he care much for swing, already evolving through the work of Benny Goodman, Duke Ellington, Count Basie, Artie Shaw, and others into the definitive popular musical form of an age that Ellington described as "jazz-shaped," filled with the "sudden turns, the shocks, the swift changes of pace (all jazz-shaped) that serve to remind us that the world is ever unexplored, and that while a complete mastery of life is mere illusion, the real secret of

24. Quoted in Furnas, op. cit., p. 426.
25. Figures in Kenneth J. Bindas, *All of This Music Belongs to the Nation: The WPA's Federal Music Project and American Society, 1935–1939*, p. 10.
26. Figures from William F. McDonald, op. cit., p. 630.
27. Quoted in Bindas, op. cit., p. 64.

the game is to make life swing."[28] Sokoloff, however, saw nothing to admire in swing. "I like to dance when I am dancing," he said, "but to compare it to music, why, it is like comparing the funny papers with the work of a painter."[29]

Sokoloff's personal prejudices notwithstanding, the FMP could not ignore the more popular forms of American music and hope to retain the public support it needed, and it must be said that it probably put more musicians and singers to work at the local level through its non-classical productions than its more formal work. Marching bands, swing bands, hillbilly (Blue Grass) bands, cowboy bands and singers, and even jazz bands and ensembles managed to get on the FMP's regular payroll. So did blacks and Hispanics. Black choruses offered to largely black audiences everything from choral works by Brahms to Thomas Dorsey's gospel blues, while black symphony orchestras in several cities brought them classical music; some of the more adventurous groups, however, like the Richmond Colored Orchestra of Virginia, often alternated between classical and swing pieces during their performances, and Chicago's Negro Dixie Orchestra went so far as to bring jazz *into* classical compositions, punctuating standard concertos and symphonies with spectacular riffs and solos. In California and the Southwest, the FMP supported dozens of *Tipica* orchestras that played both traditional and classical Spanish and Mexican music.

The FMP also sponsored numerous festivals around the country that emphasized traditional forms of popular American music, from folk songs to fiddling, and in 1938 began an annual three-day, nationwide American Music Festival built around Washington's Birthday. With the support of the WPA's Joint Committee on Folk Arts, FMP researchers gathered sheet music and made hundreds of recordings of folk music among the hill people of the Appalachians, the black people of the South, and Native American and Mexican American people in New Mexico and other southwestern states.

Between October 1935 and August 1939, the FMP sponsored 224,698 performances attended by nearly 150 million people.[30] This

---

28. Quoted in David W. Stowe, *Swing Changes: Big-Band Jazz in New Deal America*, p. 1.
29. Quoted in Bindas, op. cit., p. 13.
30. See ibid., p. 108.

astonishing figure lends some credence to the belief of many people at
the time that the program must have raised the nation's musical consciousness to a measurable degree while feeding thousands of hungry
musicians—though even an enthusiastic endorsement given by *Musical
America* had to remain in the realm of speculation. The program's rami-
fications, it said in its issue for May 25, 1937, "are so many, the quality
and worth of what has been undertaken and its manner of achievement
so diverse . . . it is inconceivable that so much should be going on without its playing some constructive part in the country's musical progress,
no matter how transient or ephemeral, or inferior in quality, the great
bulk of this welter of accomplishment may be."[31]

Like the other Federal One programs, the Federal Writers Project
believed it had a higher duty than just the employment of indigent
writers, though it never aspired to such theoretical heights as the FAP's
pursuit of immortality. Henry Alsberg, who had headed up similar programs in the FERA and CWA, was a good deal more interested in
telling Americans about America. The people of the United States, Alsberg would tell a congressional committee in 1938,

> have concentrated so actively on the exploitation of our natural
> resources for industrial and agricultural purposes that until re-
> cently . . . we have not thought it worthwhile to spare the time to
> chart our cultural, scenic, archeological, or even industrial or com-
> mercial facilities. Scattered throughout the large territory of the
> United States are hundreds of communities with distinctive features
> and with special values, but for lack of knowledge of them scholars
> and educators, tourists and merchants, sportsmen and recreation
> hunters have ignored the natural and cultural advantages of the
> United States.[32]

To rectify this ignorance, the Washington office of the FWP
assigned for each state a general editor to supervise a team of writers,
editors, historians, art critics, and other professional workers to compile

31. Quoted in ibid., p. 109.
32. Quoted in William F. McDonald, op. cit., p. 695.

and compose guides that would illuminate each state's geology, geography, prehistory, history, folklore, literature, music, art, architecture, agriculture, industry, commerce, urban life, black history and life (at least in those states where significant numbers of African Americans lived), and scenic attractions and provide detailed, road-by-road highway guides and maps to each of them as well. The state editors were by no means autonomous. They would be monitored by field supervisors sent out to look over their shoulders from time to time, then report back to the Washington office on their progress, or lack thereof. Every word written by the state teams was expected to conform to complex standards and regulations developed in Washington and to be produced on firm schedules, though the consequent supervisory strain on the folks in Washington became so great that regional administrative and editorial offices ultimately were created to relieve some of the pressure.

The obstacles to producing anything of value in such a system were formidable. The bureaucratic maze was torturous, and the presence of so many people authorized to express editorial opinions and impose cultural standards guaranteed administrative incoherence and confusion. Furthermore, while many state editors displayed the highest standards of professionalism, many were appointed to satisfy political needs and tended to be no more competent than most such appointees ever are. San Francisco FWP writer Miriam Allen de Ford expressed a common frustration in the inevitable verse:

> I think that I have never tried
> A job as painful as the Guide,
> A guide which changes every day
> Because our betters feel that way,
> A guide whose deadlines come so fast
> Yet no one lives to see the last,
> A guide to which we give our best
> To hear: "This stinks like all the rest!"
>
> There's no way out but suicide
> For only God can end the Guide.[33]

33. Quoted in Penkower, op. cit., p. 33.

Nevertheless, beginning in 1937 with *Washington: City and Capital*, a massive volume whose comprehensiveness and intellectual rigor made it one of the most enduringly reliable sources for the history and folkways of the nation's capital, the FWP produced and published guides to every state in the Union, as well as equally ambitious guides to Los Angeles, San Francisco, New York City, New Orleans, Philadelphia, and Puerto Rico. Most of these were adequate at best, but some achieved true excellence and many continue to be reprinted in original or revised form today—thanks to the skills of state editors like novelist Vardis Fisher of Idaho, historian Ray Allen Billington of Massachusetts, and physician Mabel S. Ulrich of Michigan, and a pantheon of down-on-their-luck writers, among them men and women who would go on to become some of the most accomplished authors in twentieth-century America, such as John Cheever, Ralph Ellison, Richard Wright, Conrad Aiken, Margaret Walker, Nelson Algren, Zora Neale Hurston, Mari Sandoz, Saul Bellow, and Kenneth Rexroth.

While the total number of people who worked on the FWP averaged only between 4,500 and 5,200 a year (and less than 10 percent of these were professional writers), for the guide series alone the agency's contribution to the cultural inheritance of the nation outweighed its minuscule effect on the country's unemployment figures.[34] Cultural and literary critic Alfred Kazin believed that the American Guide series "resulted in an extraordinary contemporary epic. Out of the need to find something to say about every community and the country around it, out of the vast storehouse of facts behind the guides . . . there emerged an America unexampled in density and regional diversity."[35]

The FWP did not stop with guides. Its mandate, according to a WPA press release at the beginning, included "the preparation of a limited number of special studies in the arts, history, economics, sociology, etc., by qualified writers on relief."[36] Out of this vague directive issued some remarkable ancillary products, including local histories, folklore collections, and thousands of interviews. Working with the WPA's Joint Committee on Folk Arts, FWP researchers in every corner of

34. Figures from ibid., p. 62.
35. Quoted in Mangione, op. cit., p. 365.
36. Quoted in ibid., p. 47.

America collected ballads, tales, poetry, colloquialisms, and other material; in all, about 14,000 manuscripts of folklore were produced.[37] A nationwide "life-history" project began collecting the oral histories of thousands of ordinary Americans; many of these were included in *These Are Our Lives*, an anthology of interviews conducted in Tennessee, North Carolina, and Georgia, which was published in 1938 to good reviews and is still a standard source for the period.

The FWP's auxiliary programs also included an earnest effort to offset perhaps the single greatest flaw in the American Guide series: the callous and prejudicial treatment of African Americans in all the guides to the southern states, and the condescending, stereotypical view taken of blacks in many of the guides for the northern states. Under the direction of folklorist Alan Lomax, and later Benjamin Botkin, researchers interviewed about 3,000 surviving former slaves to obtain a portrait of life in the pre–Civil War South, compiling an oral history archive that would be used by historians for decades to come.[38]

It is not likely that the FWP did much to raise the literary consciousness of the nation, but it did go a long way toward preserving some of its cultural roots, and for those writers and would-be writers who participated, it served handsomely its more mundane purpose of temporary support. "If we want to have poets in this country," Malcolm Cowley wrote in *Poetry* magazine, "we will have to keep them alive."[39] Few of the writers who joined the ranks of the FWP were serious poets, but most of them looked upon it as nothing short of

37. Figure in Penkower, op. cit., p. 154.
38. The FWP was also ordered to adopt the Historical Records Survey as part of its family of projects, at least for a time. The survey, an attempt to catalog and evaluate the archival resources of the United States—all of the United States, from churches to police precincts, city halls to the United States Congress—originated during the months of the Civil Works Administration, but since March of 1934 had been lost in an administrative limbo. In November 1935, it was transferred to Federal One and put under the wing of the FWP, apparently because no other agency was willing or able to take it in. Henry Alsberg accepted the project without major complaint, but in truth had little interest in it, often dipping into its budget to finance other FWP programs and generally treating it like the unwanted child it was; he and the survey's director, Luther Evans, remained at loggerheads until the HRS finally was taken out of Alsberg's care and given an identity of its own in Federal One in November 1936. See William F. McDonald, op. cit., pp. 759–89.
39. Quoted in "Federal Poets Number," *Poetry* (July 1938).

salvation. "Men who hadn't had a job for years," novelist Anzia Yezierska remembered, "fondled five- and ten-dollar bills with the tender-
ness of farmers rejoicing over a new crop of grain."[40] New York
newspaperman James McGraw would not have argued with her. "After
being on relief for several years," he recalled, "or just getting handouts
here and there, or small writing jobs—some of us were writing pornog-
raphy to stay alive—we were all joyful at the prospect of getting a
weekly salary and doing work that had some connection with our
skills."[41]

While she hardly ignored the similar desires of unemployed theater
people, the Federal Theater Project's director, Vassar's Hallie Flanagan,
had modernist ambitions that were quite as grandiose as those of the
FAP. Her obligation, she believed, was not merely to get as many as
12,000 actors, vaudeville performers, stagehands, playwrights, designers, and other theater people off the relief rolls every year but to supervise the creation of "a national theatre [sic] and building a national
culture."[42] To both ends, the FTP established twelve regional theater
centers from Boston to Los Angeles, Birmingham to Iowa City. Each
center not only launched productions in its headquarters city, and put
together touring companies to take these and other productions on the
road, but helped private and public theater groups in the towns of its
region to undertake productions of their own. Where such groups did
not exist, the centers encouraged the formation of independent theater
companies. There were dozens of German- and Italian-language productions and scores of Yiddish productions. Fifty-eight traveling troupes
carried shows to the wilderness camps of the Civilian Conservation
Corps. A children's theater division developed dozens of traditional
puppet and marionette shows and produced original plays and musicals, including an adaptation of *Pinocchio* that proved so popular that it
inspired Walt Disney to do his own animated movie version. A radio
division produced more than 3,000 productions a year for the Federal
Theatre of the Air. Uncounted tableaux and skits produced for local

40. Anzia Yezierska, *Red Ribbon on a White Horse*, p. 161.
41. Quoted in Mangione, op. cit., p. 158.
42. Quote from Joanne Bentley, *Hallie Flanagan: A Life in the Theatre*, p. 190.

schools and community centers promoted hygiene, literacy, and other socially important concerns.[43]

The overwhelming majority of the 396 standard dramatic productions the FTP supported were quite as middlebrow and predictable—and often as inept—as the bulk of the programs of Federal One. But if most of FTP's theatrical gallimaufry was unremarkable, some was innovative enough to raise eyebrows. Like the rest of the WPA's divisions, the FTP devoted considerable energy and resources to the needs of African Americans, particularly in the development of black theater projects in most major cities, including such southern cities as Birmingham, Raleigh, and Greensboro. Most productions in the various black projects were just as ordinary as those among white units, although the production of *The Swing Mikado*, a jazzy, window-rattling adaptation of the Gilbert and Sullivan standard by Chicago's Negro Unit, ran for more than five months in Chicago and is still one of the best-remembered productions of the entire FTP. But it was the Negro unit in New York's Harlem, where John Houseman and Orson Welles built upon decades of work by the Lafayette Theater Company, that produced the most renowned black show of the era. This was *Macbeth*, a free-spirited adaptation of Shakespeare's tragedy set in nineteenth-century Haiti with a voodoo theme. The production featured an all-black cast, including a group of genuine voodoo drummers from Africa, direction by Welles, and music by Virgil Thomson. It opened to a packed house at the Lafayette on March 14, 1936, while an estimated 10,000 people teemed in the street outside. The reviews were generally good, except that from the conservative Percy Hammond in the *Herald Tribune*, who panned the production as one more wretched excess from the New Deal. The next night, Hallie Flanagan claimed, the voodoo drummers filled the theater "with unusual drumming and with chants more weird and horrible than anything that had been heard on the stage."[44] A few days later, Hammond caught pneumonia and died. While it apparently killed no more critics, the black *Macbeth* ran for

---

43. Unless otherwise indicated, my discussion of the individual works of the Federal Theater Project is from ibid.
44. Quote in ibid., p. 227.

seven months in New York, then toured to eight other cities around the nation, including Dallas, where it enlivened the state's Centennial Exposition for ten days.

Another gaudy success from the FTP was *It Can't Happen Here*, an antifascist play adapted by Sinclair Lewis and Jack Moffit from Lewis's novel. The novel had already been turned down by Hollywood, whose moguls, most fresh from their crucial participation in the defeat of Upton Sinclair, had no interest in a book claiming that the United States was just as vulnerable to the evils of fascism as any other country. "A novel so highly controversial and in such scabrous bad taste that it suffered rejection for screen production by all the important motion picture companies," columnist Harold Lord Varney had written in Hearst's *Los Angeles Examiner*, "*It Can't Happen Here* is now to be given a nationwide staging UNDER THE GONFALON OF THE UNITED STATES GOVERNMENT ITSELF . . . PROPAGANDA—naked and unconcealed."[45] Lewis's play was not the only standard FTP production to earn the charge that the Project was in the hands of New Deal leftists (as, in fact, much of it was). Other productions, including a version of Shakespeare's *Julius Caesar* in which the cast wore black shirts, got their share of conservative criticism, but nothing matched the reaction that greeted the FTP's most startling innovation: "The Living Newspaper." Designed to educate the general public on current affairs, the form employed pantomime, puppetry, reenactments, crowd scenes, visual projection, and other devices to replicate the simplicity and impact of the daily American newspaper and, as the staff of the New York Living Newspaper Unit put it, "break through the technological barriers of decadent stagecraft as well as the ideological barriers of decadent thought."[46]

The barriers of decadent stagecraft and thought were first broken with *Triple A Plowed Under*, an interpretation of the New Deal's agricultural programs that had recently been invalidated by the Supreme Court; in the finest proletarian tradition, the play concluded with farmers and unemployed factory workers linking arms in a final tableau to demonstrate unity against their oppressors. This theatrical pamphlet

45. Quoted in Hallie Flanagan, op. cit., p. 117.
46. Quoted in Stuart Cosgrove, "Introduction" to Lorraine Brown, et al., eds., *Liberty Deferred and Other Living Newspapers of the 1930s*, p. x.

opened in New York on March 14, 1936, playing there for nearly three months and doing similarly well in five other cities. Others soon followed, including *Injunction Granted*, a union-friendly presentation of the ongoing labor struggle; *Power*, which celebrated the New Deal's commitment to government hydroelectric projects; and the single most successful of the nine "Living Newspaper" productions, *One-Third of a Nation*, a vivid, crowded (195 characters were played by 67 actors), and uncommonly effective dramatization of the continuing problems of unemployment, housing, and hunger, which opened in New York on January 17, 1938, and ran for nine months, while separate performances were given in nine additional cities.

During the four years of its life, the FTP brought nearly 64,000 performances of plays, musicals, operettas, folk and ballet dances, vaudeville skits and songs, and even circus shows to the cities and towns of America, estimating that total attendance reached more than 30.3 million.[47] Such incipient luminaries as Arthur Miller, Arlene Francis, Will Geer, Joseph Cotten, and Burt Lancaster (as an acrobat) were kept off the relief rolls at one time or another by FTP work relief. That was all well and good, Hallie Flanagan declared in a statement that invoked the artistic convictions of the entire Federal One program probably better than anything ever written about it. Aside from its "primary and most important function, that of enabling people to live decently and happily by the practice of their profession," she said, the FTP's "greatest achievement" was in the

> creation of an audience of many millions, a waiting audience. This audience proved that the need for theatre [sic] is not an emergency. Either the arts are useful to the development of the great numbers of American citizens who cannot afford them—in which case the government has no reason to concern itself with them; or else the arts are useful in making people better citizens, better workmen, in short better-equipped individuals—which is, after all, the aim of a democracy—in which cast the government may well concern itself. . . .
>
> Creating for our citizens a medium for free expression such as no other government can assure, and offering the people access to the

47. Figures from Flanagan, op. cit., "Appendix," p. 435.

arts and tools of a civilization which they themselves are helping to make . . . is at once an illustration and a bulwark of the democratic form of government.[48]

MEMBERS OF CONGRESS, most of whom were suspicious of artists on general principles anyway, as legislators often are, regularly expressed doubts about the legitimacy of the whole federal arts program, and the Federal Theater Project's identifiably leftist inclinations would get it into serious trouble before long—though the irrepressibly upbeat Flanagan would claim that such criticism was just one more indication that the theater still had "tremendous power to stir up life and infuse it with fire. . . . No one argues over a dead art or a dead issue."[49] That may have been true, but the congressional arguing had begun from the moment the WPA itself was created, usually during those periods when the administration came to Congress asking for the WPA's annual appropriation, and not all of the discussion was confined to the FTP's political shading or to the questionable character of the artistic community in general. Conservative congressmen and their allies believed the entire WPA—or at least most of it, and certainly those portions of it devoted to helping artists and other white-collar types—was little better than an enormous boondoggle. For such as these, the folkloric image of lazy workers leaning on their shovels was no joke. "Millions for Expense, But Not One Cent for Efficiency," cried a headline in the *Chicago Daily News*, and when Berton Braley, resident versifier for Hearst's *New York American*, lampooned the New Deal's spending habits, it was almost certainly the billions of dollars under the control of the WPA that he had in mind: "So New Deal expenditures constantly mount./The cost? Oh, why bother to weigh it,/Since no one has troubled to check the account/Or figured who's going to pay it?"[50] Even some of FDR's supporters worried about what Hopkins and his people

48. Ibid., pp. 372–73.
49. Ibid., p. 333.
50. Headline in *Chicago Daily News* (December 6, 1935); poem in Berton Braley, *New Deal Ditties, or, Running in the Red with Roosevelt*, p. 26.

were up to. "I'm sick of voting blank checks," Senator Bennett Champ Clark, a Democrat, complained at one point.[51]

Clark and others may have been reluctant to vote the WPA's annual appropriations, but for most of the decade enough of them did so to keep the agency alive, though often pinched. Whatever their reservations, few politicians were yet ready to challenge a powerful public sentiment in favor of the WPA, especially potent, unsurprisingly, among the vast majority of those whom its programs had helped. This came home with a certain force in the spring of 1936, when diminishing funds forced Hopkins to issue a call for an across-the-board cut of 10 percent in all expenditures for the rest of the fiscal year. The uproar of complaint was immediate, including a flood of letters from WPA workers themselves. "Please continue this W.P.A. program," one group wrote on April 5, 1936. "It makes us feel like an American citizen to earn our own living. Being on the dole or relief roll makes us lazy and the funds are not enough to live decent on. . . . So we as W.P.A. workers in Battle Creek Michigan, appeal to you as our *Great Leader* to continue this great cause for Better citizens in Battle Creek Michigan."[52] In Washington, the United States Conference of Mayors urged Hopkins to rescind his order as soon as possible, while in New York City an emergency meeting of more than 400 social workers called the WPA a manifestation of "the essence of democracy" and sent a resolution protesting the cuts.[53]

Not all WPA workers were inclined to be quite so docile as those in Battle Creek, and demonstrations, sit-downs, strikes, marching picket lines, and other turmoil erupted on WPA project jobs and in front of agency offices all over the country—many engineered by the Workers' Alliance, a former Socialist union now dominated by Communists. Some of the actions were of major dimensions. Chief among them were those in New York City, where WPA administrator Victor F. Ridder, a notorious martinet, announced on March 4 that 10,000 jobs would be

51. Quoted in Adams, op. cit., p. 94.
52. Quoted in Robert S. McElvaine, ed., *Down and Out in the Great Depression: Letters from the Forgotten Man*, p. 127.
53. Quoted in Millett, op. cit, p. 53.

294 THE HUNGRY YEARS

cut by the end of the month and another 40,000 by the end of June, stating further that the first to go would be "loafers" and "shirkers."[54] Almost instantly, picket lines ringed the Port Authority building on Eighth Avenue, where the WPA's main offices occupied the tenth floor, while WPA employees inside the building seized the offices and held them until routed by police. Outside, the picket lines not only interfered with the coming and going of WPA officials but travelers as well, since the building was also the city's main bus terminal. When police were called in to keep the building open, fights between club-wielding patrolmen and WPA workers became almost daily affairs, disturbing reminders of all the labor violence that had erupted in 1934.

In New York and elsewhere, disruptions and work stoppages fell off once Congress gave the WPA another chunk of operating money at the beginning of the fiscal year in July, but the point had been made: with all its faults and confusions of complexity, for millions of Americans, the WPA was neither a boondoggle nor a refuge for political scoundrels; it was a plain necessity, one worth fighting to keep. And when in October 1936, Harry Hopkins stood up before an audience in the San Francisco Opera House who had gathered to hear a program by the WPA-sponsored San Francisco Symphony and Choir, it doubtless was to all of those millions, not just the audience before him, to which he made his vow: "I am proud of what I have done," he shouted. "I am terribly proud, and as long as I have anything to do with it, I'LL NEVER LET YOU DOWN."[55]

The applause, it was said, made the opening strains of "The Star-Spangled Banner" almost impossible to hear.

54. Quotes in Millett, op. cit., p. 52.
55. Quoted in McJimsey, op. cit., p. 99.

13

The Lions of Labor

While Hopkins and his colleagues in the Works Progress Administration set about building a new architecture of relief for those who did not have jobs, the leadership of the labor movement was struggling through a snarl of contending factions to ensure that at least some who did have jobs would also enjoy greater control over what they were paid and the conditions under which they had to work. Section 7(a) of the National Industrial Recovery Act had given organized labor a taste of opportunity it had not enjoyed since World War I, and by the beginning of 1935 the movement had blossomed, establishing new unions, increasing union membership hugely, and otherwise exercising its new-found hope, often with the clatter and cry of violence. But it still possessed no real power.

It never would, the UMW's beetle-browed John L. Lewis said, as long as industry maintained its dominance over labor. There was much talk about the "partnership" of capital and labor that the NIRA had established, Lewis had told a largely conservative audience at San Francisco's Commonwealth Club on October 10, 1934, but, he warned,

"Labor cannot, and will not, and should never be content until its partnership becomes a real one and not merely one in theory. To oppose such
a movement is . . . not only a crime against labor—it is a social blunder
which may lead to the toppling over of our whole economic edifice."
The world, he said, was "seething with new ideas and new desires,"
among them the belief that there must be created "a better organized
economic system, in which there will be no unemployment of those
who wish to work, a more equitable distribution of income, and far
more intelligent use of the earth's natural resources."[1] In almost precisely a year, Lewis, no friend of Communists (though willing enough
to use them), indeed on most nonlabor issues a card-carrying conservative, would be instrumental in achieving a metamorphosis in the
labor movement that may have fallen short of the proletarian revolution
dreamed of by the CP/USA, but was nonetheless crucial in shaping the
future of American society.

    In its pursuit of a new measure of power, the labor movement was
abetted by a profoundly labor-friendly contingent in the United States
Congress, led by Senator Robert F. Wagner. Wagner had been born in a
tiny village near Wiesbaden, Germany, in 1877, and did not come to
this country until 1886. His family settled in Yorktown, Manhattan's
German colony, and every member had to work at something in order
to keep food on the table. It was only by dint of the kind of blind perseverance and dogged labor by which so many immigrants had crawled
out of their circumstances that Bob Wagner had managed to get
through school and obtain a law degree—and ultimately a place in the
political firmament of New York's Tammany Hall. That connection
sent him to the New York State Assembly, where he became, with Al
Smith, one of that body's most progressive-minded legislators. In 1926,
he was elected to the Senate of the United States, and, with the advent
of the New Deal, he became one of its most steadfast congressional
allies and chairman of the original National Labor Board. "My boyhood
was a pretty rough passage," he once remarked. "I came through it, yes.
But that was luck, luck, luck! Think of the others!"[2]

1. Quoted in Dubofsky and Van Tine, op. cit., p. 209.
2. Quoted in J. Joseph Huthmacher, *Senator Robert F. Wagner and the Rise of Urban Liberalism*, p. 12.

Wagner had been thinking of "the others" most of his public life. As 1934 came to an end, among those he was thinking of were the workers who had found Section 7(a) of the National Industrial Recovery Act to have failed them—in spite of the heady months of organization and activism it had helped to generate. For Wagner, the job as head of the NLB had started out well enough. When several thousand workers walked off their jobs at the Berkshire Knitting Mills in Reading, Pennsylvania, after the company refused to recognize their Section 7(a) union, Wagner and the NLB had brought all parties together in August and ended the strike with a settlement prescription it was hoped would apply to other industries: all employees were rehired without discrimination, and an election was held in which the majority of workers were allowed to choose their union representation. This "Reading Formula" was then used to settle a strike in Patterson, New Jersey, as well as several small walkouts in Detroit, and, finally, it was applied to a strike of some 10,000 workers in the Weirton Steel Company of West Virginia and Ohio.

That was where the system started to break down, setting a precedent that the NLB had not anticipated: the Weirton management refused to let its employees vote for anything but the company union. This was a violation of Section 7(a), as the NLB read the law, but when Wagner asked the National Recovery Administration to penalize the company by withdrawing its Blue Eagle, nothing happened. This, in spite of Wagner's reminder that "until the promises made by the Recovery Act are given definite meaning, we cannot have happy and contented workers."[3] Hugh Johnson was unwilling to force the issue of compliance for fear of rocking the code-making boat. Encouraged by the Weirton company's success in defying the NLB, the Edward G. Budd Manufacturing Company followed suit by repudiating a board ruling with regard to its own striking employees. To Wagner's frustration, the NRA did not move against the Budd company, either.

Largely at Wagner's request, FDR issued executive orders at the end of 1933 and the beginning of 1934 that reaffirmed the administration's support of the Reading Formula. But Roosevelt failed to give the NLB any additional power to enforce the formula, nor did he put pressure on

3. Ibid., p. 162.

the NRA to do so. Worse, he refused to repudiate Johnson and NRA legal counsel, Donald Richberg, when they issued what they called a "clarification" of Section 7(a): the NRA, the statement said, would support "the right of minority groups or of individual employees to deal with their employer separately."[4] The statement was an ax-blow at the whole notion of solidarity, as sacred to unionism as the doctrine of free enterprise was to capitalism.

On March 1, 1934, Wagner expressed his frustration with administration policy by introducing a "Labor Disputes Act" that would create a permanent National Labor Board with the power to issue subpoenas, enforce its orders through the federal courts, certify bargaining agents in labor disputes, and issue cease-and-desist orders. His main concern, Wagner made clear, was that the presence of company unions as the principal bargaining agents deprived workers of the strength that came with a wider membership—a condition, he said, that was necessary "not only to uphold their own end of the labor bargain but to stabilize and standardize wage levels, to cope with the sweatshop and the exploiter, and to exercise their proper voice in economic affairs."[5]

The bill, predictably, was immediately opposed by industrial groups. "It foments class warfare," one trade association told members of Congress, while the Associated Industries of Oklahoma made Wagner the apparent minion of Lucifer himself in a newspaper advertisement stating that the bill "prohibits the practice of Christian brotherhood. It puts loyalty to labor unions above loyalty to God. The measure, in effect, would out-Stalin Stalin, out-Soviet the Russian Soviets, and create a despotism."[6] While he made no reference to God or Stalin, Charles H. Hook, president of the American Roller Company, thought Wagner should be removed from the National Labor Board immediately, since "he is unfairly prejudiced against industry and industrial management generally."[7] What was less easy to take was opposition from the Roosevelt administration, which, through Johnson and Richberg, reiterated

---

4. Quoted in Stanley Vittoz, *New Deal Labor Policy and the American Industrial Economy*, p. 141.
5. Quoted in Philip Taft, *The A.F. of L. from the Death of Gompers to the Merger*, p. 122.
6. Both quotes in Huthmacher, op. cit., p. 165.
7. Quote in Taft, op. cit., p. 23.

its support of the company union idea and dismissed Wagner's fears as insupportable. Wagner and his legislative staff worked out compromise legislation with White House staff, but the resulting bill failed to impress either labor or the Congress, and when Roosevelt's own support proved lukewarm, the proposal never even reached the floor for debate. Meanwhile, in June, with a potential steel strike in the offing, the White House New Dealers asked Congress to give FDR the authority to establish, through executive order, a mediation board with many of the powers that Wagner's bill had sought.

A resolution to that effect passed the House unanimously shortly before the scheduled adjournment of Congress, but when it got to the Senate, where Wagner had promised his support, the ever-radical Progressive, Robert M. La Follette, promptly offered Wagner's original legislation as an amendment, warning that unless it was passed with the amendment intact, "we shall have the most serious labor conditions with which the United States has ever been confronted."[8] Wagner was in a dilemma. In order to get his resolution passed, he would have to oppose his own earlier amendment. "This is really one of the most embarrassing moments of my whole political life," he said when he stood to speak against La Follette's amendment. Then, in a rejoinder to an anti-union tirade by Senator Millard Tydings of Maryland, the mild-mannered Wagner delivered himself of perhaps the most heated political statement of his career.[9] "Who is this worker we are talking about?" he asked.

> Is he some enemy of this country? Is there any reason why he, unlike other people, should be shackled in some way? He is a man of flesh and blood like you and me, with hopes and aspirations, who wants to preserve America for himself and for his children. . . . That is the man for whom I am pleading. . . . I simply want to see him get an opportunity in life, because I love this country, which gave me my opportunity, and to which I owe everything I have.[10]

8. Quoted in Patrick J. Maney, *"Young Bob" La Follette: A Biography of Robert M. La Follette, Jr.*, p. 127.
9. Quoted in Huthmacher, op. cit., p. 169.
10. Quoted in ibid., p. 170.

Wagner asked La Follette to withdraw his amendment. La Follette did so, finally, but not before extracting a firm promise from Wagner—willingly given—that even better legislation would be put into the pipeline when a new Congress was seated in 1935.

With La Follette's amendment gone, the Senate passed the joint resolution, and on June 29 Roosevelt exercised his new powers by abolishing the National Labor Board and replacing it with the National Labor Relations Board—with the ambiguity with regard to company unions versus noncompany unions intact. But the administration's true feelings appeared to be revealed all too clearly in response to a decision made by the new board. That decision had recognized a union that a majority of workers had voted to join, rather than the company union a minority had chosen. This, an NRA lawyer said, was "contrary to the President's interpretation."[11] Roosevelt did not disagree, and went on to impose severe restrictions on how the 1934 NLRB could go about its business. By the end of 1934, the board's chairman, Francis Biddle, recalled, it was clear that something had to be done. "I was convinced that the present law was unclear and imprecise; that it could not be enforced; that a new law was needed with enforceable remedies."[12] Wagner was already working on it. On February 21, 1935, as the new, presumably more radically minded 76th Congress got down to work, the senator introduced another labor bill, one of whose main purposes was to remedy the inequities "between employees who do not possess full freedom of association or actual liberty of contract, and employers who are organized in the corporate or other forms of ownership association."[13] What was good enough for industry ought to be good enough for labor. The bill also restated the powers of the National Labor Relations Board that Roosevelt had created but made the board permanent, not merely an administrative child subject to the whims of the president.

Most of the New Dealers were lukewarm, at best, in their support of Wagner's bill, feeling that the administration had gone far enough in meeting labor's demands with the National Industrial Recovery Act.

11. Quoted in Vittoz, op. cit., p. 145.
12. Quoted in ibid., p. 146.
13. Quoted in ibid., p. 148.

But after the Supreme Court invalidated Title I of the NIRA in the *Schechter* decision on May 27, killing Section 7(a) with it, that assumption vanished. On July 5, Wagner's bill was on the president's desk, and he signed it.

GIVEN RECENT HISTORY, Roosevelt's signature was by no means any guarantee that law had finally triumphed over corporate anarchy. Industry had every hope that ultimately the Supreme Court would crush the Wagner Act just as firmly as it had the NIRA. (In the end, it did not.) Whether the law could be made to work under such ambiguous circumstances was open to question, but there were those just as ready to test the proposition as the workers of 1934 had been ready to seize the opportunity provided by Section 7(a)—and, as in 1934, the New Dealers would have little control over the consequences.

In October 1935, delegates to the annual convention of the AFL gathered for deliberations in Atlantic City, New Jersey. Prominent among them was John L. Lewis. Like Senator Wagner, Lewis knew what it was to work, having learned this particular lesson in Lucas, Iowa, where as youngsters he and his brothers had joined their Welsh immigrant father in working the nearly airless pits of the Big Hill Coal and Mining Company and other mines in the district. "Unionism in the Welsh and Scottish coal-mining areas has a special quality that is part of Mr. Lewis's heritage," Jonathan Mitchell wrote in a 1936 profile of the labor leader. "It has always been hopelessly tangled up with evangelical religion. Possibly the horrors of the early Welsh coal mines, where half-naked mothers acted as draft animals in the black, suffocating galleries, served to identify unionism with the path to Heaven."[14] Lewis's own brand of perseverance had impelled him out of those pits and up the path of unionism until he became president of the UMW in January 1921. He and the UMW had managed to survive the crippling anti-union years of the twenties, and by 1935 the astonishing burst of growth that had followed the passage of the NIRA in 1934 had given both the man and his union greater power.

14. Jonathan Mitchell, "John the Giant-Killer," *The New Republic* (October 14, 1936).

Lewis would use his new prominence to insist once more that it was time to industrialize the AFL by opening its doors to workers of all kinds, and by now he had a coterie of powerful allies who agreed with him—among them David Dubinksy, president of the International Ladies' Garment Workers' Union (ILGWU); Thomas McMahon, president of the Textile Workers Union (TWU); Charles Howard, president of the International Typographical Union (ITU); and Sidney Hillman, president of the Amalgamated Clothing Workers of America (ACWA). As the 1935 convention got under way, Lewis and his coterie soon were aware that the leaders of the AFL—particularly its conservative president, William Green—were not going to move the AFL anywhere near industrial unionism. "On the contrary," David Dubinsky remembered, "they were determined to move backward at top speed."[15] Still, Lewis and the others were determined to make the AFL put its reluctance on the record. Shortly after the opening gavel of the convention, Charles Howard presented a minority resolution drafted by Lewis and the dissidents: "In those industries where the work performed by a majority of the workers is of such a nature that it might fall within the jurisdictional claim of more than one craft union," the resolution read in part, "it is declared that industrial organization is the only form that will be acceptable to the workers or adequately meet their needs."[16]

After opponents spoke against the resolution, Lewis rose to defend it. "There has been a change in industry," he reminded the convention in an extemporaneous speech that was vintage Lewis in its powerful, if sometimes tortured, poetics:

> a great concentration of opposition to the extension and the logical expansion of the trade-union movement. . . . And, whereas today the craft unions of this country may be able to stand upon their own feet and like mighty oaks stand before the gale, defy the lightning, yet the day may come when . . . those organizations may not be able to withstand the lightning and the gale. Now, prepare yourselves . . . heed

15. David Dubinksy and A. H. Raskin, *David Dubinsky: A Life with Labor*, p. 220.
16. Quoted in Saul Alinsky, *John L. Lewis: An Unauthorized Biography*, pp. 73–74.

this cry from Macedonia that comes from the hearts of men. Organize the unorganized.[17]

If they rejected the minority resolution, Lewis warned in conclusion, "despair will prevail where hope now exists [and] high wassail will prevail at the banquet tables of the mighty."[18] Eloquence done, a vote was taken and the resolution was rejected, 18,024 to 10,933.

Lewis was not quite finished. Three days later, he was in attendance when a rubber worker from Akron was arguing the question of jurisdiction for his local. William Hutcheson of the Carpenters' Union, an opponent of Lewis and his allies, interrupted the man with a shout of "point of order!"

Lewis came to the defense of the somewhat rattled rubber worker by telling Hutcheson that "this thing of raising points of order all the time on minor delegates is rather small potatoes."

This outwardly mild remark seemed to enrage Hutcheson. He stood, his three-hundred-pound bulk rising above those around him like an Irish mountain. "I was raised on small potatoes," he shouted. "That is why I am so small."

Lewis and Hutcheson exchanged a few more unrecorded remarks, during which time Hutcheson may or may not have called Lewis a "bastard" (accounts vary). Lewis scampered over a few empty auditorium chairs, jumped up, and slugged Hutcheson, who fell, Lewis on top of him. By the time the fight could be broken up, Hutcheson was bleeding profusely and had to be led from the hall. "Lewis," according to a reporter, "casually adjusted his tie and collar, relit his cigar, and sauntered slowly through the crowded aisles to the rostrum."[19]

The little lion of labor had wanted a moment of drama to heighten the importance of what was about to happen next, and it was generally believed he had cold-bloodedly engineered his scuffle with Hutcheson. At any rate, with newspapers still trumpeting the incident, Lewis

17. Quoted in ibid., pp. 74–75.
18. Quoted in Dubofsky and Van Tine, op. cit., p. 220.
19. My account of the fight is based mainly on that in Alinsky, op. cit., pp. 75–76. The reporter's quote is from Dubofsky and Van Tine, op. cit. p. 220.

joined Dubinsky, Howard, Hillman, and a few others at a breakfast meeting at the President Hotel the day after the convention adjourned, where they agreed that the future of industrial unionism lay with them, not with the leadership of the AFL. Three weeks later, most of the same men met again at UMW headquarters on K Street in Washington, D.C., to form the Committee for Industrial Organization, an ad hoc organization that would work within the AFL to promote industrial unionism's goals. Lewis would be its president.

In the beginning, the CIO liked to present itself as the loyal opposition, but William Green and the AFL executive council suspected insurrection (with good reason). In late November, Green sent a letter to Lewis and the rest of the CIO organizers warning them to disband. Lewis responded by noisily resigning his position as vice president of the AFL, then followed that up on December 7 with a well-publicized letter that offered Green the chairmanship of the new organization, saying that the AFL president "would have the satisfaction of supporting a cause in which you believe inherently and of contributing . . . to the achievement of an enlarged opportunity for the nation's workers."[20]

Such cheeky behavior infuriated Green, but, like Lewis's assault on Hutcheson, it enchanted the nation's press, and the CIO's name was spread across the land repeatedly over the weeks of the dispute. Lewis capitalized on the publicity by launching an organizing drive, traveling to Detroit, Cleveland, Toledo, and other industrialized areas to address cheering throngs of workers. When Green and the AFL's executive council continued to demand that Lewis and his organization stop what they were doing, and stop it immediately, he either ignored them or repudiated their authority to tell the CIO what to do.

The predictable schism came in June 1936, when Lewis stepped into the vacuum created by the AFL's reluctance to launch a major organizing drive among steelworkers. Lewis offered the services of the CIO to the Amalgamated Association of Iron, Steel and Tin Workers. The steel union hesitated for fear of alienating Green and the AFL, but Lewis would have none of it, giving the union twenty-four hours to decide. "We're tired—want action," Lewis telegraphed Mike Tighe, president of the union. "I think we're going to help steelworkers with

20. Quoted in Dubofsky and Van Tine, p. 225.

or without you. If you spurn it, we'll announce to the country and you can do your own explaining."[21] Tighe capitulated, signing an agreement that gave the CIO organizing authority and the right to create a Steel Workers Organizing Committee that Lewis would run. All of this, of course, had been done without the slightest authorization from the AFL, and in July Green filed an official complaint with the AFL board, charging the CIO with "dual unionism" and general insubordination. The charges were approved, to no one's surprise, and the leaders of the CIO were instructed to take their respective unions out of the new organization or face expulsion from the AFL. They chose expulsion. Two years later, the split would be formally ratified and the organization renamed the Congress of Industrial Organizations.

While Lewis single-mindedly steered the CIO to independence, the newly formed United Rubber Workers' Union in Akron, Ohio, gave the organization a splendid opportunity to demonstrate its superiority to the AFL and establish its credibility with workers throughout the nation. Things had been bubbling in Akron for quite a while. Back in the summer of 1934, rubber workers at the General Tire Company plant had organized under the provisions of Section 7(a), then had taken things into their own hands when the company refused to agree on a contract—and in the process the union reintroduced one of the oldest and most useful tactics in labor's arsenal. Rex D. Murray, a rubber union officer, described it:

> I walked through the plant and gave [the workers] the signal to shut it down. That's when it started. And as fast as I could walk from one department to another, throughout the plant, that's when it went down. And one of the plant guards was following me from about the time I got to the second department, telling me I couldn't do it. "You have to stay in your own department." I said, "I'll go back to my department in a little while!" and I just kept walking, one floor to the other. When I gave them the signal they pulled the switches and shut it down.[22]

21. Quoted in ibid., p. 237.
22. Quoted in Daniel Nelson, op. cit., pp. 138–39.

This forthright action was called a "sit-down," a tactic first applied in the United States by the IWW during a 1906 strike against a General Electric plant in Schenectady, New York, and while the Akron rubber workers only held the plant for about twenty-four hours before leaving and forming picket lines outside the place, the device had gotten management's attention. After three weeks of the usual run of conflict between strikers and strikebreakers, General Tire and the union came to an agreement. On July 18, the rank and file had ratified the pact and one of the few successful Section 7(a) strikes of 1934 had ended.

By 1935, however, the rubber workers in the federal unions of Akron felt the need of cohesion if they were not only going to hold the limited gains of 1934 but have the strength to counter a powerful company-union presence that had been established during the war years, dominated by the Industrial Assembly of the Goodyear Company plants. In the summer of 1935, union membership actually began to decline even as the tire industry plucked the fruits of a substantial economic recovery. From a low of forty million in 1932, new tire sales had been rising every year, and by the end of 1935 would surpass fifty million. Encouraged by the sudden comfort of stock dividends, the big tire companies had sustained a constant anti-union program, luring workers away with such devices of enlightened self-interest as employee benefits, institutionalized grievance procedures, and other inducements designed to promote the notion that labor and management were embraced within a large, benign partnership.

Management's program seemed to be working. Facing defeat by attrition, late in the summer of 1935 Akron locals turned to William Green and asked that the AFL establish and help finance one big rubber workers' union. The AFL's executive council agreed, and in September an organizing convention was held in Akron. It was not quite the love fest of gratitude that Green might have hoped for, however, as he learned when he proposed that he and the executive council be allowed to follow their usual procedure of arbitrarily choosing and appointing the officers of the new union. "[It] is not a question of democracy," he explained; "it is a question of what to do while we are passing through a probation period."[23] To Green's chagrin, his proposal was roundly

23. Quoted in ibid., p. 167.

defeated by voice vote. The AFL president acquiesced in the astonishing desire of the workers to elect their own union officials, but not with much grace, and his studied arrogance did little to soothe relations between the rank and file of Akron and the national office of the AFL.

Still, the rubber workers had their own union now, and they were prepared to act. The sit-down had already proved its utility, and when truck tire builders at the Firestone Company plant wanted to object to a piece-rate reduction in January 1936, they simply shut off their machines and sat down to play cards for a few days until the company came around. Truck tire workers in the Goodyear and Goodrich plants followed suit a few days later. The Firestone and Goodrich incidents were swiftly settled. Not so the Goodyear conflict, which soon escalated into a major strike.

When the Goodyear strike began, it was the CIO, not the AFL, that immediately stepped in to help. The new union body not only sent Adolph Germer and Powers Hapgood, both old colleagues of Lewis in the United Mine Workers, to work with the strikers on tactics and strategy and help with public relations but it contributed $3,000 to the strike fund—and in those (or any other) times there was no gesture of support that was more quickly understood or more profoundly appreciated than cold cash. When Goodyear's Industrial Assembly stepped up its public relations campaign, the CIO brought in its own labor journalist, McAllister Colman, to counter with a storm of professionally written press releases, pamphlets, and newspaper and radio advertisements.

The ILGWU sent Rose Pesotta, its vice president and one of David Dubinsky's most experienced organizers, and other CIO unions sent people in on a regular basis to aid with advice and encouragement and to assure the workers that they were not alone in their struggle. Pesotta, who helped organize rallies, amateur theatricals, and labor sing-alongs to boost morale, was especially impressed with the contribution women were making. Women represented only about 20 percent of the industry's labor force, but the auxiliary support of sisters, wives, and daughters of union workers was essential, particularly in the care and feeding of pickets, and Pesotta found the women as determined as the men. "We got them [the company] unawares this time," one woman told her, "before they had a chance to prepare gas bombs and barbed wire against us, and if they call the militia against us, why we will stick it out all the same."[24]

By comparison to the contributions of the CIO, the AFL, the United Rubber Workers' ostensible parent, did almost nothing to aid and abet the strike, sending only one organizer into town; he did not stay long after being generally snubbed by the workers. So it was that when the strike finally was settled at the end of March, it was the CIO, not the AFL, to which the workers had looked for guidance in the final negotiations that had given them most of what they had wanted— including a thirty-six-hour workweek in the tire and tube division and forty hours in all other departments, union shop committees with the power to deal with foremen, and recognition on an equal footing with the Industrial Assembly, a concession that effectively destroyed the old company union. "Their joy was unbounded," Rose Pesotta reported after watching the strikers stage a victory parade. "Not since Armistice Day in 1918 had there been such jubilation in Akron."[25] Four months later, when it seemed clear that more strikes in the rubber industry would be inevitable, the URW officially gave its allegiance to the CIO.

WITH ITS METTLE tested in the Akron strike, the CIO was poised to launch organizing drives that Lewis hoped would not only give it equal power with the AFL in the labor movement but dominance over it. In the interest of reaching this goal, Lewis was willing to put aside some old rivalries, including that with William Z. Foster, whose Trade Union Unity League—and especially its National Miners Union—had been irritating the UMW's leader for years. Foster and the Comintern proved more amenable than Lewis might have supposed.

In spite of all the hunger marches, demonstrations, mass meetings, violence, and other forms of leftist pandemonium with which the CP/USA had agitated the Republic for five years, by the middle of the decade it had become abundantly clear that the dream of Communist

24. Quoted in Philip S. Foner, *Women and the American Labor Movement: From the First Trade Unions to the Present*, p. 322.
25. Quote in ibid., p. 323.

revolution in this country was not likely to be carried to triumph on the backs of the working classes. Through William Z. Foster's TUUL, the party had established numerous small labor organizations, like the Maritime Workers' Industrial Union in San Francisco or the National Textile Workers' Union in the cotton mills of the South, but while many of these had launched strike actions on their own and had been important allies of non-Communist unions in many areas during the turbulent months of 1933 and 1934, they had never grown to be more than minor players when compared to the established AFL organizations.[26] The great mass movement to the party among working people that the Comintern had assumed was merely a matter of time simply had not developed; fewer than half of all Communists in the United States belonged to any kind of union even in the radical atmosphere of 1934.

Nevertheless, the CP/USA had been able to colonize (as Foster put it) AFL trade unions with its people. Most of these "factions," in party parlance, remained isolated and often powerless within the unions they had infiltrated, but the Comintern nevertheless had concluded that burrowing from within was the party's best hope of controlling the American labor movement. In December 1934, the Comintern made it official, instructing Foster to dissolve the TUUL and ordering TUUL unions to seek respectability within the AFL (as many, seeing the handwriting on the wall, had done on their own already). Foster was not especially happy about the decision to kill his child, but, good party man that he was, acceded. "As for myself," he announced during the TUUL's last convention in March 1935, "I shall devote my chief attention to the work within the AFL."[27] Not for long. The new CIO's crusade to break down the elitist trade structure of the AFL—"bourgeois," the Communists might have called it—had its attractions, and not long after the CIO was officially formed at the end of 1935, Foster let it be known that the labor section of the CP/USA would support the CIO

26. For number of unions, see Fraser M. Ottanelli, op. cit., p. 54.
27. Quoted in Johanningsmeier, op. cit., p. 274. This is also my main source for the discussion of the shift in the CP/USA's labor policy, especially pp. 272–75. See also Ottanelli, op. cit., p. 49–55.

with "every energy."[28] Before long, the party would be one of Lewis's most important allies in the CIO's nationwide organizing drive.[29]

The alliance between Lewis and Foster was no more startling than another that both Lewis and Foster were forced to establish—reluctantly and temporarily, but inevitably—with the Roosevelt administration. It was a matter of plain expedience, for it was clear that the reelection of Roosevelt was crucial to the hopes of both the party and the CIO. From the point of view of the CIO, a Republican administration would be lethal, and for all his too often troublesome labor policies, FDR was far and away the only viable alternative. The Communists were no more fond of Roosevelt than many of those in the labor movement, but what the Comintern perceived as international necessities drove them into his camp.

Both believed they had reason to worry. Even for the most optimistic of regular Democrats, Roosevelt's reelection was by no means considered a foregone conclusion by the spring of 1936. Boardroom America, for one thing, was now in full revolt. Businessmen and industrialists and their allies had demonstrated a kind of terrified passivity during the first few months of the New Deal. But most now regretted how quickly they had relinquished their nearly untrammeled power over the economy in 1933, giving it into the hands of a man whom they soon considered a traitor to the traditions that had made him—and them—what they were. Such people were not inclined to admit Roosevelt's essential economic conservatism, or hear his repeated calls for a balanced budget, or recognize his clear determination merely to refine the capitalist system—not obliterate it and replace it with something new.

Capitalist revision did not work out quite as smoothly as FDR had hoped, but it was not for lack of the sort of traditional thinking that conservative businessmen might have been expected to applaud.

28. Quoted in ibid., p. 275.
29. The symbiosis between the CIO and the CP/USA may have been a good deal more intimate than previously understood, at least according to Harvey Klehr, et al. in *The Secret World of American Communism*. "Historians have long known that John L. Lewis . . . made use of Communist organizers in the CIO's formative years," the authors write. "However, the extent to which this relationship was based on negotiation and agreement between CIO leaders and the CP/USA has long been disputed. Lewis never admitted any explicit understanding with the Communists, and most historians have

Instead, most looked upon the various regulatory programs of the New Deal as the tactics of a government out to enslave business, stifle free enterprise, pander to the demands of radicals of all stripes, and give labor the power to dictate wages, hours, and other matters most businessmen and industrialists still believed the legitimate province of enlightened capitalists. Political and economic conservatives took up the cudgel early on, and the degree of personal antagonism that erupted as they mounted their attacks was notable even for a political tradition in which character assassination had always added a certain spice to the proceedings. The most notorious expression of this phenomenon was a whispering campaign in 1935 that may have originated in the advertising department of the Edison Company in Orange, New Jersey, in an attempt to defeat passage of the Public Utility Holding Company Act. If so, the effort failed, but it left a smear of lies that spread with insidious speed. "All over the country tongues waggled," *Newsweek* said, "in smoking cars, taprooms, and country general stores rumor sprouted."[30] Roosevelt, the stories went, was pathologically insane, possibly because of his polio. One version insisted that he was hopelessly addicted to narcotics; another, that his condition was such that he was surrounded day and night by White House psychiatrists disguised as servants; another, that Senator William E. Borah had found the president in his study snipping out paper dolls; and another, that during a press conference he had started laughing uncontrollably and had to be wheeled hurriedly from the room. Hamilton Fish Jr., a right-wing Republican congressman from FDR's own district who would oppose his neighbor with virulent consistency throughout all the Roosevelt years, professed to believe every word of it. "Whom the gods would destroy," he reminded his colleagues on the floor of the House, "they first make mad."[31]

---

tended to believe that Lewis simply needed a large cadre of organizers in a hurry and made use of the ready availability of the dedicated Communist organizers on an individual basis; other scholars have seen at most an unspoken understanding between Lewis and the CP/USA. Documents in the Comintern archives show that the understanding was explicit and the result of active negotiations." (Footnote, pp. 105–6.)
30. "Whispers," *Newsweek* (July 20, 1935).
31. Quoted in George Wolfskill and John A. Hudson, *All But the People: Franklin D. Roosevelt and His Critics, 1933–1939*, p. 6.

Roosevelt was too visibly healthy in mind and overall physical condition in 1936 for such rumors to do any real damage, but throughout his presidency he, Eleanor, and selected members of his administration were constantly subject to levels of vituperation not enjoyed by any president since the days when Abraham Lincoln was called an ape. "Roosevelt is my shepherd; I am in want," one inventive screed went,

He maketh me to lie down on park benches;

He leadeth me beside the still factories.

He disturbeth my soul:

He leadeth me in the paths of destruction for his Party's sake.

Yea, though I walk through the valley of recession,

I anticipate no recovery

For he is with me;

His promises and pipe dreams they no longer fool me.

He preparest a reduction in my salary in the presence of my creditors:

He anointeth my small income with taxes;

Surely unemployment and poverty shall follow me all the days of the
    New Deal,

And I will dwell in a mortgaged house forever.

Still another neatly combined hatred of FDR and Eleanor with racism and anti-Semitism:

WHAT MAN SAID TO 'THAT' WOMAN?

"You kiss the negroes

I'll kiss the Jews,

We'll stay in the White House

As long as we choose."[32]

Not all conservative sentiment could be dismissed as merely odious, however. There was a very real ideological rift that separated Roosevelt from many of those who had once supported him most enthusiastically. "We belong to a generation that has lost its way," journalist and politi-

32. Both poems in ibid., pp. 25, 35.

cal philosopher Walter Lippmann wrote. "Unable to develop the great truths which it inherited from the emancipators, it has returned to the heresies of absolutism, authority, and the domination of men by men."[33] In this harsh summary, Lippmann was including the rise of fascism in Italy and Germany and the increasing totalitarianism of Joseph Stalin's monolithic view of what a Communist state was supposed to be, but to Lippmann and other conservative Democrats, FDR and the New Dealers had distorted the progressive impulse that had placed the president in office and were corrupting the freedom of the individual by investing government with a power that reeked of collectivist tyranny. "It is the choice of Satan," Lippmann said, "offering to sell men the kingdoms of this world for their immortal Souls."[34]

The ponderous Lippmann and such others as former FDR budget director Lewis Douglas, who had resigned in frustration over FDR's stubborn insistence that he could somehow reconcile the contradictory goals of budget balancing and free-spending relief programs (he never could), generally contented themselves with the issuance of a "Statement of Principles," written by Lippmann, as a means of shaping FDR's future course. The "enormous concentration of power in the hands of appointed officials," the statement read in part, ". . . can lead only to waste, confusion, bureaucratic rigidity, and the loss of personal liberty."[35] But the more reactionary wing of disaffected Democrats, led by Al Smith, former New York governor and Roosevelt's old political mentor, formed what they called the American Liberty League early in 1934 and began to eye the Democratic nomination in 1936. "Let me give this solemn warning," Smith told an NBC radio audience in January 1936, "there can only be one capital, Washington or Moscow. There can be only one atmosphere of government, the clean, pure, fresh air of free America, or the foul breath of communistic Russia."[36]

While the Liberty League fed on the stubborn bitterness of the corporate community and conservative Democrats, keeping up a steady

33. Walter Lippmann, *The Good Society*, p. 21.
34. Ibid.
35. Quoted in John Morton Blum, ed., *Public Philosopher: Selected Letters of Walter Lippmann*, p. 350.
36. Quoted in Arthur Schlesinger Jr., *The Politics of Upheaval*, p. 519.

patter of complaint in the press and on the radio, and the Republicans chose Kansas Governor Alfred M. Landon as the best candidate to throw at Roosevelt in 1936, a startling alliance was forming on the darkest fringe of the extreme Right. Francis Townsend's Old-Age Revolving Pension plan campaign had not vanished with passage of the Social Security Act in 1935, as Roosevelt might have hoped, and after Huey Long's assassination it gained a valuable ally in the form of Gerald L. K. Smith. Smith had been thrown out of what remained of the Share Our Wealth movement when he attempted to seize power over the organization after his beloved leader's death, then had announced his support of Georgia Governor Eugene Talmadge as a dark horse Democratic presidential candidate. "Roosevelt is rapidly becoming the most despised President in the history of the country," Smith slavered before the 130,000 people who attended a "Talmadge Grass Roots Convention" in Macon late in January 1936. "We're going to turn that cripple out of the White House. . . . He and his gang are in the death rattle. We have only to put the cloth of the ballot over his dead mouth."[37] Talmadge liked Smith's sentiments well enough but was jealous of the ex-minister's popularity, and Smith was soon forced out of the Talmadge ranks. He refused to vanish. In June 1936, he attended a congressional committee hearing that was looking into the Townsend Plan (even with Social Security in place, Townsendites in Congress were pushing additional old-age legislation). When Townsend abruptly left the witness table after the questions got too sharp for comfort, Smith leaped to the doctor's side and helped him out of the crowded room. Shortly afterward, he was at Townsend's side again at a press conference to announce that "we here and now join hands in what shall result in a nationwide protest against this Communistic dictatorship in Washington."[38]

The means by which that goal might be reached, Smith felt, was a third-party candidate. Townsend agreed, and to engender support for the idea, the two turned to Father Charles E. Coughlin, in whom they found a ready ear. The Radio Priest's disillusionment with Roosevelt had bloomed into furious contempt by 1936. In November 1934, Coughlin had organized the National Union for Social Justice, and

37. Quoted in Bennett, op. cit., p. 138.
38. Quoted in ibid., p. 130.

while he labeled it just another "lobbying" group, it was clear that he had larger things in mind. "This invention plays an important part in the restoration of democracy of the American people," he told a live audience of 23,000 at Madison Square Garden on May 22. "The National Union, employing not only the radio, but also utilizing the telegraph, or when time permits, the nationally owned post office, proposes to revive the meaning of democracy as it was conceived by the fathers of this country."[39] By the summer of 1935, the priest was claiming that at least 8.5 million people had expressed support for the NUSJ, and in January 1936 he maintained that active membership in thousands of local NUSJ groups had grown to 5.2 million. While the number of active members probably was closer to a million, there were plenty of people who sympathized quietly, and there was no question that Coughlin was going to be a problem.[40] "Today I humbly stand before the American public to admit that I was in error," he broadcast early in 1936. "Despite all promises, the money changer has not been driven from the temple. . . . The slogan 'Roosevelt or Ruin' must now be altered to read 'Roosevelt and Ruin.' "[41]

Coughlin himself had been thinking along the lines of a third party for some time when Smith and Townsend approached him, and he quickly put forth his own choice as the candidate: North Dakota congressman William Lemke, an early Republican supporter of Roosevelt but now as thoroughly discontented as Coughlin. Smith and Townsend concurred, and Lemke agreed. On June 20, the congressman announced he would be the candidate of the newly formed Union Party. Coughlin took to the radio to shout the news: the Union Party, he said, meant "a new day for America. . . . Behind it will rally agriculture, labor, the disappointed Republicans and the outraged Democrats, the independent merchant and industrialist and every lover of liberty who desires to eradicate the cancerous growths from decadent capitalism and avoid the treacherous pitfalls of red communism."[42]

39. Quoted in Warren, op. cit., pp. 65–66.
40. Figures from ibid., pp. 71–72.
41. Quoted in Bennett, op. cit., p. 78.
42. Quote in Sheldon Marcus, *Father Coughlin: The Tumultuous Life of the Priest of the Little Flower*, p. 113.

As expected, Alfred Landon won the Republican nomination in
June, with Frank Knox as his running mate, and Roosevelt and Garner
were easily renominated by the Democrats a few days later with no serious challenge from Talmadge or anyone else. Roosevelt, angered by the
ugly recidivism of business and industry, accepted the nomination with
a call for eternal vigilance against the continued machinations of those
"economic royalists" who had "created a new despotism" in the past.
"Against economic tyranny such as this, the American citizen could
appeal only to the organized power of Government. The collapse of
1929 showed up the despotism for what it was. The election of 1932
was the people's mandate to end it. Under that mandate it is being
ended."[43] He then went off on a long fishing trip, seemingly oblivious
to what appeared to be tremendous odds. Not only were the regular
Republicans and the Democratic dissidents of the Liberty League dead
set against him, so were most of the old Republican Progressives who
had done much to get him elected in 1932. The radical right was firmly
fixed in the peculiar amalgam controlled by the Union Party, and Father
Coughlin continued to fill the ears of millions of rapt Americans with
frenetic, increasingly anti-Semitic and anti–New Deal diatribes while
extolling the plain Christian American virtues of the candidate from
North Dakota. Business and industry, whose power to influence votes
was enormous, were almost universally against Roosevelt. So was most
of the newspaper and magazine press, whose publishers repeatedly spat
out pro-Landon, anti-Roosevelt editorials and blithely slanted the news
wherever and whenever they could overcome the liberalism of their own
reporters. While conditions slowly improved, the nation's economy was
still in a depressed state. The NRA had failed. Strikes and violence still
punctuated the land. Some polls showed a marked decline in Roosevelt
support among voters, and many of the New Dealers were frantic with
worry. The president "smiles and sails and fishes and the rest of us worry
and fume," Interior Secretary Ickes fretted in his diary on July 18.
"With even our own private polls showing an alarming falling off in the
President's vote, the whole situation is incomprehensible to me."[44]

43. Quoted in Rosenman, op. cit., 5: p. 231.
44. Harold L. Ickes, *The Secret Diary of Harold L. Ickes: The First Thousand Days, 1933–
1936*, pp. 639–40.

It was in this context that the Comintern had decided that the CP/USA must come out in support of Roosevelt's election—or, perhaps more accurately, in support of Landon's defeat. "Landon and Knox are the candidates of the camp of reaction," the CP/USA's general secretary, Earl Browder, explained during a conference at the Institute of Public Affairs at the University of Virginia. "They were handpicked by William Randolph Hearst, chief exponent of fascism in America. They are supported by the Liberty League, by Morgan, by the du Ponts, by the Rockefellers, by all the monarchs of monopoly, collectively known as Wall Street."[45] Browder was not acting on his own, of course. By 1936, the Comintern had directed a major shift in the policies of the CP/USA. Adolf Hitler's sudden assumption of power in Germany in 1933 and the continued reign of Benito Mussolini in Italy—coupled with "Il Duce's" vicious conquest of Ethopia in 1935—had convinced the Soviet Union that the greatest immediate need throughout the world was a "Popular Front" against the rise of fascism. Throughout Europe, Communist organizations were admonished to form coalitions with Socialists and other distinctly antifascist groups in order to create large "proletarian" political blocs to overthrow present systems of government. In the United States, the Comintern had told Browder, that union of effort—known here as the "People's Front"—required that the party soften its image and establish a loose alliance of expedience with the Democrats to assure the election of Roosevelt in 1936 as the lesser of two evils. Browder's task in this shift called for some ingenious rhetorical tap dancing, and at one point he found himself proclaiming that "we Communists are proud that we can truly say that Communism is the Americanism of the twentieth century," and that in joining to defeat Landon and elect Roosevelt, "the American people are but carrying on their glorious revolutionary traditions, which are the most hallowed heritage of our people."[46] As instructed, Browder also attempted

---

45. Earl Browder, *The People's Front*, p. 109.
46. Ibid, pp. 113–14. Another aspect of the Comintern's transformation of strategy was less well known—though it was instinctively suspected by Roosevelt's conservative and right-wing opponents. During the party's ninth annual nominating convention in June 1936, at which time Browder was anointed the CP/USA's presidential candidate, a resolution was passed emphasizing a new order. "The Communist Party is not a conspirative [sic] organization, it is an open revolutionary Party, continuing the

to forge a merger with the CP/USA's adversary, the Socialist Party, and get it to join the Communists in the anti-Landon campaign, but was rejected by Norman Thomas and the rest of the Socialist old guard, who considered Landon and Roosevelt equally despicable.

John L. Lewis himself was no unconditional fan of Roosevelt. In these years, he always had in the back of his mind the possibility of someday forging a national farmer-labor party along the lines of the coalition that had been so powerful in Minnesota. Consequently, he was at first reluctant to form any sort of firm alliance with the New Deal. But, like the Communists, the labor movement had little choice in 1936. Lewis swallowed his hesitancy, going so far at one point as to tell Roosevelt, "Command me at any time I can be of service."[47] FDR issued no commands, but Lewis and the CIO made themselves of considerable service. Lewis not only went on the stump for Roosevelt himself on several occasions but the CIO established the great ancestor of the polit-

---

traditions of 1776 and 1861; it is the only organization that is really entitled by its program and work to designate itself as 'sons and daughters of the American revolution.' " (Quoted in Browder, op. cit., p. 112.) But the Party was conspiring energetically, not least by placing as many people as it could in the warrens of the New Deal to help shape policy wherever possible and gather information that might prove useful to the CP/USA or the Soviet Union. Most of these people were under orders to keep their Party memberships secret. They were told by their cell leaders that they must take on different names for use within the Party so that no one member could identify another should he be questioned by authorities. Hope Hale Davis, an AAA employee who had joined the Party in 1934 as the People's Front was getting under way, remembered other inconveniences her cell leader ("Charles") enumerated: "We must keep away from any place where leftists might gather. We must avoid, as far as possible, associating with radicals, difficult as that would be in Washington. Even liberals, outspoken ones such as Gardner Jackson, Charles said, looking my way, were out of bounds. This saddened me. Pat [Gardner's nickname] had been so kind a friend." (Hope Hale Davis, *Great Day Coming: A Memoir of the 1930s*, p. 71.) Harvey Klehr, et al., in *The Secret World of American Communism* suggest that the infiltration of secret Communists was considerable, particularly in the AAA, the NLRB, and Senator Robert M. La Follette's Civil Liberties Subcommittee, which investigated violations of labor rights and employer violence. "The benign view," they write, "is that those Communists who did work within the government were present only as individuals and never acted in concert, were not supervised by the CP/USA or a Soviet agency, and did not provide the party with information and, further, that their communism did not affect the content of their work or the activities of any government agencies" (p. 96). Not necessarily so, the authors say, though they do not analyze in any detail what effect the Communists might have had on specific policies and actions.

47. Quoted in Dubofsky and Van Tine, op. cit., p. 252.

ical action committees of a later day—Labor's Non-Partisan League, designed, as Sidney Hillman put it, as a means of "organizing for the first time the political power of the men and women who toil."[48] In spite of its calculatedly neutral title, which deceived no one, the Non-Partisan League and its fifty-nine international unions with a membership of more than two million were devoted entirely to the reelection of Franklin Delano Roosevelt. They demonstrated that support not merely by working door to door in the labor precincts of the nation but by the contribution of hundreds of thousands of dollars, much of it directly to the Roosevelt campaign and most of it—nearly $600,000—from Lewis's United Mine Workers of America.[49] The AFL, meanwhile, true to its traditions, maintained an official neutrality, although it did go so far as to allow George Berry of the Printing Pressmen's Union to serve as chairman of the Non-Partisan League.

The support of the CP/USA, however oblique, was welcome enough, though never openly acknowledged and certainly never actively solicited by the Democrats, but it was a minor factor in the 1936 presidential race. Aid from the labor movement, and especially from the CIO, was a good deal more important (and much easier to accept), particularly in the big industrial centers, where union campaigning would help to give Roosevelt huge majorities. But in the end even this was probably unnecessary. Roosevelt may have lost forever those few capitalist leaders who had reluctantly supported him in 1932 and 1933; he may have lost the embittered Democrats and Progressives who had gathered under the flag of the Liberty League; he may have lost much of the middle class; and he certainly had lost those fringes whose prejudices and passions Father Charles Coughlin was so busily exploiting. But everything else was his—the millions of still unemployed, immigrants and the sons and daughters of immigrants, blacks who rejected "Lincoln's Party" and voted Democratic for the first time in their lives (where they *could* vote), millions of others who lived in a world of hunger and whose hopes were fixed on the figure of a man whom they believed in absolutely. Most of them were working men and women, and Roosevelt had them whether they were unionized or not. Steve Hatalla, who had

---

48. Quoted in Matthew Josephson, *Sidney Hillman: Statesman of American Labor*, p. 399.
49. Figure from Dubofsky and Van Tine, op. cit., p. 252.

been rescued from penury by his WPA job, was no union man, but he was a Roosevelt man all the way and spoke for millions when he told the reporter from *Fortune* in October 1935 that he voted for Roosevelt in 1932 and expected to vote for him again. "Roosevelt is all right, he says, he's honest and he's trying to do what he can for the poor people," the reporter wrote. "If Roosevelt hadn't beaten Hoover, he says, there would have been a revolution long ago. . . . Roosevelt does the best he can, Steve says, and maybe things will work out all right."[50]

Roosevelt had them, and they voted. More than 45.6 million people went to the polls on November 3—61 percent of all registered voters, higher than in 1932, and in some states, among them New York and Illinois, the turnout was 70 percent or more (in West Virginia, it was a staggering 84.9 percent). Nearly 28 million of them had voted for Roosevelt, and his plurality over Landon of 10.8 million votes was, as in FDR's victory over Hoover in 1932, the largest in history up to that time. Furthermore, the margin in the electoral college of 523 to 8 was greater than in any election since that of James Madison in 1820.

The CIO's support may or may not have been instrumental in giving Roosevelt a second term, but his victory was unquestionably instrumental in giving the labor organization added muscle for its challenge to organized industry and the entrenched conservatism of the AFL. The CIO's leaders, after all, could remember what Roosevelt told a crowd at Madison Square Garden just two days before the election, when in one of the most powerful political speeches he ever made he both attacked and ridiculed the business community that had risen up against him. They were sick men, he said; he had made them well, and now they "wanted to throw their crutches at the doctor. . . .

> For twelve years this nation was afflicted with hear-nothing, see-nothing, do-nothing government. The nation looked to government but government looked away. Nine mocking years with the golden calf and three long years of the scourge! Nine crazy years at the ticker and three long years in the breadlines! Nine mad years of mirage and three long years of despair! Powerful influences strive today to restore that kind of government with its doctrine that the government is

50. "Family on Relief," *Fortune* (February 1936).

best which is most indifferent. . . . Never before have these forces
been so united against one candidate as they stand today. They are
unanimous in their hatred of me—and I welcome their hatred.[51]

Roosevelt had beaten those forces as they had never been beaten before.
Perhaps labor could do the same. The first major test would come in the
automobile industry, setting in motion perhaps the best-known labor
action in our history, a strike in which the forces of capitalism, labor,
and government were joined with such drama that it has been remembered with all the passion of a great American folktale.

THE UNITED AUTO WORKERS had been formed—much like the United
Rubber Workers' Union of Akron—when delegates from a group of
Federal Unions in the automobile industry had appealed to the AFL for
a unified charter in the summer of 1935. Green and the executive council had agreed, and this time had managed to dictate the appointment
of the union's officers. That domination ended in the summer of 1936,
when delegates to the UAW's first annual convention, heavily laced
with CIO "observers" like Powers Hapgood and Rose Pesotta, had
defied the AFL leadership and voted for the right to choose their own
leaders. Homer Martin had been elected president, and the union
shortly thereafter had aligned itself with the CIO.

Roosevelt's open antibusiness election campaign of 1936, Martin
declared, was "a mandate to organize," and the union plastered leaflets
and brochures with a casual remark attributed to the president: "If I
were a factory worker, I would join a union."[52] Organizers—many of
them Communists or Socialists—were dispatched into all the cities
where automobiles or automobile parts were made.

The membership drive went slowly and erratically at first, ham-
pered by factional disputes among UAW leaders and the sort of ideological squabbling common wherever Communists, Socialists, and

51. "Campaign address at Madison Square Garden," October 31, 1936. In Samuel
Rosenman, ed., *The Public Papers and Addresses of Franklin D. Roosevelt*, 5: p. 568.
52. Both quotes in Nelson Lichtenstein, *The Most Dangerous Man in Detroit: Walter
Reuther and the Fate of American Labor*, p. 61.

other leftist lights gathered, but also by fear. The automobile industry was enjoying its share of the nation's slow but significant industrial recovery. Total manufacturing income had risen from a low of $31.8 billion in 1932 to $47.4 billion at the end of 1935; stockholders' dividends had nearly doubled. Automobile sales had more than matched that increase—from 1.1 million sales worth $616 million in 1932 to 3.8 million sales worth $1.7 billion in 1935 (more than $20 billion in 1998 dollars). The industry was as healthy as it had been at any time in years, and it was reluctant to let unions get in the way. Companies established elaborate spy systems within their plants to ferret out union organizers and get rid of them. Agitators could not be fired legally for union activity, but if they were watched long enough, they might sooner or later be observed violating one work rule or another that could then be used as justification for dismissal. The Ford Motor Company had been doing this for years, of course, but in the 1930s General Motors took the idea to new levels. It spent a million dollars a year on a spy system that employed as many as two hundred agents hired from fourteen companies specializing in the trade, including labor's longtime foe, the Pinkerton National Detective Agency.[53] GM and other companies may or may not also have had an implicit understanding with a group of thugs known as the Black Legion, a Michigan offshoot of the Ku Klux Klan that was nicknamed the "Invisible Eye of Labor" because it concentrated somewhat less on the terrorization of blacks, Jews, and Catholics than on the intimidation of suspected union organizers, whom the Black Legionnaries labeled "anti-American" and subjected to kidnappings, beatings, and, at least once, it was believed by many, death.[54]

Such levels of oppression had bred timidity, and most automobile workers were reluctant to risk their jobs to join the UAW, a group that was still in its infancy and might be incapable of protecting their livelihoods. As Homer Martin had hoped, however, the organizing drive

53. See Sidney Fine, *Sit-down: The General Motors Strike of 1936–1937*, pp. 37–38.
54. See Henry Kraus, *Heroes of Unwritten Story: The UAW, 1934–1939*, pp. 195–200. Kraus was the founding editor of the UAW's *United Auto Worker* and his history of the UAW in the thirties is unashamedly biased toward the union; nevertheless, historian Nelson Lichtenstein, among others, has cited the troubling presence of the Black Legion in the automobile labor wars (Lichtenstein, op. cit., pp. 113, 120).

picked up after FDR's victory in November, and was given an even bigger boost when a rash of brief but dramatic UAW-engineered sit-down strikes erupted in Detroit and elsewhere during the weeks following the election. Two of these—at the Midland Steel Products Company, which produced Chrysler and Ford body parts, and the Kelsey-Hayes Wheel Company, which provided Ford with most of its brake shoes and drums—had resulted in wage increases and significant changes in work rules at the two plants, demonstrating that the new union had acquired at least some muscle. By the end of December 1936, UAW organizers had managed to bring the union's membership up to about 63,000, or nearly 14 percent of the total automotive workforce.[55]

The UAW was still a minority, but a sizable one, and it was at this juncture that the union determined to challenge General Motors on a major scale. It would be a definitive moment, and the union knew it. Robert C. Travis, who had led a 1935 strike against the Chevrolet plant in Toledo, saw GM in apocalyptic terms. The company, he wrote, was "a vast army," with "all the hideous advantages of modern warfare— airplanes—poison gas—machine guns—long-range guns, and hand grenades, and last but not least, their secret service."[56] He was not far off the mark. By 1936, General Motors had far surpassed the Ford Motor Company as the giant of the industry. The company, *Fortune* magazine would gush in December 1938, was "the perfect exemplar of how and why American business is Big. Every way you can measure it, the business of General Motors is not big but colossal." Its net profits in 1936 were nearly $240 million. It had 250,000 employees in sixty-nine plants producing Chevrolets, Buicks, Oldsmobiles, Pontiacs, and Cadillacs, together with trucks, trailers, commercial vehicles, appliances, and even locomotives and airplanes. If General Motors could be made to succumb to the UAW, the union's future might be assured.

The best place to launch the crusade, it was agreed, was Flint, a town utterly dominated by GM's factories, including Fisher Body Plant No. 1—"Fisher One"—the largest auto body plant in the world. Nearly fifty thousand GM workers were employed in Flint, and the company's policy of speeding up assembly line production while cutting the labor

55. Figures in Kraus, op. cit., p. 98.
56. Quoted in Fine, op. cit., p. 92.

force had already led to a number of wildcat work stoppages. "It was always the speedup, the horrible speedup," Henry Kraus, editor of the UAW's newspaper, the *United Auto Worker*, remembered. "Flint workers had a peculiar grey, jaundiced color which long rest after the exhausting day's work did not erase. Even on Sunday when they wore their best and walked in the open one felt that one was in a city of tuberculars. It was the speedup that organized Flint."[57] Resentment of the speedup had reached explosive levels when Robert Travis, who was rapidly becoming one of the union's most effective strike leaders, visited Fisher One. He found the plant's UAW representative almost in tears with frustration. "Honest to God, Bob," the man said, "you've got to let me pull a strike before one pops somewhere that we won't be able to control!"

"You think they're as ready as that?" Travis asked.

"Ready? They're like a pregnant woman in her tenth month!"[58]

Union leaders wanted to wait until the newly elected governor of Michigan, Frank Murphy, a resolute New Dealer and a demonstrated friend of labor, took office in January 1937. But events, as the UAW representative in Fisher One had feared, soon took matters out of their hands, beginning a domino-like process that in a few weeks would take the biggest automobile corporation in the world out of the car-building business almost entirely. GM plants in Atlanta and Kansas City had been on strike since November, but both were small and the impact on the company minor. The Cleveland plant, which made the bodies for all of Chevrolet's popular two-door models, was another matter, and on December 28, after two union men had been demoted by management, a shift of 135 workers turned off their machines and sat down. Apparently inspired by the Cleveland example, at seven o'clock in the morning of December 30, fifty workers in Flint turned off their own machines in Fisher Body Plant No. 2. Fifteen hours later, Robert Travis took advantage of a rumor (perhaps fabricated) that management was going to ship dies from Fisher One to poorly unionized plants elsewhere and called a sit-down at the huge plant. The strikes at Fishers One and Two alone were enough to cripple the company, but it was further stag-

---

57. Henry Kraus, *The Many and the Few: A Chronicle of the Dynamic Auto Workers*, p. 42. (Unlike Kraus's *Heroes of Unwritten Story*, this book is more of a memoir than a history.)
58. Quoted in ibid., p. 42.

gered when walkouts and sit-downs spread through much of its corporate structure. By the end of January 1937, General Motors plants in Toledo, St. Louis, Oakland, Norwood, Ohio, and Anderson, Indiana, had been shut down, while the strikes in Cleveland, Kansas City, and Atlanta continued.

The company responded by getting an injunction from Genesee County Circuit Court Judge Edward D. Black that ordered the strikers to leave all the occupied plants and refrain from picketing or any other form of harassment of nonunion workers. The sheriff dutifully read the injunction to the workers in Fishers One and Two and served it on UAW officials, but neither the union nor the workers obeyed—and Black's credibility was shattered when the union held a press conference to announce that the judge owned 3,665 shares of GM stock. Chagrined GM attorneys took the case to another judge and waited for another injunction, in the meantime bolstering plant police and guards, while laying in extra stocks of tear gas and vomit gas and planting what spies it could in the ranks of the strikers.

For nearly two weeks, there was little violence. Inside the occupied plants, a village atmosphere prevailed among the workers, all of whom were males. All women workers had been ordered to leave the plants when the strikes started, to the resentment of many like Pat Wiseman, a woman who had labored equal hours at equal work for unequal pay in the paint shop of Fisher One for six years. "Pat, whose deep voice was eventually to command as much respect as that of any male in the union's councils," union editor Henry Kraus remembered, "spurned such womanish work as kitchen duty during the strike. If she couldn't sit in she'd picket outside and she never missed a day." At one point, a male picket asked her what she expected to get out of it. "I'll tell you why I'm doing it," Wiseman answered. "You're getting fifteen dollars a week more than I am for the same number of hours and I'll be damned if I don't work as hard as you do!"[59]

The remaining male strikers organized themselves into little communities remarkable for their determination to be considered orderly and civilized. Strike committees governed the hundreds of men who

---

59. Pat Wiseman's story is told in Kraus, *The Many and the Few*, pp. 97–98.

had chosen to remain behind in the plants, though not without the consent of the governed; a rough form of democracy prevailed in a kind of town meeting atmosphere. The men were divided up into groups which set up housekeeping together in a selected corner of a plant, often utilizing automobile seats as beds and chairs. In some plants, post offices were established, as well as game rooms and kitchens. There were committees formed to control everything from picket duty outside the plant to sanitation inspection inside. Plants were to be kept spotless by cleanup crews, and no damage to the facilities, machinery, or auto bodies was tolerated—indeed, most machinery was kept oiled and in good working condition throughout the strike. The men were ordered to shower daily, and no liquor was allowed at any time. Kangaroo courts enforced the rules, but since peer pressure usually was sufficient to keep the men in line, the courts provided comic relief more often than justice, featuring broad parodies of such proceedings and often outlandish sentences. There was, one reporter wrote of Fisher One, "more substantial humor in a single session of the . . . strikers' kangaroo courts than in a season of Broadway musical comedies."[60] Pickup bands were common, and strike meetings began and ended with songs. The old IWW standard, "Solidarity Forever," was a favorite, though scores of original lyrics were written to such familiar tunes as "Goody, Goody":

> We union men are out to win today,
> 　Goody, Goody!
> General Motors hasn't even got a chance,
> 　Goody, Goody![61]

"We are all one happy family now," one worker wrote home. "We all feel fine and have plenty to eat."[62] In truth, they did eat well. Most plants had kitchens and kitchen crews inside to provide sandwiches, but hot meals were prepared outside by the women and brought in daily under the guard of union picketers. In Flint, the Women's Auxiliary, which had been founded during a New Year's Eve dance outside

60. Quoted in Brecher, op. cit., p. 197.
61. Quoted in Fine, op. cit., p. 164.
62. Quoted in Brecher, op. cit., p. 197.

Fisher Two at the beginning of the strike, established a huge kitchen that employed 200 people and used 500 pounds of meat, 100 pounds of potatoes, 300 loaves of bread, 100 pounds of coffee, 200 pounds of sugar, 30 gallons of milk, and four cases of evaporated milk every day.[63] The Women's Auxiliary also entertained the strikers by holding mass charades and ethnic dances outside the plants, but circumstances soon gave them a more active—and a good deal more dangerous—role to play.

On January 11, guards locked the gates at Fisher Two and for the first time refused to let the evening meals be brought in to the men. The tactic apparently had been planned in advance, for pickets had no sooner broken the lock to the gate and started taking the food into the plant past the unresisting guards than carloads of police armed with tear gas and vomit gas arrived on the scene and began firing smoking canisters at the pickets. Many men inside the plant responded by shooting off their own arsenal—of hinges, canned goods, pipe sections, milk bottles, and anything else that might serve as a missile—while others stuck the nozzles of fire hoses through the plant's windows and sent arcs of freezing water down on the attacking police. The police retreated, shooting as they went and wounding thirteen pickets, then continued to fire gas at the plant and the pickets from a safe distance until midnight, when they ran out of canisters. In the middle of the fray was Genora Johnson, a twenty-three-year-old Socialist, the wife of a union man and the mother of two, who at one point jumped up on the roof of a union sound truck, grabbed the microphone, and harangued the retreating police. "Cowards!" she cried. "Cowards! Shooting unarmed and defenseless men!" She then turned to the women who had gathered. "Women of Flint! This is your fight! Join the picket line and defend your jobs, your husbands' jobs, and your children's homes!"[64]

There was no more fighting that night in what came to be dubbed the "Battle of Bulls Run," but the nature of the auto strike had changed, and so had the role of women in it. Ten days after the battle, Genora Johnson announced the formation of the Women's Emergency Brigade, which soon included 350 women. Its purpose was simple

63. Food statistics from Foner, op. cit., pp. 324–25.
64. Quoted in ibid., p. 325.

enough, Johnson told a reporter for the *New York Times*. The women intended "to be on hand in any emergency and to stand by our husbands, brothers, and sons. We will form a picket line around the men, and if the police want to fire, then they'll just have to fire into us."[65] Soon, brigades were formed in other GM cities, complete with officers, colorful berets and armbands, and two-by-fours crudely tapered into clubs.

The women of the Flint brigade got their first serious taste of action on February 1, when strike leaders decided to seize Chevrolet Plant No. 4, so far unaffected by the strike. To draw the attention of the police and GM guards away from Chevrolet No. 4, a diversionary attack was launched on the smaller Chevrolet No. 9. The Women's Emergency Brigade was crucial to the tactic—though only Genora Johnson was aware that the action was a diversion when she led her brigade down to the plant to aid the men in seizing it. "We formed in a line and marched right ahead," a member of the brigade remembered. "We carried the American flag before us. Of course we got gassed but we had been gassed before, nothing was going to stop us. We were going to protect our husbands."[66] The device worked. Several hundred police were diverted to Chevrolet No. 9 by the attack, and by the time they realized that Chevrolet No. 4 was the real target, Johnson had formed a line of brigade members across the plant's entrance. Linked arm in arm, the women were able to hold the police off long enough for the men inside to battle their way to control, floor by floor. When it was clear that the attack had been successful, the women re-formed into a picket line that slowly circled the entire plant, their massed voices singing "We Shall Not Be Moved." Two days later, the UAW declared February 3 to be "Women's Day," and several hundred red-bereted women marched down the streets of Flint to Fisher One and the other plants under strike to cheer their men. Meanwhile hundreds of sit-downers rushed to the roofs of the plants to cheer their women, the whole scene witnessed by as many as seven thousand spectators. It was, one observer said, "one of the most amazing labor demonstrations ever seen in America."[67] Over

65. Ibid.
66. Quoted in Garrison, op. cit., p. 278.
67. Foner, op. cit., p. 327.

the next ten days, the women paraded and demonstrated regularly in the streets of Flint and many of the other GM towns.

By then, General Motors was in a world of financial trouble. Before the strikes, it had been producing more than two thousand cars a day; now it was down to twenty or twenty-two. At an average wholesale price of about a thousand dollars a vehicle, it was losing nearly two million dollars in potential sales every day. It had won another injunction against the union, effective February 5, but the strikers showed no sign that they would obey it, while the police and the company's own guards were manifestly incapable of dislodging the workers, and liberal Governor Murphy was profoundly reluctant to use National Guard troops to get them out. "I am not going to do it," he is said to have remarked to a friend. "I'm not going to go down in history as 'Bloody Murphy'! If I sent those soldiers right in on the men there'd be no telling how many would be killed."[68] For weeks, GM had refused to negotiate until the plants were evacuated. Now it was clear that the men were not going to leave on their own and neither the federal government nor the state government was going to force them out. Succumbing to the inevitable, GM's general manager, William Knudsen, agreed to meet with the CIO's John L. Lewis, who had been asked by the UAW to represent the union in its negotiations with the company.

Lewis had not been silent, of course. He had made it clear to GM that the CIO would not ask the strikers to leave the plants, and he had publicly demanded of Roosevelt that his administration take an active hand in ending the stalemate—along the way reminding the president of his debt to labor. "The administration asked labor for help . . . and labor gave its help," he had told reporters during a press conference on January 21. Now, he said, the "economic royalists" of GM "have their fangs in labor. The workers of this country expect this administration to help the workers in every legal way, and to support the auto workers in the General Motors plants."[69] But Roosevelt had gone no further than to encourage Labor Secretary Perkins in her efforts to get the two sides together.

68. Quoted in Fine, op. cit., p. 294.
69. Quoted in Dubofsky and Van Tine, op. cit., p. 264.

Now they were. The haggling ground on for days, mediated by a perpetually nervous Frank Murphy—a man whose bushy red eyebrows were almost a match for those of the labor leader. Slowly, steadily, Knudsen began giving ground. "We've got 'em by the 'balls,'" Robert Travis told Lewis during a break; "squeeze a little."[70] Lewis squeezed, and on the morning of February 11, the settlement was reached, though he and Knudsen did not put their official signatures to it until noon. Covering seventeen plants that had been struck, the accord stipulated that GM would consent to the dismissal of its court injunction, that all striking workers would be allowed to return to work without discrimination, that the company would begin negotiations on a labor contract with the UAW on February 16, that it would recognize the union as the only legitimate bargaining agent for the workers for a period of six months, and that it would not in any way interfere with the right of its workers to join (a tacit agreement to end its spy system). For its part, the union agreed to evacuate all company properties, not to engage in union organizing on company premises (though the agreement noted that "this is not to preclude individual discussion"), and not to strike during the contract negotiations.[71] It was as close to a complete victory as the UAW could have hoped to get.

"This strike isn't over till these boys say so," Bud Simons, Fisher One's strike leader, told reporters when the agreement was announced.[72] At Fisher One and the other occupied plants that day, strike leaders read the terms of the agreement to their men, who then voted whether to accept or reject it. At each plant, the approval was nearly unanimous, after which the men began packing up. At Fisher One, the evacuation began in the gloaming of five o'clock in the afternoon. The plant had stood as the symbol of union determination for forty-four days, and now it became the core of celebration. Thousands gathered outside the gates. As the men came out, cigars in the corners of their mouths and "Solidarity Forever" on their lips, flares were sent up like fireworks and confetti danced and glittered in the light. "Never had anything like this been seen in Flint," Rose Pesotta remembered. "To great numbers of work-

70. Ibid., p. 270.
71. Quote in Kraus, *The Many and the Few*, p. 283.
72. Ibid., p. 287.

ers, the UAW victory was more important than the ending of World War I, for it meant a freedom that they had never known before. . . . I suddenly realized that my face was wet. Tears of gladness were streaming down my cheeks."[73]

"WHAT'S THE USE of kidding ourselves?" one worker was reported to have said after voting for the agreement. "All that piece of paper means is that we got a union. The rest depends on us. For God's sake, let's go back to work and keep up what we started here!"[74] To an astonishing degree, they did. All was not peace after the settlement of February 11. As UAW negotiators and GM officials met to work out the union's first contract, enlivened workers initiated brief but disruptive—and illegal—sit-downs and work stoppages at several plants, often without the knowledge or consent of union leaders. The UAW pointed to recalcitrant GM managers as the villains, GM pointed to the union and its inability to control its own people, and the agitation probably weakened the position of the union negotiators, for the contract that resulted fell a good deal short of getting the union everything it had wanted.

But it was a beginning, however flawed, and it would be enough for many UAW locals to engineer agreements with their individual firms for higher wages, shorter hours, recognition of seniority, and grievance procedures that gave the men some control over their work on the floor. "The inhuman high speed," one worker reported, "is *no more*. We now have a voice, and have slowed up the speed of the line. And are now treated as human beings, and not as part of the machinery."[75] UAW membership flowered—from about 88,000 at the end of February to 166,000 at the end of March, 254,000 at the end of April—and by the middle of October the union was claiming nearly 400,000 members, making it one of the largest of all the CIO unions.[76] Big enough to take on the Chrysler Corporation next, and after a sit-down strike in March, during which Governor Murphy once again played the part of mediator,

73. Quoted in Page Smith, op. cit., p. 740.
74. Quoted in Kraus, *The Many and the Few*, p. 287.
75. Quoted in Fine, op. cit., p. 328.
76. Figures in ibid., p. 327.

the union won recognition and concessions from Chrysler similar to those with GM. The Hudson, Reo, Packard, and Studebaker companies fell to the union over the next several months, until only the Ford Motor Company was left out of the UAW's fold—and it, too, would succumb when war became imminent in 1941.

"When they tie a can to a union man—/Sit down," a UAW lawyer wrote after the GM sit-downs, and for a time the tactic became epidemic in the labor movement. There were 4,740 strikes in the United States in 1937, and 477 of them were of the sit-down variety.[77] In Detroit at one time or another, workers occupied the Newton Packing Company plant and turned off the refrigeration; clerks sat down at the Crowley-Milner and Frank & Sedar department stores, as well as at Woolworth's five-and-dime stores; the Durable Laundry Company was closed down by its black women employees; women barricaded themselves in at three tobacco plants for three weeks; eight lumberyards were occupied; the Yale & Towne Lock Company was shut up; and four hotels were closed down. In Chicago, there were sixty sit-down strikes among waitresses, candy makers, truckers, cab drivers, office workers, and the motormen on the underground freight railroad system. Women seemed to take to the device with a special enthusiasm. "The auto victory showed us how," one said.[78] Hosiery workers sat down at mills in Reading, Pennsylvania, meatpackers in Chicago, counter waitresses in the Woolworth, Grand, and H. L. Green five-and-dimes in New York, thousands more in hospitals, drugstores, restaurants, hotels. "Armed insurrection—defiance of law, order and duly elected authority—is spreading like wildfire," a group of worried Bostonians wired their senators. "It is rapidly growing beyond control."[79] Not quite. By the end of the year, with once-strong public support declining rapidly, use of the tactic faded just as rapidly as it had blossomed.

A far more lasting effect of the GM story was the enhanced position and power of the CIO. One of its smallest unions had taken on and defeated one of the giants of industry, and John L. Lewis had been there to dictate the terms of the settlement. Among those watching events

77. See ibid., p. 331.
78. Quoted in Foner, op. cit., p. 331.
79. Quoted in Fine, op. cit., p. 332.

were the executives of United States Steel; they were enjoying their first profitable year since 1930, and the daily losses that GM suffered as the sit-downs continued were not lost on them. Almost a month before the GM settlement was reached, U.S. Steel's chairman, Myron Taylor, began secret negotiations with Lewis in the Mayflower Hotel in Washington. The secret talks were interrupted when Lewis began negotiations with GM on February 4, but resumed again on February 17, and on March 1 Lewis presented Philip Murray, head of the CIO's Steel Workers Organizing Committee, with a fait accompli: Taylor had agreed to recognize the SWOC as the sole bargaining agent for its union workers. On March 2, Murray and U.S. Steel's president, Benjamin Fairless, signed an official agreement to that effect.

U.S. Steel was "Big Steel." "Little Steel," an informal collective of smaller competitors, was not so easily conquered, although the SWOC did manage to get a contract out of the Jones & Laughlin steelworks in Aliquippa, Pennsylvania, on May 14. The rest of "Little Steel," including Bethlehem Steel and Republic Steel, refused to negotiate, but for all their newly won power, CIO leaders were reluctant to call a general strike against the companies, fearing that after months of labor conflict all over the country, the resources of both the SWOC and the CIO were too depleted to get the job done. Once again, grassroots unionists forced the issue. "We've had a hell of a time holding the men in," one SWOC plant organizer told Philip Murray during a conference on May 26. "If I go back without word to go out . . . I will get my throat cut."[80] Murray and the CIO finally called a strike.

The CIO's leadership had been right to worry. Little Steel, led by Republic, whose president, Tom Girdler, was as rigid an antiunion executive as anyone in the land, fought the union every step of the way, importing thousands of strikebreakers, hiring hundreds of guards, and enlisting the aid of local police (sometimes arming and feeding them as well). When about two thousand workers, including their wives and children, demonstrated peacefully outside Republic Steel's gates in South Chicago during a Memorial Day picnic, guards and police opened fire without warning. After the crowd had been sent running from the field in panic, ten people lay dead in the grass, while dozens of

80. Quoted in Zieger, op. cit., p. 61.

the wounded writhed in agony as policemen prowled among them, beating them with billy clubs. Similar conflicts erupted in Cleveland, Massillon, and Youngstown, Ohio, bringing Little Steel's death toll to eighteen. By the middle of July, the SWOC had little money and less energy left; it could get only one agreement out of a single Inland Steel plant, and strikers slowly returned to work without contracts.

The CIO—and the AFL, for that matter—had had reason to cheer in April when the Supreme Court validated the constitutionality of the National Labor Relations Act, which freed up the National Labor Relations Board to begin serious investigations into charges of violence and other violations of labor's rights. But for the rest of the decade, labor victories were few and came with little of the passion and glory that had punctuated the intoxicating years between 1933 and 1937, when workers found themselves embroiled in what millions believed was nothing less than a definitive class struggle that would see Americans finally freed of the degradation of wage slavery. The future would prove more mundane and exhausting, as workers sought to improve their lot on a shop-by-shop basis, while their leaders constructed elaborate bureaucratic structures and embroiled themselves in almost constant doctrinal and territorial wrangles that both enervated the movement and tainted its reputation. And the Roosevelt administration, ostensibly the champion of labor, would remain lukewarm and conflicted.

But something important had happened, something that changed the face of industrial America forever. By October 1937, the CIO was claiming 4 million members in some six thousand local unions. Together with the 2.9 million members still claimed by the AFL, it meant that nearly 7 million American workers now belonged to unions, nearly 18.5 percent of the total nonagricultural labor force—a minority, certainly, but by far the largest minority in our history up to that time. Just as important, the relationships among industry, labor, and the government had been transformed by the currents that had been loosed with passage of the National Industrial Recovery Act in 1933 and given legal validation by the passage of the National Labor Relations Act of 1935. No longer would most employers feel privileged to exploit their workers—any workers, including nonunion workers—in the callous traditions of the past. Neither public opinion nor the workers themselves would tolerate it—and the economic costs of ignoring that fact could be considerable. No longer could the government pretend that it had no role to play in protecting the rights of workers, however confused and vacillating it could still be in fulfilling that obligation. And no longer would labor need to feel deprived of power, voice, and respect in American society, however elusive its goals of full equality with management and the middle class, and however raddled with disunity and discontent it might remain.

Industrial America, of course, was not all of America, and if the pressures of the depression years and the response of the people and the New Dealers who professed to represent them had reshaped the character of urban and industrial America and changed forever the symbiosis between the country's citizens and their government, these pressures had done no less for the other America, the America where dreams were linked with land, where hope was defined by the shape of clouds and the smell of rain in the wind.

III

THE PLOUGHLAND CURVE

To see this ploughland curve as a graph of history,
The unregarded sweat that has made it fertile,
Reading between the furrows a desperate appeal,
From all those whose share in them was bitter as iron,
Hearing the young corn whisper
The wishes of men that have no other voice,

Only then am I able to know the difficult
Birth of our new seed and bear my part of the harvest.

—C. Day Lewis, from "A Prologue"
The New Republic (April 10, 1935)

14

Revolt in the Heartland

For years, Theresa Von Baum and her husband had worked the eighty acres of their Nebraska farm diligently. And when her husband died, Theresa continued working it with their sons, enduring season after season of killing frosts, destructive rains, inadequate rains, grasshopper infestations, crop disease, and the always uncontrollable vagaries of the market until all these forces combined to ruin her. She could no longer meet the payments on a mortgage of $442. Her local bank carried her for a while and then the bank collapsed, and on October 6, 1932, the receiver of the mortgage announced a forced sale of all her livestock and farm equipment.

But something happened. On the day of the sale, 2,500 farmers showed up. A committee of twelve surrounded the receiver and escorted him into Mrs. Von Baum's kitchen. "We'll give you $100 for that mortgage," the group's leader said. "We don't intend to have that woman sold out."

"Nothing doing," the receiver replied. "I'll postpone the sale."

"No, you won't," the chairman declared. "We'll hold it ourselves."

Helpless, the receiver stood by and watched as Mrs. Von Baum's ten cows were auctioned off for 35 cents apiece, her twenty-four shoats for a total of 75 cents, her six horses for a total of $5.60, and her hay binder, corn planter, and disc plow for 25 cents each. All the animals and equipment were then turned over to Mrs. Von Baum, after which the farmers took up a collection, which, with the proceeds from the sale, came to $101.02. They handed the money to the receiver. Probably counting heads and coming to the conclusion that forcing the issue was not likely to get him a cent more—and might get him a broken nose, or worse—he accepted the money as payment in full for the mortgage, got in his car, and drove back to town.[1]

The little rebellion in Mrs. Von Baum's farmyard has been cited as Nebraska's first expression of what would come to be called "penny auctions" or "Sears, Roebuck sales" and take place over much of the Midwest in the next few months, manifestations of unresolved angers that simmered just as hotly in the bosoms of heartland farmers as they did in those of San Francisco longshoremen. The anger had always been there, but never had it been so deeply felt or as widely expressed as it was during the months between the summer of 1932 and the fall of 1933, as hard times exposed one more of the widening gaps between dream and reality in the culture of cultivation. From the hog farms of the Ohio River Valley to the cotton plantations of the Mississippi Delta, from the wheat fields of North Dakota to the fruit orchards of California, the strains of the Great Depression tested as never before the validity of one of the oldest and most revered icons in our history.

For more than a century and a half, the farmer—or, more accurately, the *idea* of the farmer—had lain at the mythic heart of America's view of itself, and the small family farm had been perceived as the ideal social unit for the preservation of democratic ideals. For most Americans, that fond vision still obscured the fact that by the 1930s, economic imperatives and an often overweening ambition had made many farmers as vulnerable to the gyrations of the market as the most rawly

---

1. Mrs. Von Baum's story was first told in Edwin C. Hill, *The American Scene* (1933), pp. 150–52. Hill identified her as "Mrs. Von Bonn," but John L. Shover uses "Von Baum" in "The Penny-Auction Rebellion," *The American West* (Fall 1965), and this seems the more likely spelling.

unschooled urban speculator. And in spite of a succession of federal laws designed to encourage the growth of the small family farm—the preemption acts of the 1840s, the Homestead Act of 1862, and the Reclamation Act of 1902 chief among them—the thrust of history was toward bigness: the size of the average farm increased from 139 acres in 1910 to 157 acres by 1930, while the total number of farms declined by 71,000 in the same period. Farm machinery grew in dimensions and sophistication, enabling corporate wheat farmers, for instance, to harvest hundreds of acres a day, with combines the size of small buildings crawling over the landscape, cutting the wheat, threshing it, and spewing out the grain in a single operation. Increasingly powerful and affordable tractors enabled even small farmers to work their land more swiftly and efficiently and inspired many to expand their operations, acquiring and working ever-larger units. Capital-intensive and debt-heavy agribusiness farmers banded together into cropwide organizations that differed from manufacturing trade associations only in the character of the product. "We no longer raise wheat here," one California grower said, "we manufacture it. . . . We are not husbandmen, we are not farmers."[2]

Roughly a quarter of America's population of 123 million people still lived on farms in 1930, but at the turn of the century the figure had been more than 41 percent. The number of individuals who owned their own farms had declined by nearly half a million between 1910 and 1930, while those who lived on and worked land owned by others— renters, or tenant farmers, as they were called—increased by more than 300,000 in those same twenty years. In the Deep South, tenant farmers and sharecroppers outnumbered farm owners by more than a million, while in California and other parts of the Far West, wage laborers, most of them migrants, accounted for nearly 50 percent of the total farm population of nearly a million.[3] With few exceptions, the remaining family farmers, brutally overworked, their numbers and importance declining, the fate of their farms and families vulnerable to whatever

2. Quoted in Harvey Green, *The Uncertainty of Everyday Life, 1915–1945*, p. 41.
3. Migrant labor assumptions are extrapolated from tables in the Research Division, Works Progress Administration, *Rural Regions of the United States*, pp. 119–30. All other farm statistics are from *The Historical Statistics of the United States*.

providence might bring them in the way of weather and what politicians and the financial community might bring them in the way of economic insecurity, had little time and less energy to devote to the finer points of democratic tradition. Tens of thousands of them would be driven off their farms in the first few years of the depression to join the desperate, wandering throngs of the largest internal migration in American history, while in the ragged plantation world of the Deep South and the "factories in the fields" of the Far West, democracy was rendered irrelevant, subverted at the grass roots by class warfare far more savage and repressive than anything urban America had yet experienced.

The belief that they could somehow take hold of this agonizingly complex and desperately confusing social and economic issue and unravel its mare's nest of problems may have been the most touchingly optimistic of all the many ambitions of the New Dealers. Unfortunately, as with many of their hopes, much of what they tried would prove to be so bound up in a snarl of conflicting instincts and ideologies that it either fell short of what was planned for it or actually made things worse. In probably no other area of national concern was the difference greater between the theories being shaped into policy in late-night Washington offices and the actual experience of real people suffering the consequences of a dream become nightmare.

MUCH OF WHAT infuriated and frustrated the farmers of the Midwest in the early 1930s could be laid to weather conditions and natural events over which neither they nor anyone else had any control, but at the heart of their resentment was a conviction that the farmer had, once again, gotten the short end of the economic stick. All through the incandescent prosperity of the twenties, they had seen their fortunes steadily decline, hostage, most believed, to the national infatuation with stock speculation against which farm leaders had railed. Now that the investment mania had ended in precisely the disaster they had feared and predicted, it was they who were suffering more than any other single group. And, as usual, no one east of the Mississippi River Basin either understood or cared about their particular plight.

These complaints held more than a few grains of truth, but the indictment tended to ignore the role many farmers had played in bringing themselves to such a sorry condition. Farmers were no more immune to the seductions of possibility than any other segment of society, and in the years of World War I and the first few months that followed it, thousands had succumbed with a greed no less feral than that which had infested eastern brokerage houses—and with much the same result.

The temptation had been considerable. As the terrible engine of war began grinding across the European landscape in August 1914, all but obliterating the ability of the warring nations to feed themselves, the demand for American-grown food swelled to unprecedented levels. The United States, Henry C. Wallace, editor of *Wallace's Farmer* (and father of FDR's secretary of agriculture), wrote, had a "moral responsibility to feed the hungry people of the world," and farmers cheerfully accepted the obligation, planting and harvesting more and more bushels of wheat and other grains, raising and shipping ever-increasing numbers of hogs and other livestock, while prices for all agricultural products rose in an exhilarating demonstration of the principles of supply and demand.[4] When the United States entered the war in April 1917, setting up a Food Administration for War that put in place artificially high price supports to encourage even more production, farmers could be forgiven for believing that it was impossible to lose money.

More and more of them began expanding production, buying new equipment, purchasing new acreage and putting it to the plow. When they did not have the money themselves, they went to the federal land banks established in 1916, capital-heavy insurance companies, and local private banks—many of them so new they had been created by farmers who had made so much money in the first couple of years of the boom that they decided to get out of farming, which they knew, and into banking, which they did not. All three were more than happy to fuel the boom with new money. And, much like the allure of the great lottery on Wall Street, the appeal of the midwestern farming boom was

4. Quoted in Theodore Saloutos and John D. Hicks, *Agricultural Discontent in the Middle West, 1900–1939*, p. 89.

not confined to those directly involved in the business of planting and growing. "Bankers and lawyers, doctors and ministers left their offices and clients and drove pell mell over the country to procure options and contracts upon this farm and that, paying a few hundred dollars down," one observer remembered. "Not to be in the game marked one as an old fogy, while paper profits were pyramided and Cadillac cars and pleasure trips to the cities took the place of Fords and Sunday afternoon picnics."[5]

Wheat and hogs, wheat and hogs, became a kind of midwestern mantra for success. The demand for both was higher than that for any other product, and the statistics the two produced were enough to strike wonder into the heart of anyone. In 1913, American wheat farmers had produced 751 million bushels on 52 million acres at a price of 79 cents the bushel; in 1919, the figures were 952 million bushels on 73.7 million acres at $2.16 the bushel. In those six years, gross sales had risen from a little over $593 million to more than $2 billion (in equivalent 1998 dollars, an increase of $13.2 billion), an astonishing return. The figures for hog production were less spectacular, but inarguably gratifying—12.2 billion pounds, bringing in $91.9 million in 1913; 13.9 billion pounds garnering $227.8 million in 1919. Gross income for all farm products rose from $7.9 billion in 1913 to nearly $18 billion in 1919—$169.2 billion in today's money—and for one of the few times in the history of American agriculture, parity—that magical statistical point at which the cost of production was matched by the amount of return—not only had been reached, it had been exceeded. Farmers now were getting more in than they were paying out. And as a recovering Europe clamored for food at war's end, the levels of prices and production remained high well into 1920, even after the government removed its price supports.

European demands for relatively expensive American food began to decline as cheaper wheat from Australia and Canada and cheap beef and other meat products from Argentina and elsewhere came in on suddenly submarine-free shipping lanes. An anti-inflation Federal Reserve announced an end to the easy credit of the war years. Prices sank every

5. Remley J. Glass, "Gentlemen, the Corn Belt!" *Harper's Monthly Magazine* (July 1933).

bit as dramatically as they had risen: by 1923, wheat had fallen from $2.16 the bushel to 93 cents, while hogs that had brought $22.18 a head in 1919 were down to $12.29. The slide continued throughout the rest of the decade, net farm income dropping from the 1919 high of $9.6 billion to a shade over $4.5 billion by 1930, while taxes and production costs rose so high that the average farmer was now paying out more than he took in. Frantically, farmers attempted to counter falling prices with higher levels of productivity, borrowing money to finance expansion and continuing to mine the soil for money crops like wheat. By 1930, the debt load of the agricultural sector had climbed to more than $9.6 billion (by comparison, the entire federal debt was only $16.5 billion).

Agriculture probably was in a worse position than any other segment of the economy when the full weight of the depression struck. Prices that had seemed low in 1930 had become grotesque parodies by 1932—wheat down to a pitiful 38 cents a bushel, for example; hogs to $6.31 a head. And if the prices of everything the farmer had to buy had also fallen, few of his costs had declined proportionately; parity had become an improbable statistical dream. The average per-acre value of American farms fell from a high of $69.31 in 1920 to $29.68 by the end of 1932; there had never been such a decline. In Iowa, in the very heart of the heartland, the value of the average farm had fallen from more than $35,000 in 1920 to less than $20,000 by the end of 1930 (and by 1935 would be down to a little over $11,000). More and more Iowa farmers began selling their places for whatever they could get, and as sales proliferated, desperation gave birth to one of the oddest (if short-lived) public relations campaigns on record.

It all started with Indianola newspaper editor Don Berry. "The general opinion seems to be that every farmer wants to sell out and go home to his wife's folks," a Des Moines banker had complained to Berry early in 1931. "As a matter of fact, I'll bet that 90 percent of the farms in Iowa couldn't be bought at present prices."

Berry got to thinking about that claim when he returned to Indianola. He talked things over with a fellow editor and folks in the local Rotary and Lions club organizations, then began printing up signs reading "THIS FARM IS NOT FOR SALE," with a slug line below the title: "This Is the Land of Three Square Meals a Day." Committees from the two service organizations began distributing the free signs around the county to any farmer willing to nail one to a stake and plant the thing on his roadside property line. "The signs do not mean that these farms wouldn't be sold at any price," Berry noted, "but simply that they aren't on the market at these prices or anything like them. They mean that farmers aren't alarmed and tramping over one another in a wild rush to unload their land on anyone who'll take it. . . . [They] are reminding themselves and the rest of us that in the long run a good piece of farm land always has been, always will be a dependable asset and a fine place to make a home."

By the end of the summer the not-for-sale signs were all over the county. "Constant thinking and talking about troubles had begun to take the joy out of living in this neighborhood," one farm woman explained. "We were all tired of that state of mind so we welcomed this chance to count our blessings for a change. And it's surprising how much better we have all felt since."[6]

Therapy by slogan was not enough to stave off disaster, and by 1933 there were few of the brave "NOT FOR SALE" signs to be seen. Tens of thousands of farmers in Warren County and elsewhere had indeed sold their land and left the heartland. Among those who remained, the fear of failure remained high. The farm foreclosure rate for the nation reached 54.1 per thousand by 1933; nearly 150,000 farms were being lost to foreclosure every year. The situation was worst in Iowa, where the rate had reached 78.3 per thousand—roughly 17,000 farms a year were going under in the Hawkeye State.[7] "We lawyers of the Corn Belt have had to develop a new type of practice," one Iowa attorney wrote in the summer of 1933, noting that one-third of the court cases filed now had to do with foreclosures.

6. Warren County's story is related in "They Tell the World 'This Farm IS NOT For Sale,'" *The Farmer's Wife* (October 1931).
7. Foreclosure rate figures for the United States from Milton S. Eisenhower, ed. *Yearbook of Agriculture 1934*, p. 710. Iowa foreclosure rate from John L. Shover, "Depression Letters from American Farmers," *Agricultural History* (July 1962). Number of Iowa farms affected extrapolated from figures in Donald P. Wood, *Historical Statistics of the States of the United States: Two Centuries of the Census, 1790–1990*, p. 165. As usual, all other statistics from *Historical Statistics of the United States*.

I have represented bankrupt farmers and holders of claims for rent, notes, and mortgages against such farmers in dozens of bankruptcy hearings and court actions, and the most discouraging, disheartening experiences of my legal life have occurred when men of middle age, with families, go out of the bankruptcy court with furniture, team of horses and a wagon, and a little stock as all that is left from twenty-five years of work. . . . And the powers that be seem to demand that these not only accept the situation but shall like it.[8]

There were plenty of farmers who were willing neither to accept nor to like the situation. One of their principal spokesmen was a sometime Campbellite minister in Iowa by the unlikely name of Milo Reno, a political being straight out of the radical Greenbacker and Populist movements of the nineteenth century. Tireless and obsessed, with bright wild eyes behind a pair of dark-rimmed spectacles and a head of hair that perched on the top of his head like a large pad of tattered steel wool, Reno had become one of the most effective evangelical speakers that a long tradition of rural protest had ever produced. By the end of the decade, he had risen to the presidency of the militant Iowa Farmers' Union, part of the National Farmers' Union, itself an aggressive competitor as representative of the farmers' interests with the National Grange, the Non-Partisan League, the Farmer-Labor Party, and the American Farm Bureau Federation.

From his base in the Iowa Farmers' Union, Reno had led resistance to a state public health law requiring that all dairy cattle be tested for bovine tuberculosis. Reno and his protesters claimed that the test was notoriously unreliable and therefore useless in the fight against the spread of the disease to the human population, that in the hands of incompetent or corrupt veterinarians cows would be mistakenly (or not so mistakenly) condemned and confiscated, and that the animals' carcasses would be turned over to meat-packing companies at hugely reduced prices. "FAKE, FAKE, FAKE" the placard of one demonstrator read during a protest march through downtown Des Moines. "Vets condemn our cattle/And to the packers take/Fake, Fake, Fake." The whole

8. Remley J. Glass, op. cit.

procedure virtually guaranteed the illegal seizure of private property, they claimed, and before their rebellion was put down in the fall of 1931, outbreaks of violence had caused the governor of Iowa to call out the National Guard.[9]

The tuberculosis protests reinforced the growing conviction on the part of Reno and other agricultural reformers that farmers must be prepared to "strike," to withhold the production and sale of their livestock and produce in order to win necessary reforms. Their primary goal was the creation of a federally mandated pricing structure that would guarantee coverage of the farmer's cost of production, one of the stipulations of the McNary-Haugen bill, agricultural reform legislation that had been unsuccessfully promoted in various forms through much of the twenties. "Concede to the farmer production costs," Reno exhorted a radio audience, "and he will pay his grocer, the grocer will pay the wholesaler, the wholesaler will pay the manufacturer and the manufacturer will be able to meet his obligations at the bank. Restore the farmers' purchasing power, and you have reestablished an endless chain of prosperity and happiness in this country."[10]

In May 1932, the Iowa Farmers' Union organized a national convention in Des Moines to discuss the ways and means of striking, and out of this convention came the Farmers Holiday Association, with Milo Reno as its president. With the slogan "Stay at Home—Buy Nothing—Sell Nothing," a strike, or "holiday"—as in bank holiday—was planned to begin on July 4.[11] "[The] national Farmers Holiday Association," Reno announced, "is appealing to the individual farmers, to the cooperative groups, and to all farm organizations to forget their differences and join in a united effort to correct the situation before it is everlastingly too late to save the farm home, that has been builded by the sweat, the toil, the sacrifice, of those who occupy them."[12] That said, and with Farm Holiday organizers having laid the groundwork in several other midwestern states, the national strike began—though not until the end of August.

9. See Saloutos and Hicks, op. cit., pp. 437–41. Placard poem quoted on p. 439.
10. Quoted in John L. Shover, "Populism in the Nineteen-Thirties: The Battle for the AAA," *Agricultural History* (January 1961).
11. Quoted in Saloutos and Hicks, op. cit., p. 442.
12. Quoted in Valelly, op. cit., p. 88.

The strike was meant to be a simple—and peaceful—matter of individual farmers' banding together and refusing to sell their goods for a month or so. But Reno and other Farm Holiday officials had little control over what might happen on the ground. The movement lasted longer than planned and in many areas degenerated into sporadic violence. From Wisconsin to Nebraska, picketers armed with pick handles and the occasional rifle set up roadblocks to stop the movement of produce, strewing highways with nail-studded planks and sometimes seizing and destroying truckloads of goods. Dairy trucks were particularly attractive targets of opportunity, and milk was spilled in many a roadside ditch. "We can get five hundred men together in any spot in a couple of hours," Will Daniel, a local activist who had organized milk picket lines near Sioux City, boasted. "I suppose we'd be foolish if we started anything away from home; you know a rooster can fight best on his own dung-hill."[13] In one of the largest single demonstrations, as many as 1,200 pickets blocked all five highways leading to the huge produce market in Omaha, Nebraska, through Council Bluffs, Iowa, on August 26, while County Sheriff P. A. Lainson surrounded himself with several dozen special deputies armed with six machine guns, 100 baseball bats, and 100 pick handles, and declared that he and his men were there "to kill people if we must, though we don't want to."[14] No one was killed in Council Bluffs as a result of the strike that day, but during a gun battle outside Sioux City, Iowa, a few months later, five men were wounded and one was killed. Elsewhere, there were plenty of bruised bones and broken heads on both sides before the demonstration gradually wound down as fall 1932 wore into winter 1933.

The intensity of the violence that attended the holiday belied the fact that probably no more than 10 percent of the region's farmers ever participated in the movement. As usual, local officialdom tended to ascribe the uprising to outside agitators sent in by the CP/USA to stir up the folks. The Communist-led United Farmers League was, in fact, something of a power in a few regions—most notably, northeastern South Dakota, where in the fall of 1931 the legendary Ella Reeve ("Mother") Bloor, one of the party's most ubiquitous organizers, had

13. Quoted in Page Smith, op. cit., pp. 292–93.
14. Quoted in the *New York Times* (August 27, 1932).

helped orchestrate a well-publicized UFL relief caravan in 1931.[15] Still, the vast bulk of the demonstrators were local people who did not need the Communists to furnish them with passion or the willingness to express it.

However dramatic, the strike accomplished little; farm prices did not increase, and Hoover was adamant in his opposition to legislation that would guarantee the "cost of production" to the farmer: as he had indicated with his response to the Bonus Marchers that summer, he was not a man to give in to the demands of protesters. But the anger did not go away with the end of the strike, and in its next manifestation it did produce measurable results. By the end of 1933, more and more local Farmers Holiday Association groups were spending less time in stopping the movement of crops than in preventing mortgage foreclosures, as Theresa Von Baum's neighbors had done when they held the "penny auction" sale in Nebraska that fall. It was a popular tactic, one that not only allowed farmers to demonstrate their solidarity but at the same time vent their spleen against a favorite target. "Shoot the banker if he comes on your farm," North Dakota governor William "Wild Bill" Langer had declared during his 1932 election campaign. "Treat him like a chicken thief."[16] Penny auction farmers shot no bankers, but anti-foreclosure actions appeared throughout the Midwest—as many as seventy-six in the months of January and February 1933 alone.[17] The ubiquitous Meridel LeSueur was on hand for one such passive-aggressive rebellion when several farms were announced for auction in a Minnesota courtroom packed to the windowsills with farmers. Each time the court clerk nervously read off the name of a farm, he was greeted with gravid silence. Only once, she reported, was there a response. "I bid a hundred dollars," someone said. "There was a single moment," LeSueur remembered, "then above the massed heads the kicking body of a man rose in the room, his arms and legs squirming. . . . [T]hey

15. For the United Farmers League and its role, see Allan Mathews, "Agrarian Radicals: The United Farmers League of South Dakota," *South Dakota History* (Fall 1973).
16. Quoted in Catherine McNicol Stock, *Main Street in Crisis*, p. 140. As Stock notes, "Wild Bill" was an appropriate nickname. Langer was soon indicted for misappropriating CWA money. Although he was reelected in spite of the indictment, his election was later recalled.
17. The estimate is John L. Shover's in "The Penny-Auction Rebellion."

handed him upon solid outstretched arms to the door, and he was emitted on a solid band of lifted horny hands down the stairs, and I do not know what became of him after that. He didn't bid any more. Neither did anyone else. The clerk came to the end of the list, made a gesture that he had done his duty and to hell with it."[18]

The Iowa state legislature, for one, took the point, and on February 17, 1933, passed a mortgage moratorium law, while in Minnesota eight days later Governor Olson issued a decree establishing a one-year moratorium on farm mortgage foreclosures. By April Nebraska, Wisconsin, South Dakota, North Dakota, Arkansas, Oklahoma, Kentucky, and Illinois had all followed suit. These laws helped to reduce the number of farm foreclosures, but they did not apply to mortgages that were delinquent at the time of passage and did not include chattel foreclosures. Direct action continued even as Franklin Roosevelt was inaugurated and began assembling his New Deal army to take on the crisis of the depression, and in a few instances—most of them in Iowa—demonstrations escalated into something a good deal uglier than the often grim, but generally peaceful, farmyard gatherings that had typified the antiforeclosure movement.

In Wilbur, Nebraska, demonstrators had to be driven out of the Saline County sheriff's office with tear gas on March 14. Ten days later, a Harlan, Iowa, attorney was seized and held prisoner until he agreed to let a family pay rent to his client rather than be thrown off the farm after foreclosure. On April 27, several dozen farmers broke through a line of deputies guarding the O'Brien County Court House in Primghar, Iowa, forced a receiver to accept a token payment, then made the receiver, the sheriff, and each of the deputies kneel and kiss the American flag (a news photograph of this scene became one of the most durable images in the national iconography).

Later that same day, a hundred farmers entered the courtroom during a mortgage hearing in Le Mars, Iowa, grabbed the judge, drove him out of town, then stopped by a telephone pole on a lonely road. The crowd discussed the merits of hanging the judge or merely dragging him behind a speeding automobile for a while, then settled on the more prudent course of dumping a hubcap full of grease on his head,

18. Meridel LeSueur, *North Star Country*, p. 274.

stripping his pants from him, filling them with gravel, tossing them into a ditch, and leaving their victim by the side of the road. That night, the sheriff of Plymouth County wired Governor Clyde Herring: "Situation beyond control of civil authorities. Demand militia."[19] The governor obliged, not only sending troops but declaring martial law. Fifty-seven participants in the Primghar and Le Mars incidents were arrested, though most received token sentences, the judge in this case apparently sharing the opinion of Wallace Short, a minister and publisher of a Sioux City labor newspaper, the *Unionist and Public Forum*, that "at such times men turn their backs on the question of what is legal, and act with energy and conviction on their sense of what is right."[20] Milo Reno certainly agreed: "The farmers of that community have been God-fearing, law-abiding members of society up until the present. [Any] acts of violence and law violations that have been committed have been due to some intolerable wrong under which the people have been suffering."[21]

"WE HAVE THE right to ask the federal government for aid and assistance in times of great emergency," William Loriks, an official in the National Farmers' Union, declared early in 1933. "It is the duty of government to come to [our] aid."[22] Henry Wallace had only a little more regard for the Farmers' Union, than he held for the Farmers Holiday Association, which he characterized at one point as a "misery-ridden, desperate farm group," but he would never have denied the validity of the claim on government aid.[23] "I am going to Washington, March 4, to serve as Secretary of Agriculture in the Cabinet of President Roosevelt," he wrote in his final editorial for *Wallace's Farmer*, which he had inherited from his father. "I remember how my father left home twelve years ago to take a similar position under President Harding. . . . While the situation of the world and of agriculture is far more desperate today than it

19. Quoted in Shover, "The Penny-Auction Rebellion."
20. Quoted in Rodney D. Karr, "Farmer Rebels in Plymouth County, Iowa, 1932–1933," *Annals of Iowa* (winter 1985).
21. Quoted in DiLeva, op. cit.
22. Quoted in Stock, op. cit., p. 141.
23. Ibid.

was then, I have an advantage he did not have—a chief who is definitely progressive, entirely sympathetic toward agriculture, and completely determined to use every means at his command to restore farm buying power."[24]

Wallace also had around him in the Department of Agriculture men who were more than ready to make policy and in Congress a body of legislators equally ready to translate policy into law. But which policy into what law? There was no dearth of choices. For every proposal offered by Wallace's economic advisers there was a counterproposal that either modified or rejected the first proposal, then was modified or rejected by a third, and while the planners kicked up foam in a sea of theory, *Business Week* reported on March 29, 1933, lobbyists poured into Washington, "farm leaders representing every shade of opinion, every commodity, and every locality," together with "grain dealers, meat packers, the millers, the cotton converters, and the hundreds of business elements affected by farm legislation."

Out of the confusion emerged the proposed Agricultural Adjustment Act of 1933, which displayed, *Business Week* noted in that same issue, "all the earmarks of a document hastily drawn to the specifications of divergent and conflicting groups." However complex, the substance of its three titles was neatly summarized by *Wallace's Farmer*:

As soon as the bill passes, three big horses will be ready to work for the farmer.

The first horse is the section of the bill that provides for increasing farm buying power by paying farmers to reduce production to effective demand.

The second horse is the section that cuts interest rates on many farm mortgages and makes possible the scaling down of the principal on many more.

The third horse . . . is inflation.[25]

Few in or out of Congress argued with the need to take the pressure off farm mortgages, and while Title II of the legislation was hardly the

24. Quoted in Russell Lord, *The Wallaces of Iowa*, pp. 324–25.
25. Quoted in Saloutos and Hicks, op. cit., p. 466.

moratorium that many had demanded, its refinancing stipulations would help to rescue many farmers from foreclosure, and its easy credit provisions would go a long way toward keeping many others from sliding into bankruptcy. On the other hand, while virtually every agricultural interest supported some sort of inflationary policy that would make money more easily available and at the same time drive prices up, that provision of the bill was a harder sell. After much legislative tinkering and congressional wrangling, the amendment that finally got tacked on to the final version of the bill authorized the president, at his discretion, to issue up to $3 billion in new U.S. notes, to fix the weight of gold and silver in U.S. coinage and in doing so to regulate the price of both metals, and to accept silver in payment of foreign debts. In effect, the country not only would go inflationary, it would go off the gold standard. Among those most vigorously opposed to the amendment was Director of the Budget Lewis Douglas, who argued that any attempt to institute "controlled" inflation was doomed to ensure that prices would, in fact, spiral out of control and that to abandon the gold standard was to ensure nothing less than "the end of Western Civilization."[26] End of Western civilization or not, most of those in the administration and in the Democratic Congress supported the provision, and engineered inflation became Title III of the bill.

By far the most controversial section of the bill, however, was its first. Title I established a "domestic allotment" program for the basic agricultural commodities of wheat, cotton, field corn, hogs, rice, tobacco, and milk. Through voluntary contracts with the government, the producers of these commodities would agree to maintain production levels established by the Department of Agriculture. The theory was that by reducing production, the farmer would be increasing demand, which, in turn, gradually would raise prices to levels that would assure parity. In exchange, and until such natural parity was reached, the government would pay him the difference between what he might make in current prices for his product and what the parity price would have been. To finance the benefit payments, the law would

26. Quoted in Davis, op. cit., p. 107. Douglas would later resign over this and other economic issues.

impose a tax on processed goods equivalent to the difference between the current farm price and the fair exchange value.

One glaring flaw here, of course, was the fact that in an era in which people were rumored to be starving to death on every street corner, the government was proposing to pay farmers *not* to produce food. It was a public relations quagmire, of which fact Wallace was perfectly aware. On March 9, the secretary met with brain-truster Rexford Tugwell, Russell Lord, Washington correspondent for *The Country Home* magazine, and the magazine's managing editor, Andrew Wing, to discuss the situation. Wallace, Lord remembered, "was searching, characteristically, for a moral justification" for the domestic allotment plan. Lord offered a letter from an Arkansas farm woman who liked the idea of domestic allotment just fine. "We can rest part of our land each year," she had written, "and we can find time to rest ourselves. We can use the time that we used to spend in speeding up production in living and developing our own possibilities as human beings. We will have more time for our children, and more time for reflection, books, music, travel, sociability, and even art."

The somewhat romantic Wallace, rarely slow to embrace any scheme that promised the perfection of the human spirit, was delighted. "That is fine," he said. "It is true. We must make a religion of that!"

Tugwell was appalled. "My God, Henry, no!" he exclaimed. "Rationalize any way we have to, we can't make a religion out of growing or making fewer goods with this whole country and the whole world in bitter need."

Wallace, Lord recalled, glanced at him and Wing a little impishly. "They get awfully scared here when I as much as mention religion," he said. "But on this I guess Rex is right."[27]

The farm bill, introduced on March 16, was argued as furiously as any measure the New Dealers presented. Anti-inflation forces and defenders of the gold standard objected to the title granting the president monetary powers. Hard-line conservatives maintained that the bill was an unwarranted, pernicious, and probably communistic attempt to interfere with the farmer's God-given right to grow as much as he

27. The meeting is described in Lord, op. cit., pp. 328–29.

wanted of whatever he wanted whenever he wanted to grow it. "Cost of production" advocates said the domestic allotment system would be too bureaucratic to comprehend and administer and would not raise prices sufficiently in any event. Those friendly to meat packers and other processors despised the processing tax, while those representing consumer groups pointed out that the tax would simply be passed on to those who bought the finished product on the shelf. Nevertheless, the need to do something and do it soon ultimately overcame the multitude of obstacles. As *Business Week* admitted in commenting on earlier domestic allotment legislation, while it might seem economically unjustifiable to "tax the city dweller to maintain a decent standard of living on the farm," economic rationality might be irrelevant in the face of social and political needs. "It might well seem important to us to preserve in our country the one large class of property owners, the greatest body of entrepreneurs, the one stable and rooted element. It might seem worth a high cost—and it might be cheaper than to add them to the breadlines of the cities."[28] The bill was passed and signed into law by Roosevelt on May 12, 1933.

IT WAS THE pigs that first got Wallace and his new Agricultural Adjustment Administration (AAA) in trouble—and for precisely the reasons he had feared. After weeks of negotiation, the corn-hog division of the AAA still had not worked out industry-wide contracts with farmers and processors over how many pigs might be allowed to go to market. At the same time, hog prices were going down while hog numbers were going up, including a disproportionate number of "piggy [pregnant] sows," which, when they came full term, would swell the inventory even more. By early July, *Wallace's Farmer* was warning that "we are headed straight for big trouble in hogs, unless we get busy with a reduction program."[29]

The AAA responded in the middle of August with an emergency purchase program, which over the next several months bought a little

28. "Three Farm Roads," *Business Week* (February 15, 1933).
29. Quoted in Roger C. Lambert, "The Illusion of Participatory Democracy: The AAA Organizes the Corn-Hog Producers," *Annals of Iowa* (fall 1974).

over 6 million hogs at prices that ranged between $6 and $9.50 per hundredweight, including a bonus of $4 for piggy sows weighing 240 pounds or more.[30] The animals were removed from the normal marketing stream. Those too small to be butchered and processed for meat and turned over to the Red Cross and other charitable agencies were rendered into "tankage," which could then be converted into fertilizer, grease, and other commercial by-products.

From the beginning, the program was something of a mess. Neither meat packers nor tankage processors were able to handle the sheer number of animals that were suddenly funneled into their systems in St. Paul, Sioux City, St. Joseph, Kansas City, Omaha, and Chicago. Tankage that could not be sold or stored was dumped into the Missouri and Mississippi Rivers. Carcasses with meat still on them were reported floating in the rivers or piled up and left to rot behind packing plants. The AAA admitted to much of the tankage disposal, noting that it had authorized the processors to get rid of the excess as economically as possible, but never did recognize the existence of floating bodies.

In the public perception, it was not pollution that was the problem, but waste, as rumor built upon fact to discredit the entire program. The outcry was widespread and vehement. A woman wrote in to condemn the slaughter of helpless "expectant mothers," while attorney Clarence Darrow said it was a crime to "kill little pigs and throw them out on the prairies to decay while millions are hungry." One of the hungry agreed. "How the pigs would help us," he wrote from Indiana, "if we could only get them to feed and kill, if only two-thirds of the people who are without meat could get [some] this winter and the coming summer there would be but little surplus. . . . I am only asking our leader to consider sparing the flesh and food that nature has given us."

Wallace attempted to stand firm. "I cannot say it too strongly," he declared during a press conference in Des Moines. "Nobody will starve if we reduce hog production; but farmers will go without the necessities of life if we don't." It simply was not logical, he would later add, to expect agriculture to "survive in a capitalistic society as a philanthropic enterprise" or to believe that "every little pig has the right to attain before slaughter the full pigginess of his pigness," but even Wallace was

30. Figures from Eisenhower, ed., op. cit., p. 39.

clearly uncomfortable, while AAA administrator George N. Peek appeared to squirm a bit when he admitted that "it does seem shocking to kill these small hogs. But, on second thought, is it any less shocking to kill them some months later when they are in the prime of youth?"[31]

In actuality, some of the pigs were going for relief food, but that aspect of the program was too casually administered to do the job effectively and too obscure to still the outrage. Among those who objected to the waste was legal counsel Jerome Frank, a liberal-minded lawyer who had fought urban corruption in Chicago and New York and was now one of the leaders of the "Little Brain Trusters" grouped under Wallace and Tugwell in the Department of Agriculture—including agricultural journalist Chester Davis and planners and economists Mordecai Ezekiel, Louis Bean, and Gardner Jackson. Frank recommended that the meat processed from the hog slaughter be turned over to Harry Hopkins at the Federal Emergency Relief Administration and made a formal part of its distribution network. Peek objected to the idea, insisting that Hopkins should buy his relief meat on the open market in order to help raise prices. But the FERA was buying no commercial meat and had no intention of starting. Hopkins liked the idea of getting it from the AAA's domestic allotment program. So did Tugwell. The three men got together and outlined a distribution program, then took the proposal to Roosevelt at Hyde Park. Roosevelt approved it immediately and on September 21 authorized the purchase of $75 million worth of surplus agricultural commodities for relief purposes. A little over a week later, he established the Federal Surplus Relief Corporation, which over the next several months would buy and distribute through the FERA about 100 million pounds of hog meat, among other products. Soon, thousands of head of cattle and tons of clothing would be added to the program. Though he had not thought of the program himself—and his AAA administrator Peek disliked it—Wallace was happy to take credit for its success a few months later. "To many of us," he wrote, "the only thing that made the hog slaughter acceptable was the realization that the meat and lard salvaged would go to the unemployed."[32]

---

31. All hog-killing quotes from Roger C. Lambert, "Slaughter of the Innocents: The Public Protests AAA Killing of Little Pigs," *Midwest Quarterly* (April 1973).
32. Henry Wallace, *New Frontiers*, p. 184.

If Wallace had hoped that the creation of the Federal Surplus Relief Corporation would significantly reduce the weight of criticism leveled against the AAA from the beginning, he was disappointed. Rumors of ghastly waste and the pointless "slaughter of the innocents" continued well into 1934, exacerbated by the fact that the hoped-for rise in market prices did not materialize. And throughout its existence in the FERA, the surplus food program would be locked in constant bickering with AAA officials, livestock producers, and packers over the number of animals purchased and the prices paid. In 1935, the program would finally be moved from the FERA to the Department of Agriculture, restructured, renamed the Federal Surplus Commodities Corporation, and taken out of the business of relief entirely.

Reaction to the wholesale murder of pigs and difficulties with the FERA remained only two of the agency's problems as AAA officials nobly struggled to forge some decently workable farm program in spite of odds that seemed to grow longer with every passing day. More than ten million acres of cotton were withdrawn from production in the first few months of the program—much of it literally plowed under—and another nine million acres of wheat. Prices for both commodities did rise about 47 percent within a few weeks, but much of this was the result of speculation, not scarcity, and growth remained sluggish; wheat would not hit a dollar a bushel again until 1936, and even that would soon fall off, while cotton would get no higher than a little over twelve cents a pound for the rest of the decade. What was more, the initial impact of the National Recovery Administration's wage regulations and price agreements had been to raise the farmer's costs. "Agriculture did not make the progress expected in reducing the disparity between agricultural and nonagricultural prices," Wallace's report for the year admitted, then went on to wax optimistic, nevertheless. Nonagricultural prices were bound to go down as the NRA program stabilized, the secretary insisted, while "agricultural prices on the other hand should continue to advance with adjustments in farm production and increases in consumer buying power."[33]

33. Henry A. Wallace, "The Past Year in Agriculture," in Eisenhower, ed., op. cit., p. 13.

The prediction would not pan out in the long run, and in the short run the problems already visible were enough to punctuate the rest of 1933 with discontent. The Farmers Holiday Association began calling for a code system for agriculture similar to that for businesses in the NRA—only in this case it would include "cost of production" guarantees—and encouraged further strike actions. Milo Reno himself worried that "the whole program of the Brain Trust is in the direction of Russian Communism, German Fascism, or Italian Dictatorship. . . . What in the name of God are we finally coming to? It will require the energy of every American citizen to save this republic from destruction."[34] In an attempt to force wheat prices higher, Governor "Wild Bill" Langer of North Dakota instituted a short-lived embargo on the shipment of wheat from his state that, while attention-getting, was as illegal as it was ineffective. Farmers complained about AAA "regimentation" and bureaucratic entanglements and maintained that the county agricultural agent, ostensibly devoted only to the interests of the farmer, had become a political tool, a "rural ward-heeler."[35] Wisconsin milk farmers, who had already undertaken short but relatively violent strikes in February and May, banded together one more time in October, picketing roads, dumping milk cans, and burning two cheese factories before running out of energy three weeks later. Five western governors met in November to demand that the federal government license all processors to pay fair exchange rates to farmers for their produce and to institute production quotas for each individual farmer.

Patience was what the Department of Agriculture urged in a press release on November 4; the checks would be in the mail, and the checks would make all the difference: "There has been no opportunity as yet to send out checks to the corn and wheat regions of the west and northwest. The wheat checks are now beginning to move and the corn-hog benefit checks will begin to flow out into the country about January. Corn loan money will become available in a few weeks."[36] By the end of the year, more than $131 million in allotment checks had, indeed, gone

34. In John L. Shover, ed., "Depression Letters from American Farmers," *Agricultural History* (July 1962).
35. Quoted in Saloutos and Hicks, op. cit., p. 491.
36. Quoted in ibid, p. 485.

out (by the end of 1934, payments would reach more than $600 million), and while the bulk of the money had gone to cotton farmers (most of whom had signed contracts almost immediately), there was enough money spread around the Midwest among corn-hog farmers and wheat farmers to make an impression on people who had not been able to rub two coins together in their pockets for years. Additionally, the Farm Credit Administration—the agency created to administer the AAA's mortgage program—had upped its staff from 212 people in the middle of May to more than 5,000 by the fall, and reports had it that they were processing $2.5 million a day in loans and refinancing agreements.[37] "The farmer," *Fortune* magazine remarked with approval in January 1934, "has had something done for him. As contrasted with other classes in the community, he has had a great deal done for him. . . . And whatever the final outcome of the Agricultural Adjustment Act as an economic experiment, whatever its ultimate effect on agriculture, there can be little reasonable doubt but that its immediate political effect will be sedative."[38]

Fortune's writer was close to the mark. Strikes and holiday actions gradually diminished, and while the AAA would not at any time have universal—or even general—support from midwestern farmers, with unrest erupting here and there in the years to come, the Midwest would never again experience anything like the uprisings of 1933. A functional symbiosis between the federal government and mainstream agriculture had been established, a bond that would grow so powerful that not even the Supreme Court of the United States could effectively sever it—though it tried. In January 1936, after hearing *United States vs. Butler et al.*, the court invalidated the AAA, the majority opinion stating that "Congress has no power to enforce its command on the farmer to the ends sought by the Agricultural Adjustment Act."[39] The administration and Congress responded first with the Soil Conservation and Domestic Allotment Act of 1936, which established a cooperative system of crop reduction, with payments to accommodating farmers com-

37. See "Bryan! Bryan! Bryan!" in *Fortune* (January 1934).
38. Ibid.
39. Quoted in Joseph M. Rowe Jr., *"United States vs. Butler, et al.,"* in James S. Olson, ed., *Historical Dictionary of the New Deal: From Inauguration to Preparation for War*.

ing from a processing tax. Not enough farmers cooperated, however, and crop surpluses continued to mount. In 1938, another Agricultural Adjustment Act was passed, this one establishing a quota system to maintain prices and providing financial assistance through a Commodity Credit Corporation, a Federal Crop Insurance program, and a Surplus Reserve Loan Corporation. In March 1938, the government sponsored farm elections to approve the quotas it had established. The quotas were overwhelmingly approved, and the government was in the agriculture business to stay.

But if the New Dealers could take some cautious satisfaction from what they had been able to accomplish among the corn-hog and wheat farmers of the Midwest, in other fields there would be too much pain, too much death, and too little hope to let them rest very comfortably in their fine progressive certitudes.

15

Further Down the Country

While the great majority of local protest movements in the thirties were homegrown and usually led by people without any particular leanings toward the left—often by people with no politics at all—social eruptions were relentlessly attributed to the work of Communist agitators by most politicians and virtually all of the press. This was as true of rural agitation as it was of unrest in the cities. The Communists themselves did little to rectify this misperception—and, in fact, they frequently could be found lurking in the background or agitating at the center of the turmoil, usually taking credit for it whether they had contributed anything or not. Trouble was where they lived, after all, and presumably there should have been no more fruitful an environment for their work than among black people and organizations. That it did not turn out that way was one of the greatest disappointments of the American party's history.

The Comintern had targeted the black community early. In 1924, its executive committee declared that the main task of the American party in regard to what it called the "Negro problem" must "consist of

fighting against . . . prejudices, and in energetic action for the equality
of rights. . . . It is only under such conditions that it will be possible to
draw the Negro masses in America into a general fight for the dictatorship of the proletariat."[1] Nevertheless, the party had not been overwhelmed by applications from African Americans, even after James
Ford, a black party official, was nominated as William Z. Foster's running mate in the 1932 presidential campaign. (Foster and Ford finished
dead last with a little over 100,000 votes.) As late as 1936, the number
of card-carrying black party members would be less than 4,000. Robert
L. Vann, editor of one of the oldest and most influential black newspapers, the *Pittsburgh Courier*, thought he knew why. "We have our serious
doubts that the average American Negro understands communism," he
wrote a little arrogantly in the April 1932 issue of *Crisis*, the NAACP's
journal. "Communist leaders are confused also. They think the radicalism of the present-day Negro fits him precisely for Communism. This is
error. The radical Negro is . . . intelligent; he knows what he wants. He
also knows he does not want Communism."[2] In his *Amsterdam News*,
Harlem editor William Kelly pointed out that black people had no reason to cheer for the dictatorship of the proletariat when that proletariat
was made up from the "same ignorant white class in the North and
South which now fails to respond to just and intelligent appeals for
racial and religious tolerance—the same ignorant white working class
which forms the backbone of every lynching mob."[3]

  Some black intellectuals were willing to think about it, however,
and many, like poet Langston Hughes and novelist Richard Wright,
nurtured relationships with the party that had all the character of a
long, passionate engagement that doesn't quite make it to the altar;
they never became card-carrying members. None had a longer or more
fervent alliance than Paul Robeson, the former All-American and Phi
Beta Kappa from Rutgers College who had become an internationally
acclaimed singer and actor by the early thirties. During Robeson's tour

1. Quoted in Wilson Record, *The Negro and the Communist Party*, p. 55.
2. Quoted in Theodore G. Vincent, *Voices of a Black Nation: Political Journalism in the Harlem Renaissance*, p. 207.
3. Quoted in James Goodman, *Stories of Scottsboro: The Rape Case That Shocked 1930s America and Revived the Struggle for Equality*, p. 71.

of the Soviet Union in 1934, he said that he felt "like a human being for the first time since I grew up. Here I am not a Negro but a human being. Before I came I could hardly believe that such a thing could be. . . . Here, for the first time in my life, I walk in full human dignity."[4] Robeson never lost his fondness for communism and would be hounded because of it for most of his life, but even he never joined the party.

If relatively few joined, many blacks appreciated the party's readiness to put action behind its words. "The Communists appear to be the only party going our way," Carl Murphy, editor of the Baltimore *Afro-American*, wrote. "Since the abolitionists passed off the scene, no white group of national prominence has openly advocated the economic, political and social equality of black folks. . . . The Communists are going our way, for which Allah be praised."[5] J. E. Mitchell, editor of the black *St. Louis Argus*, agreed: "The communists say that they are for the equal protection of the law for all citizens alike, and many of their followers have gone to jail and suffered to demonstrate their belief."[6]

Much of the esteem that the CP/USA had earned from Murphy, Mitchell, and other blacks stemmed from the willingness of the party's organizers to challenge the class structure, and nowhere was that willingness demonstrated more vividly than when it seriously disturbed two of the most emotionally charged of the Deep South's most peculiar institutions: the psychological amalgam of guilt, fear, and sexual insecurity that underlay white terror of black rape; and an agricultural system that differed from antebellum slavery only in that people could not actually be sold at the auction block. While the party's role in agitating both would soon enough diminish, it could take grim satisfaction in having helped to churn up the kind of feral apprehensions that W. J. Cash noted when discussing the black rebellions of the early thirties in *The Mind of the South*: "[The] white South delighted to say and believe that it knew the black man through and through. And yet even the most unreflecting must sometimes feel suddenly . . . that they were

4. Quoted in Martin Bauml Duberman, *Paul Robeson: A Biography*, p. 190.
5. Quoted in Vincent, op. cit., p. 203.
6. Quoted in Goodman, op. cit., p. 72.

looking at a blank wall. . . . What was back there, hidden? What whispering, stealthy, fateful thing might they be framing out there in the palpitant darkness?"[7]

ON MARCH 25, 1931, some of the boxcars on the Chattanooga Southern freight to Memphis were occupied by transient youths, both African American and white, hoping to find work. One of them was Haywood Patterson, a nineteen-year-old black man traveling with three companions. As the train dipped down into northwestern Alabama, Patterson would recall, he was hanging on to the side of a car when a white youth stepped on his hand while walking along the roof.

"The next time you want by," Patterson said to the other, "just tell me you want by and I let you by."

"Nigger," the white tramp replied, "I don't ask you when I want by. What you doin' on this train anyway?"

"Look, I just tell you, the next time you want by you just tell me you want by and I let you by."

"Nigger bastard, this a white man's train. You better get off. All you black bastards better get off!"[8]

A fight broke out and spread to other cars on the line, as blacks and whites wrestled, punched, and jumped off to throw rocks at one another when the freight slowed to a crawl on the steepest grades. Finally, most of the white transients had been tossed off, losers in what should have been an ordinary, soon-forgotten brawl.

But some of the whites went to the sheriff in nearby Stevenson and filed a complaint of assault. The sheriff wired this news down the line, and when the freight arrived at Paint Rock, Alabama, it was met by every white man in town who owned a gun. Patterson and eight other black transients were seized, tied together with a plow rope, put in the back of a flatbed truck, and carried into the county seat of Scottsboro to be arrested and arraigned. But not just on charges of assault and battery. By then, two white female transients named Victoria Price and Ruby Bates had been discovered on the same train, and the principal charge

7. W. J. Cash, *The Mind of the South*, p. 319.
8. Dialogue in Goodman, op. cit., p. 3.

now was rape. The women claimed that all nine of the black youths had ravished them at knifepoint. Indictments came down swiftly—although for a while it seemed that a trial was not going to be necessary. On the night of the arrests, a reporter for the *Huntsville Daily Times* reported that it appeared that "the entire population of the little county seat, augmented by hundreds of visitors, surrounded the two-story dilapidated jail."[9] It was a lynch mob, M. L. Wann, the county sheriff decided. But unlike many of his fellow sheriffs, who would have thrown up their hands and turned the young men over to the mob without much thought of resistance, Sheriff Wann wired the governor for the National Guard. Twenty-five armed troops were sent over from the National Guard Armory in Guntersville twenty miles away. That, combined with uncommonly cold weather, was enough to prevent a lynching.

Regional newspapers did little to cool the public temper, however. A story in the *Chattanooga News* on March 26 called the nine youths "beasts unfit to be called human," and its publisher editorialized the next day that "we still have savages abroad in the land, it seems," while the *Huntsville Daily Times* described the alleged crime as "the most atrocious ever recorded in this part of the country, a wholesale debauching of society."[10] Under such circumstances, a fair trial for any of the men seemed out of the question. Further, the attorneys appointed by the court to defend the nine had been given almost no time to prepare their cases even had they been interested in doing so—and since one had a serious drinking problem and another was described by a reporter as a "doddering, extremely unreliable, senile individual who is losing whatever ability he once had," that seemed unlikely.[11]

The four trials that ensued were swift and ludicrous. While Victoria Price, a lively sort with a background that included charges of prostitution and running a speakeasy, kept the courtroom enthralled with her luridly detailed accounts of the alleged rape and brought frequent bursts of laughter with her sharp tongue and rude wit, she and her companion, the much more subdued and confused Ruby Bates, contradicted

9. Quoted in Dan T. Carter, *Scottsboro: A Tragedy of the American South*, p. 8.
10. Quotes in ibid., p. 20.
11. Quoted in ibid., p. 18.

themselves and each other repeatedly. So did other witnesses for the prosecution, as well as several of the defendants, who, understandably terrified, randomly and a little hysterically accused one another of the crime at various points. The prosecution offered no hard physical evidence to support the charges of rape.

None of it mattered. Within two days, eight of the defendants were found guilty; the ninth, thirteen-year-old Leroy Wright, escaped conviction when the judge declared a mistrial because seven of the jury men insisted that the child should be given the death penalty even though the prosecution had recommended life in prison. There was no disagreement with regard to the remaining eight defendants; on the afternoon of April 9, each was sentenced to death.

"The people in the court cheered and clapped after the judge gave out with that," Haywood Patterson, the oldest and toughest of the defendants, remembered. "That courtroom was one big smiling white face."[12]

There soon were other white faces in the vicinity of Scottsboro, and they were not smiling. While the National Association for the Advancement of Colored People and other organizations dithered over how to respond to the verdicts (for a while, the NAACP worried that the men might actually be guilty), and white southerners congratulated themselves on having tried the defendants instead of lynching them, the American Communist Party's Central Committee issued a southern call to arms. On April 10 in the *Daily Worker*, it denounced the convictions as a legal travesty perpetrated by and for the ruling class of the South. "We demand," it said, "a united front of all working and farming masses of this country to stop the legal lynching at Scottsboro. . . . Let the southern ruling class know that we will tolerate their crimes against our class and against the persecuted Negro race no longer!"[13] The Central Committee then announced it was putting the resources of its legal arm, the International Labor Defense (ILD), at the disposal of the Scottsboro Boys, and began a publicity campaign that helped to stir up wholesale revulsion and a flood of letters, which poured into the offices

12. Haywood Patterson and Earl Conrad, *Scottsboro Boy*, p. 14.
13. Quote in Philip S. Foner and Herbert Shapiro, *American Communism and Black Americans: A Documentary History, 1930–1934*, p. 252.

of Alabama authorities from all quarters and classes of people in the country and the world. (These included outraged missives from such unlikely fellow protesters as rock-ribbed New England conservative Hamilton Fish and the scientist Albert Einstein.)

TO NORTHERN LIBERALS and radicals, the Scottsboro case was a living demonstration of the primitive repression that characterized the caste-ridden South. And as the cycle of trials and appeals continued through the decade and on into the 1940s, it would remain a definitive liberal shibboleth, the fate of the "Scottsboro Boys" cited in church pews and civil rights demonstrations well into the 1960s. At least one historian has given the case credit for having helped "revive the great struggle for freedom and equality waged by white people and black people together from the beginning of abolitionism to the end of Reconstruction."[14] In its early years, the case even helped to enhance the reputation of the Communist Party among mainstream liberals, the ILD at one point earning an accolade from the American Civil Liberties Union. "You have done a job," the ACLU's president, Roger Baldwin, said, "that no other agency could do or would do, not only in arousing world-wide opinion and protest but in the selection of counsel for skillful handling of the moves in court."[15]

Others noted that for all its work on behalf of the Scottsboro prisoners, the CP/USA was clearly not acting out of the purest altruism. The case made for invaluable publicity, and the party's national headquarters took every advantage of it, leading to charges of cynicism. "The Communists profess to be interested in uniting the white and the black 'proletarians' of the South," Elmer Davis wrote in *Harper's Monthly* magazine, "but everything they do has the effect of further inflaming the white proletariat against the black proletariat, and of spreading among Negroes the conviction that the Communists only want to use them for machine-gun fodder."[16] In truth, relationships between the ILD and other individuals and organizations that had come to the aid of the boys

14. Goodman, op. cit., p. 391.
15. Quoted in Klehr, op. cit., p. 338.
16. Elmer Davis, "Makers of Martyrs," *Harper's Monthly* magazine (August 1933).

did not run smooth. The ILD had staked out its territory early and fought to hold it for the party's own purposes, a rigidity that irritated many with an interest in the case. The ILD destroyed its own credibility to a large degree, however, when two of its representatives were arrested for attempting to bribe one of the women witnesses in 1934. The defendants constantly argued among themselves about who should represent them, and it was only after much bickering that, in 1935, the various parties agreed to the formation of a Scottsboro Defense Committee, which would include representatives from the ILD, the NAACP, the ACLU, the League for Industrial Democracy (founded by Socialist Norman Thomas), and the Methodist Federation for Social Service. It was this collective body, not the Communist Party, that would steer the future conduct of the case.[17]

Still, if the role of the party in the Scottsboro affair was viewed with mixed feelings in the liberal North, among most African Americans in the South there was a good deal less ambivalence. They had reason to share the belief that the Scottsboro trials were precisely representative of southern justice, and they tended to admire the Communists for coming to the aid of the defendants before anyone else. That admiration became an effective promotional tool when party organizers began intensifying their fieldwork in the South, particularly in the steelmaking town of Birmingham, Alabama, which offered familiar territory to a movement spawned in the working-class warrens of the urban North. The depression had hit the industries of Birmingham as hard as those of any city in the country, and by 1931 the party had organized and led enough hunger marches, Unemployed Council rallies, and other demonstrations to thoroughly alarm the authorities—who were particularly unnerved by the party's deliberate use of the racial issue to stir up support among blacks (a tactic that also tended to limit the party's

17. A summary of subsequent events in the Scottsboro saga might be useful: The Alabama Supreme Court upheld the convictions of 1931. The case was then taken to the U.S. Supreme Court, which on November 7, 1932, reversed the verdicts. A second series of trials was conducted; the men were again convicted. Once again, the convictions were appealed to the Alabama Supreme Court, which once again upheld them, then once again to the U.S. Supreme Court, which once again reversed them. A third series of trials began on January 20, 1936. The first defendant, Haywood Patterson, was swiftly convicted, as expected—but this time, the jury recommended seventy-five years in prison. After a long postponement, the remaining seven defendants were

influence with southern white workers, most of whom remained locked in ancestral prejudices). "Communists Tell Negroes to Force Social Equality throughout the South," read a typical headline in the *Birmingham News*, and if the power of the party was greatly exaggerated, its appeal to blacks was real.[18] Nevertheless, party membership in Birmingham never exceeded 500 people. The party found a more fruitful arena for agitation in the Mississippi Delta, which bordered both sides of the big river from Natchez to Memphis, and in the "Black Belt"—so called not for its people but for its dark-soiled bottomlands—which stretched from northwestern and central Georgia through central and northwestern Alabama to the middle of Mississippi. Most of this was cotton-and-corn country, where the Deep South did not get any deeper. It was a mosaic of big and little plantations whose resemblance to the antebellum world depicted with such moist romanticism in *Gone With the Wind*—both the most popular book and most popular movie of the entire decade—lay only in the size of many of its farms and the conditions of servitude that characterized the lives of the people who worked them. Almost everywhere in this American subculture, conditions were uniformly miserable, in spite of a self-generated mythic image—one probably held to and promulgated all the more fiercely because it was so demonstrably false, and, by the end of the twenties, annoyingly challenged by northern intellectuals and social critics.

At its most refined, the dogma postulated the kind of rural utopia defended in *I'll Take My Stand: The South and the Agrarian Tradition* (1930), a collection of essays by twelve white southern writers who, John Crowe Ransome said in his introduction, "all tend to support a Southern way of life against what may be called the American or prevailing way; and all as much as agree that the best terms in which to

---

scheduled for trial in July 1937. One was convicted and sentenced to death; one was given ninety-nine years; one was given seventy-five years; one had his charge reduced to assault and received twenty years for it—and all charges against four of the men were dropped. It would take another eleven years of agitation before four of the convicted men finally were pardoned. Haywood Patterson escaped from a work gang in 1948, was rearrested after a fatal barroom brawl in 1950, charged with manslaughter, convicted, and died in prison in 1952 at the age of thirty-nine.

18. Quoted in Robin D. G. Kelley, *Hammer and Hoe: Alabama Communists During the Great Depression*, p. 29.

represent the distinction are contained in the phrase, Agrarian *versus* Industrial." According to this nativistic reaction to a changing world, the only good society was one "in which agriculture is the leading vocation, whether for wealth, for pleasure, or for prestige," and that the South represented the best of what such a world could offer.[19]

For white farm owners, perhaps. Robert Penn Warren did mention the question of race and inequity in his contribution, offering up Booker T. Washington's life as the ideal to which black people might aspire, but neither he nor any other contributor in the book touched on the failures of an economic system that had created a culture of dependency and subjection. The literary agrarian might believe the typical plantation owner acted out of a benevolent paternalism that ensured he would care for the people who worked his land as he would his own children, but a more nearly accurate measure of common attitudes could be taken from a November 1930 report made by the district manager of the Mississippi Staple Cotton Cooperative Association, in which human beings were equated more or less with draft animals. "Every planter that we know," he wrote, "is very much concerned with feeding his stock and tenants at a minimum cost. . . . We know of one . . . who has a schedule by which he believes he can take care of his livestock for 15 cents a day and his tenants for $4.50 per month per head."[20]

Gross insensitivity aside, the worry implied by the report was real enough, for the economic foundation on which the plantation world was built was fragile at best, debt-ridden, overextended, and little able to withstand natural or financial disasters—and in the early depression years, it had suffered both killing drought and economic collapse. Not since the glory days of World War I, in fact, when cotton prices had soared to as high as forty cents a pound, with a consequent orgy of overproduction that had spilled into the twenties, had anyone made much money in the growing of southern cotton.

In 1936 (the same year that *Gone With the Wind* was published, as it happened), the government issued a portrait of the plantation economy

---

19. Twelve Southerners, *I'll Take My Stand: The South and the Agrarian Tradition*, pp. ix–xix.
20. Quoted in Rupert D. Vance, *Human Geography of the South: A Study in Regional Resources and Human Adequacy*, p. 271.

in the early 1930s that stood in shabby contrast to the genteel vision of southern agrarianism offered in *I'll Take My Stand*, illuminating both the marginal character of the business and the social structure it supported. The average size of a typical plantation, the study found, was 907 acres. Of this land, 385 acres were under cultivation, 170 of them in cotton, most of the rest in corn. The remaining uncultivated land was taken up with woodlands, fallow lands, unreclaimed "waste" lands, and pasture. The plantation supported a landlord-owner and his family (though about 10 percent of the plantations had resident managers who operated the farms for absentee owners) and fourteen resident families. Eight of these were sharecropper families who, in exchange for half the value of the crop, furnished their labor and half their own fertilizer; the landlord furnished the other half of the fertilizer, in addition to land, housing, fuel, tools, work stock, seed, and feed for the animals. Three of the families worked for straight wages. Two of the families were tenant farmers, who furnished their labor, three-fourths or two-thirds of the fertilizer they used, and everything else but housing and land, in exchange for either three-fourths or two-thirds of the crop, depending on the terms of their agreement. The final family was that of a renter, who got the entire value of the crop he harvested in exchange for a fixed amount in cash or ginned cotton paid as rent to the landlord.

Twelve of the families were African American; the remaining two were white. The landlord, of course, was white. The study revealed that of the 835,000 black males engaged in agriculture in the South in 1930, only 107,000, or 12.8 percent, owned their own land, even though blacks accounted for nearly 40 percent of the total of 2.1 million males in the industry. The division between white and black was a little more even when it came to tenancy and sharecropping; in 1930, 581,000 whites and 486,000 blacks were either tenant farmers or sharecroppers. But for black or white, owner, tenant, or sharecropper, it was not a life calculated to enrich the body, mind, or bank account—not by 1930s standards, at least. The average plantation in 1934 was worth about $28,700; it had long-term indebtedness to the tune of $11,700 and a net annual income of $6,000, some $3,400 of which was divided up among the sharecroppers and tenant farmers, leaving the owner himself with $2,600. That was a good deal better than the earnings of his

sharecroppers, who earned an average of $312 per family, and his ten-
ants, who earned $417, but it still was not the stuff that dreams were
made on. In fact, in spite of the difference in income, the owner-landlord
of the typical plantation did not live that much better than his tenants
and sharecroppers. His house, the report calculated with bland statistical insistence, would have an average of 4.8 rooms; his white tenants
would have 4.3 rooms, and his black tenants, 3.6 rooms. Only 60.9 percent of all owners' houses had screens, and only 30.2 percent of tenants'
houses had them. More than 21 percent of the owners had no sanitary
facilities at all, and 66.7 percent had only "unimproved" outdoor facilities—privies. White tenants enjoyed about the same ratios, while 30.9
percent of black tenants reported no facilities and 66.7 percent also used
privies. Virtually all water for all parties came from individual wells,
and the incidence of groundwater contamination was suggested by the
fact that the 1930 death rate from typhoid of 12.9 per 100,000 people
in the seven cotton states was more than two and a half times the
national average. Other diseases abounded as well: 25.2 per 100,000
people died of pellagra (the national average was 2.8) and 16.5 died of
malaria (the national average was 1.9).[21]

This feeble and diseased infrastructure supported a labor system
that approached peonage, as landlords, particularly those living nearest
the cusp of financial ruin, routinely gouged and cheated their sharecroppers and tenants. Mysterious charges would appear when settling-up
time came around; or bills that the tenants had run up at the plantation
stores many landlords kept would somehow eat up what little profit
they had earned; or cash advances made by the landlord during the year
would add up to more on his books than the tenant (who, generally
illiterate, had no books) could remember having received, while the
interest rates the landlord charged for such advances, as one observer
noted, ran anywhere "from 25 percent to grand larceny"; or cotton and
other money crops would deliberately be underweighed or underval-
ued.[22] Some plantations did not even pay off in U.S. currency. The

21. All statistics on plantation economy, labor force, and living conditions from T. J.
Woofter, et al., *Landlord and Tenant on the Cotton Plantation* (WPA Research Monograph
V, 1936).
22. Quoted in Neil R. McMillen, *Dark Journey: Black Mississippians in the Age of Jim
Crow*, p. 132.

owner he worked for in Augusta, Arkansas, cropper George Stith remembered, "had a mint of his own called 'brozeen.' When he paid you off and credited your money, you got his money called brozeen. Now he wasn't the only one. . . . [Each] plantation had a different brozeen, but you could spend Wilson brozeen only at a Wilson store."[23] In an environment in which black people who complained overmuch ran the risk of becoming the "strange fruit" of the bitter blues song, there was little recourse for the tenant but to move on. The average black sharecropper family drifted from one plantation to another every three years in search of better living and working conditions.

Gracie Turner and her family, for example, had managed to stick a little longer in one place than the average, but she had still moved around more than she had ever wanted to. "I wish I could have me one acre o' land dat I could call mine," she told an interviewer in the mid-1930s. The interviewer may have been a little too meticulous in attempting to record every nuance of Mrs. Turner's speech, but the literalness could not stifle the tough old woman's pain and spirit, and her words spoke for the experience of tens of thousands like her. Mrs. Turner and her husband had been sharecropping for forty-nine years and had seen virtually nothing but work and too many children for their trouble. "Dat's all dey is to expect—work hard and go hongry part time—long as we lives on de other man's land. Dey ain't nothin' in sharecrappin', not de way it's run." And as she told it, the way it was run made a story that would have elicited shouts of "Amen!" if she had been speaking to a group of her own:

We left Mr. Jake Anderson 'cause he didn't treat us right. . . . Every settlement day me and him had a round. I'd tell him he had too much charged against us, and he'd say I was the fussin'est woman he ever saw, and to go to de devil! De last year we was wid him we made 'leben bales o' cotton and three hund'ed bags of peas. When we settled, we didn't have accordin' to his figgers but five dollars for our part o' the crap. . . . We left him.[24]

23. Quoted in Sue Thrasher and Leah Wise, eds., "The Southern Tenant Farmers Union," *Southern Exposure* (winter 1974).
24. Quoted in W. T. Crouch, ed., *These Are Our Lives*, pp. 20–22.

Gracie Turner and her husband never did find a landlord who would do right by them, and neither did most of those, black and white, who found themselves trapped in the net of plantation poverty. Thousands moved restlessly from plantation to plantation, county to county, across the river and back again, in a relentless search for security and fairness, living out the lyrics in "'34 Blues," one of many songs that Charley Patton wrote as the representative Delta bluesman, a troubador emulated by men like "Muddy Waters," "Big Bill" Broonzy, Robert Johnson, and Son House—all of whom, like Patton, took their texts from the numinous land that bordered both sides of the Mississippi for two hundred miles:

> Further down the country it almost make you cry,
> Further down the country it almost make you cry
> (my God, Children)
> Women and children flaggin' freight trains for rides.

> And it may bring sorrow, it may bring tears,
> It may bring sorrow, Lord, it may bring tears,
> Oh, Lord, oh Lord, spare me to see a brand new year.[25]

Believing them too loose a group of people ever to be effectively organized, the CP/USA generally ignored plantation workers until January 1931, when about 500 drought-stricken Delta farmers—many of them tenants and sharecroppers and many of them black—got together late one afternoon and "invaded" the community of England, Arkansas, demanding food for their families. "We are not going to let our children starve," a farm leader shouted. "We want food and we want it now."[26] They got it, too, and their action suggested to party organizers that tenants and sharecroppers actually were capable of united action. Party headquarters in Birmingham responded with a statement that encouraged farmers all over the South to join together: "Call mass meetings in each township and on each large plantation. Set up Farmers Relief

25. Quoted in William Barlow, *Looking Up at Down: The Emergence of Blues Culture*, p. 38.
26. Quoted in the *New York Times* (January 4, 1931).

Councils at these meetings. Organize hunger marches on the towns to demand food and clothing from the supply merchants and bankers who have sucked you dry year after year."[27]

Efforts were launched to form a union, but white reluctance to join with blacks stalled the drive until a young African American schoolteacher in Tallapoosa County named Estelle Milner—one of several women who would play a major, though generally unacknowledged part in the movement—spread the word among local black sharecroppers, who asked the party for help. Organizer Mack Coad, a black steelworker traveling under the name of "Jim Wright," was sent down to the Alabama Piedmont country and the result was the Croppers' and Farm Workers' Union (CFWU), created in the spring of 1931.

The tiny union proceeded with care, spreading the word mostly by leaflets left in mailboxes or tacked on to porch railings and even impaled on tree branches. By July, while still generally confined to Tallapoosa County, the new union had grown to about 800 members—too many for the comfort of local plantation owners and the police and politicians who served their needs. On July 15, eighty black sharecroppers gathered in a vacant house outside the town of Camp Hill to hear Mack Coad and other organizers talk about the union and the Scottsboro defendants. County Sheriff Kyle Young deputized a group of vigilantes and led a raid on the meeting, breaking it up and beating several people in the process. The vigilantes then converged on the home of Tommy Gray, an outspoken black member of the union, and beat him and his family, fracturing his wife's skull. The next night, another meeting brought forth 150 people. When Sheriff Young attempted to lead an attack against this meeting, too, he was met outside by Tommy Gray's brother, Ralph. Shotgun blasts were exchanged. Young, wounded in the stomach, was rushed to a hospital. Gray, his legs full of shot, was carried to his home by union members. The vigilantes attacked the house, driving off the union men. One of the white men rammed a pistol into Ralph Gray's mouth while the wounded man lay on his bed and pulled the trigger. The vigilantes then torched the house, carried Gray's body into town, and threw it on the steps of the county courthouse,

27. Quoted in Kelley, op. cit., p. 38.

where ragged clots of white men kicked it and used it for target practice for several hours. Other citizens of Camp Hill entertained themselves by attacking the black section of town, beating, killing, looting, and burning. Coad escaped to Atlanta, but the luckless Estelle Milner suffered a fractured vertebra. Dozens of blacks were arrested, and five union members were charged with assault with intent to murder. Fearing that they might be creating another Scottsboro case, however, authorities ultimately dropped all charges.

In August 1931, the handful of surviving unionists reorganized into the Share Croppers' Union (SCU), and with the martyrdom of Ralph Gray as a rallying point, the new union grew to about 600 members within the next several months, largely through the organizing work of Eula Gray, Ralph Gray's niece. In spite of her demonstrated competence, the regional party chief, Nat Ross, soon replaced her with male organizer Al Murphy (for all the slogans regarding equality, the leadership of the CP/USA in the South as elsewhere was only a little less sexist than the bourgeois society from which much of its leadership had sprung). "He wanted us to organize," Tallapoosa County farmer Ned Cobb remembered of Murphy's work, "and he was with us a whole lot of time, holdin' meetin's with us. . . . We had the meetin's at our houses or anywhere we could have em where we could keep a look and a watchout that nobody was comin in on us. Small meetins, sometimes there'd be a dozen, sometimes there'd be more, sometimes there'd be less—niggers was scared, niggers was scared, that's tellin the truth."[28] Scared or not, Cobb and the others displayed the stubborn courage of the desperate. "I didn't think about gettin shot and I didn't think about not gettin shot," he remembered. "I thought this: a organization is a organization and if I don't mean nothin by joinin I ought to keep my ass out of it. But if I'm sworn to stand up for all the poor colored farmers—and poor white farmers if they'd takin a notion to join—I've got to do it. Weren't no use under God's sun to treat colored people like we'd been treated here in the state of Alabama. Work hard and look how they do you."[29]

28. Theodore Rosengarten, *All God's Dangers: The Life of Nate Shaw*, p. 297. "Nate Shaw" was the pseudonym given Ned Cobb by Rosengarten, who worked Cobb's oral memoirs into one of the truly great narratives of American life.
29. Ibid., p. 309.

As membership in the union continued to increase, authorities once again took action, this time just before Christmas 1932. The battle took place in Reeltown, fifteen miles southwest of Camp Hill. On December 19, Tallapoosa County Deputy Sheriff Cliff Elder and three other officials attempted to serve a writ of attachment on a local farmer's work stock; armed union members drove them off. That brought out Sheriff Kyle Young, recovered by now from his stomach wounds. He deputized another band of vigilantes and, with the enthusiastic participation of much of the county's white male citizenry, proceeded over the next few days to wage warfare against not merely the union but virtually the entire black population in the town. Hundreds were beaten or shot or thrown out of their homes, at least twenty were arrested on various charges, and two union leaders who had been ·shot were left untreated in their cells and later died.

The savagery that had been loosed on Reeltown appalled much of the respectable South, and even in white Birmingham some sympathy for the plight of the sharecroppers was expressed, the *Birmingham Post* offering an interesting comparison in its editorial condemning the affair. "The cause of the trouble was essentially economic rather than racial," it said. "The resistance of the Negroes at Reeltown against officers seeking to attach their livestock bears a close parallel to battles fought in Iowa and Wisconsin between farmers and sheriff's deputies seeing to serve eviction papers. A good many white farmers, ground down by the same relentless economic pressure from which the Negroes were suffering, expressed sympathy with the Negroes' desperate plight."[30] In January 1933, a mass funeral for the two union leaders was held in Birmingham. The caskets, draped with red flags and other Communist paraphernalia, were loaded into a hearse for the journey up to Grace Hills Cemetery. The hearse was followed by an estimated 3,000 people, most of them black. Among them was recent party convert Hosea Hudson, who, like many, had been brought to communism by its support of the Scottsboro defendants. "All the police in town was at the funeral," he remembered. "Everybody was saying anybody could of went on downtown, take everything they wanted, because seems like all the police in town was out there in North

30. Quoted in the *Daily Worker* (December 31, 1932).

Birmingham. . . . That was one time one Negro funeral was recognized in Birmingham."[31]

If the violence had been intended to annihilate the union, Young and those who supported him were frustrated not merely by the toughness and persistent loyalty of the organizers, Communist and non-Communist alike, but by an unwitting collusion between the federal government and many southern plantation owners. Early in the summer of 1933, the AAA had set in motion its cotton-reduction program, and by the end of the year had contracted with a little over a million cotton producers to "withdraw" 10.4 million acres from cultivation; since most of the year's crop had already been planted, this meant plowing the cotton under. In exchange, farmers would get straight cash payments of $7 an acre for land producing 100 to 124 pounds an acre and $20 an acre for land producing 275 pounds or more. Some $110 million in benefits were paid out.[32]

According to the law, tenants and croppers were to share in this bounty, the tenants on any given farm dividing up 50 percent of the payment and the croppers, 25. But it did not take much effort for many plantation owners to adjust the figures to suit themselves; they had been doing it for years, after all. According to Lorena Hickok in one of her reports to Harry Hopkins, "hardly any tenants ever got any of the cotton reduction money. The landlords always could present bills for the entire amount, and the tenants, being illiterate and never knowing exactly what they did owe the landlords, were just out of luck."[33] It got even easier to bilk them in 1934, when the law was amended to include a complicated schedule of "rental" and "parity" payments that enabled landlords to further confuse things in their favor.

Getting cheated was bad enough. Getting displaced was worse. If the plantation owner had no crop either to plant or to harvest, he certainly had no need for sharecroppers or tenants. No one knows precisely how many families moved off the land as the direct result of crop reductions—but some indication of the total numbers involved by 1935 is

31. Quoted in Nell Irvin Painter, *The Narrative of Hosea Hudson: His Life as a Negro Communist in the South*, p. 154.
32. Figures in Henry A. Wallace, "The Year in Agriculture," in Milton Eisenhower, ed., op. cit., p. 30.
33. Quote in Lowitt and Beasely, eds., op. cit., p. 212.

suggested by the 1936 government report on plantation labor. "A further idea of the importance of displacement of tenants as a factor in the
relief situation," it said, "may be obtained when it is noted that in
Eastern Cotton Area counties in June 1935 unemployed croppers and
other tenants accounted for 37 percent of the agricultural relief cases, or
approximately 20,000 families in the whole area."[34]

The people being victimized, of course, had no idea how many they
were, but they did know that they were hurting, and thousands turned
to the Share Croppers' Union in desperation and hope. "The SCU in
places where [it] has been slack," an organizer wrote from Camp Hill,
"[is] beginning to wake up and people don't wait for the comrades to
come as they used to."[35] By the end of 1934, after a series of brief
picking-season strikes, which had resulted in some substantial wage
increases in spite of being suppressed swiftly and violently, SCU membership rose to a high of 8,000. But it was a hollow kind of growth, for
the SCU never did include more than the tiniest minority of total farmworkers in the South and an even tinier minority of the white farmers.
It remained an almost entirely black union, and with the exception of
the handful of party members in Birmingham and elsewhere in the
region, received almost no support or sympathy from local communities—quite the opposite, in fact, as the full weight of this preeminently
racist society was brought to bear against it. As a result, SCU leaders
spent much of their time in a lonely, dogged struggle merely to survive,
leading the occasional strike (some with marginal success, some with
total failure, none without bloodshed) and otherwise stubbornly perse-
vering in the face of the rigid despotism and chronic violence of plantation society. By 1936, membership had dribbled away to almost
nothing, and what was left of the union merged into the similarly
anemic Alabama chapter of the Communist-led National Farmers'
Union—though not before seeking immortality by revising the words
to the old country hymn "Give Me That Old Time Religion":

> Give me that old Communist spirit,
> Give me that old Communist spirit,

34. Woofter, op. cit., pp. 160–61.
35. Quoted in Kelley, op. cit, p. 54.

It was good enough for Ralph Gray,
And it's good enough for me.[36]

Generally speaking, the struggle of the Share Croppers' Union might as well have taken place in Afghanistan, for all the attention it got outside the South. The union was black, it was small, and it was controlled by the Communists, and if its chronicle demonstrated the extraordinary reserves of marrow-deep courage that men and women could draw upon when faced with great need—the same levels of bravery that a later generation of southern black people would find in the battle for civil rights—the story remained largely unknown or ignored outside the Deep South.

From the point of view of the CP/USA, which had midwifed the birth of the SCU, probably the most painful aspect of the union's relative anonymity was the fact that the better-known and marginally more successful sharecroppers' movement of the era was the child of a small group of Socialist Party members in the little Delta town of Tyronza, Arkansas—and that the despised Norman Thomas, the Socialist Party's perennial candidate for president, had been instrumental in its creation. Harry LeLand Mitchell, owner of a dry-cleaning shop, had filed the first Socialist charter in the state of Arkansas. Henry Clay East, whose gas station sat next door, became one of Mitchell's most fervent converts, and the two friends gathered regularly with anywhere from 50 to 150 other socialists in the Tyronza Odd Fellows Hall. Among the usual topics of discussion was the plight of the sharecroppers of the region.

Mitchell and East, meanwhile, were convinced that it was only the lack of information that kept Henry Wallace and the Department of Agriculture from acting to help. They persuaded fellow socialist William R. Amberson, a professor of physiology at the University of Tennessee across the river in Memphis, to take on the task of researching and preparing a report. Amberson himself sought help from Socialist Norman Thomas, who had stated publicly that the AAA's domestic allotment program was a travesty that proposed to assure "prosperity

36. Quoted in Lowell K. Dyson, "The Southern Tenant Farmers Union and Depression Politics," *Political Science Quarterly* (June 1973).

through starvation."[37] Thomas agreed to finance the report. What was more, he managed a brief side trip to Tyronza while on a speaking tour in February 1934. During that visit, East remembered, "We took him out to the Norcross plantation, and he went in there and Norcross had this barn with concrete floors and running water for his hogs. Then he goes out to these sharecropper houses and there was no screens and there was flies and holes in the floor and roof and everything."

"What you need here is a union," Thomas told Mitchell and East over noontime dinner that day.[38] The frenetic Socialist leader then went spinning off to finish the rest of his speaking tour, though not without letting Henry Wallace know what he thought. The plantation system, he wrote the secretary, was "one of the most abominable and indefensible systems of landlordism in the world." Thousands, he said, "are either driven out on the roads without hope of absorption into industry or exist without land to cultivate by grace of the landlord in shacks barely fit for pigs. . . . Has the administration any plans . . . other than pious hopes . . . ? Shall they starve quietly so as not to interrupt our much predicted return to 'prosperity'?"[39] Wallace eventually replied, saying that the situation was being investigated. Indeed, it was, but not very energetically. Chester Davis, who had become director of the AAA after George Peek resigned early in 1934 because of what he disparaged as the New Deal's program of "socialized agriculture," had little sympathy for the sharecroppers, and while he did send a man down with orders to look into matters, the investigator was not motivated to do much digging. Nor did he, according to Mitchell, who reported to Thomas in March that the man spent a few hours in town, then before leaving "requested that there not be any more complaints . . . and also that since the 'landlords are all your friends and these sharecroppers are a shiftless lot there is no use of being concerned about them.'"[40] After more prodding by Wallace, Davis sent a whole team down in May, but cautioned its members that "this work you are to do in investigating

37. Quoted in W. A. Swanberg, *Norman Thomas: The Last Idealist*, p. 158.
38. East and Thomas quotes in Thrasher and Wise, op. cit.
39. Quoted in Swanberg, op. cit., p. 159.
40. Quoted in ibid., p. 160.

and adjusting difficulties must be done in such a way as not to reflect unfavorably upon the work which has already been done by these local authorities."[41] The team's report, unsurprisingly, found little wrong with either the way the AAA was being administered or the manner in which plantation owners dealt with their tenants and sharecroppers.

Not long thereafter, Mitchell and East took Thomas's casual dinnertime suggestion and made something of it. On July 11, they organized a night meeting at a schoolhouse outside town. That in itself was less remarkable than the fact that the meeting was racially mixed, black men who had witnessed or been victimized by white persecution standing elbow to elbow with white men who may have perpetrated the violence or, at least, had let it happen. There was some discussion about whether the men should organize a single integrated union or two separate but presumably equal bodies. Then, a seventy-one-year-old black man spoke. He had been a member of the short-lived Progressive Farmers and Household Union of America. Founded in nearby Elaine, Arkansas, after World War I, this black organization was destroyed by a massive countywide assault by armed whites in October 1919. At least twenty-five African American tenants and sharecroppers were killed (some estimates put the figure closer to a hundred). So this sharecropper's words carried weight among the men who huddled together in the pale yellow glow of kerosene lanterns.[42] "For a long time now," he said, "the white folks and the colored folks have been fighting each other and both of us have been getting whipped all the time. We don't have nothing against one another but we got plenty against the landlord. The same chain that holds my people holds your people too. If we are chained together on the outside we ought to stay chained together in the union."[43]

So they were, and the organization whose chains they forged that night was called the Southern Tenant Farmers' Union (STFU). Its first president was a white man, J. R. Butler, and its first vice president was a black man, the Reverend E. B. McKinney, and its official song, adopted

41. Quoted in Donald H. Grubbs, *Cry from the Cotton: The Southern Tenant Farmers Union and the New Deal*, p. 36.
42. For the "Elaine Massacre," see George Brown Tindall, *The Emergence of the New South, 1913–1945*, pp. 152–54.
43. Quoted in Grubbs, op. cit., p. 88.

somewhat later, included a chorus whose lyrics would become part of an anthem known to millions in another generation: "Just like a tree that's planted by the water,/ We shall not be moved."

The STFU, unlike the Share Croppers' Union, was not ignored by Washington, D.C., particularly after the union filed suit in federal court against Hiram Norcross, whose facilities Norman Thomas had explored. Norcross had promptly evicted his tenants when they joined the union, replacing them with nonunion workers. While the case was pending, AAA general counsel Bernard Frank sent his own investigator into the region. Mary Conner Myers's report—almost certainly supportive of the STFU's claims of wholesale illegal evictions and other wrongdoing on the part of landlords—vanished without explanation once it was sent to Chester Davis's office. Frank then joined with Gardner Jackson and a few other radical allies in the AAA and tried to implement an interpretation of the law that would effectively prohibit those receiving domestic allotment payments from evicting their tenants. When he got word of the action, Davis asked Wallace to let him fire Frank and the others for insubordination. Wallace complied.

The "purge" of the AAA in February 1935 left the Southern Tenant Farmers' Union with few friends in the Department of Agriculture, and it is not impossible that events in Washington encouraged the series of violent attacks on the union that erupted almost simultaneously. This new anti-union campaign had begun in January 1935, when Ward Rodgers, a radical young graduate of the Vanderbilt Theological Seminary and one of the STFU's best speakers, was arrested by the local prosecutor in Marked Tree, Arkansas, on charges of "criminal anarchy." He was swiftly convicted, and sentenced to six months in jail. That violated Rodgers's constitutional rights alone, but on February 1, plantation society showed sharper teeth when two white radicals who had tried to speak at a sharecroppers' meeting in a church near Gilmore, Arkansas, were dragged from the building by a plantation riding-boss and several cohorts, thrown into a car, pistol-whipped while being driven around, then thrown out on the road.

Six weeks later, Norman Thomas returned to Arkansas for a speaking tour in the southeastern part of the state. He was accompanied by the STFU's new president, Harry Mitchell, and Howard Kester, head of the Fellowship of Southern Churchmen and, like Rodgers, a Vanderbilt graduate. When he attempted to speak before a crowd of about 500 sharecroppers in Birdsong, Thomas and his entourage were surrounded by a gang of thirty or forty armed and drunken thugs. According to Mitchell's later account, one of the armed men shouted, "There ain't gonna be no speaking here. We are the citizens of this county and we run it to suit ourselves. We don't need no Gawd-Damn Yankee Bastard to tell us what to do."[44] Thomas and Kester were seized, forced back into their car, and told to leave the county forthwith. They left.

In March, night riders drove by the homes of several union leaders in Marked Tree, and sprayed the houses with bullets. Among the homes hit was that of F. T. Carpenter, the lawyer who had filed suit against the AAA over the Norcross evictions. Carpenter and his family were unhurt, but the family of Reverend E. B. McKinney, the STFU vice president, was not so lucky. A similar attack resulted in the wounding of two of McKinney's children. By the end of the month, most of the union men had taken their families and moved across the river to the relative safety of Memphis.

It was a dark time for the little union. In spite of the STFU's Socialist origins—and Mitchell's deep suspicion of Communists (he would later claim to have been the target of a Communist assassination attempt)—the union did receive sporadic and limited financial aid from the Organization of Agricultural Workers, a Communist group attempting to unite all farmworker organizations into a single body. But for the most part, the STFU was on its own, supported mainly by its meager dues of ten cents a month. It had courted the AFL but been rejected, and was devoid of even legal sanction by the presumably labor-friendly Roosevelt administration. Section 7(a) of the National Industrial Recovery Act had not specifically excluded farm-labor unions from its protection, but neither had the New Dealers paid much attention; Henry Wallace, in particular, remembering the midwestern agitation of Milo Reno and his counterparts, had no affection for the idea of agricultural unionism. And whatever solace the STFU might have found even in Section 7(a) was rendered moot in May 1935, when the Supreme Court invalidated most of Title I of the NIRA, including its labor pro-

44. Quoted in Robert P. Ingalls, "Anti-Labor Vigilantes: The South During the 1930s," *Southern Exposure* (November/December 1984).

visions, on the grounds that the act gave the Executive Branch unconstitutional powers. The administration responded with the National
Labor Relations Act, but a powerful lobbying effort on the part of the
American Farm Bureau Federation and other owner groups saw to it
that agricultural labor would find no refuge here, either—the new law
stipulated that its provisions did not include any individual employed
as an agricultural laborer.

The situation had been no more comforting to the union in other
areas of the New Deal architecture. The plight of sharecroppers and tenants was one of the concerns that Rexford Tugwell cited in early 1935,
when he urged that the various rural rehabilitation programs then
being administered by the Federal Emergency Relief Administration
and other bodies be transferred to a new agency in the Department of
Agriculture called the Resettlement Administration. FDR had agreed,
issuing an executive order that created the RA, with Tugwell in charge,
shortly after the "purge" of Jackson and the Agriculture Department
dissidents. But the RA's programs would concentrate almost entirely on
long-range efforts to reform agriculture in general and would do little
to alleviate the immediate problems of the sharecroppers. Nor did the
RA give the STFU any more support—actual or symbolic—than had
the National Labor Relations Act.

The union may have been shorn of even a semblance of federal
recognition or financial health, but Mitchell nevertheless called for a
strike vote against the cotton growers at the end of August 1935. The
membership approved Mitchell's proposal by 11,186 to 450 (according
to Mitchell, at least, who later admitted that he may have inflated the
figures, though not by much). Thousands of cotton-pickers that season
sat on their sagging porches and claimed sickness or simply disappeared
to hunt or fish, holding out for an increase in their piece rate from fifty
cents to a dollar a hundred pounds. It was the height of the picking season, and the desperate owners finally agreed to compromise at seventy-
five cents by the beginning of October, though not before utilizing
every legal and illegal tool at their disposal, including more violence.
The union accepted the offer, and the strike was called off.

By then, the union had achieved a national identity. It became a
cause, like the fate of the Scottsboro defendants, and while the STFU
would never come close to cutting the bonds that had tied poor blacks

and whites to the rigid confines of the plantation system for nearly a century, it would help persuade a glacially reluctant Congress and a not very enthusiastic president to at least recognize the existence of a problem and to make efforts to correct it—however halting and imperfect they turned out to be.

In no small part because of the efforts of Gardner Jackson, one of the employees of the AAA's legal division who had been fired by Davis during the 1935 unpleasantness, the STFU's travails became common currency in the liberal press and among radicals everywhere in the country. After his dismissal, Jackson had formed the National Committee on Rural Social Planning and was soon functioning as a de facto lobbyist and public relations agent for the union. His efforts were joined to those of Norman Thomas, who had continued to publicize the sharecroppers' lot at every opportunity (though he was in no hurry to return to Arkansas); the American Civil Liberties Union, which had taken up the cause of getting Ward Rodgers released; and a growing number of other organizations and individuals—including columnist Drew Pearson, Supreme Court Justice Louis Brandeis, and Library of Congress librarian Archibald MacLeish.

The list also included many religious people, who found in the sharecroppers' story an appealingly stark demonstration of need. To the young radicals of the Protestant theological schools, the sharecroppers' fight against oppression was the perfect metaphor to define what was wrong with the nation and what must be done to set it right. It was this conviction that had brought Ward Rodgers, Howard Kester, and other Social Gospel graduates to Arkansas from the Vanderbilt Theological Seminary to work and suffer for the union. It was this conviction that brought contributions from individual churches and many religious organizations, including theologian Reinhold Niebuhr's Committee on Economic and Racial Justice. It was this conviction that brought ministers from various denominations down to see the situation for themselves and then return to their churches to spread the word. Bowery missionary Dorothy Day was one of them, and while she had no church to preach in, she did have the pages of *The Catholic Worker*, where she was soon begging alms for the union: "I have seen the bare poverty of the union headquarters where three people are doing this work of fighting for the oppressed. They sleep in cots at the headquarters, they have neither heat nor telephone. . . . I spent a week with them and can vouch for their honesty."[45]

Publicity was flamed into a genuine bonfire of attention in 1936 when a young black union member named Willie Hurst was murdered—apparently to keep him from testifying that he had seen sheriff's deputies beating some members of the STFU during the 1935 cotton strike—and again in the summer when two vocal white supporters of the union, Willie Sue Blagdon and the Reverend Claude Williams, were forced to the side of the road while on their way to Memphis, pulled from their car, and flogged. Both the Hurst and the Blagdon-Williams incidents—well publicized in the northern press and even in some of the southern press—were seized by Jackson, Thomas, and other reformers and shaken at the New Deal as two more good reasons why the government should step in and do something about the situation.

The administration responded in the fall of 1936 by forming the President's Special Committee on Farm Tenancy and, in early 1937, the committee issued recommendations calling for the complete restructuring of the Resettlement Administration and some kind of effort to promote land ownership by small family farmers—including former sharecroppers and tenants. Congress then passed the Bankhead-Jones Farm Tenancy Act of 1937, which created the Farm Security Corporation to provide long-term, low-interest loans that would enable poor farmers to buy their own land. Wallace scrapped the Resettlement Administration (Tugwell had resigned from the government by then) and established the Farm Security Administration to assume its responsibilities, including the administration of the Farm Security Corporation's loan program.

Vigorously promoted and funded, the farm purchase program might have helped to break the hold of the plantation system on the region's economy and people. In fact, there would never be enough money, and the political power of the South was still so strong that neither the Department of Agriculture nor the administration was willing to challenge tradition in any substantial way. Only a fraction of the South's sharecropper and tenant population would ever be helped, and

45. Quoted in William Miller, *Dorothy Day: A Biography*, p. 287.

even then this assistance would not be enough to bring most of them out of a depressed and generally degraded condition in both the Delta and the Black Belt for years to come.

Reporter Ernie Pyle, off on one of his regional exploring expeditions, stopped off in Coffee County, Alabama, in 1939, where he found that about 600 out of the county's total of 4,200 or so farmworkers had been enrolled in the FSA's farm ownership program, being supplied with small government-built or remodeled houses, a bit of land, and loans to pay for both. The FSA, Pyle reported, "didn't hand out much on a silver platter. For instance, they didn't put bathrooms in the houses." That would have been useless, FSA county administrator W. L. McArthur told him. "Lots of [the workers] won't even use privies now. What would they do with a bathroom? Wait till they get healthy and out of debt and grow up to a bathroom. Then they can put one in themselves."

The problem, McArthur and the other white, southern-born FSA workers insisted, was less in the land or the plantation economy than in the people, some white, most black, who displayed a lack of character they called "sorryness." "It's not submarginal land that puts us in our sorry shape," one man told Pyle. "It's submarginal people." Such class prejudices did not suggest that the government's tenant-farmer programs, however well intended or ambitious in their goals, would ever go far in bringing the people up from economic slavery. Certainly, Pyle did not think so. "One night, there in Alabama," he wrote,

> I went to see a movie called *St. Louis Blues*. Dorothy Lamour was in it . . . and the setting was on the Mississippi, and it was all very romantic and full of the lovely old things of the South. I came away in the dumps, thinking that I was all wrong, and that Hollywood was right. I should have written about Coffee County as romantic, and full of guitars, and happy, happy Negroes, and sweeping bows to the ladies. Maybe I should—I don't know. But Hollywood has never seen all the pale dead people walking slowly around the red clay countryside.[46]

46. Pyle's visit to Coffee County is recounted in *Home Country* by Ernie Pyle, pp. 363–68.

The STFU fared no better. The strike of 1935 would be the only clear-cut victory the union would ever enjoy. In 1937, it would align itself with the newly formed and radical United Cannery, Agricultural, Packing, and Allied Workers of America (UCAPAWA), which the leaders of the Organization of Agricultural Workers had finally helped to bring into existence. But Mitchell, jealous of his own power and fearing domination of the STFU by the Communists in the UCAPAWA, pulled the STFU out of the larger union in 1939. The STFU, isolated from the rest of the labor movement, as poor as its people and increasingly fractured by internal rivalries and Mitchell's erratic management, inexorably declined, until the union's crusade to join southern blacks and whites in a common struggle to free themselves from economic subjugation sputtered to an ember that World War II would snuff out forever.

16

---◆---

¡Huelga!

More than half a continent west of the bottomland soils of the Delta where the Southern Tenant Farmers' Union was born, another kind of agricultural revolt developed, one whose eruptions surpassed in breadth, longevity, and violence those of any other farming region in the country. In one of the clearest demonstrations of class war in the era of the Great Depression, field-workers of the Communist Party joined and helped guide grassroots activists in a rebellion against a statewide economic oligarchy embarked on a systematic campaign to discredit, dismantle, and destroy all opposition to its rule. This campaign enjoyed the full support of the political establishment, state and local police, the judiciary, financial institutions, and most of the press, and gave the decade perhaps its most troubling glimpse of a home-grown fascism.

While there were forays into such coastal areas as the Salinas Valley near Monterey or the Sonoma and Napa Valleys north of San Francisco, the principal arenas for the conflict were the huge irrigated farms of California's Imperial Valley, San Joaquin Valley, and Sacramento Valley, the three most important agricultural regions in the second most important agricultural state in the nation. (Only Iowa, with annual crop sales of $621 million in 1930, topped California's production of $608 million, and not even Iowa could match the bewildering variety of the Golden State's cornucopia, which included some 200 different crops.) There was little here that would have appealed to the southern romanticism of a Margaret Mitchell. The kinds of novels that rural California inspired were more along the lines of Frank Norris's bitter 1901 tract, *The Octopus*, or the more graceful but still angry depression fables of John Steinbeck, especially *In Dubious Battle*, *Of Mice and Men*, and his Pulitzer Prize–winning epic, *The Grapes of Wrath*. What Norris and Steinbeck wrote about in these books, after all, was not a rural way of life in the American grain—or even the Southern grain—but the dehumanizing character of an industry whose "factories in the field," as journalist, attorney, and social worker Carey McWilliams described them, were the agricultural equivalents of Henry Ford's River Rouge complex in Detroit.

If sharecropping and a one-crop economy had characterized much of southern agriculture, then land monopoly, absentee ownership, and migrant labor defined much of California's. By the thirties, agricultural economist Paul S. Taylor could write that "37 percent of the large-scale farms of all types in the United States—those with gross incomes of approximately $30,000 or more—are in California. In that state are 41 percent of the large-scale dairy farms, 53 percent of the large-scale poultry farms, and 60 percent of the large-scale truck farms of the United States. . . . The number of these large-scale farms in California is less than 3,000 and they comprise hardly more than two percent of all farms in that state. But they produce nearly 30 percent of all California agricultural products by value."[1] Twenty-five percent of California's land was owned by only 2 percent of its farmers, including such unlikely cultivators of the earth as Standard Oil, Shell Oil, the Southern Pacific Railroad, and the Transamerica Corporation, the parent company of the 483-branch Bank of America.[2] Even those corporations whose principal

1. Paul Schuster Taylor and Dorothea Lange, *American Exodus: A Record of Human Erosion*, p. 145.
2. Figures from Kevin Starr, *Endangered Dreams: The Great Depression in California*, p. 63.

business was farming, such as the Kern County Land Company or the Miller & Lux Land Company, were entities whose owners and executives had rarely if ever seen their holdings, either leasing them out or leaving them in the hands of resident managers.

For the most part, the profit margin ruled in such boardroom agriculture, encouraging monoculture, where costs and revenues could be most easily calculated and controlled and where volume could help to offset market fluctuations. Entire farms were given over to the cultivation of various "money" crops—one or two thousand acres in orange trees in the San Bernardino Valley, for example, or five thousand acres in cotton in the San Joaquin Valley, or twelve thousand acres in grapes in the Sacramento Valley. Such monoculture, in turn, required a large and cheap labor force, particularly at harvest time, and since the agricultural labor pool of the white population had been thin from the outset (too many superior jobs to be had in a state still building its population and its economy), California growers had learned to depend upon successive waves of cheap and generally tractable immigrant labor—Chinese in the nineteenth century; Hindus, Japanese, and Koreans after the turn of the century; and Filipinos in the first few years after World War I.

By 1930, however, Mexican Americans, or Chicanos, dominated California's traditional migrant labor pool. Like the blacks of the South, they were a much abused people, though their story had its own peculiar wrinkles. While the families of many Mexican Americans had been in this country for generations, a substantial percentage of Chicano workers were immigrants—this, in spite of the otherwise rigid stipulations of the Johnson-Reed Immigration Act of 1924, which attempted to reverse immigration history. During World War I, sentiment in favor of restricting the immigration of "undesirable" European immigrants had begun to develop, a movement that the tumultuous postwar years accelerated. Some of the pressure for restrictions had come from organized labor, which feared competition for jobs, but most was applied by nativist bigots who detected the odor of Bolshevik radicalism, Jewish economic conspiracies, Middle European genetic deficiencies, and southern European degeneracy on every non–Anglo-Saxon immigrant. There was, above all, a growing fear that the pure "Nordic" race on whom the greatness of the nation allegedly rested was being defiled by the "migration of lower human types," as Lothrop Stoddard had put it in his well-received 1920 polemic, *The Rising Tide of Color Against White World-Supremacy.*[3]

The Johnson-Reed Act of 1924, the editors of *The American Year Book* for 1928 noted with approval, "fairly marks the turning point when the immigration policy of the American people became primarily biological and only secondarily economic," then went on to mention casually one important consequence of the restrictions on European immigration: "The southwestern part of the United States . . . is supplying its rising demand for common labor with Mexicans who are now free to come into the United States without quota limitation, and who find ready employment because of the lack of European immigrant competitors."[4]

Thanks largely to vigorous lobbying on the part of the industry that depended upon their muscle and sweat, Mexican immigrants were allowed into the country, and in the decade of the twenties, the Mexican-American population of the United States would grow by about 500,000, bringing the total to 1.5 million. Much of the increase was due to immigration, as tens of thousands were tempted north by the labor demands of the war and postwar years—though precise figures are almost impossible to establish; for example, U.S. authorities estimated that 62,709 Mexicans entered this country in 1923, while Mexican authorities put the figure at 100,562, and such discrepancies continued throughout the period; then as now, of course, there was no accurate measure of those who had slipped across the border without bothering to register with officials.[5]

By whatever numbers, most Chicano immigrants gravitated toward the fields of Texas, Arizona, southern Colorado, and California. In the off-seasons, they joined the resident populations of the little *barrios* that had sprouted in the smaller railhead and mining towns or the growing Mexican-American *colonias* in the big cities. The biggest *colonia* was in Los Angeles, where the Chicano population increased from 33,644 in

3. Quoted in J. C. Furnas, *Great Times: An Informal Social History of the United States, 1914–1929,* p. 54.
4. Albert Bushnell Hart and William M. Schuyler, eds., *The American Year Book: A Record of Events and Progress for the Year 1928,* p. 472.
5. For immigration figures, see Ricardo Romo, "Responses to Mexican Immigration, 1910–1930," *Aztlan-International Journal of Chicano Studies Research* (spring 1975).

1920 to 97,116 in 1930, making the city the "Mexican capital" of the United States, exhausting the bounds of the original Mexican-American settlements around the old Plaza and spreading out into the neighborhoods of East Los Angeles.[6]

Thousands of immigrants headed farther north to work the sugar beet fields of Michigan and the other Great Lakes states, while thousands gave up stoop labor as a career, moving to Chicago, East Chicago, Gary, and Detroit to look for work in steel mills, automobile plants, and other industries. By 1930, there were 19,362 Chicanos living in Chicago, some 9,000 in East Chicago and Gary, and another 8,000 in Detroit and its environs, where the allure of the Ford Motor Company had reached into the towns of northern Mexico to call young workers to the "wonderful city of the magic motor." Miguel Muñoz had followed it in 1923. "I am a young Mexican, twenty-five years old," he wrote to the company, "single, and I have left my home at Monterrey, Mexico, to come up to Detroit. . . . I want to work for the Ford Motor Company because it is the best business on earth and there must be . . . permanent employment and a good future for a man who wants to work."[7]

In Ford's plants and elsewhere, this little-known contingent of the Midwest's industrial labor force, like the more visible but no less oppressed black workers, did the dirtiest work for the most abysmal wages and in the worst of working and living conditions, ignored or held in contempt by organized labor; indeed, the AFL (with John L. Lewis particularly vocal), fearing that cheap Chicano labor would undercut local wages, spent a good deal of its energy in a vain effort to get immigration from Mexico banned altogether. It would have been smarter had the AFL exploited the Mexican Americans' own traditions, for trade unionism had been a powerful force in Mexico itself for decades. Indeed, both resident and immigrant Chicanos in the American Southwest had been organizing and leading strikes in the railroad,

6. Population growth in Los Angeles from Ricardo Romo, *East Los Angeles: History of a Barrio,* p. 80.
7. Quoted in Zaragosa Vargas, "Life and Community in the 'Wonderful City of the Magical Motor': Mexican Immigrants in 1920s Detroit," *Michigan Historical Review* (spring 1989). Population figures from Vargas, and from Neil Betten and Raymond A. Mohl, "From Discrimination to Repatriation: Mexican Life in Gary, Indiana, During the Great Depression," in Norris Hundley, Jr., ed., *The Chicano,* pp. 124–42.

mining, and other industries of the region, without the aid of the AFL or any other Anglo organization, since the nineteenth century.[8]

The AFL let the opportunity slide, joining its voice to a chorus of discrimination that could be heard even among those whom Anglo-Saxon xenophobes would have dismissed as being genetically inferior themselves. "I resent the Mexicans being brought in here, allowed to migrate freely while others are restricted," a second-generation Serbian woman complained to a social researcher in Flint, Michigan, in 1930. "My cousins can't get in and yet they bring these lower elements in."[9] Prejudice was most virulent in the areas where Mexican Americans lived in the greatest numbers, of course—in southern California, for instance, rigid discrimination in housing would exist unchallenged for decades, and the segregation of theaters and other public places was common throughout the region. But during the anti-alien years of the twenties, the Chicano population also came under national scrutiny. In 1924, the future novelist Kenneth Roberts (*Arundel*, *Northwest Passage*), one of *The Saturday Evening Post*'s most prolific feature writers, did a series for the magazine on the immigration question, and while he expressed contempt for all people not of Anglo-Saxon stock, he reserved special malice for the Mexican Americans in Los Angeles and managed to parrot every myth and misstatement that was put in his ear by his Anglo informants. In East Los Angeles, he said, one could "see the endless streets crowded with the shacks of illiterate, diseased, pauperized Mexicans, taking no interest whatever in the community, living constantly on the ragged edge of starvation, bringing countless numbers of American citizens into the world with the reckless prodigality of rabbits."[10]

This calumny, or versions of it, became the essential public image of the Mexican-American population in the United States (in some quarters, it remains), and if it seemed to echo another tradition of prejudice, the similarity was recognized even then. "[B]ecause of the very dark color of most Mexicans," a social worker in Gary, Indiana, wrote in

8. For Chicano experience in organized labor efforts, see Rodolfo Acuña, *Occupied America: A History of Chicanos*, pp. 190–201.
9. William Albig, "Opinions Concerning Unskilled Mexican Immigrants," *Sociology and Social Research* (September–October 1930).
10. Kenneth Roberts, "And West Is West," *The Saturday Evening Post* (March 15, 1924).

1924, "Americans have the same racial feelings they have for the colored."[11]

By the end of 1930, rank prejudice joined with economic paranoia to overshadow—temporarily, at least—the desire of the agricultural industry to keep its labor pool intact. Cities hard put to meet their welfare obligations began to look upon the seasonal influx of unemployed agricultural laborers with some resentment, and against the stories of people earnestly striving to help their fellow human beings through the hardest time most of them could remember must be placed the Mexican-American repatriation effort of 1931–1934.

The depression had hardly got under way before the president's Emergency Committee for Employment had targeted immigration policy as one way to curtail the oversupply of labor. Following the committee's recommendation, in September 1930 Hoover invoked the "likely to become a public charge" provision of the Johnson-Reed Immigration Act to bring immigration nearly to a halt. Between September of 1930 and the end of January 1931, only 10,000 visas were approved, and in February 1931 only 3,147 immigrants got into the United States, fewer than in any month since 1820.[12] Labor Secretary William M. Doak—whose responsibilities included the Immigration and Naturalization Service—was pleased. "My conviction is that by a strict limitation and a wise selection of immigration," he said when the new policy was announced in September 1930, "we can make America stronger in every way, hastening the day when our population shall be more homogenous."[13] In the meantime, he believed, it would be useful to weed out some nonhomogenous types. Doak requested necessary funds from Congress on January 6, got the money, and launched a series of nationwide raids that ultimately resulted in the deportation of 18,142 people the INS had discovered to be illegals.[14]

Doak had not singled out any particular nationality in his efforts, but there were plenty of people who would, and in the Southwest, the

11. Quoted in Betten and Mohl, op. cit.
12. See Irving Bernstein, *The Lean Years: A History of the American Worker, 1920–1933*, p. 305.
13. Quoted in Acuña, op. cit., p. 138.
14. Figure from Camille Guerin-Gonzales, *Mexican Workers and American Dreams: Immigration, Repatriation, and California Farm Labor, 1900–1939*, p. 80.

word "alien" was synonymous with "Mexican." When Congressman Martin Dies of Texas (who would become the founding chairman of the House Subcommittee on Un-American Activities) declared in the *Chicago Herald-Examiner* that the "large alien population is the basic cause of unemployment," for example, the aliens he had in mind were Chicanos, and his solution was simple: keep them out and send those already here back to where they came from.[15] The House Committee on Immigration and Naturalization had held hearings on the subject as early as the spring of 1930, while over in the Senate legislators began considering a bill that would have limited Chicano immigration to 1,900 people a year. The sentiment that lurked behind both efforts had been revealed when Vanderbilt University geneticist Roy I. Garis, echoing Kenneth Roberts, told the House committee that the minds of Mexican Americans "run to nothing higher than animal functions— eat, sleep, and sexual debauchery. . . . Yet there are Americans clamoring for more of this human swine to be brought over from Mexico."[16]

That level of sociopathic aversion was common anywhere Mexican Americans lived, but so, too, was the continuing desire for cheap migratory labor among the industrial farmers of California and the Southwest, and their lobbying efforts successfully killed anti-immigration legislation specifically directed against Mexican Americans, just as they had managed to keep Mexicans excluded from the stipulations of Johnson-Reed. Just the same, hard times and prejudice began to reverse immigration trends. In Gary, Indiana, for instance, many Mexican Americans willingly began packing up and leaving on their own in 1930. "[T]here was no other way out," one of them recalled. "We were happy to leave."[17] But as Gary's unemployment and relief problems increased, citizens and city officials alike made it clear that Mexicans probably ought to leave whether they wanted to or not. Relief checks were frequently withheld from Chicano applicants, and a steady hammering of anti-Mexican-American propaganda in the press and increased discrimination in job applications made life even more uncomfortable

15. Quoted in Betten and Mohl, op. cit., p. 131.
16. Quoted in Acuña, op. cit., p. 137.
17. Quoted in Abraham Hoffman, "Stimulus to Repatriation: The 1931 Federal Deportation Drive and the Los Angeles Mexican Community"; in Norris Hundley Jr., ed., *The Chicano*, p. 137.

than usual. Private donations were raised to finance the journey to Mexico as a further inducement, but many who left under such circumstances did not seem to be particularly grateful for the generosity of their Anglo neighbors. "This is my country," one young woman born in the United States remarked, "but after the way we have been treated I hope never to see it again. . . . As long as my father was working and spending his money in Gary stores, paying taxes, and supporting us, it was all right, but now we have found we can't get justice here."[18]

Gary's example was followed in many midwestern and southwestern cities, from St. Paul to El Paso, but nowhere more enthusiastically than in Los Angeles. Here, the atmosphere had been hostile from the beginning of the depression, largely because of Charles P. Visel, chairman of the overstressed Los Angeles relief committee. Visel had swiftly estimated that 20,000 to 25,000 Mexican illegals lived in southern California. "You advise please," he had then wired Colonel Arthur M. Woods, national coordinator for the PECE, on January 6, 1931, "as to method of getting rid. . . . We need their jobs for needy citizens."[19]

The method devised by Visel, in consultation with Wood and Doak, was designed, in Visel's candid words, "to scare many thousand alien deportables out of this district which is the result desired."[20] Throughout February 1931, a publicity campaign flooded such Spanish-language newspapers as *La Opinion* with announcements that the means of transportation would be provided to any Chicano willing to return to Mexico; at the same time, a generally anti-Mexican-American newspaper campaign was launched in Anglo publications, while authorities began a series of raids and arrests—"scareheading," as Visel described the tactic.[21] None would be so widely publicized in the Chicano press, however, as that which began on the afternoon of February 26, when immigration agents and Los Angeles police surrounded the *Placita*, the heart of the original eighteenth-century pueblo and a popular gathering place. Four hundred people were held in the little park for more than an hour while their papers were checked; eleven Mexicans, five Chinese,

18. Statistics and quote in Betten and Mohl, op. cit.
19. Quoted in Hoffman, op. cit., p. 112.
20. Quoted in ibid.
21. Quoted in Guerin-Gonzales, op. cit., p. 81.

and one Japanese were officially detained (nine of the Mexicans were released the next day).

It was not much of a take, but screaming headlines in *La Opinion* and other Spanish-language newspapers, followed by many other, smaller raids in the days that followed, in which a total of about 4,000 people were seized and questioned (though only 389 were deported), had the desired effect. Over the next three years, 13,332 Mexican Americans boarded "repatriation" trains sponsored by Los Angeles County and 3,492 did the same in San Bernardino County, while tens of thousands more throughout southern California—as many as 75,000 by the end of 1931 alone—made it back to Mexico on their own.

Carey McWilliams, on hand to watch the first trainload of *repatriados* leave Union Station, later wrote that "repatriation was a tragicomic affair: tragic in the hardships occasioned; comic because most of the Mexicans eventually returned to Los Angeles, having had a trip to Mexico at the expense of the county."[22] Many returned, certainly, but not most: before repatriation, the Bureau of the Census reported, there were 650,000 immigrant Mexican Americans in the United States; by 1940 that figure had been cut in half. Nevertheless, Paul Taylor noted bluntly in the May 1931 issue of *Survey Graphic*, "The Mexicans are here, from California to Pennsylvania, from Texas to Minnesota," and the effort to return them all to Mexico was fruitless: "No such exodus is probable. The representatives of our two cultures will remain in juxtaposition in large and widespread areas of the United States, with contacts of varying types and degrees of intensity. The stamp of the Mexican migration will be visible for generations."[23]

THE MEXICAN AMERICANS were here and most of them were not going to go away. Many, deprived of representation among Anglo unions even after passage of the National Industrial Recovery Act in 1933, since it did not include the agricultural industry in its labor provisions, organized themselves. The effort began conservatively, largely because the post-revolutionary Mexican government under President Lazaro

22. Carey McWilliams, *Southern California Country*, p. 317.
23. Paul S. Taylor, "Mexicans North of the Rio Grande," *Survey Graphic* (May 1931).

Cárdenas feared radicalism among its own workers and worried that leftist labor agitation might spill back across the border. This was first demonstrated just north of the Mexican border in the mercilessly "reclaimed" desert sink of California's Imperial Valley, whose spreading fields of lettuce, peas, cantaloupes, watermelons, and other crops were irrigated with Colorado River water via the Imperial Canal and planted, plucked, and packed by a seasonal army of workers, most of them Mexican American, with a sprinkling of Filipino, Hindu, and Anglo laborers among them.

In April 1928, workers in El Centro had created *La Union de Trabajadores del Valle Imperial* (Imperial Valley Workers Union), only to have the organization swiftly dominated by Mexican-American merchants and labor contractors who had a comfortable relationship with Anglo growers and farm-managers and close ties to the Mexican government—and, consequently, little interest in seriously disrupting the status quo. In May, the association presented a petition asking for better rates for cantaloupe pickers. The petition was rejected, and the growers refused to negotiate. The leadership of the union did nothing, and when a number of individual members reacted by initiating wildcat strikes, the leaders sent a letter to the newspapers denouncing the militant workers and bemoaning the harm they had done to "the good name of this society."[24] Meanwhile, Imperial County Sheriff C. L. Gillett put together a force of forty deputies and started arresting strikers on a wholesale basis. More than sixty ended up in jail, with bail set impossibly high at anywhere from $500 to $1,000. (The point made, most of the men ultimately would be released.) At the suggestion of the Mexican consul, Carlos Ariza, the union soon changed its name to something a little less threatening; it was now the *Associación Mutual del Valle Imperial* (Mutual Aid Society of the Imperial Valley).

The wildcat cantaloupe strikes had been broken almost immediately, but when growers cut wages for vegetable and fruit pickers in January 1930, the workers struck again. This time, the leaders of the

24. Quoted in Gilbert G. Gonzalez, "Company Unions, the Mexican Consulate, and the Imperial Valley Agricultural Strikes, 1928–1934," *Western Historical Quarterly* (Spring 1986).

renamed union attempted to direct the strike instead of denying it, but did so with such timidity that many Mexican-American workers were ready to listen when Communist TUUL organizers Frank Waldron, Harry Harvey, and Tsuji Horiuchi moved in from Los Angeles to fill the vacuum. It was the beginning of a five-year labor campaign in the fields of California and would provide perhaps the single most telling glimpse of the CP/USA at its best, when in the name of an indisputably oppressed class and with a minimum of self-serving politicizing, field workers risked their lives repeatedly, demonstrating reserves of courage and determination that transcended the inhuman dialectics of party dogma. Even in their ultimate failure, these astoundingly dedicated people left the residue of something identifiably brave in their passage.

Hiding in the Brawley and El Centro *barrios* during the day and at night proselytizing among "the shacks and hovels of workers who were always glad to see us," as Harvey remembered it, spinning the crank of an old mimeograph machine at breakneck speed and sending a storm of broadsides into the fields, the trio of TUUL organizers soon gathered enough supporters to establish a local of the Agricultural Workers Industrial League (AWIL), created in Cleveland the year before and still so unformed that it was described by William Z. Foster as a union "in embryo."[25]

The leaders of the Mutual Aid Society reacted by joining with the local chamber of commerce to condemn the Communist agitators, while the Mexican ambassador in Washington ordered the consul in El Centro to ask the workers to exercise "all moderation in their attitude." Meanwhile the Hoover administration sent mediator Charles T. Connell into the valley to help settle the strike in the industry's favor, which he managed to do on January 17.[26] "The Mexican Mutual Aid Association [sic] exercised a baleful influence over the strike from the beginning," *The Daily Worker* claimed with some justification on January 23. "The Mexican workers, the largest majority of the strikers, were tricked into following it. . . . The Mexican workers are beginning to see what

25. Quotes in Cletus E. Daniel, *Bitter Harvest: A History of California Farmworkers, 1870–1941*, pp. 111, 113.
26. Quoted in Gonzalez, op. cit.

was done to them and will soon organize in the AWIL."[27] Many in fact did, and, armed with a growing membership, the AWIL organizers began planning a major strike for the cantaloupe-picking season in May, holding mass meetings of agricultural workers from all over the valley in April. A conference to "lay the basis for an industrial union of agricultural workers to be organized on a national scale" was scheduled for April 14 in El Centro.[28]

The conference had barely gotten under way before the authorities moved to put an end to the proceedings. More than a hundred workers and union organizers were arrested, chained together in a long line, and marched off to jail. Eight of the TUUL leaders were convicted of criminal syndicalism and given sentences that ranged from three to forty-two years to two to twenty-eight years, though the magistrate presiding would have given them even more time had it been up to him. "The court considers them," Superior Court judge Von H. Thompson noted in a recommendation to the state prison board, "of no use or benefit whatever but on the contrary, a decided menace to society and civilization in general; that under these circumstances any prison term less than life for each defendant is quite moderate."[29]

A life sentence for union organizing was a little stiff even in those times, even in California. The prison board fixed the sentences at five years, and by early 1933 the leaders had all been paroled (though two, including Tsuji Horiuchi, were deported soon after their release). Nevertheless, the cantaloupe strike never did materialize, and the TUUL's organizing drive had effectively been stifled. While the AWIL maintained a presence in the Imperial Valley and other agricultural regions of the state, it received little support from either the national office of the CP/USA or the headquarters of District 13 in San Francisco, both of which through the first three years of the depression were more concerned with organizing hunger marches and other expressions of support for the urban unemployed. Not that District 13 was in a position to organize much of anything. Taking in California, Arizona, and

27. Quoted in Porter Chaffee, "A History of the Cannery and Agricultural Workers Industrial Union," unpublished WPA report, p. 64. In Paul S. Taylor Papers, Bancroft Library, University of California at Berkeley.
28. Quoted in ibid., p. 68.
29. Quoted in ibid., p. 90.

Nevada, it was so low in the Communist hierarchy as to be considered the Siberia of the CP/USA. When Party president Earl Browder decided that Samuel Adams Darcy, the Ukraine-born head of the ILD, was becoming a thorn in his side (Darcy had called the party's national leaders "middle-class rejects who couldn't make it in the bourgeois world," and former accountant Browder had no doubt exactly whom the young rebel had in mind), he sent Darcy to head up District 13 in December 1930.[30] Upon his arrival, Darcy found a total membership of about three hundred people and a war chest of six dollars.[31]

But Darcy was gifted, energetic, and committed. Within the next four years he would rebuild district membership to respectable levels (and would help guide the party's limited but useful participation in the waterfront strikes of 1934), even though it would never be very well funded, either through its local membership or from national headquarters. He also recognized a missed opportunity in California's factories in the field, whose singularly downtrodden workers, he realized, were "willing to fight the battle of nothing-to-lose," and he urged the leaders of the party's little agricultural union (which had renamed itself the Agricultural Workers Industrial Union, or AWIU, by then) to launch a statewide membership drive, rather than merely rushing to join grass-roots actions, as they had done in the Imperial Valley.[32]

Events soon frustrated that goal, as the scene of conflict moved from the Imperial Valley into the northern counties of the state. When 2,000 cannery workers in the Santa Clara Valley near San Jose went on strike in July 1931 after employers instituted a 20 percent cut in wages, the AWIU moved in immediately to get control of the situation, even changing its name in an attempt to enhance its position; now it was called the *Cannery* and Agricultural Workers Industrial Union (CAWIU). The new name stuck, but the strike quickly collapsed when the farmers brought in carloads of strikebreakers, and the authorities deputized members of the local American Legion to join with the police in breaking up demonstrations and aiding in mass arrests. A similarly swift and dismal fate befell a CAWIU-seized strike of 1,500 pea-pickers

30. Quote in Daniel, op. cit., p. 131.
31. Figures in ibid., p. 132.
32. Quoted in ibid., p. 133.

who had spontaneously walked off the job near Half Moon Bay in May 1932 when employers cut the piece rate from seventy-five cents a crate to as little as forty cents.

The CAWIU may have been defeated and its organizers regularly bloodied, but recruitment and organization continued, much of it the work of a stubborn quintet of uncommonly talented agitators: CAWIU president Patrick Chambers (whose real name was John Ernest Williams), field representatives W. D. ("Bill") Hamett and Patrick Callahan, talented fund-raiser Jack Warnick, a graduate student at the University of California at Berkeley, and his wife, a diminutive twenty-year-old woman named Caroline Decker, whose brief but animated career as a California strike leader was prototypical of the Communist chapter of the migrant labor movement. Remembered by her fellow radical Porter Chaffee as "a dazzling blonde" who could "electrify" an audience, Decker was the child of fully radicalized parents, having cut her activist teeth in the Pittsburgh branch of the Young Communist League, and while still a teenager she had helped to organize coal miners in Pennsylvania and Harlan County, Kentucky.[33] "As far as I was concerned," she remembered, "I considered myself a communist from the time I was sixteen years old. . . . I was prepared to give my life, and I did give a great deal of it."

In June 1932, Decker was named executive secretary of the CAWIU and sent by Darcy to its headquarters in San Jose, a ramshackle old Workers' Hall that would seem to support her description of the union as little more than "an idea in somebody's head." Here, she found "a beaten-up old typewriter, Pat Chambers, and a couple of other people—and that was the union." No matter. "Mostly," she recalled, "the workers came to us," walking into the union office to "get membership books and go back to organize the local." There were letters, too, including one from a Colorado sheepherder, asking her to tell him how to organize his trade. "I wrote a four-page letter," she remembered, and upon rereading it many years later, "I sat on the floor and just howled. Now, it was earnest and it was not stupid, but what the *hell* did

33. Quoted in Ann Loftis, *Witnesses to the Struggle: Imaging the 1930s California Labor Movement*, p. 43.

we know about sheepherders? It was that kind of thing. We cared very much, and we tried."[34]

One of the new locals served some 400 Mexican-American, Filipino, Japanese, and white pruners and fruit-pickers in the orchards of Vacaville north of San Francisco. When Frank Buck, a just-elected congressman and the owner of the largest orchard in the district, went back on a campaign promise to raise wages to $1.40 for an eight-hour day and instead dropped them to $1.25 for a nine-hour day, the CAWIU initiated its first fully planned strike at the beginning of the pruning season in November 1932, demanding an eight-hour day, a $1.50 daily wage, and recognition of the CAWIU. "We would have to starve working," one pruner remarked, "so we decided to starve striking."[35]

The owners countered with an offer of $1.20 for eight hours and refused to negotiate with the union, and the strike soon took on the ritual character that would become standard through much of the decade. Strikebreakers were brought in by the farmers, only to be effectively resisted by massed picket lines, many of them composed of women and children. Vacaville preachers railed against the union from their pulpits, one going so far as to encourage his parishioners to handle matters by "the system that is used south of the Mason and Dixon line."[36] The CP/USA branch of the Workers' International Relief sent in food and medical supplies, while the ILD offered legal help. Strike leaders were arrested, jailed, and occasionally beaten by town police, county sheriffs, or state highway patrolmen, and a vigilante force of nearly 200 deputized civilians was organized, demonstrating its usefulness most dramatically when, as one observer reported, "a masked mob of forty men in a score of cars . . . took six strike leaders out of the Vacaville jail, drove them twenty miles from town, flogged them . . . clipped their heads with sheep clippers, and poured red enamel over them."[37] Many Filipino workers, given special attention by the vigilantes, ultimately

34. Author's transcription of a tape recording in the Oral History Department of the Bancroft Library, University of California at Berkeley. Unless otherwise noted, all Decker quotes are from this source.
35. Quote in Carey McWilliams, *Factories in the Fields*, p. 215.
36. Quote in Daniel, op. cit., p. 138.
37. Quote in McWilliams, op. cit., p. 215.

fled the area, while other strikers, "feeling the pinch of hunger," drifted
back to work by the end of December; still, the CAWIU held on for two
months before voting to end the strike at a mass meeting on January 20.[38]

The workers had won nothing but pride in having maintained the
strike longer than anyone might have expected, and the union had
gained nothing but experience. But pride and experience were invaluable commodities, and both were put to vigorous use in the months
ahead, as the CAWIU led or played a significant part in strikes among
pea-pickers and cherry-pickers south of Oakland, peach-pickers in the
Sacramento Valley, grape-pickers in the San Joaquin Valley, pear-pickers
in the Santa Clara Valley, berry-pickers in the San Fernando Valley, and
sugar-beet workers on the South Coast. In all, more than thirty individual strikes spilled across the fields and orchards of the state in the spring
and summer of 1933, and in most of them the CAWIU was a visible
force. Decker, a powerful speaker for all her size, gave forth eloquently
at union rallies, while Hamett, Chambers, and Callahan (who at one
point had his skull fractured and his jaw broken by police) talked
among the workers, seeking out the most militant among them and
helping them to establish themselves as leaders and recruit local membership. "In remote garages and sheds, hastily made over into halls by a
few wooden benches," Orrick Johns remembered in *Time of Our Lives*
(1937), "the workers would be huddled together under a single light,
discussing their problems with remarkable coolness. Looking over those
halls of swarthy men and women, I saw faces that reminded me of the

38. Quote in Daniel, op. cit. The estimated 30,000 Filipino agricultural laborers in
California had always had their own distinctive share of prejudice directed against
them. Unlike the Mexican-American population, which tended to travel and settle in
family groups, most of the Filipinos were men whose families had remained in the
islands, and they were not immune to ordinary human needs. On Saturday nights, they
liked to dress up and go looking for women: "little brown men attired like Solomon in
all his glory," as one sublimely racist justice of the peace in Monterey County described
them, "only a decade removed from the bolo and the breechcloth, were strutting like
peacocks through the towns of the region to attract white and Mexican girls." Encouraged by such public declarations of sexual insecurity, anti-Filipino riots and demonstrations had taken place in Exeter, Watsonville, Stockton, Salinas, San Jose, and San
Francisco between December 1929 and February 1930, leaving one Filipino dead and
scores injured. (Quote and Filipino experience in Starr, *Endangered Dreams*, p. 64.)

ruined faces in Michelangelo's Day of Judgment on the walls of the Sistine Chapel. . . . They were a desperate and a courageous people, compelled to exist as primitively as the . . . Indians, and asking little."[39]

And getting precious little—though something. While actual union membership probably never got beyond 2,000 people, and only a handful of the strikes ended in even partial victories (the thoroughly trounced grape-pickers' strike near Fresno in September was not even that), most nonunion workers came to accept the CAWIU as their de facto leader, and the constant threat of work stoppages had raised the hourly wage for most agricultural workers from a low of fifteen cents to twenty-five cents throughout much of the industry by the end of the summer. Had work been available the whole year, that might have been enough to enable a three-worker family laboring eight hours a day six days a week for fifty-two weeks to earn nearly double the $972 that a University of California study determined was needed to meet minimum "health and decency" standards for an average family in California. Work was not available all year long, of course, but only for a few weeks during the peak planting, pruning, and picking seasons, and a study of 775 Mexican-American families two years after the wage increase found that the average family still earned only $289.[40] Regardless, twenty-five cents was indisputably better than fifteen cents, and the CAWIU could and did take credit for this improvement, using its newly won prestige to increase its membership and influence among the workers. The little union would need both, for by the end of September 1933, it was preparing to launch and lead the largest agricultural labor strike in American history.

AT ISSUE IN September 1933 in California, as it had been among the tenants and sharecroppers of the Deep South, was cotton, particularly that grown on the ranch-sized spreads of the southern San Joaquin Valley. There was a bumper crop that year, the Department of Agriculture reporting that California's 208,000 cotton-growing acres (about half in

39. Quote in McWilliams, op. cit., pp. 216–17.
40. Quote and figures from Guerin-Gonzales, op. cit., p. 120.

the San Joaquin Valley) produced 497 pounds an acre, the highest yield in the nation—and one grower had gotten 600 pounds, a national record.[41] What was more, the average price per pound had jumped from a little over six cents in the spring to anywhere from ten to twelve cents by the harvest season in the fall. Unfortunately, fully three-fourths of the crop had been contracted out in April to Japanese buyers at seven cents a pound, so many growers would be in no position to take advantage of the autumn prices. On the other hand, many would get a share in the $100 million expected to be paid out by the Agricultural Adjustment Administration's cotton-reduction program by the end of the year, and the CAWIU and the pickers it represented were not greatly moved by grower complaints that while they were willing to raise the rate from the forty cents per hundredweight they had paid in 1932, they could not offer more than sixty cents.

It had not been that long since 1929, when the price per hundredweight had been $1.50 and a family could hope to eke out a decent living by filling three or even four hundred-pound sacks a day. Still, the union would not be unreasonable, a gathering of twenty-five CAWIU locals decided on September 18; it would ask for no more than a dollar a hundredweight, union recognition, and an end to the labor contract system, which kept Mexican-American workers at the mercy of middlemen more inclined to represent the desires of the growers than the needs of the workers. The growers refused all demands, and even before the official strike call on October 4, CAWIU workers began coming in off fields throughout the San Joaquin Valley. Within a few days, somewhere between fifteen and twenty thousand farm laborers, 95 percent of them Mexican Americans, were on strike in a hundred-mile belt of boll-heavy cotton fields and bleak little ginning towns that checkerboarded the valley from below Arvin in the south to above Corcoran in the north.

This was no isolated fruit-pickers' strike. This was a major assault on a multimillion-dollar business at the beginning of its picking sea-

41. The 600-pound record is cited in Paul S. Taylor and Clark Kerr, "Documentary History of the Strike of the Cotton Pickers in California, 1933," appended to *Violation of Free Speech and Rights of Labor*, a report issued by Senator Robert M. La Follette's Subcommittee on Education and Labor, United States Senate, 1939; other figures in Milton Eisenhower, ed., op. cit., p. 460.

son, and the growers and farm managers of the valley reacted with predictable rigidity. On October 6, they refused a state offer to mediate,
although the CAWIU had agreed. At a meeting in the town of Pixley,
north of Bakersfield, a Farmers' Protective Association was formed with
600 members and plans to grow to two thousand. One of its first acts
was to threaten local merchants. "We, the farmers of your community,"
an association-sponsored newspaper advertisement read, "upon whom
you depend for support, feel you have nursed too long the viper at your
door. The Communist agitators must be driven from the towns by you,
and your harboring them further will prove to us your non-cooperation
with us and make it necessary for us to give our support and trade to
another town."[42] Nonunion pickers were brought up from Los Angeles
and the Imperial Valley, and plans were laid by a number of growers to
start importing strikebreakers from Texas and other southern Plains
states. Working families who refused to go back into the fields were
summarily evicted by county authorities from grower-owned workers'
camps. "We protect our farmers here in Kern County," one member of
the sheriff's department said by way of explanation. "They put us in
here and they can put us out again, so we serve them. But the Mexicans
are trash. . . . We herd them like pigs."[43] Vigilante groups were organized and armed with pick handles and guns. Meetings were held to
discuss means of starving out the workers so that they would be forced
to renounce the strike and return to work.

Aided and abetted by the CAWIU, strikers responded by gathering
in their own camps, forming local strike committees, and trucking
masses of pickets from farm to farm, a tactic not unlike that of sending
out the "flying squadrons" that would prove so effective during the
eastern textile strikes of the following year. At each farm, the trucks and
automobiles would stop, strikers spilling out to set up their lines and
exhort any field-workers they might find to join the strike—sometimes
blowing a Mexican call to arms on a bugle to get their attention. When
nothing else worked, women strikers frequently went into the fields to
taunt and challenge the workers face-to-face—sometimes with violence. Roberto Castro, one of the strike leaders, claimed that women

42. Quote in Taylor and Kerr, op. cit.
43. Quote in Guerin-Gonzales, op. cit., p. 121.

were used on the theory that they were less likely to be injured, but one woman remembered it otherwise. "The men always hold back because they are men and all," she said. "But the women, no. The men couldn't make us do anything. . . . The same women who were in the trucks, who were in the . . . picket line . . . these women went in and beat up all those that were inside picking cotton. . . . They tore their clothes. . . . Ohhh! It was ugly! It was an ugly sight! I was just looking and said, 'No, no.' I watched the blood flowing from them."[44]

Even more blood flowed on the afternoon of October 10, when armed growers in Pixley seized sixteen CAWIU pickets and held them prisoner. A crowd of strikers rallied to protest the action of the growers, Pat Chambers climbing on a truckbed to harangue the workers. "This is no time for a backward step," Chambers shouted, according to a reporter for the *San Francisco News*. "We must fight and show the farmers a solid front. We will match the farmers with their own violence. Let them start something—and we will finish it." When the rally ended and the workers began walking toward strike headquarters, they were confronted by a group of growers.

"Suddenly a farmer fired into the crowd," the reporter wrote. "A few fusillades rang out from the other farmers. The strikers broke, ran into their red brick building. All but a few. They lay in their own tracks where the farmers' bullets had dropped them. Some lay very still. Others weakly pulled themselves up on their elbows, tried to crawl to safety out of the line of fire."[45] Two of the still forms were dead—Dolores Hernandez, a striker, and Delfino Davila, an assistant to the Mexican consul in Visalia.

At almost the same moment that shots echoed over the unharvested cotton fields of Pixley, growers and union pickets clashed in the town of Arvin ninety miles to the south—and by the time this incident was over, another Mexican American, striker Pedro Subia, had been killed.

Nine strikers were arrested immediately for contributing to the death of the worker in Arvin; the next day, eight farmers were arrested

44. "Mrs. Valdez," as quoted in Devra Weber, "*Raiz Fuerte*: Oral History and Mexicana Farmworkers," footnote, pp. 222–23; in Daniel Cornford, ed., *Working People of California*.
45. *San Francisco News* (October 11, 1933).

for the deaths of the workers in Pixley, while Pat Chambers (on a complaint filed by one of the Pixley accused) was arrested for criminal syndicalism. All parties accused of murder ultimately would be tried and acquitted; the Chambers trial, held in December, would end in a hung jury, and in February 1934 the government would decide not to retry him and he would be released. Meanwhile, Governor James Rolph put together a fact-finding committee to look into the affair, while George Creel, NRA administrator for the region, began efforts to persuade the growers and workers alike to accept a picking rate of seventy-five cents a hundredweight (though he made it clear that the federal government would never endorse the Communist-run CAWIU as the bargaining agent for the workers).

While Chambers languished in the Tulare County Jail in Visalia, Caroline Decker was left in charge of the continuing strike. Her headquarters were in Corcoran, outside of which sprawled the largest of the several shabby workers' camps that now pocked the valley like latter-day Hoovervilles. The Corcoran camp held nearly 4,000 people on thirty acres of leased but uncultivated Santa Fe railroad land (neither the railroad nor the leasor, fearing public outrage, chose to evict them). Conditions were grim. There was little water and less food, no sanitation, and only sporadic medical attention. In the week following the Pixley and Arvin shootings, five infants died of malnutrition. This was too much even for Governor Rolph, who had no sympathy for radicals and, at best, a casual attitude toward justice.[46] On October 12, he ordered R. C. Branion, the state administrator for the Federal Emergency Relief Administration, to get food to the workers. Branion claimed that he could not do so until the strikers agreed to arbitrate (false—FERA head Harry Hopkins had decreed that unemployed strikers were to be fed just like anyone else). "Arbitration, hell!" Rolph was said to have shouted. "We're not going to force these strikers into arbitration by starving them out. Not in my state!"[47]

---

46. In November, after a mob took a pair of alleged murderers from a San Jose jail and hanged them, Rolph would enthusiastically endorse the action: "This is the best lesson California has ever given the country," he boasted, adding that the lynchers had "pioneer blood in their veins." Quoted in *Time* (December 3, 1933).

47. *San Francisco Chronicle* (October 13, 1933).

The FERA set up shop in a converted pool hall in Corcoran, and food and milk supplies were ready for distribution on October 15, but fear and ideology briefly threatened to keep them from the hungry. When relief administrators asked the standard questions regarding citizenship and car licenses, Mexican-American strike leaders feared that they were ruses by which their people could be deported or forced to accept the sixty cents a hundredweight being offered by the growers. They refused to let the supplies be distributed. FERA officials went to Pat Chambers in the county jail in Visalia for help. He sent the officials to Decker, who agreed to go into the camp and discuss the situation with the Chicano strike leaders. "Do you know you might get arrested for being seen with me?" she teasingly asked one of the FERA women as they got into the government car. Decker "caused quite a furor" when she entered the camp, FERA field agent C. W. Burr reported, she "was chucked on the chin by several Mexicans and went gaily off with the delegates."[48] When she returned, she announced that the strike committee had voted to accept the supplies if the offending questions could be eliminated from the application forms. The FERA people agreed, but it took a mass meeting to resolve all doubts before recipients began lining up to get the food on the afternoon of October 16.

On October 19, when Governor Rolph's investigation team arrived in Visalia to hold hearings, Decker led a force of marching Mexican-American workers to the county courthouse where the investigators received them. The Visalia hearings, extensively covered by the California press and in such national publications as *The Nation* and the *New York Times*, gave added inspiration to the strikers. Norman Thomas came to observe. Ella Winter, the ex-wife of renowned muckraker Lincoln Steffens and co-founder of the League Against War and Fascism, testified for the workers. Liberal elements around the state held meetings, went into the camps to observe conditions for themselves, organized relief caravans. James Cagney and other stars sent money and made public statements in support of the strike. "I think the cotton strike differed from any other agricultural strike that had ever taken place," Decker remembered, "in that it got international coverage. . . .

48. FERA field agent C. W. Burr, "Report on Cotton Strikers, Kings County," n.d. In Paul Schuster Taylor papers. Decker quoted from same source.

More people were concerned. . . . I'm sure it had some effect on the strike to have that kind of support, to have truckloads of clothes coming in, truckloads of food coming in. It gave [strikers] a lot of courage."[49]

It also put pressure on growers and government officials to find some way to end the walkout. Reports circulated that some individual growers, their crops threatened with rot, had agreed to pay as much as the dollar a hundredweight demanded by the CAWIU. On October 24, the state fact-finding committee issued its official report and recommended that a uniform rate of seventy-five cents be instituted. NRA administrator George Creel urged the growers to accept the recommendation, and after some internal disagreements, most did on October 25. Creel then addressed a meeting of strikers—though still refusing to deal directly with Decker and the other CAWIU leaders—and warned them that federal relief would be denied any workers who did not accept the settlement, while growers gathered a force of men outside the Corcoran camp and promised to evacuate it by force if the workers did not comply. The workers still refused to go back to the fields, but before the growers could make good their threats to the Corcoran camp, CAWIU leaders persuaded the central strike committee during a mass meeting on the morning of October 27 that there was nothing more to be gained by continuing the strike. Decker, "a blonde slip of a girl, twenty-one years old, the acknowledged leader of 12,000 strikers," as a *San Francisco Examiner* reporter described her, emerged from the "crude strike headquarters" and "electrified mediators with the word that the strike was over."[50]

THE CALIFORNIA COTTON strike settlement was at least a partial victory for the workers, but two of the CAWIU's principal goals, union recognition and an end to the contract labor system, were not included in the agreement. It was especially galling to the union's leaders that the federal government refused to deal with the CAWIU directly. "It is clear to the workers," the central strike committee complained in an official after-strike statement probably written by Decker, "that the government

49. "Caroline Decker Gladstein" tape recording.
50. *San Francisco Examiner* (October 27, 1933).

will not recognize any union which has a militant policy of struggle in the interests of the working class."[51] The charge had merit. "Certainly we cannot countenance communistic and radical agitation that strikes at our democratic institutions," George Creel had written to the manager of a cotton operation before the settlement. "The NRA gives no aid or comfort to those who would destroy the foundations of American democracy."[52]

The Roosevelt administration certainly gave neither aid nor comfort to the CAWIU when the union led a major strike among 5,000 lettuce workers in the Imperial Valley early in January 1934. As it had done during the strikes of 1930, the Mexican government stepped in to help the growers out. Consul Joaquin Terrazas, who had resurrected the old Imperial Valley Workers' Union as a competitor to the CAWIU (promptly and accurately described by the CAWIU as a company union), warned Chicano laborers that they faced deportation if they continued to side with the Communists. Mass arrests and numerous vigilante actions were applied by growers and county authorities regardless of any constitutional questions; indeed, the prevailing attitude with regard to civil rights was clarified in February when the Imperial County Board of Supervisors passed a highly questionable ordinance designed to make picketing or other strike actions illegal anywhere near public thoroughfares. "The Board of Supervisors hereby declares," the ordinance concluded with breathtaking gall, "that it would have passed this Ordinance . . . irrespective of the fact that any one or more section, subsections, sentences, clauses, or phrases be declared unconstitutional."[53] The campaign was so overwhelmingly resolute that the CAWIU called the lettuce strike off on January 18 without having won a single concession.

The growers, however, made it clear that this single victory was not enough; they would not be satisfied with anything less than the

51. Quoted in Daniel, op. cit., p. 217.
52. Quoted in ibid., p. 212.
53. Among other stipulations, the ordinance made it unlawful "for any person within the County of Imperial, State of California, by the use of boisterous, loud, profane, obscene, or abusive language . . . to induce or influence or attempt to induce or influence any person to refrain from entering any field, farm or ranch, works, factory, place of business or employment. . . ." Presumably, such bad language could be illegal in

destruction of the CAWIU and an end to all radical agitation. Draco-
nian antiunion repression continued. In spite of impassioned pleas from
many people in and out of the valley—including investigators sent in
by the American Civil Liberties Union—neither the federal nor the
state governments did anything in response until January 23, when
ACLU attorney A. L. Wirin was abducted by a gang of vigilantes,
beaten, robbed, stripped of his shoes, and driven out on to the empty
desert floor and left to walk barefoot eleven miles to the nearest town.

This incident, fully reported by most of the national press, persuaded Senator Robert F. Wagner, head of the National Labor Relations
Board, to send a three-man commission into the valley to investigate.
The commission spent a few days in the valley, then issued a report that
verified the terrible conditions under which migrant workers labored
and condemned the lawlessness of the valley's growers and county officials. While it did not endorse the activities of the CAWIU, the commission did recommend that the federal government "encourage the
organization of workers, in order that collective bargaining may be effective in matters of wages and conditions, both working and living, and
that the right to strike and peacefully to picket shall be maintained."[54]

Senator Wagner thanked the commissioners most sincerely for their
efforts, but the NLRB made it clear that the Roosevelt administration
was no more eager to take on the politically potent growers of California
over the question of their treatment of mostly Mexican American
migrants than it was to challenge the equally powerful oligarchy of the
South over its treatment of mostly black sharecroppers. That reluctance
was reemphasized in March, when, after another attempted CAWIU
strike had resulted in a new explosion of repression in the valley, Secretary of Labor Frances Perkins decided that the people of Imperial
County, as she later recalled it with the innocent arrogance of the confirmed Progressive, "were like children and children take comfort in

---

either English or Spanish. Source: "An Ordinance Making It Unlawful to Obstruct a
Public Highway of the County of Imperial, State of California, and to Prevent Unlaw-
ful Hindrance or Interference with Any Person Traveling Upon Any Highway in Said
County," Imperial County Board of Supervisors, February 17, 1934. (In Paul Schuster
Taylor Papers, op. cit.)
54. Quoted in Daniel, op. cit., p. 234.

authority."[55] So at the end of March she sent recognized authority figure General Pelham G. Glassford into the heart of California's agribusiness maelstrom.

Glassford, who had resigned as head of Washington's Metropolitan Police Department after the Bonus Army riots of 1932, arrived early in April, hoping to stave off a threatened strike of the cantaloupe harvest. Almost immediately, he blasted the CAWIU as an organization whose "only objective is to create dissension, destroy private property and foment a strike" and rejected proposals that an election be held to determine whether workers would rather belong to the CAWIU or the company union that Terrazas had put together (now once again called the Mutual Aid Society of the Imperial Valley).[56] That pleased the growers. They were not at all happy, however, when in June Glassford turned his scorn in their direction, charging that a "small group of growers and shippers who have set themselves up to rule Imperial Valley desire only to fog the issue with their doctrines of violence, intimidation, and suppression of the workers. Instead of setting an example of law, order, sanity, and reform, they are breeding violence and discontent among the workers." Such farmers were, he added, perhaps "the most dangerous 'reds' ever to come to Imperial Valley."[57]

Aside from having mortally offended both sides, nothing came of the general's investigation—though the cantaloupe strike was thwarted. The Labor Department accepted his report with gratitude, and the Roosevelt administration continued to mend its political fences, doing nothing about migrant labor in California. In March 1934, the growers of the Imperial Valley joined those from other parts of the state to form the Associated Farmers of California, whose transparent and unembarrassed goal was the elimination of all union activity and the suppression of any form of radical dissent in the agricultural industry.

Unimpeded by state or federal authority; richly endowed by its own members, most of whom had close if complex ties to the state's entire financial structure; given tactical support by local sheriffs and police and, when necessary, the California Highway Patrol, a force operated

55. Frances Perkins, oral memoirs, 4: p. 405.
56. Quoted in Daniel, op. cit., p. 243.
57. Ibid., p. 248.

almost autonomously by its fervently anti-Communist chief, E. Raymond Cato; abetted by city and county governments all too eager to pass any law the growers might deem useful and to violate any statute on the books that might interfere with the due process of the industry's goals; and encouraged by a wave of anti-Communist sentiment that resulted from the waterfront strike in San Francisco that year, the Associated Farmers proceeded to extinguish CAWIU unionism. In May, a CAWIU-led fruit-pickers' strike in Contra Costa County was so swiftly and completely beaten down that the TUUL union lost most of its local members to a late-coming, non-Communist union cobbled together by the AFL.

Far worse than that humiliation were the events of July 20, when, as Carey McWilliams reported, raiding parties led by Sacramento County district attorney Neil McCallister and armed with "sawed-off shotguns, handcuffs, blackjacks, rubber hoses, billies, riot clubs, gas bombs, and accompanied by news reporters and photographers from the *Sacramento Bee*," smashed into (and smashed up) the CAWIU's headquarters in the Workers Center and School in Sacramento and arrested Pat Chambers, Caroline Decker, and another two dozen suspected radicals, charging one and all with criminal syndicalism.[58]

Eighteen were tried and eight were convicted on April 1, 1935, concluding the longest trial in the state's history. Among those convicted were Chambers and Decker, depriving the CAWIU of its two brightest and most effective leaders and rendering it all but helpless. They and the others were sentenced to five years in jail, though the eight verdicts would be reversed on appeal and the prisoners released two years later. The youthful Decker served her time in the women's facility in Tehachapi. By the time she was freed, her passion for communism had guttered out. "That's a long time for a young person," she remembered, and her reading while in prison had steered her away from the CP/USA. "I couldn't find the democracy" in the party's ideology, she said, and while she remained a constitutional liberal the rest of her life, "I was persona non grata to both sides, the left and the right, but that suited me just fine."[59]

58. McWilliams, *Factories in the Field*, p. 228.
59. "Caroline Decker Gladstein" interview.

Even if she had wanted to return to the CAWIU in 1937, there would have been nowhere for her to go. By then, the union, the migrant worker's first best hope of release from the net of economic oppression, was as moribund as Decker's love of the party, a casualty of its own national leadership's neglect, together with anti-Communist delirium, corporate greed, a virulent despotism, undisguised racism, and a federal government that would not be moved to action until some of its own kind found themselves trapped in the same merciless web. Those who made up this newest wave of California's migrant labor force were, most of them, United States citizens born and bred, but if their credentials were as impeccably American as those of any self-styled patriot willing to swing a pick handle for the Associated Farmers, the circumstances of their migration made them the spiritual kin of all those who had come before them. "These people are not handpicked failures," economist Paul Taylor wrote at the end of the decade. "They are the human materials cruelly dislocated by the processes of human erosion. They have been scattered like the shavings from a clean-cutting plane, or like the dust of their farms, literally blown out. And they trek west, these American whites, at the end of a long line of immigrant Chinese, Japanese, Koreans, Negroes, Hindustanis, Mexicans, Filipinos, to serve the crops and farmers."[60] Most of these migrants were driven by their own kind of desperation to trade the known for the unknown, negotiating an uneasy bargain with hope as the dreams they left behind them lay ravaged—not only by the vagaries of the national economy but by what is still considered the most devastating ecological disaster in American history.

60. Paul Schuster Taylor and Dorothea Lange, *American Exodus: A Study in Human Erosion*, p. 148.

17

◆

An Evil in the Season

The great drought that had put the people of the lower Mississippi River Valley dead up against it in 1930, sorely testing Herbert Hoover's faith in self-reliance and sending sharecroppers swarming into England, Arkansas, to demand food at gunpoint, had not ended; it had merely shifted. By the spring of 1931, it was the upper Midwest that began to suffer, and over the next three years the misery spread south and west into every state between the Front Range of the Rockies and the Ohio and Mississippi River valleys. There was a brief respite for some states in 1932, but between June of 1933 and May of 1934, the plains states experienced the lowest rainfall on record, while from the Flathead Range in Montana to the San Juans in southern Colorado, winter snowfall in the Rockies ranged from one-third to one-half of normal—and in New Mexico the Sangre de Cristos received little more than a dusting.

With drought came heat, more heat than millions had ever experienced even in the plains, where the most ordinary summer could be a torment. Temperatures in the summer of 1934 were high enough to peel the varnish off the furniture, according to regional lore. In Vinita, Oklahoma, in the northeastern corner of the state, thermometers registered 117 degrees Fahrenheit on July 24, the highest temperature in more than twenty years and the thirty-sixth day in a row that it had been above 100 degrees. Omaha, Nebraska, hit 107 that same day; Independence, Kansas, 112; St. Louis, Missouri, 110.2 (the highest since 1871).[1] In Grafton, North Dakota, two drugstore counter waitresses emulated folklore when they cooked a cheese sandwich by grilling it on the sidewalk outside the store.[2] The urban death toll from heatstroke and related traumas rose to an estimated 700 people, 37 in Chicago alone.[3]

Rivers grew thin and brackish; some creeks vanished entirely. Lakes, ponds, and reservoirs shrank, the receding waters painting dead white smears of sediment on their shores like rings in a bathtub. City water supplies became so loaded with concentrated salts and other chemical spices that many were left unpotable; Fort Smith, Arkansas, for example, was spending about $2,000 a day on bottled water by August. "Water hasn't been drinkable for a month," a visiting reporter was told. "Makes you sick to wash your teeth in it."[4] Freshwater marshes were dessicated. Grasslands were so dry they rattled in the wind. Fish, frogs, toads, and salamanders died by the millions, while whole populations of resident and migratory bird species and other wild creatures plummeted. Paradoxically, in the northern plains the heat and dryness hatched billions of grasshoppers, which emerged from their underground sites like a biblical scourge, clouds of insects darkening the sky and eating everything from corn on the stalk to garments hung on clotheslines. Gasoline stations did a good business in grasshopper screens designed to keep the insects from clogging automobile radiators with their bodies. Locomotive wheels spun crazily on rails gone greasy with grasshopper carcasses. At one point, the air was so thick with grasshoppers in Mott, North Dakota, that the town had to turn on its

1. Figures from the *New York Times*, July 25, 1934.
2. Story is told in Catherine McNicol Stock, *Main Street in Crisis*, p. 23.
3. Figures from the *New York Times*, July 25, 1934.
4. Quoted in Charles Morrow Wilson, "Saga of Drought," *The Commonweal* (September 14, 1934).

streetlights and create bonfires on the corners, while over in Killdeer insects crackled and slithered four inches deep in the streets.[5]

Everywhere in the agricultural checkerboard of the heartland, crops not already eaten by grasshoppers shriveled under the withering blight of the sun, and livestock grew skeletal and frantic with thirst and hunger, in some places "dropping dead in their tracks from the heat."[6] Journalist Meridel LeSueur took an exploratory bus trip across Minnesota and into North Dakota, "trying not to look at the ribs of the horses and the cows, but you got so you couldn't see anything but ribs, like beached hulks on the prairie, the bones rising out of the skin. You began to see the thin farmer under his rags and his wife as lean as his cows." Everyone on the bus, she remembered, "talked about horses, cattle, seed, land, death, hunger," while the vehicle rattled through the paper-dry landscape and people pointed out the windows at land now owned by insurance companies "and we saw it splitting open like rotting fruit after years of decay and erosion, exposing the gashed core."[7]

From eastern Wyoming, Lorena Hickok reported to Harry Hopkins on September 9, 1934: "I saw range that looked as though it had been gone over with a safety razor."[8] In Utah, the water level in many irrigation ditches fell from ten inches to an inch and a half, and in the summer ranges of the mountains, one cattle rancher claimed, forage was "as scarce as the stubble on an old man's chin."[9] In oil-rich states like Texas, Oklahoma, and Wyoming a new drilling frenzy erupted—but this time derricks were built and tempered steel bits were sent corkscrewing hundreds of feet into the earth's crust to tap into dwindling aquifers, not pools of oil.[10]

There was an "evil in this season," wrote James Agee in *Fortune*, the words accompanying a numbingly effective portfolio of drought photographs by Margaret Bourke-White. It was a time, he wrote, when

5. For Mott and Killdeer, see Stock, op. cit., pp. 21–22.
6. Quoted in ibid.
7. LeSueur, *North Star Country*, pp. 261–62.
8. In Lowitt and Beasley, eds., op. cit., p. 334.
9. Quoted in Leonard J. Arrington, "Utah's Great Drought of 1934," *Utah Historical Quarterly* (Summer 1986).
10. See the *New York Times*, July 25, 1934.

much of the northern hemisphere was "little better than a turning hearth, glowing before the white continuous blast of the sun."[11] Farm families looked to the sky every day, taking the measure of each distant towering cloud to see what it might promise of hope—until for some even hope became an anguish. "The heat was like a hand on the face all day and night," Josephine Johnson wrote in her autobiographical novel of 1934, *Now in November*. "When everything was finally dead, I thought that relief from hope would come, but hope's an obsession that never dies."[12]

Then there was the wind, as much a part of the geography of the plains as the buffalo grass through which it rippled. In a good season, the wind provided its own measure of beauty. Wallace Stegner remembered it as "grassy, clean, exciting," with "the smell of distance in it. . . . In collaboration with the light, it makes lovely and changeful what might otherwise be characterless."[13] In a drought, the wind became instead an enemy collaborating with sun and heat to annihilate loveliness and test the limits of human patience. "A high wind is an awful thing," Meridel LeSueur wrote in describing what she experienced in 1934; "it wears you down, it nags at you day after day, it sounds like an invisible army, it fills you with terror as something invisible does."[14]

It was not just the wind itself that scraped at the nerves in this evil season, but the burden it carried, the direct consequence of generations of disregard for what the land could and could not be expected to do. It

11. "The Drought: A Post-Mortem in Pictures," *Fortune* (October 1934). Agee would later join with photographer Walker Evans to produce *Let Us Now Praise Famous Men*, a text-and-photograph survey of tenant farmers that would become as enduring a document of the depression years as John Steinbeck's story of Dust Bowl refugees, *The Grapes of Wrath* (1939)—though, like Steinbeck's novel, it appeared too late to do the subjects themselves much good. It might have been otherwise. *Let Us Now Praise Famous Men* was originally conceived in 1936 as a *Fortune* magazine project, but after Bourke-White and novelist Erskine Caldwell produced their own well-received study of tenant farmers, *You Have Seen Their Faces* (1937), *Fortune* let the Agee-Evans assignment slide, and they ended up converting the material into a book that was not published until 1941.

12. Josephine Johnson, *Now in November*, pp. 143–44.

13. Wallace Stegner, *Wolf Willow: A History, a Story, and a Memory of the Last Plains Frontier*, p. 7.

14. LeSueur, op. cit., p. 265.

was a lesson that should have been learned long before, of course, as far back as 1864, when, in *Man and Nature*, George Perkins Marsh had cited the nations of antiquity to demonstrate how entire empires could disintegrate once their land had been abused beyond redemption. In this country, Marsh's warnings had been validated during the ecologically ruinous 1880s. Out on the High Plains, millions of cattle, half-starved because the western range had been packed with animals and brutally overgrazed for years, perished during the winter of 1886–87 in what was called the "Big Die-Up"; when the spring winds swept the land clean of snow, carcasses dotted a landscape that Theodore Roosevelt, anticipating Lorena Hickok, described as "a mere barren waste; not a green thing could be seen; the dead grass eaten off till the country looked as if it had been shaved by a razor."[15] The lesson was driven home again when heavy rains repeatedly spilled off the timber-stripped slopes of the Appalachians, lifted rivers out of their banks, and put the streets of Pittsburgh and other eastern cities under several feet of water that same decade—and, in 1889, blew away a dam and destroyed the city of Johnstown, Pennsylvania, killing 2,295 people.

Some heed had been taken. Under Gifford Pinchot and other leaders of the Progressive Movement (including Theodore Roosevelt himself), 148 million acres of uncut forests in the West were placed under the management of the U.S. Forest Service in the five years that followed the agency's creation in 1905, while in 1911 the government began a purchase program that would put several million acres of abused eastern forests under the same protective mantle. In the western forests, both logging and grazing were monitored and controlled, at least when compared to the cut-and-run traditions of the past, but not as much could be said for the millions of acres of unforested land on the Great Plains that still lay open to livestock use and intensive agriculture, even in areas where the land had not fully recovered from the abuses of the 1880s. It was on these plains that much of the agricultural boom of the war years and the twenties had been played out, and by the thirties much of the land had been broken and exposed by repeated plowing, leached of its nutrients by constant planting and replanting, grazed down to the dirt by cattle and sheep, its topsoil skinned off in sheets or

15. Quoted in Edmund Morris, *The Rise of Theodore Roosevelt*, p. 372.

gullied by water erosion during wet years. And it was on these lands that the sun had been doing some of its most devastating work during the drought years.

So now the wind: It came down on all that exposed and crippled land, scooped up hundreds of millions of tons of it as dust, then boiled it all up into choking clouds that rolled across entire states and at least twice—in May 1934 and March 1935—sailed so high into the jet stream that airborne earth from the Great Plains darkened eastern cities in the daytime and dusted the decks of transatlantic liners. Newspaper cartoonist J. N. "Ding" Darling, an avid conservationist who had just been named head of the U.S. Biological Survey, was in Manhattan during the 1934 storm, which carried an estimated 350 million tons of soil and spread it like a gritty fog as far south as Savannah and as far north as Buffalo. "The sun," he remembered, "was not visible through its murky depths. The lights in the office buildings and on the streets were turned on and gave the appearance of twilight." An archaeologist who was with him marveled that "in America it should take just one generation to reduce its prolific nature to a condition like the Gobi Desert, which was a million years in the making."[16]

However dramatic, the jet-stream storms of 1934 and 1935 gave the East the barest taste of what had become a commonplace misery in the plains states—though as the decade wore on, the most severe storms occurred more frequently on the southern plains. Especially during the spring of 1935, a season long remembered. On March 15, after portions of Texas, Oklahoma, and Kansas already had experienced two weeks of intermittent dust storms, a big one swept down from southeastern Colorado and for the next several days shut much of Kansas down in a gloom of dust. That storm had no sooner abated when another piled across the southern plains from Oklahoma on March 24, this one destroying half the wheat crop in Kansas before sweeping up into Nebraska and killing virtually all that state's wheat. Then came the sudden "black blizzard" of April 14, which concentrated most of its terrific energy in Kansas, stranding hundreds of travelers, burying and killing one child, and lasting so long that its gale-force winds (in some storms they

16. Both quotes in Richard Lowitt, *The New Deal and the West*, pp. 34–35.

reached sixty or seventy miles an hour) and light-obliterating dust inspired apocalyptic terror among many, particularly when they were accompanied by a drop in temperature of nearly fifty degrees in a matter of hours. "This is ultimate darkness," one victim wrote in a daily log. "So must come the end of the world."[17]

It may not have been the end of the world, but for thousands of people from Texas to North Dakota—a region a newspaperman was reputed to have been the first to call the "Dust Bowl"—the assault of a succession of filthy storms "roiling in . . . the sunlight turning smoky, shadows gone, distance vanishing, the sky blown out," must have seemed at least the end of a world that could be endured, certainly for women who prided themselves on the comfort and cleanliness of homes they had made in a land hard to civilize under the best of circumstances.[18] Fighting the dust was virtually impossible, so finely was it ground and so powerful were the winds that drove it. "Wearing our shade hats, with handkerchiefs tied over our faces and Vaseline in our nostrils," farm wife Caroline Henderson wrote during some of Oklahoma's worst storms, "we have been trying to rescue our home from the accumulations of wind-blown dust which penetrates wherever air can go. It is an almost hopeless task."[19] Windows and doors were plugged with wet rags or hung with layers of wet blankets. Still, the dust seeped in, filling the air like steam, covering everything in sight, from tabletops to bedspreads. A house too tightly closed for too long also lost oxygen, and when the point of suffocation was reached, a window somewhere had to be opened, letting in even more dust. After a storm had passed, it took hours, sometimes days, to rid the house of dust, and then would come another storm, more filth to pile on the floors and furniture, mix with condensation and seep down the walls in long black smears, clog the hair, turn to grit on the teeth: "the snow-not-snow on the window sills and the clouds of it coughing up out of the upholstered chairs and dribbling down the walls like meal on a bin side so that a

17. Quoted in Donald Worster, *The Dust Bowl*, p. 17. Much of my discussion of the character, origin, and extent of dust storms is from this source; see pp. 12–25.
18. Quote in "The Grasslands," *Fortune* (November 1935).
19. Caroline Henderson, "Letters from the Dust Bowl," *The Atlantic Monthly* (May 1936).

woman would go crazy cleaning her house three times in a single day and still the shoe tracks on the floor."[20]

Meals were particularly difficult. Women learned to put up water and milk in tightly sealed Mason jars at the first sign of a storm so that the liquids would not become an undrinkable sludge. When the time came to use the jars, holes were punched in the tops and the drinks were sucked up through straws. Bread could be kneaded in a dresser drawer covered with a cloth into which two holes had been cut so the bread-maker's hands could do the work. Everything that could be baked, was baked, the closed oven door providing some measure of protection. Pan-fried meat was cooked on as high a heat as possible, so the air rising above it would lift the dust away. Everything was eaten the instant it left the stove in the few precious moments before grime covered it. Even so, dust was ingested like a condiment with every meal.

Sometimes, however determined and ingenious a woman might be, despair overwhelmed her, as it did one who found herself alone when she heard the wind begin a "low sighing moan through the cottonwood trees."

> My heart seemed to leap into my throat; I felt sick and weak. . . . I went back into the house, hastily covered the table with newspapers and an old cloth, covered the water pail, covered all the unwashed cooking utensils, made my bed and spread an old denim comfort over it. . . . Next I put on an old stocking cap to protect my hair, an old jacket to comfort my shaking body, and sat down by the kitchen range with my feet on the oven door.
>
> The room soon filled with a dust haze through which the coal-oil lamp made a pale light, and for the first and only time during the dust storms I abandoned myself to an orgy of weeping.[21]

An epidemic of what local folks called "dust pneumonia" broke out across the plains, and while medical people were divided on the question of whether the dust storms had actually caused a new form of pneumonia, the annual death rate among those with asthma, tuberculosis, or

20. Quote in "The Grasslands."
21. Quoted in Stanley Vestal, *Short Grass Country*, pp. 198–99.

bronchitis rose to 99 per 100,000 people in western Kansas, compared to an average of 70 per 100,000 for the entire state—and 80.5 infants per 100,000 died in the same region, almost eighteen more than the state average—while doctors warned of airborne silicosis, "probably the most widespread and insidious of all hazards in the environment of all mankind."[22]

Farm animals suffered terribly. Horses and mules could be protected somewhat by masking their eyes and muzzling them with feed bags or gunny sacks, but even then the dust could drive them frantic. Half-wild range cattle could not be protected at all. The rims of their eyes filled with dust; the dust mixed with tears to form mud; the mud cemented their eyelids closed and they were blinded, letting the wind and dust herd them in darkness until they piled up in fence corners or gullies, much as they had done during the killing blizzards of the "Big Die-Up" in the 1880s. They died now, too, from thirst and exhaustion and injury, but also from the dust itself. It clogged their nostrils and their throats, and when it did not kill them directly from suffocation, it made it impossible for them to eat, even when something could be found to eat. Hogs also starved; their swill thickened like fresh cement and the animals could not get it down. Chickens smothered in their henhouses.

It was a time for horror stories, like that of the Kansas child whose body was found tangled in barbed wire, or that remembered by Montana rancher Philip Long, who was on the road in his automobile when a storm forced him to slow to a crawl. The wind was tremendous, the air as full of flying thistles as it was of dirt, and even with his windows rolled up the interior of the car was so full of dust that he could hardly breathe. When he spotted the headlights of another vehicle through the murk, he slowed even more, then stopped when he realized that the other car was not moving. It seemed empty, but he got out of his car and staggered over to be sure. The vehicle was an old touring car whose windshield had long since vanished, leaving its front open to the wind. Huddled down on the front seat were a man and woman, with several children on the floor in back. "Leaning against the face-cutting wind," Long recalled, "I looked closer and gasped in amazement for those faces

22. Figures and quote in Worster, op. cit., p. 21.

looked like porcupines. Their faces were driven so full of briars from the whistling thistles that they all, even the little ones, looked like they had a week's growth of whiskers. How they must have suffered before they were forced to stop."[23]

Such stories became part of each family's collective memory—as did the jokes with which the toughest of them tried to counter disaster. A farmer sitting on his porch in Nebraska in the middle of a dust storm was asked what he was doing, one story went. "I'm counting the Kansas farms as they go by," he answered. In another, a Texas farmer said he was on his way to Kansas to pay his taxes because that was where his farm had gone. A man insisted that he had shot ground squirrels as they burrowed their way up through the air. You could tell that a "duster" was imminent, some claimed, by the sound of sneezing rattlesnakes. One motorist was said to have stopped when he spotted a man in the road. The man was buried upright in dust, with only his head and his ten-gallon hat showing, but when asked if he would like a ride into town, the buried stranger answered that he didn't need one; he was on a horse. In the middle of her photographic assignment for *Fortune* magazine, during which occasion she had spent a good deal of time traveling by air, Margaret Bourke-White was told of a pilot who had been forced to parachute out of his plane in the middle of a storm; it had taken him six hours to shovel his way to the ground.

"Hello there, Bill," one Oklahoman said to another. "What do you know for certain?"

"Nothin'."

"Well, I know it's windy and dusty. It's got so we get a half a day between the Spring Dust Storm and the Summer Dust Storm, and then we get a day and half between the Summer Dusts and the Fall Dusts."

"When better dust storms are made," the editor of the *Dodge City Globe* wrote, "the Southwest will make them."[24]

23. Philip S. Long, *Dreams, Dust, and Depression*, p. 33.
24. Quoted in Worster, op. cit., p. 24. The Margaret Bourke-White story is told by Vicki Goldberg in *Margaret Bourke-White*, p. 156. The "conversation" between Oklahomans is from Lange and Taylor, op. cit., p. 103. The rest of the Dust Bowl jokes are taken from a variety of sources, especially Vestal, op. cit.

. . .

JOKES WERE GOOD therapy, perhaps, but even the most rambunctious humor could not obscure what drought, heat, and dust had brought to the economy of the Great Plains. "By the middle of last August," the October 1934 issue of *Fortune* declared, "a good third of our part of the continent was one wide crisp. The great map in the Washington office of Relief Administrator Harry Hopkins showed 1,400 counties in twenty-two states, of which 1,100 were counted as harmed beyond all help. . . . Some 5,300,000 people—about 17 percent of our farming population—and their properties and their crops and their livestock and their lean wallets were . . . at the mercy of the sun, the dry wind, the blown dust, the handsome rainless clouds."[25]

There were no farmland riots now. Nature had a way of wearing down the most stubborn Populist. On a visit to North Dakota in October 1933, Lorena Hickok was told in Bismarck that she still would find a good deal of unrest in the countryside. "I can't say that I did," she reported to Harry Hopkins. "They seemed almost too patient to me. I went to see one farmer who was supposed to be a chronic kicker. I found him doing the family washing! His wife died five years ago and left him with eight children. . . . With an expression of utter hopelessness on his face he was puttering around the old washing machine. The rolls on the wringer were entirely worn away—right down to the iron bars."[26] Instead of riots, there now were long lines at federal relief offices in town or temporarily set up in lonely one-room schoolhouses or drafty roadside churches, where farmers and ranchers had learned to swallow their pride, endure the dull humiliation of the investigators' prying questions, and, like their urban counterparts, accept what the government could give them to keep their families going. In October 1933, nine out of every one hundred rural families were receiving the $10 to $18 a month available through FERA payments; by October 1934 the number had risen to 13.7, and by February 1935 to 15.2. In the "cut-over" regions of Michigan and Wisconsin, nearly 40 percent of all rural

25. "The Drought," *Fortune* (October 1934).
26. Quoted in Lowitt and Beasley, eds., op. cit., p. 58.

families were on relief by February 1935, and in the "spring wheat" areas of the Dakotas more than 30 percent.[27] For most, the money was barely enough for survival. "If things don't change and get worse," a South Dakota farm wife wrote to the *Dakota Farmer* magazine in February 1935, "we plan to live on our small income of $1 a week, besides $3.60 which we receive from the relief every week. . . . If these plans don't work out, we won't need to make any more plans."[28]

"Seven cent cotton and forty cent meat," a bit of doggerel went, "How in the Hell can a poor man eat?"[29] Most farm families stuck it out in spite of being "burned out, blowed out, eat out," their diets reduced to "little or nothing, boiled down."[30] To leave voluntarily, Oklahoman Caroline Henderson thought, "to break all . . . ties for the sake of a possibly greater comfort elsewhere—seems like defaulting in our task. We may *have* to leave," she acknowledged. "But I think I can never go willingly or without pain that as yet seems unendurable."[31] Thousands more felt they had no choice but to endure the pain of leaving, some of them from foreclosed farms and ranches that had been in their families for generations, more from places on which they had sharecropped or lived as tenants—and it was not always drought, dust, and grasshoppers that drove them out. There was, for example, the tractor. By the end of 1934, there were more than a million gasoline-powered tractors on American farms, almost 100,000 of them purchased since 1930 and nearly 70 percent of them manufactured by International Harvester. It was no small thing to buy one of these beasts. The cost of an I-H Farmall-30, which the company said was the best model for a 320-acre "horseless" farm, was $1,025 in 1933 (almost one-fourth the cost of all equipment on an average mechanized farm of that size), but worth every penny in long-term savings to those who could afford it.[32] In a survey of 302 "representative" farms in the Southern Plains, for example, a gov-

27. Figures from A. R. Mangus, *Changing Aspects of Rural Relief*, p. 24.
28. Quoted in Dorothy Schweider, "South Dakota Farm Women and the Great Depression," *Journal of the West* (October 1985).
29. Quoted in Walter J. Stein, *California and the Dust Bowl Migration*, p. 10.
30. Sayings from Vestal, op. cit., p. 192.
31. Henderson, op. cit.
32. The $1,025 price tag would be the equivalent of nearly $13,000 in 1998 dollars. International Harvester information from "International Harvester," *Fortune* (August 1933).

ernment study determined in 1934 that while a single farmer using a horse or mule was cultivating an average of 211 acres of cropland, his tractor-equipped neighbor was able to work an average of 529 acres.[33] More than twice the cultivated land with no increase in labor cost was not a calculation hard to understand, and if an owner had a tractor or two, what did he need with tenants or sharecroppers?

Complicating the equation was the government's crop-reduction program under the AAA, which withdrew from cultivation an estimated 9.6 million acres of wheat land and 10.3 million acres of cotton land.[34] Owners who signed AAA agreements were not supposed to evict their tenants and sharecroppers, but many did, justifiably confident that little or nothing would be done (the "purge" in the Department of Agriculture in early 1935 was assurance enough of that). "I let 'em all go," one Oklahoma cotton farmer allowed. "In '34 I had I reckon four renters and I didn't make anything. I bought tractors on the money the government give me and got shet o' my renters. You'll find it everywhere all over the country thataway. I did everything the government said—except keep my renters. The renters have been having it this way ever since the government come in."[35] Which is not to say that the government went out of its way to admit any culpability here. *Migration of Workers*, a Labor Department report issued later in the decade, never did address the question directly, though in a footnote with regard to Oklahoma it revealed that "the breakdown of tenancy, as well as drought, may be responsible for part of the heavy migration from Oklahoma. . . . A large number of the interstate migrants appear to have come from the cotton-raising portion of the State which was least affected by the drought."[36]

No one knew then precisely how many people left the land by choice or compulsion (it was hardly in the interest of the AAA to keep careful statistics on the number of human beings its programs had helped to displace), and no one knows to this day. In the plains states,

33. "Acreage Operated by Specified Number of Men, With or Without Tractors, on Selected Farms in Representative Counties in the Southern Plains, 1934," in *Farming Hazards in the Drought Area*, p. 189.
34. Figures from Eisenhower, ed., op. cit., pp. 30–35.
35. Quoted in Lange and Taylor, op. cit., p. 80.
36. Quoted in Stein, op. cit., p. 13.

alone, however, as many as 3.5 million people may have left by 1940.[37] Exactly where they went is nearly as hard to track. Some merely drifted into the largest nearby town, joining with clots of the urban unemployed in Hoovervilles that had never quite gone away. Typical was an encampment of about 2,000 people that spread out next to the stockyards in Oklahoma City, where one rural refugee remembered his family living in a shack "made up of old automobiles, old lard cases, buckets, paste board, just anything that we could get to build one out of."[38] Tens of thousands moved from county to county, state to state, lost in a maze of searching. Paul Westmoreland, who in later life ended up as "Okie Paul," a popular disk jockey in Sacramento, California, remembered that his family had been "starved out" of Oklahoma even before the drought years and had kept on wandering all through the first half of the decade. To Shamrock, Texas, first, to pick cotton; then to Gallup, New Mexico; then from there to Coolidge, Arizona, living off jackrabbits—"Hoover Hogs," they called them—black-eyed peas, and some pork for side meat. In their old Model-T truck, "We made twenty-five miles an hour," he remembered, "maybe a hundred miles a day going down Route 66, and every other road too, looking for work. We went back to Oklahoma—every good Okie left more than once—and tried again and failed again. Did that more than once until finally we left for good, right down 66, splitting it wide open for six or seven days to Arizona. The wind was blowing, it was dry, the cotton wouldn't come up, everything went wrong."[39]

37. North Dakota lost more than 3 percent of its population between 1930 and 1940 (38,910 people), South Dakota nearly 7 percent (49,586), Nebraska 5 percent (62,179), Kansas 4 percent (79,971), and Oklahoma 2.5 percent (59,606). Vermont, which showed a drop of a mere 380 people, was the only other state to lose population in the 1930s. As Donald Worster notes in *Dust Bowl*, however, citing a 1941 U.S. House report, *Interstate Migration*, such raw population figures do not accurately reflect the actual movement of population: "In net loss through migration—outflow minus inflow—Oklahoma was the easy leader: 440,000, or 18.4 percent of its 1930 population," Worster writes. "The net loss in Kansas was 227,000. . . . Almost a million plains people left their farms in the first half of the decade, and 2.5 million left after 1935" (pp. 48–49).
38. Quote in James Gregory, *American Exodus: The Dust Bowl Migration and Okie Culture in California*, p. 15.
39. Quote in "Route 66: Ghost Road of the Okies," by Thomas W. Pew, Jr., *American Heritage* (August 1977).

"It didn't seem to matter where you were during those depression years," Lois Phillips Hudson remembered of her own family's experience in North Dakota. "After you'd been in one spot for a while, you decided things couldn't be quite so bad anywhere else, and so you moved." Other tens of thousands ultimately headed to the farthest West, often in January. "If a family was going to sell out," Hudson wrote, "it was that time of year that would make them decide. Christmas and New Year's over. Nothing to look forward to but snow till April. . . . A time of year when the Pacific Coast temperatures . . . seemed unbelievable. . . . My own family had gone from North Dakota to Seattle and back, and we were destined to go again to Seattle in another couple of years."[40] Between 1930 and 1940, the Pacific Northwest states received 115,000 migrants from the Northern Plains, and another 65,000 from the Southern Plains. "Drive out on any of the main highways of our state," Senator William Borah of Idaho remarked, "and you will see cars, sometimes almost caravans, fleeing from the devastations of the drought."[41]

But the state with the greatest appeal to the suddenly landless was California. There was nothing new in this. In the eighty-odd years since the discovery of gold, California had experienced several periods of spectacular growth, millions of people heading for the state in search of wealth, health, climate, opportunity. The most recent spurt had brought more than a million new people to the state in the twenties. Most of these had been from the East and Midwest, but nearly a quarter of a million had come from the states that would be the most badly hit during the years of drought, and when the hardest of the hard times came, word of what California might offer spread like a grass fire from west to east through networks of family and friends.[42] The California migration began in the early part of the decade, then blossomed into another major movement after the spring of 1935, when the big dust storms of that season were followed by another period of lethal drought that peaked to a particularly brutal level in 1936 and continued high through the rest of the decade.

40. Lois Phillips Hudson, *Reapers of the Dust: A Prairie Chronicle*, p. 95.
41. Quote in Richard L. Neuberger, *Our Promised Land*, p. 34.
42. For numbers, see Gregory, op. cit., p. 6.

Between June of 1935 and the end of the summer of 1936, more than 86,000 people from the drought states entered California, and another 120,000 would arrive by March of 1938.[43] Like the members of the Westmoreland family, most of them came out on U.S. Route 66, "the path of a people in flight," as novelist John Steinbeck described it in *The Grapes of Wrath*, "the mother road, the road of flight."[44] The images of caravans rattling down that dusty highway with everything the families owned roped or wired to their crotchety old flivvers and trucks, backseats and truckbeds full of wild, shy children, remain pinned in the national memory so firmly by two generations of folklore and popular history that even for some of those who witnessed the movement firsthand the images sometimes do not seem quite real. They were real, though, and so were the fears and hopes that drove people to make that hot, uncertain journey, often in pitiable ignorance. Ralph Richardson, who owned a small gas station and grocery store along the highway in Montoya, New Mexico, remembered that many had no idea they had a desert to cross. He put up a sign on a cholla (a species of cactus) on the side of the road: "CARRY WATER OR THIS IS WHAT YOU'LL LOOK LIKE." As many as fifty vehicles would camp around his store at night, many of the people reduced to begging for work or bartering to pay for gasoline or groceries to get them another hundred miles west. "They even offered to leave the dog, the cat, and the canary for gas," he recalled. "Frightened, those people were frightened, and they came through here thinking they were headed for the promised land where they'd say, 'Everything's going to be all right.' I warned them about those ideas, but they went on."[45]

Most of the refugees, many of whom came from urban areas in the first place and had at least a little money in their pockets, found places for themselves or joined already established family members in and around most of the cities of the state, providing another contingent to California's already polyglot demographics. Those who had no other

43. Figures from Worster, op. cit., p. 50; Paul Schuster Taylor and Tom Vasey, "Drought Refugees and Labor Migration to California, June–December, 1935," *Monthly Labor Review* (February 1936); and Paul Schuster Taylor, "Refugee Labor Migration to California, 1937," *Monthly Labor Review* (April 1939).
44. John Steinbeck, *The Grapes of Wrath*, p. 160.
45. Quote in Pew, op. cit.

choice—a minority, though a large one—ended up as part of the traditional stream of migratory laborers who followed California's crops from
field to field, season to season. Though most had come from Missouri,
Arkansas, Texas, Kansas, and Oklahoma, once they made it to California, they usually were lumped together simply as "Okies." It was not
a term of endearment. California was still a state in which only a minority could claim membership in an outfit that called itself the Native
Sons of the Golden West and in which annual "Iowa Picnics" brought
thousands of transplanted midwesterners to Long Beach every year to
memorialize the great migration of the 1920s. But that fact did not
diminish the resentment and fear many residents—however recent
themselves—felt when this newest influx of out-of-staters spilled across
the border. Many counties and cities worried that their welfare programs would be overwhelmed, though most required at least a full year
of residence before anyone could apply for aid.

No municipality worried as much as Los Angeles. Early in 1935,
the city put together a Committee on Indigent Alien Transients, such
transients being conveniently defined as those "entering the state of
California without visible means of support and whose legal residence is
foreign to the state of California."[46] On February 3, the committee
raised no objections when Los Angeles Police Chief James Davis sent
126 Los Angeles policemen to the state's sixteen most important entry
points, where for more than two months they stopped every vehicle,
including buses, and turned back anyone who did not have proof of
money or employment.

National ridicule, coupled with a suit filed by the American Civil
Liberties Union and a decision by California's attorney general, who
declared the action unconstitutional, soon put an end to the chief's
"Foreign Legion" blockade. But if the "Okies" could not legally be
turned back at the border, there was nothing to keep them from being
vilified once they got into the state, and many residents—particularly
those in the agricultural areas—heaped contempt upon the outsiders in
the time-honored fashion of most human societies, so much so that
Okies often competed with Mexican Americans as favorite targets of
bigotry. The migrants were "shiftless trash who live like hogs," one

46. Quoted in Starr, op. cit., p. 176.

doctor in Visalia commented, while another was a little kinder when he said, "There is nothing especially wicked about them—it's just the way they live. There is such a thing as a breed of people. These people have lived separate for too long, and they are like a different race." They were, a schoolteacher said, "Adult Children."[47]

Scorned or not, most of those who straggled into California and the other far western states in the thirties were there to stay.

"I want to go back to where we can live happy, live decent, and grow what we eat," an Oklahoma refugee mother of eleven told Paul S. Taylor.

But they would not be returning to Oklahoma, her husband reminded her. "I've made my mistake, and now we can't go back. I've got nothing to farm with."[48]

THE OKLAHOMA REFUGEE would find nothing to farm with in California, either. What he did find, what tens of thousands like him found as they rattled down the Grapevine into the San Joaquin Valley or made their way into the desert blast of the Imperial Valley, was the same agricultural oligarchy that had done its best to maintain Mexican-American migrant workers at the level of seventeenth-century peons— but an oligarchy that welcomed the Oklahoman's presence even as most of the valley's residents held him in contempt. By the middle of the 1930s, with the Cannery and Agricultural Industrial Workers Union all but obliterated by state action in 1934 and 1935, many Mexican-American workers had opted to stay on relief during the harvest season rather than accept picking rates below what they believed decent. This could have presented the growers with a major dilemma: in order to get sufficient labor to harvest their crops—particularly on the 600,000 acres of cotton land enjoying bumper-crop production after the great strike of 1933—they might have had to increase wages to attractive levels. The new migrants rescued them from this odious recourse. Thousands of these people had not had work of any kind for years, and state and county welfare laws would keep them off the relief rolls for at

47. Quoted in Gregory, op. cit., pp. 100–101.
48. Quoted in Lange and Taylor, op. cit., p. 128.

least a year after their arrival. They would take anything they could get, and did. As the San Joaquin Valley Agriculture Labor Bureau put it, "the labor that came voluntarily from the drought area came at the opportune time."[49]

Not for the continued good health of agricultural unionism. There was not much left of the CAWIU by 1936 to begin with, and the newcomers merely added to the union's woes. While many had Populist instincts (they would give the state's certifiably weird "Ham-and-Eggs" movement at the end of the decade much of its political strength), they were not leftists, these people.[50] Most were fundamentalist Christians, self-consciously patriotic, conservative, and self-described "just plain folks" who had neither experience nor interest in unions. "Those people . . . didn't like unions," relief worker Helen Hosmer remembered. "They would squat on their knees and sift the dirt in their hands and say, 'All we want is a little bit of this land; that's all we ask is a little bit of this. A little bit of this good dirt.'"[51] They had demonstrated little or no interest in the socialistic Southern Tenant Farmers' Union back east even when they had heard of it and were not much inclined to get involved with the openly (indeed proudly) communistic CAWIU. "I ain't no Communist," one of them declared firmly. "I hold the American flag's just as good here and now as when Betsy Ross finished her stitchin' and handed it over to George Washington. What's good over in Russia don't mean it's good for us."[52] Finally, the presence of Chicanos at all levels of the CAWIU did not make it any more attractive to a people who embraced most of the

49. Quoted in Stein, op. cit., p. 40.
50. Promoted by Los Angeles advertising men Willis and Lawrence Allen, the movement proposed the creation of a special state bank with its own currency to be paid to pension-age Californians at the rate of "$30 Every Thursday." "Ham-and-Eggs!" was the cry raised to begin and end meetings of the movement's many groups (some compared it to the "Sieg Heil!" of Nazi Germany). The Allens managed to get the proposal on the California ballot in both 1938 and 1939, and in both elections it was only narrowly defeated. Wartime prosperity ultimately killed the movement. (See Winston and Marian Moore, *Out of the Frying Pan.*)
51. Randall Jarrell, oral history interview: "Helen Hosmer: Radical Critic of California Agribusiness in the 1930s," Regional Oral History Office, University of California at Santa Cruz.
52. Quoted in Gregory, op. cit., p. 154.

prejudices common to the rest of white America. While a handful did join the CAWIU and, after 1937, the United Cannery, Agricultural, Packing and Allied Workers of America, there were not many refugees from the beleaguered heartland of America visible in the few strikes— most of them swiftly put down—that erupted in California's fields for the rest of the decade.

There was one exception that tested the rule: the Salinas lettuce strike of 1936. While the AFL had studiously ignored most California migrant labor, it had authorized the creation of the Fruit and Vegetable Workers Union. The union was dominated by white workers, who far outnumbered Mexicans and Filipinos in the packing trades, and a substantial number of the new arrivals therefore found it acceptable. So it was that on August 28, when Salinas lettuce growers broke off negotiations with the union and ordered a lockout—the union countering by declaring a strike—it was the first time since the IWW-led "riots" of 1913 in the hop fields of Wheatland that Anglo-Americans had faced off against Anglo-Americans in a major conflict in California's bloody fields.

The Associated Farmers of California, which had helped the local growers to plan the lockout, was at the height of its power by 1936. It turned its full arsenal on the union, aiding in the organization of a coalition that included the Grower-Shipper Vegetables Association; Colonel Henry Sanborn of the U.S. Army Reserve (though he acted surreptitiously, setting up a secret headquarters in a Salinas hotel room); Chief E. Raymond Cato, head of the California Highway Patrol (acting not at all surreptitiously); the Citizens Association of Salinas; the county sheriff's office; and city and county officials. On September 16, when pickets attempted to block the movement of trucks loaded with lettuce picked by scabs (most of them recently arrived Anglo migrants), they were gassed and beaten by police and routed. That night, a thousand-man *posse comitatus* was organized; armed with ax handles, it was sent out into the streets of the town on patrol. Fields and packing sheds were armed camps; Salinas itself crawled with county sheriff's deputies, municipal and state police, and deputized vigilantes; and for weeks strikers watched helplessly while long caravans of lettuce-loaded trucks were accompanied out of town by phalanxes of highway patrol vehicles. The strike did not end until November 3, when the movement collapsed and men began drifting back to work.[53]

THE FRUIT AND VEGETABLE WORKERS UNION had been beaten as badly as any union in California ever had been. But the victory came at a cost in public relations that the Associated Farmers and the rest of the California agricultural machine had not previously suffered. The Salinas strikers were not Communist-led Chicanos of questionable citizenship whose plight could be safely ignored; the vast majority of men and women being gassed and beaten in Salinas were white and native-born, and what was done to them became a matter of headlines, no matter how hard the Associated Farmers tried to portray the entire strike as one more act of traitorous Communist subversion. Paul Smith, the *San Francisco Chronicle's* executive editor, for one, had flown his own plane down to investigate the situation during the second week of the strike. "Tension permeated every corner of the community," he would write in a series of articles entitled, "It Did Happen in Salinas" (a title suggested by Sinclair Lewis's antifascist novel, *It Can't Happen Here*). He found armed deputies and other questionable types infesting the town everywhere he looked. His dismay did not diminish when one of his own reporters was beaten by thugs and warned that any *Chronicle* newsman they found could expect the same. Smith flew the injured reporter to a hospital, then returned, managing to escape a beating and file his stories. "For a full fortnight," he wrote, "the 'constituted authorities' of Salinas have been but the helpless pawns of sinister fascist forces which have operated from a barricaded hotel floor in the center of town."[54] Protest meetings and broadsides throughout the state deplored the actions of the authorities, while the American Civil Liberties Union urged the U.S. attorney general to look into Colonel Sanborn's clearly illegal participation, and Gary Cooper, Humphrey Bogart, James Cagney, and other stars expressed anger and sent money.

53. For a good account of the Salinas lettuce strike of 1936, see Starr, op. cit., pp. 179–88.
54. Quoted in ibid., pp. 187–88.

The Mexican and Filipino strikers of the previous three years had enjoyed no such statewide upwelling of concern. But by 1936, America's non-Mexican migrant population was becoming a New Deal metaphor. The anguish of the drought, dust, and displacement years did not go unremarked in Washington, D.C., and the New Dealers would make certifiably valiant attempts to relieve suffering and mend the ravages of time, nature, and human stupidity (some of the stupidity their own, of course, as in the unanticipated—and never properly acknowledged—effects of the AAA crop-reduction program). Most of them never seriously questioned their belief that the ingenuity of human enterprise could mend the most difficult human problems— even if they had to take on the natural forces of the earth itself. "I have been so moved by the distressing effects of a widespread drouth," the president remarked in a speech delivered while on a cross-country train tour in August 1934, "and at the same time so strengthened in my belief that science and cooperation can do much from now on to undo the mistakes that men have made in the past and to aid the good forces of nature and the good impulses of men instead of fighting against them."[55]

Generally speaking, it would prove more difficult to invoke the spirit of cooperation and build on the good impulses of human beings—whom the New Dealers would find (then, as always) maddeningly unpredictable and not easily squeezed into sociopolitical molds— than it would be to harness the tools of science to aid the good forces of nature. But, everlasting believers in the progressive impulse, the New Dealers would try both, with predictably mixed results. In a largely successful attempt to stem wind erosion on the Great Plains, a Prairie States Forestry Project—commonly known as the Shelterbelt Program—would spend $14 million and employ thousands of CCC workers to plant 220 million trees in a hundred-mile-wide "shelterbelt" through North Dakota, South Dakota, Nebraska, Kansas, Oklahoma, and Texas from the Canadian border to the Texas Panhandle.[56] Early in 1933, the Interior Department established the Soil Erosion Service, and by the summer of 1934 it had forty erosion control demonstration proj-

55. Quoted in Davis, op. cit., p. 396.
56. See Allan J. Soffar, "The Forest Shelterbelt Project," *Journal of the West* (July 1975).

ects on some four million acres divided among thirty-one states; later moved to the Department of Agriculture and renamed the Soil Conservation Service, the program would go on to rescue millions of acres of ruined farmland—though without making any real attempt to control production on those lands, leaving millions of acres vulnerable to the same frenzy of overproduction and consequent "soil mining" that had helped to produce the Dust Bowl in the first place.[57]

If the nation's farmland was in trouble, so was its grazing land. More than half the public grasslands of the West were overgrazed and eroded by the end of 1933, capable of carrying fewer than 11 million out of the 22.5 million cattle and sheep they might have supported.[58] Further, it was becoming clear that the rapidly spreading drought was going to inflict terrible losses on cattle from the Mississippi River Valley to the Rocky Mountains and as far west as Arizona. There was, the AAA estimated, a surplus of anywhere from eight to ten million head of cattle alone, and by December 1933 the industry, long antagonistic to any sort of federal "interference," was ready to adjust its position.[59] "Traditionally independent though he be, whether he likes it or not," warned F. E. Mollin, secretary of the American National Livestock Association, "the cattleman today is very much in the 'new deal,' entirely unable to cope single-handedly with forces."[60]

What the cattlemen wanted, and what the government ultimately gave them in the Jones-Connally Farm Relief Act of 1934 (which included an appropriation of $200 million in drought relief money), was not an orchestrated animal-reduction effort like that of the corn-hog program in the Midwest, but a simple purchase program that would reduce the number of existing animals without interfering with any cattleman's desire to keep his cows popping out more calves. Unlike the dismal fate of "piggy sows" in the AAA's corn-hog program, no

57. For a good discussion of the Soil Conservation Service's weaknesses, see Donald Worster, *The Wealth of Nature: Environmental History and the Ecological Imagination*, pp. 71–83.
58. See Joe A. Stout, "Cattlemen, Conservationists, and the Taylor Grazing Act," *New Mexico Historical Review* (December 1970).
59. For numbers, see Roger C. Lambert, "Drought Relief for Cattlemen: The Emergency Purchase Program of 1934–1935," *Panhandle-Plains Historical Review* (1972).
60. Quoted in ibid.

pregnant bovine mothers would be murdered, and while cattlemen agreed to the creation of a "Committee of Twenty-Five" to control future production, true oversight would prove impossible. One Department of Agriculture wag (there weren't many) did, however, send a memorandum to Henry Wallace suggesting that one way to get the ranchers to curtail production might be to "allow the bulls and cows to run together, but put roller skates on the hind feet of all the bulls."[61] Nevertheless, nearly 600,000 cattle were being shot or shipped every week within a few months. Goats and sheep were added to the list, and before long thousands of those animals also became government issue. Before shutting the program down entirely at the end of January 1935, when even the cattle industry had to admit that it was no longer needed, the government bought nearly nine million cattle—so many, that market prices were on the rise, soon surpassing the twenty-dollar maximum per head provided by the AAA.

The cattle-purchase program—even though it reduced the number of grazing animals significantly for a while—would have done little to help the land itself if the livestock industry had been left to return to the unchained habits of the past, as many conservation-minded folk feared it would do. Among them was Senator Edward J. Taylor of Colorado, who had come to the conclusion that saving the West's grasslands was a job "too big and interwoven for even the states to handle with satisfactory co-ordination. On the western slope of Colorado and in nearby states I saw waste, competition, over-use, and abuse of valuable range lands and watersheds eating into the very heart of western economy. . . . Erosion, yes, even human erosion, had taken root. The livestock industry . . . was headed for self-strangulation."[62]

Early in 1934, Taylor introduced legislation that called for 173 million acres of vacant and otherwise unappropriated public domain lands outside Alaska to be withdrawn from entry by any existing land laws (the various homestead acts, the General Mining Law of 1872, etc.). Eighty million acres of these lands were to be divided up into

<hr/>

61. Quoted in ibid. Most of my discussion of the cattle-purchase program is from this source.
62. Quoted in Louise Pfeiffer, *The Closing of the Public Domain*, p. 217. For more on the background of the act, see Lowitt, op. cit., pp. 64–71.

grazing districts that also would include national forest grazing lands. The livestock industry would be allowed to graze animals on these district lands, but for the first time would be required to pay for the privilege—five cents per cow per month. The program would be managed by a Division of Grazing in the Interior Department, and on the local level by district managers selected from the local population, with the aid and advice of local advisory boards consisting of seven cattlemen and seven sheep men appointed by the holders of grazing permits in the region, with a Division of Grazing employee appointed by the Interior Department.

As the bill came up for hearings, many livestock organizations weighed in against it. A. A. Jones, head of the Arizona Wool Growers Association, went so far as to testify that "there isn't any such thing in the Southwest as overgrazing," while Arizona Senator Henry F. Ashurst complained that "it ought, at least, to be the policy of Congress not to destroy a state. You gave birth to Arizona some years ago. Now you propose to break her limbs, crack her skull, and starve her to death."[63] Officials in the U.S. Forest Service also opposed the bill as written, fearing, among other things, that the permit system and the advisory boards would give the industry too much power. But opposition was not unanimous even in the livestock industry. Stockman Farrington Carpenter of northwest Colorado spoke for many others when he said the bill was the industry's "only chance against being completely wiped out of existence."[64] Moreover, the Taylor Grazing Act was the only measure likely to get through a Congress whose public land committees were occupied almost entirely by western congressmen and senators, most of whom were supported by the livestock industry, and it was a measure that Roosevelt wanted, however imperfect it might have been. On June 28, 1934, he signed it, and on November 24, he issued an executive order withdrawing the first 80 million acres (an additional withdrawal of 62 million acres would be made in December 1935), while Interior Secretary Harold L. Ickes appointed Farrington Carpenter head of the Division of Grazing, then went on the road to promote the new agency's

63. Both quotes in Joe A. Stout, "Cattlemen, Conservationists, and the Taylor Grazing Act," *New Mexico Historical Review* (October 1970).
64. Quoted in ibid.

virtues. "In more ways than one," he told an assembly of stockmen in Denver on February 12, 1935, "the Taylor Grazing Law is not merely a regulatory measure to upbuild and maintain the public range and to control its use in the interest of the stockmen of the nation. It is a Magna Charta upon which the prosperity, well-being, and happiness of large sections of this great western country of ours will in the future depend."[65]

Ickes believed it, and so it might have been in a perfect world. The Division of Grazing (commonly called the Grazing Service) did erect some useful guidelines for the future management of the public grazing lands that especially foresightful ranchers were happy to follow, and this redounded to the benefit of some land in some areas. But the Forest Service critics had been right to worry about the permit system. The grazing permits were regarded as property, and any attempts to revoke or reduce them were viewed as assaults on private property rights. Not that the managers of most grazing districts were inclined to do anything of the sort. They were local people who had to answer to their neighbors for their actions, and even if they disagreed with the advice offered by the industry-weighted boards looking over their shoulders, few were brave enough to contradict it. On most of the grazing lands of the West, short-term profit (or the hope of it) continued to come at the expense of long-range protection, a condition that would prevail even when the Division of Grazing was wedded to the General Land Office to create the Bureau of Land Management (BLM) in 1946. Nearly sixty years after passage of the Taylor Grazing Act, a study undertaken by the Natural Resources Defense Council and the National Wildlife Federation could estimate that no fewer than 100 million acres of BLM grazing land were still in "unsatisfactory" condition.[66]

SENATOR TAYLOR HAD talked about "human erosion" when discussing the need for his grazing legislation. It was a term the New Dealers could understand. Taylor doubtless thought of the phrase principally as just one way of describing the economic effects of drought and over-

65. Quoted in T. H. Watkins, *Righteous Pilgrim*, p. 481.
66. See George Wuerthner, "How the West Was Eaten," *Wilderness* (spring 1991).

grazing, but many people in and out of the administration would have cheerfully expanded its scope to embrace not just economic deprivation but social, psychological, and even spiritual loss—particularly when it came to the matter of human beings and the land. Roosevelt himself had an almost mystical faith in the healing character of the land. "There is space, freedom and room for free movement," he had declared in a speech delivered while he was still governor of New York. "There is contact with earth and with nature and the restful privilege of getting away from pavements and from noise." It was this sentiment that lay behind Roosevelt's enthusiastic support for the expansion of the National Park System in the Department of the Interior during his presidency (he would dedicate seven new national parks, two new national monuments, and one national seashore, adding more than seven million acres to the system). But actually living on the land and taking sustenance from it was even better, he believed: "There is an opportunity for permanency of abode, a chance to establish a real home in the traditional American sense."[67]

He was hardly alone in this conceit. A largely middle-class back-to-the-land movement had been ebbing and flowing for decades in the United States (it still does), and the depression had given new life to this philosophical hangover from the pre-industrial age. In *Flight from the City* (1933), back-to-the-lander William Borsodi, an advertising man who had renounced his faith in Madison Avenue, urged creative Americans like himself to abandon their city-bound, materialistic lives and reconnect with the spiritual enrichment "which comes from contact with nature and from the growth of the soil, from flowers and fruits, from gardens and trees, from birds and animals."[68] On a more practical level, M. G. Kains, a practicing farmer all his life, argued in *Five Acres and Independence* (1934) that "the farm is the safest place to live," and that when a wage earner's savings "melt away," he begins to "appreciate the advantages of a home which does not gobble up his hard-earned money but produces much of its upkeep, especially . . . food for his

67. "Address before the American Country Life Conference on the Better Distribution of Population Away from Cities," Ithaca, New York, August 19, 1931. In Samuel Rosenman, ed., *The Public Papers and Addresses of Franklin D. Roosevelt* 1: p. 511.
68. Quoted in Furnas, op. cit., p. 317.

family."[69] Thousands of people had, in fact, fled the city to try their hands at subsistence farming, most in the limited, stone-pocked soils of New England and upstate New York. Some few managed to survive the experience; most failed and found themselves floundering in at least as much distress as they had endured when they were surrounded by sterile concrete. But the idea still seemed realistic to Roosevelt when he became president, and on April 17, 1933, he wrote Senator George Norris of Nebraska, an old Progressive and longtime supporter: "I would really like to get one more bill, which would allow us to spend $25 million this year to put 25,000 families on farms at an average cost of $1,000 per family. . . . Will you talk this over with some of our fellow dreamers on the Hill?"[70]

Norris obliged, and language to that effect had been inserted into a section of Title II of the National Industrial Recovery Act, thus creating the Subsistence Homestead program. The program had a threefold purpose, according to PWA administrator Harold L. Ickes, into whose bailiwick the effort fell: "[D]ecentralization of industry; the opening up of congested factory areas; and a demonstration of the social benefits of a sound community life based on a combination of part-time industrial employment and small-scale farming."[71]

Underfunded from the beginning and, for all his stout words, never vigorously supported by Ickes, the Subsistence Homestead program never did amount to much. By the end of the decade, just 10,938 dwellings had been constructed, and only a handful of projects ever became viable communities.[72] In April 1935, to Ickes's delight, the program was shifted into the newly created Resettlement Administration under Rexford Tugwell, where it swiftly became another cog in the machinery of a Tugwellian vision that would have transformed how all

69. Quoted in ibid.
70. Quoted in Joseph Lash, *Eleanor and Franklin*, p. 394.
71. Harold L. Ickes, *Back to Work*, pp. 191–92.
72. Perhaps the Subsistence Homestead program's proudest achievement was Aberdeen Gardens, a 150-family project near Newport News, Virginia. It was the only Subsistence Homestead community that was not only built for African Americans but *by* African Americans. William C. McNeill, its chief construction engineer, was a black man, and every laborer on the job was black, as was the community manager. While

Americans lived on the land. Tugwell had little faith in the ability of untutored human beings to use the land intelligently. The typical farm, the New Deal's principal intellect had written in 1930,

> is an area of vicious, ill-tempered soil with not a very good house, inadequate barns, makeshift machinery, happenstance stock, tired, overworked men and women . . . and all the pests and bucolic plagues that nature has evolved . . . a place where ugly, brooding monotony that haunts by day and night, unseats the mind.[73]

He had not substantially changed that opinion by 1935. The "family farm" so dear to American tradition (and Roosevelt's philosophy) simply did not work anymore as an economically viable means to create community, Tugwell believed; what it created was poverty. But neither did massive corporate agriculture, as practiced in California and other western states, serve to create healthy communities; what it created was an ever-widening gap between rich and poor. Something new had to be tried, something that would combine ancient rural values with modern scientific know-how. "I'm for decentralization, for simplicity of life, along with a recognition of the complexity of industrial and scientific civilization," he wrote grandly in his syndicated newspaper column. Somehow, it must be possible to "approximate that no-riches, no-poverty kind of life in which I grew up. I'd certainly set the sleighbells ringing in thousands of village streets if I could."[74]

First, buy people out and take them off overworked and abused land—most of it in the Dust Bowl states—which would then be permanently retired and allowed to return to a natural state or be used exclusively for pasturage (this aspect of the program had already been

---

the town never reached full occupancy in the depression years and did not attain the level of self-sufficiency dreamed of for these homesteads, it did promote a sense of community among its families and proved one of the most successful black housing projects in the country. (See Kifer, op. cit., pp. 168–78.)

73. Quoted in David Myhra, "Rexford Guy Tugwell: Initiator of America's Greenbelt New Towns, 1935–36," in Donald A. Krueckenberg, ed., *The American Planner: Biographies and Recollections*, p. 234.
74. Quoted in Davis, op. cit., p. 487.

initiated, though on a relatively tiny scale, by the Rural Rehabilitation Division of the Federal Emergency Relief Administration).[75] Then, resettle as many as half a million families on better land in small, carefully planned and professionally managed agricultural communities, where they would cultivate the fields of a modernist Arcadia through cooperative effort and according to scientific principles. Furthermore, let suburbia itself be transformed by taking people out of city slums and decrepit tenant-farmer hamlets and putting them into modestly sized communities surrounded entirely by woodlands and fields. Let these communities be planned so as to emphasize affordable housing, open space, parks, trails, and recreation areas, with all city government services and commercial establishments relegated to a central area and all highways kept on the outskirts. They would be called Greenbelt Towns.

However fine Tugwell's dreaming, both the resettlement program and the Greenbelt Towns proved of marginal importance. Constantly ridiculed in and out of the Congress as ludicrous yet vaguely dangerous socialistic experiments, neither program would be given enough money to establish more than a few model communities. Resettlement was particularly difficult; aside from a lack of money, the New Deal planners too often encountered a deep reluctance on the part of many farm folk to leave their land, however used up it might be, in order to let themselves be transplanted to a strange place among strange people. "They'll have to take a shotgun to move us out of here," one New Mexico farmer said. "We're going to stay here just as long as we damn please."[76] Most did. In the end, only about four million acres of land were purchased (at a cost of $14 million), only 4,441 families were resettled, and only three collective farms were established—at Lake Dick, Arkansas; Walker County, Alabama; and Casa Grande, Arizona.[77] None flourished. The

75. In 1934, for example, 202 families from the "cut-over" lands of northern Minnesota, Wisconsin, and Michigan had been moved up to the Matanuska Valley east of Anchorage, Alaska, where they were given forty-acre farms, complete with houses and farm buildings, with thirty-year, 3 percent government loans and liberal repayment policies. Most defaulted and departed in a few years, though a small farming community remains to this day, known mostly for growing vegetables as big as basketballs. See Orlando W. Miller, *The Frontier in Alaska and the Matanuska Colony.*

76. Quoted in Worster, *Dust Bowl*, p. 42.

77. Figures from James S. Olson, ed., *Historical Dictionary of the New Deal*, p. 419; and Lowitt, op. cit., p. 39.

three Greenbelt towns that the Suburban Resettlement Division of the Resettlement Administration managed to put into place—Greenbelt, Maryland, near Washington, D.C.; Green Hills, Ohio, near Cincinnati; and Greendale, Wisconsin, near Milwaukee—fared somewhat better, but in time each would succumb to the sprawl and communal disintegration typical of suburbs in the decades after World War II.

While he remained in office (he would leave government in 1937), Tugwell fought a good fight to preserve his visions. As with most of the New Dealers, he was fully aware of the value of publicity, and when an erstwhile young documentary filmmaker by the name of Pare Lorentz came to him not long after the RA's creation, he was receptive. What Lorentz proposed was a series of films to demonstrate the need for the New Deal's various programs. Tugwell agreed, and the first film, *The Plow That Broke the Plains*, centering on the ecological and human effects of the Dust Bowl years, was issued the following year. With imagery of uncommon visual power, a stirring score by Virgil Thomson, and a semipoetic narration written by Lorentz and voiced through the mellifluous larynx of Thomas Chalmers, the film was premiered at the Rialto Theater in New York (sharing the bill with the Clark Gable–Claudette Colbert classic *It Happened One Night*, which could not have hurt attendance). It was received with critical enthusiasm and subsequently became a "short subject" seen by millions in neighborhood theaters; it remains one of the most enduring artifacts of the New Deal.

While Lorentz was still putting a production team together for *The Plow That Broke the Plains*, another kind of documentarian was setting up shop in the RA—Roy Stryker, who persuaded Tugwell to establish a Historical Section in the agency's Information Division. What Stryker was after was history shot on the wing by photographers, and he assembled a team that at one time or another would include such artists as Walker Evans, Arthur Rothstein, Ben Shahn, Berenice Abbott, Russell Lee, Carl Mydans, and Marian Post Wolcott. For nearly ten years, going far beyond their mandate to document merely the programs of the RA, these photographers would wander the United States, shooting Arkansas farmers and Pittsburgh steelworkers, eroded land and smoking factories, black sharecroppers and Polish autoworkers, Japanese artichoke-pickers and Italian fishermen, rural villages and urban sprawl, state fairs and unemployment office lines, dam-builders, CCC workers, housewives, office clerks, and union organizers, producing hundreds of thousands of pictures and covering every breed of American short of gang lords and plutocrats. There was no question as to the purpose of such images; Stryker's office used them as propaganda to advertise the virtues of the New Deal in official reports and press releases, handing them out freely to illustrate newspaper and magazine articles, and the photographers were hardly unaware of this—indeed, most of them heartily approved. They were not reluctant to choose those subjects they knew would satisfy Stryker, nor were they above arranging compositions and cropping prints to get the message across as vividly as possible. But the essential truth of the images remained undiminished by manipulation, and they became the icons that still speak to Americans of what the Great Depression was like with a sense of heightened reality and incomparable immediacy. They also proved one of the most important weapons in the government's imperfect war against the ravages of circumstance and human failing.

That war came to the factory-like farm fields of California in part through the lens of another photographer who would go on to become one of Stryker's most famous and productive emissaries. Her name was Dorothea Lange, a marginally successful portrait photographer who had achieved some measure of national repute with a single photograph published in the liberal magazine *Survey Graphic*—"White Angel Bread Line," showing an elderly man in a breadline, hunched over a cup of coffee and staring into nothingness with a hollow-eyed and hopeless look. This photograph, like most of her later work, demonstrated Lange's belief that "it is in the nature of the camera to deal with what *is*" and that it was the duty and opportunity of photographers like her to "speak more than of our subjects—we can speak with them; we can more than speak about our subjects—we can speak for them."[78] In January 1935, she was hired by the California State Emergency Relief Administration (SERA) at the urging of University of California economist Paul S. Taylor (he had written the *Survey Graphic* article her photograph had helped to illustrate), new field director of the SERA's Rural Rehabilitation Division and the recipient of a research grant to study California

78. Quoted in Charles J. Shindo, *Dust Bowl Migrants in the American Imagination*, p. 43.

migrant life. For the next several months, often with Taylor at her side, Lange traveled the agricultural regions of the state from the Imperial to the Sacramento Valleys with her big boxlike Graflex, concentrating on the migrant labor camps, the "Little Oklahomas" that had clustered along highways and irrigation ditches outside the rural towns. Some were owned and operated by local farmers, their conditions ostensibly monitored by the State Housing and Immigration Division, but few of these met even the most primitive standards of decency. Other settlements, where people had simply decided to stop because they could go no farther, were worse.

There was much to photograph, and little of it needed artistic manipulation for effect. The impromptu camps especially were rural slums constructed out of whatever came to hand—tin, cardboard, bed-sheets—filthy, overcrowded, exposed, fly-blown in the summer, battered by freezing rain and wind in the winter, ridden with diphtheria, typhus, and other diseases in all seasons. In most, there was never enough water, no toilets save for the rare outhouse or the occasional irrigation ditch (which often served to supply what drinking water there was). "The outside appearance of most dwellings is repellant," a relief worker said in describing a typical squatter "shacktown" outside Sacramento: "decay has rotted scrap construction material and the overflow piles of sodden junk help prepare the visitor for a sordid look within the household. Even in mid-day the interior is dark, but the noxious odors are strong of dampness, rot, stale atmosphere. Some shacks contain nothing but a bedroll."[79]

When Lange returned to Sacramento, her photographs were included in a report put together by Taylor and Harry Drobish, director of the Rural Rehabilitation Division. Drobish took the report to his superiors at the SERA with the recommendation that they apply for a grant from the FERA to build as many as twenty federal camps for migrants, emphasizing with some force that

THIS PROJECT MEETS A NEED CLEARLY AND PUBLICLY RECOGNIZED BY FEDERAL AND STATE AUTHORITIES, AND BY CIVIC BODIES IN CALIFORNIA.

79. Quoted in Stanley Crouch, "Housing Migratory Workers," Paul Schuster Taylor papers, Bancroft Library, University of California at Berkeley.

IT IS AN IMPORTANT STEP TOWARD REHABILITATION OF A SUBMERGED
GROUP, TOWARD BETTER INDUSTRIAL RELATIONS IN A STRIFE-TORN
FIELD, AND TOWARD TRAINING OF THOUSANDS OF MEN, WOMEN AND
CHILDREN IN BETTER STANDARDS OF AMERICAN CITIZENSHIP.[80]

In the late spring of 1935, the SERA and FERA both agreed to
launch the migrant housing program with model camps at Marysville
and Arvin. These were ready for occupation by the end of the year, complete with tents and cabins for as many as 230 families, communal
cooking sheds, sewing rooms, nurseries, first aid dispensaries, and "sanitation" buildings with showers, toilets, and laundry facilities. The
camps, whose residents were encouraged to write constitutions and participate in management committees, were offered up as examples of
democracy at work. In fact, most camp managers—like the managers of
the tenant-farmer programs in the South—thought of their charges as a
little simpleminded, and themselves as good fathers looking out for
their best interests—and, not incidentally, the labor needs of the California farmer. "A camp manager must at all times be in charge of the
camp to maintain conditions of sanitation and order," Irving Wood,
director of the camp program, said in a paper delivered to a public housing conference. "He can aid the employment services to make available
to growers an adequate supply of workers," and while the program
desired "to avoid paternalism and regimentation," it was expected "that
camp managers will protect the camp population from abuses by contractors, peddlers and others."[81] Cleanliness, health, order, and protection from abuse were not to be sneered at, of course. And for most of the
migrants who managed to get into such camps the improvement over
their previous condition was welcome, even if the paternalism got a little hard to take.

Shortly after the Marysville and Arvin camps were finished, the
housing program was placed under the aegis of the Resettlement
Administration. In 1937, after creation of the Farm Security Administration to replace the Resettlement Administration, the program was
expanded dramatically. By 1941, there would be thirteen federal camps

80. Quoted in Shindo, op. cit., p. 26.
81. Ibid., p. 28.

in California (many with such added facilities as recreation halls), together with six mobile tent-camps that could be moved around the state as needed, and five hundred permanent "garden homes" with running water and electricity that migrants could rent from the government for as little as $8.20 a month. An estimated 45,000 migrants were living in one or the other form of federal housing at the end of that year.[82]

It was by no means enough. It never would be, in spite of a groundswell of national publicity that ultimately would build this group of Americans into a depression symbol. Even before Pare Lorentz released *The Plow That Broke the Plains*, Dorothea Lange, working by now for the Resettlement Administration, had passed a pea-pickers' camp on her way home after a month in the field in early 1936. Some undefined instinct made her stop and return to the camp, where she found a mother and her children huddled in the rain under a flap of canvas. "She said that they had been living on frozen vegetables from the surrounding fields, and birds that the children killed," Lange recalled. "There she sat in that lean-to tent with her children huddled around her, and seemed to know that my pictures might help her, and so she helped me."[83]

Lange took the resulting series of photographs to the *San Francisco News*, which splashed a couple of them across the top of a page of its March 10 edition under the headline, "Ragged, Hungry, Broke, Harvest Workers Live in Squalor," later reporting that "the chance visit of Government photographer" had led to shipments of food that rescued "2,500 men, women, and children."[84] One of the photographs that did not appear in the news story was published later that year in *Survey Graphic* (again with an article by Taylor) and yet again in the popular weekly magazine *Midweek Pictorial* ("Look in Her Eyes," the caption read), and ultimately it would become one of the most famous and frequently published photographs in American history—"Migrant Mother," a Madonna-like image of a woman with haunted eyes, a hand

82. See Starr, op. cit., p. 236.
83. Dorothea Lange, "The Assignment I'll Never Forget," *Popular Photography* (February 1960). See also, Paul S. Taylor, "Migrant Mother: 1936," *The American West* (May 1970).
84. Both quotes in *San Francisco News* (March 10, 1936).

at her mouth in worry, an infant on her lap, and two of her other children hiding their faces against her neck. For millions of Americans, it was and remains the living representation of the Great Depression.

Other kinds of imagery were in the offing. In August 1936, the *San Francisco News* asked John Steinbeck (*In Dubious Battle*, his novel about the agricultural labor wars, had just been published) to do some articles on the migrants. The resulting series, "The Harvest Gypsies," was filled with excruciating details about the filth and desperation the migrants faced with numb endurance. One family he found living in a tent "the color of the ground," whose canvas was so rotten "the flaps and sides hang in tatters," the inside of the tent "full of flies clinging to the apple box that is the dinner table, buzzing about the foul clothes of the children, particularly the baby, who has not been bathed nor cleaned for several days."[85] The series ran for a week that October and was republished two years later as *Their Blood Is Strong* by the Simon J. Lubin Society, an organization devoted to improving the lot of the migrants and pulling the beards of the Associated Farmers of California, mostly in its newsletter, *The Rural Observer*, edited by a sprightly young social activist named Helen Hosmer.

By then, Steinbeck had finished *The Grapes of Wrath*, published in 1939. An ambitious sprawl of a book, this biblical epic traced the movements of the fictional Joad family from its foreclosed farm in Oklahoma to the endless fields of the San Joaquin Valley, giving a literary dimension to the life of the migrants as powerful as the visual offerings of Pare Lorentz's *The Plow That Broke the Plains* and the work of Roy Stryker's relentless battalion of photographers. The book was widely reviewed, opinions ranging from the ecstatic to the disdainful (in Oklahoma, unsurprisingly, outrage over Steinbeck's depiction of the Joads predominated). Among the reviewers was Eleanor Roosevelt: "Now I must tell you that I have just finished a book which is an unforgettable experience," the First Lady wrote in her syndicated column, "My Day," on June 28. "*Grapes of Wrath* by John Steinbeck both repels and attracts you. The horrors of the picture, so well drawn, made you dread sometimes to begin the next chapter, and yet you cannot lay the

85. John Steinbeck, *Their Blood Is Strong*, p. 3.

book down or even skip a page."[86] By the end of the year, the novel had sold 430,000 copies, making it one of the largest sellers of the decade, and has never been out of print since.

The year 1939 also saw the publication of *Factories in the Field*, by Carey McWilliams (by then, director of the California Housing and Immigration Division and struggling to improve the state's supervision of an estimated 5,600 nonfederal migrant camps holding as many as 160,000 people at peak season). Part journalism, part history, and all high-toned anger, McWilliams's book did not sit well with the Associated Farmers and its allies, who immediately perceived a conspiracy in the fact that his book came out so close to *The Grapes of Wrath*. "Reds Blamed for Books on Migrant Labor," ran a headline in William Randolph Hearst's *San Francisco Examiner*, provoking a spate of denunciations and denials, including novels named *Grapes of Gladness* and *Plums of Plenty*.[87] The paranoia only grew more intense with the publication that same year of *An American Exodus*, which combined Dorothea Lange's photographs with Paul Taylor's prose, interviews, and statistics as a kind of documentary equivalent of the Steinbeck novel.

The following year saw the arrival of John Ford's film version of *The Grapes of Wrath*, one of the most popular movies of the era. Itinerant songwriter and singer Woody Guthrie, an Oklahoma-born radical troubador following an erratic career as a Los Angeles radio performer and local recording star, saw the film in New York. At the request of an RCA Victor Records executive, who knew an opportunity when he saw it, Guthrie composed "Tom Joad," a ballad version of the film's story line. "Tom Joad," along with such better-known Guthrie songs as "Dusty Old Dust (So Long, It's Been Good to Know You)," "Dust Pneumonia Blues," and "Do Re Mi," were issued together in *Dust Bowl Ballads*, an album produced by RCA Victor in May 1940. "They are 'Oakie' songs," Guthrie wrote in his liner notes to the album. "'Dust Bowl' songs, 'Migratious' songs, about my folks and my relatives, about a jillion of 'em, that got hit by the drouth, the dust, the wind, the

86. Quoted in Warren French, ed., *A Companion to "The Grapes of Wrath,"* p. 131.
87. Quote and novel references in Carey McWilliams, "A Man, a Place, and a Time: John Steinbeck and the long agony of the Great Valley in an age of depression, oppression, frustration, and hope," *The American West* (May 1970).

banker, and the landlord, and the police, all at the same time."[88] The album did not sell widely, but it swiftly became popular among leftists, and in time its songs would be regarded as an essential part of the migrant story.

The sea of publicity that spilled out of California in the last two years of the decade was climaxed by a series of congressional hearings sponsored by Congressman John Tolan at the urging of Paul Taylor. All during 1940, Tolan's Select Committee to Investigate the Migration of Destitute Citizens held hearings around the country, from Oklahoma City to Los Angeles, San Francisco to Washington, D.C., listening to testimony and collecting evidence that corroborated fully and in exquisite detail the story told by Taylor and Steinbeck, Lange and Lorentz, John Ford and Woody Guthrie and all the other reformers. The committee's 1941 report, *Interstate Migration*, described by historian Kevin Starr as "documentary art of the highest order," sent the growers into yet another paroxysm of furious denial.[89]

It was much too late by then. The image of the Dust Bowl migrants was firmly fixed in the American imagination. The denials also were irrelevant—as was the *Interstate Migration* report itself. The migrants immortalized by book, photography, film, song, and government report were already entering a new cycle of history. The New Dealers had been no more successful in fitting these contrary Anglo-Saxon farmers into the mold of sedate and obedient citizen-laborers than the CP/USA had been in persuading them to join the rest of the proletariat to pull down capitalism and stamp it into ruins. This new wave of migrants, like most Americans, entertained dreams of becoming part of the capitalist system—or at least part of the comfortable middle class—and they were not particularly interested in spending the rest of their lives working some corporate farm. They might not have been able to break the monopoly on land and get a "little bit of this good dirt" for their own, but as soon as the wartime boom began, the vast majority of them fled California's factories in the field for the factories of war as swiftly as they had arrived—leaving a vacuum filled, once again, by Chicanos.

88. Quoted in Shindo, op. cit., p. 181.
89. Starr, op. cit., p. 270.

They were tough and enduring, the Okies, and most would make a new life in this new place, helping to shape its future, particularly when they captured it whole and gave it to Ronald Reagan as governor thirty years later, as folklorist John Greenway would note.[90] Their psychic strength perhaps derived from their unity in hope and in their roles as targets of prejudice and economic dispossession—but possibly it was fortified just as much by what Lois Phillips Hudson thought was a kind of mourning that idealized the places they had left behind. "We cherish our griefs over those green fields," she wrote, "because our griefs seem to prove that what we grieve over must once have existed. . . . and in a way none of us ever really leaves those fields that made us. It is from those lost fields that we go on shyly, silently calling to each other."[91]

90. See John Greenway, "Woody Guthrie: The Man, the Land, the Understanding," *The American West* (fall 1966).
91. Hudson, op. cit., p. 97.

18

A Perfect Laboratory

R efugees from the Dust Bowl had been forced off the land mainly by an accident of climate (with some unanticipated help from New Deal agricultural policies), but even before the first "Okies" and their fellow travelers had begun streaming across California's border, much of an entire regional population was being picked up and moved by a federal program as deliberate as it was astonishing in its ambition and long-lasting in its consequences.

Among those affected was Mrs. Cora Hill Trent. On a summer afternoon in 1933, she stood on the porch of her farm between the Clinch and Powell Rivers in Union County, Tennessee, and watched Dewey Bowman, a neighbor boy, ride up on his horse in a breathless state. "It's a coming!" he shouted.

"What's a coming?" Cora asked.

"That *thing*!" the boy said. "That *thing* is a coming."[1]

---

1. Oral history interview with Cora Hill Trent, p. 17; Tennessee Valley Authority Oral History Collection.

Mrs. Trent remembered being amused by the boy's inability to say what that "thing" was, though she and the rest of her neighbors scattered throughout the valley of the Clinch River knew its name well enough and had been waiting for its beginning with both excitement and anxiety for several months. It was Norris Dam, the first installment of a dream whose breadth and ambition surpassed anything else that ever sprouted in the fecund imaginations of the New Dealers: the Tennessee Valley Authority (TVA). To Mrs. Trent, whose great-great-grandfather had settled the Clinch River Valley at the end of the eighteenth century, this land was home. But to the New Dealers, it was "the perfect laboratory for an experiment in regional planning," as agricultural economist Stuart Chase described it, and before they were done, they would harness the Tennessee River and many of its tributaries, transform the region's environment, and uproot Mrs. Trent and tens of thousands of other people who had lived on the land for generations.[2]

The TVA was not by any means the only gargantuan river-basin project the relentless resource planners of the New Deal undertook. In the West, the Bureau of Reclamation not only completed Boulder (later Hoover) Dam, begun during the Hoover administration, but would go on to plug up the lower Colorado River with three more dams to develop electricity and provide drinking water for burgeoning Los Angeles and irrigation water to perpetuate the agricultural factories of the Imperial Valley. On the Columbia River, the Corps of Engineers' Bonneville Dam produced cheap electricity for most of the Pacific Northwest, while the Bureau of Reclamation's Grand Coulee Dam provided irrigation water for a million undeveloped acres in eastern Washington. In California, the bureau took over the bankrupt state Central Valley Project, designed to irrigate the agribusiness empires of central California. In Montana, the Corps of Engineers constructed Fort Peck Dam on the Missouri River, the largest earth-fill dam in the world, for power, irrigation, and flood control. In other western states, a plethora of similar, if less ambitious projects was undertaken by both agencies.

2. Stuart Chase, *Rich Land, Poor Land: A Study of Waste in the Natural Resources of America*, pp. 263–64.

None of these western projects, no matter how large or technically challenging they were, or how important their long-range impact on the West's future growth would be, could truly compare with the TVA. The Tennessee River was a thousand-mile stream that curled southwest through Tennessee from its headwaters in the northeastern part of the state, swung west through the northernmost section of Alabama, then curved north, paralleling the Mississippi River before joining the Ohio River near Paducah, Kentucky. Fed by scores of tributaries that snaked down through the ancient Appalachians, the Tennessee drained more than 40,000 square miles and was the main stem of one of the most important river systems in the eastern third of the United States. To match those dimensions, the dams and related structures that the TVA would erect over a ten-year period rivaled those in the West in numbers, complexity, scope, and cost. Moreover, most of the western projects were constructed in near-wilderness regions, and while natural land-scapes that had lain virtually untouched by human ambition since their evolution were now forever trammeled, the numbers of those humans physically disrupted by the projects were minimal—though some Native American populations did feel the impact, particularly in the Pacific Northwest, where ancient fishing traditions were severely affected.

Not so with the projects of the TVA. They would embrace the land and water resources of seven states that had been settled for nearly two centuries, turning them to ends that, the planners firmly believed, would greatly enhance the economic, social, and even spiritual quality of life of the 2.5 million people who lived there, most of them poor, nearly two million of them rural, and all of whom felt the impact of the TVA almost immediately. Nothing—not the western river projects, not the human reclamation programs of the Resettlement Administration, not Tugwell's Greenbelt Towns—so precisely demonstrated the relent-lessly utopian instincts of the New Deal at its best (and worst). "Here, struggling in embryo," as Stuart Chase put it, was "perhaps the promise of what all America will be some day."[3]

The Tennessee Valley, Chase might also have observed, was what much of all America used to be. Even before the American Revolution,

3. Ibid., p. 287.

Daniel Boone had opened up the Wilderness Road through the Cumberland Gap from Virginia into the well-named "dark and bloody ground" of Kentucky, and down the Wilderness Road the ancestral pioneers had rumbled, most of them first- or second-generation Scotch-Irish or English, with their wagons, horses, cattle, sheep, pigs, dogs, seed corn, and children, spilling into the valleys and mountain coves of the plateau whose rivers flowed toward the Ohio. Over time, settlement crept into more and more of the Appalachians' places, the people scattering and overwhelming local populations of Indians in vicious skirmishes, then eking out a life on thousands of corn-stubble farms and raising up tiny, scattered villages. Insular and clannish and deeply suspicious of anyone and anything outside the ring of family—a crotchety paranoia reinforced by all the gore that had accompanied their conquest of the mountains—the people built a life that was unique and enduring, Protestant to the bone, and, like most such "island" cultures, rich in language and tradition, myth and music. But economically poor, dreadfully poor even by the standards of the depression years, which only exacerbated their condition. By the 1930s, many of the region's people had been sucked into the maw of the coal industry, itself a relentless engine of working-class poverty, and those who remained to work and overwork ancestral farms found themselves on what promised to be a long slide into cultural oblivion.

But not if the planners and dreamers of the New Deal had anything to say about it, and few had more to say than Roosevelt himself. He had sensed the possibilities of the valley even before he assumed the presidency. On January 21, 1933, he had been given a tour of the valley by Nebraska Senator George Norris, who had long envisioned a system of federal flood-control and electric power-producing dams for the region. To Norris's astonished delight, Roosevelt not only took his point immediately but ran with it during an informal talk later that day in Montgomery, Alabama. The valley, Roosevelt said, provided "the opportunity to accomplish a great purpose for the people of many States and, indeed, for the whole Union." The government could set an "example of planning, not just for ourselves but for the generations to come, tying in industry and agriculture and forestry and flood prevention, tying them all into a unified whole over a distance of a thousand

miles so that we can afford better opportunities and better places for living for millions of yet unborn."[4]

Roosevelt and Norris had not been the first to be struck by the possibilities of the river, though for decades its promise had been stifled by
an apparently insurmountable obstacle. It was called Muscle Shoals, a
point just north of the thickly wooded ridge of La Grange Mountain in
the northwestern corner of Alabama. Here, where the Tennessee turned
north, it surged across a rocky bed so shallow that it made navigation
almost impossible in an age when waterway transportation was crucial
to any region's economic development. By the turn of the century, however, with the growing importance of electricity in the nation's life, the
inconvenience of Muscle Shoals was beginning to be viewed as an
opportunity. In 1906, the newly formed Muscle Shoals Hydroelectric
Company proposed that Congress authorize the federal government to
join it to build three hydropower dams.

Congress declined, but in 1916, when war with Germany seemed a
distinct possibility, the National Defense Act of 1916 did authorize the
president to choose a site or sites "for the production of nitrates or other
products needed for munitions of war and useful in the manufacture of
fertilizers."[5] Large amounts of phosphate and electricity were essential
to the production of nitrates. The Tennessee Valley had substantial
phosphate deposits hidden in the hills; Muscle Shoals held plenty of
potential power; and when war was indeed declared in 1917, Wilson
chose the Tennessee River site for nitrate plants and a dam.

As it happened, the war ended before the first dam—later named
after Wilson himself—and one nitrate plant were completed and before
the remaining nitrate plant could get into full production. The Harding administration, not much for federal public works projects, considered the whole Muscle Shoals complex a white elephant and offered it
for sale. There were no takers until Henry Ford stepped up in July 1921
and offered to pay $5 million for the nitrate plants—far below what
they had already cost—so that he could manufacture fertilizer (no
munitions would be forthcoming from the fervently antiwar Ford). He

4. Quoted in Rosenman, ed., op. cit., 1: pp. 888–89.
5. Quoted in Donald Davidson, *The Tennessee,* 1: *The New River: From Civil War to TVA,*
p. 81.

also promised to finish two of the proposed dams, including the still incomplete Wilson, but only if he could then lease them from the government for a hundred years at extraordinarily cheap rates. It would be worth it, Ford assured Congress, for he would create a whole new world here. He envisioned a linear city straddling the curves of the river for seventy-five miles, with once destitute farmers combining enlightened subsistence farming with good factory jobs in the nitrate plants and other bustling manufacturing concerns, all in the wholesome setting of small-town life. Profit to the Ford Motor Company, Ford insisted, was irrelevant. "We can here do an epochal thing," he exclaimed at one point, "literally, I mean it—an epochal thing."[6] The region's boomers, who had been profoundly disheartened when the government decided to get out of the nitrate business, were captivated by the implication that Ford would build a new version of Detroit in the heart of the southern Appalachians. They bought up land in anticipation of the inevitable boom and took to wearing "I Want Ford to Get Muscle Shoals" lapel buttons, while a popular ditty warbled, "Henry Ford went to Muscle Shoals,/To bring to the people of the South pure gold./Let him have it, says O My Lord!/The Lord's ridin' in Heaven on a Henry Ford."[7]

Senator George Norris, however, was mortally offended by the deal. "No corporation ever got a more unconscionable contract" than that which Ford was offering to cut with the government, he declared.[8] Nor did he trust Henry Ford to do anything that would redound to the benefit of anyone but Henry Ford. Muscle Shoals, Norris believed, should be developed by the federal government and only the federal government, producing cheap power to light the lives of people too long trapped in the gloom of candles, coal oil lamps, and flickering fireplace light. Norris gathered his fellow Progressives around him and led a fight in Congress that proved so forceful that Ford ultimately withdrew his offer. During the next several years, Norris twice got legislation through Congress for the federal hydropower development of Muscle Shoals and other sites on the river; President Coolidge pocket-vetoed one Norris bill in 1928, and Hoover vetoed another outright in 1931,

6. Quoted in Lacey, op. cit., p. 212.
7. Button quote in ibid., p. 211; ditty quoted in Davidson, op. cit., p. 184.
8. Quoted in Lacey, op. cit., p. 213.

stating his firm belief that "the power problem is not to be solved by the Federal Government going into the power business."[9]

Franklin Roosevelt disagreed, and Roosevelt the silviculturist probably knew more about electric power than Hoover the engineer. As governor of New York, FDR had vigorously criticized private utility companies for the exorbitant rates they routinely charged, rates that made it all but impossible for ordinary people to afford electricity, particularly in rural regions. Roosevelt did not advocate that public power companies should replace all private efforts everywhere, but he did believe that the government had a duty to see to it that rates should be democratically affordable and that the near monopoly of private utility trusts should be broken. To these ends, he proposed the development of public power sites by public entities. The power generated would be sold under contract to private companies who would be regulated so as to limit what they could charge their customers; the cost of building and maintaining the public dams and generating facilities would be used as a "yardstick" by which a fair profit for the private distributor would be determined (though critics would contend that such "yardsticks" did not take into consideration the higher capital costs that private companies would have to absorb). Moreover, he encouraged municipalities and other public entities to build their own transmission lines to deliver energy directly to the consumer, where appropriate.[10]

These goals had been part of Roosevelt's campaign rhetoric in the summer and fall of 1932 and would inspire his creation of the Rural Electrification Administration in 1935, and they surely were on his mind when he appropriated Norris's vision in January 1933—with the senator's entirely cheerful acquiescence. And they remained on April 10, when FDR sent one more message to the frantically overworked Congress of the Hundred Days, this one requesting legislation that would establish a "Tennessee Valley Authority—a corporation clothed with the power of government but possessed of the flexibility and initiative of a private enterprise. It should be charged with the broadest duty of planning for the proper use, conservation, and development of

9. Quoted in Roy Talbert Jr. *FDR's Utopian: Arthur Morgan of the TVA*, p. 74.
10. For a good summary of FDR's power principles, see Thomas K. McCraw, *TVA and the Power Fight, 1933–1939*, pp. 26–36.

the natural resources of the Tennessee River drainage basin and its adjoining territory for the general social and economic welfare of the Nation."[11] Those "natural resources" included hydropower, and private power companies, knowing potential competition when they saw it, immediately sent up a howl. Chief among them was Commonwealth Southern, the corporate descendant of Samuel Insull's utility empire and the largest private company in the region, whose president, Wendell Willkie, testified before Congress that the government's plan to sell power directly to the consumer would constitute an unfair business practice, a kind of government theft; to "take our market," he said, "is to take our property."[12] Congress was not persuaded; both houses passed the bill, and Roosevelt signed it into law on May 18. While Willkie's Commonwealth Southern and other private power companies would fight to kill the TVA and other federal power projects for many years to come, they would never be able to get the government out of the power business.

Administrative responsibility for the Tennessee Valley Authority would reside in its board of directors. As chairman, Roosevelt appointed Arthur E. Morgan, a hydraulic engineer, social and educational theorist, teetotaler, devout agnostic, erstwhile playwright, and self-described moralist who had served as president of Antioch College since the early 1920s. He had rescued the small college from financial failure, but he was certifiably racist, nakedly elitist, hypersensitive, paranoid, and utterly without humor. "I tell you, Henry, humor's dangerous," the protagonist of Morgan's never-performed play, *The Seed Man; or, Things in General*, declaims at one point. "A man of dignity and responsibility must beware of it."[13] By 1933, his inflexible moralizing about everything from student sexual habits to an insufficiently noble sense of purpose displayed by the faculty had left the college in administrative turmoil. The new job could not have come at a better time.

Roosevelt would come to regret his decision to appoint this peculiar man, but at the beginning he was taken by Morgan's enthusiasm and largeness of vision. Indeed, as reported in the *New York Times* in

11. Quoted in Rosenman, op. cit., vol. 2, p. 122.
12. Quoted in Davis, op. cit., p. 93.
13. Quoted in Talbert, op. cit., p. 85.

December 1933, Morgan's dreams for the Tennessee Valley were not so different from those which had bubbled in Henry Ford's mind in the early 1920s (and which FDR had admired): "Go to Pittsburgh," Morgan told audiences in Tennessee, "go to Detroit and look on the rows on rows of hovels occupied by the workers of the big mills, and you will say, 'I don't want to see anything like that in Chattanooga.' We are looking to a valley inhabited by happy people, with small hand-work industries, no rich centres, no rich people, but everybody sharing in the wealth."[14]

Morgan's dreaming did not stop at this benign tableau, however. "He was a zealot who believed so strongly in the things he believed in," Charles J. McCarthy, a senior attorney for the TVA recalled, "that it was impossible for him to accept the concept that someone could disagree with him and not be a dishonest, 'bad person.' I can picture him burning perfectly innocent people at the stake and feeling that he was doing a great thing."[15] The proper goal of the New Deal, Morgan believed, was the creation of a "new social and economic order," and as he told the TVA's first clutch of employees in July 1933, the main order of business in the valley would be "a full and wholesome development of the region and its people in accord with wise design." To do this, their work must be rooted in ethics, which would require "actual changes in deep-seated habits, social, economic, and personal," reached through "deliberate, conscious effort."[16] And while he was confining his remarks to how the employees themselves must change, the chairman left little doubt that his deepest ambition was to transform the economic structure and moral atmosphere of the entire valley, perhaps thinking of it as a somewhat larger version of Antioch College.

To assist him in designing this new human order, Morgan chose as his fellow board members David Lilienthal and Harcourt A. Morgan (no relation). Lilienthal, only thirty-three, as ebullient as Arthur Morgan was somber, had graduated (like several of the New Deal's best and brightest young lawyers) from Harvard Law School under the tutelage

14. Quoted in Walter L. Creese, *TVA's Public Planning: The Vision, the Reality*, p. 76.
15. Oral history interview with Charles J. McCarthy, p. 4; Tennessee Valley Authority Oral History Collection.
16. Quotes in Talbert, op. cit., p. 111.

of Felix Frankfurter, then had gone on to specialize in public utility issues. In 1931, Wisconsin Governor Philip La Follette had appointed him to the State Utility Commission. Harcourt A. Morgan—"H. A." or "Doctor" to his colleagues—was appointed to take on the TVA's agricultural work. Born and reared in Canada, Morgan had come to the United States to study entomology and horticulture at Cornell in 1891 and had stayed. In 1919, he was named dean of the University of Tennessee's College of Agriculture and the same year became the university's president, a position he held until joining the TVA.

With the agency's administrative triumvirate in place, the work of the Tennessee Valley Authority began in a flourish of high-minded cooperation and flying dust.

WITHIN THREE YEARS, the TVA was employing an army of 13,000 people—laborers, engineers, architects, planners, sociologists, scientists, foresters, chemists, agronomists, architects, economists, clerks, and bottle washers. Roughly 9,000 of these were laborers, and almost all of the workforce for the TVA's construction projects was drawn from the valley's population of farmers and miners, together with working people from Knoxville, Chattanooga, and other cities in the region.[17] It was no good for the nation's unemployed to come streaming down to the Tennessee hills to find work, the *Florence* (Alabama) *Times* warned: "Despite the fact that some . . . outsiders have obtained employment in the valley, most of them have not and are being speeded on their way as rapidly as possible, because of the fact that there are still thousands and thousands of persons in the basin who are without work of any kind of a permanent nature."[18] TVA field representatives traveled from town to town in the region to hold employment interviews, and everywhere they went they were nearly overwhelmed by applicants. In Dayton, Tennessee, field representative Marshall A. Wilson had no sooner registered at the Aqua Hotel and gone into the restaurant for dinner than a crowd of jobless men gathered in the lobby, watching him through the glass doors of the dining room. "I went to my room on the second floor,"

17. Figures from Chase, op. cit., pp. 276–77.
18. Quoted in Creese, op. cit., p. 7.

he remembered, "and they followed me. I locked the door and waited for nearly an hour, expecting the mob to disperse; some did but some did not. Finally, I let them in, one at a time, and talked with them until midnight."[19] The avidity was understandable: quite aside from the fact that the region had one of the highest rates of unemployment in the nation, the TVA maintained a thirty-three-hour workweek and wages that were substantially higher than those in much of the country—forty-five cents an hour for unskilled laborers, for example—and recognized all unions.[20]

But not the needs of the black population. In the TVA, as in most New Deal programs, dedication to the highest standards of the Republic declined to the point of collapse south of the Mason-Dixon line. "In TVA the South is in the saddle," John P. Davis and Charles H. Houston reported to the NAACP after a swing through the valley in July 1933.[21] "We are trying to employ black people in about the same proportion that they bear to the population," Morgan insisted during a June 1934 speech in Knoxville.[22] But they never did. Black people in the counties surrounding Norris Dam, for example, comprised 4.5 percent of the population, but the employment of blacks in this region never got beyond 2.7 percent in any given year and was usually much lower.[23] As always, discrimination was exercised most diligently by the locals, especially by post office clerks who refused to hand out TVA employment application forms to black people. When black applicants insisted, they were often told that if they filled out the applications, they would be "signing up with the government for four years," just as if they were enlisting in the army.[24]

As an example of pure and sometimes imaginative landscape reclamation and river basin engineering, however, the work that the valley's army of technicians and laborers accomplished was indisputably impressive, even in an age replete with such marvels. Much of the work

19. Marshall A. Wilson, *Tales from the Grass-Roots of TVA, 1933–1952*, p. 15.
20. For wages, see Talbert, op. cit., p. 117.
21. Quoted in Sitkoff, op. cit., p. 50.
22. Quoted in Arthur E. Morgan, *The Making of the TVA*, p. 74.
23. See Nancy L. Grant, *TVA and Black Americans: Planning for the Status Quo*, p. 48.
24. Quoted in ibid., p. 49.

was astonishingly primitive in character, suggesting scenes out of
ancient Egypt as the pyramids rose over the desert at Giza. Thousands
of laborers, for example, were divided into "squads" of 200 or more and
marched into the six principal reservoir sites, armed with long crosscut
saws, shorter bucksaws, and brush hooks to cut down millions of trees
in swaths a mile wide, buck the felled trees clear of their branches, cut
them into logs, then stack everything into great piles for burning. For
months, the smoke from millions of burning trees shrouded the ancient
hills like morning mist. Elsewhere, similar armies toiled in rock quarries twenty-four hours a day like members of chain gangs, breaking
stone with sledgehammers and loading it into hundreds of mule carts
that carried the rock to crushers, where it was pulverized for mixing
with cement. Everywhere that winter 1933–34, "it was rough, it was
hard, it was cold," laborer Sydney Izlar remembered. "One morning,
when we were working, it was three degrees above zero. . . . I remember
the cafeteria would make us lunches and they'd always have a big fat
jelly sandwich with peanut butter. . . . And I remember many mornings you'd bite into that jelly sandwich and there'd be icicles."[25]

In less than eight years, beginning with Norris Dam (named after
the senator) on the Clinch River in the northeastern quadrant of the
state—1,860 feet long and 265 feet high and notable for the modernist
lines and graceful monumentalism of its Art Deco design—the TVA
erected seven "superdams" to go along with Wilson Dam (which had
finally been finished by the Corps of Engineers in 1925), together with
generating facilities capable of producing a total of 1.3 million kilo-
watts; built spillways and other flood control components; and dredged,
diked, and constructed complex lock systems to facilitate river transportation. By 1941, the Tennessee River Basin already was the single
most thoroughly trammeled major watershed in the world (and the
TVA would go on to add seventeen more dams by the early 1950s).[26]
The river soon was navigable along most of its length, and commercial

25. Oral history interview with Sydney O. Izlar, p. 11; Tennessee Valley Authority
Oral History Collection.
26. For TVA construction, see John H. Kyle, *The Building of the TVA: An Illustrated
History*.

traffic, totaling only twenty-two million ton-miles in 1931, would rise to almost a hundred million by 1941. And in 1937, when the worst flooding since 1927 ravaged much of the Mississippi River Valley, the streams of the Tennessee Valley—including the main-stem river—remained under control, a fact New Deal and TVA publicists were quick to point out.

But the transformation had not come without human costs. At each proposed reservoir site, TVA assessors established an estimated value for privately owned farms and other properties that would be flooded. Those estimates were then reviewed by a local nonpartisan committee, which recommended a price to be paid to the owner for his property. While TVA representatives were carefully trained to walk and talk softly in an effort to reduce the impact of the inevitable, it was a "take it or leave it" proposition; if the owner refused the offered price, condemnation proceedings would be set in motion. Even though she conceded that the prices that the TVA offered were fair and sometimes even generous, that it pursued condemnation infrequently and only as a last resort, and that it worked hard to help people find new homes, the removal process, Nashville journalist and regional historian Mary French Caldwell remembered, was "a restless, unhappy time. . . . The TVA, had it paid one thousand times the amount which it gave these people for their homes, could not repair the damage it has done. A fine people has been uprooted and their seed has been scattered to the winds."[27]

Well, not to the winds, perhaps (only 5 percent of those removed ever left the Tennessee Valley), but certainly to high ground. Although a full appeals process was available, the TVA reported that by 1946—by which time 13,449 families had been removed from the region's farmland, 65 percent of them tenants, the remainder property owners—just 5.4 percent of their acquisitions had been challenged, virtually all such appeals made by absentee owners (who could afford the time and legal fees).[28] Perhaps because the reality of the valley's poverty was too profound and the possibility of a second chance too attractive, contention

27. Mary French Caldwell, *The Duck's Back: A Report on Certain Phases of the Socialistic Experiments Conducted by the Federal Government in the Tennessee Valley*, pp. 63–64.
28. Figures from Donald Davidson, op. cit., pp. 255–56, and Philip Selznick, *TVA and the Grass Roots: A Study of Politics and Organization*, p. 104.

was rare and actual resistance even more rare—this, among a people not unfamiliar with violence. There were notable exceptions, however. Marshall Wilson, who had become something of a troubleshooter for the TVA by 1935, recalled a heart-stopping moment with a farmer named William Henry Hawkins. The old man and his wife had refused to leave their home after condemnation. Wilson and an assistant drove out to the farm to talk to the man. "We stopped the car about fifty yards from the house," Wilson remembered, "and, as we got out of it, [Hawkins] stepped from behind a . . . tree, holding a large axe in his hand. He ordered us to leave. We tried to explain that we intended no harm, but had come to ask if there was anything we could do to help him; however, the more we talked the more infuriated he became. He stepped to the car, raised his axe above his head and it started down toward the hood until I grabbed it from him."[29] Wilson managed to calm the man, who was later removed without incident—though he was ultimately committed to the Eastern State Hospital for the Insane in Knoxville.

Still, most of the valley's residents accepted removal with the stoicism of E. R. Lindamood of Long Hollow, Tennessee, whose farm had been established by his father in 1859. "It's one of these here things you've got to make the best of," the seventy-year-old patriarch told a reporter for the *Knoxville News-Sentinel*. "It's like a citizen's lot when the country is in war. . . . Our Congress has passed a law . . . this TVA . . . and we must do the best we can by it. It behooves me to be submissive."[30] In fact, removal was hardest on the old, not only physically but emotionally. "I don't want to move," seventy-three-year-old Nancy Longmire told Marshall Wilson. "I am old. I don't care to make new friends or see new places. I want to sit here and look out over these hills where I was born. My folks are buried down the road a piece and our babies are over there on the hill under the cedars."[31] And if some were delighted to get the government money (many farms were mortgaged up to the roof beams, and their owners otherwise would never have been able to get out of debt), for young or old, willing or unwilling, the process of removal and relocation was wrenching. "Oh it was so sad our

29. Wilson, op. cit., pp. 75–76.
30. *Knoxville* (Tennessee) *News-Sentinel* (October 28, 1934).
31. Quoted in Wilson, op. cit., pp. 83–84.

having to leave each other, you know," Mrs. Trent remembered with a pain she could still feel nearly sixty years later. "We were so close to each other, all neighbors, you know, and belonged to the same church. We'd known each other and had to leave each other for good. That was sad. You can imagine how it would be. If you lived in a place all your life, and your neighbors had lived there all your life and a lot of them were kinfolks, then to have to separate forever. That's the way it was with us."[32]

In the land that would be inundated by the reservoir behind Norris Dam, the often sorrowful complications of removing the living were compounded by having to remove the dead as well. There were more than 5,000 graves in the region, most in church graveyards, but many in family burial plots and other sites scattered through the land. TVA officials at first proposed that the agency disinter the dead and rebury them in one huge national cemetery, but quickly backed off when church groups and others objected that this would violate long-held church and community traditions. "Funerals in rural communities," a reporter wrote in the *Chattanooga Sunday Times* in 1936, summarizing the TVA disinterment program, "are far more solemn and impressive than in the busy rush and bustle of the Metropolis. The stroke of death makes a far wider circle than in the city throng." To the extent possible, then, people wanted to rebury their dead near them, for "the fixed and unchanging features of a rural community also perpetuate the memory of a friend or neighbor. . . . Such was the typical situation in the Norris Reservoir area; each mound held some perpetuating and enduring memory for the individual community circle."[33] In the end, the TVA dropped the notion of a national cemetery, agreeing to pay the "reasonable cost" of disinterment and reburial of each individual and that reburial would take place "in the same general or a similar environment as much as possible."[34] In September 1934, after nearly a year of legal and administrative entanglements—and as the elegant concrete wall of

32. Oral history interview with Cora Hill Trent, p. 45.
33. Quoted in Michael J. McDonald and John Muldowny, *TVA and the Dispossessed: The Resettlement of Population in the Norris Dam Area*, p. 198.
34. Quoted in ibid., p. 212.

Norris Dam neared completion—the people of the Norris Basin began gathering their dead.

IF REMOVAL OF human beings (dead or alive) would be seen as a sorrowful necessity at best, most people of the valley welcomed the TVA's agricultural programs and the reforestation projects of its Forestry Division. Both were needed. Drought and wind-driven dust storms carried plenty of emotional power, but in the Tennessee Valley, as elsewhere, nothing seemed to wound the agricultural reformists of the era more profoundly than the sight of farmland that had been gullied by water erosion. Here was waste, abuse, and ignorance given momentous form, the grim work of generations of large and small farmers who had cultivated the land to the point of degradation. They had plowed hills too steep to be suitable as farmland and had compounded that mistake by plowing up and down, ignoring the contours of the land. Vertical plowing allowed rainwater to run freely and sometimes fiercely down the rows, taking the soil with it. Many also had failed to follow rest-and-rotation methods, thus leaching land of nutrients so completely that even when some farmers replanted it in grass or grain in attempts to hold the soil together after harvesting (as many did not), little or nothing would grow. Not even natural ground cover could return, which left the soil vulnerable to the force of moving water.

By 1934, water had been responsible for most of the devastation inflicted on an estimated 234 million acres of agricultural land in the United States.[35] "The resultant erosion was appalling," British biologist Julian Huxley wrote after his first sight of America.

> It was brought home to me when, surveying the turbid flow of the Tennessee River, I was told that there were men still living who remembered it as a clear blue stream. Up till that moment I had taken the pea-soup appearance of so many American rivers for a fact of nature; the realization that it was a recent man-made phenomenon

35. See Donald Worster, *The Wealth of Nature: Environmental History and the Ecological Imagination*, pp. 71–83.

was staggering. Here, under my eyes, was the basic productivity being stripped from a vast area and hurried along to sterile waste in the sea.[36]

The traditional subsistence economy of the Tennessee River Valley had done particularly terrible wreckage in the 150 years since the people had crept over the mountains. By 1935, the Tennessee State Planning Commission reported that three million acres of the state's agricultural land had been gullied into uselessness, while sheet erosion had stripped anywhere from 75 to 100 percent of the topsoil from another eleven million acres.[37] Forests everywhere had been savagely cut, both by settlers and by corporate "timber miners" who had snaked railroads into the mountains in the late nineteenth and early twentieth centuries to pull out billions of board feet of timber. In many regions, slopes had been so denuded that they could no longer retain rainfall, and the water sped off the mountains, taking millions of tons of naked earth with it.

In the end, however, Harcourt Morgan would be more successful in reclaiming wrecked farmland and reforming traditional cultivation practices than the TVA's foresters would be in rebuilding the region's forests. Morgan, like most of the farmers he worked with, thought of trees in terms of woodlots conveniently scattered on hills otherwise given over to pastureland. He had little interest in forest health as such—a strange lack in a man who was otherwise a little ahead of his time in ecological matters—and while the CCC's "soil soldiers" and TVA foresters managed to plant seedlings on thousands of acres, the reforestation program never did get either the support or funding it needed, and E. C. M. Richards, the head of the Forestry Division, ultimately resigned in frustration. "The eroding hillsides, the burning forests, the valley's streams flowing red with mud," he claimed in 1938, "wait for a clear-cut policy decision on water protection by the Board of Directors of the TVA."[38] A "clear-cut" policy never would emerge, and

36. Julian Huxley, *TVA: Adventure in Planning*, p. 10.
37. See Federal Writers Project, *Tennessee*, pp. 23–24.
38. E. C. M. Richards, "The Future of TVA Forestry," *Journal of Forestry* (July 1938).

by the 1950s the TVA had abandoned responsibility for everything but those forest fringes that bordered its reservoirs.

Farming was another matter. Harcourt Morgan may not have understood forests, but he did understand farming—and farmers. Unlike Rexford Tugwell, Morgan still believed in the viability of the family farm—if properly cultivated and managed under guidelines he and his TVA division would establish. First, he purchased phosphate-bearing lands in the valley, started mining the nitrate-rich deposits, got the army's old wartime plants up and running (with power from Wilson Dam at Muscle Shoals), and began to manufacture fertilizer. At the same time, rather than attempt to impose reform regulations outright, he established a complex cooperative arrangement that included county agents of the Agricultural Extension Service and advisers from such regional land-grant colleges as the University of Tennessee and Alabama Polytechnic Institute, as well as local farming organizations. Before county-by-county gatherings of farmers, TVA representatives explained the program: the farmers could vote among themselves to nominate one of their number to take part in a demonstration farm project. For promising to use TVA fertilizers and to farm his land under the direction of advisers appointed by the TVA (usually county extension agents), the chosen farmer would get his fertilizer for nothing (though he had to bear the cost of shipment). His success, the theory went, would inspire other farmers in the county to go and do likewise.

And with it all would come cheap power, federal power. All "surplus" TVA power—power not needed to run the TVA's own facilities—would be delivered, first, to local municipally owned companies or cooperatives, and only after that to private companies like Commonwealth Southern. Quite aside from what it promised the farming household in terms of mere conveniences (such as light), it was assumed that electricity, like fertilizer and intelligent cultivation, would create a new Arcadia. "Electricity makes your labor more productive: the one-mule farm becomes the electric farm," R. L. Duffus explained in the *New York Times.*

You build a big walk-in electric refrigerator, either alone or with your neighbors, and in it you store your meat and other perishable products until the market can absorb them at a good price. As your cash income increases you can spend more on your land, on yourself and your family. You will be able to pay your taxes, and your community can support better roads, schools and other public services. The vicious cycle of crop failures, defaulted taxes, poverty and community decay will be reversed.[39]

Even at its most primitive level, as a naked lightbulb dangling crudely from the ceiling of a single room, the arrival of electricity had a profound emotional impact on people. "It seemed like this old hillside just lit up when we got electricity," one farm woman remembered.[40] And as people began wiring up more and more rooms and buying radios, refrigerators, and other appliances—all powered at rates that in some areas came to as little as two dollars a month—amazement gave way to dependence. But this particular part of the TVA's rural dream was not easily realized. Large private utility companies threw every legal obstacle they could find into their fight against the federal delivery of federal power to rural cooperatives; moreover, few farm organizations could afford the capital necessary to finance customer delivery systems, even when organized into cooperatives. In the Tennessee Valley, as elsewhere in America, it would take the formation of the Rural Electrification Administration in 1935 before farmers could seriously begin to form cooperatives capable of tapping into the TVA's rapidly growing power grid, and even then only 14.5 percent of the valley's farms would be electrified by 1941.[41]

Otherwise, the TVA's agricultural efforts were largely successful. True, the offer of free fertilizer and training to go along with it was not

39. The New York Times (April 19, 1936).
40. Quoted in William U. Chandler, The Myth of TVA: Conservation and Development in the Tennessee Valley, 1933–1983, p. 57.
41. Many municipalities, unlike rural areas, often could afford to build their own delivery systems. Commonwealth Southern fought against the municipal use of TVA power, too, but some cities in the region made things difficult for themselves by balking at charging their customers the cheap rates mandated by the TVA act. Often, "the conservative-type members of the city board or council," recalled Edward Falck, Director of Rates and Research for the TVA, "had the idea that they could tack on a big fat

unanimously accepted or admired. "I've run through three farms and pretty well used up this one," a Tennessee son of the soil reportedly told a county agent. "You can't tell me nothing about farming."[42] And Mary French Caldwell spoke for many of her generation when she rejected what she believed to be the federal paternalism that came with the federal handout. "Tennesseans have never needed . . . the New Dealers to show them the way to a 'fuller and happier life,'" she snorted. "It is our country and our natural resources and, in the words of Andrew Jackson, 'By the Eternal,' we have the right to run it as we please without outside interference."[43] She had a point, at least as regards paternalism. The statement of one TVA supervisor may not have been typical, but it probably was symbolic of an ongoing problem of attitude. "The farmers who live on the small farms in this area," he said in a report, "are mostly ignorant and inefficient and are not capable of conducting a demonstration for the benefit of their neighbors."[44] Nevertheless, by 1946 the TVA's agricultural division would be monitoring nearly 7,000 demonstration farms on more than 1.1 million acres, and if the demonstration farm program never did persuade the majority of the region's farmers to mend their ways, soil erosion was significantly reduced in many areas of the valley, and production rose so significantly that between 1935 and 1940 the average value of a Tennessee farm rose by nearly 25 percent.[45] By then, TVA publicists were cheerfully citing such success stories as that of J. W. Davis of Birchwood, Tennessee, who had despaired when he lost 300 acres of his farm to a TVA reservoir, but by the end of the decade was raising more dairy cattle on his new place than he had on the old one. "I thought we would starve to death," he said. "I started to

---

margin of profit and have the electric system pay . . . rather than have landowners be taxed . . . for the maintenance of the municipal institutions, schools, and police and so forth. We would not just sell electric power to the municipalities and permit them to charge whatever they might please. We had some really tough battles when we met to negotiate contracts." (Oral history interview with Edward Falck, p. 15; Tennessee Valley Authority Oral History Collection.) Rural electrification figures from Chandler, op. cit., p. 57.
42. Quoted in Chase, op. cit., p. 281.
43. Caldwell, op. cit., p. 53.
44. Quoted in Selznick, op. cit., p. 136.
45. Figures from Davidson, op. cit., p. 294.

leave [the valley], and I would have, too, if I could have found the land I wanted. Now I'm glad I didn't."[46]

BUT THE TVA vision—at least as Arthur Morgan defined it—was more than just a matter of spreading concrete and fertilizer in order to "turn the Tennessee Valley into 40,000 square miles of pastoral, prosperous land," as the *Washington Post* put it on February 18, 1934. At the heart of that prosperity would lie communities whose residents would embrace all the amenities that modern planning could offer them and at the same time maintain the best of those cultural values inherited from their mountain ancestors. Even before work began on Norris Dam on October 1, planners in the TVA's Town Planning and Housing Division had laid out and begun building the nearby village of Norris. The village was designed to house those who would be working on Norris Dam, but chairman Morgan and his planners were determined that it was not going to be just another transient workers' town or in any way remind folks of the ghastly coal mining hamlets that pocked the skin of the mountains like blackheads (in fact, the first one hundred residents were striking coal miners and their families, who were trucked over from Wilder, Tennessee). Designed by Earle Draper, who had planned several mill towns in the Carolinas and Georgia, Norris was to be a permanent town, based, as he put it, "upon the orderly combination of industrial work and subsistence farming."[47] It would be a model for the kind of communities the residents of the valley could expect to see sprouting throughout the region.

While a utilitarian clutch of barracks was constructed on the edge of town to house unmarried workers, most of the dwellings in the village were designed for families. A thousand homes were planned, though only 249 were ever built (as with most of the New Deal's socially ambitious projects, there would never be quite enough money available). While many of the homes that did get constructed were made of cinder block—and looked it—many others combined an ingenious and generally attractive blend of modern architectural modes and

46. Quoted in ibid., p. 298.
47. Quote in Talbert, op. cit., p. 118.

materials with the region's traditional rural architecture, which was primitive but functional—and, for many residents, comfortably familiar. Rents ranged from fourteen to eighteen dollars a month, with an option to buy. The houses were situated along gently curving streets with a great deal of open space all around, and landscaping preserved resident trees wherever possible. "The first thing we did," Draper remembered, "was to select sites and then make the streets and utilities conform to [them]. . . . The most important thing . . . was the relation of the house to the site, the type of house that we'd use, and the relation to adjacent houses so that there would be no interference with privacy."[48] A town commons lay easily accessible to all, as was the school, a shopping center, a community center, and an athletic field. Twenty-five-cent meals were available to all families at the town cafeteria, and each family was reserved a four-acre plot outside the town for subsistence farming.

Even though it remained unfinished—and thoroughly Jim Crow, like everything else in the TVA—as a physical exercise in town building, Norris Village may have been one of the best ideas the New Deal ever had. Attractive and comfortable, the community clearly was made to house human beings, not just a workforce, and was properly respectful of human needs. Above all, of course, the houses were electrified top to bottom. "Women who have lived all their lives in cabins on run-down farms," the Asheville (North Carolina) Citizen remarked, "will be moved into modern homes on fertile land and these houses will be equipped with every comfort that cheap electricity can provide."[49]

This is not to say that the town fathers—which, it should be noted, were the directors of the TVA, Arthur Morgan chief among them—were promoting idleness. The town's residents were encouraged to improve themselves along Morganic lines. One of the advantages of the thirty-three-hour workweek, he said later, was that it provided "time to train people in many forms of household skills and activities. . . . Learning to make gardens, to raise poultry, to make furniture and clothing, and to take part in social activities enlarged the lives of those involved

48. Oral interview with Earle Sumner Draper Sr., p. 24; Tennessee Valley Authority Oral History Collection.
49. Quote in Walter L. Creese, TVA's Public Planning: The Vision, the Reality, p. 255.

and was greatly appreciated by them."[50] One house was set aside as a training center in the domestic arts, while machine tooling, welding, and electrical engineering were taught in a trades training center. Traditional mountain crafts from quilting to furniture-making and wrought-iron blacksmithing were promoted, part of a national urge to revive folk arts and crafts everywhere—a campaign with which the First Lady herself was deeply involved. The big Norris school (proudly air-conditioned) offered adult education courses and a good-sized library that all residents could use. As a means of getting practical training in business, the school's younger students were offered the Norris School Cooperative, which ran a bank, a cafeteria, an insurance company, a store, and a communal garden. Churchly matters were attended to in the school auditorium, which held democratically nondenominational services every Sunday. (The absence of any of the usual Christian edifices, one suspects, stemmed from Morgan's fear that if he allowed Presbyterians or other denominations to build, he would have to accept local sects as well, including those featuring glossolalia, rolling in the aisles, or consorting with rattlesnakes, none of which would have enhanced the town's image as a modernist secular miracle.)

Norris, in Morgan's vision, was to serve the same purpose as one of Harcourt Morgan's demonstration farms—to stand as a place where the ideal of community could be refined and then spread throughout the region, if not the entire country. "When the various cultural and economic projects that I proposed were introduced into the TVA program," he remembered in 1974, "they were looked upon by some people as quite foreign to such a development and were referred to as 'vagaries.' However, the development of a program that was inclusive of all elements of cultural, economic, and legal values was not a temporary course. The efforts then made grew in variety and importance and have become important factors in the overall development of the Tennessee Valley."[51]

Not quite, but Morgan was defending his place in history and perhaps can be forgiven the exaggeration. He did not survive as chairman of the TVA long enough to see his communal goals for the Tennessee

50. Morgan, op. cit., p. 121.
51. Ibid., p. 155.

Valley get much beyond the sociological drawing board. From the beginning, he had clashed with Lilienthal over the question of power production—or, more accurately, over the degree to which the TVA should exercise control of its distribution. Lilienthal was adamant that the agency should adhere to the policy of providing TVA power to public utilities first and private utilities second, and that those private companies that did receive federal electricity should be regulated diligently as to the prices charged their customers. Above all, he did not trust Wendell Willkie and Commonwealth Southern, particularly after the company violated a mutual agreement that it and the TVA would not compete directly in certain agreed-upon areas. Even after what Lilienthal considered an outright betrayal, however, Morgan continued to believe that the larger social goals of the TVA should not be imperiled by any political reaction that the squabble with Commonwealth Southern might produce and that the TVA's stand on power distribution was negotiable.[52] Morgan did not get on particularly well with his namesake in the TVA's agricultural program, either. In this relationship, the conflict stemmed from the chairman's fear that Agricultural Extension agents and local agricultural groups were exercising too much influence over H. A. Morgan's programs, while H. A. insisted that the support of such bodies was utterly necessary to the program's success. Both H. A. and Lilienthal were also offended by what they perceived to be the chairman's arrogance and his uncertain grasp of democratic ideals. Not without some reason. At one point early in the TVA's life, the chairman had suggested that critics might be correct in calling the agency "undemocratic." If so, he insisted, it did not really matter. "In a perfect government," he said in a typically blithe declamation, "there would be some elements of communism, some of democracy, some of technocracy, and some of dictatorship," but the important thing was "a strong and passionate commitment to serve the common good."[53]

The bickering at the top brewed departmental balkanization, jealousy, the formation of bureaucratic gangs loyal only to their own factions or beliefs, and, above all, great confusion as to overall policy

52. See McCraw, op. cit., pp. 47–90, for the best single summary of the difference of opinion between Morgan and Lilienthal.
53. Quoted in Davidson, op. cit., p. 324.

within various levels of the agency, as well as Congress and the White House. The contention did not come to a head until 1938, when Lilienthal and H. A. joined to urge the chairman's departure upon the president. Morgan fought back, bitterly and in public, but to no avail; on March 23, Roosevelt removed him; shortly afterward, FDR appointed H. A. Morgan chairman—and Lilienthal, in his turn, would take H. A.'s place three years later.

Although supremely practical, Lilienthal was still a New Dealer down to his marrow, and as late as 1944 was moved to cite the TVA as a prime example of what technologists could do. "When they have imagination and faith," he said, "they can move mountains; out of their skills they can create new jobs, relieve human drudgery, give new life and fruitfulness to worn-out lands, put yokes upon the streams, and transmute the minerals of the earth and the plants of the field into machines of wizardry to spin out the stuff of a way of life new to this world."[54]

The yoking of rivers and the moving of mountains could not be gainsaid, but there was little left of the TVA's vision of social perfectionism by the time Lilienthal's words got into print. The population of Norris plummeted after the construction of Norris Dam and its facilities, leaving only maintenance and administrative staff with the need for housing. It would not grow again until the beginning of World War II, after which time the town swiftly lost its socially adventurous character and became just another suburb of Knoxville—albeit an uncommonly attractive one. The war also crippled Harcourt Morgan's campaign to revolutionize family farming. The draft sucked away farm labor, and the wartime economy's demand for large amounts of staple crops encouraged increased mechanization and capital investment from outside the region. All of this put the small family farmer at a disadvantage—even when he did not borrow heavily in order to get in on the wartime lottery himself, as many did.

But if the TVA did not erect a new social order or revive Jeffersonian ideals, what it did do, on a colossal scale, was produce electricity, and it was electricity from the TVA's growing congeries of dams, like that generated at Boulder Dam on the Colorado, and Bonneville and Grand Coulee on the Columbia, that was to power much of the nation's

54. David Lilienthal, *TVA: Democracy on the March*, p. 3.

machinery of war. Electricity and phosphates would make munitions and incendiaries on the banks of the Tennessee, and near another newly planned town called Oak Ridge, TVA power would soon help a new breed of technicians toy with the atomic structure of matter to produce uranium 235 and 238.

This, too, was a new world, perhaps, but it probably was not the world that Senator George Norris had in mind when he looked back at the TVA's progress in 1941 from the vantage point of his eighty years and the beginning of a new decade: "It seems, when I think it over," he said, "that it is too good to be true. It seems almost like a dream."[55]

And so it was. So it all was.

55. Quoted in McCraw, op. cit., p. 161.

DISMANTLING
THE DREAM, 1939

Early in January 1939, Missouri sharecropper Walter Johnson took to the road. "Mr. O.A. Reeves sent Me a Written Notice to Me at Night About 9 oclock by a Deputy Constable," Johnson later wrote to Lorenzo Green, an assistant professor of history at Lincoln University who had interested himself in the plight of the sharecroppers. The notice, dated January 3, had given Johnson twelve days to get off the land, he said. Johnson had taken the document to the state's attorney's office, but was told by the attorney that "Mr. Reeves had give me plenty of time and That he Would Advise Me to Move . . . so I begain to Walk looking for a place and I could Not fine no place and I had no Money for Mr. Reeves had Not settle with Me and a deal of others."[1]

Johnson was not alone that early January. Throughout the rich bottomlands of the Missouri "Bootheel" country, people had begun packing up what little they owned, piling it in the beds of their old wagons or stuffing it into decrepit automobiles. Some had only a horse or mule or two on which to tie their possessions. Some, like Johnson, had nothing but their own backs on which to carry their lives; many, like Johnson, had already been cheated out of what they were owed on the previous season's crop; and all, like Johnson, were being evicted from the land so that the owners would not have to worry about sharing the government's AAA cotton payments in the unlikely event that the government ever tried to force them to do so.

There were hundreds of evictees, and most straggled out to the junction of U.S. 60 and U.S. 61, the latter the main highway between St. Louis and Memphis (today's I-55), joining with friends and relatives to set up camp on the roadside. They had nowhere else to go, but the Reverend Owen H. Whitfield, a black vice president of the Southern Tenant Farmers' Union, thought that there might be some publicity value in an otherwise ugly situation and encouraged other evictees to gather by the roadside. After retelling the story of Moses leading the Jews out of Egypt, Whitfield explained to one congregation that "we also must make an Exodus. It's history repeatin' itself."[2] Soon, an estimated one thousand people were strung along the two highways in a ragged little extruded community, with little food and less shelter and in full view of hundreds of motorists every day. Whitfield directed STFU organizer Howard Kester to establish a relief center down in Blytheville, Arkansas, to collect the foodstuffs, clothing, and money that began pouring into the region from all over the country, then smuggle the goods in to the people at night past state troopers who had been posted to keep STFU workers away from the refugees.

While Missouri governor Lloyd C. Stark insisted that the demonstration was fabricated by outside agitators, including, he hinted darkly, Communists in the Farm Security Administration, Whitfield and the STFU publicized the event as one more instance in which the greed and racism of plantation society had combined with the callous ineptitude of government programs to produce human misery. Newspaper stories and newsreel coverage carried the tale of the encampment and its cause to most of the nation for several days.

1. Quoted in Herbert Aptheker, ed., *A Documentary History of the Negro People of the United States,* 4: *From the New Deal to the End of World War II,* p. 361.
2. Quoted in Louis Cantor, "A Prologue to the Protest Movement: The Missouri Sharecropper Roadside Demonstration," *Journal of American History* (March 1969). This is the source for most of my discussion.

On January 12, the temperature dropped to near freezing and it began to snow on the huddled roadside refugees, two inches accumulating within a few hours. The next day, a state health inspector ordered that the people be removed on the grounds that the encampment was a health hazard. Most of the evictees went as peacefully as they had done when vacating their croppers' shacks, though state troopers had to be used to force some out, including about a hundred families that the authorities moved to a site in the middle of the Birds Point–New Madrid Spillway near the Mississippi. The place was little better than a bog, but it was well out of sight of highway traffic. The croppers called it "Homeless Junction," while an FSA investigator pointed out that if health reasons had been the reason to break up the roadside encampment, the spillway was an odd choice, since conditions there were every bit "as conducive to serious epidemic sickness, if not more so."[3] By April, Whitfield had managed to raise enough money to buy ninety acres of land near Poplar Bluff, and many of the evicted families ultimately settled on the tract.

At the end of the year, after a second wave of evictions, Whitfield warned Governor Stark that another highway demonstration was likely. Stark conferred with state and federal agencies, then called a conference that included FSA officials, planters, and STFU representatives. The group formed a committee to investigate the croppers' situation, and the threatened demonstration was called off. The FSA ultimately established a modest housing program in the Bootheel area and spent about $500,000 to help 11,000 families, but people continued to be evicted. Wallace refused to use his influence to help stop the evictions, nor would he change the parity payment system so that croppers could be guaranteed their legal share, even when several Mississippi plantation owners put their signatures to a letter of petition stating that *they* agreed the system was unfair. Wallace insisted that because of the "wide variation in tenancy arrangements," final decisions on who got what had to remain with local committees "in order that each individual case be considered on its own merits."[4]

3. Quoted in ibid.
4. Quoted in ibid.

. . .

THE ROADSIDE DEMONSTRATION of January 1939 was the last major expression of the frustration that had combined with hope to give birth to the Southern Tenant Farmers' Union earlier in the decade. For a brief moment in history it had seemed barely possible that through working together these people would be able to force a federal government that had promised them much to lend a hand in removing the ancient weight of institutional oppression. But as the outcome of the roadside demonstration made clear, there were limits to what organizing among themselves could accomplish for the blacks of the plantation South and even greater limits on how far the government was willing to go in opposing the social and economic system that kept them locked in "sorryness."

Their story, then, was in some important respects a chronicle of disappointment. So were many others. Indeed, as the tenth anniversary year of the Great Crash wore on, it seemed increasingly probable that the decade of the Great Depression, with all its often deadly turmoil and contention, its clashing philosophies and tumultuous political shifts, would end in an ambiguous whimper.

No social phenomenon demonstrated this curve of history more precisely than the fate of black American hopes, which by 1939 had been stifled quite as thoroughly in the canyons of northern cities as they had in the soils of the rural South. During the early years of the depression era, when the nation seemed to be stumbling toward revolution, black faces had been common among the hunger marchers and others who agitated in anger and despair; the democracy of want was color-blind, at least much of the time, and the sense of empowerment such street citizenship brought must have been as compelling for black men and women as for white. Yet organized anger had proved a transient phenomenon, for all the CP/USA's hope that it would turn the nation on its head, and the power it promised was illusory—or, at best, circumscribed. The "Don't Buy Where You Don't Work" movement, for example, one of the best-known expressions of black grassroots sentiment in the depression, was only marginally successful in spite of its brief popularity. Begun in 1929 in the "Black Belt" of Chicago—where a severe recession had presaged the Great Depression itself—this crusade to boycott local merchants who did not hire black help quickly spread to other northern cities, being adapted as it went to fit local conditions. In Cleveland, for instance, shipping clerk John O. Holly took the idea and with a few friends transformed it into the Future Outlook League, an organization whose long-term goal was to establish an entirely self-sufficient system of black capitalism within the city. With the boycott, he said, "We are teaching Negroes (even children) to trade with Negroes first and second with those who are employing Negroes. The men and women who are being placed in the various stores of today will take the place of the white man and be the merchants of tomorrow, with the experience acquired under the white man's instructions."[5] Cleveland's FOL did manage to encourage the development of a number of black businesses—laundries, bakeries, restaurants, dry goods stores, and the like—but a major overhaul of the system evaded it. Other branches of the movement had smaller ambitions, the principal goal being merely to use the power of the black dollar to enforce fair hiring practices, and in some black communities the effort had some measurable impact. In Harlem, Adam Clayton Powell Jr., assistant pastor of the Abyssinian Baptist Church, became the most effective promoter of the Citizens League for Fair Play campaign. Until Judge Samuel Rosenman enjoined the league's pickets, Powell, with the flash and determination that would later make him one of the most powerful congressmen in Washington, forced many businesses on 125th Street not only to hire black and Hispanic workers but to treat people of color with unaccustomed decency. Before Powell, Harlemite Marion Warner remembered,

You couldn't even try anything on in 125th Street. You could go in there to buy something, but you couldn't sit down. You couldn't go to the five-and-ten and sit down and have a soda. Adam Clayton Powell opened up that street. I saw it myself. He would go up and down 125th Street and talk to these people and tell them not to go in there if you can't sit at the counter or if you can't buy this or that. He raised

5. Quoted in Christopher G. Wye, "Merchants of Tomorrow: The Other Side of the 'Don't Spend Your Money Where You Can't Work' Movement," *Ohio History* (winter/ spring 1984).

hell, and they were losing money because people weren't going in there to buy, so they finally opened up.[6]

Nevertheless, by the middle of the decade the "Don't Buy Where You Don't Work" movement had accomplished relatively little, and just how far black people in Harlem felt they still had to go on the road to economic equality had been suggested by what had happened on the night of March 19, 1935. A Puerto Rican boy was caught trying to steal a knife in a five-and-dime store on 125th Street that afternoon. The boy was questioned by police for a while inside the store, then released out a back door to avoid confrontation with the crowd that had gathered on the street in front, feeding on rumors that the boy was being beaten. Early in the evening, someone threw a bottle through the plate-glass window of the store. The crowd swiftly turned into an uncontrollable mob, piled into the store to loot it, then turned to the other stores along the street, breaking into them, too, carrying off whatever could be lifted. The authorities sent in scores of police and police reserves, but it was not until early the next morning that the violence finally was put down. Some 250 shops were wrecked and looted, 125 arrests made, more than 100 people had been injured, and 3 killed. It was the worst racial uprising in Harlem's history up to that time, and while the usual cry of Communist instigation was raised by much of the national press, the riot's true cause was Harlem's poverty, at least according to some. "Every night," the New York Herald Tribune editorialized the day after the riot, "Harlem has its petty stabbings and fist-fights. But yesterday the air crackled with animosity. . . . The factors lying behind this situation are rooted in the economic problems of a poverty stricken area within which a vast population is squeezed."[7] Writing in the April 13 edition of the Afro-American, Nannie Burroughs, a Harlem resident, disagreed. It wasn't economics, she said, it was racism: "Day after day, year after year, decade after decade, black people have been robbed of

6. Quoted in Jeff Kisseloff, You Must Remember This: An Oral History of Manhattan from the 1890s to World War II, p. 317.
7. Quoted in Thomas Kessner, Fiorello La Guardia and the Making of Modern New York, p. 370. My account of the Harlem riot of 1935 is from this source, pp. 365–70. See also Cheryl Lynn Greenberg, Or Does it Explode? Black Harlem in the Great Depression, pp. 3–6.

their inalienable rights. They have been goaded, hounded, driven around, herded, held down, kicked around and roasted alive. . . . In Harlem the cornered rats fought back. The worms turned over and turned around."[8]

Once the New Deal began, many black people had found relief and even a species of opportunity in the Civilian Conservation Corps, the Civil Works Administration, and the amalgam of programs embraced within the Works Progress Administration. Robert Weaver, Ralph Bunche, William Hastie, and a handful of other black individuals had won unprecedented positions of responsibility in many of the executive departments of the administration, and the so-called Black Cabinet, with Mary McLeod Bethune at its spiritual center, had provided African Americans with their first taste of influence in the White House itself—indeed, it was the first time in history that black spokesmen were regularly welcomed within its doors. Still, in spite of the dedication of such individuals as Eleanor Roosevelt, the National Youth Administration's Aubrey Williams, WPA director Harry Hopkins, and Interior Secretary Harold L. Ickes, the New Dealers as a whole would never be able to bring themselves to deal seriously with the consequences of discrimination both within and without the programs of the government, as Henry Wallace's timidity in the question of sharecroppers' rights had demonstrated. But Wallace's vacillation was not the most graphic example of what was and was not possible for blacks in the New Deal world.

Shortly after the first Scottsboro trial had concluded in 1931, newspapers in Scottsboro and other parts of the South had congratulated folks for not resorting to lynching in spite of the fact that, as the *Scottsboro Progressive Age* put it, "if ever there was an excuse for taking the law into their own hands, surely this was one." Indeed, "in the face of one of the most atrocious crimes ever committed in this section," the *Jackson County Sentinel* claimed, southerners had "shown the world that they believed in justice, regardless of color."[9] There was little reason for such journalistic smugness. Lynching was still a major problem in the

8. Quoted in Gerda Lerner, ed., *Black Women in White America: A Documentary History,* p. 409.
9. Both quotes in Page Smith, op. cit., p. 546.

United States generally, and in the South it was nearly epidemic, as it had been for decades. Its stubborn presence was such an affront to those intellectual and business leaders of the region who were promoting the vision of a "new" South that in 1930 the Commission on Interracial Cooperation assembled a Southern Commission on the Study of Lynching under the chairmanship of George Fort Milton of the University of Virginia.

The commission's report, written by researcher Arthur F. Raper and published as *The Tragedy of Lynching* in 1933, had stated at the outset that "until America can discover and apply means to end these relapses to the law of the jungle, we have no assurance that ordered society will not at any moment be overthrown by the blind passion of an ever-present mob."[10] The report then went on to offer up numbers and details in a case-study litany made all the more repulsive by its matter-of-fact presentation: Between 1889 and 1933, 3,745 people had been lynched in the United States—almost all in the southern states—ranging from a high of 255 in 1892 to a low of 8 in 1932; of this number, 2,954 had been black, 791 white; 1,406 of the victims had been accused of murder and 878 of rape or attempted rape (of white women, it should be noted, not black women), but 67 had been lynched merely for "insult to whites"; torture was common and included the cutting off of fingers, toes, and genitalia, the pulling of teeth and nails, evisceration, and being dragged behind automobiles; hanging was the preferred means of execution, but burning while alive was also popular; after death, bodies were frequently mutilated, dismembered, dragged around, or propped up and shot at for sport; finally, "of the tens of thousands of lynchers and onlookers," Raper wrote, "the latter not guiltless, only forty-nine were indicted and only four have been sentenced."[11] Nor could the South

10. Arthur F. Raper, *The Tragedy of Lynching*, p. v.
11. Figures from ibid., appendices, pp. 469–84; quote, ibid, p. 2. While the guilt of those accused of serious crime was irrelevant—whether guilty or not, their deaths were homicides—it is almost certain that a substantial number of those lynched were innocent of any crime. In a later deposition made for Gunnar Myrdal's classic study, *An American Dilemma: The Negro Problem and Modern Democracy* (1944), Raper stated that "case studes of nearly one hundred lynchings since 1929 convince the writer that around a third of the victims were falsely accused" (vol. 1, p. 561.) The level of cruelty

take comfort in the notion that such expressions of rabid vigilantism were fast-fading anachronisms; in 1933, the year after Raper's report was completed, twenty-eight people were lynched.[12]

Condemned as vile even in most of the South, lynching was a prime candidate for federal legislation, and the National Association for the Advancement of Colored People had been centering its time and resources on that goal for years. So had Jessie Daniel Ames, a white Texas feminist, one of the most influential members of the League of Women Voters and a power in the Democratic Party. Ames entertained a special contempt for the common assertion among southerners that lynching, however unfortunate, was just an extreme expression of the need to protect southern white women from the rapacity of black men. Since the vast majority of the victims were never accused of any form of assault on white women, the excuse, she said, was a dog that would not hunt, no more logical an idea than the belief that some sort of irresistible force drew black men and white women together. "[The] crown of chivalry," she once noted "has been pressed like a crown of thorns on our heads. . . . I have always been curious about the . . . white mentality which as far back as I can remember assumes that only segregation and the law against intermarriage keep . . . white women from preferring the arms of Negro men."[13] In 1930, Ames founded the Association of Southern Women to Prevent Lynching, which by the middle of the decade would persuade more than 40,000 women from every county in the American South to sign a national call to reform: "We declare lynching an indefensible crime . . . hateful and hostile to every ideal of religion

---

involved, Myrdal himself wrote, suggested that sexual obsession may well have been "a background factor in lynching. . . . The atmosphere around lynching is astonishingly like that of the tragic phenomenon of 'witch hunting' which disgraced early Protestantism in so many countries. The sadistic elements in most lynchings also point to a close relation between lynching and thwarted sexual urges" (ibid., p. 562). Well, it was the heart of the Freudian age, in which virtually every human impulse or action was deemed to have a sexual component, but it may be just as likely that the sadism of lynching had its origins in the kind of mindless recidivistic savagery that occasionally bubbles up from the human species' dim past, as Carl Jung might have suggested. Or not.

12. Figure in Sitkoff, op. cit., p. 269.
13. Quoted in Page Smith, op. cit., p. 829.

and humanity, debasing and degrading to every person involved. . . . We believe . . . public opinion has accepted too easily the claim of lynchers and mobsters that they were acting solely in defense of womanhood. In the light of facts, we dare no longer permit this claim to pass unchallenged."[14]

Armed with support from such people as Ames, NAACP president Walter White persuaded Senator Edward P. Costigan to introduce an anti-lynching bill in January 1934. The bill would have given the federal courts jurisdiction over cases of accused lynchers if state and local courts did not bring them to trial within thirty days, and would impose fines and imprisonment on those officers of the law found to have cooperated with the lynchers. Costigan's bill was cosponsored by Robert Wagner. "There is no greater evil than mob violence," Wagner said during a Judiciary subcommittee hearing on the bill, "and there is no reform for which I have pleaded with greater certainty of its wisdom . . . than this bill."[15] Even Wagner's powerful support was not enough. The subcommittee reported the bill favorably on March 28, but it immediately sank into legislative oblivion, kept there by a threat of filibuster from the Senate's clutch of dedicated bigots, chief among them Theodore Bilbo of Mississippi. The bill was reintroduced again in 1935, but the southerners managed to keep it from a vote once again, as they did in 1936 and 1937. The NAACP did everything it knew how to do to put public pressure on the body. White presented to Congress copies of petitions and resolutions calling for passage of the bill from state legislatures, city mayors, other politicians, doctors, lawyers, educators, more than 2,800 southern white college students representing thirty-one schools, and the names of more than 700,000 Catholic, Protestant, and Jewish church members. Reginald Marsh, Thomas Hart Benton, George Bellows, and other prominent artists all contributed work to an exhibit at the Newton Gallery in Manhattan, "An Art Commentary on Lynching." The show, the *New York World-Telegram* said, "is an exhibit which tears the heart and chills the blood," and thousands filed through

14. Quoted in Gerda Lerner, ed., op. cit., p. 472.
15. Quoted in Huthmacher, op. cit., p. 172.

it.[16] In January 1938, the bill's supporters finally got it on the floor for a vote, only to see the southerners make good on their promise, speaking against it for nearly six weeks straight. After a second attempt to gain cloture on debate failed on February 16, Costigan and Wagner knew the situation was hopeless and withdrew their legislation.

Throughout the anti-lynching campaign, Franklin Roosevelt made it clear that he personally considered lynching reprehensible, but at no time did he lend his name or active support to the Costigan-Wagner bill in any of its incarnations. He needed southern votes in both houses of Congress for pending legislation, and feared—not without reason—that an uncompromising stand on the bill would be too costly. His endorsement might or might not have been enough to move the bill past the filibuster, had he chosen to speak out or bend some political arms, but the absence of that support was a guarantee of failure. That the organized black community could spend the greater part of its energy and resources, with the support of public opinion and powerful, hardworking congressional allies behind it all the way, and still fail to win a bill that would prohibit the most glaringly un-American of all un-American activities indicated the extent to which political reality could eviscerate hope.

For now, black Americans would have to take what comfort they could in symbolism—specifically, the administration's famously enthusiastic support of contralto Marian Anderson when the singer was refused the use of the Daughters of the American Revolution's Constitution Hall for an Easter Sunday concert in April 1939. Eleanor Roosevelt resigned from the DAR in public protest, and she and Harold L. Ickes got the president's approval for the use of the Lincoln Memorial for the concert. Both the resignation and the government-sponsored concert were deliberate slaps in the face of racism, gestures which no other national administration in history would have been capable of making, and they were greeted with appropriate delight by the black community. But even as Anderson's extraordinary voice began with a rendition of "America the Beautiful" that would have brought tears to a

16. Quoted in Robert L. Zangrado, "The NAACP and a Federal Antilynching Bill," *Journal of Negro History* (April 1965).

stone that blustery Easter Sunday afternoon, a good many blacks in the integrated crowd of 75,000 gathered at the memorial must have been sorrowfully aware of the irony in the moment, an emotional paradox not unlike that which haunted Langston Hughes's poem, "Refugee in America":

> There are words like *Freedom*
> Sweet and wonderful to say.
> On my heart-strings freedom sings
> All day every day.
>
> There are words like *Liberty*
> That almost make me cry.
> If you had known what I knew
> You would know why.[17]

The ambivalent outcome of the struggle of black Americans for simple human rights and economic equality in the depression years stands as a useful paradigm, but the irony of limits frustrated other hopes as well. Eleanor Roosevelt's activism—itself unprecedented among First Ladies—had given women's issues more political visibility than they had ever before enjoyed, and women could celebrate the appointment of Frances Perkins as the first woman cabinet officer in history; Ruth Bryan Owen (to Denmark) and Daisy Harriman (to Norway) as the first women foreign ministers; and Florence Allen as the first woman to be appointed a U.S. District Court judge. Women were also appointed to positions of lesser but still significant magnitude throughout the administration, from the Department of Agriculture to the Works Progress Administration, and under the energetic Mary Dewson, head of the women's division of the Democratic National Committee, they had become a force to be reckoned with in the Democratic Party. Nevertheless, the overall number of women employees in the federal government between 1933 and 1939 never exceeded 19 percent of the total

17. Langston Hughes, "Refugee in America," *Selected Poems of Langston Hughes* (New York: Random House, 1990), p. 290.

workforce, and the overwhelming majority of jobs were at the paper-shuffling level.

On the face of it, for women as for blacks, the burgeoning growth of the CIO after the great sit-down strikes of 1936–1937 would seem to have provided grounds for satisfaction. The AFL remained generally backward with regard to women workers. The CIO was another matter entirely. Women had demonstrated their importance during the UAW sit-downs and had been prominent during the rash of similar strikes that erupted among businesses and industries in the months that followed. Women clearly were no longer just "auxiliary" to the CIO's branch of the labor movement, but essential. In some unions, like the ILGWU or the United Electrical & Radio Workers of America, they were a dominant force, and in many locals they held the reins of power. By the end of 1939, there would be more than 800,000 women union members in the United States—seven times as many as in 1933—and the overwhelming majority of their unions belonged to the CIO.[18]

Similarly, in spite of the fact A. Philip Randolph and his powerful Brotherhood of Sleeping Car Porters had forced William Green of the AFL to encourage the acceptance of more blacks in the AFL, that encouragement had been reluctantly given and the change that followed had been glacial. The CIO, on the other hand—not least because of its healthy contingent of Communists, Socialists, and other social and political radicals—had accepted from the beginning the notion of equality within its ranks and would prove one of the most important single supporters of civil rights in the country. Almost all CIO unions were integrated, although this was not always accomplished without conflict, particularly in those industries in which there were large numbers of European-American workers. There, blacks and first- and second-generation European Americans were in competition for the same kinds of jobs for decades, and old antagonisms and mutual mistrust, often encouraged by employers, were difficult to overcome. Nonetheless, by 1939 black union members had become an important and permanent force in the CIO (their support would be instrumental

18. For women and the CIO, see Foner, op. cit., especially pp. 330–37.

in the UAW's victory over the Ford Motor Company in 1941, for example).[19]

However gratifying the CIO's acceptance of women, blacks, and others, satisfaction necessarily was tempered by the fact that by 1939 the CIO's own hopes had been frustrated, leaving it in a condition that seemed to belie its emergence as the chief representative of organized labor in the United States. The continuing presence and influence of Communists and Socialists within the CIO kept many of its unions in a shambles of almost constant agitation, as traditionalists competed with radicals for the leadership of individual unions and the control of locals. These and other contentions inspired a string of open breaks that by the end of the decade would leave the union organization discombobulated.

David Dubinsky of the ILGWU had been concerned about Communist influences in the CIO for years. He and John L. Lewis also had disagreed over the question of eventual reconciliation with the parent AFL, which Dubinksy believed essential to the continued good health of union labor and which Lewis was reluctant to endorse. Differences between the two men came to a head on November 15, 1938, when the CIO unions gathered in Pittsburgh to formalize their withdrawal from the AFL, write a constitution for the organization, and elect its first official president—John L. Lewis, as it turned out. The ILGWU refused to participate. "We reaffirmed our opposition to dualism," Dubinksy remembered, "but promised to do all we could to promote a reconciliation [between the AFL and the CIO] while remaining independent. . . . My own view was that we were not seceding from the CIO, but that it was seceding from its original purpose of organizing the mass-production industries and assuming a new status that could only help to perpetuate the split in organized labor."[20] Dissension also struck in the burgeoning UAW. In April 1939, its conservative president, Homer Martin, climaxed his ongoing fight with the union's radical elements by splitting himself and his supporters off and defecting to the AFL.

The AFL, of course, while in an unaccustomed subordinate position now, had not vanished. It gnawed at the troubled CIO's flanks any way

19. For African Americans and the CIO, see Zieger, op. cit., especially pp. 83–85, and Sitkoff, op. cit., pp. 175–89.
20. David Dubinsky and A. H. Raskin, *David Dubinsky: A Life in Labor*, p. 238.

it could, including using the threat of CIO organization to persuade employers to sign "backdoor" contracts with AFL representatives. This tactic became especially useful when the CIO set out to duplicate in the southern textile industry its success in the steel industry by assembling a Textile Workers Organizing Committee and launching a major membership drive. While spending a good deal more than the organization could truly afford and with the financially overstressed United Mine Workers still contributing the lion's share, the CIO failed to organize more than 5 percent of the mill workers, and in many of the mills that did get organized, the AFL's United Textile Workers had the day. The CIO would survive long enough for World War II and the postwar economic boom not only to reinvigorate the organization but to bring the labor movement into a new golden age of growth, but in the waning months of the depression decade, the CIO's glittering dream of wholesale industrial unionism was shadowed by uncertainty and dissent.

THERE WAS PLENTY of uncertainty and dissent among the New Dealers themselves as the tenth-anniversary year of the Great Crash commenced—and with them a steady erosion of the power once held by those fierce liberals who had helped the president and the Congress create a legislative revolution. On January 3, the members of the 76th Congress took their seats and got down to business. More than 36 million voters had gone to the polls in November 1938, breaking the off-year election record of more than 32 million set in 1934; but this time there was little overall celebrating among the New Dealers, no talk of mandates, no cries of "Boys, this is our hour!" as Harry Hopkins reportedly had done in the aftermath of November 1934. The Democrats still controlled both houses, but the Republicans were gaining on them, having won seventy-five new seats in the House and seven in the Senate, and conservative Democrats had gained in power. The more radical Democrats who remained not only had seen their own influence diminish but had lost several of their leftist allies as well. In short, unlike the two previous Congresses, the 76th was by no stretch of the imagination a Roosevelt captive.

In large part, Roosevelt had no one to blame but himself. Once the 1936 elections had been put safely behind him, the president, who had never forgiven the Supreme Court for invalidating most of both the National Industrial Recovery Act and the Agricultural Adjustment Act, spent much of 1937 in a clearly vindictive and constitutionally questionable attempt to "pack" the Supreme Court with enough liberal justices to overcome what he believed to be a destructive reactionary bent. Legislation that would give him the authority to increase the membership of the court was introduced in Congress early in February 1937, and FDR's stubborn pursuit of this goal threw much of his administration into turmoil and alienated many members of Congress who wondered, with columnist Walter Lippmann, whether the president was "drunk with power."[21] The "court-packing scheme," as the conservative press tended to characterize it, would not have had much of a chance in Congress under the best of circumstances, and what slim possibility there was of its acceptance had vanished when majority leader Joe Robinson, FDR's reluctant spear-carrier on the question in the Senate, died of a heart attack on July 14, 1937. Shortly afterward, the Senate voted 70–20 to recommit the legislation, effectively killing it. In the meantime, the Supreme Court had stolen some of the president's thunder by validating the constitutionality of both the Social Security Act and the National Labor Relations Act, while soon reaching several other decisions that ultimately gratified the New Dealers.

Even while the president's ill-conceived restructuring of the Supreme Court was getting under way, his sudden return to the old dream of a balanced budget almost certainly helped bring on a recession in the fall of 1937, and it proved to be the most precipitous economic plunge in American history—a consequence that did nothing to enhance his increasingly troubled relations with Congress. In 1936 and well into 1937, every "economic indicator," as economists liked to put it, suggested that the nation was on the road to a "broad recovery," according to Lachlin Currie of the Federal Reserve Board.[22] Unemployment had fallen from a high of nearly 13 million in 1932 to 7.7 million, the average annual wage for factory workers had risen from $1,086 to $1,376, and corporate income had climbed from $5.3 billion to more

21. Quoted in Ronald Steele, *Walter Lippmann and the American Century*, p. 319.
22. Quoted in Allen Brinkley, *The End of Reform: New Deal Liberalism in Recession and War*, p. 24.

than $13 billion. Railroads were adding trains. Steel production had reached 80 percent of capacity, construction work had doubled. Factories all over the country were humming, adding shifts and employment regularly, even when hampered by strikes.[23] Big businessmen, the *New York Times* reported on January 3, 1937, were "showing more optimism than they have at any time in recent years." Surely, Roosevelt felt, supported with all his being by Treasury Secretary Henry Morgenthau, the national economy no longer needed anywhere near the levels of federal "pump-priming" that it had been receiving since 1933. Now was the time to tackle the deficit such tactics had created. Now was the time to balance the budget. "Business conditions have shown each year since 1933 a marked improvement over the preceding year," he had said in his annual message to Congress on January 6, 1937. "These gains make it possible to reduce for the fiscal year 1938 many expenditures of the Federal Government which the general depression made necessary."[24] And on April 20, he submitted a budget request for fiscal 1938 that would assure that the balance would be achieved—at a tremendous cost to the "emergency" programs born during the first three years of the administration. Funding to the WPA alone was cut from $1.7 billion in fiscal 1937 to a little over $1.3 billion for fiscal 1938, while employment in the agency dropped by half a million jobs between the beginning and the end of calendar 1937. The PWA lost 140,000 jobs in the same period, the CCC and NYA more than 200,000.[25]

It probably would be too much to say that the president's spending cuts were the principal cause of the slump that first began to be felt late that summer, but they certainly did not ease an already troubled situation. The economic recovery that pundits had been celebrating since the middle of 1936 was real enough, but not very deep. Reassured by the government's FIDC program, people were banking more and spending less. But even those with decent jobs had less to spend in 1937, anyway, for it was during that year that the first Social Security deductions began to take a nip out of paychecks; while the impact of the deductions varied from individual to individual, the sudden loss of some $2 billion

23. For steel and construction figures, see ibid.
24. Quoted in Kenneth S. Davis, *FDR: Into the Storm, 1937–1940*, p. 9.
25. All figures from Howard, op. cit., table 1, appendices, pp. 854–57.

in disposable income was a measurable blow to the overall economy.[26] Consumer buying simply was not keeping pace with increased production (as in the months preceding the Crash of '29), and by the fall of 1937, most backlog orders had been filled and inventories started to accumulate. Production began to slide, prices to decline, unemployment to rise, plants to close, and confidence to deteriorate. Then came the "Black Tuesday" of October 19, a too vivid reminder of all the black days of the stock market just eight years before. In a sudden burst of panic selling, nearly 7.3 million shares were traded on the New York exchange that Tuesday, more than on any day since the "Black Tuesday" of 1929. "This country again faces a very serious business and financial crisis," the Federal Reserve's Fiscal and Monetary Advisory Committee warned the president that evening. "To put it bluntly, we face another depression. . . . Plants are closing down every day. Thousands and thousands of industrial workers are being laid off every day. Forward orders are being canceled. . . . Prices are falling. . . . Such movements gather their own momentum, and feed upon themselves."[27]

Toward the end of March 1938, the stock market had lost nearly half its value. Unemployment had grown by nearly four million, corporate profits had dropped by 78 percent, and industrial production was down 40 percent.[28] Then, on March 25, the stock market took yet another sudden dive. "*Government is scared*, alarmed, more conscious of possibility of continuing depression than it has been at any time previously," *Kiplinger's Washington Newsletter* reported on March 26. "This applies to Congress, to executive officials, even to the President."[29] Fear and confusion indeed reigned on the Potomac, not least in the mind of the president. Henry Morgenthau, Jesse Jones of the Reconstruction Finance Corporation, and other fiscal conservatives urged him to hold firm to his budget cuts in spite of what had already become known as the "Roosevelt Recession." Harry Hopkins (soon to be secretary of commerce), Marriner Eccles of the Federal Reserve, and other advocates of government spending begged him to restore much of the federal fund-

26. Figure from Davis, op. cit., p. 140.
27. Quoted in Brinkley, op. cit., p. 29.
28. Figures from ibid.
29. In The Kiplinger Washington Editors, Inc., op. cit., p. 47.

ing he had stripped from the budget. In the end, Roosevelt succumbed to the pressure to spend. On April 14, he sent a request to Congress for increased federal appropriations and loans to the tune of $3 billion, and that night took to the airwaves for his twelfth "Fireside Chat" to explain the situation to the people. "This recession has not returned us to the disasters and the suffering of the beginning of 1933," he emphasized in a manner not unlike that of a man whistling past a graveyard:

> But I know that many of you have lost your jobs or have seen your friends or members of your families lose their jobs, and I do not propose that the government shall pretend not to see these things. . . . I said in my message opening the last session of the Congress that if private enterprise did not provide jobs this spring, government would take up the slack—that I would not let the people down. We have all learned the lesson that government cannot afford to wait until it has lost the power to act.[30]

Congress, whose members had been hearing from suddenly angry constituents in this election year, had learned the lesson well enough; it gave Roosevelt what he asked for, and by the beginning of 1939, the stimulus of federal money appeared to have turned the economy around and sent it limping slowly back in the direction of recovery. In the meantime, however, the president's misguided attack on the Supreme Court, followed by the recession for which he had to assume at least some responsibility—many blamed him for it, in any event—had badly damaged the administration. Both Roosevelt and the New Dealers in general had lost the seeming invulnerability that had graced them up to this point, and in both the Congress and the country at large their ability to get things done had been crippled. This result had been brought home most forcefully in April 1938 when, by a narrow margin, the House rejected a much desired reorganization bill that would have restructured much of the executive department in the interests of efficiency and increased presidential autonomy. Among those who voted against the bill were 108 Democrats. "Twelve months ago," *The New Republic*'s "TRB" wrote on April 27, "such a vote would have been

30. Quoted in Buhite and Levy, eds., op. cit., p. 113.

unthinkable. The wounds it has created in the liberal bloc cannot be easily healed." For the rest of the 1938 congressional session, the president would get only one major piece of domestic legislation passed—the Fair Labor Standards Act of 1938, which established a minimum wage and fixed the workweek at forty-four hours (gradually reduced to forty).

Clearly, it was not a good time for the president to muddy his relations with Congress further. But he did. He had not been willing to forgive the Supreme Court for its actions against the NRA and the AAA, and now he was no more inclined to turn the other cheek when it came to those in Congress who had opposed his attempt to reshape the court to his liking and had helped to defeat his reorganization bill. For the first time, the president decided not merely to take an active role in the congressional elections but to try to sculpt the outcome, at least with regard to those conservative Democrats who had fought him on issues close to his heart. He gave liberal Democrat Claude Pepper of Florida a public endorsement in February, and when Pepper won that early primary handily, Roosevelt apparently assumed his voice alone had been enough to assure the victory and that he would get similar results elsewhere. He went on the air with a "Fireside Chat" on June 24, not only castigating the Republicans as "Copperheads"—a reference to those Democrats who had opposed Abraham Lincoln's war policies—but making it perfectly clear that conservatives in general, whether Republican or Democrat, did not "recognize the need for government to step in and take action," that they would have America "return, in effect, to the kind of government that we had in the 1920s." Such people, he said, had abandoned creative thought: "I know that neither in the summer primaries nor in the November elections will the American voters fail to spot the candidates whose ideas have given out."[31] He then concentrated his personal efforts on the defeat of nine conservative Democratic senators, including Millard Tydings of Maryland, Walter George of Georgia, and Ellison ("Cotton Ed") Smith of South Carolina.

The press called it a "purge," the American political equivalent of the terrible cleansing that Stalin had initiated in the Soviet Union in 1936 to consolidate his power. But Stalin had murdered or sent to

31. Quotes in ibid., pp. 133–35.

gulags tens of thousands of presumed political dissidents—throwing many members of the CP/USA into a crisis of conscience that would reverberate for the rest of the decade—while Franklin Roosevelt achieved little more than his own political humiliation. The purge was a disaster. Only James Fay of New York managed to survive a Roosevelt recommendation that year, defeating John J. O'Connor. The rest of those whom Roosevelt had targeted for defeat won, leaving the contingent of liberal Democrats in both houses of Congress bereft of much of their power, and the Republicans with a sudden pool of potential allies with whom they might combine to make Roosevelt's life miserable. "I knew from the beginning that the purge could lead to nothing but misfortune," disaffected Postmaster General James A. Farley remembered, "because in pursuing his course of vengeance Roosevelt violated a cardinal political creed which demanded that he keep out of local matters. . . . I trace all the woes of the Democratic party, directly or indirectly, to this interference in purely local matters."[32]

Farley had despised Roosevelt for some time when he wrote those words (1948), but the indictment was valid. From this point forward, nearly every piece of domestic legislation or administrative action supported or undertaken by the president and the liberal Democrats would face diligent scrutiny and often vigorous opposition in Congress—and nothing would survive without having been amended, sometimes beyond recognition. Nor could Roosevelt assume any longer that he could stop legislation he did not like. In spite of his opposition and that of most liberal Democrats, for example, the House authorized the creation of the Special Committee to Investigate Un-American Activities in 1938, the first version of what would later be institutionalized as the House Un-American Activities Committee, with Martin Dies of Texas chairman and J. Parnell Thomas of New Jersey self-appointed head ferret.

Things got worse. When, in January 1939, the president submitted his $9 billion budget for fiscal 1940, with a request for $875 million to keep the WPA going from February through June, the House immediately cut $150 million from the WPA appropriation and the Senate approved the cut on January 27. When Roosevelt submitted another

32. James A. Farley, *Jim Farley's Story: The Roosevelt Years*, pp. 146–47.

version of the reorganization bill that had been defeated in 1938, the new Congress promptly dismembered it, threw away some of the president's most desired provisions, then reassembled the remainder and passed it. The law required that the administration submit to Congress reorganization plans to implement the law's provisions, and on April 25 and May 9, Roosevelt's planners did so. Both were accepted and scheduled to go into effect on July 1. Among other major provisions were two that cut particularly deep into the structure of some of the New Deal's most hallowed programs. A newly created Federal Security Agency, for example, would take under its wing both the NYA division of the Works Progress Administration and the formerly independent CCC. The WPA itself would be renamed the Works Projects Administration and be placed under the control of another new administrative body, the Federal Works Agency, which also took over Harold L. Ickes's Public Works Administration.

Nor was Congress entirely done with the WPA. The suspicious political coloration of Federal One's programs for artists, writers, musicians, and theater people became the special interest of Martin Dies and J. Parnell Thomas of the House Subcommittee on Un-American Activities after the spring of 1938, with the Federal Writers' Project and the Federal Theater Project coming under particularly close scrutiny. In June, Dies began hearings on the question of Communist influence in Federal One, and the investigation continued for the rest of the year—although by October, Dies himself was sufficiently persuaded of the subversive character of both the FWP and the FTP to tell one reporter that the two were "doing more to spread Communist propaganda than the Communist Party itself."[33] In April, inspired by the Dies committee, the House Subcommittee on Appropriations passed a resolution that would require the investigation of *all* WPA projects for possible subversion and placed Representative Clifton Woodrum in charge of a committee to do so.

By June, the Woodrum Committee had entertained its own share of testimony and given its recommendations to Congress. Legislation was crafted and introduced as part of the Emergency Relief Appropriations Act for fiscal 1940. The bill would strip $125 million from the WPA

33. Quoted in Penkower, op. cit., p. 195.

and give it to the PWA, now tucked into the Federal Works Agency. All WPA workers who had been on the federal payroll for more than eighteen months would be dismissed. All future WPA workers would be required to sign a loyalty oath. And while the Federal Writers' Project, the Federal Arts Program, and the Federal Music Project would be allowed to continue, they would be required to win state sponsorship of their programs after September 1 or be dissolved. The Federal Theater Project did not get even that much of a reprieve; it was to be discontinued the minute the legislation went into effect. The House passed the bill almost immediately, and while opponents put up a struggle in the Senate, the legislation was approved just before the end of the fiscal year. Roosevelt, who was in no position to veto a bill whose funds were needed to finance relief efforts for the next year, reluctantly signed it into law. "What is this America of ours, after all?" one outraged editorial writer asked. "Is it made up only of buildings and roads and sewers? Is there such a thing as the soul of America, and if so, is this American soul capable of appreciating only the things of cement and stone?"[34] Hallie Flanagan and the rest of the staff of the Federal Theater Project probably would have answered in the affirmative. After getting the word from Washington on June 30 that the FTP would be abolished the next morning, the cast and crew of the New York production of the long-running and enormously popular *Pinocchio* at the Ritz Theater changed the play's happy ending for its final performance. They turned the little boy back into a puppet. The cast then chanted, "So let the bells proclaim our grief that his small life was all too brief," tore down the scenery in full view of the audience, and laid the puppet in a casket on which was printed an epitaph: "BORN DECEMBER 23, 1938; KILLED BY ACT OF CONGRESS, JUNE 30, 1939."[35]

Curtain.

FROM NOW ON, it would be war and the fear of war that would color the national consciousness far more brightly than the struggle to overcome the Great Depression, war that would increasingly occupy the attention

34. Quoted in ibid., p. 210.
35. Quoted in Flanagan, op. cit., p. 365.

of both Roosevelt and the Congress. War, in fact, had never been long out of the minds of most Americans since October 1935, when Italy's Benito Mussolini had sent troops into Ethiopia against the ill-equipped forces of Emperor Haile Selassie; it would take the Italians just a little over six months to defeat Selassie's army and annex the country. If one had been of a suitably oracular cast of mind in November of 1935, in fact, it might have been possible to discern the shape of the future in the toy counter displays of the big chain stores—Woolworth's; Marshall Field; W. T. Grant; Sears, Roebuck; and the like. It was a good season for war toys, *Fortune* magazine reported in its December issue. The toy industry, the magazine said, was in a "pretty state of confusion" about the surge in miniature weapons of war:

> Manufacturers and retailers piously insist that they are making no profits out of war and that they have noticed no abnormal increase in sales. But the counters of chain stores . . . are overflowing with tanks and soldiers and cannons. . . . The only toy seller who is frank about appreciating the increase in business is the W. T. Grant Co. which is particularly proud of having scooped the chain-store field with Ethiopian soldiers. Until Grant could get ready-made Ethiopians, it colored up part of its regular stock of white soldiers with chocolate paint.[36]

The Italian conquest of Ethiopia was the first major conflict in the march to international war that proceeded with such inexorability over the next several years that it sometimes seemed as if it was merely a continuation of the 1914–1918 conflagration, which had left the nations of Europe littered with so much human and institutional wreckage. And if in the Christmas season of 1935 the cunning tin and cast-iron replicas of war were spilling over the countertops of American department stores, it was merely a prelude to the months to come. Here we would see war and the fear of war mix with the culture, politics, and economy of this nation in a confused kaleidoscope of ideology, contention, decency, and ugliness that in the end would simply overwhelm the protocols of depression by which the country had been living since 1930.

36. "Mars in the Nursery," *Fortune* (December 1935).

The Italian invasion of Ethiopia had inspired sympathy in this country; events in Spain brought forth more than sympathy. In February 1936, a coalition of Communists, Socialists, and other radical elements rose up in revolution, forced King Alfonso XIII to flee the country, took over Madrid, and under the leadership of General Emilio Mola Vidal, held free elections, forming a Republican government and electing Manuel Azana its president. In July, a "nationalist" coalition of monarchists, clergy, fascists, and conservative business interests joined under General Francisco Franco to launch a civil war against the Republicans. Franco was given advice, money, munitions, fighters and bombers, even pilots, by Nazi Germany and fascist Italy, since both Hitler and Mussolini saw Spain as an excellent training ground; the Soviet Union, more circumspect, though no less interested in the outcome, secretly sold arms to the Republicans, or Loyalists, as they were also called.

What with the Soviet connection and the prominence of Communists in the new Spanish government, the CP/USA, as might have been expected, was probably the most vigorous domestic supporter of the Republicans. But not all Americans who empathized were Communists, or even radicals. William Allen White, the old Progressive Republican and lifelong editor of the *Emporia Gazette* in Kansas, called Franco and the Nationalists "the rats of Spain."[37] And among the New Dealers, such otherwise disparate types as Henry Wallace, Henry Morgenthau, Harold Ickes, and Assistant Secretary of State Sumner Welles, among many others, were militantly concerned, though they could not persuade Roosevelt to aid the Republicans even to the extent of allowing them to buy arms in this country. However much he might have deplored the fascist revolt, FDR did not want to risk offending Germany and Italy.

For millions of Americans, the Spanish Civil War stood as nothing less than the apotheosis of good locked in bloody combat with evil, and Spain became the first international arena in which the old antagonism between liberalism and conservatism in America was acted out. Anthropologists Ruth Benedict and Franz Boas, religious philosophers Harry Emerson Fosdick and Reinhold Niebuhr, President James R.

37. Quoted in Walter Johnson, *William Allen White's America*, p. 513.

Angell of Yale and President Mary E. Wooley of Mount Holyoke and
scores of other university presidents, deans, and professors all signed
protests, letters, public statements, and other documents supporting
the Republicans and excoriating the monarchists. On the other side
stood conservative politicians from both parties, the American Catholic
Church, most of whose leaders saw the Republicans as the enemies of
God Himself, and most of the publishers and editors of most of the
newspaper and magazine press, who entertained special horror over
the distinctly leftist nature of the Spanish government. No one despised
the Republicans more than Henry Luce, whose *Time* magazine went out
of its way to describe Republican President Azana as "frog-faced" and
"obese and blotchy," while characterizing his government as "a regime
of Socialists, Communists, and rattle-brained Liberals."[38]

For Americans, it was a writer's war. Ernest Hemingway, John Dos
Passos, Martha Gellhorn, Meyer Levin, Archibald MacLeish, Lillian
Hellman, Malcolm Cowley, Wallace Stevens, Dorothy Parker, Granville
Hicks, Edmund Wilson, Mary McCarthy, Lewis Mumford, and scores of
others all wrote about the war in both fiction and nonfiction; many
went to Spain themselves, some joining the hundreds of Americans who
became soldiers in the Abraham Lincoln and Washington battalions of
the Fifteenth International Brigade. Martha Graham choreographed
ballets written in tribute to the Spanish struggle, while out in Hollywood Franchot Tone, Joan Crawford, Darryl F. Zanuck, and other
motion picture notables were given private screenings of *The Spanish
Earth*, a pro-Republican documentary with music by Virgil Thomson,
and in New York Benny Goodman unsheathed his clarinet at a benefit
for the cause.

But if most intellectuals and a few politicians identified powerfully
with the plight of the Republicans, when Madrid finally fell to the
Nationalists on April 3, 1939, most Americans who paid the moment
much heed at all were just as relieved that the war was over as they had
been saddened by its outcome. Roosevelt had been entirely correct in
his assumption that there was a powerful antiwar sentiment in the
country, one which would not have supported an overt act against the
Nationalists or for the Republicans any more than it would have toler-

38. Quoted in W. A. Swanberg, *Luce and His Empire*, pp. 137–38.

ated involvement in the Ethiopian conflict. The loss of democracy in Spain was not worth a war.

Nor, it seemed, was the loss of an American gunship. In 1931, the increasingly militant Empire of Japan, an island nation with few natural resources of its own, had invaded China and seized Manchuria for its raw materials. An uneasy peace had prevailed between China and Japan for several years after the Japanese coup, but in August 1937, war between the two nations erupted. On December 12, the *Panay*, a U.S. Navy gunboat that had been sent to China to look after the interests and safety of American citizens and American shipping, was unexpectedly attacked and sunk by Japanese planes while stationed on the Yangtze River. One American civilian and two sailors were killed, and eleven others wounded. While expressing outrage over the incident, the great bulk of White House mail and telegrams over the next several days also pleaded with the president not to go to war over the matter. He did not, accepting instead Japanese apologies and reparations for the attack.

In Europe, Hitler began his final chesslike moves toward conquest of the continent. In March 1938, Austrian Nazis ousted that country's chancellor, after which Hitler sent in an army of occupation and claimed that Germany and Austria were now united. Six months after the Austrian *Anschluss*, Mussolini and Hitler met with British Prime Minister Neville Chamberlain and French Prime Minister Edouard Daladier in Munich. Hitler demanded the Sudetenland, which included a large part of Czechoslovakia, as his price for peace. The French and British ministers agreed and came away with what Chamberlain insisted was "peace in our time."

In this country, an increasingly vocal and powerful contingent of isolationists in and out of Congress clamored for continued American neutrality, no matter what might happen in Europe or Asia, and Roosevelt assured everyone that the United States had no intention of getting entangled—not even to the extent of helping to rescue German Jews. While the Nazis had not yet come up with the "final solution" to the Jewish "problem," it was becoming general knowledge that in Germany Jews were increasingly persecuted, while the government passed laws that systematically stripped them of their rights. Thousands began getting out of the country as best they could, but most would find no refuge in the United States, which refused to increase its "quota" of permitted Jewish immigration. Refusal continued even after the horror of *Kristallnacht* on November 9, 1938, when the assassination of a Nazi official led to government-sanctioned rioting in both Germany and Austria that left hundreds of Jews dead and perhaps 60,000 under arrest and in concentration camps. Americans generally deplored the outrage against the Jews, but there was no sudden nationwide demand that the government lift immigration quotas and let them in. Indeed, this country had its own "Jewish problem," though it might be more accurate to say that Jews in the United States had an "American problem." Anti-Semitism had always been endemic in the United States, and in the uncertain times of 1938 and 1939, with the country still feeling the effects of the "Roosevelt Recession" and much of the world appearing on the verge of collapse, ambitious bigots had little difficulty tapping into deep wells of prejudice. Father Charles Coughlin, for example, had long since abandoned any semblance of gentility in his anti-Jewish crusade. His political hopes may have gone down to ruin in the 1936 elections, but he had found new energy in something he called the Christian Front, which organized neighborhood anti-Semites into platoons of thugs to promote bigotry and intimidation. Meanwhile Coughlin himself continued to clog the ether with ever more vituperative declamations against Jews, New Dealers, and Communists, all of which, he intimated, were pretty much one and the same thing. He had better things to say about William Dudley Pelley's Silver Legion, another virulently anti-Semitic group traveling under the guise of Christianity, as well as the German-American Bund, the Nazi government's principal propaganda machine in the United States.

While the government checked the locks on the nation's doors, and outbursts of anti-Semitic violence punctuated urban life from time to time, the world lurched closer to war with every passing week. On March 15, 1939, German troops occupied Moravia and Bohemia in Czechoslovakia; the entire country was now under Nazi control, while Hitler's ministers dismissed protests from Great Britain and France as lacking "every political, moral and legal basis."[39] On April 7, Mus-

39. Quoted in Leon Bryce Bloch and Charles Angoff, eds., *The World Over in 1939*, p. 523.

solini's troops invaded Albania. On April 15, Roosevelt wired Hitler and Mussolini, asking them to commit to a ten-year moratorium on war and to attend an international peace conference; his proposal was spurned by both fascist leaders. On April 24, the U.S. House of Representatives approved for fiscal 1940 a War Department appropriation of more than $508 million, the largest in American history, and while this was ludicrous when compared to the billions Hitler had spent to assemble his war machine since taking power in 1933, it was the first hint that even the isolationist-minded Congress feared that the United States might not be able to avoid what each day appeared more inevitable.

By the end of August, Hitler was ready. To keep his eastern flank free from threat, he had negotiated a nonaggression pact with the Soviet Union on August 24, an agreement that, like Stalin's purge of dissidents in 1936, plunged American Communists into a quandary—"I felt like I had been hit by a bolt of lightning," one remembered—though the official line from the CP/USA was the strained contention that by "compelling Germany to sign a nonaggression pact, the Soviet Union not only tremendously limited the direction of Nazi war aims, but thereby bolstered the possibilities for peace in the world."[40] And early in the morning of September 1, after staging a mock violation of German territory by Polish troops, Hitler told his *Wehrmacht* that "the Poles refused my peace offers and don't respect our frontiers. . . . We must face force with force," then launched a devastatingly effective blitzkrieg on a country that still fought wars on horseback.[41] On September 3, as they had vowed they would do if Hitler invaded Poland, both Britain and France declared war on Germany. That night, Franklin Roosevelt went on the air with what legitimately could be called the last "Fireside Chat" of the New Deal. Like all the others, the talk was designed to comfort and enlighten the public in a time of worry, but this time it was to pledge that the flames that were now beginning to flicker in Europe would not reach these shores. "I hope the United States will keep out of this war," he said. "I believe that it will. And I give you assurance and reassurance that every effort of your government will be directed toward that end.

40. Both quotes in Ottanelli, op. cit., pp. 182, 183.
41. Quoted in Bloch and Angoff, eds., op. cit., p. 758.

"As long as it remains within my power to prevent, there will be no blackout of peace in the United States."[42]

He hoped. All America hoped.

AN ENDING, THEN, from the well of my own memory: I was lying on a somewhat threadbare rug on the floor of the living room in our tiny frame house in southern California—the family's first—reading a comic book. My father was off on a fishing trip, my infant brother taking a nap in the next room. My mother and I were alone with the big Philco console, the most splendiferous piece of furniture we owned, listening to the Sunday-afternoon cowboy music broadcast from KFXM up on the hill half a mile away. My mother was ironing and humming along with the music from time to time. In recollection, the moment seems suffused with a comfortable blurred reality, like a scene out of an old movie.

I was a child of the depression. My mother and father carried its scars and would do so all of their lives. They had never been desperately poor, but neither had they been comfortably poor. And if they were among those fortunate enough to live in southern California—if you had to survive an economic depression, southern California, with its benign climate and its nearly deranged worship of possibility's dogmas, was probably the best place in the world in which to do it—they were never unconscious of the depression or immune to its effects. For most of the era, they lived too close to the last segment of Route 66 not to be aware on almost a daily basis of the growing numbers of refugees from the Dust Bowl rattling gravely down the road. They knew that what these "Okies," "Arkies," "Texies," and "Mexies" still faced was a grinding route up Cajon Pass in the San Bernardino Mountains, across the desert on old Highway 138, which dipped and rose from one scattered desert town to the other like a roller coaster for mile after mile, and finally, decrepit automobiles smoking and wheezing by now, over Tejon Pass in the Tehachapi Mountains and down the twisting, dangerous "grapevine" of Highway 99 into the lower San Joaquin Valley, in whose sprawling agribusiness empires they hoped (vainly, as it happened) eco-

42. In Buhite and Levy, eds., op. cit., p. 151.

nomic redemption lay. Some had settled right here, though, including my best friend, Terry, whose own family lived just down the alley; we would race home after school every day to hear *The Lone Ranger*, then take our handmade wooden pistols and inner-tube rubber ammunition and hunt each other down in the miniature wilderness of the vacant lot a block away.

My father had a fairly decent job in a comic-printing plant by then, but he had started life as a family man by playing the banjo in a little western swing outfit—Tommy Watkins and His Western Band—that toured the desert hamlets under the aegis of the New Deal's Federal Music Project. Often, my mother had accompanied him, and sometimes, carefully arranging the tiny bundle that was me on a couple of chairs, she would join in the dancing. They were Roosevelt Democrats to the core. My father was proud of the fact that he held one of the first Social Security cards issued in 1937, the program's first year, and he has kept that card tucked in several generations of wallets ever since. When he helped to organize the printing plant after World War II, the memory of the often violent and repressive labor struggles of the depression years was never far from his mind; there would be an almost clandestine air to the meetings that gathered in the living room of the house while the men argued themselves into commitment, knowing that it could cost them their jobs. Or worse (there were death threats).

We had not been unaware that Europe was burning across the sea. Ever since 1940, like millions of others, we had listened, fixated, to the sepulchral voice of Edward R. Murrow intoning "This . . . is London," then going on to describe the horror of the bombings whose explosions could be heard muffled in the background. And I can remember the day when my father got his draft notice, and the relief that had brought my mother to tears when my father's eyesight had been declared too bad to let him go to soldiering. Once, an Army Air Force pilot in the nearby air base had gone crazy, stolen a bomber, and flown back and forth across our little town at rooftop level. I will never forget my terror as I tried to bury my tiny body in the grass in the backyard as the big brown plane screamed over me so close I could imagine it swooping just an inch or two lower and smashing the life out of me. I still dream about it.

But there was only a warm quiet this Sunday afternoon—until the music rolling out of the Philco was interrupted by a news flash about the Japanese and Pearl Harbor. I had no idea where Pearl Harbor was or why anyone would want to attack it, but I had only to look at my mother's face to know that it was important enough for me to remember the moment for the rest of my life. Her normally full lips, lacquered in bright lipstick in the fashion of the time, were pressed into a thin red line and her lower jaw was trembling. Her eyes were narrowed, and I watched in awe as a tear spilled out of the corner of one of them. I had rarely seen my mother cry. I wanted to ask her what was wrong, but was afraid, as if the answer would be too large and terrible to be endured.

Suddenly, she turned the radio off, took my hand, and told me to come with her. We went to the room that I shared with my still sleeping brother. Silently, still quietly crying, she began to pick up my small collection of toys, one at a time, looking at the labels on their bottoms, then putting some of them in a separate pile. The process did not take long, and when done she gathered up the pile of tin automobiles, airplanes, cap pistols, badges, boats, figurines, flutes, and other childish treasures and carried them into the backyard to the incinerator my father had contrived from an old ink drum brought home from the shop.

She started a fire with some trash and a big kitchen match, and when it was going well handed me some of the toys. "I want you to help me do this," she said. "I don't want any Jap toys in this house." I had no idea what she meant, but as was true of so many instructions laid down by adults, it was clear to me that this was something I was going to have to do, whether I understood it or not. As she tossed in each "Made in Japan" toy, so did I, one at a time, until they were all consumed or shriveled, the acrid smoke of their immolation rising into the southern California air like incense. Like memory.

A NOTE ON
STATISTICS AND MONEY

◆───

With regard to the statistics that ornament (some might say, clog) *The Hungry Years*, I will insist that there are no lies and even fewer damned lies among them, to twist Benjamin Disraeli's words. This is because—unless otherwise indicated in the text or notes—all figures I have used are taken from one of the noblest publications ever to tumble off the presses of the U.S. Government Printing Office: *Historical Statistics of the United States, Colonial Times to 1970* (two volumes; U.S. Department of Commerce, Bureau of the Census, 1975). No historian should be without these tomes (but get a really big bookshelf).

It is just as necessary to pay my debt to another, much smaller but no less noble publication. Whenever I make comparisons in the book regarding the equivalent value of money then and now, I am relying on the composite commodity price index tables compiled by John J. McCusker in "How Much Is That in Real Money? A Historical Price Index for Use as a Deflator of Money Values in the Economy of the United States" (*Proceedings of the American Antiquarian Society*, October 1991), as brought up to date for me by Carolyn Alkire (though neither Mr. McCusker nor Ms. Alkire should be held responsible for any errors I may have made while using their figures). In these tables, the "multiplier" used to determine the equivalent value of money between 1998 and any year under discussion in this book ranges from a low of 8.11 (1920) to a high of 12.57 (1933). Thus, $5,000 in

1920 would be the equivalent of $40,550 in 1998, while $5,000 in 1933 would be the equivalent of $62,850.

For the sake of convenience, we can say that the average "multiplier" for the decade of the twenties is 10.38. For the four years between the end of 1931 and the end of 1935, the worst years of the depression, the average is 12.14, while between the beginning of 1936 and the end of 1939, the average is 11.58, showing a slow recovery in the economy (though one interrupted by the recession of 1937–38). As for the general reliability of such figures, I can only quote from McCusker himself, who says, "We should be fortunate indeed if the data were good enough to allow us to be within ten percent of the true mathematical figure." Ten percent will have to do.

SOURCES

◆

In many instances, I have relied upon contemporary published materials, government documents, and primary sources in the preparation of this book, but as the footnotes amply demonstrate, my debt to the hundreds of scholars who have gone before me into the often murky world of the Great Depression is too large to be properly acknowledged. The following list of sources is very long indeed, but it still does not include every book or article that at one time or another has fallen into my hands and been mined ruthlessly in search of the useful fact, illuminating statistic, or compelling quote—or has simply served as one more indispensable guide to the character of a land and time that are no more. If there is a more impressive body of scholarship that has been produced anywhere on any subject, I do not know what it might be.

GENERAL SOURCES

Government Publications

Eisenhower, Milton S., ed. *Yearbook of Agriculture, 1934*. Washington: U.S. Department of Agriculture, 1934.

Tennessee Valley Authority. *The Scenic Resources of the Tennessee Valley: A Descriptive and Pictorial Inventory*. Washington, D.C.: Government Printing Office, 1938.

U.S. Congress. *History of Employment and Manpower Policy in the United States. Parts I and II: Depression Experience, Proposals, and Programs.* Washington, D.C.: Government Printing Office, 1965. U.S. Department of Labor, Bureau of Labor Statistics. *Strikes in the United States, 1880–1936,* by Florence Peterson. Bulletin No. 651, August 1937. Washington, D.C.: Government Printing Office, 1938. U.S. House, Special Committee on Un-American Activities. *Investigation of Un-American Propaganda Activities in the United States.* 76th Cong., 3rd sess. Washington, D.C.: Government Printing Office, 1940.

Works Progress Administration, Division of Social Research. *Changing Aspects of Rural Relief.* Research Monograph XIV. Washington, D.C.: Government Printing Office, 1938; *Comparative Study of Rural Relief and Non-Relief Households,* by Thomas C. McCormick. Research Monograph II. Washington, D.C.: Government Printing Office, 1935; *Farmers on Relief and Rehabilitation,* by Berta Asch and A. R. Mangus. Research Monograph VIII. Washington, D.C.: Government Printing Office, 1937; *Farming Hazards in the Drought Area,* by R. S. Kifer and H. L. Stewart of the Bureau of Agricultural Economics. Research Monograph XVI. Washington, D.C.: Government Printing Office, 1938; *Landlord and Tenant on the Cotton Plantation,* by T. J. Woofter Jr. et al. Research Monograph V. Washington, D.C.: Government Printing Office, 1936; *The Plantation South, 1934–1937,* by William C. Holley, Ellen Winston, and T. J. Woofter Jr. Research Monograph XXII. Washington, D.C.: Government Printing Office, 1940; *Rural Families on Relief,* by Carle C. Zimmerman and Nathan L. Whetten. Research Monograph XVII. Washington, D.C.: Government Printing Office, 1938; *Rural Regions of the United States*, by A. R. Morgan. Washington, D.C.: Government Printing Office, 1940; *Rural Youth on Relief*, by Bruce L. Melvin. Research Monograph XI. Washington, D.C.: Government Printing Office, 1937.

Dissertations, Unpublished Manuscripts, Archival Materials

Blackside, Inc., and the Civil Rights Project. "The Blackside Interviews." Boston, 1991–1993.

Carlson, Lewis H. "J. Parnell Thomas and the House Committee on Un-American Activities, 1938–1948." Ph.D. dissertation, Michigan State University, 1967.

Chaffee, Porter M. "A History of the Cannery and Agricultural Workers Industrial Union." Works Progress Administration, Federal Writers Project. Oakland, Calif.: 1938.

Gladstein, Caroline Decker. Untranscribed tape recording, Oral History Department, Bancroft Library, University of California at Berkeley.

Helmbold, Lois Rita. "Making Choices, Making Do: Black and White Working Class Women's Lives and Work During the Great Depression." Ph. D. dissertation, Stanford University, 1982.

Jarrell, Randall. "Helen Hosmer: A Radical Critic of California Agribusiness in the 1930s." Santa Cruz, Calif: Regional Oral History Office, University of California at Santa Cruz, 1992.

Kerr, Clark. "Self-Help: A Study of the Cooperative Barter Movement of the Unemployed in California, 1932–1933." M.A. thesis, University of California at Berkeley, 1933. Kifer, Allen Francis. "The Negro Under the New Deal, 1933–1941." Ph.D. dissertation, University of Wisconsin, 1961.

Perkins, Frances. Oral Memoirs. Oral History Research Office, Butler Library, Columbia University, New York.

Paul Schuster Taylor Papers, Bancroft Library, University of California at Berkeley.

Tennessee Valley Authority Oral History Collection, Tennessee Valley Authority Library, Knoxville.

Books

Allen, Frederick Lewis. *The Big Change: America Transforms Itself, 1900–1950.* New York: Harper & Brothers, Publishers, 1952; *Since Yesterday: The Nineteen-Thirties in America, September 3, 1929–September 3, 1939.* New York: Harper & Row, 1940. Appel, Benjamin. *The People Talk: American Voices from the Great Depression.* Reprint of 1940 edition. New York: Simon & Schuster, 1982. Arnold, Eleanor, ed. *Buggies and Bad Times: Memories of Hoosier Homemakers.* Rushville, Ind.: Indiana Extension Homemakers Association, 1985.

Badger, Anthony J. *The New Deal: The Depression Years, 1933–1940.* New York: Hill & Wang, 1989. Banks, Ann, ed. *First-Person America.* New York: Alfred A. Knopf, 1980. Barnouw, Erik. *A History of Broadcasting in the United States.* Vol. 1: *A Tower in Babel, to 1933.* Vol 2: *The Golden Web, 1933–1953.* New York: Oxford University Press, 1966, 1968. Beatty, Jack. *The Rascal King: The Life and Times of James Michael Curley, 1874–1958.* Reading, Mass.: Addison Wesley, 1992. Bendiner, Robert. *Just Around the Corner: A Highly Selective History of the Thirties.* New York: E. P. Dutton & Co., 1968. Berger, Meyer. *The Eight Million: Journal of a New York Correspondent.* New York: Simon & Schuster, 1942. Bergman, Andrew. *We're in the Money: Depression America and Its Films.* New York: New York University Press, 1971. Best, Gary Dean. *The Nickel and Dime Decade: American Popular Culture During the 1930s.* Westport, Conn.: Praeger, 1993. Binder, Frederick M., and David M. Reimers, eds. *The Way We Lived: Essays and Documents in American Social History. Vol. 2: 1865–Present.* Lexington,

Mass.: D. C. Heath, 1992. Bird, Caroline. *The Invisible Scar*. New York: David McKay, 1966.

Chandler, Lester V. *America's Greatest Depression, 1929–1941*. New York: Harper & Row, 1970. Chernow, Ron. *The House of Morgan: An American Banking Dynasty and the Rise of Modern Finance*. New York: Atlantic Monthly Press, 1990; *The Warburgs: The Twentieth-Century Odyssey of a Remarkable Jewish Family*. New York: Random House, 1993. Collier, Peter, and David Horowitz. *The Fords: An American Epic*. New York: Simon & Schuster, 1987. Congdon, Don, ed. *The Thirties: A Time to Remember*. New York: Simon & Schuster, 1962. Conot, Robert. *American Odyssey*. New York: William Morrow & Co., 1974. Cordell, William H., ed. *Molders of the American Thought, 1933–1934*. Garden City, N.Y.: Doubleday, Doran & Co., 1934. Corey, Lewis, *The Crisis of the Middle Class*. New York: Covici. Corey, Lewis, Friede, 1935; and Kathryn Coe, eds. *American Points of View, 1934–1935*. Garden City, N.Y.: Doubleday, Doran & Co., 1936. Crane, Milton, ed. *The Roosevelt Era*. New York: Boni & Gaer, 1947.

Daniels, Jonathan. *The Time Between the Wars: Armistice to Pearl Harbor*. Garden City, N.Y.: Doubleday & Co., 1966. Dawley, Alan. *Struggles for Justice: Social Responsibility and the Liberal State*. Cambridge: Harvard University Press, 1991.

Ellis, Edward Robb. *A Nation in Torment: The Great American Depression, 1929–1939*. New York: Capricorn Books, 1971. Epstein, Daniel Mark. *Sister Aimee: The Life of Aimee Semple McPherson*. New York: Harcourt Brace Jovanovich, 1993.

Filler, Louis, ed. *The Anxious Years: America in the Nineteen Thirties—A Collection of Contemporary Writings*. New York: G. P. Putnam's Sons, 1963. Flink, James J. *The Automobile Age*. Cambridge: MIT Press, 1988. Freedman, Samuel. *The Inheritance: How Three Families and America Moved from Roosevelt to Reagan and Beyond*. New York: Simon & Schuster, 1996. Friedman, Milton, and Anna Jacobson Schwartz. *A Monetary History of the United States, 1867–1960*. Princeton, N.J.: Princeton University Press, 1963. Furnas, J. C. *Stormy Weather: Crosslights on the Nineteen Thirties: An Informal History of the United States, 1929–1941*. New York: G. P. Putnam's Sons, 1977.

Galbraith, John Kenneth. *A Journey Through Economic Time: A Firsthand View*. Boston: Houghton Mifflin, 1994. Ginns, Patsy Moore. *Snowbird Gravy and Dishpan Pie: Mountain People Recall*. Chapel Hill: University of North Carolina Press, 1982. Goldberg, Vicki. *Margaret Bourke-White: A Biography*. New York: Harper & Row, 1986. Goldman, Eric F. *Rendezvous with Destiny: A History of Modern American Reform*. New York: Alfred A. Knopf, 1953. Goslin, Omar, and Ryllis Goslin. *Our Town's Business*. New York: Funk & Wagnalls Company, 1939. Gosnell, Harold F. *Machine Politics: Chicago Model*. Chicago: University of Chicago Press, 1937. Green, Harvey. *The Uncertainty of Everyday Life, 1915–*

1945. New York: HarperCollins, 1992. Green, Stanley. *Ring Bells! Sing Songs! Broadway Musicals of the 1930's.* New York: Galahad Books, 1971.

Hendrickson, Kenneth E., Jr., ed. *Hard Times in Oklahoma: The Depression Years.* Oklahoma City: Oklahoma Historical Society, 1983. Horan, James D. *The Desperate Years: A Pictorial History of the Thirties.* New York: Bonanza Books, 1962. Howe, Quincy. *The World Between the Wars: From the 1918 Armistice to the Munich Agreement.* New York: Simon & Schuster, 1953. Hoyt, Edwin P. *The Tempering Years.* New York: Charles Scribner's Sons, 1963.

Jellison, Charles A. *Tomatoes Were Cheaper: Tales from the Thirties.* Syracuse, N.Y.: Syracuse University Press, 1977.

Kazin, Michael. *The Populist Persuasion: An American History.* New York: Basic-Books, 1995. Kindleberger, Charles P. *The World in Depression, 1929–1939.* Berkeley: University of California Press, 1986. The Kiplinger Washington Editors, Inc. *Kiplinger's "Looking Ahead": 70 Years of Forecasts from "The Kiplinger Washington Letter."* Washington, D.C.: The Kiplinger Washington Editors, Inc., 1933. Kisseloff, Jeff. *You Must Remember This: An Oral History of Manhattan from the 1890s to World War II.* New York: Harcourt Brace Jovanovich, 1989. Kuhn, Clifford M., Harlon E. Joye, and E. Bernard West. *Living Atlanta: An Oral History of the City, 1914–1948.* Athens: University of Georgia Press, 1990.

Lacey, Robert. *Ford: The Man and the Machine.* Boston: Little, Brown and Co., 1986. Laver, James. *Between the Wars.* Boston: Houghton Mifflin Co., 1961. Leach, William. *Land of Desire: Merchants, Power, and the Rise of a New American Culture.* New York: Pantheon Books, 1993. Leighton, Isabel, ed. *The Aspirin Age: 1919–1941.* New York: Simon & Schuster, 1949. Leonard, Stephen J. *Trials and Triumphs: A Colorado Portrait of the Great Depression.* Boulder: University of Colorado Press, 1993. LeSueur, Meridel. *North Star Country.* New York: Book Find Club, 1946. Lynd, Robert S., and Helen Merrell. *Middletown in Transition: A Study in Cultural Conflict.* New York: Harcourt, Brace & Co., 1937.

McDonald, Forrest. *Insull.* Chicago: University of Chicago Press, 1962. McElvaine, Robert S., ed. *Down and Out in the Great Depression: Letters from the "Forgotten Man."* Chapel Hill: University of North Carolina Press, 1983; *The Great Depression: America, 1929–1941.* New York: Times Books, 1984. McWilliams, Carey. *Southern California Country: An Island on the Land.* New York: Duell, Sloan & Pearce, 1946. MacDonald, J. Fred. *Don't Touch That Dial! Radio Programming in American Life from 1920 to 1960.* Chicago: Nelson-Hall, 1979. Marchand, Roland. *Advertising the American Dream: Making Way for Modernity, 1920–1940.* Berkeley: University of California Press, 1985. Marquis, Alice G. *Hopes and Ashes: The Birth of Modern Times, 1929–1939.* New York: The Free Press, 1986. Marty, Martin E. *Modern American Religion. Vol. 2: The Noise of Conflict, 1919–1941.* Chicago: University of Chicago Press, 1991. Meyer, Donald.

The Protestant Search for Political Realism, 1919–1941, 2d ed. Middletown, Conn.: Wesleyan University Press, 1988. Mitchell, Broadus. *Depression Decade: From New Era through New Deal, 1929–1941.* 1947. Reprint, New York: Harper Torchbooks; Harper & Row, 1969.

Nichols, David, ed. *Ernie's America: The Best of Ernie Pyle's 1930s Travel Dispatches.* New York: Random House, 1989.

O'Neal, Hank. *A Vision Shared: A Classic Portrait of America and Its People, 1935–1943.* New York: St. Martin's Press, 1976.

Parrish, Michael E. *Anxious Decades: America in Prosperity and Depression, 1920–1941.* New York: W. W. Norton, 1992. Pells, Richard H. *Radical Visions and American Dreams: Culture and Social Thought in the Depression Years.* New York: Harper & Row, 1973. Phillips, Cabell. *From the Crash to the Blitz, 1929–1939.* New York: Macmillan Co., 1969. Pyle, Ernie. *Home Country.* New York: William Sloane Associates, Inc., 1947.

Reddig, William M. *Tom's Town: Kansas City and the Pendergast Legend.* Philadelphia: J. B. Lippincott, 1947. Rogers, Agnes, and Frederick Lewis Allen. *I Remember Distinctly: A Family Album of the American People, 1918–1941.* New York: Harper & Brothers, Publishers, 1947. Rothbard, Murray N. *America's Great Depression.* Kansas City, Mo.: Sheed & Ward, Inc., 1975.

St. Johns, Adela Rogers. *The Honeycomb.* Garden City, N.Y.: Doubleday & Co., 1969. Shannon, David A. *Between the Wars: America, 1919–1941.* Boston: Houghton Mifflin Co., 1979, ed. *The Great Depression.* Englewood Cliffs, N.J.: Prentice-Hall, Inc., 1960. Simon, Rita James, ed. *As We Saw the Thirties: Essays on Social and Political Movements of a Decade.* Chicago: University of Chicago Press, 1967. Skidelsky, Robert. *John Maynard Keynes: The Economist as Saviour, 1920–1937.* New York: Viking Penguin, 1994. Sklar, Robert. *Movie-Made America: A Social History of American Movies.* New York: Random House, 1975. Smith, Page. *Redeeming the Time: A People's History of the 1920s and the New Deal.* New York: McGraw-Hill, 1987. Starr, Kevin. *Endangered Dreams: The Great Depression in California.* New York: Oxford University Press, 1996. Steel, Ronald. *Walter Lippmann and the American Century.* New York: Random House, 1980. Stowe, David W. *Swing Changes: Big Band Jazz in New Deal America.* Cambridge: Harvard University Press, 1994. Sward, Keith. *The Legend of Henry Ford.* New York: Atheneum, 1968.

Terkel, Studs. *Hard Times: An Oral History of the Great Depression.* New York: Random House, 1970. Tindall, George Brown. *The Emergence of the New South, 1913–1945.* Vol. 10 of *The History of the South.* Baton Rouge: Louisiana State University Press, 1967. Tipple, John. *Crisis of the American Dream: A History of American Social Thought, 1920–1940.* New York: Pegasus, 1968.

Warner, W. Lloyd, and Paul S. Lunt. *The Social Life of a Modern Community*. New Haven: Yale University Press, 1941. Watkins, T. H. *The Great Depression: America in the 1930's*. Boston: Little, Brown, 1993. Wecter, Dixon. *The Age of the Great Depression, 1929–1941*. Chicago: Quadrangle Books, 1971. White, William Allen. *Forty Years on Main Street*. New York: Farrar & Rinehart, Inc., 1937. Wigginton, Eliot, ed. *Refuse to Stand Silently By: An Oral History of Grass Roots Social Activism in America, 1921–1964*. New York: Doubleday, 1992. Wilson, Charles Morrow. *Roots of America: A Travelogue of American Personalities*. New York: Funk & Wagnalls Co., 1936. Wilson, Edmund. *The American Earthquake: A Documentary of the Twenties and Thirties*. Garden City, N.Y.: Doubleday & Co., 1958. Winslow, Susan. *Brother, Can You Spare a Dime? America from the Wall Street Crash to Pearl Harbor: An Illustrated Documentary*. New York: Paddington Press, 1979.

Article

Webbink, Paul. "Unemployment in the United States, 1930–40." *American Economic Review* (February 1941).

SOURCES BY SUBJECT

THE TWENTIES AND THE CRASH OF '29

Books

Allen, Frederick Lewis. *Only Yesterday: An Informal History of the Nineteen-Twenties*. New York: Harper & Brothers, 1931.

Brooks, John. *Once in Golconda: A True Drama of Wall Street, 1920–1938*. New York: Harper & Row, 1969.

Cowing, Cedric B. *Populists, Plungers, and Progressives: A Social History of Stock and Commodity Speculation, 1890–1936*. Princeton, N.J.: Princeton University Press, 1965.

Galbraith, John Kenneth. *The Great Crash, 1929*. Boston: Houghton Mifflin, 1955.

Jacobson, Matthew. *The Money Lords: The Great Finance Capitalists, 1925–1950*. New York: Weybright & Talley, 1972.

Klingaman, William K. *1929: The Year of the Great Crash*. New York: Harper & Row, 1989.

Lynd, Robert S., and Helen Merrell. *Middletown: A Study in Modern American Culture*. New York: Harcourt, Brace & Co., 1929.

Morris, Joe Alex. *What a Year!* New York: Harper & Brothers, 1956.

Olien, Roger M., and Diana Davids Olien. *Easy Money: Oil Promoters and Investors in the Jazz Age.* Chapel Hill: University of North Carolina Press, 1990.

Perrett, Geoffrey. *America in the Twenties: A History.* New York: Simon & Schuster, 1982.

Shachtman, Tom. *The Day America Crashed.* New York: G. P. Putnam's Sons, 1979. Sloat, Warren. *1929: America Before the Crash.* New York: Macmillan Publishing Co., 1979. Starr, Kevin. *Material Dreams: Southern California Through the 1920s.* New York: Oxford University Press, 1990. Stockbridge, Frank Parker, and John Holliday Perry. *Florida in the Making.* New York: The de Bower Publishing Co., 1926.

Thomas, Gordon, and Max Morgan-Witts. *The Day the Bubble Burst: A Social History of the Wall Street Crash of 1929.* Garden City, N.Y.: Doubleday & Co., 1979. Tygiel, Jules. *The Great Los Angeles Swindle: Oil, Stocks, and Scandal During the Roaring Twenties.* New York: Oxford University Press, 1994.

Vickers, Raymond B. *Panic in Paradise: Florida's Banking Crash of 1926.* Tuscaloosa: University of Alabama Press, 1994.

EARLY DEPRESSION YEARS

Books

Agar, Herbert. *Land of the Free.* Boston: Houghton Mifflin Co., 1935. Allsop, Kenneth. *Hard Travellin': The Hobo and His History.* New York: New American Library, 1967. Anderson, Edward. *Hungry Men* (novel). London: William Heinemann, Ltd., 1935.

Ballads of the B. E. F. New York: Coventry House, 1932. Bartlett, John Henry. *The Bonus March and the New Deal.* Chicago: M. A. Donohue & Co., 1937. Bremer, C. D. *American Bank Failures.* New York: Columbia University Press, 1935.

Corey, Lewis. *The Decline of American Capitalism.* New York: Covici, Friede, 1934.

Douglas, Jack. *Veterans on the March.* New York: Workers Library Publishers, 1934.

Eichengreen, Barry. *Golden Fetters: The Gold Standard and the Great Depression, 1919–1939.* New York: Oxford University Press, 1992.

Friedman, Milton, and Anna Jacobson Schwartz. *The Great Contraction, 1929–1933.* Princeton, N.J.: Princeton University Press, 1965.

Garraty, John A. *The Great Depression: An Inquiry into the Causes, Course, and Consequences of the Worldwide Depression of the Nineteen-Thirties, as Seen by Contemporaries and in the Light of History.* New York: Harcourt Brace Jovanovich, 1987. Graham, Maury, and Robert J. Hemming. *Tales of the Iron Road: My Life as King of the Hobos.* New York: Paragon House, 1990.

Harris, Sara, with Harriet Crittenden. *Father Divine: Holy Husband.* Garden City, N.Y.: Doubleday & Co., 1953. Hastings, Robert J. *A Nickel's Worth of Skim Milk: A Boy's View of the Great Depression.* Carbondale: Southern Illinois University Graphics and Publications, 1972. Hill, Edwin C. *The American Scene.* New York: Witmark Educational Publications, 1933.

Leuchtenberg, William E. *The Perils of Prosperity, 1914–32.* Chicago: University of Chicago Press, 1958. Lisio, Donald J. *The President and Protest: Hoover, Conspiracy, and the Bonus Riot.* Columbia: University of Missouri Press, 1974.

Meltzer, Milton. *Brother, Can You Spare a Dime? The Great Depression, 1929–1933.* New York: New American Library, 1977. Minehan, Thomas. *Boy and Girl Tramps of America.* New York: Grosset & Dunlap, 1934. Morgan, Murray. *Skid Road: An Informal Portrait of Seattle.* New York: The Viking Press, 1951. Mullins, William H. *The Depression and the Urban West Coast, 1929–1933: Los Angeles, San Francisco, Seattle, and Portland.* Bloomington: Indiana University Press, 1991. Murphy, Mary. *Mining Cultures: Men, Women, and Leisure in Butte, 1914–41.* Urbana: University of Illinois Press, 1997.

Pratt, George K. *Morale: The Mental Hygiene of Unemployment.* New York: The National Committee for Mental Hygiene, 1933.

Ringel, Fred J., ed. *America as Americans See It.* New York: The Literary Guild, 1932.

Seldes, Gilbert. *The Years of the Locust (America, 1929–1932).* Boston: Little, Brown & Co., 1933. Smith, Gene. *The Shattered Dream: Herbert Hoover and the Great Depression.* New York: William Morrow & Co., 1970. Smith, Richard Norton. *An Uncommon Man: The Triumph of Herbert Hoover.* New York: Simon & Schuster, 1984. Soule, George. *The Coming American Revolution.* New York: Macmillan, 1934. Sternsher, Bernard. *Hitting Home: The Great Depression in Town and Country,* rev. ed. Chicago: Ivan R. Dee, Inc., 1989.

Trolander, Judith Ann. *Settlement Houses and the Great Depression.* Detroit: Wayne State University Press, 1975.

Warren, Harris Gaylord. *Herbert Hoover and the Great Depression.* New York: Oxford University Press, 1959. Waters, W. W., as told to William C. White. *B.E.F.: The Whole Story of the Bonus Army.* New York: The John Day Co., 1933. Watts, Jill. *God, Harlem U.S.A.: The Father Divine Story.* Berkeley: University of California Press, 1992. Werner, M. R. *Privileged Characters.* New York: Robert M. McBride, 1935. Woodruff, Nan Elizabeth. *As Rare as Rain: Federal Relief in the Great Southern Drought of 1930–31.* Urbana: University of Illinois Press, 1985.

Articles

Barber, Clarence L. "On the Origins of the Great Depression." *Southern Economic Journal* (January 1978). Baskin, Alex. "The Ford Hunger March—1932." *Labor History* (summer 1972). Billington, Monroe, and Cal Clark. "Clergy Reaction to the New Deal: A Comparative Study." *Historian* (August 1986). Blackwelder, Julia Kirk. "Letters from the Great Depression: A Tour Through a Collection of Letters to an Atlanta Newspaperwoman." *Southern Exposure* (fall 1978).

Chafe, William H. "Flint and the Great Depression." *Michigan History* (fall 1969).

Eisenberg, Philip, and Paul F. Lazarfeld. "The Psychological Effects of Unemployment." *Psychological Bulletin* (June 1938).

Garraty, John A. "Unemployment During the Great Depression." *Labor History* (spring 1976).

Handy, Robert T. "The American Religious Depression, 1925–1935." *Church History* (winter 1976–77). Heleniack, Roman. "Local Reaction to the Great Depression in New Orleans, 1929–1933." *Louisiana History* (fall 1969). Hinckley, Ted C. "Depression Anxieties Midst a Pasadena Eddy." *The Pacific Historian* (winter 1983). Hine, Robert V. "Foreclosure in Los Angeles." *The Pacific Historian* (winter 1983). Holch, Arthur. "When Rubber Checks Didn't Bounce." *American Heritage* (June 1961).

Katzman, David M. "Ann Arbor: Depression City." *Michigan History* (December 1966).

Lamoreaux, David, and Gerson G. Eisenberg. "Baltimore Views the Great Depression, 1929–33." *Maryland Historical Review* (fall 1976). Larson, Lawrence H., and Barbara J. Cottrell. "Omaha and the Great Depression: Progress in the Face of Adversity." *Journal of the West* (October 1985). Leab, Daniel J. "'United We Eat': The Creation and Organization of the Unemployed Councils in 1930." *Labor History* (fall 1967).

Maxwell, Margaret F. "The Depression in Yavapai County." *The Journal of Arizona History* (summer 1982). Morgan, Iwan. "Fort Wayne and the Great Depression: The Early Years, 1929–1933." *Indiana Magazine of History* (June 1984). Mullins, William H. "Self-Help in Seattle, 1931–1932: Herbert Hoover's Concept of Cooperative Individualism and the Unemployed Citizens' League." *Pacific Northwest Quarterly* (January 1981). Murray, Gail S. "Forty Years Ago: The Great Depression Comes to Arkansas." *Arkansas Historical Quarterly* (winter 1970).

Olson, James S. "The Depths of the Great Depression: Economic Collapse in West Virginia, 1932–1933." *West Virginia History* (April 1977). O'Neal, Bill. "The Personal Side of the Great Depression in East Texas." *East Texas Historical Association* (summer 1980).

Rosenzweig, Roy. "Organizing the Unemployed: The Early Years of the Great Depression, 1929–1933." *Radical America* (July/August 1976).

Weaver, John D. "Bonus March." *American Heritage* (June 1963). Whisenhunt, Donald W. "The Transient in the Depression." *Red River Valley Historical Review* (spring 1974).

FRANKLIN D. ROOSEVELT AND THE NEW DEALERS

Books

Abbott, Philip. *The Exemplary Presidency: Franklin D. Roosevelt and the American Political Tradition.* Amherst: University of Massachusetts Press, 1990. Adams, Henry H. *Harry Hopkins: A Biography.* New York: G. P. Putnam's Sons, 1977. Alsop, Joseph, and Turner Catledge. *The 168 Days.* Garden City, N.Y.: Doubleday, Doran & Co., 1938.

Barber, James G., and Frederick S. Voss. *Portraits from the New Deal.* Washington, D.C.: Smithsonian Institution Press, 1983. Biles, Roger. *A New Deal for the American People.* DeKalb: Northern Illinois University Press, 1991. Blum, John Morton. *From the Morgenthau Diaries: Years of Crisis, 1928–1938.* Boston: Houghton Mifflin, 1959; *From the Morgenthau Diaries: Years of Deadly Urgency, 1938–1941.* Boston: Houghton Mifflin, 1965. Braley, Berton. *New Deal Ditties: or, Running in the Red with Roosevelt.* New York: Greenberg, 1936. Brinkley, Alan. *The End of Reform: New Deal Liberalism in Recession and War.* New York: Alfred A. Knopf, 1995. Brown, Dee. *When the Century Was Young.* Little Rock, Ark.: August House Publishers, 1993. Buhite, Russell D., and David W. Levy, eds. *FDR's Fireside Chats.* Norman: University of Oklahoma Press, 1992.

Carter, Boake. *"Johnnie Q. Public" Speaks! The Nation Appraises the New Deal.* New York: Dodge Publishing Co., 1936. Carter, John Franklin (the Unofficial Observer). *The New Dealers.* New York: The Literary Guild, 1934. Clarke, Jeanne Neinaber. *Roosevelt's Warrior: Harold L. Ickes and the New Deal.* Baltimore: Johns Hopkins University Press, 1996. Conkin, Paul K. *The New Deal.* New York: Crowell, 1967.

Davis, Kenneth S. *FDR: The New York Years, 1928–1933.* New York: Random House, 1985; *FDR: The New Deal Years, 1933–1937.* New York: Random House, 1986; *FDR: Into the Storm, 1937–1940.* New York: Random House, 1993. Degler, Carl N. *The New Deal.* Chicago: Quadrangle Books, 1970.

Eliot, Thomas H. *Recollections of the New Deal: When the People Mattered.* Boston: Northeastern University Press, 1992.

Farr, Finis. *FDR.* New Rochelle, N.Y.: Arlington House, 1972. Feis, Herbert. *1933: Characters in Crisis.* Boston: Little, Brown & Co., 1966. Fraser, Steven, and Gary Gerstle. *The Rise and Fall of the New Deal Order, 1930–1980.* Princeton,

N.J.: Princeton University Press, 1989. Freidel, Frank. *Franklin D. Roosevelt: Launching the New Deal*. Boston: Little, Brown, 1973; *Franklin D. Roosevelt: A Rendezvous with Destiny*. New York: Little, Brown & Co., 1990.

Garrett, Charles. *The La Guardia Years: Machine and Reform Politics in New York City*. New Brunswick, N.J.: Rutgers University Press, 1961. Graham, Otis L. Jr., and Meghan Robinson Wander, eds. *Franklin D. Roosevelt, His Life and Times: An Encyclopedic View*. Boston: G. K. Hall & Co., 1985. Graubert, Judah L., and Alice V. Graubert. *Decade of Destiny*. Chicago: Contemporary Books, 1978.

Hamby, Alonzo L., ed. *The New Deal: Analysis and Interpretation*. New York: Weybright & Talley, 1969. Hofstadter, Richard. *The Age of Reform from Bryan to FDR*. New York: Alfred A. Knopf, 1965. Hoover, Herbert, et. al. *Surplus Prophets: In Their Own Words*. New York: The Viking Press, 1936. Hurd, Charles. *When the New Deal Was Young and Gay*. New York: Hawthorne Books, Inc., 1965. Huthmacher, J. Joseph. *Senator Robert F. Wagner and the Rise of Urban Liberalism*. New York: Atheneum, 1968.

Ickes, Harold L. *The Secret Diary of Harold L. Ickes: The First Thousand Days, 1933–1936*; *The Inside Struggle, 1936–1939*; *The Lowering Clouds, 1939–1941*. 3 vols. New York: Simon & Schuster, 1952–1954. Irons, Peter H. *The New Deal Lawyers*. Princeton, N.J.: Princeton University Press, 1982.

Jacob, Charles E. *Leadership in the New Deal: The Administrative Challenge*. Englewood Cliffs, N. J.: Prentice-Hall, 1967.

Kyvig, David E., ed. *FDR's America, 1933–1945*. St. Charles, Mo.: Forum Press, 1976.

Lash, Joseph P. *Dealers and Dreamers: A New Look at the New Deal*. New York: Doubleday, 1988; *Eleanor and Franklin*. New York: W. W. Norton, 1971. Leuchtenberg, William E. *The FDR Years: On Roosevelt and His Legacy*. New York: Columbia University Press, 1995; *Franklin D. Roosevelt and the New Deal*. New York: Harper & Row, 1963; ed. *Franklin D. Roosevelt: A Profile*. New York: Hill & Wang, 1967. Lord, Russell. *The Wallaces of Iowa*. Boston: Houghton Mifflin, 1947. Louchheim, Katie. *The Making of the New Deal: The Insiders Speak*. Cambridge: Harvard University Press, 1983.

McJimsey, George. *Harry Hopkins: Ally of the Poor and Defender of Democracy*. Cambridge: Harvard University Press, 1987. Martin, George. *Madam Secretary: Frances Perkins*. Boston: Houghton Mifflin, 1976. Miller, Nathan. *FDR: An Intimate History*. New York: Doubleday, 1983. Moley, Raymond, and Eliot A. Rosen. *The First New Deal*. New York: Harcourt, Brace & World, Inc., 1966. Morgan, Ted. *FDR: A Biography*. New York: Simon & Schuster, 1985.

Norris, George W. *Fighting Liberal: The Autobiography of George W. Norris*. New York: The Macmillan Co., 1945.

Ohl, John Kennedy. *Hugh S. Johnson and the New Deal.* De Kalb: Northern Illinois University Press, 1985.

Perkins, Dexter. *The New Age of Franklin Roosevelt, 1932–45.* Chicago: University of Chicago Press, 1957. Perkins, Frances. *The Roosevelt I Knew.* New York: Viking, 1946.

Rosen, Elliot A. *Hoover, Roosevelt, and the Brains Trust: From Depression to New Deal.* New York: Columbia University Press, 1977. Rosenau, James N. *The Roosevelt Treasury.* Garden City, N.Y.: Doubleday & Co., 1951. Rosenman, Samuel I. *The Public Papers and Addresses of Franklin D. Roosevelt.* 5 vols. New York: Random House, 1938.

Schlesinger, Arthur A., Jr. *The Age of Roosevelt: The Crisis of the Old Order, 1919–1933; The Coming of the New Deal; and The Politics of Upheaval.* 3 vols. Boston: Houghton Mifflin Co., 1957–1959. Schwarz, Jordan A. *The New Dealers: Power Politics in the Age of Roosevelt.* New York: Alfred A. Knopf, 1993. Sherwood, Robert E. *Roosevelt and Hopkins: An Intimate History.* New York: Harper & Brothers, 1948. Smythe, Ray. *Memo to F.D.R.* Washington, D.C.: Columbia Publishers, 1935. Sternsher, Bernard, ed. *The New Deal: Doctrines and Democracy.* Boston: Allyn & Bacon, 1966; *Rexford Tugwell and the New Deal.* New Brunswick, N.J.: Rutgers University Press, 1964.

Tugwell, R. G. *The Brain Trust.* New York: Viking Press, 1968; *The Democratic Roosevelt: A Biography of Franklin D. Roosevelt.* Garden City, N.Y.: Doubleday & Co., 1957.

Watkins, T. H. *Righteous Pilgrim: The Life and Times of Harold L. Ickes, 1874–1952.* New York: Henry Holt & Co., 1990. Wharton, Don, ed. *The Roosevelt Omnibus.* New York: Alfred A. Knopf, 1934. White, Graham. *FDR and the Press.* Chicago: University of Chicago Press, 1979. Winfield, Betty Houchin. *FDR and the News Media.* New York: Columbia University Press, 1994. Wolfskill, George, and John A. Hudson. *All But the People: Franklin D. Roosevelt and His Critics, 1933–1939.* New York: The Macmillan Co., 1969.

Zinn, Howard, ed. *New Deal Thought.* Indianapolis: Bobbs-Merrill, 1966.

NEW DEAL PROGRAMS

Books

Adams, Grace. *Workers on Relief.* New Haven, Conn.: Yale University Press, 1939. Adams, John A., Jr. *Damming the Colorado: The Rise of the Lower Colorado River Authority, 1933–1939.* College Station: Texas A & M University Press, 1990. Alsberg, Henry R., ed. *America Fights the Depression: A Photographic Record of the Civil Works Administration.* New York: Coward-McCann, 1934. American Public Works Association. *History of Public Works in the United States, 1776–1976.*

Chicago: American Public Works Association, 1976. Anderson, Nels. *The Right to Work*. New York: Modern Age Books, 1938. Armstrong, Louise V. *We Too Are the People*. Boston: Little, Brown & Co., 1941.

Bauman, John F., and Thomas H. Coode. *In the Eye of the Great Depression: New Deal Reporters and the Agony of the American People*. De Kalb: Northern Illinois University Press, 1988. Bentley, Joanne. *Hallie Flanagan: A Life in the American Theatre*. New York: Alfred A. Knopf, 1988. Bindas, Kenneth J. *All of This Music Belongs to the Nation: The WPA's Federal Music Project and American Society*. Knoxville: University of Tennessee Press, 1995. Brown, Lorraine, ed. *Liberty Deferred and Other Living Newspapers of the 1930s*. Fairfax, Va.: George Mason University Press, 1989. Bustard, Bruce I. *A New Deal for the Arts*. Seattle: University of Washington Press in association with National Archives and Records Administration, 1997.

Caldwell, Mary French. *The Duck's Back: A Report on Certain Phases of the Socialistic Experiments Conducted by the Federal Government in the Tennessee Valley*. Nashville, Tenn.: privately printed, 1952. Chandler, William U. *The Myth of the TVA: Conservation and Development in the Tennessee Valley, 1933–1983*. Cambridge, Mass.: Ballinger Publishing Company, 1984. Chase, Stuart. *Rich Land, Poor Land: A Study of Waste in the Natural Resources of America*. New York: Whittlesey House, 1936. Coles, Robert. *Dorothea Lange: Photographs of a Lifetime*. New York: Aperture, 1982. Creese, Walter L. *TVA's Public Planning: The Vision, the Reality*. Knoxville: University of Tennessee Press, 1990. Curtis, James. *Mind's Eye, Mind's Truth: FSA Photography Reconsidered*. Philadelphia: Temple University Press, 1989. Cutler, Phoebe. *The Public Landscape of the New Deal*. New Haven, Conn.: Yale University Press, 1985.

Davidson, Donald. *The Tennessee*. Vol. 2 of *The New River: Civil War to TVA*. 1948. Reprint, Nashville: J. S. Sanders & Co., 1992. Davis, Maxine. *They Shall Not Want*. New York: The Macmillan Co., 1937.

Flanagan, Hallie. *Arena*. New York: Duell, Sloan and Pearce, 1940.

Heinemann, Ronald L. *Depression and New Deal Virginia: The Enduring Dominion*. Charlottesville: University of Virginia Press, 1983. Hewes, Laurence. *Boxcar in the Sand*. New York: Alfred A. Knopf, 1957. Holland, Kenneth, and Frank Ernest Hill. *Youth in the CCC*. Washington, D.C.: American Council on Education, 1942. Hopkins, Harry L. *Spending to Save: The Complete Story of Relief*. New York: W. W. Norton, 1936. Hosen, Frederick E. *The Great Depression and the New Deal: Legislative Acts in Their Entirety (1932–1933) and Statistical Economic Data (1926–1946)*. Jefferson, N.C.: McFarland & Company, 1992. Houseman, John. *Run-Through: A Memoir*. New York: Simon & Schuster, 1972. Howard, Donald S. *The W.P.A. and Federal Relief Policy*. New York: The Russell Sage

Foundation, 1943. Hoyt, Ray. *We Can Take It: A Short Story of the C.C.C.* New York: The American Book Co., 1935. Hubbard, Preston J. *Origins of the TVA: The Muscle Shoals Controversy, 1920–1932.* 1961. Reprint, New York: W. W. Norton & Co., 1968. Hurley, F. Jack. *Portrait of a Decade: Roy Stryker and the Development of Documentary Photography in the Thirties.* Baton Rouge: University of Louisiana Press, 1972. Huxley, Julian. *TVA: Adventure in Planning.* Cheam, England: The Architectural Press, 1943.

Ickes, Harold L. *Back to Work: The Story of the PWA.* New York: The Macmillan Co., 1935.

Jackson, Charles O. *Food and Drug Legislation in the New Deal.* Princeton, N.J.: Princeton University Press, 1970. Johnson, Hugh S. *The Blue Eagle from Egg to Earth.* Garden City, N.Y.: Doubleday, Doran & Co., 1935. Jones, Jesse H., with Edward Angly. *Fifty Billion Dollars: My Thirteen Years with the RFC (1932–1945).* New York: The Macmillan Co., 1951.

Kessner, Thomas. *Fiorello H. La Guardia and the Making of Modern New York.* New York: McGraw-Hill Publishing Co., 1989. King, Judson. *The Conservation Fight: From Theodore Roosevelt to the Tennessee Valley Authority.* Washington, D. C.: The Public Affairs Press, 1959. Kornbluh, Joyce L. *A New Deal for Workers' Education: The Workers' Service Program, 1933–1942.* Urbana: University of Illinois Press, 1987. Krueckeberger, Donald A. *The American Planner: Biographies and Recollections.* New York: Methuen, 1983. Kyle, John H. *The Building of TVA: An Illustrated History.* Baton Rouge: Louisiana State University Press, 1958.

Lacy, Leslie Alexander. *The Soil Soldiers: The Civilian Conservation Corps in the Great Depression.* Radnor, Pa.: Chilton Book Co., 1976. Lehman, Tim. *Public Values, Private Lands: Farmland Preservation Policy, 1933–1985.* Chapel Hill: University of North Carolina Press, 1995. Lewis, Helen Matthews, Linda Johnson, and Donald Askins. *Colonialism in Modern America: The Appalachian Case.* Boone, North Carolina: The Appalachian Consortium Press, 1978. Ligutti, Luigi G., and John C. Rawe. *Rural Roads to Security: America's Third Struggle for Freedom.* Milwaukee: The Bruce Publishing Company, 1940. Lilienthal, David. *TVA: Democracy on the March.* New York: Harper & Brothers, 1944; *The Journals of David E. Lilienthal. Vol. 1, The TVA Years, 1939–1945.* New York: Harper & Row, 1964. Lindley, Betty, and Ernest K. Lindley. *A New Deal for Youth: The Story of the National Youth Administration.* New York: Viking, 1938. Lorentz, Pare. *FDR's Moviemaker: Memoirs and Scripts.* Reno: University of Nevada Press, 1992. Lowitt, Richard, and Maurine Beasley, eds. *One Third of a Nation: Lorena Hickok Reports on the Great Depression.* Urbana: University of Illinois Press, 1981. Lubov, Roy. *The Struggle for Social Security, 1900–1935.* 2d ed. Pittsburgh: University of Pittsburgh Press, 1986.

McDonald, Michael J., and John Muldowny. *TVA and the Dispossessed: The Resettlement of the Norris Dam Area*. Knoxville: University of Tennessee Press, 1982. McDonald, William F. *Federal Relief Administration and the Arts: The Origins and Administrative History of the Arts Projects of the Works Progress Administration*. Columbus: Ohio State University Press, 1969. McGraw, Thomas K. *TVA and the Power Fight, 1933–1939*. Philadelphia: J. B. Lippincott, 1971. Malone, Michael P., and Richard W. Etulain. *The American West: A Twentieth Century History*. Lincoln: University of Nebraska Press, 1989. Mangione, Jerre. *The Dream and the Deal: The Federal Writers' Project, 1935–1943*. Philadelphia: University of Pennsylvania Press, 1983; *An Ethnic At Large: A Memoir of America in the Thirties and Forties*. Philadelphia: University of Pennsylvania Press, 1978. Marling, Karal Ann. *Wall-to-Wall America: A Cultural History of Post-Office Murals in the Great Depression*. Minneapolis: University of Minnesota Press, 1982. Meltzer, Milton. *Dorothea Lange: A Photographer's Life*. New York: Farrar, Straus, Giroux, 1978. Miller, Orlando W. *The Frontier in Alaska and the Matanuska Colony*. New Haven, Conn.: Yale University Press, 1975. Millett, John D. *The Works Progress Administration in New York City*. Chicago: published for the Committee on Public Administration of the Social Science Research Council by Public Administration Service, 1938. Morgan, Arthur. *The Making of the TVA*. Buffalo, N.Y.: Prometheus Books, 1974.

Neuberger, Richard L. *Our Promised Land*. Reprint of 1938 edition. Moscow: University of Idaho Press, 1989. Nixon, Edgar B., ed. *Franklin D. Roosevelt and Conservation, 1911–1945*. 2 vols. Hyde Park, N.Y.: General Services Administration, National Archives and Records Service, Franklin D. Roosevelt Library, 1957.

Olson, James S. *Saving Capitalism: The Reconstruction Finance Corporation and the New Deal, 1933–1940*. Princeton, N.J.: Princeton University Press, 1988.

Penkower, Monty Noam. *The Federal Writers' Project: A Study in Government Patronage of the Arts*. Urbana: University of Illinois Press, 1977. Philip, Kenneth R. *John Collier's Crusade for Indian Reform, 1920–1954*. Tucson: University of Arizona Press, 1977. Prichett, C. Herman. *The Tennessee Valley Authority: A Study in Public Administration*. Chapel Hill: University of North Carolina Press, 1943.

Reiman, Richard A. *The New Deal and American Youth: Ideas and Ideals in a Depression Decade*. Athens: University of Georgia Press, 1992. Rose, Nancy E. *Put to Work: Relief Programs in the Great Depression*. New York: Monthly Review Press, 1994.

Schwartz, Bonnie Fox. *The Civil Works Administration, 1933–1934: The Business of Emergency Employment in the New Deal*. Princeton, N.J.: Princeton University Press, 1984. Selznick, Philip. *TVA and the Grass Roots: A Study of Politics and Organization*. Berkeley: University of California Press, 1984. Smith, Douglas L. *The New Deal in the Urban South*. Baton Rouge: Louisiana State University

Press, 1988. Stevens, Joseph E. *Hoover Dam: An American Adventure.* Norman: University of Oklahoma Press, 1988.

Talbert, Roy, Jr. *FDR's Utopian: Arthur Morgan of the TVA.* Jackson: University of Mississippi Press, 1987. Trout, Charles H. *Boston, The Great Depression, and the New Deal.* New York: Oxford University Press, 1977. Tweton, D. Jerome. *The New Deal at the Grass Roots: Programs for the People in Otter Tail County, Minnesota.* St. Paul: Minnesota Historical Society Press, 1988.

Vittoz, Stanley. *New Deal Labor Policy and the American Industrial Economy.* Chapel Hill: University of North Carolina Press, 1987.

Wallace, Henry. *New Frontiers.* New York: Reynal & Hitchcock, 1934. Whitman, Willson. *Bread and Circuses: A Study of Federal Theatre.* New York: Oxford University Press, 1937; *David Lilienthal: Public Servant in a Power Age.* New York: Henry Holt & Co., 1948. Wilson, Marshall A. *Tales from the Grassroots of TVA, 1933–1952.* Knoxville, Tenn.: privately printed, 1982. Worster, Donald. *The Wealth of Nature: Environmental History and the Ecological Imagination.* New York: Oxford University Press, 1993.

Yezierska, Anzia. *Red Ribbon on a White Horse.* New York: Charles Scribner's Sons, 1950.

Articles

Bauman, John F., and Thomas H. Coode. "Depression Report: A New Dealer Tours Eastern Pennsylvania." *Pennsylvania Magazine of History and Biography* (January 1980). Beddow, James B. "Depression and New Deal: Letters from the Plains." *Kansas Historical Quarterly* (summer 1977). Blakey, George T. "Kentucky Youth and the New Deal." *Filson Club History Quarterly* (January 1986). Bremer, William A. "Along the 'American Way': The New Deal's Work Relief Programs for the Unemployed." *The Journal of American History* (December 1975).

Culbert, David H. "The Infinite Variety of Mass Experience: The Great Depression, W.P.A. Interviews, and Student Family History Projects." *Louisiana History* (winter 1978).

Droze, W. H. "TVA and the Ordinary Farmer." *Agricultural History* (January 1979).

Fulgham, Luisa J. "Roosevelt Feeds the Hungry: The Federal Surplus Relief Corporation, 1933–1935." *Red River Valley Historical Review* (fall 1982).

Hendrickson, Kenneth E., Jr. "The National Youth Administration in South Dakota: Youth and the New Deal 1935–1943." *South Dakota History* (spring 1979); "Relief for Youth: The Civilian Conservation Corps and the National Youth Administration in North Dakota." *North Dakota History* (fall 1981).

Ingram, Earl. "The Federal Emergency Relief Administration in Louisiana." *Louisiana History* (spring 1973).

Jackson, Donald Dale. "They Were Poor, Hungry, and They Built to Last." *Smithsonian* (December 1994). Johnson, Charles W. "The Army and the Civilian Conservation Corps, 1933–42." *Prologue* (fall 1972).

Koch, Raymond L. "Politics and Relief in Minneapolis During the 1930s." *Minnesota History* (winter 1968). Kuhn, Cliff. "Reminiscences: Interviews with Atlanta New Deal Social Workers." *The Atlanta Historical Journal* (spring 1986).

Lambert, Roger C. "Drought Relief for Cattlemen: The Emergency Purchase Program of 1934–35." *Panhandle-Plains Historical Review* (1972); "The Illusion of Participatory Democracy: The AAA Organizes the Corn-Hog Producers." *Annals of Iowa* (fall 1974); "Slaughter of the Innocents: The Public Protests AAA Killing of Little Pigs." *Midwest Quarterly* (April 1973). Leff, Mark. H. "Taxing the 'Forgotten Man': The Politics of Social Security Finance in the New Deal." *Journal of American History* (September 1983). Leotta, Louis. "Abraham Epstein and the Movement for Old Age Security." *Labor History* (summer 1975); "Want and Plenty: The Federal Surplus Relief Corporation and the AAA." *Agricultural History* (July 1972).

Mitchell, Virgil L. "Louisiana Health and the Civil Works Administration." *Red River Valley Historical Review* (winter 1982); "The Louisiana Unemployed and the Civil Works Administration." *Red River Valley Historical Review* (summer 1980). Morgan, Iwan. "Fort Wayne and the Great Depression: The New Deal Years, 1933–1940." *Indiana Magazine of History* (December 1984).

Patterson, James T., ed. "Life on Relief in Rhode Island, 1934: A Contemporary View from the Field." *Rhode Island History* (August 1980); "Mary Dewson and the American Minimum Wage Movement." *Labor History* (spring 1964).

Ray, Joseph M. "The Influence of the Tennessee Valley Authority on Government in the South." *American Political Science Review* (October 1949). Rosenstrater, Roger. "Roosevelt's Tree Army." *Michigan History* (May/June 1986).

Shapiro, Edward. "The Southern Agrarians and the Tennessee Valley Authority." *American Quarterly* (winter 1970). Shover, John L. "Populism in the Nineteen-Thirties: The Battle for the AAA." *Agricultural History* (January 1961). Soffar, Allan J. "The Forest Shelterbelt Project, 1934–1944." *Journal of the West* (July 1975). Sobczak, John N. "The Politics of Relief: Public Aid in Toledo, 1933–1937." *Northwest Ohio Quarterly* (fall 1976). Stout, Joe A., Jr. "Cattlemen, Conservationists, and the Taylor Grazing Act." *New Mexico Historical Review* (October 1970). Swain, Martha H. "'The Forgotten Woman': Ellen S. Woodward and Women's Relief in the New Deal." *Prologue* (winter 1983); "Pat Harrison and the Social Security Act of 1935." *Southern Quarterly* (October 1976).

Wade, Michael G. "'Farm Dorm Boys': The Origins of the NYA Resident Training Program." *Louisiana History* (spring 1986).

MIGRANTS, SHARECROPPERS, AND OTHER AGRICULTURAL MATTERS

Books

Caldwell, Erskine, and Margaret Bourke-White. *You Have Seen Their Faces*. 1937.
Reprint, New York: Derbibooks, 1975. Cash, W. J. *The Mind of the South*. New
York: Alfred A. Knopf, 1941. Cason, Clarence. *90 Degrees in the Shade*. Chapel
Hill: University of North Carolina Press, 1935. Collins, Henry Hill, Jr. *Amer-
ica's Own Refugees: Our 4,000,000 Homeless Migrants*. Princeton, N.J.: Princeton
University Press, 1941. Cornford, Daniel, ed. *Working People of California*.
Berkeley: University of California Press, 1995.

Daniel, Cletus E. *Bitter Harvest: A History of California Farmworkers, 1870–1941*.
Berkeley: University of California Press, 1981. Daniel, Pete. *Breaking the Land:
The Transformation of Cotton, Tobacco, and Rice Cultures Since 1880*. Urbana: Uni-
versity of Illinois Press, 1985. Daniels, Jonathan. *A Southerner Discovers the
South*. New York: Macmillan, 1938. Dunbar, Anthony P. *Against the Grain:
Southern Radicals and Prophets, 1929–1959*. Charlottesville: University of Vir-
ginia Press, 1981.

Egerton, John. *Speak Now Against the Day: The Generation Before the Civil Rights
Movement in the South*. New York: Alfred A. Knopf, 1994.

Federal Writers Project, Works Progress Administration. *These Are Our Lives: As
Told by the People and Written by Members of the Federal Writers' Project of the Works
Progress Administration in South Carolina, Tennessee, and Georgia*. Chapel Hill:
University of North Carolina Press, 1939. Flynt, Wayne. *Poor But Proud:
Alabama's Poor Whites*. Tuscaloosa: University of Alabama Press, 1989. French,
Warren, ed. *A Companion to "The Grapes of Wrath."* Reprint of 1963 edition.
New York: Penguin Books, 1989.

Gregory, James N. *American Exodus: The Dust Bowl Migration and Okie Culture in
California*. New York: Oxford University Press, 1989. Grubbs, Donald H. *Cry
from the Cotton: The Southern Tenant Farmers' Union and the New Deal*. Chapel
Hill: University of North Carolina Press, 1971. Guerin-Gonzales, Camille.
*Mexican Workers and American Dreams: Immigration, Repatriation, and California
Farm Labor, 1900–1939*. New Brunswick, N.J.: Rutgers University Press,
1994.

Hudson, Lois Phillips. *Reapers of the Dust: A Prairie Chronicle*. Boston: Little, Brown
& Co., 1964. Hull, William H. *The Dirty Thirties: Tales of the Nineteen Thirties
During Which Occurred a Great Drought, a Lengthy Depression and the Era Commonly
Called the Dust Bowl Years*. Minneapolis: published by the author, 1989.

Johnson, Gerald W. *The Wasted Land.* Freeport, N.Y.: Books for Libraries Press, 1937. Johnson, Josephine. *Now in November* (novel). 1934. Reprint, New York: The Feminist Press of the City University of New York, 1991.

Kirby, Jack Temple. *Rural Worlds Lost: The American South, 1920–1960.* Baton Rouge: Louisiana State University Press, 1987. Klein, Joe. *Woody Guthrie: A Life.* New York: Alfred A. Knopf, 1980.

Lange, Dorothea, and Paul S. Taylor. *American Exodus: A Record of Human Erosion.* New York: Reynal & Hitchcock, 1939. Loftis, Anne. *Witnesses to the Struggle: Imaging the 1930s California Labor Movement.* Reno: University of Nevada Press, 1998. Long, Philip S. *Dreams, Dust and Depression.* Calgary: Cypress Publishing, Inc., 1972. Low, Ann Marie. *Dust Bowl Diary.* Lincoln: University of Nebraska Press, 1984.

McMillen, Neil R. *Dark Journey: Black Mississippians in the Age of Jim Crow.* Urbana: University of Illinois Press, 1989. McWilliams, Carey. *Factories in the Field: The Story of Migratory Farm Labor in California.* Boston: Little, Brown & Co., 1939; *North from Mexico: The Spanish-Speaking People of the United States.* Philadelphia: J. B. Lippincott, 1949. Martin, Robert. *Howard Kester and the Struggle for Social Justice in the South, 1904–1977.* Charlottesville: University Press of Virginia, 1991. Miller, Marc S., ed. *Working Lives: "The Southern Exposure" History of Labor in the South.* New York: Pantheon Books, 1980.

Raper, Arthur S. *Preface to Peasantry: A Tale of Two Black Belt Counties.* Chapel Hill: University of North Carolina Press, 1936. Rochester, Anna. *Why Farmers Are Poor: The Agricultural Crisis in the United States.* New York: International Publishers, 1940. Rohrer, Wayne C., and Louis H. Douglas. *The Agrarian Transition in America: Dualism and Change.* Indianapolis: The Bobbs-Merrill Co., 1969. Rosengarten, Theodore. *All God's Dangers: The Life of Nate Shaw.* New York: Alfred A. Knopf, 1974.

Saloutos, Theodore, and John D. Hicks. *Agricultural Discontent in the Middle West, 1900–1939.* Madison: University of Wisconsin Press, 1951. Shindo, Charles J. *Dust Bowl Migrants in the American Imagination.* Lawrence: University of Kansas Press, 1997. Snyder, Robert E. *Cotton Crisis.* Chapel Hill: University of North Carolina Press, 1984. Stein, Walter J. *California and the Dust Bowl Migration.* Westport, Conn.: Greenwood Press, 1973. Steinbeck, John. *Their Blood Is Strong.* San Francisco: The Simon J. Lubin Society, 1938. Stock, Catherine McNicol. *Main Street in Crisis: The Great Depression and the Old Middle Class on the Northern Plains.* Chapel Hill: University of North Carolina Press, 1992. Svoboda, Lawrence. *An Empire of Dust.* Caldwell N.J.: Caxton Press, 1940.

Taylor, Paul Schuster. *On the Ground in the Thirties.* Layton, Utah: Peregrine Smith Books, 1983. Terrill, Tom E., and Jerrold Hirsch, eds. *Such As Us: Southern*

Voices of the Thirties. Chapel Hill: University of North Carolina Press, 1978.

Vance, Rupert B. *Human Geography of the South: A Study in Regional Resources and Human Adequacy.* Chapel Hill: University of North Carolina Press, 1932.

Vestal, Stanley. *Short Grass Country.* New York: Duell, Sloan & Pearce, 1941.

Woofter, T. J., Jr., and Ellen Winston. *Seven Lean Years.* Chapel Hill: University of North Carolina Press, 1939. Worster, Donald. *Dust Bowl: The Southern Plains in the 1930s.* New York: Oxford University Press, 1979; *Rivers of Empire: Water, Aridity, and the Growth of the American West.* New York: Pantheon, 1985.

Articles

Arrington, Leonard J. "Utah's Great Drought of 1934." *Utah Historical Quarterly* (summer 1986). Auerbach, Jerold S. "Southern Tenant Farmers: Socialist Critics of the New Deal." *Arkansas Historical Quarterly* (summer 1965); "Southern Tenant Farmers: Socialist Critics of the New Deal." (Altered version.) *Labor History* (winter 1966).

Daniel, Cletus E. "Agricultural Unionism and the Early New Deal: The California Experience." *Southern California Quarterly* (summer 1977). Diepenbrock, David A. "Florence Wyckoff, Helen Hosmer, and San Francisco's Liberal Network in the 1930s." *Ex Post Facto: The History Journal* (spring 1994). Dewitt, Howard A. "The Filipino Labor Union: The Salinas Lettuce Strike of 1934." *Amerasia Journal* (fall 1978). Dileva, Frank D. "Attempt to Hang an Iowa Judge." *Annals of Iowa* (July 1954). Dinwoodie, D. H. "Deportation: The Immigration Service and the Chicano Labor Movement in the 1930s." *New Mexico Historical Review* (July 1977). Dyson, Lowell K. "The Southern Tenant Farmers Union and Depression Politics." *Political Science Quarterly* (June 1973); "Was Agricultural Distress in the 1930s a Result of Land Speculation During World War I? The Case of Iowa." *Annals of Iowa* (spring 1971).

Erickson, Erlaing A. "A North Dakota Farm Auction in the Great Depression." *North Dakota Quarterly* (winter 1971).

Gonzalez, Gilbert G. "Company Unions, the Mexican Consulate, and the Imperial Valley Agricultural Strikes, 1928–1934." *Western Historical Quarterly* (spring 1986); "Labor and Community: The Camps of Mexican Citrus Pickers in Southern California." *Western Historical Quarterly* (August 1991). Gordon, Lawrence. "A Brief Look at Blacks in Depression Mississippi, 1929–1934: Eyewitness Accounts." *Journal of Negro History* (fall 1979). Greenway, John. "Woody Guthrie: The Man, the Land, the Understanding." *American West* (fall 1966).

Hogland, A. William. "Wisconsin Dairy Farmers on Strike." *Agricultural History* (January 1961). Hurt, R. Douglas. "Letters from the Dust Bowl." *Panhandle-Plains Historical Review* (1979).

Ingalls, Robert P. "Anti-Labor Vigilantes: The South During the 1930s." *Southern Exposure* (November/December 1984).

Karr, Rodney D. "Farmer Rebels in Plymouth County, Iowa, 1932–1933." *Annals of Iowa* (winter 1985).

McWilliams, Carey. "A Man, a Place, and a Time: John Steinbeck and the Long Agony of the Great Valley in an Age of Depression, Oppression, and Hope." *The American West* (May 1970). Mathews, Allan. "Agrarian Radicals: The United Farmers League of South Dakota." *South Dakota History* (fall 1973).

Naison, Mark D. "Claude and Joyce Williams: Pilgrims of Justice." *Southern Exposure* (winter 1974).

Pew, Thomas W., Jr. "Route 66: Ghost Road of the Okies." *American Heritage* (August 1977). Pratt, William C. "Rural Radicalism on the Northern Plains, 1912–1950." *Montana: The Magazine of History* (winter 1992). Purdy, Virginia C., ed. " 'Dust to Eat': A Document from the Dust Bowl." *Chronicles of Oklahoma* (winter 1980–81).

Schweider, Dorothy. "South Dakota Farm Women During the Great Depression." *Journal of the West* (October 1985). Shover, John L., ed., "Depression Letters from American Farmers." *Agricultural History* (July 1962); "The Penny-Auction Rebellion." *American West* (fall 1965). Stein, Walter J. "The 'Okie' as Farm Laborer." *Agricultural History* (January 1975). Street, Richard Steven. "The 'Battle of Salinas': San Francisco Bay Area Press Photographers and the Salinas Valley Lettuce Strike of 1936." *Journal of the West* (April 1987).

Taylor, Paul Schuster. "Migrant Mother: 1936." *American West* (May 1970). Thrasher, Sue, and Leah Wise. "The Southern Tenant Farmers' Union." *Southern Exposure* (winter 1974).

Venkataramani, M. S. "Norman Thomas, Arkansas Sharecroppers, and the Roosevelt Agricultural Policies, 1933–1937." *Mississippi Valley Historical Review* (September 1960).

Wise, Leah. "The Elaine Massacre." *Southern Exposure* (winter 1974). Wuerthner, George. "How the West Was Eaten." *Wilderness* (spring 1991).

The Labor Movement

Books

Alinsky, Saul. *John L. Lewis: An Unauthorized Biography*. New York: G. P. Putnam's Sons, 1949.

Bernstein, Irving. *A Caring Society: The New Deal, the Worker, and the Great Depression*. Boston: Houghton Mifflin Co., 1985; *The Lean Years: A History of the American Worker, 1920–1933*. Boston: Houghton Mifflin, 1960; *The Turbulent*

Decade: A History of the American Worker, 1933–1940. Boston: Houghton Mifflin, 1970. Boyer, Richard O., and Herbert M. Morais. *Labor's Untold Story.* New York: United Electrical, Radio & Machine Workers of America, 1980. Brecher, Jeremy. *Strike!* San Francisco: Straight Arrow Books, 1972. Brody, David. *In Labor's Cause: Main Themes on the History of the American Worker.* New York: Oxford University Press, 1993; *Workers in Industrial America: Essays on the Twentieth Century Struggle.* 2d ed. New York: Oxford University Press, 1993. Brooks, Robert R. R. *When Labor Organizes.* New Haven, Conn.: Yale University Press, 1937. Brooks, Thomas R. *Picket Lines and Bargaining Tables: Organized Labor Comes of Age, 1933–1955.* New York: Grosset & Dunlap, 1968. Buffa, Dudley W. *Union Power and American Democracy: The UAW and the Democratic Party, 1935–1972.* Ann Arbor: University of Michigan Press, 1984.

Carnes, Cecil. *John L. Lewis: Leader of Labor.* New York: Robert Speller Publishing Corp., 1936. Caudill, Harry. *Night Comes to the Cumberlands: A Biography of a Depressed Area.* Boston: Little, Brown & Co., 1963. Cohen, Elizabeth. *Making a New Deal: Industrial Workers in Chicago, 1919–1939.* Cambridge: Cambridge University Press, 1990.

Dayton, Eldorous L. *Walter Reuther: The Autocrat of the Bargaining Table.* New York: The Devin-Adair Company, 1958. Dubinsky, David, and A. H. Raskin. *David Dubinsky: A Life with Labor.* New York: Simon & Schuster, 1977. Dubofsky, Melvin, and Warren Van Tine. *John L. Lewis: A Biography.* New York: Quadrangle Books/The New York Times Book Company, 1977. Dulles, Foster Rhea. *Labor in America: A History.* New York: Thomas Y. Crowell Co., 1949.

Eliel, Paul. *The Waterfront and General Strikes, San Francisco, 1934.* San Francisco: Industrial Relations Department, Industrial Association of San Francisco, 1934.

Faue, Elizabeth. *Community of Suffering and Struggle: Women, Men, and the Labor Movement in Minneapolis, 1915–1945.* Chapel Hill: University of North Carolina Press, 1991. Fine, Sidney. *Sit-down: The General Motors Strike of 1936–1937.* Ann Arbor: University of Michigan Press, 1969. Foner, Philip S. *Women and the American Labor Movement: From the First Trade Unions to the Present.* New York: The Free Press, 1979. Fraser, Steven. *Labor Will Rule: Sidney Hillman and the Rise of American Labor.* New York: The Free Press, 1991. Friedlander, Peter. *The Emergence of a U.A.W. Local, 1936–1939: A Study in Class and Culture.* Pittsburgh: University of Pittsburgh Press, 1975.

Gartman, David. *Auto Slavery: The Labor Process in the American Automobile Industry, 1897–1950.* New Brunswick, N.J.: Rutgers University Press, 1986.

Hall, Jacquelyn Dowd, et al. *Like a Family: The Making of a Southern Cotton Mill World.* Chapel Hill: University of North Carolina Press, 1987. Hodges, James

A. *New Deal Labor Policy and the Southern Cotton Textile Industry, 1933–1941.* Knoxville: University of Tennessee Press, 1986.

Jones, Alfred Winslow. *Life, Liberty, and Property: A Story of a Conflict and a Measurement of Conflicting Rights.* Philadelphia: J. B. Lippincott Company, 1941. Josephson, Matthew. *Sidney Hillman: Statesman of American Labor.* Garden City, N.Y.: Doubleday & Co., 1952.

Kahn, Kathy. *Hillbilly Women.* Garden City, N.Y.: Doubleday & Co., 1973. Kraus, Henry. *Heroes of Unwritten Story: The UAW, 1934–39.* Urbana: University of Illinois Press, 1993; *The Many & The Few: A Chronicle of the Dynamic Auto Workers.* Los Angeles: The Plantin Press, 1947.

Leighton, George R. *America's Growing Pains: The Romance, Comedy and Tragedy of Five Great Cities.* New York: Harper & Brothers, 1939. Levine, Rhonda F. *Class Struggle and the New Deal: Industrial Labor, Industrial Capital, and the State.* Lawrence: University of Kansas Press, 1988. Lichtenstein, Nelson. *The Most Dangerous Man in Detroit: Walter Reuther and the Fate of American Labor.* New York: BasicBooks, 1995. Lynd, Robert S., and Helen Merrell, eds. *Rank and File: Personal Histories by Working-Class Organizers.* 1973. Reprint, Princeton, N.J.: Princeton University Press, 1981.

McKenney, Ruth. *Industrial Valley* (novel). New York: Harcourt, Brace & Co., 1939. Markowitz, Gerald, and David Rosner, eds. *"Slaves of the Depression": Workers' Letters About Life on the Job.* Ithaca, N.Y.: Cornell University Press, 1987. Meier, August, and Elliott Rudwick. *Black Detroit and the Rise of the UAW.* New York: Oxford University Press, 1979. Minton, Bruce, and John Stuart. *Men Who Lead Labor.* New York: Modern Age Books, 1937.

Nelson, Bruce. *Workers on the Waterfront: Seamen, Longshoremen, and Unionism in the 1930s.* Urbana: University of Illinois Press, 1988. Nelson, Daniel. *American Rubber Workers and Organized Labor, 1900–1941.* Princeton, N.J.: Princeton University Press, 1988. Newell, Barbara Warne. *Chicago and the Labor Movement: Metropolitan Unionism in the 1930s.* Urbana: University of Illinois Press, 1961.

Peterson, Joyce Shaw. *American Automobile Workers, 1900–1933.* Albany: State University of New York, 1987.

Quin, Mike (Paul William Ryan). *The Big Strike.* Olema, Calif.: Olema Publishing Co., 1949.

Reuther, Victor G. *The Brothers Reuther and the Story of the UAW: A Memoir.* Boston: Houghton Mifflin Co., 1976.

Salmond, John A. *Gastonia, 1929: The Story of the Loray Mill Strike.* Chapel Hill: University of North Carolina Press, 1995. Shackelford, Laurel, and Bill Weinberg, eds. *Our Appalachia: An Oral History.* New York: Hill & Wang, 1977.

Stolberg, Benjamin. *Tailor's Progress: The Story of a Famous Union and the Men Who Made It*. Garden City, N.Y.: Doubleday, Doran & Co., 1944. Sulzberger, C. L. *Sit Down with John L. Lewis*. New York: Random House, 1938.

Taft, Philip. *The A. F. of L. in the Time of Gompers*. New York: Harper & Brothers, 1957; *The A. F. of L. from the Death of Gompers to the Merger*. New York: Harper & Brothers, 1959. Tyler, Gus. *Look for the Union Label: A History of the International Ladies' Garment Workers' Union*. Armonk, N.Y.: M. E. Sharpe, 1995.

Walker, Charles Rumford. *American City: A Rank-and-File History*. New York: Farrar & Rinehart, 1937.

Zieger, Robert H. *American Workers, American Unions, 1920–1985*. Baltimore: Johns Hopkins University Press, 1986; *The CIO, 1935–1955*. Chapel Hill: University of North Carolina Press, 1995.

Articles

Ansley, Fran, and Brenda Bell. "Strikes at Davidson and Wilder." *Southern Exposure* (winter 1974); eds. "Miners Insurrections/Convict Labor." *Southern Exposure* (winter 1974); and Florence Reece. "'Little David Blues' and Interview with Tom Lowry." *Southern Exposure* (winter 1974). Auel, Lisa Benkert. "Not Without Protest: Life in the Appalachian Coalfields." *Prologue* (summer 1991).

Bernanke, Ben S. "Employment, Hours, and Earnings in the Depression: An Analysis of Eight Manufacturing Industries." *American Economic Review* (March 13, 1986). Blantz, Thomas E. "Father Haas and the Minneapolis Truckers' Strike of 1934." *Minnesota History* (spring 1970).

Findlay, James F. "The Great Textile Strike of 1934: Illuminating Rhode Island History in the Thirties." *Rhode Island History* (February 1983).

Hall, Jacquelyn Dowd, Robert Korstad, and James Leloudis. "Cotton Mill People: Work, Community, and Protest in the Textile South, 1880–1940." *The American Historical Review* (April 1986). Herring, Neill, and Sue Thrasher. "UAW Sitdown Strike: Atlanta 1936." *Southern Exposure* (winter 1974).

Nelson, Daniel. "Origins of the Sit-Down Era: Worker Militancy and Innovation in the Rubber Industry, 1934–1938." *Labor History* (spring 1982). Nyden, Linda. "Black Miners in Western Pennsylvania, 1925–1931: The National Miners' Union and the United Mine Workers of America." *Science & Society* (spring 1977).

Reynolds, Douglas. "Engines of Struggle: Technology, Skill, and Unionization at General Motors, 1930–1940." *Michigan Historical Review* (spring 1989).

Weisbord, Vera Buch. "Gastonia 1929: Strike at the Luray Mill." *Southern Exposure* (winter 1974). West, Kenneth B. "'On the Line': Rank and File Reminiscences of Working Conditions and the General Motors Sit-Down Strike of 1936–37." *Michigan Historical Review* (spring 1986).

COMMUNISTS, DISSIDENTS, AND OTHER RADICALS

Books

Baigell, Matthew, and Julia Williams, eds. *Artists Against War and Fascism: Papers of the First American Artists' Congress*. New Brunswick, N.J.: Rutgers University Press, 1986. Baritz, Loren, ed. *The American Left: Radical Political Thought in the Twentieth Century*. New York: Basic Books, 1971. Bart, Philip, et al., eds. *Highlights of a Fighting History: 60 Years of the Communist Party, USA*. New York: International Publishers, 1979. Bennett, David H. *Demagogues in the Depression: American Radicals and the Union Party, 1932–1936*. New Brunswick, N.J.: Rutgers University Press, 1969. Brinkley, Alan. *Voices of Protest: Huey Long, Father Coughlin, and the Great Depression*. New York: Alfred A. Knopf, 1982. Browder, Earl. *Communism in the United States*. New York: International Publishers, 1935; *The People's Front*. New York: International Publishers, 1938.

Carroll, Peter N. *The Odyssey of the Abraham Lincoln Brigade: Americans in the Spanish Civil War*. Stanford, Calif.: Stanford University Press, 1994. Carter, John Franklin (the Unofficial Observer). *American Messiahs*. New York: Simon & Schuster, 1935. Christman, Henry M., ed. *Kingfish to America: Share Our Wealth—Selected Senatorial Papers of Huey P. Long*. New York: Schocken Books, 1985. Cohen, Robert. *When the Old Left Was Young: Student Radicals and America's First Mass Student Movement, 1929–1941*. New York: Oxford University Press, 1993. Cornell, Thomas C., and James H. Forest, eds. *A Penny a Copy: Readings from the Catholic Worker*. New York: Macmillan, 1968. Coughlin, Rev. Charles E. *Eight Lectures on Labor, Capital, and Justice*. Royal Oak, Mich.: The Radio League of the Little Flower, 1934. Cowles, Virginia. *Looking for Trouble*. New York: Harper & Brothers, 1941. Cowley, Malcolm. *The Dream of the Golden Mountain: Remembering the 1930s*. New York: Viking Press, 1980.

Davis, Hope Hale. *Great Day Coming: A Memoir of the 1930s*. South Royalton, Vt.: Steerforth Press, 1994. Dennis, Peggy. *The Autobiography of an American Communist: A Personal View of a Political Life, 1925–1975*. Berkeley, Calif.: Creative Arts Book Co., 1977. Diggins, John Patrick. *The Rise and Fall of the American Left*. New York: W. W. Norton & Co., 1992. Draper, Theodore. *The Roots of American Communism*. New York: Viking Press, 1957. Dreiser, Theodore, et al. *Harlan Miners Speak: Report on Terrorism in the Kentucky Coal Fields Prepared by Members of the National Committee for the Defense of Political Prisoners*. New York: Harcourt, Brace & Co., 1932. Duberman, Martin Bauml. *Paul Robeson: A Biography*. New York: Alfred A. Knopf, 1989.

Fast, Howard. *The Naked God: The Writer and the Communist Party*. New York: Praeger, 1957. Folsom, Franklin. *Impatient Armies of the Poor: The Story of Collective Action of the Unemployed, 1808–1942*. Boulder: University Press of Colorado,

1991. Foner, Philip S., and Herbert Shapiro, eds. *American Communism and Black Americans: A Documentary History, 1930–1934.* Philadelphia: Temple University Press, 1991. Foster, William Z. *From Bryan to Stalin.* New York: International Publishers, 1937; *Pages from a Worker's Life.* New York: International Publishers, 1939.

Garrison, Dee. *Mary Heaton Vorse: The Life of an American Insurgent.* Philadelphia: Temple University Press, 1989. Gerassi, John. *The Premature Fascists: North American Volunteers in the Spanish Civil War, 1936–1939.* New York: Praeger, 1986. Gornick, Vivian. *The Romance of American Communism.* New York: Basic Books, 1977. Guttman, Allen. *A Wound in the Heart: America and the Spanish Civil War.* New York: The Free Press of Glencoe, 1962.

Halper, Albert. *Good-bye, Union Square: A Writer's Memoir of the Thirties.* Chicago: Quadrangle Books, 1970. Haywood, Harry. *Black Bolshevik: Autobiography of an Afro-American Communist.* Chicago: Liberator Press, 1978. Healey, Dorothy, and Maurice Isserman. *Dorothy Healey Remembers: A Life in the Communist Party.* New York: Oxford University Press, 1990.

Johanningsmeier, Edward P. *Forging American Communism: A Life of William Z. Foster.* Princeton, N.J.: Princeton University Press, 1994.

Kelley, Robin D. G. *Hammer and Hoe: Alabama Communists During the Great Depression.* Chapel Hill: University of North Carolina Press, 1990. Klehr, Harvey. *The Heyday of American Communism: The Depression Decade.* New York: Basic Books, 1984; Klehr, Harvey, John Earl Haynes, and Fridrikh Igoravich Firsov. *The Secret World of American Communism.* New Haven, Conn.: Yale University Press, 1995. Kramer, Dale. *Heywood Broun: A Biographical Portrait.* New York: Current Books, 1949.

Long, Huey P. *Every Man a King: The Autobiography of Huey P. Long.* New Orleans: National Book Co., Inc., 1933; *My First Days in the White House.* Harrisburg, Pa.: Telegraph Press, 1935.

Miller, William D. *A Harsh and Dreadful Love: Dorothy Day and the Catholic Worker Movement.* New York: Liveright, 1973. Mitchell, Greg. *The Campaign of the Century: Upton Sinclair's Race for Governor of California and the Birth of Media Politics.* New York: Random House, 1992. Moore, Winston, and Marian T. Moore. *Out of the Frying Pan.* Los Angeles: DeVorss & Co., 1939.

North, Joseph. *No Men Are Strangers.* New York: International House, 1958.

O'Neill, William L. *A Better World: The Great Schism: Stalinism and the American Intellectuals.* New York: Simon & Schuster, 1982. Ottanelli, Fraser M. *The Communist Party of the United States: From the Depression to World War II.* New Brunswick, N.J.: Rutgers University Press, 1991.

Painter, Nell Irvin. *The Narrative of Hosea Hudson: His Life as a Negro Communist in the South.* Cambridge: Harvard University Press, 1979. Preston, William, Jr. *Aliens* and Dissenters: Federal Suppression of Radicals, 1903–1933. Cambridge: Harvard University Press, 1963. Putnam, Jackson K. Old-Age Politics in California: From Richardson to Reagan. Stanford, Calif.: Stanford University Press, 1970.

Record, Wilson. The Negro and the Communist Party. Chapel Hill: University of North Carolina Press, 1951. Richmond, Al. A Long View from the Left: Memoirs of an American Revolutionary. Boston: Houghton Mifflin Company, 1972.

Shipman, Charles. It Had to Be Revolution: Memoirs of an American Radical. Ithaca, N.Y.: Cornell University Press, 1993. Sinclair, Upton. I, Candidate for Governor: And How I Got Licked. Pasadena, Calif.: published by the author, 1935. Swados, Harvey, ed. The American Writer and the Great Depression. Indianapolis: Bobbs-Merrill Co., 1966. Swanberg, W. A. Norman Thomas: The Last Idealist. New York: Charles Scribner's Sons, 1976.

Thomas, Hugh. The Spanish Civil War. New York: Harper & Row, 1961. Thomas, Norman. After the New Deal, What? New York: Macmillan, 1936; As I See It. New York: The Macmillan Co., 1932. Townsend, Dr. Francis E. New Horizons (An Autobiography). Chicago: J. L. Stewart Publishing Company, 1943.

Valelly, Richard M. Radicalism in the States: The Minnesota Farmer-Labor Party and the American Political Economy. Chicago: University of Chicago Press, 1989.

Warren, Frank A. Liberals and Communism: The "Red Decade" Revisited. Indianapolis: Indiana University Press, 1966.

Zinman, David. The Day Huey Long Was Shot: September 8, 1935. New York: Ivan Obolensky, 1963.

Articles

Bubka, Tony. "The Harlan County Coal Strike of 1931." Labor History (winter 1970).

McCoy, Donald R. "The National Progressives of America, 1938." The Mississippi Valley Historical Review (June 1957).

Naison, Mark D. "Communism and Black Nationalism in the Depression: The Case of Harlem." Journal of Ethnic Studies (summer 1974); "Communism and Harlem Intellectuals in the Popular Front: Anti-Fascism and the Politics of Black Culture." Journal of Ethnic Studies (spring 1981).

AFRICAN AMERICANS, MEXICAN AMERICANS, AND OTHER MINORITIES

Books

Acuña, Rodolfo. Occupied America: A History of Chicanos. New York: Harper & Row, 1981. Adamic, Louis. From Many Lands. New York: Harper & Brothers, 1940; Two-Way Passage. New York: Harper & Brothers, 1941. Alvarez, Robert R., Jr.

Familia: Migration and Adaptation in Baja and Alta California, 1800–1975. Berkeley: University of California Press, 1987. Anderson, Jervis. *This Was Harlem: A Cultural Portrait, 1900–1950*. New York: Farrar, Straus & Giroux, 1982. Aptheker, Herbert. *A Documentary History of the Negro People in the United States*. Vol. 3: *1910–1932, From the NAACP to the New Deal*; Vol. 4: *1933–1945, From the New Deal to the End of World War II*. New York: The Citadel Press, 1990.

Brundage, W. Fitzhugh. *Lynching in the New South: Georgia and Virginia, 1880–1930*. Urbana: University of Illinois Press, 1993.

Camarillo, Albert. *Chicanos in a Changing Society: From Mexican Pueblos to American Barrios in Santa Barbara and Southern California, 1848–1930*. Cambridge: Harvard University Press, 1979. Carter, Dan T. *Scottsboro: A Tragedy of the American South*. Baton Rouge: Louisiana State University Press, 1969. Cooper, Wayne F. *Claude McKay: Rebel Sojourner in the Harlem Renaissance*. Baton Rouge: Louisiana State University Press, 1987. Corwin, Arthur F., ed. *Immigrants—and Immigrants: Perspectives on Mexican Labor Migration to the United States*. Westport, Conn.: Greenwood Press, 1978. Couto, Richard A. *Ain't Gonna Let Nobody Turn Me Round: The Pursuit of Racial Justice in the Rural South*. Philadelphia: Temple University Press, 1991.

Davis, Allison, Burleigh B. Gardner, and Mary R. Gardner. *Deep South: A Social Anthropological Study of Caste and Class*. Chicago: University of Chicago Press, 1941. Dinnerstein, Leonard. *Antisemitism in America*. New York: Oxford University Press, 1994. Drake, St. Clair, and Horace R. Clayton. *Black Metropolis: A Study of Negro Life in a Northern City*. Chicago: University of Chicago Press, 1993.

Feingold, Henry L. *The Jewish People in America: A Time for Searching—Entering the Mainstream, 1920–1945*. Baltimore: Johns Hopkins University Press, 1992. Fields, Harold. *The Refugee in the United States*. New York: Oxford University Press, 1938. Foner, Philip S., and Ronald L. Lewis, eds. *The Black Worker: A Documentary History from Colonial Times to the Present*. Vol. 5: *The Era of Post-War Prosperity and the Great Depression, 1920–1936*. Philadelphia: Temple University Press, 1981.

Garcia, Mario T. *Mexican Americans: Leadership, Ideology, & Identity, 1930–1960*. New Haven, Conn.: Yale University Press, 1989. Gerber, David A., ed. *Anti-Semitism in American History*. Chicago: University of Illinois Press, 1986. Goodman, James. *Stories of Scottsboro*. New York: Pantheon Books, 1994. Grant, Nancy L. *TVA and Black Americans: Planning for the Status Quo*. Philadelphia: Temple University Press, 1990. Green, Constance. *The Secret City: A History of Race Relations in the Nation's Capital*. Princeton, N.J.: Princeton University Press, 1967. Greenberg, Cheryl Lynn. *"Or Does It Explode?": Harlem in the Great Depression*. New York: Oxford University Press, 1991.

Hundley, Norris, Jr., ed. *The Chicano*. Santa Barbara, Calif.: Clio Books, 1975.

Johnson, Charles S. *Growing Up in the Black Belt: Negro Youth in the Rural South*. Washington, D.C.: American Council on Education, 1941. Johnson, James. *Black Manhattan*. Introduction by Sondra Kathryn Wilson. 1930. Reprint, New York: Da Capo Press, 1991.

Kirby, John B. *Black Americans in the Roosevelt Era: Liberalism and Race*. Knoxville: University of Tennessee Press, 1980.

Lee, Albert. *Henry Ford and the Jews*. New York: Stein & Day, 1980. Lerner, Gerda, ed. *Black Women in White America: A Documentary History*. New York: Random House, 1972.

Moore, Joan W., with Alfredo Cuellar. *The Mexican Americans*. Englewood Cliffs, N.J.: Prentice-Hall, 1970. Myrdal, Gunnar. *An American Dilemma: The Negro Problem and Modern Democracy*. 2 vols. New York: Harper & Brothers, 1944.

Naison, Mark. *Communists in Harlem During the Depression*. Urbana: University of Illinois Press, 1983.

Patterson, Haywood, and Earl Conrad. *Scottsboro Boy*. Garden City, N.Y.: Doubleday & Co., 1950.

Rampersad, Arnold. *The Life of Langston Hughes*. Vol. 1, *1902–1941: I, Too, Sing America*. New York: Oxford University Press, 1986. Raper, Arthur S. *The Tragedy of Lynching*. Chapel Hill: University of North Carolina Press, 1933. Reisler, Mark. *By the Sweat of Their Brow: Mexican Immigrant Labor in the United States, 1900–1940*. Westport, Conn.: Greenwood Press, 1976. Romo, Ricardo. *East Los Angeles: History of a Barrio*. Austin: University of Texas Press, 1983.

Sitkoff, Harvard. *A New Deal for Blacks: The Emergence of Civil Rights as a National Issue*. Vol. 1, *The Depression Years*. New York: Oxford University Press, 1978. Sterner, Richard, et al. *The Negro's Share: A Study of Income, Consumption, Housing, and Public Assistance*. New York: Harper & Brothers, 1943.

Trotter, Joe William, Jr., ed. *The Great Migration in Historical Perspective: New Dimensions of Race, Class, and Gender*. Bloomington: Indiana University Press, 1991.

Walker, Margaret. *Richard Wright, Daemonic Genius: A Portrait of the Man, A Critical Look at His Work*. New York: Warner Books, 1988. Witchen, Elsie. *Tuberculosis and the Negro in Pittsburgh: A Report of the Negro Health Survey*. Pittsburgh: Tuberculosis League of Pittsburgh, 1934. Wright, Richard. *12 Million Black Voices: A Folk History of the Negro in the United States*. New York: Viking Press, 1941.

Articles

Betten, Neil, and Raymond H. Mohl. "From Discrimination to Repatriation: Mexican Life in Gary, Indiana, During the Great Depression." *Pacific Historical*

Review (August 1973). Black, Allida M. "Championing a Champion: Eleanor Roosevelt and the Marian Anderson 'Freedom Concert.'" *Presidential Studies Quarterly* (fall 1990).

Cantor, Louis. "A Prologue to the Protest Movement: The Missouri Sharecropper Roadside Demonstration of 1939." *Journal of American History* (March 1969). Clayton, Ronnie W. "The Federal Writers' Project for Blacks in Louisiana." *Louisiana History* (summer 1978). Cole, Olen, Jr. "African-American Youth in the Programs of the Civilian Conservation Corps in California, 1933–42: An Ambivalent Legacy." *Forest & Conservation History* (July 1991).

Dalfiume, Richard M. "The 'Forgotten' Years of the Negro Revolution." *Journal of American History* (June 1968).

Foreman, Clark. "The Decade of Hope." *Phylon 12* (2d quarter, 1951).

Gower, Calvin W. "The Struggle of Blacks for the Leadership Positions in the Civilian Conservation Corps: 1933–1942." *The Journal of Negro History* (April 1976). Greenbaum, Fred. "The Anti-Lynching Bill of 1935: The Irony of 'Equal Justice—Under Law.'" *Journal of Human Relations* (3d quarter, 1967).

Hamilton, Dona Cooper. "The National Urban League and New Deal Programs." *Social Service Review* (June 1984). Hoffman, Abraham. "Stimulus to Repatriation: The 1931 Federal Deportation Drive and the Los Angeles Mexican Community." *Pacific Historical Review* (May 1973). Hoffmann, Edwin D. "The Genesis of the Modern Movement for Equal Rights in South Carolina, 1930–1939." *Journal of Negro History* (October 1959). Holmes, Michael S. "The Blue Eagle as 'Jim Crow Bird': The NRA and Georgia's Black Workers." *Journal of Negro History* (July 1972); "The New Deal and Georgia's Black Youth." *Journal of Southern History* (August 1972).

Pacifico, Michele F. "'Don't Buy Where You Can't Work': The New Negro Alliance of Washington." *Washington History* (spring/summer 1994).

Romo, Ricardo. "Responses to Mexican Immigration, 1910–1930." *Aztlan-International Journal of Chicano Studies Research* (spring 1975). Ross, B. Joyce. "Mary McLeod Bethune and the National Youth Administration: A Case Study of Power Relationships in the Black Cabinet of Franklin D. Roosevelt." *Journal of Negro History* (January 1975).

Vargas, Zaragosa. "Life and Community in the 'Wonderful City of the Magic Motor': Mexican Immigrants in 1920s Detroit." *Michigan Historical Review* (spring 1989).

Wolters, Raymond. "Section 7a and the Black Worker." *Labor History* (summer 1969). Wright, Richard. "With Black Radicals in Chicago." *Dissent* (spring 1977).

Zangrando, Robert L. "The NAACP and a Federal Antilynching Bill, 1934–1940." *Journal of Negro History* (April 1965).

WOMEN'S ISSUES

Books

Chafe, William H. *The Paradox of Change: American Women in the 20th Century.* New York: Oxford University Press, 1991.

Dubofsky, Melvin, and Stephen Burnwood, eds. *Women and Minorities During the Great Depression.* New York: Garland Publishing, 1990.

Kessler-Harris, Alice. *Out to Work: A History of Wage-Earning Women in the United States.* New York: Oxford University Press, 1982.

Lerner, Gerda. *The Female Experience: An American Documentary.* Indianapolis: Bobbs-Merrill, 1977.

Scharf, Lois. *To Work and to Wed: Female Employment, Feminism, and the Great Depression.* Westport, Conn.: Greenwood Press, 1980; and Joan M. Jensen, eds. *Decades of Discontent: The Women's Movement, 1920–1940.* Westport, Conn.: Greenwood Press, 1983.

Ware, Susan. *Beyond Suffrage: Women and the New Deal.* Cambridge: Harvard University Press, 1981.

Articles

Bennett, Sheila Kishler, and Glen H. Elder Jr. "Women's Work in the Family Economy: A Study of Depression Hardship in Women's Lives." *Journal of Family History* (summer 1979). Bolin, Winifred D. Wandersee. "The Economics of Middle-Income Family Life: Working Women During the Great Depression." *The Journal of American History* (June 1978).

Helmbold, Lois Rita. "Beyond the Family Economy: Black and White Working-Class Women During the Great Depression." *Feminist Studies* (fall 1987); "Downward Occupational Mobility During the Great Depression: Urban Black and White Working Class Women." *Labor History* (spring 1988).

Strom, Sharon Hartman. "Challenging 'Woman's Place': Feminism, the Left, and Industrial Unionism in the 1930s." *Feminist Studies* (summer 1983).

THE IMPENDING CONFLICT

Books

Adams, Henry H. *Years of Deadly Peril: The Coming of the War, 1939–1941.* New York: David McKay Co., 1969.

Bloch, Leon Bryce, and Charles Angoff, eds. *The World Over in 1939.* New York: The Living Age Press, 1940.

Canedy, Susan. *America's Nazis: A Democratic Dilemma.* Menlo Park, Calif.: Markgraf Publications Group, 1990.

Dallek, Robert. *Franklin D. Roosevelt and American Foreign Policy, 1932–1945*. New York: Oxford University Press, 1979.

Higham, Charles. *American Swastika*. Garden City, N.Y.: Doubleday & Co., 1985.

Jonas, Manfred. *Isolationism in America, 1935–1941*. Ithaca, N.Y.: Cornell University Press, 1966.

Ketchum, Richard M. *The Borrowed Years, 1938–1941: America on the Way to War*. New York: Random House, 1989.

Perrett, Geoffrey. *Days of Sadness, Years of Triumph: The American People, 1939–1945*. Madison: University of Wisconsin Press, 1973. Porter, David L. *The Seventy-Sixth Congress and World War II, 1939–1940*. Columbia: University of Missouri Press, 1979.

Wiltz, John E. *From Isolation to War, 1931–1941*. New York: Thomas Y. Crowell Co., 1968.

ACKNOWLEDGMENTS

———◆———

Given the nearly eight years it has taken me to complete this book, I probably have lost track of a good many people who have helped along the way. My apologies for any oversights. A few have been along for the entire ride, however, and I could not forget them if I tried. Chief among these is my wife, Joan, to whom *The Hungry Years* is appropriately and gratefully dedicated (among other things, the title was her idea); as ever, I could not possibly have staggered through to completion without her. If Joan has held me up by one arm, the other has been firmly in the grasp of my editor, Marian Wood, whose patience has been exemplary and for whose loving guidance and diligent, creative criticism there will never be praise enough; her vision has been instrumental in the shaping of this book, as it has been for so many other books, including my previous Henry Holt volume, *Righteous Pilgrim: The Life and Times of Harold L. Ickes, 1874–1952*. Maxwell Perkins, eat your ghostly heart out. Behind us all has been Carl Brandt, my agent of more than fifteen years, whose own patience and insight have been as crucial as the occasional boot in the rear he has provided to keep me moving. Ralph Hone, who shares the dedication with my wife, did not advise me directly on this book, but in the more than forty years since we used to share illicit cigarettes in his office at the University of Redlands, his sweet wisdom has enriched my professional life and made our long friendship a constant joy—not least because it includes his dear wife, Harriet.

I will always owe a special portion of thanks to the late Henry Hampton of Boston's Blackside, Inc., for access to and permission to quote from the extraordinary series of interviews its production teams did for the 1993 PBS-TV documentary, *The Great Depression*. I am similarly indebted to Blackside's team of researchers, whom I sent prowling into the recesses of the Harvard University Library for dozens of journal articles.

Thanks to Nancy J. Proctor, librarian of the Tennessee Valley Authority in Knoxville, who directed me into the rich maw of the TVA's oral history archive and led me to several other rewarding sources as well, and to my friend David Wilcove, who helped me borrow his grandfather, Jack Yellen; and to the staff of the Bancroft Library at the University of California at Berkeley, out of whose trove of manuscripts, oral histories, and other resources I have been making a living for more than thirty-five years. A similarly large chunk of gratitude goes to The Wilderness Society's economist, Carolyn Alkire, whose updating of comparative financial figures (in "A Note on Statistics and Money") has been invaluable. It is not the only debt I owe the folks at The Wilderness Society. From the spring of 1982 to the fall of 1997, that estimable organization not only gave me the time and resources to pursue the muse of history but provided me with a platform called *Wilderness* magazine from which I was privileged to launch editorial sorties against those who would corrupt America's legacy of land and wildlife—which, as it happened, Franklin Roosevelt and the New Dealers had done so much to preserve. The experience of those years remains fixed in my heart. My new friends and colleagues at Montana State University—especially Michael Malone, Gordon Brittan, Thomas Wessel, and Dorothy Bradley—have been no less supportive of my historical expeditions than my friends and colleagues at The Wilderness Society, and have even encouraged me to shoot off the occasional environmentalist missile from my silo in Bozeman, too.

Finally, memories of Hutch and Wally continue to light my way. Rest well, old friends.

INDEX

Greenbelt Towns, 450–51, 462

"Greenfield Village," 10–11

Greenway, John, 459

gross national product, 8, 44, 47

Guild of New York Newspaper Men and Women, 220

Guthrie, Woody, 457–58

Haas, Francis J., 230, 231

Hahn, Emily, 65–66

Haight, Raymond, 250–51

Haile Selassie, Emperor, 512

Hall, Arthur F., 84–85

Hamett, W. D., 406, 408

Hammett, Dashiell, 277

Hammond, Percy, 289

Hanson, Ole, 113

Hapgood, Powers, 307, 321

"Happy Days Are Here Again" (song), 15, 32, 86, 153

Harding, Warren G., 8, 12, 147, 352

Harding administration, 464

Hardwick, Thomas W., 113

Harlan County, Kentucky, 176–77, 212–15, 406

Harlan County Coal Operators Association, 212

Harlem, 63, 77, 92, 289, 493–95

Harriman, Daisy, 500

Harris, Sam, 155

Hart, Moss, 155

Harvey, Harry, 403

Hastie, William, 168, 495

Hastings, Robert J., 62

Hatalla, Steve, Jr., 242–44, 245, 319–20

haves/have-nots disparity, 47–48

Hawley-Smoot Tariff Act, 51

Hays, Will, 205–6

Healey, Dorothy, 116

Hearst, William Randolph, 59, 66, 203, 246, 290, 292, 317, 457

heat, 421–22, 423, 431

Hedgman, Anna Arnold, 63

Heffernan, Joseph L., 58, 101

Heller, Samuel A., 57

Hellman, Lillian, 514

Hemingway, Ernest, 514

Herring, Clyde, 352

Hickok, Lorena, 176–78, 181, 380, 423, 425, 431

Hicks, Granville, 514

Hill, Edwin C., 140

Hillman, Sidney, 186, 210, 216, 220, 221, 302, 304, 319

Hine, Robert, 75

Historical American Buildings Survey, 180

Hitler, Adolf, 50, 137, 317, 513, 515, 516, 517

Hodson, William, 158

hogs/hog farmers, 344, 345, 356–58, 361, 362, 443

Holly, John O., 493

Hollywood, 203, 290

home-improvement projects, 74–75, 80

Home Owners Loan Act, 151

"Homeless Junction," 491

homelessness, 57, 58, 60–62, 65, 70–71, 72

Homestead Act of 1862, 341

Hook, Charles H., 298

Hoover, Herbert, 11–14, 41, 76, 125, 146, 162, 182, 320, 350, 398, 421, 465–66

and BEF, 134, 136, 137, 138, 140, 141

PHOTOGRAPH
ACKNOWLEDGMENTS

◆

Page 2: The Ford Motor Company's River Rouge plant, Dearborn, Michigan, 1927. From the "Rouge Series" by Charles Sheeler (Henry Ford Museum and Greenfield Village Research Center).

Page 34: "White Angel Bread Line," San Francisco, 1934. Photograph by Dorothea Lange. (Copyright © The Oakland Museum of California, City of Oakland. Gift of Paul S. Taylor.)

Page 142: "Hands and Cards, Representing New Deal," 1933. Photograph by Theodor Horydcak (The Library of Congress).

Page 336: "Migrant Mother," San Joaquin Valley, California, 1936. Photograph by Dorothea Lange (The Library of Congress).

Page 486: Black workers perform at safety meeting, Wilson Dam, Alabama, 1942. Photograph by Arthur Rothstein (The Library of Congress).